NOBLE SAVAGES

The Savage Club and The Great War 1914–1918

James Wilson

Productions

PUBLISHED BY JH PRODUCTIONS
FOLKESTONE
KENT
UNITED KINGDOM

jhproductions@gmx.co.uk

Plate section:
Savage Club War Memorial by James Wilson © The Savage Club 2018.
Jasper Myers Richardson's grave at Étaples Cemetery by Aran Wilson © 2018 all rights reserved.
Thiepval monument by Sam Wilson © 2018 all rights reserved.
Lance Thackeray's grave by Helen Sheridan © 2018 all rights reserved.
Savage Club menus © The Savage Club 2018.
AK Harvey-James's grave, Savage Club candidate books, The Cenotaph, two views of Étaples Cemetery, Harry Alexander's grave and Charles Scott-Gatty's grave by James Wilson © 2018 all rights reserved.

A catalogue record for this book is available from the British Library.

ISBN 978-1-5272-2965-5

Typeset in Caslon, Spectral and Verona Serial by JH Productions.

For

Aran and Sam

and

In memory of all members of the Savage Club
who served in the Great War of 1914–18

Voices of Savages Past

Savages on the Great War

I held a council at 10.45 to declare war with Germany. It is a terrible catastrophe but it is not our fault. An enormous crowd collected outside the Palace; we went on the balcony both before and dinner. When they heard that war had been declared the excitement increased and May and I with David went on to the balcony; the cheering was terrific. Please to God it may soon be over and that He will protect dear Bertie's life.

King George V (honorary Savage from 1901–1910)

You are ordered abroad as a soldier of the King to help our French comrades against the invasion of a common enemy. You have to perform a task which will need your courage, your energy, your patience. Remember that the honour of the British Army depends on your individual conduct.

It will be your duty not only to set an example of discipline and perfect steadiness under fire, but also to maintain the most friendly relations with those whom you are helping in this struggle. The operations in which you are engaged will, for the most part, take place in a friendly country, and you can do your own country no better service than in showing yourself in France and Belgium in the true character of a British soldier.

Be invariably courteous, considerate and kind. Never do anything likely to injure or destroy property, and always look upon looting as a disgraceful act. You are sure to meet with a welcome and to be trusted; your conduct must justify that welcome and that trust.

Your duty cannot be done unless your health is sound, so keep constantly on your guard against any excesses. In this new experience you may find temptations both in wine and women. You must entirely resist both temptations, and, while treating all women with perfect courtesy, you should avoid any intimacy.

Do your duty bravely. Fear God. Honour The King.

Field Marshal Lord Kitchener, letter to soldiers, 1914

The men that marched and sang with me
Are most of them in Flanders now:
I lie abed and hear the wind
Blow softly through the budding bough.
And they are scattered far and wide
In this or that brave regiment;
From trench to trench across the mud
They go the way that others went.
They run with shining bayonet
Or lie and take a careful aim
And theirs it is to learn of death
And theirs the joy and theirs the fame.

Edward Shanks, 'The Comrades', 1915

Many of us have never recovered from the losses of that dreadful period, though somehow or other at the time we all had to keep a straight upper lip and carry on.

Cecil Aldin, Time I Was Dead

We were in the Cambrai Salient, in support in the old Hindenburg Line. Close to us was a road where there were a ration dump and every other sort of dump. Everybody in the sector went through us to get rations, ammunition, stores, etc.

There was just room in the trench for two men to pass. Snow had been on the ground for weeks, and the bottom of the trench was like glass.

One night at stand-to the Drake Battalion crowded past us to get rations. On their return journey the leading man, with two sandbags of rations round his neck and a petrol can of water in each hand, fell over at every other step.

Things were further complicated by a party of R.E.'s coming down the line with much barbed wire, in which this unfortunate "Drake" entangled himself.

As he picked himself up for the umpteenth time, and without the least intention of being funny, I heard him say: "Well, if I ever catch that nipper of mine playin' soldiers, I won't 'arf knock 'is blinkin' block orf."

AMB (late Artists Rifles), Savage Club, WC2,
quoted in Ian Hamilton (ed), The Best 500 Cockney War Stories

Between the Ancre and the Somme a large part of the finest youth of the Empire fell with that of France and Germany, mingled on the same desolate field. There were few families now which had not felt a loss; this War of the Great Powers had invaded many sunlit islands. As men of the highest talent are often the bravest, many fell on both sides who were marked by Nature to lead their countries in years to come, in art and in letters and along the paths of thoughtful statesmanship, so that their deaths came to be felt by each country not only at the time, but twenty years later, when they would have naturally come into their own, and the torn and pitted land on which they fell had long lost any sign of its scars.

Herbert Asquith, Moments of Memory

The thing the Allies are really fighting against is a spirit, a tradition, a creed. That spirit and that creed have always directed the policy of Prussia. They now direct the policy of Germany. In so far as the Emperor represents them we are at war with the Emperor. In so far as the governing class of Prussia represents them we are at war with the governing class of Prussia. In so far as the German peoples accept them and are prepared to fight for them we are at war with the German peoples.

In a word this war is at bottom a religious war.

Cecil Chesterton, The Prussian Hath Said In His Heart

Somehow distance, and the years, soften for us the jagged edges of discomforts outlived. The wind and the rain; the interminable mud; the torment of being chivvied and badgered about by soldiers, sailors, police and civilians alike ...

Flanders seems afar now; its worries and discomforts all faded and remote. There remains supreme over all other things, that exulting thing, that feeling of life lived; life sought out and faced; life hot, strong and undiluted; the Male animal's conception of romance.

Basil Clarke

We only walk with reverence this sullen mile of mud
The shell-holes hold our history, and half of them our blood.

AP Herbert, 'Beaucourt Revisited'

We had seen much that was obscene at Gallipoli, the Somme and Passchendaele, but nothing shameful. Would the war have been less shameful if we had lost it, if the British Fleet had steamed over to Heligoland to surrender or scuttle, if the people under British rule had been handed over to the gentle Germans? How I dislike these anaemic belittlers of our past!

AP Herbert

Heeding no advantage, asserting no virtue, claiming no righteousness, the August volunteers marched away, the vanguard of a generation doomed to die untimely ... There was no estimating the extent to which creative thought was depleted, or the cost to learning, literature and science of the destruction of so many strong and cultivated intelligences.

Reginald Pound, The Lost Generation

As it went, it wasn't a question of "if I get killed", it was merely a question of "when I get killed", because a battalion went over 800 strong, you lost 300 or 400, half the number, perhaps more. Now it wasn't a question of saying, "I am one of the survivors, hurrah, hurrah", because you didn't go home … Out came another draft of 400 and you went over the top again.

There was an awful feeling of a great black cloud on top of one the whole time, there seemed to be no future …! think one lost one's sensitivity. You lived like a worm and your horizon was very limited to "shall I get back in time for the parcel to come? Shall I ever get back to eat that cake that I know mother has sent me?" You certainly lived one day at a time. I didn't dare think of tomorrow It was general abject misery. I think your imagination became dulled. I think in the end you just became a thing.

Arnold Ridley, The Train and Other Ghosts

Savages on the Savage Club

Of all the clubs in existence, for those who seek refuge from the sins and sinners of this wicked world, the Savage Club is the most famous. These Savages are the most civil and civilised of all the races of humanity.

Lieutenant-Colonel John Mackenzie Rogan

The Savage Club's unwritten rule is that, whoever you are, you are nobody once you're inside. It is observed.

Basil Boothroyd

Our Brother Savages were men famed in the Arts and I was thrilled to lunch there and listen to so much wit and wisdom. It was a refreshing change from the hurly-burly of show business.

Bud Flanagan

A focus, a centre, a gathering place, a resort, a haunt, a retreat, a rendezvous, a head-quarters; such are the many definitions of the word club in my book of reference, and all these varied things has the Savage Club been to me at one time or another during my forty-six years of membership … The Savage Club was then, as it still is, a kaleidoscope of every kind of being, human and inhuman. It sponsored crankism together with high literary, artistic, musical and scientific achievement, characters of all kinds galore.

To be a good Savage one must certainly not show over-sensitiveness about anything. The man who cannot take rather biting if good-natured banter will never survive in our club. But we are more sensitive than were the members of the now extinct Yorick Club whose authorised way of addressing an audience when proposing a toast in their club was: "Sons of gentlemen and members of the Yorick Club!" By the by, the Savage Club's definition of a gentleman is a man who can take another man's money in a pleasant way.

Mark Hambourg

It was, it is, I suppose an entertainment without its like in the world – all freely and proudly given, by Savage or guest, for the love of the Club, by tired men just come from stage or concert, by old men who feel they have entertained enough, by young men at the peak who could charge a fortune for a song or a turn.

AP Herbert

No account of my life could be complete without a lengthy reference to my association with the Savage Club. Here I have spent my laborious leisure for the last thirty-odd years and have found friends that no man could hope to better.

It was in 1916 that I was first taken there by George Baker, now the Hon Secretary of the Club, at the time when he and I were soldiering together on the City Road front. I was his guest, and even now I remember the profound impression that the Club, then in the Adelphi, made on me. I was exhilarated by the walls covered with paintings and drawings of illustrious members, the indefinable atmosphere of good fellowship, a feeling that here all men were equal, no matter what the rank or profession; the blending of tradition with the present, and the stimulation of meeting those famous in the arts. From the window of the dining-room I looked upon a panorama of London's river that to me, a Cockney, was thrilling.

Joe Batten

In the Savage Club I was able to mix with numbers of great doctors, eminent scientists, actors, writers, musicians, artists – sensible, hard-working men, all busy at their arts or professions, all men of the world, and generally speaking all possessed of X-ray eyes and capable of stripping a high-brow of all poses, affectations, and pretentions. There is no other collection of men in the world to compare with it. There are field-marshals and fiddlers, mummers and millionaires, and when they enter those dignified doors in Carlton House Terrace they leave all differences behind them and meet their fellow members on common ground. I found myself in an atmosphere I loved. It reminded me somewhat of the early art days before the War, when tolerance and artistic camaraderie were accepted facts among practising artists.

CRW Nevinson

Contents

Foreword

by Alan Williams

Noble Savages is about the extraordinary record of eminent individuals who were members of the Savage Club over its long history. James Wilson has written about some of those members who fought in the First World War, a war in which, as he says, a million British and Empire troops never returned, and for those that did, it was not to the land fit for heroes that politicians had promised.

It is James Wilson's aim in this book to remember those members of the Savage Club who fought for King and Country. And he does it superbly.

In total, 147 members of the Club served in that conflict and the author has chosen a selection who became well known in their later careers and who were without doubt fascinating and interesting men.

The first qualification to be a Savage is to fall into one of the membership categories: science, art, music, drama or literature. Law became a category much later although the Club had lawyers of distinction, as this book vividly reveals, who had fallen into other categories.

James Wilson has made an important contribution to Savage history with this book. His impeccable research has thrown up some Savage Club gems. There have been many books about the Club: Aaron Watson's history of 1907, and the later history by Percy V Bradshaw (1958), are remarkable works. Later writings, too, of Alan Wykes (with Matthew Norgate) of 1976, and John Wade in 2007, show the 'indefinable atmosphere of good fellowship, a feeling that all men were equal no matter what rank or profession, and the blending of tradition with the present', as Joseph Batten put it so well in his book of 1956. Indeed, there can be no other Club in the country that has had the distinction of four future Kings of England chairing Club dinners.

Noble Savages joins that succession of histories in a very real and profound way. It is the first time that a number of eminent members have been researched in depth and their contribution to society has been placed against the background of a Club which was a very significant part of their lives.

The Club, of course, has a library and all books have either been written by members of the Club or are books about members of the Club. The names of James Agate and Eric Midwinter frequently appear. Indeed, to show James Wilson's versatility, three books in the library are written by him.

James is an accomplished author and his latest book will bring further distinction to our library.

Alan Williams
Chairman of the Savage Club 2015–2018

Preface

I have long been fascinated by the First World War. Like most people with ancestry in New Zealand and England, I had several relatives who served in different capacities during the conflict. Most notably, on my mother's side my great uncle Sydney Ellis died in August 1915 at Gallipoli, serving with the Otago Battalion; while on my father's side my great-grandfather Joe Jarvis fought on the Western Front with the Royal Artillery and was wounded by poison gas, the effects of which stayed with him until his death in 1957.

For the past three decades I have been overloading my bookshelf with works on the war, and I have also made numerous trips to the battlefields of the Western Front. I have written a few short pieces on the conflict in two of my previous books, but this is the first time I have attempted anything on the present scale.

Throughout the project I have had the assistance of an expert general staff. Quite a few of the discussions herein were based on conversations I have had with fellow enthusiasts, including my brother John Wilson and two Brother Savages, Neil Harris (who is also my brother-in-law) and Andrew Riddoch (a First World War author and accredited Battlefield Guide). John also read the book front to back several times and offered comments on everything from punctuation to the discussions of broad strategy.

My mother Penny Wilson also proofread the entire book and offered many insights, using her training in science and in classical music when vetting the relevant chapters. More importantly, she knew the Great War generation, who formed the elderly in her youth, and she had many memories of their character and culture – taciturn men and women of duty, for whom it was the height of bad form to grumble about their lot or, equally, to brag about their achievements. Instead, 'service before self' was their overarching creed.

My two sons, Sam and Aran, were dragooned into helping with various aspects of putting the book together, and accompanied me as an expeditionary force to the Western Front for research and photographs. Our most recent trip was in August 2018, where (accompanied by Neil and Annette (his wife; my sister)) we took pictures of the graves of Savages buried in France, the Vimy Ridge monument and the great Lutyens memorials at Thiepval and Étaples.

I am grateful to all the Savages who provided encouragement as I went along, of whom there are too many to mention.

Special thanks are due to Alan Williams for writing the foreword.

I must also acknowledge the help I received from the online community of the Great War Forum. Time and time again, all I had to do was float a name, and within a day, two or three people would find the relevant online records.

The final mention concerns Helen Sheridan, who held every rank going in the editorial army I deployed – assisting with the research, editing, proof-reading every page, sourcing many illustrations, typesetting, designing the cover, and a host of other tasks too many to mention. The book would never have been the same otherwise. Helen's support through a major change in real life while I was writing the book was all the more valuable; that deserves a book of its own.

All mistakes are my sole responsibility.

James Wilson
The Savage Club
1 Whitehall Place
London

August 2018

Introduction

Great monuments to great men

> "Let us now praise famous men"—
> Men of little showing
> For their work continueth,
> And their work continueth,
> Broad and deep continueth,
> Greater than their knowing!

Rudyard Kipling, Stalky & Co[1]

Three things struck me when I first became acquainted with the Savage Club. The first was the magnificent setting, nestled away in the Victorian splendour that is the National Liberal Club. The second was the conviviality and erudition one invariably found of an evening within those surrounds. The third was the extraordinary record of eminent individuals who had belonged to the Club over its long history.

Almost from my first days as a member, I had in mind writing some sort of celebratory sketch of the individualists, the raconteurs, the *bon viveurs*, the heroes and – should I manage to find any – the villains who have graced the different premises of our redoubtable Club over the past 160 years.

The problem was not deciding what to write, but rather deciding what – and who – *not* to write about. A comprehensive history of the Club and its members was beyond my resources. So I had to decide upon a theme. In that respect I was prompted by a sight found on the wall just inside entrance of the Clubroom. There, to the lower left of the desk with the log book, hangs the Great War memorial – the list of the fallen of the Club, just like those found in so many of Britain's cities, towns, villages and institutions. The Savage's list is mercifully

---

1 Kipling was channelling *Ecclesiasticus (Sirach) 44:1–15*, which begins 'Let us now sing the praises of famous men, our ancestors in their generations.'

short compared with some other First World War memorials. But it has the unique distinction for a non-military club of no fewer than *two* field marshals. The first is Lord Kitchener, whose image appeared on one of the most iconic wartime images in history, imploring his fellow citizens 'Your country needs you'. The second is Field Marshal 'Bobs' Roberts, the epitome of the soldier of Empire, a veteran of India, Afghanistan and the Second Boer War and the subject of three Kipling poems. Some investigations disclosed that two other field marshals of the same era – Robertson and Byng – were also Savages, as was Admiral Jellicoe, the commander of the British fleet at the Battle of Jutland, the most significant naval battle of the First World War.

But the Savage Club has never been confined to lords and colonels. Instead, it has only ever asked of its candidates that they should fall into one of the categories of membership – science, art, music, drama and literature[2] – and (informally) be a clubbable sort. That has always led to a much more interesting membership than simply a military or political establishment full of tailor's dummies or party hacks. And it means that the Savage memorial has a second unique feature for a club of the early twentieth century, since its members included 'other ranks' – as low as Private Cecil Chesterton – along with the two field marshals.

Continuing my research, hidden in the cupboard behind the wall, near the entrance, I found candidate books and lists of members from years past.

Given all the great names in this book, visiting the Club in the first half of the twentieth century would have been quite an experience. One might have arrived and found oneself at the bar in conversation with a Nobel Prize-winning scientist. Then one might have been joined by a stand-up comedian, a leading surgeon, a Victoria Cross winner, a great artist, an esteemed novelist, a virtuoso musician, a well-known actor, or an MP of any political stripe.

The diversity of membership also meant it was possible to piece together interesting and improbable interactions across history. Several of the Savage authors started their careers writing for the Oxford student publication *The ISIS Magazine*, founded by Brother Savage Mostyn Pigott. Brother Savage EH Shepard met the Prince of Wales at the Italian front at Christmas 1917, where the Prince was apparently amused by Shepard's 'slightly dishevelled appearance'.[3] I wonder if the Prince would have been more surprised to know that Shepard would later join the same club as him, along with the Prince's assistant on the Western Front, the future light entertainer Chesney Allen.

Immediately after the war, before he was demobbed, Shepard met and was very impressed by Ernest Hemingway. I doubt he suspected that one day

---

2   Law was added as a category much later, in 1956.

3   James Campbell, *Shepard's War: E. H. Shepard, the Man Who Drew Winnie-the-Pooh* (Michael O'Mara, 2015, Kindle edn).

Hemingway would write a novel featuring an invented cocktail named pejoratively after a British field marshal who was also a member of the same club.[4] Shepard also illustrated the children's classic *Wind in the Willows*, whose author, Kenneth Grahame, was Brother Savage Lord Moulton's son-in-law. Meanwhile, the secretary of Brother Savage JM Barrie of *Peter Pan* fame[5] from 1917, Cynthia Asquith, happened to be the wife of the Great War veteran Brother Savage Herbert Asquith (son of the prime minister who led Britain into the conflict). Barrie was also a good friend of Brother Savage Robert Falcon Scott, and godfather to Scott's son Peter, and one of those to whom Scott wrote in his final hours in Antarctica. One could cite many more instances of small degrees of Savage separation.

I was therefore soon in possession of a list of individuals united by the common theme of all being Club members who served in the First World War.

There was one final First World War prompt: the magnificent 1915 portrait of Sir Winston Churchill by the staircase in the National Liberal Club. I discovered that the story behind the painting was as engaging as the image itself, yet it had been strangely ignored by many of Churchill's biographers.

A century may have passed since the epic tragedy of the First World War, and there are no survivors left.[6] Our society and its standards, attitudes, institutions and values have changed substantially since those times, but they also changed substantially *because* of the war and its even more disastrous successor, the Second World War. For those reasons it has always been important to study the war, its origins and the course of world events it involved. But there is another reason. The men who fought the First World War made an extraordinary sacrifice. Almost a million British and Empire troops did not come home. Millions more were wounded, physically and psychologically. They were promised, but did

---

4   I refer to Field Marshal Bernard 'Monty' Montgomery, the best-known British general of the Second World War, whose fame derived from his victory at El Alamein and his command of Allied troops at D-Day. In Hemingway's novel *Across the River and into the Trees*, Colonel Cantwell gives an order to the waiter in Harry's Bar while he is entertaining a young lady:
   "Two very dry Martinis. Mongtomerys. Fifteen to one."
   The waiter, who had been in the desert, smiled and was gone.

5   Barrie was a member of the Savage, the Garrick and various other clubs, but very infrequently attended any of them, making his appearance at the Savage something of a coup for the Club. On 8 January 1922, he wrote to Sir Arthur Quiller-Couch, 'A few years ago I was elected to another club and went into it for the first time with a member who said he knew I didn't go much to my other clubs but hoped I would come oftener here, to which my reply, "Dear Sir, I *have* now been oftener here than to my other clubs".' See Viola Meynell (ed), *Letters of J. M. Barrie* (Charles Scribner's Sons, 1947), pp 8, 23. Despite his reticence, he was the special guest at a Savage Club dinner on 2 April 1930.

6   Pedants' corner: 'veterans' is not a term British men of that generation would have used; they would have said 'ex-servicemen' (in New Zealand it was 'returned servicemen', and 'RSA' (Returned Servicemen Association) halls were a common sight in most New Zealand towns and suburbs in my youth). 'Veteran' was a word imported from America later in the twentieth century.

not receive, a land fit for heroes upon their return. Above all, they asked one thing of future generations: that we remember them. Lawrence Binyon famously decreed in the fourth verse of his poem 'For the Fallen':[7]

> They shall grow not old, as we that are left grow old:
> Age shall not weary them, nor the years condemn.
> At the going down of the sun and in the morning
> We will remember them.

This book is my own modest contribution towards fulfilling that request.

The scope of the book

This book is not intended as a general history of the First World War. Broad themes do come up throughout, but I have looked at them as a way of setting the individual stories in context.

In total, 147 Savages served in the conflict[8] and it was not possible to write about every one of them. I chose to write about all those whose names were on the memorial, and a selection of others who also served in the conflict but who were much better known for their later careers, often a world away from the mud and blood of the Western Front. I claim no logic or authority for the final selection beyond saying that I chose the people I found the most interesting to research.

Accordingly, I like to think of the book as no more than a first volume, or at the least a first edition with much scope for addition should I have occasion to revise it. In Appendix III, I have listed a number of other interesting Savages of the day, who fell outside the selection I made for the main body of the book but deserved at least the equivalent of a mention in despatches.

I have aimed to set out a short biographical sketch for each person, and to identify controversies in which they were involved: the sort of thing that might – and, in my happy experience, often does – form the basis of a cut and thrust discussion of an evening in the Club. The strategies of Jellicoe at Jutland and Robertson and Haig on the Western Front, for example, have been the subject of robust academic and popular debate ever since their respective battles closed.

Although the individuals considered here all excelled in their fields, my focus has been confined to their service in the Great War. Their later lives, however

---

7 Binyon wrote the poem while sitting on the cliff-top looking out to sea on the Cornish coast-line in September 1914, and hence very early on in the conflict, but after the first important British engagement, the Battle of Mons on 23 August 1914.

8 The figure is from the Imperial War Museum: http://www.iwm.org.uk/memorials/item/memorial/65279. I doubt whether it would include all of the people who became members afterwards, as was the case for the majority in this book.

interesting, are necessarily covered in truncated form only. Throughout I have noted biographies and other sources in the footnotes, so readers can easily find out more about each.

The book is not intended to be a hagiography. At times we have to confront some uncomfortable realities, be it the less important matters of Billy Bennett and Dennis Wheatley not quite being the heroes they were occasionally made out to be, or the more serious fact of Henry Williamson and Collin Brooks acting as Nazi apologists.

To impose a logical structure, I have separated people into different categories corresponding to the field in which they are best remembered: war reporters, generals, the Savage dead, authors, entertainers (musicians, conductors, actors and composers), artists, scientists, lawyers, politicians, royalty and future leaders; albeit many excelled in more than one field.

I felt the outstanding literary men ought to be permitted to speak for themselves: reading the original words of authors of the likes of Henry Hamilton Fyfe, Sir Percival Phillips, Perceval Gibbon and Henry Williamson describing events they witnessed would be much more moving than any potted summary a later author might construct. For a number of chapters, therefore, the book functions effectively as an anthology. For others, the surviving details of their Great War service is rather sketchy, with few extant primary sources. In those cases I have instead written a more general summary of the units in which they served or the battles in which it was known they participated.

I have not assumed more than a rudimentary knowledge of the conflict. I have used some standard abbreviations such as 'BEF' the for British Expeditionary Force,[9] 'NLC' for the National Liberal Club, 'demobbed' for demobilised, and have used 'Great War' and 'First World War' interchangeably. Here and there I have added footnotes explaining some of the key figures and the key battles. At the end of the book, in Appendix I, I have set out a timeline of the key events

---

9   The British Expeditionary Force was technically the name of the British Army on the Western Front for the duration of the First World War, but the term is normally used only in reference to the small (by the standards of the day) professional force sent to France at the start of the conflict, and often only to the army present until the end of the First Battle of Ypres on 22 November 1914. By the end of 1914, following major engagements at Mons, Le Cateau, the Aisne and Ypres, the initial force had been effectively wiped out, though it had served its purpose of helping the French stop the Germans from reaching Paris and knocking France out of the war.

An alternative date for the end of the BEF was 26 December 1914, at which point it was divided into the First and Second Armies (followed later in the war by a Third, Fourth and Fifth Army).

Famously, the German Kaiser Wilhelm II dismissed the original BEF as a 'contemptible little army', a badge the British adopted with pride, hence members of the original BEF calling themselves the 'Old Contemptibles'. It appears now that the Kaiser never used the term, and it was probably the creation of British propaganda; if so, it certainly worked as intended.

for readers not so familiar with the broad narrative of the conflict. Finally, in the footnotes throughout the book, I have set out some further reading for anyone who wishes – as I hope they will – to learn more of the Savages and the part they played in what remains the most bloody conflict in British history.

Joseph Batten wrote of the 'profound impression that the Club had on me and I was exhilarated by the walls covered with paintings and drawings of illustrious members, the indefinable atmosphere of good fellowship, a feeling that all men were equal no matter what the rank or profession, and the blending of tradition with the present.'[10] I hope that this book captures some of that spirit.

The objective

I have painted on such a large canvas that the book is necessarily composed of broad sweeps interspersed with a few anecdotal stories, rather than a dense monograph on a discreet subject. If it fills a few gaps in fellow Savages' knowledge I will consider it a qualified success. If it inspires them to read further on any of the subjects herein, I will consider it a complete success. And if they then corner me in the Savage Club bar of an evening and challenge a few of my arguments and conclusions, I will consider it to have exceeded my expectations.

---

10 Joseph Batten, *Joe Batten's Book: The Story of Sound Recording* (Rockliff Publishing Corp, 1st edn 1956, Kindle edn, 2012).

NOBLE SAVAGES

The Savage Club and The Great War 1914–1918

CHAPTER 1

The National Liberal Club 1914-1918

Introduction

Before looking at the Savage Club itself in wartime, it seems appropriate to start with a few words about clubs generally, and in particular how the Savage Club's present host club, the National Liberal Club (NLC), fared from 1914–18.

It is a moot point how influential club life remains in twenty-first century British politics. If anything, most controversy nowadays concerns *perceived* rather than actual influence. For example, David Cameron resigned from White's when he was elected prime minister, though possibly more as an attempt to dissociate himself from the elitist image of his Eton and Oxford background rather than because he feared it would be argued he was actually running the country via an unseen cabal within its cloisters.

Either way, it is true that many fewer members of parliament today are members of London gentlemen's clubs than was the case during the Great War.[1] This is especially so in the case of the NLC, which has long ceased to be the exclusive preserve of the descendants of the Liberal Party. By way of contrast, at the turn of the twentieth century, the NLC had over 6,000 members and the Liberal Party was the chief opposition to the Tories. In those days, the clubhouse formed a hotbed of political activity. In his novel *The New Machiavelli*, HG Wells described a scene there:

---

1 The Carlton Club played a central role for the Tory Party, while the rebuilding of the Houses of Parliament themselves drew very heavily on London clubs. The architect of the Houses of Parliament, Charles Barry, had worked on the Reform Club and The Travellers Club, whilst MPs wanted a recreation of the comforts found in their clubs, such as smoking rooms and, of course, bars.

> My discontents with the Liberal party and my mental exploration
> of the quality of party generally is curiously mixed up with certain
> impressions of things and people in the National Liberal Club. The
> National Liberal Club is Liberalism made visible in the flesh—and
> Doultonware. It is an extraordinary big club done in a bold, wholesale,
> shiny, marbled style, richly furnished with numerous paintings, steel
> engravings, busts, and full-length statues of the late Mr. Gladstone;
> and its spacious dining-rooms, its long, hazy, crowded smoking-room
> with innumerable little tables and groups of men in armchairs, its
> magazine room and library upstairs, have just that undistinguished
> and unconcentrated diversity which is for me the Liberal note. The
> pensive member sits and hears perplexing dialects and even frag-
> ments of foreign speech, and among the clustering masses of less
> insistent whites his roving eye catches profiles and complexions that
> send his mind afield to Calcutta or Rangoon or the West Indies or
> Sierra Leone or the Cape ...

He later added:

> Most clubs have a common link, a lowest common denominator in the
> Club Bore, who spares no one, but even the National Liberal bores are
> specialised and sectional. As one looks round one sees here a clump
> of men from the North Country or the Potteries, here an island of
> South London politicians, here a couple of young Jews ascendant from
> Whitechapel, here a circle of journalists and writers, here a group of
> Irish politicians, here two East Indians, here a priest or so, here a clump
> of old-fashioned Protestants, here a little knot of eminent Rationalists
> indulging in a blasphemous story sotto voce. Next to them are a group
> of anglicised Germans and highly specialised chess-players, and then
> two of the oddest-looking persons—bulging with documents and in-
> tent upon extraordinary business transactions over long cigars ...

> I would listen to a stormy sea of babblement, and try to extract some
> constructive intimations. Every now and then I got a whiff of politics.
> It was clear they were against the Lords—against plutocrats—against
> Cossington's newspapers—against the brewers ... It was tremendously
> clear what they were against. The trouble was to find out what on earth
> they were for!

It is interesting to speculate how much artistic licence Wells might have been
employing. But the place of the NLC in political life in his time was not in doubt.
It was the official club of the Liberal Party, and much of the goings-on of the
party took place within the club or were otherwise reflected in the club's activities.[2] In April 1914, for example, the club was the scene of some acerbic political
bickering over one of the great insolubles of British politics, the Irish question.

---

2 Norgate and Wykes (op cit, p 25) erroneously state that the NLC was where Sir Edward Grey
   made his famous remark on the eve of the First World War that 'The lamps are going out all
   over Europe, and we shall not see them lit again in our lifetime.' In fact Grey was in his office in
   the nearby Foreign Office.

Under the heading 'The National Liberal Club and the Army' *The Times* reported:[3]

> Lord Willoughby De Broke called attention to the following words passed at the National Liberal Club on March 31 with the Marquess of Lincolnshire in the chair: "That this meeting views with indignation the unpatriotic attempts of the Tory Party to corrupt the Army and use it as an instrument for the defeat of Parliamentary government," and moved for papers showing specific instances, if any, of corruption of the Army by the Tory Party.

The respective sides went on to exchange barbs using the genteel euphemisms common to the House of Lords then as now. The underlying question was whether the army might not blindly follow orders in Ulster, part of the fall-out from the 'Curragh incident', wherein the army had refused to move against Ulster. We will see more of the Irish question throughout the book, as it directly affected a number of the Savages of the day as well as forming an important consideration for British politics even during the First World War, not least with the Easter Rising of 1916.

The First World War

In Appendix II we will see how the Churchill portrait was moved around the NLC in parallel with how Churchill himself moved around (and out of) the party. During the First World War, Lloyd George and his colleague Brother Savage Rufus Isaacs were given a banquet in their honour at the club, in which Lloyd George mounted an aggressive anti-Tory speech. He attacked his critics, including the journalist and politician Leo Amery.[4] Amery soon retaliated, snorting that Lloyd George's speech had been to 'crow brazen defiance to the public conscience from his own dunghill at the National Liberal Club.'[5]

During the party's 1916–23 split, that 'dunghill' initially tried to follow the parliamentary Liberal Party in accepting the compromise which had Lloyd George as head of the coalition government but Asquith as head of the Liberal Party.[6] In time, though, the NLC rejected Lloyd George and sided firmly with Asquith. Both factions thought themselves the 'true' Liberal party, in a dispute

---

3   23 April 1917.
4   Leo Amery (1873–1955), Conservative Party politician and journalist. The history of the Amery family is a political tale of some magnitude. Leo was an anti-appeaser in the 1930s. During the Second World War, he stood and invoked Cromwell in the House of Commons when he exhorted Chamberlain to 'in the name of God, go' in 1940, an extraordinary demonstration of freedom of speech in wartime. At the same time he made the speech, his son John was collaborating with the Nazis, an action for which he would be hanged at the end of the war.
5   David Faber, *Speaking for England: Leo, Julian and John Amery – the Tragedy of a Political Family* (Pocket Books, 2007), pp 76–77.
6   See Malcolm Noble, 'The NLC during World War 1', *The National Liberal Club News*, Issue 73, November 2017, p 18.

that nowadays looks much like the internecine quarrelling between the various Judean peoples' groups in Monty Python's 1979 film *Life of Brian*. Partly as a result of the split, the Liberals suffered a dramatic decline after the First World War as Labour rose to become the official opposition.

Most of the NLC's Great War machinations did not take place in its normal residence, but in a temporary home at the Westminster Palace Hotel. One Whitehall Place had been requisitioned in 1916 for use as a billet for some exceptionally fortunate Canadian officers. Some NLC members allegedly preferred the new surroundings as they found the atmosphere less political.[7]

Serving officers from the Dominions and sons of members in the forces were elected as 'service members' of the NLC for the duration of the war. As well as opening up its facilities for recreational purposes, office space and accommodation, the NLC made some contributions to the men at the front. At the beginning of 1917, for example, it had raised sufficient funds to provide a refreshments hut for the Western Front, to be managed by the YMCA, but the hut was destroyed by enemy action before it had opened for business. Later the same year, there was a failed effort to improve access to club facilities for female guests.

During 1917, as the Russian Revolution started to ferment, the NLC also sent two optimistic démarches to the Tsar's regime, praising Russia's contribution to the war but expressing hope that it might be accompanied by some social change. The second such missive received the gloomy response 'At such times as these, when Russia is passing through so many grave troubles and anxieties, one appreciates all the more deeply the spirit of sympathy extended to her.'[8]

All was in vain, as the revolutionaries soon swept the Romanovs from power and took Russia out of the war. As we all know, the Allies prevailed nonetheless, and upon the Armistice being signed in November 1918, all of the combatants started to try to adjust to peacetime – save, tragically, Russia herself, whose destructive civil war continued for some years afterwards.

The aftermath

After the war, the resident Canadians were evidently not keen on giving up their rather superior lodgings, since the club held a 'farewell dinner' for them in March 1919 as a none-too-subtle hint. They did move out later that year, and left a stuffed moose head by way of thanks. The club had to close for almost the whole of 1920 to restore the premises to their pre-war splendour – ironically, just as the Liberal Party itself was dissembling amidst factional infighting and the rise of the Labour Party.

---

7   Anthony Lejeune and Malcolm Lewis, *The Gentlemen's Clubs of London* (Dorset Press, 1984), p 157.
8   Noble, op cit, p 21.

Clubland in general not only recovered from the First World War, but had some interesting additions. A cavalry officer, Herbert Buckmaster, set up his own club, 'Buck's', based on an idea he had when serving in the trenches. The club opened in 1919 and is probably best known for giving its name to Buck's Fizz, the champagne-and-orange juice cocktail the club's memorable barman, Mr McGarry, invented in the 1920s (he also invented the Sidecar Cocktail). Buck's was the model for Brother Savage PG Wodehouse's 'Drones Club,' the fictional club of his comic novels.

In the Second World War, clubs again became a valued refuge for members, not least because they were usually able to maintain a decent menu and wine list in spite of rationing. That is a story for another day, so let us turn instead to how the Savage Club itself fared in the Great War.

CHAPTER 2

The Savage Club and the Great War

Pre-First World War

In contrast with the National Liberal Club, the Savage has never had a formal affiliation with a political party, and therefore has always had a rather more varied and interesting membership than politicians and party hacks. It does share the distinction with the NLC of appearing in a nineteenth century novel by one of the eminent authors of the day: the narrator in Sir Arthur Conan Doyle's science fiction novel *The Lost World* belongs to the Club and makes several appearances at 6–7 Adelphi Terrace,[1] as well as wistfully wondering if he would 'live to sit once more on a lounge in the Savage Club and look out on the drab solidity of the Embankment' after witnessing some terrifying sights on his adventures.

The origins of the Club have been covered in several publications and do not need repeating here.[2] A vivid portrait of the Club in its pre-war days can be found in the non-fiction biography of the journalist and prolific novelist George Henty,[3]

---

1   The Club had moved there in 1889, which had proved costly due to the necessary repairs to the building. It had been quite nomadic in the early days, moving five times in its first decade. It lasted at the Adelphi until 1936, when it moved to Carlton House Terrace.

2   See Aaron Watson (ed) *The Savage Club: a medley of history, anecdote and reminiscence* (privately printed, 1907) with an introduction by Mark Twain; Percy Bradshaw's *Brother Savages and Guests: A History of the Savage Club 1857–1957* (WH Allen & Co Ltd, 1958); and *Not So Savage* by Matthew Norgate and Alan Wykes (Jupiter Books, 1976). I will draw on Bradshaw's book the most in these pages. (Bradshaw himself became a Savage in October 1922, under the category of literature.)

3   George Alfred Henty (1832–1902). Henty was best known for his historical adventure stories written in the late nineteenth century. They were as jingoistic and prejudiced as one would have expected. He was phenomenally successful: one estimate is that he sold 25m books during his lifetime (see Brian Thompson, 'A boy's own story', *The Guardian*, 7 December 2002). Nowadays, Henty's work is not much remembered, probably because he was extremely

written by his contemporary author George Manville Fenn (1831–1909). Fenn wrote:[4]

> [Henty] was, of course, a member of various yachting clubs; but coming to literary gatherings, he early became a member of the world-known Savage, which he joined in its old days, and his was a familiar, quiet, thoughtful face at the weekly dinners, while he was a welcome and trusted chairman at the gatherings of the committee. Later, without giving up his membership, he joined, consequent upon some little tiff, the select band of the oldest members, who formed what, if they had been members of Saint Stephen's, would have been called the Cave of Adullam. Here, however, the little branch or lodge was dubbed the Wigwam, whose cognisance, still printed on the circulars which announce the chairman and the date of the next dinner, is a clever sketch of a Red Indian's wigwam ...
>
> On the whole, though, perhaps from its propinquity to the newspaper world, Henty was most frequently seen at that centre of which the late Andrew Halliday wrote that the qualification for admission was to be "a working-man in literature or art, and a good fellow." Of course the rendezvous meant is the Savage Club—that place "apart from the chilling splendour of the modern club," —the club over which so many disputes have taken place amongst its members as to its title, as to whether it borrows from poor, improvident Richard Savage, or from its supposed Bohemian savagery. Be that as it may, it is certainly the spot where the bow of everyday warfare is unstrung and set aside.
>
> It has long been the custom here to invite to dine at the social Saturday evening gathering pretty well everyone who has become famous, and whose name is upon the public lips, and these invitations have been accepted by warrior and statesman, by our greatest artists and travellers, whether they have sought to discover the Boreal mysteries or to cross the Torrid Zone. Even those who have become great rulers have not disdained to accept "Savage" hospitality, and upon such nights some popular or distinguished member of the club is called upon to take the chair. Now it so happens that there is extant a copy of the menu of a dinner, drawn by one of the cleverest members, which depicts in quaint, characteristic, and light-hearted fashion the imaginary proceedings and post-prandial entertainment connected with the aforesaid unstrung bow. In the case in question Lord Kitchener was the guest, fresh from his victories in the Sudan, and no better chairman could have been chosen than the popular war correspondent, George Henty, whose portrait and that of the famous general occupy the centre of the dinner card represented here.

---

politically incorrect by today's standards. Nevertheless, his reputation lasted at least until the 1970s: in Norgate and Wykes, op cit, p132 it is said 'Henty had (and probably still has) a tremendous following for his boys' adventure stories, all of which featured clean-limbed action and glowing cheeks'. Henty was also a distinguished war correspondent, and we will return to him in that context.

4　George Manville Fenn, *George Alfred Henty: the story of an active life* (book on demand, Kindle edn, original publication 1901).

It would be difficult to over-estimate the interest of such a typical meeting at the club, one which had naturally drawn together a crowded gathering of men who had more or less deeply cut their names upon the column popularity, if not fame.

The name of the general and war correspondent attracted to that dinner a distinguished company; the singer possessed of sweet tenor voice or deepest bass; the musician who excelled as pianist or who could bring forth the sweetest tones from the strings; the flautist; the skilful presti-digitator who puzzled the gathering with the latest Egyptian card trick, but who will amuse no more; the clever actor ready to give expression to some recitation, serious or laughable; the delineator of quaint phases of life; the artist whose works have provoked thought and admiration in the picture galleries; the scientist with the secrets of his laboratory gradually developing into life-saving and labour-economising reforms; to say nothing of the keen-visaged diplomatist whose range covers the mysteries of the chancelleries of Europe and cabinets where whispers are sacred and policies are shaped; and the writer to whom the wide world is but the sunning ground of cogitation.

At the club's improvised concerts and entertainments all are ready to amuse or be amused; even the learned judge and the argumentative counsel who takes his brief from some clever lawyer, now his compan-ion for the evening, meet the eye of physician or surgeon upon common ground.

Later, the deeply-engaged actor, when his part is at an end, comes in straight from the boards, bringing with him the buoyancy and imag-inativeness of the strange fantastic realm where he is so popular—a realm so different from all others, although merely divided from the commonplace world by a row of lights.

Here all are friends, gathered by the attractions of music, song, and repartee. Men who have striven greatly all their lives and have gained much, and maybe lost something too, are here in good fellowship. Irksome trammels for the time are cast aside, permitting one and all to partake of what seems to be like a whiff of ozone or a breath from the pine-scented Surrey hills, after the contracted arena of the struggle for life.

On the particular occasion referred to above, supported as he was by those who had shared his past and been his companions and the witnesses of many a deadly battle, Henty was thoroughly at home; and it was a happy choice of a chairman which brought him to preside on that November evening when Kitchener was the special guest.

It was only a few short months after Kitchener's crowning victory at Omdurman, which had finally crushed the Dervish power and set Slatin and his fellow captives free, and established law and order at Khartoum and through the immense territories which separate that city from Cairo. It was, therefore, a bright idea that inspired Oliver Paque, to give him his *nom de plume*, in his merry caricature to depict the gallant general as a *beau sabreur* leading a charge at full gallop and riding in to the feast. He is seen, as the illustration shows, leaping triumphantly through a circus paper hoop supported by a swarthy Sudanese, and the tatters of the paper ingeniously form the map of Africa. Right through Africa he leaps, as it were, into the fire of cheers and applause that greet him—into the smoke of the "Savage" pipe of peace, started by the chairman.

But that memorable night is not so far back in the Hinterland that one has any need to strain the memory assiduously for the leading details of historic incidents sketched in upon the menu card. The tattered indication of a map recalls Major Marchand and his march across desert and through forest and swamp to Fashoda. There are pleasant suggestions, too, in the tribute paid to the chairman by the artist's pencil, which playfully deals with the fame the chairman had reaped by his books. Boys are shown eagerly reading his thrilling tales of history and adventure, a young mother is depicted admonishing a lad who is engrossed in some stirring work, while the list of titles—*A Dash for Khartoum, True to the Old Flag, Through the Fray, By Right of Conquest, Held Fast for England*—is alone a tribute to the sturdy chairman, for thought titles only they illustrate the feelings of a patriotic man.

The pen-painter of the merry scene, indeed, notwithstanding the grotesqueness of the work, has contrived to suggest by many a happy touch little peculiarities in the individualities of his subjects. Thus he gives a wonderful likeness of such a familiar member as Dan Godfrey, the well-known band-master of the Guards, who is shown leading the concert in heroic bearskin what time Handel's march of 'The Conquering Hero' is blown by one of the most popular humourists of the club. The name of another member—Slaughter—seems by the irony of fate to be singularly apposite at a war correspondent's banquet, while the drum and cymbals and the tom-tom tell their own tale as beaten by members whose faces are familiar to those behind the scenes. Everything, in short, tended to make this dinner a great success.

Sometimes when taking the chair, however, at one of these club dinners, Henty would fancy that the attendance was not so good as it might have been, and attributing it to a want of popularity, he would turn to the writer and whisper with almost a sigh, "Another frost!" This quaint bit of dramatic slang is, of course, popularly used in the theatrical world when the British public displays a tendency not to throng the seats, and there is a grim array of empty benches to crush all the spirit out of the actors in some clever piece. It was quite a mistake, though, to use it in connection with Henty's dinners, for he was always surrounded by plenty of warm-hearted friends whose presence and sunshiny aspect were sufficient to set the wintry chill of unsociability at defiance.

None of the above would be wholly out of place in a twenty-first century edition of *Drumbeat,* and it therefore provides some indication of the Club's continuity in a world that has otherwise changed out of much recognition.

As can be gleaned from Fenn's account, a number of famous people passed through the doors of the Savage Club as guests. One of the most notable appearances was by Gladstone, while he was in the middle of his 'Midlothian campaign'.[5] On 14 June 1879 he wrote in his diary:[6]

> 6-11. Attended the dinner of the Savage Club. Too long and the clouds of tobacco were fearful. In other respects most interesting. It was impossible to speak ill of so quick and sympathetic an audience. I returned thanks for Literature & was (like the ensemble) too long; but nothing could exhaust their patience.

The *Spectator* magazine had some more details of the occasion:[7]

> Mr Gladstone, in responding on behalf of "Literature" on Saturday, at the Savage Club, made some terse and amusing remarks on the tendency of any special life, like the political, to temper the cunning of those who led it to its own sphere, and unfit it for any other sphere. He had been told by a great oculist, Mr Alexander, that when invited to play in a cricket match he had decidedly refused, and refused on the ground that it would cost him £5,000 a year. To accustom his hand to handling the bat and driving the ball, would have been to unfit it for removing cataracts, or performing those other delicate operations in which success depends on the most exquisite delicacy of touch. And so it was also in a different world; the rough play of politics demoralised a man for the finer departments of literature.

The next day Gladstone recorded himself as being 'laid up with deranged liver & bowels'. His doctor prescribed castor oil and tactfully laid the blame on 'eight hours of heat & on preserved peas'. Gladstone's biographer Roy Jenkins thought a simpler explanation was that he had a crashing hangover.

For another example of eminent guests, Cecil Harmsworth MP[8] wrote in his diary for 10 December 1910:

> Fifty-third Annual Dinner of the Savage Club at the Hotel Cecil, Sir George Reid, High Commissioner for Australia, in the Chair.

---

5   The Midlothian campaign was a series of foreign policy speeches made by Gladstone that together formed what some have called the first modern political campaign. They unified the Liberal Party under Gladstone and led to his second ministry the following year. See Richard Price, *British Society 1680 – 1880: Dynamism, Containment and Change* (Cambridge University Press, 1999), p 289.

6   Roy Jenkins, *Gladstone* (Pan Macmillan, 1995, 2012 Kindle edn).

7   *Spectator,* 21 June 1879, p 3.

8   First Baron Harmsworth (1869–1948). He was the younger brother of the press barons Lord (Alfred) Northcliffe and Lord Rothermere. Although he played a role in the early development of the Harmsworth press, Cecil mostly worked as a Liberal MP, representing Droitwich from 1906 to 1910 and Luton from 1911 to 1922. See Andrew Thorpe and Richard Toye (eds), *Parliament and Politics in the Age of Asquith and Lloyd George: The Diaries of Cecil Harmsworth MP, 1909–22* (Camden Fifth Series) (Cambridge University Press, 2016). Harmsworth clearly enjoyed the dinner, for he was nominated for membership of the Club in December 1910, and elected in June 1911.

I attend as guest of Mr E. W. Roper and in obedience to an urgent invitation of the Committee two days ago I propose the toast of the "Savage Club coupled with the name of Sir G. Reid". A brilliant assembly including General French[9] and Field Marshal Lord Grenfell.[10] We adjourn afterwards to the Club house in the Adelphi.

In June 1913, the well-attended Savage Club ladies' dinner offered some genial thoughts on gender relations:[11]

> The chairman [the Earl of Dunraven] in proposing the health of the ladies, said that he had been told there were sometimes some little differences of opinion as to the relative capacity of the two sexes to perform certain unimportant and insignificant duties, but there was not and could not be any possible difference of opinion as to the fact that in the great republic of letters and art they were perfectly equal. It was the individual who counted. He thought that mere man was under a certain disadvantage in the fact that by his totally illogical devotion to logic and his intense desire to have everything brought down to demonstrable facts he lost in the much greater field of intuition.
>
> MRS ALICE PERRIN spoke of the various conceptions of what was meant by "a lady", the old notion being that a lady was a woman who did not work with her hands. So far as a man was concerned it had been said that an unmarried man lived as a gentleman and died like a dog, while a married man lived like a dog and died as a gentleman.

It should be remembered that women did not even have the vote at the time, or the opportunity to work in the professions, or protection against discrimination in such employment as they were able to secure – hence the rise of the Suffragettes, who by the time of the Savage dinner were undertaking not just peaceful protests, but also those involving burning of public buildings, vandalising art in public galleries and hunger strikes resulting in force-feeding. Perhaps most dramatically of all, on the very same day as the Savage dinner, Emily Davison died from the injuries she had sustained at the Derby a few days earlier when staging what modern writers would call a 'direct action' protest against George V's horse Anmer.[12]

9　Field Marshal John Denton Pinkstone French, 1st Earl of Ypres (1852–1925), commander of the British Expeditionary Force at the outbreak of the First World War and effectively sacked at the end of 1915; we shall return to him more than once. He was made a peer in 1916, sardonically remarking that he should have been Lord St Omer – 'sent home-r' – since he had effectively been sacked from command at the end of 1915, and an earl in 1922.

10　Francis Wallace Grenfell (1841–1925). He was made a field marshal in 1908, the year of his retirement.

11　*The Times*, 9 June 1913. Note the scale of the dinner: over 300 guests attended; the venue was the Connaught Rooms.

12　The traditional recounting of events, as repeated in history lessons worldwide, was that Davison stepped out onto the course and deliberately threw herself under the royal runner as the field negotiated Epsom's sharp downhill bend known as Tattenham Corner. While modern

Distinguished dinners such as those mentioned above persuaded the author Nigel Cross that the Club had become 'almost respectable' by the First World War.[13] Nevertheless, not every historian of London clubs has been entirely complimentary about the early days of the Savage. Phillip Waller, in *Writers, Readers and Reputations: Literary Life in Britain 1870–1918*, was rather disparaging. Having quoted Brother Savage Andrew Halliday, editor of *The Savage Club Papers* (1868), on the Club's origins as 'a place of reunion, where, in their hours of leisure, they might gather together and enjoy each other's society, apart from the publicity of that which was known in Johnson's time as the "Coffee House", and equally apart from the chilling splendour of the modern club', he then wrote rather condescendingly:[14]

> This account ... was a virtual admission that its members' literary attainments and/or social positions had been deemed below par for The Club and other institutions of comparable standing in mid-Victorian England. That doubtfulness was personified by one of the founders, George Sala;[15] and it originally met in Vinegar Yard, across from the pit entrance to Drury Lane Theatre. Brother Savages revelled in a self-description as "intellectual Bohemians", but their attempt to demonstrate to other clubs what they were missing, by producing an annual volume of miscellaneous stories and essays, proved embarrassing when a gap of over a quarter of a century opened up between publication of the second Savage Club Papers in 1869 and the third in 1897.

Waller dismissed the quality of the 1897 publication as 'beta and below' and said 'Henry de Mosenthal, a Fellow of the Institute of Chemistry, contributed a dull history of dynamite. This rather epitomised the whole: the world of Literature was not going to be detonated by Savages.'

Since nineteenth century members included writers of the calibre of

---

observers disagree as to the extent of Davison's field of vision, and therefore her ability to target Anmer, the consensus now seems to be that her purpose was to either attach a Suffragette scarf to a horse's bridle or disrupt the race generally, not to pull a horse down as alleged in the immediate aftermath or die in the cause of the Suffragette movement. Interestingly, the historical revision has involved hi-tech video analysis as three British Pathé cameras covered the race. See for example Elizabeth Crawford, *The Women's Suffrage Movement: A Reference Guide 1866–1928* (UCL Press, 2003), Michael Tanner, *The Suffragette Derby* (The Robson Press, 2013) and Vanessa Thorpe, 'Truth behind the death of suffragette Emily Davison is finally revealed', *The Observer*, 26 May 2013.

13 Nigel Cross, *The Common Writer: Life in Nineteenth-Century Grub Street* (Cambridge University Press, 1988), p 108.

14 Oxford University Press, 2006, pp 515–516.

15 Sala was a controversial sort in his earlier days. One of his contemporaries wrote in 1870 that he was 'often drunken, always in debt, sometimes in prison, and ... totally disreputable'. Sala successfully sued the writer for libel. See Peter Blake, *George Augustus Sala and the Nineteenth-Century Periodical Press: The Personal Style of a Public Writer* (Routledge, 2016), p 4.

WS Gilbert, JM Barrie,[16] Weedon and George Grossmith,[17] and Jerome K Jerome,[18] as well as less-remembered polymaths such as Professor Francis Elgar,[19] I think his criticisms a bit harsh, even if early Club publications were infrequent and of uneven quality. However modest and bohemian the origins, there is little doubt the Savage had made its way to respectability by the early twentieth century. Ironically, it received a rebuke for having gone *too far* in that direction from none other than Oscar Wilde, who complained 'I never enter the Savage Club. It tires me so. It used to be gentlemanly Bohemian, but ever since the Prince of Wales became a member and sometimes dines there, it is nothing but savagely snobbish.'[20] One wonders how much Wildean humour was at play there but, either way, the Savages of the day might have laughed off the insults. Aaron Watson wrote in his 1907 book of the Club:[21]

> In the Savage Club, it must be admitted, there is as little mutual admiration—or, at any rate, as little inclination to express it—as is to be found among any assembly of mortal men. Rudeness, based on real friendship, and such as only a very real friendship can tolerate, are much more common than compliments. Instead of log-rolling, the Savages are somewhat given to baiting their brethren. It is all done in the way of good-fellowship, but with a frank understanding that it is not good Bohemian form to be thin-skinned.

Jerome had a good anecdote illustrating the sentiment, concerning the Canadian novelist and British politician Gilbert Parker,[22] of whom he

---

16 Barrie joined in May 1889. At the time he was very proud of his membership, and wrote to a friend afterwards 'To think of it, and I was once obscure': Lisa Chaney, *Hide-And-Seek With Angels: The Life of JM Barrie* (Hutchinson, 2005). Barrie joined the Garrick the following year and a number of other clubs too, though he rarely went to any. In a short private autobiography of his early years (*The Greenwood Hat, being a memoir of James Anon 1885–1887*), he noted how he came closer to attending the Savage than any other, since he lived very near the Club while it was in the Adelphi, enabling him to watch members come and go 'as if I were in a lofty private box'. See Barrie, *The Complete Works of JM Barrie* (Delphi Classics, 2013, Kindle edn).

17 Co-authors of the 1893 comic novel *Diary of a Nobody*.

18 See Carolyn W de la L Oulton, *Below the Fairy City: A Life of Jerome K Jerome* (Victorian Secrets, 2012), p 98. Incidentally, arguably the most famous of all nineteenth-century authors, Charles Dickens, was not a member, but assisted with early fundraising efforts by the Club and his son served as Club Treasurer for three years.

19 Professor Francis Elgar FRS, FRSE, LLD (1845–1909), a brilliant naval architect and talented author, whose work was particularly distinguished in the technical field of ship stability. He joined the Club in March 1886.

20 Quoted in Barbara Black, *A Room of His Own: A Literary-Cultural Study of Victorian Clubland* (Ohio University Press, 2012), p 269.

21 Aaron Watson, op cit, p 14.

22 Gilbert Parker MP, LLD, DCL (1862–1932). Parker began as a teacher in his native Canada but gained later fame in Britain as a romantic novelist. During the war, he was employed by the British as a propagandist to try and get the Americans onside. His efforts, known as the 'White Papers,' were sent into *The New York Times* in 1914. Gilbert employed quotes from the works of Kipling, Wells, Bernard Shaw and others as well as his own rather purple prose.

said 'there was a feeling that after his marriage he had become more impressive than was needful.' Jerome continued:[23]

> I remember one evening at the Savage Club. He had kindly looked in upon us, on his way to some reception. He moved about, greeting affably one man after another. Eventually he came across Odell, an old actor; his address now is the Charterhouse, where Colonel Newcome heard the roll call. Odell was an excellent raconteur, one of the stars of the club. Sir Gilbert laid a hand upon his shoulder.
>
> "You must come down and see me, Odell," he said. "Fix a day and write me. You know the address. B—Court."
>
> "Delighted," answered Odell. "What number?"

The best riposte to Savage critics is the words of the Savage members found throughout this book. They show conclusively that, regardless of its origins, the Club flourished in the Edwardian period and up to the Second World War, attracting many of London's literary, scientific and artistic *haute société*.

First World War

When the war began, the Club's management committee was anxious to 'do its bit'. It resolved that up to 25 staff officers in London would be invited to accept honorary membership. It further resolved that no enemy alien would be permitted to enter the Club, either as member or guest, for the duration of hostilities. That proved to be no empty gesture: one Dr Sven Hedin was stricken from the membership due to his 'antagonistic attitude towards Britain', while a Dr Hans Plehn was removed on the ground that he was an enemy alien.[24]

Some wartime hardships found their way to the Club, although it has to be said that surviving menu cards do not disclose much in the way of privation. In August 1914, Scotland Yard decreed that no intoxicating liquors should be consumed after 11pm and in October 1914 the cut-off time was changed to 10pm.

---

23 Jerome K Jerome *The Complete Works of Jerome K Jerome* (Delphi Classics, 2013, Kindle edn). Odell seems to have turned into a major liability for the Club after a while, since he was forever running up a bar tab he was unable to pay, and regularly offering the weakest of excuses and promises to the committee.

24 Meanwhile, the German-born Herman Oelsner, who held a chair in Romance languages at Oxford from 1909 to 1913, was charged in October 1914 with failing to register and residing within a prohibited area without a permit. *The Times* reported that he had offered various documents which the court felt insufficient to establish his identity, and ordered an adjournment. It added 'Applying for bail, which was refused, the professor gave the names of university professors and members of the Savage Club.' Oelsner wrote to the paper shortly afterwards, complaining that he had not given any names of professors or the Savages to the court, but added that he had been treated 'with the utmost courtesy'. See *The Times*, 27 and 29 October 1914. On the latter date he appeared in court again and on that occasion was released on bail, the bench being satisfied as to his identity but ordering a copy of his father's naturalisation certificate.

In 1915, the Club committee proposed that town members be asked to pay a voluntary War Tax of £1 1s 0d and country members 10s 6d. Later the same year, a number of members decided to raise a special reserve fund to preserve the Club during the war years, by taking up life memberships of £52 10s 0d.

In the autumn of 1915, the Club resolved to bring together some brief recollections and sketches by members, to celebrate the completion of a quarter of a century's occupation of the premises at Adelphi Terrace, and to mark Thomas Catling's[25] fortieth year in the position of honorary auditor to the Club. A special committee was appointed, and many old and new members sent in literary, pictorial, and musical contributions.

In January 1916, a notable occasion took place in the form of a dinner with Louis Raemaekers, the great Dutch artist and cartoonist, as the special guest. Raemaekers had been living in his home country of the Netherlands when the war broke out. As a neutral country, the Netherlands received many Belgian refugees in the first few months following the German invasion. Raemaekers began drawing graphic descriptions of the refugees themselves and of the German atrocities that they described to him. His work became famous across the world, and obtained much respect given that the audience knew it was based on first-hand testimony. Anti-German propagandists in Britain, France and America therefore drew extensively on his work.

Raemaekers moved to London in 1915. At his Savage dinner, Brother Savage Lance Thackeray was in the chair – one of the very last social occasions Thackeray attended before his death. Thackeray presented one of his own drawings. Raemaekers drew what *The Times* called 'an admirable and characteristic portrait of the Kaiser' in about three minutes at the start of the dinner, and also presented it to the Club. Thackeray then announced 'Everybody knows Raemaekers and his indictment of Germany, and we give him the only compliment we can pay to anybody', following which all present sang 'For he's a jolly good fellow'. *The Times* reported further:[26]

> Mr Raemakers also made a short and sprightly speech in English in which (alluding to the fact that former guests of the club on similar occasions had been the explorers Peary and Shackleton) he gave a fanciful description of his own explorations in the infernal regions, where he had found devil busy plotting to overthrow the Allies, a task which he found so difficult that he now had the presumption—"Gott mit uns"—to apply to the Almighty for help.

---

25 Thomas Catling (1838–1920), journalist and author.

26 *The Times*, 31 January 1916. Note Raemaekers mentioning the legendary Savage explorers; after his time would come, among others, Aimé Félix Tschiffely (who joined the Savage Club in September 1937), and Sir Francis Younghusband, who was made an honorary life member of the Savage Club in 1923.

The dinner was also recalled in the foreword to a 1917 collection of Raemaekers'
work, by Brother Savage J Murray Allison:[27]

> What he actually saw with his own eyes he does not tell. But a hundred
> of his early cartoons bear witness to the burning impression made upon
> his soul. Raemaekers, like others who have seen them, cannot speak of
> these unnameable horrors, but can only express his consuming pity or
> his white-hot rage in the medium that lies nearest his hand. On one
> occasion only has he publicly referred to his experiences in Belgium.
> It was at a dinner given him by the artists and literary men of London
> at the Savage Club, where, pointing to the portraits and trophies of
> Peary, Scott, Nansen, Shackleton, and other explorers which hang on
> the walls, he said: "I, too, have been an explorer, Gentlemen. I have
> explored a hell, and it was terror unspeakable."

At about the same time as the Raemaekers dinner, the Savage Club found itself
in the unenviable position of being a litigant in the Chancery Division of the
High Court.[28] The case came about through some peculiarly Savage circumstances. Brother Savage David Louis, not otherwise well known to history, died
leaving a substantial estate. In his will he left various chattels to his friends, dona-
tions to a number of charities including the Salvation Army and the vicar of
St James's, Piccadilly, and then £650 to the Savage Benevolent Fund. The will had
two memoranda, the second of which went on to explain:

> I have frequently noticed gloomy looks dispelled by the simple expres-
> sion, 'Have a drink, old chap.' Now I should like to be able to say this to
> some Brother Savages for ever, and therefore I have directed in my will
> that a sum to yield twenty-six pounds a year be placed at the disposal
> of the Benevolent Fund for that purpose.

> This will enable a few Savages to have a drink or smoke with Louis
> every day, to be consumed by himself, to the extent of not more than
> sixpence any one member per day; a day to start at 2pm, and, at the
> closing of the club for the day any balance from day to day may be
> added to that available for the next day throughout the week, but any
> balance from a week remaining on Monday morning shall be devoted
> to the usual purposes of the Benevolent Fund.

---

27 Louis Raemaekers, *Raemaekers' Cartoons of the Great War vol 1* (Abela Publishing, 2014).
    Raemaekers' publication in America formed part of the concerted propaganda efforts on the
    part of the British and French to bring American public opinion onside. It was accompa-
    nied by a lecture tour of the country by Raemaekers himself, which was a great success: as
    well as his speaking engagements, he met President Woodrow Wilson and former President
    Theodore Roosevelt. He also signed a contract to work with the papers of William Randolph
    Hearst, one of America's most controversial media magnates (and the model for Orson Welles'
    masterpiece Citizen Kane), to great surprise since Hearst's papers were generally sympathetic
    to the Germans. Raemaekers knew that, and reasoned his work would provide an antidote to
    the pro-German line of the papers.
28 *Re Louis – Louis v Treloar*, Times Law Reports, *The Times*, 18 February 1916.

In connexion with this fund I should like, in the first instance, amongst my many old friends, Billy Barrett, E. J. Odell, Muddock, and Hugh Moss to have the first call each day, but this is not to be cumulative, that is, if any one of these old friends does not exercise his right the moneys so available go to the general fund the next day, and so on until the Monday of the next week.

It is hard to imagine a will more in keeping with the spirit of the Savage Club. Unfortunately, the trustees were unsure as to its validity, since the second memorandum had been expressly stated not to form part of the will. It is not clear from the law report of the case why that was so; it seems contradictory on the part of Louis or his advisers. Whatever the explanation, the trustees had to apply to the High Court seeking a declaration that the directions in the second memorandum were valid. Their application was opposed by the Salvation Army and the vicar of St James's.

The trustees argued that the second memorandum, although not admitted to probate, was a contemporaneous document referred to in the will and identified, and could be looked at for the purpose of construing the bequest.

The Salvation Army argued that the memorandum was not incorporated in the will, and its contents had not been communicated to the trustees of the Benevolent Fund until after Louis' death, and therefore the trusts should fail and the £650 given to the residue of the estate. The vicar of St James's supported that argument.

Sadly for the Savages, Mr Justice Neville ruled against the trustees. The law stated that where a bequest was made on trusts not declared in the will, evidence of the trusts were admissible if they were communicated to the legatee before the death of the testator. There had been no such communication in Louis' case. Secondly:

> The cases showed that where a document was incorporated by reference in a will it formed part of the will. Here the testator had expressly directed that the memorandum was not to form part of his will and it had not been admitted to probate, and when he wished a document to be incorporated he had said so, because he had directed that the first memorandum should form part of his will. Therefore the contents of the second memorandum were expressly excluded from the will and could not be taken into consideration for the purpose of construing the will.

The case therefore failed and the money passed under the residuary gift to the other charities.

More enjoyably, the Club double-celebratory publication begun in 1915 was finished in March 1916. It was entitled *A Savage Club Souvenir* and was in the form of a hardcover book, 244 pages long with illustrations, dedicated to Thomas Catling.[29] A copy along with a portfolio containing the original drawings and manuscripts was presented to Catling on 11 March, at a dinner presided over by Yeend King.[30]

In 1917, the effect of German submarine warfare on British imports was starting to be felt. On 22 February, Club members received an unwelcome message:

> On and after Monday, 25th inst., members will be able to obtain meat dishes in the Club only on production of their Meat Card. Meat will only be served at luncheon, and will consist as nearly as possible of 5oz and 2½oz. of uncooked meat, and the waitress will detach a whole or half coupon according to the item ordered. Those who desire to obtain all or part of their meat ration in the Club should complete the attached form and return it to the Secretary at once.

Despite those difficulties, it seems that the Club prospered financially during the war. Assets exceeded liabilities by an average of more than £2000 per year from 1908 to 1918. Saturday dinners continued throughout the conflict and the annual and ladies' dinners were all well attended. Evidently, people needed the escapism of the Club in those darkest of times.

The attitude of the Club in remaining open was consistent with that of the West End generally: restaurants and theatres in Covent Garden did a prosperous trade throughout the war. No fewer than 150 illegal nightclubs opened up in Soho alone during the conflict. Moreover, the shows in the West End were rarely serious drama, especially as the war went on, and instead 'a frilly array of pantomimes, musicals, revues and farces.'[31]

Not all were in agreement with the need for such distractions. WG Grace, the great Victorian cricketer, famously wrote an article not long after hostilities broke out in which he declared that the playing of cricket should be suspended forthwith. Shortly after Grace's article appeared, Brother Savage Lord Roberts uttered similar sentiments when he told a New Army battalion of the Royal Fusiliers: 'I respect and honour you more than I can say. My feeling towards you is one of intense admiration. How very different is your action to that of the men, who can still go on with their cricket and football, as if the very existence of our nation

---

29 See *A Savage Club Souvenir* (privately printed, 1916), p ix.
30 Henry John Yeend King (1855–1924), an important Victorian genre and landscape artist. He studied under William Bromley and in Paris under Leon Bonnat and Fernand Cormon. He lived in London most of his life but specialised in scenes of rustic genre and the countryside, rather than the more austere industrial cities of the day. His *Times* obituary described him as 'a real Bohemian, with a wonderful collection of funny stories, which he told well' – the model Savage, in other words.
31 Richard Morrison, 'It's time we learnt a lesson from the Great War – and cheered up', *The Times*, 29 December 2017.

were not at stake.'[32] *The Times* thundered 'We view with indignation and alarm the persistence of Association Football clubs in doing their best for the enemy' while Sir Arthur Conan Doyle weighed in with his own injunction 'If the cricketer has a straight eye let him look along the barrel of a gun. If a footballer has strength of limb let them serve and march in the field of battle.'

Then there were those who indulged in what would nowadays be called 'virtue signalling' – making pointless gestures involving no contribution to the real problem and no real hardship on their part. The august-sounding members of the Library Commission of the Wandsworth Borough Council, for example, resolved to ban the circulation of all works of fiction during the period of the war. They prompted an indignant exchange of correspondence in *The Daily Telegraph*.[33]

Such killjoys should have remembered the genius that was *The Wipers Times*,[34] the sublime satirical publication produced in the trenches by serving soldiers who endured the full horrors of war, yet were still able to make jokes about whether they were being 'offensive enough'. The paper regularly ran spoof letters which perfectly captured a suburban British pettifogging mentality that will be instantly recognisable to readers of *The Daily Telegraph* in the present day. Here are just two examples:

> Sir,
>
> Whilst walking along the Rue de Lille the other night, a gentleman (sic) coming in the opposite direction accosted me quite abruptly with the words "Who are you?" When I told him not to be so inquisitive he became quite offensive, and assumed a threatening attitude. This incident was repeated several times before I had reached the Square. I endeavoured to find a constable, but could not. Where are our police, and what are they doing? Have any more readers had the similar unpleasant experience?
>
> Yours, etc,
>
> TIMIDITY

> Sir,
>
> Several noted farmers have complained of wanton injury done to their fields. They cannot catch the offenders, and the irritating frequency with which they find neat round holes dug in their fields has led them to prepare a strongly worded protest. They are supported by the Mayor of Wulverghem, and wish me to ask you if they may also rely on you.
>
> Yours, etc.
>
> RIGHT IS MIGHT

---

32 Andrew Riddoch and John Kemp, *When the Whistle Blows: The Story of the Footballers' Battalion in the Great War* (Haynes Publishers, 2008), p 22. As they go on to recount, professional footballers created their own 'Pals Battalion' later on.

33 See Gavin Fuller (ed), *The Telegraph Book of Readers' Letters from the Great War* (Aurum Press, 2014), pp 175–80.

34 *The Wipers Times* (Conway Publishing, 2013).

The Savage Club, by remaining open for business throughout, was clearly of the same mentality as *The Wipers Times* and the West End, realising that anyone would go stir crazy if they had nothing other than the war in their lives.

Club dinners were hosted for a number of important military figures. Admiral Sir Percy Scott[35] was the special guest in 1915. In 1916, a dinner was held with Lord Moulton chairing and guests comprising military representatives from France, Russia, Belgium, Romania, Italy and Japan – an occasion particularly noteworthy since it was extremely rare for Moulton to allow himself any time away from his war duties.

In 1917, Sir John Jellicoe was in the chair, only a year after he had been on board HMS *Iron Duke* commanding the Grand Fleet in the Battle of Jutland. In the same year, the Club featured in an interesting vignette when one Edward Pearce, aged 50, was charged with wearing military uniform without lawful authority. He had been seen in the Savage Club wearing the uniform of a captain in the New Zealand Medical Corps, to which he was not entitled.[36]

The Club suffered one further hardship as the war proceeded to its end in 1918, in the form of a whisky shortage. It was somewhat ironic given that General Haig's family were well-known whisky distillers. Percy Bradshaw later mused 'it was resolved that consumption should be limited to four bottles per day until further notice. Some of our veterans never fully recovered from this blow. A little later, the price of our house-dinners was raised to four shillings for members and five shillings for guests.'[37]

The Savage Great War Memorial Plaque

After the war, the Savage, like most institutions, commissioned a memorial plaque for its members who had died in uniform during the conflict. The Savage chose the famous sculptor Brother Savage Albert Toft (1862–1949) to design and build the plaque.

Toft came from a family of Staffordshire artists in pottery and silverwork. He was apprenticed to the Wedgwood pottery as a young man, and in 1879, he won a National Scholarship to the National Art Training Schools (the predecessor of the Royal College of Art), where he studied under Edouard Lanteri. His famous non-military works included *Lilith, Spring, The Spirit of Contemplation, The Metal*

---

35 Admiral Sir Percy Moreton Scott (1853–1924). He was a brilliant engineer and one of the most foresighted admirals in history, being at the leading edge of naval gunnery, land-based artillery, depth charges and anti-aircraft fire. Following the Japanese victory at Tsushima, he had been one of the proponents of big gun ships – the thinking which led to HMS *Dreadnought* – and as early as 1919 he argued in print that the aircraft carrier should replace the battleship. See Percy Scott, *Fifty Years in the Royal Navy* (John Murray, 1919), p 332.

36 *The Times*, 20 November 1917, p 5.

37 Bradshaw, op cit, p 75.

Pourer and *The Bather*. He was elected to the Art Workers Guild in 1891 and published a book, *Modelling and Sculpture*, in 1911. He became an exponent of the 'New Sculpture' movement. According to the Tate Gallery website:[38]

> New sculpture is a name applied to the sculptures produced by a group of artists working in the second half of the nineteenth century.
>
> The term was coined by critic Edmund Gosse in an 1876 article in *Art Journal* titled *The New Sculpture* in which he identified this new trend in sculpture. Its distinguishing qualities were a new dynamism and energy as well as physical realism, mythological or exotic subject matter and use of symbolism, as opposed to prevailing style of frozen neoclassicism. It can be considered part of symbolism.
>
> The keynote work was seen by Gosse as Lord Fredrick Leighton's *Athlete Wrestling with a Python*, but the key artist was Sir Alfred Gilbert[39] followed by Sir George Frampton. An important precursor was [the] Michelangelesque work of Alfred Stevens.

The best known example of the movement was Gilbert's statue of Eros (actually Anteros) which quickly became a legendary landmark at Piccadilly Circus.[40]

In his later years, Toft was elected a Fellow of the Royal Society of British Sculptors. He excelled at portrait busts. His one of Gladstone, made in 1888 and housed in the NLC to this day, was thought to be the best anyone made of the Grand Old Man of Victorian politics.[41] He also made busts of fellow Savages including George Odell,[42] Sir Henry Irving and Lord Kitchener.

Toft also made memorials commemorating the Second Boer War, such as the Welsh National Memorial in Cardiff. He was therefore an obvious choice following the First World War when so many more war memorials were tragically required across the nation. Among other works, Toft created the Royal Fusiliers (City of London Regiment) Memorial at Holborn Bars,[43] the Chadderton

---

38 http://www.tate.org.uk/art/art-terms/n/new-sculpture.

39 Brother Savage Sir Alfred Gilbert RA (1854–1934).

40 The proper name for the sculpture is the Shaftesbury Memorial Fountain, erected in 1892–1893 to commemorate the philanthropic works of the Victorian politician and philanthropist Lord Shaftesbury. It was originally placed in the centre of Piccadilly Circus but after the Second World War was moved to its now familiar position at the Southeastern side. Gilbert's winged nude at the top is usually and wrongly called Eros, when it is actually a statue of his brother, Anteros. The fact of a nude sculpture caused some controversy initially but the public was largely untroubled.

Gilbert was also responsible for the tomb of Albert Victor, Duke of Clarence in St George's Chapel, Windsor, and The Queen Alexandra Memorial, Marlborough Gate, London, now a Grade 1 listed building. When Gilbert died in 1934, Toft attended his funeral as a representative of the Savage Club (see *The Times*, 8 November 1934).

41 'Grand old Man' or 'the G.O.M.' was one of the affectionate nicknames bestowed upon Gladstone by his supporters, though Disraeli suggested the initials stood for 'God's Only Mistake'. Gladstone was also known as 'The People's William'.

42 Presented to the Club at the end of the Great War, in November 1918, by Sir George Frampton.

43 An exact copy stands as the 41st Division Memorial at Flers in France.

War Memorial in Oldham, and the Monument to Captain Albert Ball VC, the legendary fighter ace, in the grounds of Nottingham Castle.[44] In conjunction with a firm of architects, he created the seated bronze allegorical figures representing the Navy, Army, Air Force and Women's Services as an integral part of the design of the Hall of Memory in Centenary Square, Birmingham.

Toft has been described as 'socially gregarious', and a 'stalwart of the Savage Club, figuring prominently in their affairs, frequently presiding over their House Dinners'.[45] After his fame increased he liked to give the Club's address as his own.[46] He was, therefore, the natural and obvious choice to commemorate the fallen Savages.

The plaque was unveiled at the Club on 5 July 1922 by the guest of honour, Brother Savage Field Marshal Sir William Robertson. The event was commemorated in *The Times* newspaper the following day.

The names on the Savage plaque were appropriately set in alphabetical order and not divided into officers and other ranks. They were (as set out on the plaque itself):

2nd Lt Harry Alexander

Pte Cecil Chesterton

Capt AK Harvey-James (*A Scott Craven*)

FM The Earl Kitchener

2nd L^t A Wyatt Papworth

L^t C^{ol} JM Richardson

FM The Earl Roberts

Major Charles CS Scott-Gatty

Lce Cpl Lance Thackeray

---

44 Captain Ball was the highest scoring British flying ace at the time of his death in May 1917 and he was fourth overall at the end of the war. As well as the Victoria Cross, Ball was posthumously given the *Croix de Chevalier, Légion d'honneur* from the French government.

Ball crashed behind enemy lines, with no sign of battle damage; he had most probably become disorientated as many pilots had before him. The Germans, well aware of Ball's eminence, buried him in Annoeullin with full military honours. They erected a cross bearing the inscription *In Luftkampf gefallen für sein Vaterland Engl. Flieger Hauptmann Albert Ball, Royal Flying Corps* ('Fallen in air combat for his fatherland English pilot Captain Albert Ball'), just as the British buried the Red Baron, Manfred Von Richthofen, with much ceremony when he was shot down over their lines.

45 Norgate and Wykes reproduced two of the menus for Toft's dinners (op cit, pp 88–89), including a striking one from 7 December 1918 which depicted Toft chiselling a triumphalist female figure holding a sword aloft – the dinner scheduled less than a month after the end of the Great War.

46 See http://www.glasgowsculpture.com/pg_biography.php?sub=toft_a. Toft died in 1949.

CHAPTER 3

Savage War Reporters

War reporting in the Great War generally

The Allies at the Germans lunged
And won a fight at (name expunged);
But French's Army was defeated
Upon the field of (name deleted).

Brother Savage Reginald Pound

War has been the subject of reportage since at least the time of Thucydides. Modern war reporting as we would recognise it, however, began properly during the Crimean War in the 1850s with the great *Times* journalist William Howard Russell. It was Russell's description of the 93rd Highlanders at the Battle of Balaclava as a 'thin red streak topped with steel' which led to the phrase 'the thin red line' entering the vernacular. And it was his report of the Charge of the Light Brigade in the same battle – 'At 11:35 not a British soldier, except the dead and dying, was left in front of those bloody Muscovite guns' – which inspired Tennyson's famous poem.

Thereafter, reporters were increasingly to be found in various hot spots across the globe. Prominent among them was none other than the founder of the Savage Club, George Augustus Sala, who joined *The Daily Telegraph* in 1857 in the same year that he started the Club. A few years later Sala reported for *The Telegraph* on the American Civil War, some engagements of which were practically a spectator sport. He published a book of his experiences as well, which he dedicated to William Russell.[1] Before the end of the century Winston Churchill and the future Savage Percival Phillips also attained fame in Britain and America respectively with their reporting from various conflicts.

In July 1901, the Savage Club held a 'welcome home' dinner for its war correspondents from South Africa – HHS Pearse, Melton Prior, George Lynch and Charles Hands. Hands, a veteran reporter who had earlier covered the Spanish-American War, had been severely wounded in a battle near Maritsani involving the relief force on the way to Mafeking. Elsewhere he was noted for writing on America's Cup yacht racing and the tour by Kaiser Wilhelm II of the Holy Land in 1898. Perhaps most significantly, he was the person who coined the term 'Suffragette', when writing for the not-renowned hotbed of feminism the *Daily Mail*.[2] As a *Mail* reporter he also wrote strongly in support of the miners during an industrial dispute, something else which might come as a surprise to modern readers of the paper.[3]Lynch, meanwhile, wrote a book of his experiences, *Impressions of a War Correspondent*,[4] and described his craft in the introduction:

> There are few people in the world who have more opportunity for getting close to the hot, interesting things of one's time than the special correspondent of a great paper. He is enabled to see "the wheels go round;" has the chance of getting his knowledge at first hand. In stirring times the drama of life is to him like the first night of a play. There are no preconceived opinions for him to go by; he ought not to, at least, be influenced by any prejudices; and the account of the performance is to some extent like that of the dramatic critic, inasmuch as that the verdict of the public or of history has either to confirm or reverse his own judgment. There is a peculiar and unique fascination about this reading of contemporary history, as it grows and develops while one peers with straining eyes through one's glasses. There is something like a first night, too, about the way the critics view things. Sometimes great difference of opinion. I recollect the afternoon of Nicholson's Nek—Black Monday, as it was afterwards called—when we returned into Ladysmith half the correspondents seemed to be under the impression that the day had been quite a successful one; while, on the other hand, one had headed his despatch with the words, "Dies Iræ, dies illa!" To get to the heart of things; to see the upspringing of the streams of active and strenuous life; to watch the great struggles of the world, not always the greatest in war, but the often more mighty, if quiet and dead silent, whose sweeping powerfulness is hidden under a smooth calmness of surface—to watch all this is to intimately taste a great delicious joy of life. The researches of the historian of bygone

---

1   George Augustus Sala, *My Diary in America in the Midst of War (two volumes)* (Tinsley Brothers, 1865).

2   See: http://www.npg.org.uk/collections/search/group/1102/Suffragettes.

3   Sarah Lonsdale, *The Journalist in British Fiction and Film: Guarding the Guardians from 1900 to the Present* (Bloomsbury Academic, 2016), pp 29–30.

4   George Newnes Ltd, 1903. The book has been digitised and was easily found free online at the time of writing.

times are fascinating—absorbingly fascinating, although he is always handicapped by remoteness; but the historian of to-day—of his day—this day—whose day-page of history is read by hundreds of readers, the day after has set to him a task that calls for all, and more than all, that he can give—stimulates while it appals, and would be killingly wearying if it were not so fascinatingly attractive. That close contact with the men of this struggling world, and the men who do things, and shove these life-wheels round, warms up in one a great love for one's kind—a comrade feeling, like that which comes from being tent-mates in a long campaign. Two o'clock in the morning wake to the tramp, tramp of men marching in the dark—marching out to fight—and the unknown Tommy you march beside and talk to in low voice, as men talk at that hour, is your comrade unto the day's end of fighting; when returning, to the sentries' challenge you answer "A friend," and, dog-tired, you re-enter the lines, welcomed by his sesame call, "Pass, friend; all is well."

Thus, by 1914, the British public were used to up-to-date reporting on global conflicts, and would have expected journalists to accompany the British Expeditionary Force to the Front. But there was an immediate problem: Lord Kitchener had despised the press ever since his time in the Sudan, when they had had the temerity to bestow something less than lavish praise on him. (Upon arrival at Khartoum, he had barked 'Get out of my way, you drunken swabs!' at the assembled reporters.) And, as we will see in the next chapter, he was incandescent at his future Brother Savage, Edgar Wallace,[5] gaining a scoop about the conclusion of the Boer War.

In August 1914 the British government established the War Office Press Bureau under Brother Savage FE Smith, later Lord Birkenhead and well known to present day Savages as the subject of one of the National Liberal Club's most famous anecdotes.[6] The Bureau was intended to censor news and telegraphic

---

5 Richard Horatio Edgar Wallace (1875–1932). Born an illegitimate child, he left school aged 12. He joined the British Army at 21 and worked as a war correspondent during the Second Boer War, where he managed a major scoop to the fury of Lord Kitchener as we will see in the next chapter. After the war he returned to London and started writing thrillers. He became an incredibly prolific writer: as well as his reporting, he wrote some 18 stage plays, 957 short stories, and over 170 novels.

For an entirely random piece of trivia, the infamous murderer Dr Crippen was reading *The Four Just Men*, a murder mystery by Wallace, when spotted by Captain HG Kendall on the steamship *Montrose* trying to flee to America with his mistress, Ethel LeNeve. Kendall recorded that when the fact of them discussing the Wallace book was wirelessed to England and published, 'it made Edgar Wallace's name ring, so agog was everybody in England over the Crippen case.' See Kendall, 'The Arrest of Dr Crippen', quoted in Bailey (ed), *Scrapbook 1900–14* (1957). Wallace joined the Savage Club in March 1905.

6 If anyone has not heard the story or seen the plaque commemorating it in the NLC, the story goes that Smith used to stop off at the club and use the facilities each morning on the way from his chambers in the Temple to the House of Commons. Eventually, the porter asked if he was aware it was a private club. 'Good lord!' Smith replied, 'I didn't know it was a club as well!' – said

reports from the British Army and then issue permissible copy to the press. Soon, though, Smith was exasperated by Kitchener's attitude, complaining that 'He rather thinks he is in Egypt where the press is represented by a dozen mangy newspaper correspondents whom he can throw in the Nile if they object to the way they are treated.'[7] But Smith went too far when he signed off a report by *The Times'* correspondent Arthur Moore which, far from exulting another dashing victory, wrote of a 'terrible defeat' conceded by the British on the Western Front near Amiens and of 'broken bits of many regiments',[8] showing that the war was not going to be all over by Christmas. The report, which became known as the 'Amiens Dispatch', was published on the front page of a special Sunday edition of *The Times* on 30 August and caused a sensation, with a hurried 'correction' following by Sunday afternoon from the War Office via the Press Bureau, and a warning to take any future 'dispatches' with caution. The editor of *The Times* correctly responded that it was the Press Bureau who had encouraged publication in the first place. Within another week, three casualty lists had been published, totalling just over 15,000 killed, missing and wounded, with the Press Bureau offering some faint mitigation by pointing out that the missing included prisoners of war.

In the wake of the controversy Smith resigned, but the episode was not heavily damaging to his career. He went on to work in France as a staff officer with the Indian Corps, before returning to England to assume a series of senior governmental legal positions.[9] One possible reason for his survival was that recruitment numbers increased dramatically after the publication of the dispatch and the subsequent casualty lists – an indication that at the beginning of the war the loss of men at the front acted more as an *incentive* for those at home to enlist, rather than frightening them off. Many who signed up did so because they were intent on avenging their fallen brothers, upholding national honour and ensuring the expected Allied victory.

Kitchener, however, had no intention of changing his ways, and his own response to the Amiens Dispatch was to introduce blanket press censorship in September 1914 and refuse all press accreditation. He had a powerful ally in Lloyd George (who, as a notorious philanderer, benefited in other respects from a more deferential press throughout his life[10]). The public would hear only what the generals wanted them to hear, which was not very much, not very often and not very accurate.

to be a reference to the Victorian tiles in the club, which reminded him of a public lavatory. Supposedly the club was then known 'The National Lavatory Club', though that name might also have referred to the tiles on the walls.

7   J Lee Thompson, *Northcliffe: Press Baron in Politics 1865–1922* (John Murray, 2000), p 226.

8   Spencer Tucker (ed), *The Encyclopaedia of World War I* (ABC – CLIO, 2005).

9   In May 1915 Smith was appointed solicitor general, and he was promoted in October 1915 to attorney general. In 1916 he was briefly placed under military arrest for arriving at Boulogne without a pass. Later the same year he prosecuted Sir Roger Casement for treason following the Easter Rising.

10   In 2017, the 95-year-old Baroness Trumpington recalled how David Lloyd George had acted towards her when she was a 17-year-old land girl. She observed that 'he would be

Percy Bradshaw's 1958 book on the centenary of the Savage Club[11] noted:

> You may need reminding that there were no news bulletins from the
> BBC to keep us continually informed of the progress of each day's
> events (it was not until ten years later that we were first thrilled by the
> magic of "2LO Calling") and our war news, during 1914–15, came from
> Parliament, through the newspapers (dominated by a rigid censorship),
> through occasional official dispatches by a Government-appointed
> "Eye-Witness", and by the brilliant war correspondence of such men
> as Philip Gibbs, and our Brother Savages Percival Phillips, Hamilton
> Fyfe, Charles Hands and Perceval Gibbon.

Kitchener did grudgingly appoint Ernest Swinton[12] as the sole official war
correspondent, who was later joined by a conscripted journalist, Henry Tomlinson.
Both were chosen by the authorities on the ground they were a safe bet – that
is, unlikely to publish material severely critical of the army. As for photography,
only army cameramen were allowed anywhere near the Front. The quality of their
pictures was generally unimpressive, and they were not above staging photographs. The same went for those responsible for moving pictures slightly later in
the war: many of the classic silent film clips shown time and again on television
and in YouTube videos in the years since were staged, or 'reconstructions' to use
a modern term.[13]

In early 1915, President (Theodore) Roosevelt wrote to the British foreign
secretary, Sir Edward Grey, warning that the ban on journalists at the Front
was damaging Britain's cause in the United States. Kitchener relented to the
extent that, in March 1915, he invited four journalists under strict supervision
to visit the British Field Headquarters during the Battle of Neuve Chapelle.
Two months later, Philip Gibbs, Percival Phillips, William Beach Thomas,
Henry Perry Robinson and Herbert Russell were given official accredited status.

---

booted, wouldn't he' if he had behaved in the same lecherous fashion in the present. See
Patrick Maguire, 'I had measure of handsy rogue Lloyd George, says baroness', *The Times*,
29 December 2017.

11 Bradshaw, *Brother Savages and Guests: A History of the Savage Club 1857–1957* (WH Allen &
Co Ltd, 1958), p 66.

12 Major-General Sir Ernest Dunlop Swinton, KBE, CB, DSO (1868–1951). Swinton had
served in South Africa and was the author of well-received books including the classic
The Defence of Duffer's Drift, the standard text on small-unit tactics for 50 years. While in France
in 1914, Swinton formed the idea for an armoured tracked vehicle. His idea was presented to
Kitchener, who ignored it, but it found greater favour at the Admiralty with Churchill, who
formed the Landships Committee. Ultimately the British were the first to deploy the secret
weapon for which Swinton claimed to have coined the secret name 'tank'. See Ian V Hogg and
John Weeks, *An Illustrated History of Military Vehicles* (Golden Press, 1980), pp 18–19.

13 A good rule of thumb is to ask where the cameraman would have to have been standing to take
the footage; if it meant he would be standing in the middle of No Man's Land whilst the bullets
were flying, the footage is in all probability a 'reconstruction'. The actual films of combat tend
to show men in the distance, well away from the cameraman.

Henry Hamilton Fyfe was added later, as was Basil Clarke. Their status gave them access to areas and people they would not have had otherwise, but it also meant their reports were vetted by the government. They were appointed initially on a 'pooled' basis, sharing their information for general distribution to all news outlets in the United Kingdom and elsewhere. Along with that stick approach, the army dangled a few carrots by way of providing them with officer status, superior food and accommodation, and various other privileges including a driver, in the hope that they might write more favourably about the campaign.

Ironically, one official censor was Charles Edward Montague, who opposed the war at the beginning, changed his mind once it started – to the extent of dying his hair to fool the officials into thinking he was young enough to enlist – but at the end wrote bitter attacks on the generals, railing against them for being public school nobodies. The following extract from his post-war writings shows his melancholy tone:[14]

> So we had failed—had won the fight and lost the prize; the garland of the war was withered before it was gained. the lost years, the broken youth, the dead friends, the women's overshadowed lives at home, the agony and bloody sweat—all had gone to darken the stains which most of us had thought to scour out of the world that our children would live in. Many men felt, and said to each other, that they had been fooled. They had believed that their country was backing them. They had thought, as they marched into Germany, "Now we shall show old Fritz how you treat a man when you've thrashed him." They would let him into the English secret, the tip that the power and glory are not to the bully. As some of them looked at the melancholy performance which followed, our Press and our politicians parading the Prussianist goose-step by way of pas de triumphe, they could not but say in dismay to themselves: "This is our doing. We cannot wish the war unwon, and yet—if we had shirked, poor old England, for all we know, might not have come to this pass. So we come home draggle-tailed, sick of the mess that we were unwittingly helping to make when we tried to do well.

A list was drawn up for the War Office of journalists thought to be on message.

Meanwhile, in Gallipoli in 1915, a 30-year-old Australian reporter was so sickened by what he saw that he wrote an 8,000-word letter directly to his friend, the Australian prime minister Andrew Fisher, stating that the latter's worst fears had been realised and that the campaign was 'undoubtedly one of the most terrible chapters in our history'. The letter has been credited with bringing the campaign to its (ignominious) end: the reporter had tried to send it to Asquith, but the letter was intercepted in France, so he sent it to Fisher instead. Asquith saw the letter anyway and had it printed as a cabinet document. Soon after, the

---

14 *Disenchantment* (Brentano's, 1922), pp 230–231. The book was one of the first prose works to attack the way the war was fought. Incidentally, Montague was the father of Evelyn Aubrey Montague, the Olympic athlete and journalist depicted in the 1981 film *Chariots of Fire*.

British commander in the theatre, General Sir Ian Hamilton, was dismissed and his replacement, Lieutenant-General Sir Charles Munro was ordered to withdraw the Allied forces from the theatre.[15] The reporter's name was Keith Murdoch, and he went on to establish a media conglomerate subsequently inherited and expanded enormously by his son Rupert. Keith had sent the letter from the offices of *The Times* in London; Rupert famously ended up owning the paper.

Back on the Western Front, despite the worst efforts of Kitchener and other officers, the reporters were able to send back some moving depictions of the battles. Gibbs, working for *The Daily Telegraph*, was furious about the censorship. He smuggled back some reports describing how grim life was in the trenches. Then he went one further by describing the poor relations between officers and other ranks. He was arrested on charges of aiding and abetting the enemy – a charge that carried the death penalty – and he was told that if he persisted in returning to the frontline he would be put up against a white wall 'with unpleasant consequences'. In the event, Gibbs received the lesser sentence of a forced return to Britain. Thanks to the connections of *The Telegraph*, he was able to return to France with full military accreditation and keep reporting for the remainder of the conflict, albeit his reports were still censored, leading him to chastise himself afterwards:[16]

> We identified ourselves absolutely with the armies in the field. We wiped out of our minds all thought of personal scoops and all temptation to write one word which would make the task of officers and men more difficult or dangerous. There was no need of censorship of our despatches. We were our own censors.

Gibbs also wrote an excellent post-war memoir, *The Realities of War* (published in

---

15 It should however be noted that the commander of the Australian contingent, Lieutenant-General Sir William Birdwoood, opposed evacuation. One other factor was Asquith's correspondence from his son, Arthur ('Oc') who was serving in the theatre and sent furious letters to his father about the poor conditions.

In the popular imagination Gallipoli is most commonly associated with the 'Anzacs' (Australia and New Zealand Army Corps), a powerful myth in the national conscience of both Australia and New Zealand – something I can attest to from having grown up in New Zealand. In truth, the Anzac legend somewhat distorts the historical record. The largest contributor to the Gallipoli campaign was Britain by a wide margin, with a substantial contribution also by France, without in any way downplaying the resolute contribution of the Anzacs. Nor was it a case of Anzac squaddies being sent to death by incompetent British generals: no generals from any nation involved covered themselves in glory during the campaign (save for Byng, who supervised the bloodless withdrawal) and the Turkish bullets did not discriminate on the basis of nationality, as can be seen by the respective casualty figures: both the Allies and the Turks suffered approximately 250,000 casualties (killed, wounded or captured). Of those killed, the British lost approximately 34,000, the French nearly 10,000 and the Indian troops 1,400. The total Anzac fatalities were about 11,500.

16 Philip Gibbs, *Adventures in Journalism* (Harper & Brothers, 1923).

the United States as *Now It Can Be Told*), in which many of his frustrations were set out in detail.

We will see shortly how Basil Clarke enjoyed a brief spell of freedom as an unofficial journalist on the Western Front at the start of the conflict, while Henry Hamilton Fyfe avoided censors by joining the Red Cross. A non-Savage journalist who also managed to avoid censorship for a time was Charles à Court Repington, a former army officer who had had to resign due to a sex scandal. He wrote for *The Times* during the war and used his previous army contacts to gain information. Most notably, he was responsible for the 'Shell Crisis' of May 1915, when the commander of the BEF, Sir John French, confided to him that the failure at Neuve Chapelle and Aubers Ridge earlier in the year had been caused by a shortage of high explosive shells, something which would be seen as squarely the fault of Kitchener, since Kitchener was minister of munitions. To make sure of things, French also leaked documents to Lloyd George, who was in Asquith's cabinet, and the senior opposition politicians Andrew Bonar Law[17] and Arthur Balfour[18] as well.

Repington's story was run in *The Times* and the *Daily Mail*, both of which were owned at the time by Lord Northcliffe.[19] Northcliffe blamed Kitchener for the death of his nephew at the Front, so had no hesitation in printing critical stories about him. The story caused an uproar in parliament, leading to Asquith dissolving the Liberal government and forming a coalition. The government might

---

17 Andrew Bonar Law (1858–1923), often referred to as 'Bonar Law', Conservative Party politician and prime minister. He headed the Conservative Party in 1914 and during Asquith's coalition government (1915–16) held the post of colonial secretary – a minor post during wartime, which Bonar Law accepted rather than allow the coalition to break. Asquith's motivation in giving him the role was that otherwise too many Conservatives would hold key wartime posts, since he considered Kitchener a Conservative. Bonar Law served in Lloyd George's war cabinet, first as chancellor of the exchequer and then leader of the House of Commons. He lost two sons during the war.

18 Arthur Balfour (1848–1930), Conservative politician. He served during the war as First Lord of the Admiralty in Asquith's coalition government and, from December 1916, foreign secretary in Lloyd George's coalition government. He remains best known for the 'Balfour Declaration' of November 1917:

> His Majesty's government view with favour the establishment in Palestine of a national home for the Jewish people, and will use their best endeavours to facilitate the achievement of this object, it being clearly understood that nothing shall be done which may prejudice the civil and religious rights of existing non-Jewish communities in Palestine, or the rights and political status enjoyed by Jews in any other country.

At the time, Palestine was an Ottoman region with a minority Jewish population. The Balfour Declaration was the modern origin of the state of Israel.

19 Alfred Harmsworth (1865–1922) was created a baronet in 1904 and in 1905 was ennobled as Lord Northcliffe, of the Isle of Thanet in Kent. In 1918 he was raised to Viscount Northcliffe, for his service as the head of the British war mission in the United States. Northcliffe is occasionally said to have been the inventor of the quote 'man bites dog', but almost certainly was not, although the exact origin of the phrase is unknown.

have ridden out the scandal if it had not come at the same time as Lord Fisher resigning as First Sea Lord; Asquith thought the two events might destroy the 'general political and strategic situation'.

Initially, Northcliffe's campaign incurred the wrath of a million *Mail* readers and several advertisers, but he recovered quickly once he was proved to have been in the right about the shells. It helped that he had been fiercely pro-British since the start of the war, so could hardly have been accused of having a treasonous mindset.

Kitchener was replaced by Lloyd George as minister of munitions, though he kept his seat in cabinet. French, meanwhile, infuriated other generals since he had been seen to meddle in politics. The failed Battle of Loos was the final nail in his coffin and he was gone by the end of 1915.[20]

Kitchener's own response to the Shell Crisis was to ban Repington from the Front. In June 1916, however, Kitchener died and Repington was allowed back to France. At the beginning of 1918, Repington became embroiled in another scandal, this time arising out of the power struggle between Lloyd George and chief of the imperial general staff, Brother Savage William Robertson. Repington was charged with having contravened the Defence of the Realm Act, Regulation 18[21] by publishing articles discussing Lloyd George's attempt to thwart Robertson by setting up a rival staff under Henry Wilson at Versailles. He was convicted and fined.[22]

During the Battle of the Somme, Major Neville Lytton established a foreign press mission at the behest of the British General Headquarters. It succeeded so well that a French reporter, M Painleve, complained that the French papers gave better accounts of what the British armies were doing than of the French operations. The French editors riposted that the British armies gave the correspondents more facilities for doing their work. In the winter of 1916–17 Sir Douglas Haig gave an interview to the foreign journalists, whose reports, when somewhat indiscreetly censored and badly translated, gave a misleading impression of what he had said. As part of the fallout, Lytton was ordered to appear before the war cabinet. He recalled that 'Lloyd George appeared to be in a towering passion', but the situation was saved by the tact of Arthur Balfour. 'Sir William Robertson said

---

20 French's memoir of his time in command, entitled *1915* (digitised and easily found online at the time of writing), was masterfully ghost-written by a reporter, Lovat Fraser, though in many places it was also an imaginative work of fiction.

21 The Act had been passed at the start of the war, and one of its regulations provided 'No person shall by word of mouth or in writing spread reports likely to cause disaffection or alarm among any of His Majesty's forces or among the civilian population.' Defence Regulation 18B later became one of the most notorious regulations in English legal history, when it was the subject of the Second World War case of *Liversidge v Anderson*. See *Trials and Tribulations*, Ch 15.

22 One other interesting fact about Repington is that he might have been the first person to call the conflict 'The First World War' in print, in a diary entry for 10 September 1918.

nothing during the meeting, but before dismissing me he said, "You see what I have to put up with every day."' Lytton then appealed to Lord Northcliffe, who 'undoubtedly maintained Haig where he was.'[23]

One notable piece of reporting from 1916 came from another Savage Club member, Hugo Buist, a pioneering motor and aviation journalist,[24] when he wrote an article for the *The Observer* on the use of the British Army's new weapon of the tank. It was published on 24 September and thus during the Battle of the Somme, very soon after the tanks had been in action for the first time (without much success, mostly due to the muddy ground and their inherent mechanical unreliability). Buist was cautiously optimistic about the new technology but at the same time under no illusions about the tank being a war-ending weapon:

> The secret of the "tanks," those heavy armoured cars that are being variously described, not inaptly, as the Dreadnoughts of the trenches for His Majesty's Land Navy, has been kept well. As a result they were able to make a debut under the most favourable conditions. While the Army at the Front had styled them "tanks," a name which is likely to stick not so much for its aptness but because of its brevity, those who had to deal with evolving the new Jules Verne arm at home have all styled it the "Hush-hush Brigade," because they had to keep so mighty secret about all they were doing ... But it must not be imagined that the advent of this new class of heavy armoured car is going appreciably to shorten the duration of the war. These monster armoured motor ferrets will have more to do with dislodging the Germans and causing them to shift their ground than with the time factor as such.
>
> The much-peppered "tanks" have done tremendous execution, and on the occasion of their being first used they did not emerge wholly unscathed. The fact that this class of machine is vulnerable, however, is not discouraging, because every weapon of war up to a super-Dreadnought also proves vulnerable when brought into action against an adequately equipped and handled foe. All that matters is the proportion of vulnerability achieved in practice. For instance, we see that the Germans are very bold with their Zeppelins—in any area—up to the point at which they begin to lose them. But you can build these very heavy armoured cars and man them in vastly greater quantities and very much more quickly than you can make Zeppelins and train crews for them.
>
> You can also make sure of the fact that when an armoured car does any damage it will be of immediate and wholly military value. For obvious reasons one cannot go into the many fascinating mechanical details of this latest and most ambitious version of what was always an obvious and inevitable mechanical weapon.
>
> Undoubtedly we shall hear more of the news of this new weapon as

---

23 Neville Lytton, *The Press and the General Staff* (Collins, 1921).

24 Hugo Massac Thomas Buist (1878–1966), life member of the Savage Club from 1909. He was the editor of *Autocar* magazine, and produced an interesting early work entitled *Aircraft of the German War*, published in 1914 by Methuen.

the war goes on, for the initial test has proved the value of it—firstly, for saving enormously the infantry employed to take enemy trenches that have been heavily shelled; and, secondly, to deal with the remaining enemy units to be found in those trenches, and especially with the deadly machine-guns and their crews there; also with those snipers who lurk in shell craters, and so forth. But the contention advanced from at least one quarter that these and other of our latter-day mechanical instruments of warfare have left our infantry with practically nothing to do, or, in any case, with "a soft job," requires to be indignantly and instantly repudiated as an utter lie. We are not advancing too cheaply, though we are quite thankful that we are advancing at a much less cost than we might have had to pay had we not equipped ourselves with a wide variety of fighting machinery for paving the way for the advance of the infantry ...

That passage was a remarkably fair and accurate appraisal of the tank in the Great War.

In 1917, Lloyd George created a propaganda body, the National War Aims Committee. At his invitation Northcliffe became director of propaganda at the Ministry of Information, while Lord Beaverbrook, owner of the *Daily Express* and *Evening Standard*, served as first minister of information. At a reception held for him at London's Savoy Hotel on 27 December 1917, Gibbs spoke of the horrors of the Front – the fact of the reception being held showed how far the image of reporters had come. Lloyd George was in attendance and later told the proprietor of the *Manchester Guardian*, CP Scott, 'If people really knew [the truth], the war would be stopped tomorrow. But of course they don't know, and can't know.'

Overall, it has to be said that the various acts of dissent and rebellion by some journalists did not reflect the actions of the majority of the press during the war. Most put up with the restrictions, partly because they reasoned it was better to be near the Front under reporting restrictions than not near it at all, and partly, one suspects, because the army favours and chaperones made for a better life than risking all in the misery and danger of the frontline. As Lytton put it:[25]

> Only at the beginning in 1914 when a disorganised handful of free lancers sent home fragments of facts relating to that dramatic retreat, and at the end in 1918 when a well-organised band of accredited correspondents, working in perfect harmony with every branch of the Army, described in detail the greatest series of victories in the history of our race, was there any sport to the business.

It all meant that much of what appeared in the newspapers was not written by

25 Lytton, 'A Great War Witness: Sir Percival Phillips' Work at the Front', *Daily Express*, 31 March 1920. Quoted in William Richard Black, *Impacts Dispatches from the World: The Life of Percival Phillips, War Correspondent* (Author House, 2012), p 136.

anyone with first-hand knowledge. Instead, most was churned out by hacks back in Britain working from official communiqués. The author Tim Luckhurst returned a damning verdict:[26]

> The correspondents failed to serve the ethical purposes of liberal jour-
> nalism to which they and their editors professed allegiance. Their
> profession lost the aura of glamour with which it had been associated.
> Moreover, though their contribution to misinforming the public was rela-
> tively small, their conduct promoted a belief among surviving members
> of the front generation that newspapers had failed to do their duty and
> were vulnerable to manipulation. It also promoted an understanding
> among military leaders and politicians that war correspondents could be
> exploited in ways that rendered them valuable as agents of state propa-
> ganda. General Francisco Franco (1892–1975), Adolf Hitler (1889–1945)
> and Benito Mussolini (1883–1945) would exploit this lesson ruthlessly
> during the wars that followed, and to deplorable effect. The dictators'
> enemies learned, too. Combat correspondents would not operate again
> with the freedom they had enjoyed before 1914. Newspaper readers
> would not expect them to speak truth to power and would be additionally
> delighted and impressed when the best among them managed to do so
> despite the barriers placed in their path.

We now turn to some notable individual Savage correspondents.

Sir Basil Clarke: war reporter, propagandist and father of modern PR

Sir Basil Clarke was one of the first British reporters to reach the Western Front at the start of the Great War, and he went on to have a variety of interesting adventures in different theatres. After his career in journalism, he worked for a time in propaganda and then found an innovative way to combine the two 'professions' when he started what was arguably the world's first modern public relations firm. He was, therefore, a most intriguing name to find in the Savage Club candidate books.

Early life

Thomas Basil Clarke was born in August 1879 in Cheshire, the son of a success-ful pharmacist. As a very young child he lost an eye in an accident, something which was not to hold him back either as a sportsman or as an adventurous news hound. After leaving school, he worked short stints for a bank and an insurance company respectively, and studied music, though he did not enjoy working for either company, nor did he complete a degree in music.

---

26 Tim Luckhurst, 'War Correspondents', *1914-1918 online*, 15 March 2016, http://encyclopedia. 1914-1918-online.net/article/war_correspondents.

At the age of 22, he moved to London hoping to play the piano for a West End theatre. By that stage he and his girlfriend, Alice, had a child, so he was starting to feel the pressure of responsibility, although curiously (given the rigid morality of the day) they did not marry immediately upon discovering she was pregnant.

Clarke's next move was teaching English in Germany for a small school run by two Frenchmen. Clarke soon fell out with them, and ended up in a fist fight with one. He had the better of the exchange until his opponent produced a revolver, at which point Clarke conceded that the fight as well as his employment was over.

Clarke returned to England and started in journalism after meeting the editor of the *Manchester Evening Chronicle* through his rugby club (he played to quite a high level in Manchester). In 1904 he joined the *Manchester Guardian* as a subeditor. In 1907 he was promoted to reporter, and soon attracted praise for his work covering a wide range of subjects, from the reified world of interviewing Sir Ernest Rutherford, the New Zealand physicist, to the physically dangerous arena of industrial disputes.[27]

In 1910, he was headhunted by the *Daily Mail* with the promise of a higher salary and no editorial control over his political views. In April 1914 he travelled to Canada for a time to report on the lives of British emigrants, but returned to England before the outbreak of war.

His life up to that point, involving international travel and obvious displays of physical courage mixed with foolhardiness, was in retrospect the perfect training for the role of a war reporter.

First World War

The Western Front

When war broke out, Clarke was sent to London to form part of the Press Bureau that had been established at Charing Cross to distribute copy.[28] He met two notable Savage Club members, Lord Kitchener and FE Smith, and was not at all

---

27 The subject in which he was most interested was the nascent science of aviation. In that context Clarke met Charles Rolls, a pioneer aviator as well as the business partner of Sir Henry Royce, and was present when Rolls was killed in an air crash. Clarke wrote a moving description of Rolls' accident, but the experience did not stop him from accepting an aeroplane ride himself some time later. See Richard Nelsson, 'Basil Clarke at the Manchester Guardian', *The Guardian*, 7 June 2013. Nelsson also writes that Clarke tried hard but failed to enlist during the Great War. I suspect that his eyesight would have been the chief problem.

28 According to the biography by Richard Evans, *From the Frontline: the Extraordinary Life of Sir Basil Clarke* (The History Press, 2013, Kindle edn, loc 999), Clarke overheard a tune being played and attempted to reprise it on the hotel piano. He was then angrily confronted by a young Ivor Novello: the tune was *Keep the Home Fires Burning*, and Novello objected to Clarke playing it as it had not yet been released.

taken with the former, whom he dismissed as 'stupid'. Nor was he taken with the degree of censorship, which was so severe the reporters started calling the office the 'Repress Bureau'. But his frustrations were short-lived, for in October he was given an expense account in the form of a hundred gold sovereigns, with orders to head to Ostend, where a German invasion was imminent. He left immediately, wearing his civilian clothes and hence wondering if he was the first man to go to war in (or under) a bowler hat.[29] By the time he reached Folkestone, the town was full of Belgian refugees who told him that Ostend had already fallen. Undeterred, Clarke pressed on to the Continent, and went on to spend three months as a self-described 'journalistic outlaw', risking arrest as an unaccredited journalist, and hence having to dodge the British authorities as well as the German shells.

Clarke had some moving encounters with the fleeing civilians before he was able to see any fighting. In negotiating his way to the Front he was helped by his own interpersonal skills (he once wrote 'You can never do more towards making the ordinary man talk and forget his original line of question than by contradicting him, and letting him convince you he is right'[30]) and the fact that soldiers were often keen to share their stories with him.[31] He was also helped by a chance meeting with an old journalist friend, Richard Reading. Reading had joined the Legion of Frontiersmen[32] and, impatient to see action, transferred to the Belgian Army. Clarke was in awe of Reading's courage: Reading had once captured two Germans whilst unarmed. He had taken the rifle from one of them and concluded proceedings by buying him a drink.[33]

Building upon Reading's connections, Clarke hitched a ride to Furnes, where he witnessed King Albert addressing troops. It was Albert who perhaps most personified the quixotic idea of 'national honour' that was such an important factor across Europe in in plunging the continent into disaster. When the German government bluntly demanded permission to cross Belgian territory in order to invade France, the Belgians refused, citing their independence and

---

29 Basil Clarke, *My Round of the War* (William Heinemann, 1917), p 2.

30 Evans, *From the Frontline*, op cit.

31 Clarke, op cit, p 10. Max Hastings in *Going to the Wars* (Pan, 2012) remarked on the same phenomenon in his time as a war reporter – that soldiers on battlefields were usually anxious to have their actions reported to people back home.

32 The Legion of Frontiersmen was a voluntary service formed in Britain in 1905 by Roger Pocock, a Boer War veteran. It was created in response to fears of an invasion of Britain and the Empire. It was based in London but had branches throughout the Empire to prepare patriots for war and to foster vigilance in peacetime. It achieved little and lost many of its members in the Great War, after which it gradually faded into obscurity.

33 Clarke, op cit, pp 18–22. Reading thereafter used the rifle himself, which required him to 'catch a German blighter or two every few days' to keep himself supplied with ammunition the gun could use, something he seemed to be doing without difficulty. Reading's demeanour did not even seem to be deflated after he was caught in an ambush and had his legs riddled with bullets, nor even later on when his ship taking him to convalesce in Australia was torpedoed. Clarke would eventually write a touching tribute to his friend upon Reading's death in 1929.

national honour. Albert declared defiantly 'I rule a nation, not a road.'[34] By the time Clarke saw him, however, Albert seemed to have lost some of his idealism. Instead, Clarke wrote,[35]

> The King looked on. The band ceased. The Chasseurs presented arms. The King, at the window, gravely returned their salute. A quick order, and they were pouring out of a corner of the square, four deep, past me and on towards the spot whence the firing came. The King waved his hand.
>
> His eyes and his mien were sad. Perhaps he was wondering, as I was, how many of those sturdy Chasseurs of France would ever come back on that road leading from the old town square. He waited till the last of them had left the square, then stood silently looking after them.
>
> Then he quietly shut the window.

The first major fighting Clarke witnessed was the Battle of Yser, in which the French and Belgians tried to prevent the Germans from crossing the eponymous canal. Clarke conceded in his private correspondence to Alice that he was unable to write about everything he saw as it was too horrific (and in any event a full description would probably have been cut down by the *Mail*), but his writing was not devoid of colour. Describing a German attack, he wrote 'The Germans came down upon the countryside in a fury of hate. The frost had hardened the marshy fields. They came on now with a clatter instead of with a squelch. And the whole afternoon the Allies were busy beating them off. The guns thumped, the machine guns tapped, and rifles cracked.'[36]

What his reports could not convey was the true nature of the strategic situation. At Yser, the Belgians opened canal locks in desperation to flood the German trenches. They succeeded in preventing the Germans crossing the canal, but at the cost of devastating substantial tracts of their own countryside. Clarke sent a triumphalist report about the Germans retreating, and the apparently improving situation meant that the censors applied a lighter touch to his copy for the next few weeks.

In spite of joining in with the false optimism of the moment, and sharing

---

34 On 24 July, the Belgian government had announced that if war came it would uphold its historic neutrality. On 31 July, Belgium mobilised its armed forces, which everyone knew were miniscule compared with the German Army and thus stood no chance. The Germans gave their ultimatum on 2 August, demanding passage through the country and German forces invaded Luxembourg. On 4 August, the Belgian government refused the demands and the British government guaranteed military support to Belgium. The German government declared war on Belgium the same day and the German Army began its assault on the Belgian city of Liège.

35 Clarke, op cit, p 25.

36 Richard Evans, 'Mail man who went to the trenches in a bowler hat and Burberry coat: Eccentric, rebellious and breathtakingly brave, Basil Clarke defied the censors to tell an unsuspecting world the true horror of WWI', *Daily Mail*, 15 January 2014.

jingoistic notions about the cause, Clarke's reports were commendably untainted by the xenophobia of the day. Moreover, after experiencing shellfire himself, he wrote a thoughtful piece on the nature of courage, a pertinent subject given the shellshock that was soon to be found throughout all the warring armies.

Clarke's next destination was a place that was to become one of those names forever etched on the British consciousness, the Belgian city of Ypres (pronounced 'Eep' by Walloons, 'Eep-er' by the Flemish and, legendarily, 'Wipers' by British squaddies). Clarke was the first reporter to visit the ruined city centre, and his moving report about the horror was, he later considered, his best exclusive of the war. 'The awful sight struck me cold', he wrote, 'The city, so silent and empty and waste, might have been unpeopled by a plague, shattered by a mad god. You looked, and still looking, could hardly believe'.[37]

Despite the devastation of Ypres, Clarke continued to believe that the Allies were gaining the ascendancy, writing in mid-December 1914 that the 'turning point in the long-drawn struggle for Flanders and Northern France has begun' and that the Allies 'know they are winning'. In amongst those inaccurate predictions, he continued to write more sober depictions of individual experiences of the war, and, significantly, also wrote of a fearsome battle which raged on Christmas Day, showing that the Christmas Truce was not at all a universal feature of the Western Front.[38]

In early 1915 Clarke described a possibly unique battle between two armoured trains, which ended in an Allied victory after they hit the German train with a shell. He also filed a restrained description of a soldier brought in with what was evidently shellshock. But his luck soon ran out when he as arrested and sent back to Britain, Kitchener's crackdown on journalists having finally caught up with him.

To the East

Within a few days of his return, the *Mail* decided to send Clarke to Greece, Bulgaria and Romania on a roving commission to explore the tensions in the region. Before leaving he had some more good fortune, when a Romanian prince who had enjoyed his pre-war writing offered help by way of letters of introduction.

Clarke found Greece severely divided over which side to back in the war. It was a febrile atmosphere in which other Savages would become embroiled, most notably Sir Compton Mackenzie, whom we will meet later as a Savage man of letters.

---

37 Evans, *From the Frontline*, op cit. Clarke's name was removed from his copy so as not to alert he authorities that the *Mail* had a rogue reporter in the area. Instead, the *Mail* pretended that the piece came from an English-speaking local resident.

38 It was not until 8 January that the *Mail* was able to draw attention to the truce, when it published a photograph obtained from another source showing British and German soldiers together in No Man's Land.

Clarke correctly predicted Greece would join the Allies, but he wrongly thought the move was imminent; in fact, the 'National Schism' precluded a declaration of war by Greece against the Central Powers until mid-1917.

Clarke moved through Serbia, Bulgaria and Romania, but although he encountered German spies and various mild forms of intrigue, he sent back little interesting copy. Thus, in mid-February 1915, he decided to try and find some fighting to report instead. He found an encounter between Russia and the Austro-Hungarian forces.[39] Afterwards he travelled to the Russian headquarters, where he learned they had been reading translations of his *Mail* reports. He described the Russian shelling of enemy positions:[40]

> I wondered whether gunners would aim as well if they could watch at close quarters as I was watching, the fall of their shells; if they could see the bodies and the faces, and could dread in the eyes the very hearts, almost, of the men they sought to kill. It is doubtful whether they would. To kill a man at a mile or two is quite impersonal—an easy matter. And the soldier fighting at close quarters has the heat of battle and the need to defend his own life to help him to kill and to wish to kill. But here on my safe hillside I had none of these aids.

In spite of that action Clarke concluded that there was insufficient newsworthy material in the region and he therefore returned home.

Blockades and the Easter Rising

Back in England, Clarke rejoined his family in Dulwich Village, a leafy area of London then as now (in fact, one of the areas of London that has probably changed the least since Clarke's day). He took time to visit Belgian refugees and to write for the *Mail* about how they had developed a taste for tea and cricket.

Soon, though, he was back on the investigative journalistic path, seeking out how wartime expenditure was affecting the economy. He wrote of the new-found prosperity many areas experienced due to increased spending, but doubted that anyone was saving enough for the inevitable hard times that would follow in peacetime. His articles also did not fully take inflation into account. But he noticed the zeal and ability the new female workforce brought to traditional male roles, albeit no-one seems to have been immune to the sexism of the time, one employer telling him he preferred female workers because they did not complain as much.

Clarke's next overseas assignment came at the end of 1915, when he went to Denmark to investigate whether the British blockade of Germany was working. By going through the lists of goods trading through Danish ports (the Danish

---

39 Evans, *From the Frontline*, op cit.
40 Ibid.

government refused permission for him to see any official statistics), he calculated that there was a flagrant flouting of the blockade, since there had been a massive increase in imports since the war had begun, which could only be explained by the additional goods heading to Germany. In January 1916 he published an article in the *Mail* alleging 'We are feeding the Germans ... ship after ship and train after train, as I have seen for myself, are still pouring the world's goods into Germany.' The British government replied with a memorandum disputing his methodology and pointing out that some of his statistical calculations were incorrect. Clarke accepted his figures contained some mathematical errors but maintained his overall thesis. But the memorandum, accompanied by a speech in parliament by Sir Edward Grey, saved the day for the government, which then established a Ministry of Blockade. Its efforts paid off eventually: by 1917, the tighter blockade was starting to have a severe effect on the German war effort, not least by undermining morale amongst German civilians. Having stirred things at home, Clarke was sent to Ireland immediately after the Easter Rising. He filed what might have been the first independent report from Dublin, in which he wrote of 'Sackville Street torn up and ramparted with overturned vehicles of every kind; of the Four Courts invested and turned, so to speak, inside out with the rebels entrenching themselves behind great piles of ancient and historic tomes and records, and of machine guns whirring from the front windows of the aristocratic and elegant Shelbourne Hotel.'[41]

It was questionable how much action he had personally witnessed, though the *Mail* was pleased with his reporting. Back in England, however, his short temper cost him his employment for a second time, when he clashed with the news editor. Although he had to go, Clarke left with Northcliffe's good wishes and a standing invitation to return.

The Somme

Now working as a freelance journalist, Clarke registered as an accredited reporter and headed straight back to action, going to France as the greatest battle in the history of the British Army was under way on the Somme. As an official journalist, he was no longer at risk of arrest, but suffered the accompanying restrictions on his movements and copy. Nevertheless, he went on to write some fine descriptions of classic Somme imagery:[42]

> In many villages German shell fire was so frequent that it was not safe to sleep anywhere ion ground level or above. To find cellar billets, therefore, saved the trouble of digging dug-outs, and the hunting for cellars was very keen. Officers and men specially told off for this duty

41 Evans, *From the Frontline*, op cit.
42 Clarke, op cit, pp 194–5, 197, 199.

would rummage about the ruins of houses, and underneath the most dilapidated and unpromising ruin might be found cellars quite intact. The stone steps leading to them might be blocked up with bricks and plaster and ash, but a fatigue party under a corporal would soon put this out of the way and lay bare a cellar which would be passed as "fit for occupation." Only too often there were gruesome finds in these cellars – from which the Germans had been driven—and if people who die a violent death leave ghost behind them our soldiers may be said to have slept amid congregations of Teuton ghosts. Not that that seemed to weigh on their minds particularly. They were very much more both-ered by the rats. These creatures were almost everywhere, and at first they were so hungry as to be ready to feed on anything from a crust to a Sam Browne belt. But after our soldiers had been in occupation of a cellar for some time the rats picked up so much waste food that they became fat and lazy, and then they would fall an easy prey to the heel of a boot or a well-aimed bully-beef tin ...

Of all his war writings, Clarke considered that his best concerned his trip accompanying the wounded from the Front back to England. He began with the stretcher bearers on the frontline, who impressed him not only with their physical fitness and courage, but also their classic English gallows humour and their banter with the wounded.

After being retrieved from the battlefield, the wounded were taken to a regi-mental aid post not far behind the line. From there they were sent to an advanced dressing station further back – but not out of range of German shelling, the patients frequently having to be rushed down to the cellars. As soon as possible, the wounded were then evacuated by motor vehicle to the main dressing station in a village further back, where there were much better medical facilities and no risk of German shelling.

The next stop was still further behind the lines, in a casualty clearing station, which was notable for having female staff. A nurse at the station Clarke visited remarked to him how much they saw the wounded men's spirits rise accordingly.[43]

There was an added luxury for the wounded at the clearing stations since they were now able to be moved by rail. The train Clarke took went first to a differ-ent clearing station, where he marvelled at the cheery banter of the wounded and how they interacted on friendly terms with wounded German prisoners. Finally he travelled with the wounded to the coast, where they boarded a hospital ship. Looking through a grimy porthole the men could make out a bleak coastline: 'eyes sparkled with moisture at the mere sight of it. Throats moved without words issuing forth. Till at last pent-up feelings found vent in one hoarse murmur: "Blighty!"'[44]

---

43 Clarke, op cit, p 281.
44 Ibid, pp 302–3.

That was the end of Clarke's time in action. He wrote up his memoirs of the conflict and published them in late 1917 – not only before the war's end, but before it was even clear who would win.[45] For the rest of the war and into peacetime he moved around different government posts.

Post-war career

In 1920, Clarke went to Ireland to head the Public Information Department in Dublin Castle, the British government's propaganda office. The office published a steady farrago of information, disinformation and misinformation at twice daily press briefings. Clarke knew that the key was for the briefings at all times to have an air of verisimilitude; if the 'news' did not seem plausible the game would be up. He certainly had his work cut out for him, given the brutality that started to take place in Ireland at the time, epitomised by the original Irish 'Bloody Sunday'. For his efforts he was knighted in 1923.

In 1924, Clarke left working for government and put all of his working experience to use in setting up what was probably the first public relations firm in the country, called Editorial Services. In September of that year, he joined the Savage Club, after being proposed by his fellow war reporter Charles Hands.

Perhaps ironically, given his role in propaganda – but less ironically given his determination to tell the truth to the public when he was at the Western Front – Clarke emphasised ethics in public relations and attempted to turn it into a profession, by developing its first code of conduct.

In 1935, he suffered a stroke, and lived in poor health for the rest of his life. He died in 1947.

Henry Hamilton Fyfe: sixty years in Fleet Street
Early life

Henry Hamilton Fyfe was one of the leading war reporters during the Great War, though his work there formed only a small fraction of a remarkably long career in Fleet Street.

Fyfe was born in London in 1869, the son of a barrister and journalist. After attending the public school Fettes, he started his career in journalism. He began at *The Times*, where he worked as a reporter and reviewer before becoming secretary to the editor, George Earle Buckle.

In 1902, he became editor of the *Morning Advertiser*, the trade publication of the Licensed Victuallers' Association. He entered a sharp disagreement with the paper's owners, but came to the notice of Alfred Harmsworth, the future

---

45 The book seems only to have become available either right at the end of 1917 or the beginning of 1918, but the copyright states 1917.

Lord Northcliffe. In 1903, Harmsworth hired Fyfe to try to sort out the *Daily Mirror*. Fyfe successfully increased the paper's circulation by turning it into a popular newspaper, making particular use of photography.

In 1907 Fyfe moved to Harmsworth's better known *Daily Mail* to work as a journalist. He flourished in the role, reporting international politics but also significant events such as Blériot's crossing of the Channel. He was still working for the paper when the First World War started. Although he was a well-established journalist, he did not join the Savage Club until March 1929.

War reports

Fyfe slated the ineptitude of politicians who had blundered into the war but not made adequate preparations for it. Still, at first he found himself caught up in the excitement, until he saw the disaster in the making that was the French Army of 1914: [46]

> To me at first it was an exciting novelty. The thrill of romance was in it still. All that I had read about war (nearly all of it rubbish) flooded my mind with ideas of pomp and circumstance, of shrewd intellects contending for advantage, of marching columns and flying cavalry doing as those intellects planned. What a fool I was! How quickly I learned that war is above all dullness; that those who direct it—or let it take its own course—are mostly pompous, incompetent dullards; that, like all other machinery, the machinery of war has escaped from the control of its users; that the task of soldiers is to cower in trench dug-outs and have hell rained upon them. However, for the moment, before I had seen anything of it, war appeared to be a tremendous event, full of colour, fine in quality; and I was going to report it.

> The whole country swarmed already with soldiers. Most of them were middle-aged, none of their uniforms fitted. They wore the absurd red trousers below the blue coat which had been in fashion since Napoleon's time. I recall a conversation with a French journalist who assured me that the army would lose all spirit if its red trousers were taken away. He would not listen to me when I said the uniform would have to be altered, as the British red coats were changed to khaki in South Africa. That was the general attitude of Frenchmen.

The French in their bright uniforms[47] were to march into an industrial-scale

---

46 I have drawn from a number of sources for the quotations, but the most useful has been the outstanding *Spartacus Educational* website (http://spartacus-educational.com/FWWfyfe.html) with its substantial amount of free primary source material.

47 The 1914 French uniforms included blue coats and red trousers for the infantry and cavalry. The French cuirassiers wore plumed helmets and breastplates. There had been attempts from 1903 to modernise their uniforms but the conservative forces and, it seems, public opinion opposed the change. Adolphe Messimy, minister of war from 1911–1912, complained about the 'blind attachment to the most visible of colours' but his words fell on deaf ears and were not repeated by his successors. The French did manage to develop a more demure outfit, known as

slaughterhouse in 1914–15. British histories of the war rightly bemoan the horrendous casualties the Empire suffered. Some perspective should be given by the French experience, though: the first month of the war cost the French a staggering 212,000 casualties (note: the figure comprises killed, wounded, captured and missing), about 20 per cent of its mobilised strength, including 40 per cent of its regular officers. By December 1914, France had lost 955,000 casualties and in 1915 she suffered 1,430,000 casualties. No fewer than 27,000 men were killed on 22 August 1914 *alone* in the Battle of the Frontiers, the bloodiest day in French military history. By way of comparison, that was more than the British lost on the first day of the Somme, and roughly the same number of French soldiers as were killed during the entire Algerian War of 1954–1962.[48]

The cause of the 22 August disaster and the incredibly high casualty figures generally was essentially the culmination of all the problems France faced in the early months of the war, before the onset of static trench warfare. France had five armies positioned from Alsace and Lorraine to the Belgian border, all of whom fought in separate assaults with no co-ordination between them. Each assault resulted in a loss of ground and many wounded being left behind. The French had not been trained for defensive warfare and had also not developed proper, modern artillery techniques. They (in common with most countries at the time) held the doctrine that ground lost had to be recovered as soon as possible, irrespective of other considerations.

Moreover, the idea of the Germans being rigid, robotic machines was the opposite of reality. It was the French Army which in 1914 had an inflexible hierarchy, requiring orders before it would deviate from any pre-existing plan. In the context of battle, that meant sending runners back and forth, which took far too long and risked the runner being killed and the message or reply never delivered. The German Army, on the other hand, allowed much more discretion in more junior officers.

The BEF was generally more capable unit for unit than any other army, being composed of professional soldiers and led by men with experience in conflicts across the Empire. The British were also highly trained in marksmanship thanks to Field Marshal Roberts. But they were simply too few in number to make a difference. Fyfe explained, with reference to the Amiens Dispatch:

'horizon-blue' because it was thought to meld with the skyline, but it was introduced too late for the start of the war in 1914. Hence the French went into battle in the bright outfits, with disastrous consequences.

From the start of 1915 the horizon-blue started to be distributed throughout the French Army. They were also the first to use steel helmets in the trenches. See Ian Sumner, *The French Army: 1914–18* (Osprey Publishing, 1995).

48 In 1914, the French suffered an average of 2,200 losses per day. In 1915, during the Artois Offensive between 9 May and 18 June, the French lost 300,000 casualties (killed, wounded or captured) to gain just four kilometres of territory.

Driving from Boulogne we saw British soldiers and we heard the whole story. Orders had been given for a hasty retreat of all the British troops in and about Amiens. What had happened? They shrugged their shoulders. Where were they going? They didn't know. What Arthur Moore (*The Times*) and I felt instantly was that we had to know. There was nothing to keep us out of Amiens now. In less than two hours we were there, listening to the sound of not very distant guns. We drove about all that day seeking for news and realizing every hour more and more clearly the disaster that had happened. We saw no organized bodies of troops, but we met and talked to many fugitives in twos and threes, who had lost their units in disorderly retreat and for the most part had no idea where they were.

That Friday night, tired as we were, Moore and I set off to Dieppe to put our messages on a boat which we knew would be leaving on the Saturday morning. They reached London on Saturday morning. They reached London on Saturday night. Both were published in *The Times* next day. (*The Times* was then published on Sunday; the *Mail* was not.)

As they gave the first news of the defeat they must in any case have caused a sensation. But the sensation would not have been so painful if Lord Birkenhead, then F. E. Smith, had not been Press Censor at the time. The despatches were taken to him after dinner. When the man who took them told me about it later on, he said, "After dinner—you know what that meant with him."

Birkenhead saw that they must be published. He saw the intention with which they had been written—to rouse the nation to a sense of the need for greater effort. But he seemed to think that it would be better to suggest disaster by the free use of dots than to let the account appear in coherent and constructive form. With unsteady hand he struck out sentences and parts of sentences, substituting dots for them, and thus making it appear that the truth was far worse than the public could be allowed to know.

When Kitchener clamped down on the press, Fyfe joined a French Red Cross detachment so he could keep reporting from the Front:

The ban on correspondents was still being enforced, so I joined a French Red Cross detachment as a stretcher bearer, and though it was hard work, managed to send a good many despatches to my paper. I had no experience of ambulance or hospital work, but I grew accustomed to blood and severed limbs and red stumps very quickly. Only once was I knocked out. We were in a schoolroom turned into an operating theatre. It was a hot afternoon. We had brought in a lot of wounded men who had been lying in the open for some time; their wounds crawled with lice. All of us had to act as aids to our two surgeons. Suddenly I felt the air had become oppressive. I felt I must get outside and breathe. I made for the door, walked along the passage. Then I found myself lying in the passage with a big bump on my head. However, I got rid of what was troubling my stomach, and in a few minutes I was back in the schoolroom. I did not suffer in that way again.

During his time with the Red Cross, he saw appalling brutality:

> What caused me discomfort far more acute—because it was mental,
> not bodily—were the illustrations of the bestiality, the futility, the
> insanity of war and of the system that produced war as surely as land
> uncultivated produces noxious weeds: these were now forced on my
> notice every day. The first cart of dead that I saw, legs sticking out
> stiffly, heads lolling on shoulders, all the poor bodies shovelled into a
> pit and covered with quicklime, made me wonder what the owners had
> been doing when they were called up, crammed into uniforms, and told
> to kill, maim, mutilate other men like themselves, with whom they had
> no quarrel. All of them had left behind many who would be grieved,
> perhaps beggared, by their taking off. And all to no purpose, for nothing
> ...We came across a group of men in varying stages of disability by the
> roadside. They greeted us joyfully. But there were a dozen of them. Our
> motor ambulances held only eight. Some of them who were almost, but
> not quite, walking cases, looked at us with pleading eyes. Somehow or
> other, after their dressings and bandages had been looked to in the red
> glare of the burning town, we squeezed eleven of them in. One we had
> to leave there. It was impossible that he could live for more than a few
> hours. To move him would have killed him at once.
>
> On a little mound we left him, a truss of straw beneath his head. His
> features were aquiline, delicate. He was unconscious, would never
> be conscious again. He murmured broken phrases. As he drove off, I
> thought I should never cease to see the butchered body, that death-
> mask on its truss of straw. Within an hour or two I was sitting with
> the rest at supper (we had not eaten since morning), talking, laughing,
> forgetting the episodes of the day. It had to be so. If we had not forgot-
> ten, we should have gone mad. Experiences that in our peaceful lives
> would have seemed too horrible for endurance now made next to no
> impression on us. So quickly is callousness bred by war.

The following year Fyfe went to the Eastern Front, where he found 'the Russian
troops, all the men and most of the officers, were magnificent material who were
being wasted because of the incompetence, intrigues, and corruption of the men
who governed the country.' He went on:

> The Russian officers, brutal as they often were to their men (many of
> them scarcely considered privates to be human), were as a rule friendly
> and helpful to us. They showed us all we wanted to see. They always
> cheerfully provided for Arthur Ransome,[49] who could not ride owing to
> some disablement, a cart to get about in.

Post-war career

After the war, Fyfe renewed his attack on politicians and slated them for the
Versailles Treaty as well as the abject failure to provide a land fit for heroes at home:

---

49 The author of *Swallows and Amazons*. He worked as a war correspondent in Russia for a radical
    newspaper, the *Daily News*. He later covered the Russian Revolution, coming to sympathise
    with the Bolshevik cause and becoming personally close to a number of its leaders, including
    Lenin, Trotsky and Karl Radek.

If all had worked together as comrades to repair the damage done and to build up better conditions than existed before - had worked at this task without resentment, recognizing that all had been to blame, there would have been employment for all and the promises of a "better world", made so glibly for recruiting purposes, could have been fulfilled. But that called for a clearness of foresight, an honesty of purpose, which the politicians in power at that time did not possess.

He also provoked the establishment with his republican-favouring 1920 play *The Kingdom, The Power and The Glory*.

Despite his political stance, he continued to enjoy good relations with the conservative Northcliffe. After Northcliffe died in 1922, Fyfe became editor of the *Daily Herald*, which saw a substantial increase in circulation under his leadership, even though he did not get on with the board. In 1926, he moved to the *Daily Chronicle*, which merged with the *Daily News* in 1930.

When Ramsay MacDonald became prime minister, he was irritated by Fyfe's work, complaining that his paper had become 'a dumping-ground for rubbish which would be put in the waste-paper basket by anyone who knew his business, or who was not out for mischief.' Fyfe riposted:

> I have had to do with so many Prime Ministers that I am not surprised by the petulant tone of your letter ... You tell me I don't know my business as an editor. Assuredly I have much yet to learn, but I have been in training for 30 years. You have been Prime Minister for eight months without any previous experience. Isn't it just possible that you have some things to learn too?

Despite their differences, Fyfe later stood as a Labour candidate in 1929 and 1931, albeit both times without success. In 1935, he published his autobiography, *My Seven Selves*,[50] in which he was unsparing about the horrors of the First World War. The book was also critical of Churchill, saying that he had missed his chance of leading the Conservative Party when he left for the Liberals in the early 1920s. Fyfe added that Churchill's staff despised him when he edited the government-owned *British Gazette* at the time of the 1926 General Strike.

In 1940, Fyfe published another book, *The Illusion of National Character*, a critique of nationalism – something of a contentious argument in the year of the Battle of Britain. He also wrote a well-received memoir of his time in the press, *Sixty Years of Fleet Street*.

He died in 1951.

---

50 Published by G Allen & Unwin Ltd, 1935.

Perceval Gibbon: man of adventure
Early life

Perceval Gibbon was born in Trelech, Wales, in 1878, the eldest son of the Rev James Morgan Gibbon.

As a young man Gibbon joined the merchant navy. He served aboard British, French, and American ships, and travelled extensively throughout Europe, America, and Africa. From an early age he wrote novels and short stories influenced by his travels, including *The Vrouw Grobelaar's Leading Cases* (1905) and *Souls in Bondage* (1904). Several of his short stories were published in British and American magazines such as *McClure's Magazine* and *Collier's Weekly*. He remained a prolific author for most of his life.[51] He joined the Savage Club in July 1905, under the category of literature.

Gibbon has been described as 'a small, lively, dark, virile and sometimes brutal man, with thick blue-black hair and a sensitive mouth' and was said to be 'well known for his forceful personality, his sharp wit and his strong views ...'[52] He certainly had a taste for danger. During the Second Boer War, while he was reporting the conflict for the *Natal Witness*, he was captured but managed to escape, like a more famous correspondent of the same war, Winston Churchill.

Gibbon remained in South Africa for a time after the war, joining the *Rand Daily Mail* in 1902. He wrote about Africans, race relations and the Boers.

In 1908, back in England, he met and became firm friends with the great novelist Joseph Conrad. Conrad told his wife Jessie just before introducing her to Gibbon 'I am sure you will like him, Jess, but be careful. He is well known for his repartee, he will give you as good as you send every time.'[53] Conrad was inspired by Gibbon's adventures and both seem to have influenced the other in their work. Gibbon supported the Conrad family when Conrad was ill in 1910. Later that year Conrad stayed with Gibbon while his family was relocating. One of Conrad's biographers wrote:[54]

> On this visit Conrad was as exhilarated by Gibbon, who shared his experience of Russia and knowledge of the sea, as he had been by Crane, for both young men had the capacity to have fun, dispel his gloom and cheer him up. Using a striking simile, Conrad told Gladsworthy: "He

---

51 Other works of Gibbon that were published in book form include a collection of verse, *African Items* (1903); the novels *Salvator* (1908) and *Margaret Harding* (1911); short stories including *The Adventures of Miss Gregory* (1912), *The Second-Class Passenger* (1913), *Those Who Smiled* (1920) and *The Dark Places* (1926).

52 Jeffrey Meyers, *Conrad, A Biography* (Cooper Square Press, 2001), p 242. See also Martin Ray, *Joseph Conrad: Memories and Impressions: an Annotated Bibliography* (Rodopi, 2007).

53 Jessie Conrad, 'A Personal Tribute to the Late Percival (sic) Gibbon and Edward Thomas', *Bookman*, 78 (September 1930), p 323.

54 Meyers, op cit, pp 241–243.

rushed me about on his side-car motor-bike, storming up hills and flying down dales as if the devil were after him. I don't know whether that is particularly good for the nerves, but on return from these excursions I felt ventilated, as though I were a bag of muslin, frightfully hungry and almost too sleepy to eat."

In 1911, Gibbon published a novel, *Margaret Harding*, dedicated to the Conrads (it was filmed many years later). Conrad returned the compliment in 1915 by dedicating his book *Victory* to Gibbon and his wife. In 1912 Gibbon also wrote a positive review of Conrad's *A Personal Record*.

He had one more interesting foreign adventure in 1912, when he went to Bulgaria to cover the Balkan-Turkish wars for the *Daily Chronicle*.

War reports

During the First World War, Gibbon reported from a number of fronts. In 1915 he spent five months in Russia. When he returned to England, he spoke highly disparagingly about the Russian conduct of the war and how they behaved towards civilians.

In 1916 he went to the Western Front, where for a time he replaced Philip Gibbs on *The Daily Telegraph*. Whilst there, he joined his future Brother Savages Percival Phillips and Basil Clarke in the reporters' mess, and was described by the latter:[55]

> Over by the far side of the fire is a short, thick-set figure with a strong square face, glowing eyes and a shock of shining black hair. You will ransack memory for a moment to think where you have seen a like face and then the memory comes in a flash. The head is like Beethoven's. It is that of Percival Gibbon. It is as a short-story writer rather than a journalist that the world knows him best; it was as a sailor, globe-trotter and adventurer that he picked up his amazing wealth of experience of men and things. And to a restless physical energy Nature has added, in him, a restless mental energy. He is in one man two contradictions, roving adventurer and student. His researches in the one capacity touch the remotest corners of the world; in the other, the remotest byways of learning. He has commanded a sailing ship, traded with savages in Central Africa, and yet found time to learn half a score of languages and to plumb the literature of Europe. He talks. It is with all the fire and emphasis of his Celtic blood. He rises and begins to walk as he talks, till with playful remonstrance – and the rudeness of good fellowship—you push him into his chair again, and tell him to "shut up" and be "cozy," all of which he bears in excellent part, returning chaff for chaff.

Gibbon's first report for *The Telegraph* was published on 24 October. The byline

---

55 Clarke, op cit, p 177.

dryly explained that Philip Gibbs was 'unfortunately temporarily indisposed' and was in England recuperating. Gibbon's report mentioned place names that have since become very familiar to any who have toured the Western Front:

> Sun at last, a clear sky of pale winter blue, and a keen edge of cold in the air—perfect war-weather after the wet and the mists of the past week. And, as if nothing else had been needed, the fighting that has been flickering around the Schwaben Redoubt and all along that precarious crest of land which runs northward from where the gaunt, dead trees stand over dead Thiepval, burned up at midday to a clear flame of battle. Upon a front of some 5,000 yards, from the corner of the Schwaben Redoubt to near the north end of that German position which is known as the Regina trench, our troops went forward in the wake of the barrage-fire, captures and held the whole of the positions which formed their objective, and added upwards of a thousand new prisoners to the population of the "cages." From west of Pozieres, where the ground slopes down by Mouquet Farm to the shallow valley below the Thiepval ridge, there was an outlook over the whole smoke-smeared panorama of battle.

On 30 October, under the heading 'The Tenacious Mud: No rest for Bavarians', he sent another report replete with imagery which became symbolic of the Western Front:

> There is no rest for the 15th Bavarians. To-day, again, for the sixth time since Monday, they have to fight for that string of shell-craters, whose lips crumbling together make some sort of a line, which is what remains of Hazy Trench. As I have related previously, this is a position opposite our lines west of Les Boeufs—lines already considerably straightened and simplified as a result of the last week's fighting—and five times already they have been bombed and bayoneted and rough and tumbled out of it, and five times they have come desperately back. Dewdrop Trench, a little to the north of Hazy, is also attacked, and already news has leaked back through the shell curtain that British troops have gained a footing in its northern end after a frightful struggle with that tenacious German ally, the mud of these fields. There was a trench between us and Dewdrop—Rainy was the name of it on the trench map—but that troubles us no longer. Rainy Trench, throughout its 180 yards of length, has ceased to exist—it and its wasps' nests have been gouged out of the ground by a week of cannonading.
>
> Men wounded in this week of white-hot fighting in the blasted fields between Les Boeufs and Le Transloy speak chiefly of the mud. They are to be found in the casualty clearing station behind the battle. The great tents lead one into the other—long, shadowy halls where the wounded lie to each side. Such tents I have seen a hundred times in Russia, but never such wounded. The Russian wounded man has always the child-like side of him most developed when he brings his hurt back to be nursed. Then it was: "Well, where have you got it?" "In the leg, sir—and God help me, it hurts a lot." But here, "Got a puncture, sir. Machine-

gun bullet while we was goin' over the top … Yes, sir, a rest was all I wanted … No, it don't hurt nothin' to speak of!"

On 11 November, he mused that things were all quiet on the Western Front (his actual headline was 'Quiet on the Somme. Enemy's dejection'):

> From Thiepval to the Butte de Warlemcourt and thence again to Les Boeufs, the front of the Somme battle has subsided to an interval of relative quiet, with only the routine shelling, the patrolling of aeroplanes, and the minor activities of trench life keeping alive the spark of war. The trains of wounded from the recent fighting have drawn out with their tiers of cigarette-smoking casualties; this is the season at which both sides, behind their melting parapets, take stock of each other.

Indeed the Somme Offensive was winding down at the time. On 22 November, Gibbon wrote about the continuing low level of activity in the sector, though without suggesting to the reader that the greatest battle in the history of the British Army had effectively come to a close:

> Slowly, by little adjustments and the enterprise of patrols, our new line to the north and south of the Ancre becomes definite. The members who held the outlying ruins of Grandcourt, lying out there among the brick-heaps waiting for the counter-attack to come rolling down on them, are now the foremost point of the troops who yesterday and last night made good their footing upon ground which extends up to and into the village. The men in the south end of Puisieux Trench, upon the ridge of that name that runs down to the channel of the Ancre, are now linked with our forces beyond the Bois d'Hollande. At a score of points lonely little groups of British soldiers, hanging to strings of shell-holes out in the open, mounting guard through the hours over their lives, have seen the line crawl up toward them and make them one with itself again. It is not battle—it is not even fighting on the scale of a mention in the official communique. It is rather a process of isolated, obscure heroisms, working like a strenuous yeast in the mud and the fire; out of it grows to sight a new firm front, a spring-board for fresh victories.

In 1917, Gibbon moved to the Italian Front, and sent back some colourful reports of that lesser-known theatre. The fighting there had begun in 1915 on the border between Austria-Hungary and Italy, with the Italians trying to seize the Austrian Littoral and northern Dalmatia, as well as the territories of present-day Trentino and South Tyrol. As with other battlegrounds of the First World War, it started with mobile engagements but soon stagnated into trench warfare. The civilians in the contested areas on both sides suffered badly, being moved to refugee camps where many died due to the dismal conditions.

By the time Gibbon arrived in the region, the Austro-Hungarians had been reinforced by some German units freed from the Eastern Front after the Russian Revolution.

On 3 September, Gibbon described a charge up a mountainside:

> The battle is swelling southward, eating Austria's strength as it goes. General Boroevic has ten divisions opposed to General Cappello's Second Army, of which a fair proportion consists of mountain troops. His line in the extreme north has been broken. He has fallen back upon such country as impedes our advance there—land that lies like a pane of splintered glass, a mere disorder of rocks and gullies, overgrown with a sparse growth of pine and fir and broken by hollows as arbitrary and unforeseeable as the Dolimas upon the Carso. The Austrians there are making as desperate resistance as they may. Opposite Tolmino and its bridgehead there is the Twenty-first Division, next southwards lies the Seventeenth Mountain Brigade, with a reinforcement of nine various battalions, and then next and still southward there are appearances of the Twenty-fourth Division, which seems lately to have replaced the Twenty-first Division of Schutzen, whose wrecked remains exist as a reserve. They stand near the village of Kal (north-east of the Bainsizza Plateau) and are supplemented with an extra brigade, consisting of the Sixty-fourth and Thirty-seventh Regiments of Schutzen ...The Italians came uphill at them from that great, almost circular, hollow between Monte Santo and the main bulk of Monte San Gabriele, which is known as the Conca di Gargaro. To attack they had a slope of one in three to ascend, against machine-gun fire and every obstacle which the elaborate military science of Austria—a military people who stand foremost in the science of war—could devise. I had stationed myself with a colleague at a point whence the actual advance upon the hill was invisible. I saw of that only the fury of the shelling, with black, rose-and-white, and emerald-green shell smokes mixing in choronomatic cadences, while the thunder of the great trench-mortars, the roar of the guns, and the echo of the bursting shells made a choir. The great hollow of Gargaro belched its condensed tides of noise out over the saddle, between Santo and Gabriele, a mile-wide trumpet, magnifying the uproar of battle to the appealing apocalyptic note of Gabriel's trumpet There were moments in that ecstasy of gunnery when "the mountains sang together" as if they themselves were at war.

On 30 November, with the headline 'Von Below's Hammer: Fruitless Blows':

> The principle of the German offensive methods is exemplified by the fighting which still proceeds along the great mountain ridge which joins the Piave valley with that of the Brenta. Monte Grappa, with its subordinate heights, is the western buttress of it, and Monte Tomba, with its outlying height, Monfenera, is the eastern, with Monte Pallone lying between them. It is a titanic barricade of crags and precipices, crevasses, and stone slides, which lies across von Below's road to the illimitable riches of the great plain below. On either hand of it the rival valleys run like roads, but where he can avail himself of them that barrier must be forced somewhere.

Below's first attempt, as I described after his efforts to cross the river had been frustrated, was at Monfenera and Monte Tomba, where he poured out Prussian and Pomeranian blood like water in effort after effort to rush the Italian defence off its feet, and start again that swift and irresistible onward movement which seems essential to any German success. He made of his best troops a hammer-head with which to drive in our front, actually weakening much of the remainder of his line in order to put an insuperable weight into the blow. How that hammer rose and fell, striking again and again, I have already told. His losses were ghastly and ours were heavy; but the Monte Tomba defences held, and the great blow failed.

Elsewhere Gibbon reported from the Isonzo, the Piave and the Carso. The Italian Front ended in October 1918 with a major Italian victory at the Battle of Vittorio Veneto (later commemorated by the name of an Italian battleship, which saw action against the Royal Navy in the Mediterranean in the Second World War), accompanied by the collapse of the Austro-Hungarian empire.

In 1918 and 1919 Gibbon served in the Royal Marines, being appointed a temporary honorary major in May 1918. Records of his time in the service are slim. In 1976, a Mr AD Harper made an official request from the Royal Marines press office. He received a reply from the Department of the Commandant General at the Ministry of Defence, stating 'I am sorry to say that, despite a great deal of research into the subject, our records are somewhat thin on this particular person' and that 'it would appear that he had neither a long nor a distinguished record of Service in the Royal Marines.' The record does show that Gibbon was appointed fleet press officer, which would make sense given his journalistic background.

The file Harper collected had Gibbon's birthdate as 1879 – the error appears elsewhere, but the census indisputably shows 1878 – and noted that he reported for the *Daily Mail*, *Daily News* and *Daily Chronicle* during the Great War, though as we have seen he was also published by *The Daily Telegraph*.

Post-war career

After the war, Gibbon wrote the text for a 48-page pictorial pamphlet *The triumph of the Royal Navy: how the German fleet came to Britain*[56] recording the surrender of the High Seas Fleet to Britain at Scapa Flow at the end of the war and its subsequent scuttling by the Germans. He was placed on the retired list of the Royal Marines on 13 May 1919.

The *London Gazette* records that Gibbon was declared bankrupt in 1919 as well. In it he is described as 'Perceval Gibbon, formerly of 122 Beaufort Mansions SW, in the county of London, but whose present place of residence the Petitioning Creditor has been unable to ascertain, a domiciled Englishman journalist.' It seems

---

56 Hodder & Stoughton, 1919. A copy is held by the Imperial War Museum in London.

his income did not match his lifestyle, or perhaps he suffered some unforeseen stroke of misfortune.

Gibbon's adventurism did not appeal to all of his fellow Brother Savages. The artist Bert Thomas recalled:[57]

> Perceval Gibbon was a quarrelsome little man who took a delight in getting people's backs up. I suffered from this on several occasions. One summer's evening at Adelphi Terrace he was in one of his specially truculent moods and Norman Tharp, the most inoffensive of men, took umbrage and suggested they both adjourned to the terrace to settle things, as Gibbon had gone too far. So, coats off, they went at it hammer and tongs and Gibbon got very much the worst of the scrap. They returned to the bar, but Gibbon once again made himself a nuisance. Back to the terrace they went for another set-to—which, by the way, was witnessed by Lillah McCarthy from an adjacent window, much to her delight. The result of this second encounter was indeed the decline and fall of Gibbon.

Quarrelsomeness and truculence aside, Gibbon led an extraordinary life, which one might have thought would have made him a lively Savage bar companion.

Gibbon died in 1926. His obituary in *The Times*[58] was perfunctory on his work as a war reporter, but complimentary on his work in fiction:

> It is as a writer of fiction, and especially of short stories, that Gibbon will be chiefly remembered. "The Vrouw Grobelaar's Leading Cases," which appeared in 1905, was undoubtedly his best collection. The shrewd, humorous old Boer widow is an unforgettable figure, and Gibbon also showed in these tales a remarkable power of hard, straightforward horror. They give, too, a striking picture of the Boer character as developed among the Kaffir population, with its rude contempt of life, narrow pride, and intense loyalty to a race creed ... his vivid imagination, his store of curious and terrible incidents which he had heard of or seen in his wanderings, and his power of leading up to a dramatic and forcible conclusion, found their best scope in magazine stories, which appeared afterwards in collections, such as "The Adventures of Miss Gregory" and "The Second-class Passenger." Gibbon was also counted among South African poets, but there his work showed too plainly the influence of Browning.

Sir Percival Phillips: war reports and a famous 'scoop'
Early life

Percival Phillips was born in 1877 in Brownsville, Pennsylvania, in the United States. He started working as a journalist at the age of 16, initially writing about

57 Bradshaw, op cit, p 87.
58 1 June 1926.

coal miners' riots in his home state. At the age of just 19 he covered the Greco-Turkish War of 1897, and the following year the Spanish-American War, thereby establishing himself as a war reporter.

In 1901 he moved to England, where he started working for the *Daily Express*. He continued to cover wars and other events across the globe, including the Russo-Japanese war of 1905, the Jamaican earthquake in 1907, the Catalonian revolution of 1909, the Portuguese revolution of 1910 and the Balkan War of 1912–23. He joined the Savage Club in 1906, under the category of literature.

War reports

Phillips was sent to Belgium at the outset of the First World War. One of his earliest despatches was on 7 August, regarding the town of Liege:[59]

> Yesterday the town presented a picture in which war and peace were strangely blended. Cavalry remounts were tethered in circles in some of the squares.
>
> The Place Lambert was filled with camp kitchens, and army cooks were stirring boiled soup for the famished soldiers, while the children of the town looked on in wonderment.
>
> The pigeons, which fled in terror from their haunts around the old palace of the archbishop, returned yesterday, and were induced to accept bits of bread from the Prussian troopers.
>
> Piles of bodies still awaiting identification lie under shrouds in the Place Marche. One body is that of a child of twelve, another is an old man in civilian clothes.
>
> Soldiers of the opposing armies mingle freely in the streets.

Phillips had an international reputation, such that two American newspapers worked a deal with the *Daily Express* later the same month to reprint his copy. Then, however, the authorities started to get chary about the press at the Front. On 27 August, Phillips complained about French censorship:

> The "fog of war" that has settled over this country screens the important movement of the allied armies as effectively as the stone wall built across France from Dunkirk to Ushant. They have closed towns that appear to ordinary civilians to be far away from the theatre of war. There is a proscribed zone, officially described by the French military authorities, into which no foreigner or native not connected with the operation may enter.

Phillips was ordered back to London as Kitchener's clamp-down on reporters took effect. Almost straight away he was made one of the accredited correspon-

---

59 Quoted in Black, op cit, p 104. The piece was published in the *Daily Express* on 10 August 1914.

dents and told he would be billeted with the BEF in France. He soon returned to Belgium by himself, but ran up against the censors once he started writing copy.

In 1915, the *Daily Express* encountered financial problems, which affected Phillips even though his expenses were fairly modest. In the spring of that year, restrictions on official correspondents were lifted slightly, enabling Phillips to join the BEF and report developments. But the clumsy hand of the censor had not been lifted. In May, he along with the other accredited correspondents of the time arrived at St Omer to find themselves unwanted by the officers based there. They were permitted to report the Battle of Loos at the outset – though not to be at the Front – but then the censors moved in and, as one of the reporters later put it, 'chopped our dispatches to meaningless pie'.[60] In those circumstances the reporters did what they could. Though they were in theoretical competition, they co-operated with one another, since no individual could begin to cover the whole Front by himself.

In 1916, Phillips was sent to Ireland to cover the Troubles, and was present for the Easter Rising. He returned to France afterwards, filing reports on one of the battles at Vimy Ridge in May, but then had to go to England as he was stricken by illness. In June 1916, he stayed at the Savage Club whilst convalescing,[61] then in Bournemouth before going to the Front in France once again. Whilst on the Somme he was described by his future Brother Savage Basil Clarke in the following terms:[62]

> Percival Phillips of the *Express*, from the outer fringe of the circle round the fire contributes now and again a snappy, dry, and almost pawky comment to the chatter. He speaks but seldom; a listener rather than a talker. But one of those delightful people whom one can describe as a "merry listener." He was a war correspondent at the age of twenty, when, with pack on shoulder, so to speak, he set off on his own account from his home in America to the Greek war, where he wrote war dispatches and sent them on approval to editors, American and British, who were forced, by their very excellence, to use them. He soon won for himself a foremost place among English journalists. A man of fine presence, great unselfishness, courtly manner, and sterling worth,

---

60 G Valentine Williams (1882–1946), *Daily Mail* reporter during the war. Since reporters were not allowed near the Front, Williams obtained a commission with the Irish Guards in December 1915. He won the Military Cross on the Battle of the Somme, where he was seriously wounded. He then joined the accredited war correspondents based at British General Headquarters and continued to serve as the accredited correspondent for the *Daily Mail* until the end of the war. Like some other reporters of the day, Williams made extra money churning out popular fiction, in his case mystery stories, publishing 28 books from 1918 until his death in 1946. Some of his reports of the First World War were collected in a book which could be found online at the time of writing: G Valentine Williams, *With Our Army in Flanders* (Edward Arnold, 1915).

61 Black, op cit, p 136.

62 Clarke, op cit, p 177–178.

he is a large contributor in a quiet way to the happiness and almost family "comfortableness" (one would have liked to borrow the word *Gemütlichkeit*) that characterised our mess.

Here are some of Phillips' reports for the latter half of the war. The censor's hand had a slightly lighter touch by that stage, though it was undoubtedly still present.

From 18 September 1916 on the Somme:

> The tense calm of the last hour before battle leaves an unforgettable impression. The preparations are finished. Everything is ready for the dawn. Expectant infantry crowd the forward trenches, rehearsing their final orders and locking home their bayonets; gunners pace idly beside their batteries, fingering their watches; empty dressing-stations put out neat piles of bandages, and skilful surgeons wait to mend the wounds of men who are still unhurt. The stage is set for the great drama, and silence, heavy and oppressive, hangs over the waiting army in the field.

From June 1917, at Messines Ridge:

> The battle itself was rehearsed bit by bit. The infantrymen who followed the equally well trained artillerymen's barrage this morning had been drilled for their journey by practice trips far from the scene that left nothing to chance. They had a wonderful model of the ridge—covering more than an acre of ground and true in every detail of contour and adornment—which could be studied for hours. I came back from witnessing the attack early this morning.

In August 1917, at Passchendaele, he wrote of the effect of the mud, one of the enduring images of the Western Front in general and that battle in particular:

> I talked today with a number of wounded men engaged in the fighting in Langemarck[63] and beyond, and they are unanimous in declaring that the enemy infantry made a very poor show wherever they were deprived of their supporting machine guns and forced to choose between meeting a bayonet charge and fight. The mud was our men's greatest grievance. It clung to their legs at every step. Frequently they had to pause to pull their comrades from the treacherous mire—figures embedded to the waist, some of them trying to fire their rifles at a spitting machine gun and yet, despite these almost incredible difficulties, they saved each other and fought the Hun through the floods to Langemarck.

In April 1918, when the Germans threw the British back during Operation Michael, thus undoing any gain the latter had made during the Battle of Passchendaele,[64] he was compelled to send a sanguine despatch:

---

63 Langemarck is now the site of the largest German cemetery on the Western Front.
64 See John Terraine, *The Road to Passchendaele: The Flanders Offensive 1917, A Study in*

Our withdrawal from Passchendaele and the ground for which so many men of the Empire have died causes the deepest regret, but it has not discouraged the soldiers, who know that in open warfare trench positions lose their former value, and that the people will regard the sacrifice in the same sensible way.

During the Battle of the Somme he had seen tanks in action, which he had described as 'Sinister, formidable, and industrious, these novel machines pushed boldly into No Man's Land, astonishing our soldiers no less than they frightened the enemy'. In April 1918, he saw a tank-on-tank clash:

> For the first time British and German tanks have met in battle, and the victory is ours. They fought yesterday in the open fields round Villers-Brettonneux, east of Amiens, where the enemy made a determined and, for the moment, a successful attack on that town and high ground round it.
>
> The German tanks led the attack, swinging on the town from the north-east and from the south, and in their wake came infantry with their machine guns and heavy mortars and light artillery.
>
> Although there were four or five tanks. they were bulky, ungainly creatures, quite unlike the British tank in appearance, with a broad, squat turret containing quick-firing guns. Hidden in the thick mist until very close to our trenches, they crawled up in the wake of an intense barrage about six o'clock in the morning.

Inevitability (Leo Cooper, 1977).

We will encounter Operation Michael on many occasions in this book, as a number of Savages saw action resisting it. It came about because the Germans realised that with the ongoing Royal Navy blockade and the entry of America into the war that they could not last much longer, but on the other hand, with reinforcements arriving from the Eastern Front following the end of Russian participation in the war, they had had a significant temporary boost to their combat power.

Operation Michael began on 21 March 1918. Within a week, three British divisions – the 16th (Irish), 36th (Ulster) and 66th (2nd East Lancashire) – each with losses of more than 7,000, had been virtually annihilated. Soon General Petain thought the cause was lost.

Despite their early gains, the Germans slowed for a variety of reasons. They lacked cavalry and tanks (the latter were too slow for fast mobile advances anyway) and the ground which they were traversing had been devastated by almost four years of war. Often their soldiers would be slowed, not emboldened, by capturing Allied supply dumps as the Germans stopped to enjoy the sort of food and drink that had become unavailable to them. Moreover, the Allies finally implemented a sound strategic organisation with General Foch appointed Generalissimo in charge of all their armies, thwarting German attempts to split the British and French, and those armies started to show the lessons of war just as much as the Germans. Operation Michael ended on 5 April. On 9 April, the Germans launched Operation Georgette, to try and throw the British First and Second armies into the sea. General Haig responded with his famous command which concluded 'There is no other course open to us but to fight it out. Every position must be held to the last man: there must be no retirement. With our backs to the wall and believing in the justice of our cause each one of us must fight on to the end. The safety of our homes and the Freedom of mankind alike depend upon the conduct of each one of us at this critical moment.' On 29 April, the Germans called a halt to Georgette as well.

They concentrated their guns on one British tank, but others came to the rescue, and in the brief duel that followed one enemy tank was put out of action by an opponent of less bulk and lighter armament and the others scuttled away.

The lesson of this first engagement between German and British tanks seems to be that we have nothing to fear from the enemy despite the greater size and armament of his machine. The crews plainly showed their unwillingness to stand when invited to fight out to a finish.

He was in Belgium in November 1918 when the Armistice was signed:

Just at eleven I came into the little town of Leuze, which had been one of the headquarters nearest the uncertain front. From the windows of all the houses round about, and even from the roofs, the inhabitants looked down on the troops and heard uncomprehendingly the words of the Colonel as he read from a sheet of paper the order that ended hostilities.

A trumpeter sounded the "stand fast". In the narrow high-street at one end of the little square were other troops moving slowly forward, and as the notes of the bugle rose clear and crisp above the rumble of the gun-carriages these men turned with smiles of wonder and delight and shouted to each other 'The war's over'.

The band played "God save the King". None heard it without a quiver of emotion. The mud-stained troops paused in the crowded street, the hum of traffic was stilled. A rippling cheer was drowned in the first notes of the Belgian hymn; the "Marseillaise" succeeded it, and the army of each ally was thus saluted in turn. I do not think that any one heard the few choked words of the old mayor when he tried to voice the thanks of Belgium for this day of happiness.

Post-war career

For his services during the war, Phillips was knighted, despite being an American.[65] In 1924, he moved to the *Daily Mail* and continued work as a foreign correspondent, covering stories across the world in the 1920s and 1930s. Much of his travel involved accompanying the Prince of Wales on royal tours including Canada in 1919, India and Japan in 1921–22 and Africa in 1928. One of his contemporaries was the journalist and novelist Evelyn Waugh, who was then working for *The Times*, the *Daily Express* and the *Daily Graphic*. Both covered the coronation of Haile Selassie in 1930.

Eventually, Phillips fell out with the *Daily Mail*'s proprietor, Lord Rothermere (he may also have disagreed with the editorial line of the paper), and moved to

---

65 The bestowing of knighthoods on non-British citizens is not as unusual as one might think; later recipients have included Bob Geldof of Band Aid fame and Norman Schwartzkopf, commander of Allied forces in the 1991 Gulf War.

its the rival, *The Daily Telegraph*, where the next memorable incident of his life occurred, extra irony being given to the saga by the fact that the *Daily Mail* then hired Waugh.

Phillips and Waugh both returned to Abyssinia in 1935. While en route, Waugh encountered an interesting character called Francis Rickett, who claimed to be carrying funds raised by the Coptic Church which he was to pass to the Red Cross in Abyssinia. Rickett also claimed that the telegrams he received continually through their travels were from his huntsmen, Rickett being the master of the Craven Hunt. Waugh correctly discerned that Rickett was not telling the truth, but instead of trying to befriend him and prise information out of him in a traditional journalistic fashion, he wrote to a contact in England and asked her to investigate Rickett there.[66] Given the length of time correspondence took between England and Abyssinia in those days, he could not have expected a reply for a month at best. He therefore left Addis Ababa with another reporter to visit the town of Harar to follow up a story about the French Count and Countess Maurice de Roquefeuil du Bousquet, who had been arrested whilst trying to pass a hidden roll of film to the Italian consul.

Phillips, more experienced and better connected than Waugh, remained behind at Addis Ababa and used all his contacts and skill to find out Rickett's true purpose. It turned out Rickett was trying to buy up the mineral rights for about half of Abyssinia for £10m, supposedly on behalf of a British and American entity called the African Exploitation and Development Corporation. *The Daily Telegraph* duly published Phillips' scoop, which began 'A few strokes of an ordinary black fountain-pen this morning performed the most momentous and far-reaching act in the history of Ethiopia, bringing her out from the Middle Ages and setting her fairly on the road of the twentieth century.'[67] The reasoning on the part of Haile Selassie in signing the contract seemed to be to acquire the protection of Britain and America against the threat of Italian invasion.

Predictably enough, it was soon discovered that the corporation was a straw entity, registered in Delaware. Mussolini was furious, whilst London and Washington quickly dissociated themselves from Ricketts and advised Selassie to disown the agreement. In short order the bargain evaporated, but not before *The Telegraph* had sold its scoop repeatedly and at the particular expense of the *Mail*.

---

66 Waugh's contact was Penelope Betjeman, the wife of John Betjeman, with whom Waugh had long been obsessed. Apparently he never got very far with her, who regarded him as unattractive and was not impressed by the obscene language he liked to use in letters to her – the Rickett request being no exception, as Waugh promised her 'Be a good girl about this and I will reward you with a fine fuck when I get back.' See Stephen Robinson, *The Remarkable Lives of Bill Deedes* (Abacus, 2008), pp 56-7.

67 Robinson, op cit, pp 56-7.

The normal response of a chastened foreign correspondent, especially in those days, would be to get inebriated at the hotel bar on expenses. Instead, Waugh chose to write the roman-à-clef, *Scoop*, based on the events. Phillips appeared in the novel in the form of the character Sir Jocelyn Hitchcock.[68]

Later in the 1930s, Phillips covered Gandhi's nationalism in India. He died in 1937, while reporting the Spanish Civil War, his final assignment as a war correspondent.

---

68 See WF Deedes, 'The real Scooped: who was who in Waugh's cast list and why', *The Daily Telegraph*, 28 May 2003. Deedes was always associated with the novel as he was a junior reporter present at the time, and has often been presumed to have been the model for the lead character.

CHAPTER 4

Savage Generals

Introduction: the Great War leadership in general

> A feeling exists that life is being thrown away on objectives
> which are not worth it ... Are we not asking too much of our
> infantry?

Sir Henry Rawlinson[1]

For many of the general public, the Great War was nothing but *Blackadder Goes Forth* writ large, with well-upholstered but tragically ignorant generals sitting in chateaux sipping champagne whilst sending millions to their death, using a reprise of Napoleonic infantry tactics wholly unsuited to the age of the machine gun. *Blackadder's* General Melchett called the Charge of the Light Brigade 'a victory for common sense', while the programme also depicted his commander

---

1   General Henry Rawlinson, 1st Baron Rawlinson (1864–1925). At the beginning of the war, Rawlinson was appointed General Officer Commanding 4th Division in France. He later took command of IV Corps. In December 1914, Rawlinson predicted that the Allies would win a war of attrition, but it was unclear whether it would take one, two or three years.

Rawlinson received several promotions before being given command of the new Fourth Army in January 1916, and he led them on the Somme later that year. He therefore has to shoulder some of the blame for the disaster of the first day, though he escaped censure at the time, because his dismissal would have been an admission that the assault had failed. Also, he would have preferred a more limited attack than Haig demanded. Later in the war, he held a senior command in the 'Hundred Days' Offensive of 1918, the success of which demonstrated that he had learned much in the intervening years.

Field Marshal Haig as determined to make whatever sacrifice was necessary in order to move his drinks cabinet six inches closer to Berlin.[2]

As ever, reality paints a more complex picture. It is true that Haig was not without critics from an early stage. Winston Churchill made some negative judgements in his history of the conflict, written in the 1920s[3] when Haig was still alive. When Haig died in 1928 he was greatly mourned, with the general public turning out in huge numbers to pay their respects. In 1936, however, Lloyd George published his memoirs,[4] which included a stinging attack on Haig, saying he was 'brilliant to the top of his army boots'. The historian Norman Stone said Haig was the greatest ever Scottish general since he was responsible for the deaths of more English soldiers than anyone else in history. More substantively, the influential military historian and strategist, Great War veteran and Brother Savage Basil Liddell Hart wrote a book in the 1930s which slated Haig's tactics.[5] We will return to Liddell Hart's work later in the book.

The generals' reputation also suffered due to the rise of the pacifist movement from the late 1920s. That movement was given a powerful literary ally and an even more powerful cinematic one in Erich Maria Remarque's *All Quiet on the Western Front*,[6] essential reading and viewing for anyone interested in the Great War.

In February 1930 a compilation of first-hand accounts was published entitled *On The Front Line*, consisting of short pieces by veterans recalling specific actions. The editor, CB Purdom, wrote in his introduction:[7]

> The impression I get from reading them [the first-hand accounts making up the book] is not that of suffering or horror, but of the senselessness of war. No one who served in it but was oppressed more or less constantly by its futility (sic). Its political effects were far-reaching; but as a method of State action we discovered it to be without any redeeming features. In the narratives printed here the War is looked at from the point of view of individual men engaged in it. These men

---

2 *Blackadder Goes Forth* was co-written by Ben Elton and Richard Curtis. Elton's uncle, as it happens, was Sir Geoffrey Elton, one of the greatest British Tudor historians. Sir Geoffrey upbraided his nephew initially for denigrating the British Army, but apparently quite enjoyed the series anyway.

3 Winston S Churchill, *The World Crisis* (RosettaBooks, 2013, Kindle edn).

4 David Lloyd George, *The War Memoirs of David Lloyd George* (Odhams Press Ltd, new edn, 1938).

5 BH Liddell Hart, *History of the First World War* (Papermac, new edn, 1992).

6 The book, originally titled *Im Westen nichts Neues*, was published in January 1929 by Propyläen Verlag in Germany and the translation, by AW Wheen, was published in English in the same year by Little, Brown and Company.

    The film was released in 1930 and was directed by Lewis Milestone. It is still in this writer's opinion one of the greatest war films of all time.

7 *On the Front Line: True World War I Stories* (edited and introduced by CB Purdom; foreword by Malcolm Brown, Constable & Robinson Ltd, 2009), p 11.

do not lose their human qualities, their courage, honesty, chivalry and spirit of self-sacrifice, but those qualities themselves are seen to lose their value, for man surrenders himself to the machine and all that makes life worth living is gone. The truth about war is that it is an evil, not only because men suffer and die in it, but because it destroys the meaning of life.

The book showed that within not much more than a decade of the war ending, there had been a shift in attitudes from those revealed in diaries and letters written during the conflict itself. Professor Richard Holmes once commented:[8]

> If you look at what veterans were writing just 10 years after the end of the war, it's quite different from what they were writing at the time.
>
> In the late 1920s, history was refracted through unemployment and the depression, and the war became a sham that wasted men's lives, but contemporary diaries and journals reflect a different image. The war was something to be endured – not in the stiff-upper-lip class sense, but as a necessary hardship in which it was still important to maintain standards.

I would also suggest, however, that during the conflict soldiers and officers alike might have wanted to spare those back home from the horror they were enduring, as well as any military reverses, whilst perhaps in their diaries too it would have been harder to admit to the futility of the conflict or any other negative personal feelings. A decade later they might have been more candid about all those things, assuming they overcame the general reticence of most veterans and their families to speak or write about the war at all after its end.

Well-known among the pacifists of the 1930s was Brother Savage Cyril Joad.[9] On 9 February 1933 he spoke at the Oxford Union 'King and Country' debate in support of the motion 'that this House will in no circumstances fight for its King and Country.' At the time, Hitler had been in power for just ten days, so would not have been perceived as the threat which he later became. The motion, passed by 275 to 153, caused a strong reaction across the press and the public. Churchill called the outcome 'abject, squalid, shameless' and 'nauseating'. The significance of the debate was much greater than an equivalent event might be today: in those pre-internet days, when only the tiniest fraction of the electorate owned a television (and very little was broadcast) and when politics was dominated by a small,

---

8   John Crace, 'Richard Holmes: officer and gentleman', *The Guardian*, 18 May 2004.

9   Cyril Edwin Mitchinson Joad (1891–1953), a popular philosopher (the term not then being a contradiction) famous for his anti-war stance. Joad had effectively evaded serving in the First World War by leaving his home in London and holing up in Wales. He railed against war during the 1930s but eventually came out in support of the Second World War, after it had started. Joad's legendary oratory and debating skills would have been a most suitable addition to the Savages of the day.

largely public school and Oxbridge elite, the reports of the debate would have been much more widely read and influential than today's Oxford Union debates or any equivalent such as debates organised by Intelligence Squared. (Ironically, Joad, who had refused to serve in the First World War, eventually came out in support of the Second World War.)[10]

Haig's legacy also came under attack due to events. Once the Second World War broke out, it is wholly understandable that many felt the sacrifices of the First World War had been a complete waste, whatever had been achieved on the battlefield.[11]

In the 1960s, the counter-culture and its growing cynicism about authority in all its forms took firmly against the Great War and its generals. The popular attitude was summed up in Joan Littlewood's musical *Oh, What a Lovely War!* adapted for the screen at the end of the decade by Richard Attenborough. (Littlewood, incidentally, was the guest of honour at a Savage Club ladies' dinner on 6 June 1964 – the twentieth anniversary of D-Day, though that was not mentioned on the menu – chaired by Henry Oscar and held at Whitehall Place.)

Both Alan Clark's *The Donkeys*[12] and Barbara W Tuchman's Pulitzer prize-winner *The Guns of August*[13] provided revisionist inspiration for Littlewood's musical. When the film rights to *Oh, What a Lovely War!* were being sold, Clark sued Littlewood's company for failing to credit the use of his research and was awarded £1000 in damages and 5 per cent of the film rights. To Littlewood's relief, though, the Haig family, anxious to defend their famous relative, failed to stop the play or the film.[14]

Their books were joined in 1963 by AJP Taylor's book *The First World War* –

---

10 The debate was followed later in the decade by a by-election in Oxford which was, very unusually, contested solely on foreign policy grounds. It was won by the pro-appeasement Conservative candidate Quintin Hogg (later Lord Hailsham), who had spoken in opposition to the motion at the Oxford Union in 1933.

11 It is worth noting at this point that fighting on the Western Front ended due to an armistice, not a full-scale surrender. There would have been some concern on the ground that the fighting would resume, while some generals – especially the much less jaded Americans – felt that they should continue with the attack until they reached Berlin. That explains why fighting continued from the announcement of the ceasefire at 5am on 11 November 1918 until it took effect at 11am.

Even on the German side, some thought that they had not been defeated and therefore considered the armistice amounted to a gross betrayal. Most notable among their number was a certain Austrian corporal by the name of Adolf Hitler.

12 Hutchinson, 1961.

13 Macmillan, 1962.

14 Matthew Sweet, 'Oh, What a Lovely War: Why the battle still rages', *The Daily Telegraph*, 1 February 2014. Sweet noted: "'The Haig family wanted to take out an injunction on us because we were denigrating their ancestor,' recalls Melvin. 'But everything that we said on stage was documented. Word for word. Lines like, 'I ask thee for victory, Lord, before the Americans arrive.' They sent their solicitors in to see the show three times a week, and had we got one word wrong they could have closed us.'"

dedicated to Littlewood – which became a best-seller. It contained a ruthless assault on the generals, the following being an illustrative passage:[15]

> The statesmen were overwhelmed by the magnitude of events. The generals were overwhelmed also. Mass, they believed, was the secret of victory. The mass they evoked was beyond their control. All fumbled more or less helplessly. They were pilots without a chart, blown before the storm and not knowing where to seek harbour.

Many continued with the same thesis: the title of John Laffin's 1988 book *British Butchers and Bunglers of World War One*[16] leaves no ambiguity as to its contents. From the 1960s onwards, there was a rise in fame of the war poetry of Wilfred Owen, Siegfried Sassoon, Rupert Brooke and the other now familiar names, most of whom were largely unknown in the immediate aftermath of the Great War.

A notable exception to the academic trend was the historian John Terraine, who remained sympathetic towards Haig throughout the 1960s. In more recent years, Paddy Griffith's *Battle Tactics of the Western Front: the British Army's Art of Attack 1916–18*[17] argued that the British Army did in fact learn quickly from the disaster of the Somme to achieve the final victory in 1918. Among others, Professor Gary Sheffield,[18] the late Professor Richard Holmes[19] and the maverick but entertaining former Gurkha officer Gordon Corrigan[20] all published books giving at least qualified praise to Haig and his fellow generals. While this chapter was being drafted, Peter Hart published *The Last Battle: Endgame on the Western Front, 1918*,[21] in which he insisted that Haig deserved credit for the astonishing Allied victories of the final months of the war. The work of all those historians has swung the academic debate back some distance from the iconoclasm of the 1960s, but one suspects that none of their efforts have been able to compete in the popular imagination with *Blackadder Goes Forth* or the anti-war poets.

My own view is that even the generals' harshest critics cannot deny their ultimate achievement but, equally, even their staunchest defenders cannot deny the terrible cost or the mistakes made as the slow learning process played out. Haig assumed command when the pre-war scenario that the British had prepared for had vanished, and when the vast majority of the hastily assembled new armies

---

15 Penguin Classics edn, 1974. The quoted passage is from the preface.

16 History Press, 2003 edn.

17 Yale University Press, 1994.

18 See for example *Forgotten Victory: The First World War: Myths and Realities* (Endeavour Press, 2001), and *The Chief: Douglas Haig and the British Army* (Aurum Press, 2011).

19 In a number of publications including *The Western Front* (BBC Worldwide, 1999) and *Tommy: The British Soldier on the Western Front 1914–1918* (Harper Perennial, 2004).

20 *Mud, Blood and Poppycock* (Weidenfeld & Nicolson, 2012).

21 Profile, 2018.

were not adequately trained or equipped. They had suffered horrendously at Loos, and would do so again at the Somme and Passchendaele. But the British Army was the only army which was in the war from start to finish and did not suffer a collapse of morale at any point. It survived all its own failed offensives, and held on during 'Operation Michael', the last throw of the German die, and went on to produce arguably the greatest series of victories in its history, in the form of the 'Hundred Days' offensive of 1918. Over that time offensive tactics evolved from a crude recreation of the Napoleonic wars to the first modern combined arms attacks involving co-ordination between aircraft, artillery, tanks and infantry, with men advancing under cover of a 'creeping barrage' that did not allow the defenders any opportunity to fire unmolested. It is as unfair as it is inaccurate that the British Army and its generals remain in the public conscience because of all the earlier defeats and stalemates, with very little knowledge of the battles which produced eventual victory.

The question is sometimes raised as to why the British and French continually mounted offensives when the nature of warfare at the time so clearly favoured defence. A partial answer is that the Germans occupied great swathes of Belgium and Northern France, and, even allowing for exaggerations in Allied propaganda, were not benign conquerors. The Allies – particularly the French, who were the senior coalition partner for most of the war – felt they could not allow the Germans to retain the captured territory.

It is also true that military doctrine among the British and French emphasised attack and recognised the consequent price that would have to be paid in casualties. Again, we return to the question of national honour and how the men of the time perceived the struggle. The historian Sir Michael Howard wrote that 'the casualty lists that a later generation was to find so horrifying were considered by contemporaries not [as] an indication of military incompetence, but a measure of national resolve, of fitness to rank as a Great Power'.[22] Ironically, one of the more incompetent generals – Hamilton, who commanded the failed Gallipoli expedition – was also one of the more humane and compassionate. He showed great sympathy for the men under his command and the terrible conditions in which they were forced to fight.[23]

---

22 Quoted in Holmes, *The Western Front*, op cit, p 35.
23 For example, he wrote in a letter to Herbert Asquith, that the Naval Division 'are stout fellows and are sticking it out well, but they are very tired … Simply put the poor fellows are worn out and some of them are as weak as cats … [Major General Sir Archibald] Paris was horrified at the youth of some of the boys who had been sent out to him, and wanted to send them home. He found one of them crying in the trenches because he was so frightened …But I told him not to send them home but to keep them for light duties in camp, and doing messages, cooking etc. etc. I assured him they would grow up and have time to fill out into fine men before the war

There were occasional mutterings from the rank and file and later from historians that Haig and the other generals were not seen at the front. The historian Wade Davis, for example, wrote scathingly:[24]

> In four years at the head of the largest army the British Empire had ever placed in the field, a force that would suffer 2,568,834 casualties in France and Belgium alone, Haig never once saw the front; nor did he visit the wounded. Long after the war Haig's son attempted an explanation: "The suffering of his men during the Great War caused him great anguish. I believe that he felt that it was his duty to refrain from visiting the casualty clearing stations because these visits made him physically ill."

Certainly it would be wrong to assume the generals of all sides were immune to the suffering over which they presided. After the war Haig devoted the remaining ten years of his life to the welfare of his former charges, being instrumental in the formation of what became the British Legion. One of his German counterparts, Marshal Von Hindenburg, despaired in his memoirs at some of the sights he had seen during wartime. Of a tactical victory over the Russians in 1915 he wrote:[25]

> On the orders of His Majesty the whole affair was called the "Winter Battle in Masuria." I must be excused a more detailed description. What is there new I could say? The name charms like an icy wind or the stillness of death. As men look back on the course of this battle they will only stand and ask themselves: "Have earthly beings really done these things, or is it all but a fable and a phantom? Are not those marches in the winter nights, that camp in the icy snowstorm, and that last phase of the battle in the forest of Augustovo, so terrible for the enemy, but the creations of an inspired human fancy?"

On the French side, the 'hero of Verdun', General Petain, had been ready to throw in the towel during Operation Michael. The memory of the appalling bloodshed of the Great War and the devastation of large parts of Northern France would ultimately lead him to accept a humiliating truce with the Germans just over twenty years later.[26]

The fact that generals were not always seen at the Front was partially a reflec-

---

came to an end.' (Quoted by Colin Clifford, *The Asquiths* (John Murray, 2002), p 319.)

24 Wade Davis, *Into the Silence: The Great War, Mallory and the Conquest of Everest* (Vintage Books, 2012), p 29.

25 Paul Von Hindenburg, *Out of My Life* (Cassell and Company, 1920).

26 Petain was convicted of treason, as was his collaborator in the Vichy government, Pierre Laval. Brother Savage Peter Ustinov wrote a play about them, *The Moment of Truth*, exploring what Ustinov saw as a cruel irony that the French celebrated the life of Napoleon, a man responsible for the deaths of hundreds of thousands of Frenchmen, yet convicted Laval and Petain for treason (and executed the former) for an action – the 1940 Armistice – which was entered into for the sole reason of trying to save the lives of (potentially) millions of French citizens.

tion of its size – several hundred miles – which combined with the regular rotation of forces meant no-one could realistically have visited all of the soldiers in all of the forward trenches even if he had tried. More importantly, it would have been inappropriate for a senior general to have done so anyway, since it was not his role to be leading from the front. Instead, he was supposed to be at the hub of communications directing the flow of battle. Also, from a crudely economic perspective, it made no sense to risk high-ranking officers more than necessary since it took much more time and expense to train a general than a private. Rudyard Kipling, in his history of the Irish Guards, wrote of an incident involving the future Brother Savage Harold Alexander:[27]

> The Germans certainly whizz-banged the working-parties generously, but the flights as a rule buried themselves harmlessly in the soft ground. We on our side made no more trouble than could be avoided, but worked on the wire double tides. In the heat of the job, on the night of the 11th January, the Brigadier came round and the CO. took him out to see Captain Alexander's party wiring their posts. It was the worst possible moment for a valuable brigadier to wander round front lines. The moon lit up the snow and they beheld a party of Germans advancing in open order, who presently lay down and were joined by more. At eighty yards or so they halted, and after a short while crawled away. "We did not provoke battle, as we would probably have hurt no one, and we wanted to get on with our wiring." But had the Brigadier been wasted in a mere front-line bicker, the CO, not to mention Captain Alexander, would have heard of it.

Finally, the statistics show that British officers were not lacking in courage or absent from the action anyway, since the casualty rate among the senior frontline commanders was strikingly high.[28]

All that said, one is entitled to ask whether the tactics of the British Army really required the death of hundreds of thousands of men before they were redeveloped and refined. A somewhat unflattering comparison was made by the late historian Sir John Keegan with the United States Army in the Second World War. America began that conflict with the seventeenth-largest army in the world – just behind Romania – and suffered painful losses in 1942 in North Africa at the hands of the experienced Germans. Yet it swiftly transformed itself into the second most powerful land army in the world (the Soviet Union, by dint of numbers and an almost total indifference to casualties, would have been the first), developing tactics that still inform modern warfare today. It is a tragedy that the new British armies of the Great War did not learn their own lessons as quickly

---

27 Rudyard Kipling (ed), *The Irish Guards in the Great War, edited and compiled from their diaries and papers* (Macmillan, 1923).

28 Of the 1,252 generals in the First World War, 146 were wounded or taken prisoner, and 78 were killed in action or died of wounds. See Professor Gary Sheffield, 'Has history misjudged the generals of World War One?', BBC online http://www.bbc.co.uk/guides/zq2y87h#orb-banner.

and at a lesser cost in lives. In that respect, one should credit their Russian allies with developing some of the first modern offensive techniques of the Great War during their Brusilov Offensive of mid-1916, even if that assault eventually petered out into the usual Great War stalemate with enormous casualties on all sides.[29]

As was inevitable with any large-scale human endeavour, there were mistakes large and small by leaders of all levels. On the Somme, the best known of the British Army's battles of the First World War, the British leaders wrongly thought their preliminary bombardment would suffice to destroy German resistance. When the men went over the top many were carrying too much equipment, walking too slowly, and were unprepared for the German machine guns which awaited them.

There were myriad other reasons for the resultant slaughter. To some extent it was down to Haig's insistence on a great push, rather than the 'bite and hold' cautious gains intended by Rawlinson. Also, the German trenches were deeper and better defended than those of the Allies, partly due to better engineering and partly due to the Germans not feeling the need for offensives to gain lost national territory. Far from being surprised by the attack, the Germans had learned much of the British intentions via the 'Moritz' system of listening devices, information provided by British POWs (including a deserter who offered much detail) and a captured British infantry tactics handbook. They therefore knew the timing of the attack and the precise methods the British would employ.

The British faced inevitable technological handicaps – poor communications (radio, for example, being in its infancy) meant the generals could not co-ordinate reserves or exploit minor breakthroughs across a wide front involving tens of thousands of men.[30] Finally, to add a cruel paradox, the best ground to attack across was the firmest and least muddy, but that was also the best ground for the Germans to fortify, for exactly the same reasons.

After the first-day disaster, the British started to develop the tactics described earlier, including the 'creeping barrage' whereby artillery would advance its firing in front of the troops, forcing defenders to remain hidden or be killed – arguably, the single most important tactical innovation of the war. Basil Clarke described

---

29 The offensive, named after the Russian General Aleksei Brusilov, involved a major Russian attack against the armies of the Central Powers on the Eastern Front. It began on 4 June 1916 and lasted until late September. The Russians began with a short, accurate, concentrated artillery barrage and focused on breaking through the weak parts of the enemy's front – the template all sides would use later in the war, notably in the German 'Operation Michael' of early 1918 and the successful Allied 'Hundred Days' Offensive later that year. See Timothy Dowling, *The Brusilov Offensive* (Indiana University Press, 2008).

30 In passing I would note that the French Army – which did much better on the first day of the Somme – did not learn the lesson about modern communications and that was a key reason for their rout in 1940, since fast communications became even more crucial in the age of mobile, mechanised warfare as developed by the German Army in the 1930s.

an intermediate tactic in action in his account of the Somme, written some weeks after the first-day disaster:[31]

> It was before daybreak on Saturday that these shell storms began. Drum fire for so many minutes or hours; then the sudden stop. Drum fire again; then the stop. Then again and again, and always the sudden stop ... So a dozen times or more; and a dozen times or more the Germans in those iron-stormed trenches must have leapt to their feet as the sudden silences came. Now for the attack! Such gun fire, so suddenly ceased, could surely portend nothing lesss! It had always done so before!

> But no attack came. From the jagged line of chalk and sand that marked for them the British parapets, watched with beating hearts and tense eyes, no line of khaki figures rose, no bristle of bayonets; not a shrapnel helmet was to be seen above them ...

> [I]n the small hours of Monday the guns blazed forth in a new tornado, things were quietly afoot in the British trenches. Men were tightening their belts, taking another hole in their helmet chin straps, relacing boots, and re-winding puttees, to make them more secure for a run. Rum was served out and the men drank it, toasting one another quietly in the dark of the trench ... Then out of the trench they crawled stealthily—on hands and knees and bellies, over the ploughed up ground, under the great arch of explosive steel that was hurtling through the air from their own guns behind.

> Almost to the very rim of that arch they crawled, almost to the German trenches where that revolving rainbow of shell met the earth, beating it, flaying it, churning it, till the very ground heaved and splashed like a yellow boiling liquid.

> Here in the last darkness of the night they waited, some with rifles ready bayoneted, others with hand bombs in canvas bags.

> There was mist on the ground. They could not be seen even if the Germans had faced the steel storm to look, which they did not.

> The sky began to lighten and gave birth to the first frail limb of day. The shell storm ceased abruptly – cut off clean, snap once again, like light cut off by the shutter of a camera.

> The men jumped to their feet and with hoarse yells sprang into the German trenches.

The British leaders also hastened the development and deployment of tanks, though the designs of the day were too crude to make a critical difference. Therein lay another reason for the terrible death toll – technology that would preclude static trench warfare today was not available then. In any modern conflict, fixed defences could be either circumvented by a mechanised army or obliterated by air attack, but the machines of war in 1914–18 were incapable of doing either.

The war at sea was a different matter. For the first half of the war, Brother Savage

---

31 Basil Clarke, *My Round of the War* (William Heinemann, 1917), pp 240–41.

Admiral John Jellicoe was in a vital strategic role as commander of the Royal Navy's Grand Fleet. Ironically, the chief criticism levelled against him over the years has been that he was *too cautious* – the direct opposite of the criticisms of the generals on land – because he did not throw his fleet at the Germans during the Battle of Jutland. A bolder approach, critics have argued, might have cost a few more ships but won a decisive victory. The distinguished naval historian Andrew Gordon portrayed the Royal Navy admirals of Jellicoe's era as unflatteringly as their counterpart generals: dull Victorian men devoid of imagination. Yet Jellicoe, like Haig, could point to a successful outcome at the end of the war – and in Jellicoe's case with a fraction of the casualties incurred on land.

Ultimately, if one really wishes to find stupidity in the men of the Great War, then the best place to look is among those who caused it. In 1910, Brigadier Henry Wilson, then commandant, staff college, and later an important early strategist on the Western Front,[32] warned his students that a large European war was coming. One student objected, claiming that only 'inconceivable stupidity on the part of statesman' could cause such a disaster. Wilson's response was to laugh: 'Haw! Haw! Haw! Inconceivable stupidity is what you are going to get.'[33]

Field Marshal Lord Roberts VC: 'the master gunner'
A trivia question

Here is a trivia question for history buffs: who was the only commoner in the twentieth century apart from Winston Churchill whose body was permitted to lie in state? The answer is Brother Savage Field Marshal Frederick Sleigh Roberts, 1st Earl Roberts, VC, KG, KP, GCB, OM, GCSI, GCIE, KStJ, VD, PC.

Although he died in France during the Great War, and hence appears on the Savage memorial, Roberts' life and career almost completely preceded the conflict. He served in the Indian Rebellion of 1857, the Expedition to Abyssinia, the Second Anglo-Afghan War and the Second Boer War. A few years before the Great War, Roberts spoke out against what he saw as the threat of German militarism. For that he was derided by much of the popular press, but he was sadly proved right, leading at least one historian of the period to argue that Roberts

---

32 Field Marshal Sir Henry Wilson (1864–1922). While director of military operations at the War Office he played an important part in drawing up plans to deploy an Expeditionary Force to France in the event of war. At the start of the Great War, he advised Sir John French, but was elbowed aside when Haig took over. As we will see, he came back to the fore at the end of the war thanks to his better relations with Lloyd George. After the war he played a leading role in the Irish War of Independence, and served for a short time as an MP. He was assassinated by the IRA in 1922.

33 Max Hastings, *Catastrophe 1914: Europe Goes to War* (William Collins, 2014, Kindle edn), loc 235.

should be held in the same retrospective esteem as the 1930s anti-appeasers such as Churchill.[34]

Forty-one years in India and a Victoria Cross

Roberts was born in 1832, into a military family in Cawnpore, India. His father was General Sir Abraham Roberts, who commanded the 1st Bengal European Regiment at the time, while his mother was the daughter of an Irish major. The young Roberts had some health issues and returned to England, where he was sent to Eton and Sandhurst. After graduating from the latter, he returned to India, where he joined the Bengal Artillery in December 1851 as a second lieutenant. He became *aide-de-camp* to his father the next year. In 1854, he transferred to the Bengal Horse Artillery and was promoted to lieutenant in 1857. He saw action in a number of different engagements, the high point being winning the Victoria Cross. His citation read:

> Lieutenant Roberts' gallantry has on every occasion been most marked.
>
> On following the retreating enemy on 2 January 1858, at Khodagunge, he saw in the distance two Sepoys going away with a standard. Lieutenant Roberts put spurs to his horse, and overtook them just as they were about to enter a village. They immediately turned round, and presented their muskets at him, and one of the men pulled the trigger, but fortunately the caps snapped, and the standard-bearer was cut down by this gallant young officer, and the standard taken possession of by him. He also, on the same day, cut down another Sepoy who was standing at bay, with musket and bayonet, keeping off a Sowar. Lieutenant Roberts rode to the assistance of the horseman, and, rushing at the Sepoy, with one blow of his sword cut him across the face, killing him on the spot.

Remarkably, Roberts' son also went on to win a VC, for the action in which he was fatally wounded at Chieveley, Natal, during the Second Boer War.[35]

Throughout the 1860s and 70s Roberts worked his way up the ranks, fighting in a succession of well-known engagements including the Umbeyla campaign of 1863, the Abyssinian campaign of 1867–1868 and the Lushai campaign of 1871–1872. It did no harm to his career prospects that he saved the life of his superior, John Nicholson, in action. In 1875, he was promoted to brevet colonel and became quartermaster general of the Bengal Army. He was given command

---

34 John Terraine, *Impacts of War: 1914 & 1918* (Leo Cooper, 1993), p 36.

35 There was some controversy because prior to then no VC had been awarded posthumously; instead the would-be recipient would get a special mention in the *London Gazette* recording that, had he survived, he would have been recommended for the award. It was assumed that the young Roberts had received special treatment because of his father (not in the sense he was undeserving, but in that they had bent the rule about posthumous awards). As a result the rule was changed allowing posthumous VCs. See Michael Ashcroft, *Victoria Cross Heroes* (Headline Review, 2006, paperback edn, 2007), pp 14–15.

of the Kurram field force in March 1878 and fought in the Second Anglo-Afghan War. His actions at the Battle of Peiwar Kotal in November 1878 earned him the thanks of parliament.

In September 1879, by then a lieutenant general, he was sent to Kabul to seek retribution for the assassination of the British envoy Sir Louis Cavagnari, who had signed the Treaty of Gandamak with Amir Mohammad Yaqub Khan earlier in the year. Roberts commanded the field army which conquered and occupied Kabul. He was then appointed commander of the Kabul and Kandahar field force. The force, consisting of 10,000 troops, crossed 300 miles of rough terrain in Afghanistan and defeated Ayub Khan at the Battle of Kandahar on 1 September 1880. Once again, Roberts received the thanks of parliament.

In total, Roberts served 41 years in India and, by the time he had finished, was known as the most popular man in England.[36]

In 1895, he began commanding British forces in the rather different environs of Ireland, a common role at the time for older generals near the end of their careers. His predecessor was another great soldier of empire, Sir Garnet Wolseley, who has often been said to be the model for the character of Major-General Stanley in Gilbert and Sullivan's *The Pirates of Penzance*.[37]

While in Ireland Roberts was elevated to field marshal. He also wrote a memoir of his time in India.[38] It was a great success, with no fewer than 34 editions published by 1901.[39] The book was written in a matter-of-fact style, largely devoid of hyperbole. Of his Victoria Cross-winning exploits, for example, he wrote:[40]

> The next moment I descried in the distance two sepoys making off with a standard, which I determined must be captured, so I rode after the rebels and overtook them, and while wrenching the staff out of the

---

36 Walter Jerrold, *Lord Roberts Of Kandahar, VC: The Life-Story Of A Great Soldier* (Facsimile Publisher, 2015, reprinted from original from 1900). See also J Morris, *Pax Britannica* (Harmondsworth, Penguin, 1968), p 237.

37 The author Michael Ainger in *Gilbert and Sullivan, a Dual Biography* (OUP, 2002) prefers General Henry Turner, uncle of Gilbert's wife, as the very model of a modern major general, since Gilbert disliked him and he fitted the caricature of the old-fashioned Victorian officer better than Wolseley. In the original production, however, the actor George Grossmith imitated Wolseley's mannerisms and appearance. Wolseley enjoyed the caricature and sometimes sang the tune to his friends and family. Incidentally, a 1929 recording of Brother Savage George Baker singing the song survives; his prodigious talent is evident.

38 Field Marshal Lord Roberts of Kandahar, *Forty-one Years in India: from Subaltern to Commander-in-chief* (1897, reprinted by Asian Educational Services, New Delhi, 2005). It was easily found online at the time of writing. One professed fan of Roberts' writing was Tony Blair, who wrote in his memoir *A Journey* how exciting and interesting he found them. Whether he learned anything from Roberts I leave for another day.

39 Michael Silvestri, *Ireland and India: Nationalism, Empire and Memory* (Palgrave Macmillan, 2009), p 97.

40 Roberts, op cit, p 215.

hands of one of them, whom I cut down, the other put his musket close to my body and fired; fortunately for me it missed fire, and I carried off the standard.

The book resonated with the values of Victorian England, the Empire and the claimed British superiority over all others. 'Play up, play up, and play the game' exhorted Henry Newbolt's jingoistic poem *Vitaï Lampada*, and no-one played the game better than Roberts. But he did not come across as an inhuman killing machine. Of one engagement he wrote:[41]

> Next day we halted while the walls were being destroyed and the place rendered indefensible. As I was superintending the work of destruction, the horrors of war were once more brought very forcibly before me by the appearance of an infirm old man, who besought me to spare his house, saying: "Yesterday I was the happy father of five sons: three of them lie there" (pointing to a group of dead bodies); "where the other two are, God only knows. I am old and a cripple, and if my house is burned there is nothing left for me but to die." Of course I took care that his house and property were left untouched.

Moreover, later in the book he had the following to say about Indian governance:[42]

> Gradually the form of Government in the United Kingdom has become representative and democratic, and it is therefore assumed by some people, who have little, if any, experience of the east, that the Government of India should be guided by the utterances of self-appointed agitators who pose as the mouth-pieces of an oppressed population. Some of these men are almost as much aliens [Roberts inserts a footnote explaining that he is referring to the Parsees, of whom he says "whose religion and customs are as distinct from those of the Natives of India as are our own."] as ourselves, while others are representatives of a class which, though intellectually advanced, has no influence amongst the races in whom lies the real strength of India. Municipal self-government has been found to answer well in the United Kingdom, and it is held, therefore, that a similar system must be equally successful in India. We in England consume animal food and alcoholic liquors, but have no liking for opium; an effort has accordingly been made to deprive our Asiatic fellow-subjects, who, as a rule, are vegetarians, and either total abstainers or singularly abstemious in the matter of drink, of a small and inexpensive stimulant, which they find necessary to their health and comfort. British institutions and ideas are the embodiment of what long experience has proved to us to best for ourselves; but suddenly to establish these institutions and enforce their ideas on a community which is not prepared for them, does not want them, and cannot understand them, must only lead to suspicion and discontent. The Government of India should, no doubt, be progressive in its policy, and in all things be guided by the immutable principles of right, truth

41 Ibid, p 218.
42 Ibid, p 250.

and justice; but these principles ought to be applied, not necessarily as we should apply them in England, but with due regard to the social peculiarities and religious prejudices of the people whom it ought to be our aim to make better and happier.

British rule in India has long ceased, but Roberts in that passage hit upon a question which has become of significance in modern day Britain, a far more multi-cultural society than in his time. The question is what constitutes 'due regard' to 'social peculiarities and religious prejudices'? We might agree with Roberts that meddling with the opium trade in nineteenth century India was unlikely to be a success, for the reasons he gave.[43] On the other hand, few would disagree that the British rulers were right to end the practice of 'suttee', under which widows threw themselves on their husband's funeral pyres. When faced with calls by Hindus to lift the ban, Sir Charles James Napier replied famously:

> You say that it is your custom to burn widows. Very well. We also have a custom: when men burn a woman alive, we tie a rope around their necks and we hang them. Build your funeral pyre; beside it, my carpenters will build a gallows. You may follow your custom. And then we will follow ours.

And therein lies the classic debate in liberal political thought – how far does one tolerate intolerance? In Britain today, most would agree that honour killings and female genital mutilation (let alone the suttee, if anyone called for its revival) should be outlawed, but there are many milder cultural practices that still offend against majority opinion, such as first-cousin arranged marriages, or wearing the full burka in public, especially in court or places with security concerns. It is a weighty debate for another time.[44]

South Africa

Returning to Roberts' career, his next great assignment was in the Second Boer War. The conflict started badly for the British. They were holed up in appalling conditions in the towns of Kimberley, Ladysmith and Mafeking whilst besieged by the Boers, tenacious fighters who knew the land and how to exploit it. The beleaguered British sent for the decorated veteran Roberts to try to retrieve the situation. In December 1899, he arrived to assume overall command of British forces, rendering the previous commander, General Buller, his subordinate. He

---

43 As a matter of interest the same misguided attempts by the Spaniards and later the USA to deprive the native South American Indians of the cocoa leaf stimulant and mushroom hallucinogens were also doomed to fail.

44 I have written about such questions in more detail in *Cases, Causes and Controversies* (Wildy, Simmonds & Hill, 2012); Ian McDougall and James Wilson (eds) *Cases that Changed Our Lives*, vol 2 (LexisNexis, 2014); *Court and Bowled*, revised edn (Wildy, Simmonds & Hill, 2017) and *Trials and Tribulations* (Wildy, Simmonds & Hill, 2015).

reached across the Empire for his staff, appointing, *inter alios*, Kitchener as chief of staff from the Sudan. He also received substantial reinforcements.[45]

Roberts immediately identified the tactical problem that British troops faced in the field: the accuracy of Boer marksmanship with modern rifles. He quickly rewrote the tactical manual, in the form of his 'Notes for Guidance', in which he demanded that the infantry adopt extended formations between 1,500 and 1,800 yards from Boer positions – more than twice the distance specified in the pre-war regulations.[46]

Roberts' larger strategy involved a two-pronged offensive. He himself led an advance across the Veldt to the Orange Free State, while Buller attacked the hills of Natal. Roberts managed to relieve Kimberley in February 1900 and capture about 4,000 prisoners in the process. Then, following his victory at the Battle of Poplar Grove, he captured the Free State capital Bloemfontein in March.

It should be noted that Roberts was not an unqualified success in the war. He attempted to reorganise the army logistics on the Indian Army model, but the result caused severe interruptions in supplies and contributed to a typhoid epidemic which went through the British lines. Nevertheless, he went on to take Pretoria in May 1900 and link up with Buller, winning the battle of Bergendal in August 1900. Unlike Kitchener, Roberts was in favour of press attention, and staged various photographs to show his triumphs.

Bergendal proved to be his final victory in the field. Thereafter, the Boers adopted an insurgent strategy rather than facing the British en masse. In response, Roberts sought to find a way of destroying the economic base and the community upon which the Boers depended. The result was the notorious 'concentration camps', established to confine the civilian population, and the burning of Boer farms.

In the years since, the fact of the 'concentration camps' has often been used to indict the British Empire and even to provide an equivocation with Nazi Germany. Some nuance, however, is required. The British did not invent the concept of civilian confinement: the Spanish used a similar method on a much larger scale to defeat the Cuban rebellion in 1896, while the United States had used camps in the Philippine-American war in 1899.

More importantly, the British camps were not intended to be 'death camps' as a deliberate policy of genocide, which is how many modern readers would understand the term 'concentration camps'.[47] Rather, the intention was to exert

---

45 His reinforcements included Lord Strathcona's Horse, a Canadian regiment formed by a fellow Brother Savage, the first Baron Strathcona.

46 Spencer Jones, '"Shooting Power": A Study of the Effectiveness of Boer and British Rifle Fire, 1899–1914', *British Journal for Military History*, vol 1, no 1 (2014).

47 The term was applied elsewhere before the Second World War as well, for example in a *Times* report of 9 September 1922, as the Turks moved on Smyrna and the Greeks took flight.

control over the civilian population upon whom the Boer guerrillas depended. Unfortunately, the British did not have the numbers or resources to run the camps properly, and hence there was much hunger and disease. One estimate has a total of 26,370 women and children dying in the camps, out of a population of about 118,000.

Roberts and Kitchener bear responsibility since they came up with the idea of the camps. But it is important to understand that they were professional soldiers given the task of winning a war. There were few alternatives available once the Boers had begun their insurgency. The British Army in Iraq in the twenty-first century encountered a similar situation: it swiftly defeated the Iraqi Army outside Basra and took the city, only to find the locals descending into gang warfare and an insurgency. Eventually the British cut a deal with the worst of the insurgent groups and left the city to stay in the airport. They were then humiliated when the reformed Iraqi Army, backed by American forces, assailed the militia head on, without bothering to involve the remaining British forces.[48] Roberts, by contrast, delivered an undisputed military victory for Britain.

In December 1900, Roberts handed command over to Kitchener and returned to England. He was ennobled as Earl Roberts of Kandahar in Afghanistan and Pretoria in the Transvaal Colony and of the City of Waterford and Viscount St Pierre. More honours followed, including – ironically in view of what was to come – the German Order of the Black Eagle by the Kaiser, when the latter visited Britain in 1901. Roberts was also one of the original recipients of the Order of Merit in the 1902 Coronation honours list. In 1901, he received another prestigious accolade when he was invited by George A Henry[49] to become an honorary life member of the Savage Club. He responded:

> Dear Mr Henry
>
> I had the pleasure of receiving your letter of the 4th inst. asking me whether I would like to be an Honorary Life Member of the Savage Club. I would indeed, and I beg that you will kindly convey my best thanks to the Committee for thinking of conferring so high and accept-able an honour on me.
>
> Yours very truly,
>
> Roberts.

---

48 The grim saga of the British involvement in Iraq was set out in much detail in the official report into the war, led by Sir John Chilcott: see http://www.iraqinquiry.org.uk/the-report/. While praising the 'great courage' of the individual troops, the report was scathing about those in command, concluding: 'It was humiliating that the UK reached a position in which an agree-ment with a militia group which had been actively targeting UK forces was considered the best option available. The UK military role in Iraq ended a very long way from success.'

49 George Henry RA (1858–1943), a Scottish painter, one of the most prominent of the Glasgow School.

And so the link between Britain's greatest soldier and arguably its most estimable gentleman's club began.

Roberts was no military Luddite. Building upon his experience in the Boer War, he pushed for the development of both the short magazine Lee Enfield rifle and the quick firing artillery gun. In all his formal military writing, he placed a heavy emphasis on marksmanship. In 1902, for example, he stated that the first goal when training a new soldier was 'to make him a good shot'.[50] In his preface to the 1904 cavalry drillbook, he wrote that 'the sword must henceforth be an adjunct to the rifle; and that cavalry soldiers must become expert rifle shots and be constantly trained to act dismounted.'[51] The result was that the BEF in 1914 made such an impression on the Germans with its accurate rifle fire that the Germans sometimes thought they were facing machine guns.[52]

Germany, the Great War and death

Roberts became a strong advocate of conscription, and travelled the country giving speeches to that effect, though they were not always well attended and not always well received. In October 1912, for example, he caused a media firestorm by speaking out about the impeding German threat, a combustible subject at any time but all the more so because the first Balkan War was under way:

> Germany strikes when Germany's hour has struck. That is the time-honoured policy relentlessly pursued by Bismarck and Moltke in 1866 and 1870. It has been her policy decade by decade since that date. It is her policy at the present hour. It is an excellent policy. It is or should be the policy of every nation prepared to play a great part in history.

He was attacked by the radical press as a warmonger, although some of the more conservative papers spoke in his defence, including, reluctantly, *The Times*. The authorities were unmoved: conscription was not introduced by Britain until after the Great War had begun, and then only when the 'old contemptible' professional army and the first great waves of volunteers had been expended on the Western Front.

---

50 Spencer Jones, *From Boer War to World War: Tactical Reform of the British Army 1902–1914* (Norman, University of Oklahoma Press, 2012), pp 92–93. And see Roberts' contribution to the *Report of His Majesty's Commissioners Appointed to Inquire into the Military Preparations and Other Matters Connected with the War in South Africa* (London, HMSO, 1903), Cmd no 1789–1792, vol 2, Q15850, p 233.

51 Richard Holmes, *The Western Front* (BBC Worldwide, 1999), p 32. See also Holmes, *Tommy: The British Soldier on the Western Front 1914–1918* (Harper Perennial, 2004), p 106. Unfortunately, the cavalry training manual as late as 1907 was still declaiming that '[i]t must be accepted as a principle that the rifle, effective as it is, cannot replace the effect produced by the speed of the horse, the magnetism of the charge, and the terror of cold steel.'

52 As recorded in various places, including the recollections of Brother Savage Henry Williamson for the BBC series *The Great War* in 1964.

It is salutary to consider how much stronger the BEF might have been had Roberts' advice been heeded several years before 1914, and whether it might have dealt the Germans a strong enough blow to prevent the stalemate that developed by early 1915 – or even whether the Germans would have been more reluctant to attack Belgium and thus risk bringing Britain into the war in the first place. On the other hand, conscription was not politically acceptable before the war and it is unrealistic to imagine Roberts could have changed that, even if he had had greater support in the press. William St John Brodrick, secretary of state for war from 1900–1903, had no success at all with the idea when he tried it.

When the war broke out, Roberts' old comrade Kitchener brought him back as colonel-in-chief of overseas forces in England. One of the first things Roberts did was prompt Admiral Percy Scott, the gunnery expert and future Savage guest, to come up with proposals for the use of 6-inch naval guns mounted for mobile use on land as long range artillery. Unfortunately, it would be more than a year before the War Office realised the merit of the idea.

In November 1914, aged 80, Roberts left for France to visit the Indian soldiers who had been deployed as part of the British Expeditionary Force.[53] Leo Amery recorded in his diary:

> I doubt if [Roberts] ever enjoyed two days more ... Meeting the Indians was a special delight to him and he insisted on stopping his car and talking to every turbaned soldier he met, and visited them in their hospitals. Old Pertab Singh [Maharajah of Jodhpur] was here to tea the day he came to us, and it was great to see the devotion in the old Indian warrior's eyes and his joy when Bobs addressed him as "dear old friend".

Not long after his arrival, Roberts caught a chill climbing to the top of the Scherpenberg near Messines to observe the trenches. He rapidly developed pneumonia and died the following evening. His death was front page news in *The Times*, which also published a hagiographic obituary.[54]

---

53   At this point it would be right to mention that some 827,000 Indian soldiers saw action in the First World War, across all the fronts, according to George Morton-Jack, *The Indian Army on the Western Front: India's Expeditionary Force to France and Belgium in the First World War* (Cambridge University Press, 2014). Shrabani Basu in *For King and Another Country: Indian Soldiers on the Western Front 1914–18* (Bloomsbury, 2015) puts the figure at over a million.

54   See *Great Military Lives: A Centenary in Obituaries* (Times Books, 2008), p 77.

    Roberts body was taken by gun-carriage in a procession in London marking his death. One of those following up Ludgate Hill to St Paul's Cathedral was Brother Savage AP Herbert, a young Oxford student at the time who was soon to join up. We will meet Herbert again as a Savage man of law.

Coda: Roberts and Kipling

Upon the death of Roberts, Rudyard Kipling wrote a poem, the first verse of which hits as squarely as a bullet fired by a marksman trained according to Roberts' methods:

> He passed in the very battle-smoke
> Of the war that he had descried.
> Three hundred mile of cannon spoke
> When the Master-Gunner died.

Kipling had not always been a Roberts fan, writing an indirect attack on him in the context of favouritism in staff appointments in the satirical poem 'A General Summary' in 1886. Roberts was not bothered and continued to act as Kipling's mentor and unofficial patron, though he was incensed by similar criticism from others in 1888.[55] In 1892, Kipling wrote a second, much more complimentary poem about Roberts entitled 'Bobs' (Roberts' affectionate nickname in the army), including the following verse:

> Now they've made a bloomin' Lord
> Outer Bobs,
> Which was but 'is fair reward—
> Weren't it, Bobs?
> So 'e'll wear a coronet
> Where 'is 'elmet used to set;
> But we know you won't forget—
> Will yer, Bobs?

But there was a sad irony: it was Roberts to whom Kipling turned to ask for a favour in bending the rules to allow Kipling's son Jack to join the army. And it was Jack's death at Loos in 1915 that eventually turned the once-jingoistic Kipling into one of the most powerful of all anti-war poets, though not before he had encouraged Brother Savage Oliver Baldwin to join up. Kipling's later anti-war verse 'Common Form' has lost none of its potency:[56]

> If any question why we died,
> Tell them, because our fathers lied.

Nor has his 'A Dead Statesman':

---

55 See Rodney Atwood, *The Life of Field Marshal Lord Roberts* (Bloomsbury, 2015) pp 156–158.

56 Kipling was also heavily involved in the creation of the war graves following the conflict, and it was he who came up with the phrase 'A soldier known unto God' for the many thousands of unidentified corpses.

I could not dig: I dared not rob
Therefore I lied to please the mob.
Now all my lies are proved untrue
And I must face the men I slew.
What tale shall serve me here among
Mine angry and defrauded young?

Had he lived, Roberts would have understood Kipling's loss, given the loss of his own son in South Africa. Indeed, there can have been little about the reality of war that Roberts did not understand, given that he was on active duty for the majority of his life. He might not be considered in the first rank of British strategic generals, but as a soldier 'Bobs' VC can have had few peers.

Field Marshal Lord Kitchener: 'Your Country Needs You'

Field Marshal Earl Horatio Herbert Kitchener is the subject of one of the most famous images in British history. It is he who points commandingly outwards in one of the great images from the Great War with the caption 'Your Country Needs You', the subject of countless reproductions, imitations and pastiches the world over, created by Kitchener's fellow Savage Alfred Leete.[57] Kitchener was chosen for the image because at the time he was the best known living soldier in Britain. As with Lord Roberts, the First World War was only the final act in a military career lasting several decades and involving active duty on three different continents.

Early life

Kitchener was born in Ireland in 1850. His father was an army officer who had bought land in Ireland after selling his commission. He seems to have been strict and eccentric in equal measure: he disdained blankets, preferring to sleep under sheets of newspaper sewn together, and on one occasion punished the young Kitchener by binding his hands and wrists and tying him to croquet hoops on the lawn.

While Kitchener was still at a young age, the family moved to Switzerland due to his mother's failing health, where Kitchener started his military training. He later went to the Royal Military Academy in Woolwich back in England. In a rather spirited youthful adventure, he managed to join a French field ambulance unit during the Franco-Prussian War in 1870, but was forced to return to Britain after he caught pneumonia during a balloon reconnaissance ride. He was

---

57 Although, as we will see in the chapter on Savage artists, the image was probably not as widely used during the war as has long been believed.

censured by the army for having violated British neutrality by his actions, though his military career continued largely unaffected.

Kitchener served in the Mediterranean and the Middle East as a surveyor, and learned Arabic whilst there. The ordinance survey to which he contributed still underpins modern maps of Israel and Palestine, and the data he and a colleague collected is still used by archaeologists and geographers in the southern Levant. Kitchener then surveyed Cyprus and Turkey before moving to North Africa, where his fluency in Arabic could be put to use.

Africa

Kitchener saw extensive action in Africa, including the battle against the Mahdi's army at Handub in January 1888 and the Battle of Toski in August 1889. In 1896, he was ordered to invade northern Sudan, ostensibly to avenge the death of General Gordon. Kitchener won victories at the Battle of Ferkeh in June 1896 and the Battle of Hafir in September 1896. Then, in 1898, he famously won the Battle of Omdurman, with a young Winston Churchill among his men. Controversy arose after a number of the enemy's wounded were killed and the grave of the Mahdi was desecrated. Nevertheless, both actions secured Kitchener a reputation for ruthlessness, while the victory at Omdurman was celebrated in November 1898 by a Savage Club dinner in his honour. The artist Herbert Johnson produced a lithograph for *The Graphic*[58] commemorating the event, entitled 'The Sirdar and the Savage Club, toasting the Conqueror of Omdurman'. Omdurman had been less a battle than a massacre: the British machine guns brought down 11,000 'dervishes' for the loss of only 48 of their own. In the same year Brother Savage Hilaire Belloc famously wrote in *The Modern Traveller*:

> Whatever happens, we have got
> The Maxim gun, and they have not

After Omdurman, Kitchener opened a special sealed letter from Lord Salisbury. It explained that avenging Gordon had only been a pretext: the real reason for the invasion of Sudan was to check the French imperial ambitions in the region. Consequently, Kitchener went to the French fort at Fashoda and demanded that the occupants leave the Sudan. The French declined and a stand-off ensued. The event became known as the 'Fashoda Incident' and almost caused an Anglo-French war, as both countries made much of it in their respective propaganda back in Europe.

In Fashoda itself, however, Kitchener's diplomatic skills came to the fore. His fluency in French was doubtless an asset. It was agreed initially that the respective

---

58 *The Graphic* was a British weekly illustrated newspaper, published from 1869 to 1932. It was highly influential in the art world, and its admirers included Vincent Van Gogh.

countries' flags would fly over the fort. But the cards turned against the French. Back in Paris it was realised that war with Britain might result in a serious defeat for the French Navy. Their hoped-for ally, Nicholas II of Russia, made clear that the French could not count on his support in a war with Britain. And there was also the risk of an opportunistic German attack on the French if the latter's eye was on the British. With all those factors in mind, the French conceded the whole of the Sudan and withdrew in September 1898. Kitchener then assumed the role of governor-general of the country.

In that role, just like Roberts with his acknowledgement of Hindu culture in India, Kitchener showed he was not simply a Blimpish Victorian imperialist lording it over what he saw as the primitive natives. He established the Gordon Memorial College, which was open to all Sudanese. He ordered Khartoum's mosques to be rebuilt and for the Islamic holy day to be made a national holiday. Moreover, he announced freedom of religion for all, and did not encourage the actions of Christian missionaries.

Second Boer War

> But we bequeath a parting tip
> For sound advice of such men,
> Who come across in transport ship
> To polish off the Dutchmen!
>
> If you encounter any Boers
> You really must not loot 'em!
> And if you wish to leave these shores,
> For pity's sake, DON'T SHOOT 'EM!!
>
> And if you'd earn a D.S.O.,
> Why every British sinner
> Should know the proper way to go
> Is: "ASK THE BOER TO DINNER!"

Lt Harry 'Breaker' Morant (1864–1902), 'Butchered to Make a Dutchmen's Holiday'

In 1899, Kitchener along with Roberts was sent to South Africa to try to retrieve the Second Boer War. He was mentioned in despatches by Roberts on several occasions. In November 1900, after Roberts returned to Britain, Kitchener assumed overall command of British forces. He continued and expanded Roberts' strategy of confining Boer civilians to concentration camps and destroying their economic base by burning farms, but the strategy turned to tragedy when the British were unable to provide adequate resources for the camps, as we saw earlier. In 1901, Emily Hobhouse from the Liberal opposition in London had made public the terrible conditions in the camps. The British High Commissioner in South Africa, Lord Milner, took over the administration of the camps from the army.

Kitchener was also involved in one of the great controversies of the British Army of the day when he signed the death warrants for Lieutenant Harry 'Breaker' Morant and Lieutenant Peter Handcock. The case had involved one English and five Australian officers from an irregular unit being court-martialled for the summary execution of 12 Boer prisoners and for the murder of a German missionary who was a suspected Boer sympathiser. The incident subsequently became the subject of books, a play and a feature film.[59] A campaign also began in the late twentieth century for the executed to be retrospectively pardoned, on the ground they were scapegoats who were executed as much for public relations as anything else. In 2010, the British Ministry of Defence refused to set aside the original verdicts.

We might observe that it is ironic that Kitchener was accused of approving the stitch-up of Morant and the others to show that Britain was concerned about Boer civilians, but also accused of murdering the latter by the use of concentration camps. Had it been his intention with the camps to kill Boer civilians, it seems improbable he would have approved punishment of others doing the same on a much smaller scale.

The war was finally ended by the Treaty of Vereeniging in May 1902. The settlement was the result of six months of haggling among British commanders and leaders in the region, amongst whom Kitchener wanted the most lenient peace for the Boers: he urged recognition of their rights and to find some form of future self-governance. Here his loathing of the press came to the fore: the press were excluded from discussions and soldiers put on guard to ensure that they did not find a way in to the tent. But he had not reckoned on Brother Savage Edgar Wallace, then working for the *Daily Mail*. One of the guards of the Boer delegation was an old and trusted friend of Wallace. He had been given three coloured handkerchiefs; red, white and blue-red for 'nothing doing', blue for 'making progress' and white for 'treaty definitely to be signed'. Each day, Wallace took a return trip to Vereeniging. The guard would walk close to the railway line and, as the train passed, would wipe his nose with one of the coloured handkerchiefs. Wallace sent his reports back to London in the form of fake financial transactions with a friend in the financial business where they were sent on to the *Daily Mail*.

On 31 May, the Boers agreed to Kitchener's proposals and travelled under strict guard to meet Kitchener in Pretoria. The guard duly blew his nose with the white handkerchief as Wallace looked on from the train, and in short order the

---

59 *Breaker Morant* (1980, directed by Bruce Beresford and starring Edward Woodward).

Daily Mail had its scoop – news of the peace treaty a full 24 hours before it was announced in the House of Commons. Kitchener was incandescent with rage, and his resultant much greater hatred of the press, as we saw earlier, would later cause considerable trouble in the First World War.

Nevertheless, peace with the Boers was secured, and one remarkable outcome was that the South African prime minister, Louis Botha became an advocate for the British during the First World War, albeit his actions prompted a Boer revolt when he moved to take German South-West Africa, while the more lasting effect of the Boer War was the sense of Afrikaans' nationalism. Kitchener, meanwhile, returned to Britain after the Boer War as a hero and was given a procession through the streets and a formal welcome at St James's Palace.

India

In 1902, Kitchener was appointed commander-in-chief in India. He tried to reorganise the Indian Army, which led to a dispute with the Viceroy, Lord Curzon. One of their points of difference was Kitchener's desire to make his own office the ultimate military decision-maker, instead of the power being split between commander-in-chief and the 'military member' of the Viceroy's office. Kitchener prevailed and Curzon resigned. But problems arose from the fact that the two offices which Kitchener now held were at the head of two separate bureaucracies, which might offer conflicting advice, placing Kitchener in a similar position to that of Pooh-Bah in *The Mikado*. Eventually he was succeeded by General O'Moore Creagh, who set about repairing relations with the Viceroy and gained the appreciative nickname 'no More K' (rhyming with his surname).

Kitchener was promoted to field marshal in September 1909. Over the next two years, he lobbied for the role of Viceroy of India, but did not have the support of the Secretary of State for India, John Morley. Morley was a disciple of Gladstone and did not want a serving soldier in the role, particularly since India had obtained limited self-governance under the Indian Councils Act 1909. Asquith had to back Morley and so Kitchener's efforts failed.

In 1911, instead of his hoped-for Indian role, Kitchener was sent to Egypt to serve as British agent and consul-general. In the same year, prompted by the Agadir Crisis, he warned that the Germans would easily defeat France in a conflict and stated that he would refuse to command a British force to support the French.

While in Egypt he befriended the Savage artist, Lance Thackeray. Thackeray later recalled that Kitchener was an avid collector of rare china and of antiques in general, and was known to be somewhat light fingered when he found something he liked, albeit he would later send a cheque for considerably more than the value of the piece, and hence silence any intended protest.[60] (Brother Savage Compton Mackenzie recalled that a piece of very fine china was once placed in front of Kitchener, the intention being to offer it to him as a present. Kitchener, not realising that, dismissed it as poor quality, since he hoped to buy it at a knock-down price. Mackenzie added: 'it is remarkable how often in Lord Kitchener's correspondence the spirit which led him to cheapen that piece of china betrays itself.'[61])

In June 1914, he became Earl Kitchener of Khartoum and of Broome in the County of Kent.

First World War

When the war was about to break out, Kitchener happened to be in Britain on leave, but was preparing to return to Egypt. He was immediately recalled to London and appointed Secretary of State for War, against his wishes (he had once said he would rather sweep the streets than serve in the War Office). He responded with advice the cabinet did not want to hear: the war would take years, would involve the raising of a giant land army, and would incur casualties in the millions. On all three counts he was tragically proved correct.

We have already discussed Kitchener's ruthless efforts at censorship during the war. As to the strategy of the war, it was obvious from an early stage that Britain's comparatively miniscule land army would not be sufficient to make any measurable difference on the Front, given the size of the German field army. A new army would have to be raised, and raised quickly. The British Army totalled 733,514 men, of whom fewer than one quarter were regulars, and half of those were based overseas across the vast spread of the British Empire. The Germans, thanks to peacetime conscription, mobilised 3.8 million men at the outset, composed of a standing army of about 700,000, with the remainder being adult males who had passed through conscription and were thus immediately available. France, by way of contrast, had a standing army of some 820,000, including about 45,000 colonial troops, and approximately 2.75 million reservists – again dwarfing the British, even if like Britain France had to deploy some of its regular army around its empire. Given all those figures, it is easy to see why the Germans regarded the British Army as no more than loose change, unlikely to stand in the way of the Schlieffen Plan (the Germans' pre-existing strategy for knocking the French out of the war) even if the British were so foolish (as the Germans saw it) as to enter the war.

---

60 As related to an American reporter by Thackeray and published in *Desert Evening News* (Salt Lake City, USA), 1 July 1916 – the first day of the Somme, when Kitchener had been dead for nearly a month and was about to be joined by almost 20,000 of his countryman in one day. Quoted in Tom Askey, *Lance Thackeray: His Life and Art* (ShieldCrest, 2016), pp 84, 91 n6.

61 Compton Mackenzie, *Gallipoli Memories* (Doubleday, Doran & Co, 1930), pp 58–59.

Within days of Britain declaring war, the press published the first of Kitchener's appeal for 100,000 volunteers. Kitchener later lent his visage to the famous recruitment poster by Brother Savage Alfred Leete, thus inadvertently securing his own immortality in Britain and fame far from British shores. 'If not a great man, he was, at least, a great poster' came the damning-by-faint-praise usually attributed to the prime minister's wife, Margot Asquith.

Initially, Kitchener pursued a sound strategy with the BEF, arguing that it should be deployed at Amiens in preparation for a counterattack once the route of German advance was known. He knew that the Belgian Army could not hold the Germans and thus to send the whole BEF there would be to throw good men after irretrievably bad. Unfortunately, his argument was mostly rejected, though a third of the BEF was withheld and thus total disaster was averted when Sir John French – the commander on the ground – withdrew rather than sending everything at the advancing Germans.[62]

Kitchener had also ordered Sir John to co-operate with the French but not to take orders from them. Kitchener was much better at dealing with the French brass (for a start, Kitchener was fluent in French which, despite his name, Sir John was not). He annoyed Sir John by wearing his field marshal's uniform when the two met, though it was probably out of habit rather than a deliberate slight. Either way, by the end of 1914 relations between them were badly soured.

Their relations worsened in January 1915, since French and others including Haig wanted the New Armies to be incorporated into existing divisions as battalions rather than sent out as entire divisions of barely trained and wholly untested troops. French appealed to Asquith, but the latter backed Kitchener. Kitchener was contemptuous of the Territorial Army, who he referred to as 'the town clerk's army' composed of 'play soldiers', so was opposed to integrating new recruits into the territorial structure. He reasoned that he would rather have men who knew nothing than those with a smattering of the wrong thing. Kitchener also worried about a possible invasion across the Channel, and so kept some of the new recruits on British soil. (We might observe that the Germans never had a realistic chance of crossing the channel in numbers in either war, as the Royal Navy would have cut them to pieces, but as with most arguments that one is easier to make in hindsight.)

In 1915, he supported the attack at Loos, acting in accordance with the wishes of the French (but not Sir John French, who along with Haig did not think

---

62 Some credit here might be due to Repington's report in *The Times*, which set out an essentially accurate map of German dispositions. Based on that report Amiens was a logical position for the British to focus upon. As for Sir John French, his biographer Richard Holmes gave a representative verdict, namely that French was out of his depth commanding on the Western Front. Holmes instead thought Henry Wilson was the real power on the staff. See Holmes, *The Western Front*, op cit, pp 38–39.

the ground suitable). The offensive was an expensive failure. Added to the 'Shell Crisis', it placed immense pressure upon Kitchener, though he stayed in the cabinet.

Kitchener believed the German line could not be broken, and backed an attack on Turkey as an alternative strategy. His own preference was an invasion of Alexandretta, a strategically important port with a large, potentially friendly Christian population, but in the event he went with the Gallipoli option, which ended in another disaster in 1915. Unlike Churchill, he retained his office, but he came under yet more pressure from different sources. His enemies included Generals Robertson and Haig, the latter wanting him to be made Viceroy of India as a means of getting him out of the way. Things became even worse for Kitchener when his advice to attack the Ottomans and seize Baghdad resulted in the British failure at Kut – arguably the worst British defeat of the entire war in terms of proportion of casualties.[63]

Despite his embattled position, in June 1916 Kitchener received a strong vote of thanks from 200 politicians who had questioned him. His work on the Home Front made small but tangible gains, including a knitting pattern that produced socks more comfortable for the soldiers – still known today as 'the Kitchener stitch'.

Kitchener had also been keeping an eye on the Eastern Front and decided to meet Tsar Nichols II and his commanders to discuss problems of money, ammunition and strategy. It was a mission he undertook with alacrity as it offered respite from the strain of his duties in London.

Death

On 5 June 1916, Kitchener was on board HMS *Hampshire* heading to Russia when she struck a mine left by a U-boat. In a force 9 gale, only 12 of the approximately 650 men on board (estimates have been as high as 725) made it to safety. Kitchener was not among them and his body was never found, even though corpses washed up on the shores of nearby Orkney for weeks afterwards. He became the highest-ranking soldier on any side to die from enemy action.

His loss, coming only days after the disappointing Battle of Jutland, was a great blow to the public. The fact that his relations with a number of politicians and other generals had been deteriorating led to conspiracy theories about his death over the following years, most of them wildly improbable and all of them devoid of evidence.[64] One of the more interesting ones was from General Ludendorff,

---

63 Charles Townshend, *When God Made Hell: The British Invasion of Mesopotamia and the Creation of Iraq, 1914–1921* (Faber and Faber, 2010).

64 In 1923, Lord Alfred Douglas, the former lover of Oscar Wilde, cooked up a ridiculous one involving Jutland, Winston Churchill and the perennial conspirator's favourite 'the Jews', wherein Churchill was supposed to have planted fake news to manipulate the stock market.

joint head of Germany's war command, who claimed that Russian communists had leaked the plans for Kitchener's trip to the Germans and that Kitchener had been assassinated because the Germans feared and respected his abilities. But Kitchener died near Scapa Flow, where the Grand Fleet was based – precisely where the Germans would have been trying to lay mines throughout the war – and it seems far-fetched to assume it was a targeted hit.

Among many monuments to his memory, the Lord Kitchener National Memorial Fund was established in 1916 to aid casualties of the war. It still exists and is used to fund university education for soldiers, ex-soldiers and their children.

Field Marshal Sir William Robertson: army legend

We have already met Field Marshal Robertson in several contexts: strategist of the Western Front, one of a number of *bêtes noirs* of Lloyd George, and the unveiler of the Savage Great War memorial. Robertson holds the extraordinary distinction of being the only person in the history of the British Army to start at the lowest rank and finish at the highest, having begun his career as a private and ended as a field marshal. For that reason alone his place in the first order of British military history is assured.

Early life and career

William Robertson was born in Welbourn, Lincolnshire, in 1860. He was the son of the village tailor and postmaster, and was educated at the local village school. He was singled out by the rector as showing promise, and was given extra tuition and encouraged to stay on beyond the minimum leaving age. Robertson left school at the age of 13 and went into service, initially for the rector's family and then for the Earl of Cardigan in Northamptonshire. He despised the work and later said he had been 'a damned bad footman.' He took one of the few routes out of domestic servitude by joining the army. He signed up in 1877 while still under age, and joined the 16th Lancers. His mother was appalled, and wrote to him saying that he was the great hope of the family and that she 'would rather bury you than see you in a red coat'.

His mother's concern reflected the low public opinion of the common soldier of the day. If it was not wholly composed of what Wellington supposedly called 'the scum of the earth', it was nevertheless true that the army drew mostly upon the less fortunate for its rank and file, due to the low pay, bad conditions and

---

Churchill sued him for criminal libel – the very same cause of action which Wilde had disastrously brought against Douglas's father, the Marquess of Queensberry, over a decade earlier. Churchill won. Douglas was sent to prison for six months and was bankrupted by the costs. It was the last ever action for criminal libel in England.

On the conspiracies regarding Kitchener's death, Jeremy Paxman wrote an interesting piece 'The strange death of Lord Kitchener', *Financial Times*, 7 November 2014.

risk of death in far-flung lands defending the red parts of the map. Robertson, used to the genteel ways of the households in which he had worked, found his fellow recruits to be coarse, foul mouthed and hard drinkers. He was so disgusted by their behaviour that he contemplated deserting on his first night, but found another recruit had stolen his civvies and beaten him to it.

Robertson soon got over his initial horror and put his mind to succeeding in the forces. He made steady if initially unspectacular progress through the ranks in the 1880s, reaching the officer class in 1888 when he became second lieutenant in the 3rd Dragoon Guards. Just as he had felt out of place amongst the coarse rankers at the start of his career, so he was uncomfortable among the officer class upon his promotion. He disliked the officers' mess and tried to keep his origins from the others there, though he was never fully able to escape the rigidity of the class system. Even when he reached the highest echelons of the army there were mutterings about his apparent lack of social graces and other traits of a 'gentleman' as then understood. He responded by deliberately dropping his 'aitches'.[65]

Despite any attendant social difficulties, Robertson's intellect and other attributes soon came to the attention of his superiors after his promotion. He was deployed to India and attached to the intelligence branch at army headquarters at Shimla, where he became fluent in Urdu, Hindi, Persian, Pashto, Punjabi and Gurkhali. In 1895, he went on the Chitral Expedition, during which he was attacked by his two native guides. He was suffering dysentery at the time, so one of the guides was carrying his sword for him while the other was armed with a shotgun. The latter fired at Robertson but missed, whereupon the other attacked him with the sword. Robertson punched him to the ground, then drew his revolver and saw both assailants off. He was awarded the Distinguished Service Order after the incident.

While in India he married Mildred Adelaide, the second daughter of Lieutenant-General Charles Thomas Palin of the Indian Army. They went on to have four children.

He returned to England in December 1896, and soon after became the first former private to be accepted into Staff College, Camberley. His contemporaries there included Douglas Haig. Both of them imbued the philosophy of their lecturer George FR Henderson who, drawing on earlier theorists such as Clausewitz, stressed the concentration of forces in the primary theatre of the enemy in order to overwhelm his main force in a decisive battle. That was the strategy both Robertson and Haig were later to pursue on the Western Front. At the college Robertson also met Frederick Maurice, with whom he would later work closely during the Great War.

Robertson qualified as a French interpreter and became fluent in German, the

---

65 Holmes, *The Western Front*, op cit, p 39.

ninth language he mastered. He passed out from staff college second in December 1898, and the following year began working in the Intelligence Department at the War Office.

During the Second Boer War, Robertson initially stayed with the Intelligence Department but later joined Lord Roberts' staff in South Africa. He was promoted to brevet lieutenant-colonel. After the war, he returned to London and resumed his old role in the Intelligence Department, becoming head of the Foreign Section. He was made a brevet colonel in 1903 and a full colonel in 1904. By that stage his abilities were rated very highly indeed by his contemporaries.

In December 1907, he was appointed chief of the general staff to Sir Horace Smith-Dorrien. In 1910 he became commandant of the Staff College, Camberley. Shortly before he assumed the role, he had visited the college with Kitchener, who criticised Wilson. It was the start of poor relations between Wilson and Robertson that was to last throughout the First World War.

In 1913 Robertson returned to the War Office to serve as director of military training, and was promoted to major-general.

In 1914, with the Home Rule Bill for Ireland due to become law, he warned the cabinet that the army would not move against the Ulster Volunteers, following the 'Curragh incident' where British officers including Hubert Gough had threatened to resign rather than deploy the army in Ulster.[66] (Sir Edward Carson,[67] leader of the Unionists, was mouthing off about 'a clean war and a clean fight'. On the Republican side, there were many prepared to give him both, with the 'clean' part being optional, and both sides stockpiled illegal weapons so fast it was feared that armed civilians outnumbered soldiers in the province.) In the event, the Home Rule Bill received Royal Assent on

---

66 In 1910, after two general elections, the Liberal government was without a majority in the House of Commons and had to rely upon the Irish Nationalists in order to keep them in power. The price extracted was a Home Rule Bill for Ireland, which predictably met with strident opposition from the Conservatives and the Ulster Unionists. It was delayed by the outbreak of the First World War. It is easy for modern readers to forget how volatile the Irish situation was heading up to the war, but it meant that some papers, such as the *Daily Express*, virtually ignored the ripples from the Balkans that were leading to Armageddon on the continent, because they so fixated with Ireland.

67 Sir Edward Carson, later Baron Carson, (1854–1935), notable lawyer and politician. In the former capacity he successfully defended the Marquess of Queensberry against Oscar Wilde in the latter's libel action; Wilde, who knew Carson from their time at Oxford together, had predicted he would conduct the case 'with all the bitterness of an old friend'. See my earlier book *Trials and Tribulations* (Wildy, Simmonds & Hill, 2015), Ch 2.

Carson became was the leader of the Irish Unionist Alliance and Ulster Unionist Party between 1910 and 1921, and is often referred to as the 'father of Northern Ireland'. He was later elevated directly from the bar to become a member of the Appellate Committee of the House of Lords, a very rare distinction.

We will encounter him again in the next chapter, in the context of the Marconi Scandal broken by Cecil Chesterton.

18 September, but was also suspended for the duration of the First World War. One result was the falling out between the senior officers and Liberal politicians. Robertson's reputation was unaffected by his part in the affair, but he and Lloyd George would become implacable enemies during the Great War.

First World War

1914-1915

Robertson was still in the role of director of military training when war broke out in August 1914. He hoped for a command in battle, but it was felt that at 55 he was too old. Instead, he was moved to the position of quartermaster general of the BEF under Sir John French. He chose Frederick Maurice, his friend from staff college days, to assist him.

Robertson excelled in the role: he feared the BEF was deployed too far forward, so arranged supply dumps further back and resupply via France rather than Belgium, which proved invaluable during the retreat from Mons. In January 1915, he was appointed chief of general staff (CGS). Maurice again accompanied him and became director of military operations at the War Office, with the rank of major-general.

As CGS, Robertson, supported by Maurice, urged commitment to the Western Front. Robertson dismissed naval operations in the Dardanelles and pointed out that casualty rates being incurred at Gallipoli were just as high as those on the Western Front, but without the possibility of defeating Germany.

The strategy of the two men was 'slow attrition, by a slow and gradual advance on our part, each step being prepared by a predominant artillery fire and great expenditure of ammunition', emphasising the importance of counter-battery, and also attacking places where the Germans would be reluctant to concede ground (for political or strategic reasons) and therefore bound to incur losses – much as the Germans reputedly selected Verdun for a great assault in 1915 because they assumed the French would sacrifice anything rather than allow it to fall.[68]

Robertson gradually lost all confidence in Sir John French. When French was forced out at the end of 1915, Robertson was favourite to succeed him in command of the Western Front. After some machinations Robertson in fact became chief of the Imperial general staff (CIGS) while Haig replaced French. Haig's appointment was one of Robertson's conditions for taking the CIGS role, given the two men's agreement on Western Front strategy. Robertson's other issue was how he would work with Kitchener; the two men were not close and Robertson did not want Kitchener undermining him. Eventually they agreed

---

68 Later historians suspect that the Germans did indeed try to capture Verdun, and came up with the story about wanting to bleed France white as a retrospective justification for their failure to do so.

that Robertson would advise the cabinet and Kitchener would retain responsibility for recruiting and supplying the army, though (against Robertson's wishes) both would sign orders jointly.

1916

Robertson set to work supporting Haig in prioritising the Western Front, and called time on the Dardanelles failure. He was also fully behind conscription and the need to put a substantial army in the field, urging ever greater call-ups. Like Haig, he had unrealistic expectations about the Somme Offensive, although he was always less in favour of major assaults than Haig, preferring a strategy of small gains and attrition. In the event, the Somme was the most costly single battle in British history in terms of life lost, and was modest in terms of ground gained, albeit some German commanders conceded that another Somme would be the end of the German Army. At least some of the blame for the size of the casualties – 57,470 on the first day alone (of whom 19,240 were killed; the rest wounded, captured or missing), 419,654 in total[69] – could be blamed upon tactical failures and material deficiencies such as the types of shell involved.

In response to Churchill's claim that the Somme Offensive had wasted resources, Robertson argued that the casualties had been small compared with French operations in the previous two years of the war and that the attack had placed German resources under great strain. When the war was over, he argued in retrospect:

> Remembering the dissatisfaction displayed by ministers at the end of 1915 because the operations had not come up to their expectations, the General Staff took the precaution to make quite clear beforehand the nature of the success which the Somme campaign might yield. The necessity of relieving pressure on the French Army at Verdun remains, and is more urgent than ever. This is, therefore, the first objective to be obtained by the combined British and French offensive. The second objective is to inflict as heavy losses as possible upon the German armies.

Reflecting his cautious nature, Robertson warned ministers that the war would likely not end before Summer 1918. He caused great consternation with that apparently pessimistic outlook, though he was ultimately proved correct. At the Savage Club's fifty-ninth annual dinner in December 1916, he issued a similarly restrained summary of events, as reported by *The Times* on 11 December:

---

69 The Battle of the Somme lasted from 1 July to 18 November 1916. Approximately 1,700,000 shells were fired onto the German lines. The French suffered 204,253 casualties and the Germans about 500,000.

Sir William Robertson, replying for the Army, said human nature was the most predominant factor in war; it came up against one at every turn—decision and indecision, courage and timidity, cheerfulness and pessimism. As regarded the war, although he quite freely admitted that they might still have a long way to go, and must be prepared to do so—as he believed they were (cheers)—yet they were getting on as well as could be expected, having regard to the bad start they had had. It was common knowledge that they had been utterly unprepared for this great war, and it was also common knowledge that in war the belligerent who got the upper hand at the start and own first blood gained a very great advantage, and one of which it was exceedingly difficult to deprive him afterwards. That was the history of all wars, and in most cases the man who got the best of the start kept it to the end; but, fortunately, there were a good many exceptions, and they were justified in hoping that there would be an exception in the present case. (Cheers.)

When he said that they had not been prepared for war he was not thinking only of the Army. It was certainly a great defect that we had at the time such a small Army; fortunately, it was very good, but it was very small. That, however, was not the only nor did he think it was the chief defect. They must, therefore, have patience, and be prepared to pay the penalty of their shortcomings. The Empire had risen to the occasion, and was determined to pay that penalty and to see the thing through. (Cheers.) That was the greatest asset they could possibly have in war, for they could not successfully prosecute war unless they had behind it proper support. It was a most valuable assistance to the men at the front to know that they had that support.

When they were inclined to be a little discouraged let them look at the other side of the picture. (Cheers.) It was of no use grumbling and thinking they never did right. The Army was improving in strength and efficiency every day, and its loyalty, fortitude, and readiness to make the greatest sacrifices were known to all of them. (Cheers.)

1917

Following the dreadful experiences of 1916, Lloyd George, secretary of state for war, was adamant that other theatres should be tried in order to avoid more endless losses on the Western Front. He considered Palestine, Italy and possibly the Balkans. Robertson held firm with his prioritisation of the Western Front and was eventually able to keep the War Cabinet in agreement. Vimy Ridge was captured by the Canadians early in the year and there was a qualified success with the use of tanks at Cambrai, both substantially due to Brother Savage Julian Byng, who we will meet again later in this chapter.

The Third Battle of Ypres (Passchendaele) was less of a success: improved British assault tactics were checked by the horrendous conditions and improved German defensive techniques, and ended with the appalling statistic of 310,000

British and 260,000 German casualties. Haig and Robertson's determination to pursue attacks on the Western Front cost both some support amongst the War Cabinet, the more so when good news came at the end of the year with the capture of Jerusalem in one of the theatres Robertson had argued against. Also, Russia had collapsed by then, freeing up substantial German resources for the Western Front, and although America had entered the war, she had not yet sent men in substantial numbers to Europe.

1918

By 1918, Lloyd George had had enough of Robertson. He dismissed Robertson's reputation as a soldier by saying he had hardly been to the trenches and had never fought at the Front. The conflict between the two led to the prosecution we saw earlier of Charles Repington and another journalist for an alleged breach of Defence Regulation 18.[70] Shortly afterwards Robertson resigned. It was announced that he had accepted the leadership of the eastern command, one of the seven 'commands' of the army in Britain.[71] His old adversary Henry Wilson replaced him as CIGS.

Following the German Operation Michael of early 1918, which almost broke the Allied line, the press blamed Lloyd George for the near-disaster. There were calls for Robertson to be recalled as CIGS. Haig suggested that Robertson be made second-in-command of the BEF, but Robertson was adamant he would be CIGS or nothing. Lloyd George later said in his memoirs that he believed Robertson was trying to topple the government and install himself as a dictator. At the time, Lloyd George was probably responsible for rumours that Robertson was forming a sort of 'axis of evil' with the likes of Asquith, Repington and Jellicoe – in other words, anyone else who had fallen out with Lloyd George.

Nonetheless, in June 1918 Robertson was appointed general officer command-ing-in-chief for home forces. He took the role seriously, visiting each regional command. Among his concerns were air power; at the time the Zeppelin and Gotha raids were the extent of strategic bombing but Robertson accurately foresaw that in future wars it would be a much greater concern.

Incidentally, one should not belittle the air raids of the First World War: although they were on nothing like the scale of the Blitz in the Second World War, some 557 civilians were killed and 1,358 injured by the approximately 50

70 The two journalists were said to have published articles discussing the controversy amongst Allied leaders over Lloyd George's plans to concentrate efforts against Turkey, and the failure to keep army manpower up to strength. Repington later wrote that Robertson had told him that he could no more afford to be seen with him than either of them 'could afford to be seen walking down Regent Street with a whore'.

71 See David R Woodward 'William Robertson' in *1914-1918-online – International Encyclopedia of the First World War*, Ute Daniel, Peter Gatrell, Oliver Janz, Heather Jones, Jennifer Keene, Alan Kramer, and Bill Nasson (eds), issued by Freie Universität Berlin, 2008.

airship raids on England during the war. They also caused about £1.5 million in damage, including destroying the famous landmark department store of Swan & Edgar on Piccadilly Circus. The later Gotha bombers carried out 27 raids, killing 835 and injuring 1,972 on the ground, and inflicting about the same value of material damage as the airships.[72] Moreover, they were an entirely new kind of terror: powered flight was only just over a decade old in 1914, and such a novelty that at the start of the war soldiers would sometimes shoot at their own planes out of curiosity,[73] while crowds would sometimes gather in England to watch the raiding planes overhead instead of seeking cover. By 1917, however, Londoners had started to use underground stations as public shelters, just as they would do during the Blitz two decades later, while the press furiously denounced Zeppelins as 'baby killers'.

Post-war career

Following the Armistice, Robertson took command of the British Army of the Rhine. There was a brief fear that Germany would not sign the Treaty of Versailles and that an insurgency might begin, but as it turned out the Germans signed without major incident. As demobilisation began, the Rhine Command was downgraded to a lieutenant-general's command and thus Robertson lost his post.

In July 1919, Churchill offered him the position of commander-in-chief, Ireland. The problem was that by that time tensions in Ireland were rising, and Robertson was thought to be too blunt for the role. In October 1919, Robertson's old adversary Wilson, still CIGS, asked Churchill to consult the Prime Minister about the appointment, doubtless knowing that Lloyd George would never back Robertson. Lloyd George suggested Robertson be made commander-in-chief, India, instead, but Rawlinson was already the fait accompli for that role. Churchill was annoyed at being overruled about Robertson so had him promoted to field marshal as a consolation prize, thus

---

72 The Germans lost 30 Airships shot down or crashed, and 62 aircraft. See Christopher Cole, EF Christopher and EF Cheesman, *The Air Defence of Great Britain 1914–1918* (Putnam, 1984); Raymond Fredette, *The Sky on Fire: The First Battle of Britain 1917–1918* (Harvest, 1976); GW Haddow and Peter M Grosz, *The German Giants: The German R-Planes, 1914–1918* (Putnam, 1962); and Edgar Jones, 'Air-raid casualties in the First World War', History of Government Blog, 19 January 2015, https://history.blog.gov.uk/2015/01/19/air-raid-casualties-in-the-first-world-war/.

73 Max Hastings, *Catastrophe*, op cit. It was long said that WG Grace, the legendary cricketer, suffered a stroke and died as a result of the shock from an early Zeppelin raid, but his most recent biographer at the time of writing, Richard Tomlinson (in *Amazing Grace: The Man Who Was W. G.* (Little, Brown, 2015)), dismisses the story as an urban myth.

completing the final step in Robertson's unique journey through the entire ranks of the British Army.

Robertson did not receive the sort of endorsement one might have expected. Wilson thought the promotion 'disgusting'. No one was waiting to meet Robertson on his return to Britain, leaving him to find a taxi home and, as he put it, join 'the long list of unemployed officers on half-pay'. He was never of substantial means, but made his retirement from the services more comfortable by some directorships in private enterprise. He also served as President of the British Legion.

In his autobiography, Robertson claimed that there had never been any material disagreement between himself and Haig over the main principles to win the war. But the two men had not been without their differences: Haig, like others, was disparaging about Robertson's social origins and the fact he was therefore not a 'gentleman' however much he achieved in his career. At a dinner after the war at which both were present, Haig paid tribute to Wilson, but not to Robertson. Robertson was infuriated.

Britain's allies were more generous: Robertson was awarded the Belgian War Cross, the Grand Cross of the Serbian Order of the White Eagle (with Swords), the American Distinguished Service Medal, the Chinese Order of Chia-Ho (1st Class), the Grand Cross of the Order of the Crown of Italy, the Russian Order of Alexander Nevsky, and the Japanese Grand Cordon of the Order of the Rising Sun.

Robertson did not become a pacifist, but the cost of the war clearly weighed upon his shoulders, and he spoke out against the expenditure of blood and treasure that the war had demanded.

He died in 1933.

Coda: Robertson and a future Savage

There was a price to be paid for the diligence and dedication that Robertson had to exhibit to make his unique ascendancy through the ranks of the army: he neither drank nor smoked. In that respect he preceded a later, even more famous general and honorary life Savage, Bernard Montgomery, albeit in Monty's case his abstinence was due to war wounds rather than choice.

Either way, there was an appropriate link between the two, for it was at a summer party after the Great War at Robertson's residence in Germany (while he was commanding the British Army of the Rhine) that a young Monty agitated to be placed in staff college. Robertson evidently saw something in the junior officer for he granted Monty's wish. Without Robertson's support Monty would never had reached the upper echelons of the British Army, and someone else would have had to become the most famous British general of the next war.

Field Marshal Byng: from 'scug' to field marshal

The last of the Savage Club's Great War field marshals was Julian Hedworth George Byng. He had a fine record as a commander during the conflict. He also gained lasting fame afterwards – albeit of an unwanted kind – when he found himself embroiled in one of Canada's great constitutional crises, which would go on to have significant influence in how the relations between Britain and her dominions were organised.

Early life and career

Byng was born into nobility: his father was the Earl of Strafford and the owner of the impressive family seat of Wrotham Park, Hertfordshire. The young Byng's position was not, however, quite as privileged as it sounded. Since he was the thirteenth child and the seventh son, his chances of inheriting the family estate were remote. Also, with such a large family, the earl's finances were more straitened than they might otherwise have been.

Nevertheless, Byng was able to attend Eton – where he almost completely failed to distinguish himself, leaving before he had entered the Sixth Form. He had no pretensions about his achievements at school except in a self-deprecatory sense: he once claimed that he had been the school's worst 'Scug', Etonian vernacular for an undistinguished pupil.

In Byng's day, commissions in the army could still be bought. His father had already purchased four for his brothers, leaving not much spare cash, so Byng went into the militia. At the end of 1879 he was commissioned as a second lieutenant into the 2nd (Edmonton) Royal Middlesex Rifles. He prospered much more in the army than he had at Eton, being promoted to lieutenant in April 1881. In his spare time his hobbies included becoming proficient on the banjo.

In 1882, the Prince of Wales wanted Byng to join his regiment, the 10th Royal Hussars. Byng could not afford it as the commission cost £600 per annum. Since, however, the offer was not one he could refuse, his family managed to come up with the money by buying, training and selling polo ponies. Byng transferred to the 10th Royal Hussars at the start of January 1883 and shortly afterwards joined the regiment in Lucknow, India, making him a contemporary of Field Marshal Roberts in the theatre.

In 1884 the Hussars were on their way back to Britain when they were diverted to the Sudan to join the Suakin Expedition. Byng took part in the charge at the first Battle of El Teb. Later, his horse was killed under him at the Battle of Tamai. Ultimately the British prevailed and managed to see off the rebels. The Hussars then resumed their journey to Britain, arriving in the latter part of April 1884. Byng was mentioned in despatches.

Back in Britain, Byng came to know the Prince of Wales's sons, Prince Albert Victor, and Prince George. Albert Victor joined the regiment. He died in January 1892, and Byng headed the pallbearers at his funeral.

In 1887, Byng became involved in a notable incident after his regiment was moved to Hounslow. He suspected that contractors were selling him inferior meat. He went to Smithfield Meat Market to learn the trade sufficiently to establish his case; having done so, the suppliers had their contract terminated. Also at Hounslow, Byng met the Victorian philanthropist Lord Rowton, who was determined to improve housing for working men in London. Rowton established a chain of hostels known as 'Rowton Houses' to replace the dilapidated lodging houses prevalent at the time. Byng had the idea of hiring retired senior soldiers to maintain order in them.

In the early 1890s, Byng studied at the staff college at Camberley, where he was a contemporary of the likes of Henry Rawlinson, Henry Hughes Wilson, Thomas D'Oyly Snow and James Aylmer Lowthorpe Haldane. He encountered Winston Churchill on one occasion as well, though Churchill was studying at Sandhurst. After graduating from staff college in December 1894, Byng commanded the A Squadron of the Hussars. He was promoted to major in May 1898.

In 1899, Byng went to the Second Boer War. He was given the local rank of lieutenant colonel and charged with raising and commanding the South African Light Horse. He served with distinction under both Roberts and Kitchener, and in February 1902 reached the rank of brevet colonel. In the same year he returned to England. He married there but was sent to India to command the 10th Royal Hussars at Mhow. He had to return to England in 1904 after severely breaking his right elbow whilst playing polo.

First World War

Not long after war broke out, Byng went to France with the BEF, where he saw action in the First Battle of Ypres. In 1915, he went to Gallipoli to supervise the Allied withdrawal. In sharp contrast with the costly, failed offensive, the withdrawal was conducted so efficiently there were no losses at all. Byng then spent time commanding the Suez Canal defences before returning to the Western Front, where he commanded the Canadian Corps.

Byng's crowning achievement in the field came when he was in charge of the successful attack in April 1917 at Vimy Ridge,[74] the first time in which

---

74 The attack was the subject of a customarily moving description by Henry Williamson, who was stationed nearby. See Williamson, 'The Battle of Vimy Ridge', *Daily Express*, 6–7 April 1967. His article was later collected in *Days of Wonder* (1987; e-book 2013, Henry Williamson Society).

all four divisions of the Canadian Expeditionary Force had participated in a battle together. The attack has been celebrated in Canada ever since as a historic achievement for a fledgling nation. It was a good example of the British and Empire forces learning from past encounters. Byng's troops were well briefed by French soldiers about the tactics used in the successful retaking of Verdun. Byng employed a very effective artillery bombardment, in contrast with the failed efforts on the Somme in 1916. Instead of simply hoping preparatory shelling would clear the wire and other obstacles, at Vimy Ridge a 'creeping barrage' was used in which troops would advance with artillery progressively firing in front of them.[75] The tactic required great precision in organisation and execution.

Later, in June 1917, Byng's forces fought the Battle of Cambrai, the most successful use of tanks in the Great War. The Allies were under severe pressure at the time: the French mutiny had rendered much of their army incapable, the Italians had suffered badly at Caporetto, the Russians had collapsed completely, and the Americans were a long way off being able to supply a meaningful contribution to the continental land armies. The British and Empire troops were thus in the best position for a substantial offensive.

Byng chose Cambrai as it was a supply point for the Hindenburg Line, and its capture would also expose the rear of the German line. He was urged to use tanks by the newly created Tank Corps.[76] Some of Byng's subordinates, however, wanted to use the refined artillery-infantry techniques, as developed at Vimy Ridge and elsewhere. Byng decided to combine both strategies.

Byng had some 476 tanks, including 378 combat tanks, at his disposal. The tanks advanced in groups of three to bridge the German trenches. The Mark IV tanks leading the assault carried fascines which they dropped in the trenches in sequence. Behind them came the infantry, moving in close column rather than the older method of extended line. The tanks also carried fascines which they dropped in the trenches, enabling the infantry to cross quickly in support.

The new tactics met with demonstrable success: the first day saw the British capture 4,200 prisoners for the loss of about 4,000 casualties and 180 tanks. They captured more ground – a breach six miles wide and 4,000 yards deep – than they had in three months at Flanders, even though they did not secure all their objectives. The success was celebrated back in Britain by ringing church bells.

Unfortunately, the slowness of the tanks, the heavy losses they incurred – more

---

75 See Alexander Turner, *Vimy Ridge 1917: Byng's Canadians Triumph at Arras* (Osprey Publishing, 2005) and Patrick Brennan, 'Julian Byng and Leadership in the Canadian Corps', in Geoffrey Hayes, Andrew Iarocci and Mike Bechthold, *Vimy Ridge: A Canadian Reassessment* (Wilfrid Laurier University Press, 2007), pp 87–104.

76 In 1916, Haig – contrary to his subsequent Luddite reputation – had ordered 1,000 new tanks and had supported the creation of a separate Tank Corps. It was headed by Major Hugh Elles. Its chief staff officer was Major JFC Fuller, an important and original military thinker, who lost credibility later in life due to his support for fascism.

from breakdown than enemy action – and, most importantly, the lack of infantry and tanks available for exploitation (horse-mounted troops proved unsuitable) meant the attack slowed after the first day's success. The Germans quickly reinforced the sector and launched counter-attacks in a manner which demonstrated that they, too, had learned from earlier battles. They employed a short, intense bombardment followed by infantry attacking using 'Hutier' infiltration tactics, comprising groups of soldiers avoiding heavily-defended areas rather than broad waves of troops traversing the whole Front.[77]

Had the British attack been intended only as a raid, as had been urged by the Tank Corps' Major Fuller, it could have been called a dramatic success. Instead, it ended looking something like a draw, with both sides suffering about 40,000 casualties and 11,000 German prisoners as against about 9,000 British, with little British land gains and in some cases small amounts of ground conceded. If nothing else, though, the respective casualty figures were a much better result than the earlier large-scale offensives on the Western Front.

After the battle, Byng was made a permanent general. Following the Armistice, he was elevated to the peerage in his own right as Baron Byng of Vimy, of Thorpe-le-Soken in the County of Essex. He retired from the military in 1919.

Governor general of Canada

In 1921, Byng was appointed governor general of Canada, reflecting his successful service with the Canadian forces during the First World War.[78] He was enthusiastic and popular for most of his tenure, but he became best known for the 'King-Byng Affair', a controversial constitutional episode that bears some similarity to the Whitlam Dismissal in Australia in the 1970s.

The King-Byng Affair remains of interest because it involves the actual use of the governor general's power which, like that of the monarch in Britain, is normally wholly theoretical. It is not beyond the realms of possibility that one day a hung parliament in Britain might drag the monarch into a similar constitutional crisis, as indeed it almost did in 1950.

The start of the affair was the Canadian federal election in October 1925, which resulted in a hung parliament comprising 101 Liberals, 116 Conservatives and 28 Progressives, Labour and Independents. The Liberal prime minister, William Lyon Mackenzie King, managed to obtain sufficient backing in the House to form a minority government.

His government did not last long: in June 1926, a no-confidence vote was

---

77 The better German tactics were named after Oskar von Hutier, a German officer, though he had no role in their development.

78 There have been various other interesting links between Canada and the Savage Club: for example, Sir Richard Squires, the former prime minister of Newfoundland (when it was still independent) joined the Club in February 1931 under the category of literature.

passed after the opposition uncovered a scandal involving customs officials turning a blind eye to US bootleg liquor (another example of alcohol finding a way to influencing the important affairs of the nation). King asked Byng to dissolve parliament and call a new election. Byng declined the advice, because a motion of censure of the government for the bootleg scandal was under debate, and there was no precedent for a request for dissolution in those circumstances. Instead, Byng asked the Conservatives to form a government under their leader, Arthur Meighen.

King resigned following Byng's refusal and Meighen duly formed a minority Conservative government. Under the rules then in force in Canada, an MP appointed to a cabinet post had to resign his seat and seek re-election in a by-election. Meighen gave up his own seat, but he tried to evade the rules for the rest of his cabinet by calling them 'acting ministers' or 'ministers without portfolio' and claiming they were therefore not obliged to resign. Unsurprisingly, the Liberals disputed the validity of that manoeuvre.

The Conservative government was short-lived: it survived four successful parliamentary votes, including one to censure the previous King government, but lost a fifth vote only a few days into their tenure. Meighen then asked Byng for a dissolution and an election, and Byng complied.

During the subsequent campaign, King emphasised the constitutional issue and sought to impugn Byng as a foreigner interfering with the rights of Canadians to govern themselves, the implication being that the Englishman Byng was acting on orders from London. His tactic succeeded: he won a substantial majority in the election, and Byng returned to Britain.

King went on to use the affair to argue for the dominions to gain further formal independence from Britain.[79] The result was the Statute of Westminster being passed by the British parliament in December 1931, at the behest of Canada, Australia, New Zealand and South Africa. The Statute left those dominions effectively wholly independent, save to the extent they themselves chose otherwise. And, in the case of Canada, governors general would thereafter not demur from the advice of Canadian prime ministers. The same applied in the other dominions, with the notable exception of Australia in 1975 when Sir John Kerr dismissed his prime minister, Gough Whitlam, and installed Malcolm Fraser as

---

79 The affair was one of the factors leading to the Committee on Inter-Imperial Relations at the 1926 Imperial Conference in London. Under the leadership of Arthur Balfour, the committee redefined the legal relationship among self-governing nations of the British Empire. King played a strong part in the work of the committee. Its report defined the group of self-governing communities composed of Great Britain and the dominions as 'autonomous Communities within the British Empire, equal in status, in no way subordinate one to another in any aspect of their domestic or external affairs, though united by a common allegiance to the Crown, and freely associated as members of the British Commonwealth of Nations.'

prime minister. On that occasion, Kerr's actions were more controversial than Byng's, but on the other hand the electorate supported his decision by returning Fraser at the next election.

Byng himself always maintained that he had acted in the interests of Canada, and he took all responsibility for his part in the affair. Upon his return to Britain, his reputation was unharmed and he was seen to have acted with dignity and probity throughout.

In the years since, there have been authoritative commentators both for and against Byng's actions. On the one hand, King's request for parliament to be dissolved while it was investigating his conduct had an obvious taint of self-interest. As against that, no Canadian governor general had previously refused the advice of the Canadian prime minister.

It seems to me that while Byng's refusal was understandable, given the appearance of a tawdry motive at stake, it would still have been better for him to have followed convention and left the opposition to make what it chose to about King's behaviour in the resultant election. Instead, Byng gifted King the opportunity to claim that a foreign governor general was defying the will of an elected Canadian politician.

In Britain, a similar situation nearly occurred in 1950, when the Labour government held a very slim majority. Sir Alan Lascelles, the private secretary to George VI, wrote to *The Times* stating that the monarch might refuse to call an election, but only if three conditions were met: (i) if the existing parliament was still 'vital, viable, and capable of doing its job'; (ii) if a general election would be 'detrimental to the national economy', and (iii) if the sovereign could 'rely on finding another prime minister who could govern for a reasonable period with a working majority in the House of Commons.' In the King-Byng affair, all three conditions appeared to have been met at the point Byng's decision was taken, but the third soon unravelled. (I have to say the first two tests at least have a disarming level of subjectivity about them.)

The affair was recalled in Canada in 2008, when the Conservatives, led by Stephen Harper, won the election with a minority. A few weeks later, the Liberals, NDP and Bloc Québécois announced an agreement to defeat the Conservatives and form a government. The agreement would make Stéphane Dion prime minister even though he had already announced his resignation as Liberal leader.

Much speculation followed as to whether the governor general, Michaëlle Jean, should allow a new election if requested by Harper. In the event, the question was never put to her. Instead, Harper asked for a prorogation of parliament, and Jean agreed. Parliament reconvened nearly two months later, Harper's government survived, and went on to win the next election with a majority.

Byng's later life in England

In January 1928, Byng became Viscount Byng of Vimy, of Thorpe-le-Soken in the County of Essex. In the same year, he was appointed commissioner of the Metropolitan Police. During his time, a number of reforms were made to the force, including the introduction of a system of promotion based on merit rather than length of service. He also took steps to improve discipline, remove inefficient senior officers and ensure policemen's beats were regularly changed to prevent criminals predicting them. Modern technology was brought in, including police boxes, more police cars and a central radio control room.

Byng left the police service in 1931 and was promoted to field marshal the following year. He died in 1935.

Coda: pour encourager les autres

Much further back in the Byng lineage was Admiral John Byng, who commanded the British at the Battle of Minorca during the French and Indian War. He became a legend in naval circles and beyond, albeit not for reasons he would have wished. His story ironically preceded, and had some influence on, the greatest sea battle of the First World War.

Minorca was a British possession, but was attacked by the French in 1756. The British government had been warned about French plans but had done nothing to reinforce the inadequate garrison. It hastily assembled a rescue force and promoted Byng from vice-admiral to admiral in order to lead it. When Byng's forces arrived, they found the French had already overrun the island, but he engaged the French fleet nevertheless.

Although the opposing sides were roughly numerically comparable, the British ships were in a poor state of repair. They also suffered from poor signalling, something which was modernised by the Battle of Trafalgar half a century later, but which again fell behind the times in the age of steam.[80]

After coming off badly in the early exchanges, Byng withdrew to Gibraltar rather than needlessly risk losing his ships. The result was humiliation for the British, quickly exploited by the French. In true managerial style, the Admiralty used Byng as a scapegoat. Byng was court-martialled under the 12th Article of War[81] and executed by firing squad in March 1757 on board HMS *Monarcque*.

---

80 See Chris Ware, *Admiral Byng: His Rise and Execution* (Pen & Sword, 2009).

81 As originally drafted, it provided:

> Every person in the fleet who, through cowardice, negligence or disaffection, shall in time of action withdraw, or keep back, or not come to the fight or engagement, or shall not do his utmost to take or destroy every ship ... [or to] assist all and every of His Majesty's ships, or those of allies, which it shall be his duty to assist and relieve; every such person so offending and being convicted thereof by the sentence of a court martial shall suffer death or such other punishment as the circumstances of the offence shall deserve

Byng remains the only British admiral to have been executed in the history of the Royal Navy. The apparent injustice of him carrying the blame was satirised by Voltaire in *Candide* in which the eponymous character witnessed an execution of an admiral at Portsmouth, and was told '*Dans ce pays-ci, il est bon de tuer de temps en temps un admiral pour encourager les autres*', or 'In this country, it is good to kill an admiral from time to time, in order to encourage the others'. The line '*pour encourager les autres*' has been in the English vernacular ever since.

Over the past two centuries, Byng's culpability has been debated on and off. His descendants have never given up hope for his redemption. In 2007, they petitioned the Ministry of Defence for a posthumous pardon along the lines of that which had been granted to those executed for cowardice during the First World War, something we look at in Chapter 9. The Ministry declined, on the somewhat questionable ground that the situations could not be compared since Byng had no relatives left who had had any knowledge of him. One suspects that the real reason was that the ministry ironically feared a pardon might '*encourager les autres*' and result in endless petitions from relatives of everyone killed by the British Army from Joan of Arc to Breaker Morant.

The chief reason for telling Admiral Byng's story is that more than a century-and-a-half after his death, another English admiral would exercise caution in battle, be hampered by poor signalling, have his reputation traduced by the fact of the enemy seizing the post-battle propaganda initiative, and would find himself having to fight battles at home against those who wanted a scapegoat for the failure to secure a decisive victory. To Admiral Jellicoe we will now turn.

Admiral Jellicoe: 'the only man who could lose the war in an afternoon'

Based on the number of gongs he managed to accumulate, the career of Admiral of the Fleet John Jellicoe, 1st Earl Jellicoe, seems to be of a piece with Roberts, Kitchener, Robertson and Byng: Jellicoe served at the apex of the Royal Navy during the First World War, and was later a popular governor-general of New Zealand. Yet he was fated to be remembered above all else for a single day – the great clash of ironclads that was the Battle of Jutland in 1916. From the moment the battle finished to the present day, over a century later, the outcome has been furiously contested by armchair admirals worldwide. As a result, Jellicoe never enjoyed the unqualified admiration of the public or his peers, either in his lifetime or since. What is especially remarkable about the battle is that almost no

---

and the court martial shall judge fit.
The final clause 'or such other punishment …' had been removed from the Article in 1745, meaning that by the time Byng's trial took place there was no discretion in sentencing: the death penalty was mandatory.

material facts are left in dispute, yet historians have still not been able to agree whether it was a tactical or strategic victory, both or neither.

Early life

Jellicoe was born in Southampton in 1859. His father was a captain in the Royal Mail Steam Packet Company. He joined the Royal Navy in 1872. In 1879, he passed out first of his term of 39 boys and was promoted to midshipman. Thereafter he climbed steadily up the ladder of naval promotions.

Jellicoe showed an early interest in gunnery, qualifying as a gunnery officer in 1883. In May 1886, he rescued the crew of a capsized steamer near Gibraltar, for which he was awarded the Board of Trade Silver Medal. In the early 1890s he served in the Mediterranean, and was on board HMS *Victoria* when it collided with HMS *Camperdown* in June 1893. He also served during the Boxer Rebellion in June 1900, where he was wounded so badly it was assumed he would not survive.

By 1914, Jellicoe held the post of Second Sea Lord. When war was declared, Churchill, as First Lord of the Admiralty, removed Admiral George Callaghan as commander-in-chief of the Home Fleet, promoted Jellicoe to full admiral and gave him command of the Home Fleet, which was renamed the Grand Fleet. Jellicoe was angered by the treatment meted out to Callaghan. He reluctantly accepted the command, but he did not forget. When Churchill was removed from office after Gallipoli, Jellicoe railed against his interference as a politician in matters normally the preserve of professional naval officers.[82]

Jutland

The background

The transformation of Germany from an historic ally of Britain to a rival was due in no small measure to the decision of Kaiser Wilhelm II and Admiral Tirpitz to build a surface fleet to rival the Royal Navy. When the Prussians had marched into France in 1870, the British had been happy to sit on the sidelines, since the Prussians had no navy to speak of.

In 1902, however, the supremacy which the Royal Navy had enjoyed for almost a century was threatened by its own innovation. The new HMS *Dreadnought* instantly rendered all other battleships obsolete, leaving all nations more or less at the same starting point. Germany began building rival Dreadnoughts with great earnest. By 1914, the German High Seas Fleet was of a size and strength that the prospect of it gaining access to the Channel ports was unacceptable to Britain,

---

82 He also apologised years later to Callaghan, who bore him no ill-will since he knew it had not been Jellicoe's choice to usurp him.

and so British admirals would have felt they could not allow the Germans to overrun France again.[83]

Thanks to Britain's shipbuilding prowess and its massive expenditure on the navy, Britain was still stronger at sea than Germany in 1914. It had a problem in that its commitments were worldwide – covering the entire Empire – whereas the Germans could concentrate their fleet locally. (American admirals face a similar problem in the twenty-first century.) Nevertheless, thanks to the Anglo-Japanese alliance in 1902, the *Entente Cordiale* with France in 1904 and the 1907 rapprochement with Russia, Britain was able to remove forces from the Far East and the Mediterranean and thereby have enough ships to retain a clear advantage over Germany in the North Sea. Britain also had greater shipbuilding capacity and so could replace any wartime losses more quickly. It was assumed by the British military and public alike that a second Trafalgar would be delivered at some point during the war.

Aside from hoping to defeat the Germans in open battle, the Royal Navy had two overarching strategic functions during wartime: first, to preserve its own trade routes, and secondly, to impose a blockade upon German imports by sea. For the Germans, their best chance of overcoming the British advantage in surface vessels was to use mines and U-boats, but they were hampered by a strategic masterstroke on the part of the British. Instead of attempting a 'close blockade' involving ships patrolling close to German waters, the Grand Fleet was based in the comparatively remote waters of Scapa Flow in Scotland. It could still prevent merchant ships reaching Germany around the Denmark Strait, or German capital ships heading in the other direction as commerce raiders, whilst being effectively invulnerable thanks to the remoteness of the location. (The English Channel was never an option for German merchant or naval ships since it was too heavily defended.)

The only problem for the British was that the chances of meeting the High Seas Fleet were slim, since the Germans were not foolhardy enough to venture out for a large-scale set battle, while Jellicoe was not going to try and tempt them by placing the Grand Fleet within U-boat range or in danger of mines without good reason.

The German counter-strategy was to try and entice parts of the Grand Fleet out here and there and meet them with a superior force, and thereby degrade

---

83 The fact of naval rivalry being a cause of the war between Britain and Germany was disputed by Niall Ferguson in *The Pity of War* (Penguin, new edn, 2012 – original published in 1988); he claimed to have established through archival research that the naval arms race was more or less over by 1912, since the Germans knew by then they could not hope to match the British ship for ship. Instead, Ferguson puts Britain joining the war down to Sir Edward Grey and Winston Churchill, and the rest of the cabinet going along with them less down to the force of their advocacy, and more for their own careers, since the Asquith government was faltering at that point. It is an interesting thesis but beyond our scope here.

the British numerical advantage over time. Among the tactics the Germans employed was to bombard British coastal towns, which they knew the British could not leave unanswered. The British responded by stationing Admiral Sir David Beatty with fast battlecruisers further south as a rapid response force to deal with German raiders. Beatty was also given Rear-Admiral Evan-Thomas's 5th Battle Squadron, composed of the modern Queen Elizabeth-class battleships, which were able to take on the strongest German ships.

Beatty was something of a cad in his personal life. Aside from a sucession of mistresses, he was married to a wealthy American woman – so wealthy that, when he was once threatened with disciplinary action, she said dismissively that she would just buy the navy another ship. At sea, he was the opposite of Jellicoe in that he was anxious to show as much aggression as possible. The Germans knew that and suspected he would fall for their intended traps. It was one such attempt that led to Jutland, at the end of May 1916.

The battle came about when the Germans sent an advance force of five modern, fast battlecruisers, commanded by Vice-Admiral Hipper, to entice Beatty south, where he would then meet the whole of the High Seas Fleet under its commander, Admiral Reinhardt von Scheer. British intelligence, which had broken German naval codes, discovered the plan. They set about implementing a counter-trap in which Beatty would lure the High Seas Fleet straight into the maw of the entire Grand Fleet. Between the two sides, 250 ships and 100,000 men left port to do battle.

The run to the south

Hipper's scouting group encountered Beatty on the afternoon of 31 May 1916. The two engaged in a running battle heading south, just as the Germans had planned. That first encounter was the worst phase of the battle for the British. Even before they reached the main German force, two of the British battlecruisers were sunk following spectacular explosions with virtually all hands lost. As the second ship went down, Beatty famously turned to his flag captain Ernie Chatfield and said 'There seems to be something wrong with our bloody ships today.'

In fact three things were wrong with them. The first was that British ships were designed for long range patrols all over the world, whereas the Germans only envisaged short sorties in the North Sea for theirs. Hence the latter did not have to bother with crew comfort and could instead add extra armour plating, stronger bulkheads and more watertight compartments. Jellicoe himself had noted the resultant superior German protection long before the war. That weakness was exacerbated in the case of battlecruisers, which were not designed to face capital ships in the first place. They were supposed to use their speed to hunt down enemy cruisers and destroyers, and to escape capital ships. To gain that speed they made sacrifices in armour.

The second problem was that the British had loosened the safety requirements around the handling of cordite, including leaving blast doors open and thus enabling the German shells to ignite whole magazines, hence the spectacular explosions. The reason for the lax British practice was an obsession with rate of fire, a crucial factor in the days of sail and cannons, but a poor second to accuracy with twentieth-century long-range guns and far too risky, as they discovered to their cost. The Germans had had a similar experience in the earlier, much smaller engagement at Dogger Bank, and had learned their lesson.

The third problem was the British shells themselves, which were much inferior to those of the Germans.

Beatty had compounded his disadvantages by steaming ahead of the 5th Battle Squadron, his most powerful ships. Evans-Thomas had lost sight of signals in the gloom – bad signalling would plague the British throughout the battle. Worse, he had never been properly briefed by Beatty. He was used to Jellicoe's cautious approach and had not been able to second-guess what the more aggressive Beatty had done.[84]

Having paid for his initial exuberance, Beatty finally stopped trying to be Nelson when he met the High Seas Fleet, and turned to draw the Germans back to Jellicoe. The Germans, assuming Beatty was running for his life, duly gave chase.

The trap and the escape

Back on his flagship *Iron Duke*, Jellicoe knew nothing of the loss of the two British battlecruisers, or much else about Beatty's engagement, but he eventually received the signal he had been waiting for since the war began: the enemy was approaching in numbers. Because the information was incomplete, he was forced to guess the German disposition, but he made the correct call when he ordered his fleet to turn to port to form a battle line, and thereby 'cross the T' of the Germans – meaning all his guns would be brought to bear while the Germans would have only their front guns with which to reply.[85] The smoke of battle and the mist combined to obscure his fleet from the Germans until the last minute.

---

84 See for example Andrew Gordon (*The Rules of the Game: Jutland and British Naval Command*, Naval Institute Press, 2013, reprint) and Arthur J Marder, *From The Dreadnought to Scapa Flow: The Royal Navy in the Fisher Era, 1904–1919. Volume III, Jutland and after (May 1916–December 1916)* (OUP, 1966) p 55.

85 Robert K Massie, *Castles of Steel: Britain, Germany and the Winning of The Great War at Sea* (Vintage, later edn, 2007) pp 611–12. See also Peter Padfield, *Battleship* (Thistle Publishing,

As the forces converged, the British lost their third battlecruiser, *Invincible*, in the same fashion as the other two: a catastrophic explosion caused by the exposure of cordite.[86] But *Invincible* was the last British disaster of the battle. It was now the turn of the Germans to be on the receiving end.

To begin with, Scheer acted with a cool head, given the sudden discovery that his fleet was facing annihilation. He ordered a well-rehearsed manoeuvre, which his ships executed almost perfectly: a 180 degree turn and retreat under a smokescreen and with the cover of a torpedo attack. For the next 20 minutes the Germans moved away from danger. Then, for reasons unclear – and on which he himself gave conflicting accounts – he performed the same manoeuvre and headed back towards the British. 'The fact is', he later conceded, 'I had no definite object', and 'if I'd done it in a peacetime exercise, I'd have lost my command'. 'No naval assault during the Great War was as useless as this second attack of Reinhardt Scheer' opined one historian,[87] while others have speculated that Scheer thought he could cross the tail of the British fleet, damage it and escape.[88]

Either way, Jellicoe had been gifted a second chance, and he did not need a written invitation. The Grand Fleet's broadsides resumed, and Scheer quickly realised the magnitude of his error. Once again he ordered his battleships to execute the 180 degree turn. He added two further orders to buy some time: his more expendable battlecruisers were to throw themselves at the British, while his destroyers were to launch a massed torpedo attack. This time the German *volte face* was not executed so precisely, and the battlecruisers soaked up some terrific punishment in what was little short of a suicide run. The torpedo attack, however, triggered Jellicoe's natural caution, and he took a defensive course before resuming the chase. The Germans gained enough of a lead to keep the bulk of their fleet out of range. Among other things, Jellicoe feared German night gunnery was superior to his own, and so would not press the attack in the dark. Beatty found and engaged some German battlecruisers, but switched his fire to some old German pre-Dreadnoughts. Although he inflicted some damage, the Germans escaped into the night.

The German situation was still perilous, since the Grand Fleet was positioned between them and home and only six hours of darkness were expected. Yet luck

---

Kindle edn, 2015).

86 On board was a great naval name, Admiral Hood, whose namesake vessel would meet a similar fate at the hands of the *Bismarck* in the next war, perhaps the most famous single loss of a British ship ever. The HMS *Hood* website (www.hmshood.com) has a wealth of information on the vessel.

87 Massie, *Castles of Steel*, op cit, pp 626–628.

88 William Koenig, *Epic Sea Battles* (Octopus Books Ltd, 1975, reprinted 2004 by Bounty Books) p 178. References are to the later edition.

stayed on the German side, as they managed to cut behind the British fleet. Some shots were exchanged, but the British did not discern that they came from the main component of the High Seas Fleet. Moreover, the signalling problems continued, leaving Jellicoe largely blind. The bulk of the High Seas Fleet thus made it home and the Battle of Jutland was over.

The numbers

The bare statistics showed that Britain lost 6,784 men and 14 ships weighing a total of 111,000 tons against German losses of 3,058 men and 11 ships weighing a total of 62,000 tons.

It is important to note that the disparity in losses was not, as is sometimes assumed, due to better gunnery on the Germans' part. In the first 75 minutes of the battle, the British managed 17 heavy hits against the Germans' 44, but in the last half hour the British scored 49 to 3. Rather, it was due to the superior German protection and better German shells. German admirals told the neutral Swedes not long after the battle that had the British shells been up to standard the High Seas Fleet would have been routed.[89]

There was a clear parallel between the British battlecruisers at Jutland and many of the Allied tanks in the Second World War. The trade-off equation for an armoured ship was the same as for a tank: speed, firepower and protection. Battlecruisers chose speed on the assumption that they would not have to fight a heavily armoured enemy, but once the shooting started they were denied that luxury and had to face whatever was in front of them. The historian Andrew Gordon's phrase that men lost their lives at Jutland in 'a costly rediscovery of the designer's terms of reference' is apposite. Sadly, they were not the last to do so. In the Second World War, the Royal Navy's most famous remaining battlecruiser, HMS *Hood*, was lost in similar fashion.[90] Then, decades later in the Falklands War, ships were lost because the exigencies of war required them to fight the enemy in front of them, rather than undertake a narrow task for which they had been designed.[91]

---

89   Richard Osborne, *Voices from the Past: The Battle of Jutland. History's Greatest Sea Battle Told Through Newspapers Reports, Official Documents and the Accounts of Those Who Were There* (Frontline Books, 2016), p 126.

90   In a letter to *The Times* of 26 May 1941 – just after her sinking – Ernie Chatfield (by then a retired former admiral of the fleet) dismissed talk of a 'lucky hit' and said that the loss was due to *Hood* being an outdated vessel, designed with a compromise between speed and armour that had long been discredited; he, at least, had learned the lessons of 1916.

91   Almost all of the ships deployed lacked point defence systems against missiles, the thinking being that they would operate defined tasks as part of a NATO fleet, instead of having to defend themselves against low flying aircraft and missiles.

The verdict

The Germans were quick off the mark in the public relations battle, immediately issuing a communiqué claiming victory based on the number of ships known to have been sunk (they withheld details of losses they thought the British would not know about). A national holiday was declared and the Kaiser trumpeted that the myth of Trafalgar had been shattered. Jellicoe, on the other hand, sent a measured explanation to the Admiralty, expressing disappointment at the German escape and frustration at the performance of his battlecruisers, admitting of the latter 'the result cannot be other than unpalatable'.[92] The British fumbled around with their own press releases and failed to announce the ringing victory the public expected.

The key as it seems to me is that it was the Germans who fled the battlefield in order to avoid annihilation. It was not a situation akin to, say, the Battle of Quatres Bas, when Wellington had always planned to withdraw towards Waterloo, or Austerlitz when Napoleon deliberately gave up the Pratzen Heights to lure the Allies into an attack. Moreover, the Grand Fleet was ready for action almost immediately afterwards but damage to the German ships took many weeks to repair. Both points suggest a British tactical *and* strategic victory.

It might be said that the Germans had never intended to hold the battlefield. But they had certainly intended to shift the strategic balance more in their favour. Despite sinking more ships than they lost, they failed to do so, judging by the readiness of the respective fleets after the battle. Moreover, even when most of their ships were repaired, the High Seas Fleet only deployed on three unremarkable occasions for the whole of the rest of the war, and never chanced another encounter with the Grand Fleet, even as the blockade began to suffocate the German war effort (and mutinied at the end of the war when asked to make a last attack on the British).[93] Instead, the Germans turned their energies to U-boats. Unrestricted submarine warfare was an important factor in the United States joining the war, which in turn was an important factor in sealing Germany's defeat. One can, therefore, see a clear chain from Jutland to victory in the entire war.

Jellicoe's fate

As for Jellicoe himself, he might not have not won a Trafalgaresque victory, but nor had he suffered a Trafalgaresque defeat. Those expecting him to act like Nelson had should have remembered that Nelson commanded only a third of

---

92 Despatch from the Commander-in-Chief No 1396/HF 0022 'Iron Duke', 18 June 1916, http://www.gwpda.org/naval/jut02.htm.

93 Particularly damaging was the fact that the Germans struggled to import enough ammonia for explosives. Food also became scarce: in desperation, the Germans devised over 800 varieties of sausage substitute, which they called 'Ersatzwurst'.

the British fleet when he went into action at Trafalgar, so could afford more risks than Jellicoe, who was responsible for the entirety of British sea power. Moreover, Jellicoe was not personally to blame for the poor signalling or for the poor design of the battle cruisers, nor for the low quality of the British shells. He was also right to have been cautious about a night encounter.

Such nuances were lost on his critics, however, and he carried the blame for not delivering the great victory that the public had expected. It is possible that had he ordered full steam ahead and damn the torpedoes as Scheer was retreating, he might have only lost a handful of ships but won a decisive victory. Equally, he might have created disaster. In all the circumstances, it was reasonable for Jellicoe to conclude that he held the whip hand the day before the battle and still held the whip hand the day after. Or, as *The New York Times* put it, the inmate had assaulted his jailor, but was still in jail.

Nevertheless, thanks to their respective public relations skills, Jellicoe was moved into a desk job as First Sea Lord in November 1916, whilst Beatty – whose poor tactics and signalling had cost British lives and prevented greater success – took over as Commander of the Grand Fleet. It was not the first and would not be the last time an officer's self-promotion abilities had masked his errors and exaggerated his achievements.

In his new role as First Sea Lord, Jellicoe had to deal with the devastating effect the U-boats were having on the British economy. He, along with others, mistakenly advised that convoys were not the answer because they constituted too large a target and the merchant ship masters would be unable to maintain the convoy anyway. It was not until August 1917 that convoys were fully adopted, by which time the U-boat threat had receded slightly anyway and Jellicoe's reputation had taken more damage. He was removed from office in December 1917.

Post-war

Jellicoe was promoted to Admiral of the Fleet in 1919, and the following year was appointed to a much less stressful role on the other side of the world, as governor-general of New Zealand. Initially he had to be content with being made a viscount whilst Beatty was made an earl, but he received an earldom in 1925 after returning from New Zealand. He died in 1935.

The better fortune Beatty enjoyed represented an unfair distortion of the praise and blame for Jutland. In the twenty-first century, Jellicoe's grandson wrote a treatise arguing that his grandfather had in fact won a great victory, at least as good as Trafalgar.[94] That might be overegging Jellicoe's achievements somewhat, but what cannot be disputed is that in the most important task given to him –

---

94 Nicholas Jellicoe, *Jutland: The Unfinished Battle: A Personal History of a Naval Controversy* (Seaforth Publishing, 2016).

the preservation of British naval superiority – he did not fail. For that, he should have had the nation's gratitude.

Coda: Jellicoe and the Savage Club

Doubtless the pressures he was under in wartime meant that Jellicoe would have been glad to enjoy the escapism of Savage Club dinners. The fifty-ninth annual dinner at the end of 1916 was chaired by Reginald Geard and attended by Sir Hedworth Meux[95] and Sir William Robertson. We have already noted Robertson's fascinating speech on that occasion. Before the speeches, the chairman proposed 'The Navy and Army'. *The Times* reported:[96]

> Sir Hedworth Meux, in reply, said he thought everyone in the Navy was very sorry that Sir John Jellicoe had left the Grand Fleet. He had done thoroughly well, and the strain on him had been very great. The Navy had complete confidence in his gallant successor, Sir David Beatty. Alluding to "the U boat danger," he remarked that a great many people did not understand what the difficulties of hunting a submarine were. While, however, it was a danger which could not be entirely removed, it could soon be mitigated, and they could only hope that it soon would be. (Hear, hear.)

In June 1917, Jellicoe was elected an honorary life member of the Savage Club and had a dinner to mark the occasion. The dinner was chaired by J Bell White[97] with the menu designed by the eminent Savage naval artist Bernard Gribble.

Jellicoe attended another house dinner in October 1917. *The Times*[98] reported: 'At the house dinner of the Savage Club on Saturday Admiral Sir John Jellicoe, who was recently elected an honorary life member, presided, and the principal guest was the Lord Dr Eliot,[99] who recently tendered his resignation as Dean of Windsor, owing to advanced age and ill health.' If one was given a time machine and offered the choice of Savage dinners past, there are few which would be higher on the list of any Great War buff.

---

95 Admiral of the Fleet The Honourable Sir Hedworth Meux GCB, KCVO (pronounced 'Mews') (1856–1929). He was one of the 'heroes of Ladysmith' in the Second Boer War. During the First World War Meux served as commander-in-chief, Portsmouth, charged with defending cross-Channel communications, including transport for the British Expeditionary Force crossing to France.

96 *The Times*, 11 December 1916.

97 Captain John Bell White CBE RNR, High Sheriff of Buckinghamshire 1918 and Member of the Inner Temple. The *London Gazette* of 1919 records him having been made Knight Commanderof the Military Division of the Most Excellent Order of the British Empire, for valuable services as Assistant to the Director of Naval Recruiting, https://www.thegazette. co.uk/London/issue/31262/supplement/4196/data.pdf.

98 8 October 1917.

99 The Very Rev Philip Frank Eliot KCVO, DD (1835–1917), an eminent Anglican clergyman during the late nineteenth and early twentieth century. He was Dean of Windsor from 1891 until his death on 1 November 1917, not long after the Savage dinner.

CHAPTER 5

The Savage Fallen

Introduction

We have already discussed the lives of two of the entries on the Savage war memorial, Field Marshals Roberts and Kitchener. We now turn to the remaining seven names on Alfred Toft's plaque of Savage Club members who fell during the conflict. They form an intriguing group, with a wide range of age, wartime rank and civilian occupation. More than that, they are the true *raison d'être* for this book: the project began because I wanted to find out more about the names on the wall.

Many of the books on the First World War are about its origins, the Kaiser, the generals, the bare statistics and the aftermath of the Treaty of Versailles. For the majority of those at the Front, however, the war was a lot less about grand strategy and a lot more about getting through another day of mud, squalor and boredom mixed with terror and the ever-present pall of death. For most of those back in Britain, the war was about privations, a suddenly intrusive state, harsh labour in the hastily assembled factories, and above all the perpetual worry that husbands, fathers, sons and brothers at the Front might not come home.

Those who would never come home were memorably recorded by John MacCrae's verse:[1]

---

1 The second verse from his poem 'In Flanders Fields', written in 1915 and hence in the early days of the war, while McCrae was serving at the front as the doctor in an artillery unit from his native Canada. Contrary to many modern inferences, the work was anything but an anti-war poem: the third verse exhorts the readers:

> Take up our quarrel with the foe:
> To you from failing hands we throw
> The torch; be yours to hold it high.

We are the Dead. Short days ago
We lived, felt dawn, saw sunset glow,
Loved and were loved, and now we lie
In Flanders fields.

What follows is intended to give some idea of how the Savage men who did not return lived, felt dawn and saw sunset glow.

Second Lieutenant Harry Alexander: model Corinthian

Harry Alexander was the model Corinthian of his day – an outstanding international sportsman who learned his craft in the privileged if uncompromising environment of nineteenth-century English public schools, and who unhesitatingly offered his services to his country when war was declared.

Early life and career

Alexander was born at Oxton, Cheshire, in January 1879. Evidently of the upper middle classes, he attended Bromborough and Uppingham School before going up to Corpus Christi, Oxford. While at Uppingham he represented the school at rugby, cricket, hockey and fives. At Oxford he won two blues for rugby, playing against Cambridge at Queen's Club in 1897 and 1898, and also played in the Freshmen's cricket match.

After leaving Oxford, he worked as a schoolmaster at Stanmore Park Preparatory School while continuing with his rugby career (since rugby union was an exclusively amateur sport in Britain in his day,[2] all players either had independent jobs or independent means). He played seven matches for England between 1900 and 1902, scoring on debut against Ireland and captaining England against Wales in January 1902. As a player he was described as 'a hard-working forward and always being in the thick of it' and 'one of the most 'painstaking and punctilious' place kickers in the game.'[3] He played club rugby for Birkenhead Park

---

If ye break faith with us who die
We shall not sleep, though poppies grow
In Flanders fields.

In other words, we would break faith with those who died if we were to fail to continue with the war and prevail. McCrae started writing the poem when he was asked to conduct the burial service of a member of his unit. He himself was killed later in the war.

2 The New Zealand tourists against whom he played were paid three shillings per day, something which caused some disgruntlement amongst British rugby authorities, especially the elitist Scottish Rugby Union.

3 Nigel McCrery, *Into Touch: Rugby Internationals Killed in the Great War* (Pen & Sword Military, 2014).

and Richmond, captaining the latter in the 1905–6 season, most notably in their match against the touring New Zealanders.[4]

Away from rugby, he was also a county hockey player, a scratch golfer, a talented ice skater and a professional singer known for his baritone voice.

First World War

In April 1915, Alexander joined the Savage Club, having been nominated in March. He had precious little time to enjoy his membership, however, since he was commissioned in the Grenadier Guards in the same year and, in October, was deployed to France. He arrived as the new British armies were engaged in their first major offensive of the war, the Battle of Loos. Alexander fought and died at the Hohenzollern Redoubt, a series of engagements from 13–19 October 1915 near Auchy-les-Mines after the main part of the battle was over.

In many ways Loos was the battle which came closest to the popular *Blackadder Goes Forth* view of the First World War, involving inept strategy culminating in soldiers marching in lines towards machine guns and being slaughtered en masse. It was the first large-scale offensive fought by the rapidly-enlarging British Army and both the leaders and the ranks were still learning their craft. Mindful of the army's inexperience and the terrain around Loos, both French and Haig were not keen on the proposed battle, but Kitchener was adamant they had to show their Gallic allies that they were capable of launching a large-scale offensive. Kitchener's attitude was shaped partly by how badly things had been going in the war for the Allies: by September 1915, both the Russian casualties on the Eastern Front and the French casualties on the Western Front had been appallingly high, the alternative strategy of Gallipoli had failed and the Germans had secured large parts of Northern France and Belgium. Moreover, Britain was still the junior coalition partner and the French commander, General Joffre, had demanded 'a large and powerful attack … executed with the hope of success and carried through to the end.'

The British attack was preceded by a substantial artillery bombardment, which nevertheless failed to cut all of the German wire or otherwise suppress all their defences. It was also the first occasion on which the British Army used poison gas, though that too failed to have the desired effect and in some places even blew back to the British lines. The British suffered terrible casualties moving forward. Worse, they were in no position to exploit such breakthroughs as were achieved, since Field Marshal French was too slow co-ordinating the reserves, while the

---

4   Known as 'The Originals', the 1905 tourists were the first New Zealand team to play outside Australasia, touring Britain, France and the United States. A 3–0 defeat against Wales was the sole loss; in my childhood there were still elderly people who complained about the referee's decision, though they could not have been old enough to have first-hand memories of the match. See Ron Palenski, *The Jersey* (Hodder Moa Beckett, 2001).

Germans quickly reinforced the sector. At one stage in the battle, 10,000 British soldiers marched as if on parade towards a murderous array of German machine guns. A German regimental diary recorded:[5]

> Never had the machine-gunners such straightforward work to do nor done it so unceasingly ... with barrels becoming hot and swimming in oil, they traversed to and fro along the enemy's ranks; one machine gun alone fired 12,500 rounds that afternoon. The effect was devastating. The enemy could be seen falling literally in hundreds, but they continued their march in good order and without interruption.

Once the survivors reached the German lines, they realised they could not cut through the barbed wire, and withdrew. The Germans were so nauseated by the sight of all the dead bodies that they ceased firing, and later called the scene the 'Leichenfeld von Loos'– the field of corpses at Loos. That particular engagement cost the British some 8,246 killed or wounded out of the 10,000 who had been involved.

The main Battle of Loos finished by early October, but afterwards the 9th (Scottish) Division managed to capture the Hohenzollern Redoubt. The Germans re-took it in a counter-attack and the British tried again. It was in that final action that Alexander was killed, on October 17. He was aged 36. His death came just two days after he reached the trenches and on only his thirteenth day of active service.[6]

The *Guards Magazine* recorded the following:[7]

> By 17th October, the 2nd and 3rd Guards Brigades were back in the front-line, preparing for an attack onto the Hohenzollern Redoubt. It began at 5am, supported by artillery and trench mortars. But in the face of intensive enfilade machine-gun fire, Lord Cavan called the attack off at 8am. The decision had clearly not been taken lightly. To quote the official history: "Some idea of the severity of the fighting may be obtained from the fact that the two Guards brigades between them made use of 15,000 bombs,[8] while both brigadiers agreed that they had experienced no more heavy shell fire during the war than between dawn and midday on the 17th October 1915."

> The Loos offensive ended the following day. The British had begun with a numerical advantage, but the ground was far more favourable to the Germans, there were shortages of heavy artillery and shells, and the use of gas created as many problems for the attacker as the defender.

---

5   Quoted in Sir John Keegan, *The First World War* (Bodley Head, 2014), p 218.
6   See Andrew Renshaw (ed), *Wisden on the Great War: The Lives of Cricket's Fallen 1914– 1918* (Wisden, 2015), p 100 and http://www.militarian.com/threads/harry-alexander-rugby-player.7374/.
7   Taken from http://guardsmagazine.com/features/Autumn2015/features_autumn15_05Battle OfLoos.html.
8   By 'bombs' they meant what modern readers would call grenades.

> The reserves had been held back from the front-line and remained under Sir John French's orders for too long, a fact that Haig wasted no time in reporting to Kitchener: "No Reserve was placed under me. My attack, as has been reported, was a complete success. The enemy had no troops in his second line, which some of my plucky fellows reached and entered without opposition ..." But by the time the reserves were ready to attack, it was too late. "... We were in a position to make this the turning point in the war ... but naturally I feel very annoyed at the lost opportunity".

Alexander is buried in the Arras Road Cemetery, Roclincourt, Pas de Calais. He left behind a wife (Louisa) and a daughter (Jean, born 1914).

Private Cecil Chesterton: crusading journalist

Cecil Chesterton was the younger brother of the better-known author Gilbert Keith (GK) Chesterton.[9] He showed much ability as a writer and journalist before his life was cut short by the war.

Early life and career

Cecil was born in London in November 1879, five years after GK. His parents were Marie Louise, *née* Grosjean, and Edward Chesterton. As with his brother, he attended St Paul's School. Edward had in mind that Cecil would follow him into business as an estate agent, and had him trained as a surveyor. When Cecil turned 21, however, he began a relationship with a much older journalist, Ada Jones, who encouraged him to follow him into her profession instead.

Jones went on to have a great influence upon Chesterton. Her socialist views were an important factor in him joining the Fabian Society in 1901, which exposed him to many of the great thinkers of the age including George Bernard Shaw and HG Wells. Chesterton also befriended the author Arthur Ransome of *Swallows and Amazons* fame.[10]

A later acquaintance of Chesterton was Brother Savage Hilaire Belloc.[11]

---

9   GK Chesterton (1874–1936) was the famous English writer, poet, lay Catholic theologian, philosopher, dramatist, journalist, orator, biographer, and literary and art critic, possibly best known for his *Father Brown* fictional detective series.

10 As we saw earlier, Ransome went to Russia during the war and spent time there in the company of another Brother Savage, Henry Hamilton Fyfe.

11 Hilaire Belloc (1870–1953), Anglo-French writer and historian. He was one of the best known and most prolific authors in England during the early twentieth century, and also served as MP for Salford from 1906 to 1910. He became a naturalised British subject in 1902, while retaining his French citizenship. He joined the Savage Club in August 1909.

    A strong Catholic, he was known for his anti-Semitism and engaged in various feuds with other public figures of the day. He had served in the French Army but by the time of the First World War was too old for front line service. Instead, during the conflict he edited a journal, *Land and Water*, which had its antecedents in country sports but from 1914–18 was dedicated

Belloc was well enough known to have the honour of being regularly spoofed as 'Bellary Hilloc' in *The Wipers Times*. Like GK Chesterton, Belloc was a believer in 'distributism', a philosophy based upon the principles of Catholic social teaching, especially the teachings of Pope Leo XIII. It was supposedly opposed to both socialism and capitalism, and bore some similarity to the anarchy espoused by Prince Peter Kropotkin.

Belloc soon persuaded Cecil to take up the distributist cause. They wrote a book about it together and started a weekly political magazine, *The Eye-Witness*. At one stage the circulation reached 100,000. Chesterton used family money to assume control of the magazine in 1912. He changed the name to *The New Witness* and installed Jones as assistant editor. In the same year he also converted to Catholicism (his parents had been irregularly practising Unitarians).

Marconi Scandal

Belloc, both Chestertons and *The New Witness* were prominent in the Marconi Scandal of 1912–13. The name Marconi remains of interest to Savages since Guglielmo Marconi himself was the guest of honour at a Savage Club dinner on 21 February 1903. The scandal was a noteworthy event for involving Savages on both sides, since one of the chief targets of Belloc and the Chestertons was the attorney general, Brother Savage Rufus Isaacs KC.[12]

The facts

Senior British military figures pressed upon HH Asquith the value of a chain of wireless telegraphy across the Empire. In early 1912, Herbert Samuel, the postmaster-general, began negotiating with several potential suppliers, including the English Marconi Company, whose managing director was Geoffrey Isaacs, brother of Rufus.

It happened that Geoffrey also sat on the board of the Marconi Company of America, and was under instruction to sell 50,000 shares in the American entity to English investors before they became available to the general public. He advised Rufus Isaacs to buy 10,000 of the shares at £2 apiece. Rufus mentioned the opportunity to the chancellor, Lloyd George, and the Liberals' chief whip, Andrew Murray. Lloyd George, being of working class origin and thus insubstantial means, had been trying to invest in shares to gain the sort of private income other senior politicians of the day enjoyed. He and Murray both purchased 1,000

---

to the progress of the war. It was the only steady employment he ever had; otherwise he enjoyed the fitful income that is the lot of most full-time writers.

12   Rufus Isaacs joined the Savage Club in March 1903, with the candidate book noting that he was 'honorary counsel to the club'. He was nominated and elected on the same day, with his seconders and supporters named only as 'the committee'; clearly he must have done the Club a good turn around that time.

shares at the same price, and on 18 April 1912 Murray also purchased 2,000 shares on behalf of the Liberal Party.

On 19 April, American Marconi shares became available in London. They opened at £3 each and ended the day at £4, the chief reason for the dramatic rise in value being the news that Samuel was negotiating with the English entity. Rufus Isaacs sold his shares, reaping a very substantial profit of £20,000, while Lloyd George and Murray sold half their shares with Lloyd George using his profit to re-invest in the company. Belloc and Chesterton started investigating how the three men had made such a windfall.

On 19 July 1912, Samuel announced that a deal had been agreed with the English Marconi Company. The mainstream press did not make anything of the deal, but first the weekly publication *Outlook* muttered about the dealings of the company, and then in a series of articles *The New Witness* alleged that Lloyd George, Isaacs, Murray and Samuel himself had used insider knowledge to make a substantial profit.[13]

Asquith – an experienced barrister – advised the accused not to sue for libel, since it would only heighten the scandal and boost the circulation of Chesterton's magazine. In parliament, however, the Tories scented blood.

The controversy

As with many a political scandal since, the chief mistake made by the alleged conspirators was less their actions at the time and more their conduct afterwards. Lloyd George and Rufus Isaacs told the House of Commons that they had never had any interest in the English Marconi Company – the truth, but not the whole truth since they did not say anything about their American holdings.

A House of Commons select committee was established to investigate the matter. It comprised six Conservatives, six Liberals (including the chair, Albert Spicer), two Irish Nationalists and one Labour MP.

In February 1913, the French newspaper *Le Matin* alleged Samuel, Lloyd George and Rufus Isaacs had purchased Marconi shares at £2 and sold them at £8. When told that was untrue, it published a retraction and apology, but nonetheless Samuel and Isaacs brought an action for libel in England. Winston Churchill, then a prominent Liberal politician, advised his colleagues to blur the political lines in the affair by instructing as counsel the barristers and Conservative politicians Brother Savage FE Smith and Sir Edward Carson. Because they were acting in the case, both barristers were precluded from speaking on the affair in the House.

Although Isaacs and Samuel won the case, the revelation about the American

---

13 Roy Jenkins, *Churchill: A Biography* (Pan Macmillan, 2001, Kindle edn).

shares arguably dented their reputations more than the libel victory restored them, because the mainstream press was now interested in the affair.

Meanwhile, Chesterton himself expected to be sued for libel by the government ministers he had named in *The New Witness*, but instead found himself facing a criminal libel charge brought by Geoffrey Isaacs. He was convicted and fined £100 plus costs. The sum was paid for by his supporters. It was seen as a victory for him since the penalty was much lower than might have been expected.

Before the select committee, the three accused Liberal MPs admitted they had purchased shares in the Marconi Company of America, but emphasised they had no business with the English entity. Lloyd George also argued he had no shares in companies which had dealings with the government. Alexander Murray was unable to appear before the Committee because he was in Bogotá, South America, but his stockbroker was declared bankrupt, meaning his records became public. They revealed Murray's dealings on his own part and on behalf of the Liberal Party. Asquith firmly supported all his ministers – not least, one suspects, because he would have worried his own future depended on the scandal dissipating.

The select committee ended up issuing no fewer than three reports, all of which agreed on the basic facts, but the conclusions were split upon party lines. The Liberal members cleared the ministers completely in the majority report, whilst the minority opposition report claimed that there had been impropriety. The chair, Albert Spicer, signed the majority report but also issued his own report in which he was critical of Rufus Isaacs for not disclosing the share purchases from the beginning. Predictably, the party-biased outcome attracted adverse comment about the composition of the committee.[14]

The aftermath

In his autobiography, published in 1936, GK Chesterton thought the event would come to be seen as a landmark in British political history:[15]

---

14 See for example the letter to *The Times* published on 13 June, 1913 from Llewellyn Archer Atherley-Jones QC (1851–1929), a radical British Liberal Party politician and barrister who eventually became a judge. Atherley-Jones pointed out that the House could have chosen a much more impartial committee. His own verdict was that the ministers were not guilty of anything, and that it had been understandable not to mention the purchase of American Marconi shares because of all the rumour and innuendo flying around at the time concerning any mention of the word 'Marconi' – though again as a Liberal party member he would be dismissed by cynics as partisan.

15 GK Chesterton, *The Autobiography of GK Chesterton* (Sheed & Ward, 1936), pp 205–206.

> It is the fashion to divide recent history into Pre-War and Post-War conditions. I believe it is almost as essential to divide them into the Pre-Marconi and Post-Marconi days. It was during the agitations upon that affair that the ordinary English citizen lost his invincible ignorance; or, in ordinary language, his innocence ... I think it probable that centuries will pass before it is seen clearly and in its right perspective; and that then it will be seen as one of the turning-points in the whole history of England and the world.

In reality his prediction did not come to pass. All of the dramatis personae survived the scandal. The accusers Belloc and Cecil Chesterton continued as successful journalists, the latter being described by Sir Desmond MacCarthy as 'the best pugnacious journalist since Cobbett.'

As for the accused, Lloyd George made a robust speech in the National Liberal Club (as, separately, did Churchill in support) ridiculing the scandal. He went on to play a pivotal role in British politics, taking over as prime minister from Asquith during the Great War. Yet he also embroiled himself in other scandals, most infamously the 'cash for peerages' practice in which he virtually codified the squalid practice of selling honours for money.[16]

Rufus Isaacs was appointed Lord Chief Justice of England and Wales in late 1913 and, somewhat bizarrely, also served as ambassador to the United States for a time during the Great War. In the 1920s he became Viceroy of India. He also became the first and so far only Jewish marquess – another Savage who rose above the prejudices of his age.

As to the two barristers, Smith and Carson, there was some controversy about them taking briefs which disqualified them from speaking on the case in parliament. The question was whether their duty as counsel to accept a brief offered (known by barristers as the 'cab rank' rule) outweighed their duty as parliamentarians to enable themselves to speak in the House on matters of interest to their constituents. In the result, neither was held to have acted improperly, and both continued their successful political and legal careers. Carson became known as the 'Father of Ulster' and was later appointed directly from the Bar to the Appellate Committee of the House of Lords.

Smith was appointed Lord Chancellor (in the days when that office had

---

16 Lloyd George established a going rate of £10,000 for a knighthood, £30,000 for baronetcy, and £50,000 upwards for a peerage. Parliament eventually responded with the Honours (Prevention of Abuses) Act 1925 outlawing the practice. Only one person was convicted under the Act, Maundy Gregory (1877–1941), Lloyd George's political fixer who worked as a theatre agent in his day job and was quite theatrical in other spheres as well. He was captured by the Germans in the Second World War and died in internment. See also Ian Ker, *GK Chesterton, A Biography* (Oxford University Press, 2011).

meaning[17]) and became Lord Birkenhead. As noted in Chapter 3, he served briefly as a censor for the War Office during the conflict.[18]

First World War

When the First World War broke out, Cecil Chesterton set to work writing patriotic material. He composed a poem for *The New Witness*, simply entitled 'France':

> BECAUSE for once the sword broke in her hand,
> The words she spoke seemed perished for a space;
> All wrong was brazen, and in every land
> The tyrants walked abroad with naked face.
>
> The waters turned to blood, as rose the Star
> Of evil fate denying all release.
> The rulers smote, the feeble crying "War!"
> The usurers robbed, the naked crying "Peace!"
>
> And her own feet were caught in nets of gold,
> And her own soul profaned by sects that squirm,
> And little men climbed her high seats and sold
> Her honour to the vulture and the worm.
>
> And she seemed broken and they thought her dead,
> The Over-Men, so brave against the weak.
> Has your last word of sophistry been said,
> O cult of slaves? Then it is hers to speak.
>
> Clear the slow mists from her half-darkened eyes,
> As slow mists parted over Valmy fell,
> And once again her hands in high surprise
> Take hold upon the battlements of Hell.

17 In Smith's time, the Lord Chancellor sat in the Appellate Committee of the House of Lords, was the head of the legal profession, and a member of the cabinet – a very British-style wearing of different constitutional hats, of the sort satirised by the character of Poo-Bah in *The Mikado*. The Blair government tried to abolish the office in the early 2000s, but failed since no-one had done their homework on what the office actually entailed. The office staggers on in much reduced form – the holder is no longer elevated to the peerage and does not sit as a judge any more. At the time of writing holders of the emaciated post have included non-lawyers such as Chris Grayling and Elizabeth Truss, neither of whom distinguished themselves in the role.

18 Before the conflict started, he received an amusing public rebuke from GK Chesterton. Smith ranted that a Welsh disestablishment bill 'shocked the conscience of every Christian community in Europe.' GK shook his head in verse at Smith's hyperbole, and replied with his poem 'Antichrist, or the Reunion of Christendom', which finished with the lines 'But the souls of Christian peoples, Chuck it, Smith!'

The poem was included in a book entitled *Poems of the Great War* published in late 1914 on behalf of the Prince of Wales's National Relief Fund.[19] The book contained a foreword by Rudyard Kipling, and all the contributions were jingoistic, pro-war efforts[20] far removed from the later war poetry from the likes of Wilfred Owen and Siegfried Sassoon for which the Great War is normally known.

Chesterton also travelled to the United States to try to persuade them to join the conflict on Britain's side. In 1915, he published a short book *The Prussian Hath Said*,[21] which contained the following forthright words in the introduction:

> It is the principal object of this book to present a certain view, which the author holds to be the true view, of the war in which this country is now engaged, to show that war in a certain perspective, as, I think, history will see it. For that purpose it is necessary to bring into sharp relief the factor which made war inevitable. That factor was, according to the view here taken, the political and military power of Prussia, the character of the Prussian monarchy, and the spirit of those who as representing Prussian ideas directed the policy of the German Empire. Prussia as it existed before the war, was incompatible with a civilised and Christian Europe. Sooner or later the one had to be crushed, if the other were not to be destroyed or (what would be worse) corrupted. That is my thesis.

He joined the Savage Club in October 1915, having been nominated in September. Surprisingly, his long-time friend and collaborator Hilaire Belloc was not his proposer or a supporter, and I cannot recognise Belloc's name among any of the supporting signatures, even though Belloc was a member already, having joined in August 1909.

In 1916, even though he was well into his thirties, Chesterton volunteered for service and enlisted as a private in the East Surrey Regiment. In 1917, when he returned to England on leave, Jones finally agreed to marry him.

He was wounded in action three times during the war. Right at the end of the conflict he fell ill, and died on 6 December 1918 from nephritis, aged just 39. GK was in no doubt it was the war which had caused his ill health, and it would

---

19   The actual publisher was Chatto & Windus, 1914.

20   The contents page leaves the reader in no doubt as to what the book was about, with titles such as 'Wake up, England' by Robert Bridges, 'To the Troubler of the World' by William Watson and 'To England: To Strike Quickly' by Maurice Hewlett.

    Of great interest to modern readers is that one contributor was Laurence Binyon, who later in the war would write arguably the most famous Great War verse of all, in his 'For the Fallen'. GK Chesterton contributed 'The Wife of Flanders', and Owen Seaman 'Pro Patria' – words now almost exclusively associated with Wilfred Owen and in a negative sense. Kipling himself contributed 'Hymn before Action'.

21   Published by Lawrence J. Gomme, 1915. At the time of writing, it was free online at: http://www.archive.org/stream/prussianhathsaid00ches/prussianhathsaid00ches_djvu.txt.

seem all concurred: the author John Pearce, for example, wrote 'He did not die in the trenches, but of no man could it more truthfully be said that he died for his country.'[22]

A year after Cecil's death, GK managed to have published a book which Cecil had been working on during the war, entitled *A History of the United States*, part of his efforts to encourage American participation. GK wrote in his introduction:[23]

> The author of this book, my brother, died in a French military hospital of the effects of exposure in the last fierce fighting that broke the Prussian power over Christendom; fighting for which he had volunteered after being invalided home. Any notes I can jot down about him must necessarily seem jerky and incongruous; for in such a relation memory is a medley of generalisation and detail, not to be uttered in words. One thing at least may fitly be said here. Before he died he did at least two things that he desired. One may seem much greater than the other; but he would not have shrunk from naming them together. He saw the end of an empire that was the nightmare of the nations; but I believe it pleased him almost as much that he had been able, often in the intervals of bitter warfare and by the aid of a brilliant memory, to put together these pages on the history, so necessary and so strangely neglected, of the great democracy which he never patronised, which he not only loved but honoured.

GK also quoted Hilaire Belloc on Cecil: 'His courage was heroic, native, positive and equal: always at the highest potentiality of courage. He never in his life checked an action or a word from a consideration of personal caution, and that is more than can be said of any other man of his time.'

Captain AK Harvey-James: of drama and duty

Captain Arthur Keedwell (AK) Harvey-James was better known as the author and poet Arthur Scott Craven. Like others on the Savage memorial, he achieved much in his chosen field in his comparatively short life.

Early life and career

Harvey-James was born in 1875. His father, Stephen Harvey-James (1849–97), had passed into the Indian Civil Service, before becoming a judge, a member of Her Majesty's Council and secretary for law to the government of India. Arthur followed him for a while by working in the civil service in India, but returned to England where he began appearing on stage under the name Arthur Scott Craven, as well as writing under that name. His published works included

22 Eagle, Solomon (John C Squire), 'Cecil Chesterton' in *Books in General, Third series* (Hodder & Stoughton, 1920), pp 119–121.
23 GK Chesterton, introduction to Cecil Chesterton, *A History of the United States* (Chatto & Windus, 1919).

Joe Skinner Or The Man with the Sneer (1907); *Alarums and Excursions* (1910); *The Last of the English: a play in four acts* (1910); *A Fool's Tragedy; The Complete Angler: A Duologue* (with John Davys, 1915) and *The Phoenix* (1918, and hence published posthumously[24]). He also acted in the 1913 silent film *Ivanhoe* as Richard I; at the time of writing a clip of him in the film could easily be found on YouTube.

At the beginning of the twentieth century he married Meliora Louisa Harvey-James, *née* Milner (1875–1944). They had two children, Basil (b 1904) and Olive (b 1906), but they separated in 1912. Olive was sent to live for a while with her paternal grandparents, by then living in Westward Ho!.[25] Harvey-James joined the Savage Club in January 1912, under the name Arthur Scott Craven, having been nominated in November 1911.

First World War

Within two days of the outbreak of war, despite being a married man aged 40, he applied for a commission in the army, as well as exhorting his friends to join up as well. His first application was rejected on health grounds, but he then went to the headquarters of the Artists Rifles and stood for nearly two days in the queue before finally being accepted. He was commissioned into the 'Buffs' (Royal East Kent Regiment), an old regiment tracing its name back to the Austrian War of Succession.[26]

---

24 Sadly I have been unable to obtain a copy; the only one I found on sale was for more than £200, and unfortunately I could not justify the outlay. The description read: 'This work (58 pp.) publishes a letter (dated May, 1916) "Dear Tommy" [Thomas Leslie Graham, the book's dedicatee]. The letters maintain a strong religious thrust throughout.'

25 Olive later recalled that Westward Ho! at the time consisted mostly of the scattered remnants of the school and was sparsely populated even in the holiday season. It had a church, but little of the other features of English village life such as a public house, farming community and rows of cottages. Many of the regular inhabitants were retired Armed Forces officers and – like her grandfather – Indian civil service officials with their families.

26 The Buffs' actual origins go as far back as 1572, when Elizabeth I sent aid to Protestant rebels in the Netherlands against Phillip II of Spain. Returning soldiers were organised into local commands. The regiment gained the name 'the Buffs' in 1744 when it came under the command of Lieutenant-General Thomas Howard, who also had command of a second regiment (later the 19th Regiment of Foot). Following the naming convention of the time both regiments would be called 'Howard's Regiment of Foot'. In order to distinguish between them they were named after the colour of their uniform facings; the Green Howards and Howard's Buffs, the latter being shortened to 'the Buffs'.

In 1782 all British regiments without royal titles were given county titles in order to aid recruitment. The Buffs became the 3rd (East Kent) Regiment of Foot. In 1881 the army was further reformed into a network of multi-battalion regiments each consisting of; two regular and two militia battalions. In 1888, it appeared along with the phrase 'Steady the Buffs!' in Kipling's novel *Soldiers Three*.

In the present day, the Buffs have been amalgamated with the Royal Hampshire Regiment to form the Princess of Wales's Royal Regiment, the most senior English line infantry regiment.

He was rapidly promoted to captain. Initially he served in desk jobs, but volunteered nonetheless for service in the frontline, where he was mentioned in despatches. He was killed in action in April 1917.[27] He is buried at St Patrick's Cemetery in Loos, in the Pas de Calais, France. The inscription on his memorial reads: 'KEEN EYES OF FAITH THAT PIERCE BEYOND THE DAY SCORNING THINGS TRANSCIENT'.

As far as I am aware, there has never been a biography of his life, but there is nevertheless some publicly available material. The Imperial War Museum has a photographic portrait of him,[28] while the Commonwealth War Graves Commission states: 'Son of Stephen and Sarah Harvey-James; husband of Louisa Harvey-James, of 28, Holland Park, Notting Hill, London.'

As well as his grave in Loos, he is remembered on the war memorial at Westward Ho!, the original home of his parents, and he is also remembered on a memorial in St Just, Cornwall. The inscription reads:[29]

> In loving memory of Arthur, Captain East Kent/Regt. (Arthur Scott Craven, poet and author)/Born 1875, killed 1917 in the First World War./ The son of Stephen and Sarah Harvey-James/Also in memory of Basil, the son of Arthur/and Louisa Meliora Harvey-James, born /1904, Killed on active service in the Second World War.

Thus the Harvey-James family was one of so many in Britain who lost members in both world wars. Harvey-James' daughter Olive, on the other hand, lived a long life (1906–2000). In her 1990 memoir *Jill of All Trades*, published under her married name of Ordish, she recalled her father's death:

> These were the Easter holidays of 1917. I was in Devon and playing with a neighbour's small son in their garden when we were summoned into the house. There, the semi-circle of grave adults filled me with apprehension. I must have done something very bad.
>
> "I am very sorry to tell you, Olive, that your father has been killed in the War."
>
> They led me, weeping, to my grandmother's house. Even amid the grief I was conscious that Granny was not unnaturally annoyed that the neighbour had broken the news to me.
>
> For years after the blow had fallen I continued to miss the presence of a father. I could not watch any realistic representation of the War, such as the film Battle of the Somme, without tears in my eyes and real pain and revulsion in my heart.

---

27 I have seen differing dates; some record his death as 14 April, others 15 April.
28 See http://www.iwm.org.uk/collections/item/object/205301949.
29 See the Imperial War Museum website: https://www.iwm.org.uk/memorials/item/memorial/40391.

Harvey-James was a close friend and fellow freemason of the actor and poet Robert Henderson-Bland. Henderson-Bland had written poems about Harvey-James before the war. After Harvey-James died, Henderson-Bland wrote the following verse dedicated to him:

> O all my youth came singing back to me
> When first I learnt that you were dead, my friend.
> What of the years when you and I did see
> In life a splendour daily spilt to mend
> Our souls grown tired of trivial delights?
> Not lost to you the glimpses of the heights,
> For you went gladly where the worst is surely best.

Second Lieutenant Alfred Papworth: much-loved architect

An outstanding Savage architect, Alfred Papworth died on the Western Front after a short but impressive career.

Early life and career

Papworth was born in 1880. His father, Wyatt Papworth, FRIBA, was a successful architect and the editor for the Architectural Publications Society in London. Alfred followed him into the same profession, being educated at the Architectural School of the Royal Academy and becoming an associate of the Royal Institute of British Architects (RIBA). He worked for three years with Arthur Cates, who became surveyor to HM Office of Woods and Forests. He then became chief draughtsman for the office of the Crown Surveyor. For his work on surveying St John's Church, Westminster, he was awarded a gold medal by RIBA and his drawings were accepted by the Victoria and Albert Museum.

In 1902, he went to South Africa to work as chief assistant for a local firm, Arthur and Wallis Reid. He spent some two years travelling the world, including visiting Japan, before returning to London in 1905. He went into partnership with Gilbert H Lovegrove as Lovegrove & Papworth. In May 1909, he joined the Savage Club.

In the 1911 census he was recorded as 'aged 31, married to Katherine Florence, a Royal Architect Assistant, born St Giles in the Field, resident 17 Upper Mall, Hammersmith, London.'[30]

---

30 See the Roll of Honour website, http://www.roll-of-honour.com/London/RoyalAcademy.html.

First World War

When the war broke out, he was another who initially joined the Artists Rifles. He later joined the Royal Engineers, with whom he received his commission as a second lieutenant in August 1916 and went to the Front in October of that year. He was killed on 2 April 1917, at the age of 37. *The Times* recorded:[31]

> He was a liveryman of the Clothworkers Company, a member of the Art Standing Committee of the RIBA, and surveyor to the Licensing Justices of Paddington, and a member of the Savage Club. In August 1915, he enlisted in the Artists' Rifles, and received his commission in the Royal Engineers in August, 1916. He went to the front on October 18, 1916. His C.O. writes:-"His loss is a great sorrow to the company as he was loved by his men and brother officers for his kindly ways, his devotion to duty, and his willingness to carry out to the last letter any order received."

As well as appearing on the Savage memorial, he is commemorated on the Royal Academy Great War memorial in Burlington House, Piccadilly. He is buried in the Aix Noulette communal cemetery extension, in the Pas de Calais, France.

Lieutenant-Colonel JM Richardson: the oldest soldier

The bare biographical details of Lieutenant-Colonel Jasper Myers Richardson seem unexceptional in the context of Great War memorials: he attended Rugby School, Cambridge University and was called to the Bar, before signing up upon the outbreak of war. He was sent to the Western Front, where he was killed by enemy shellfire in March 1918 near Bapaume.

What renders his story remarkable is his age: he was killed at 68 years old, only a few days before his 69th birthday – the oldest soldier killed in the Great War by enemy action. Older men who died during the conflict, such as Field Marshal Roberts, were not killed in action but through illness or natural causes.[32] For many years the oldest victim of combat was assumed to be Harry Webber,[33]

---

31 *The Times*, 7 July 1917, p 9.
32 The oldest was probably Captain George William Valentine Clements, a veteran of the Crimean War. He was aged 85 when he died in March 1916. His records show that he was serving as quartermaster in the 1st (Royal) Dragoons. He held a Long Service and Good Conduct Medal for his service in the Crimean War from 1853–56 (Alma, Balaklava, Inkerman and Sebastopol) and had the Turkish Medal as well.
33 Webber's story was quite something. He kept volunteering when war broke out. Initially rejected on the basis of age, he was eventually accepted. Just before he died, he wrote to his old school:

> Fifty one years ago I got my colours in the XI and last week 51 years ago was bowling against the old boys and looking on some of them as "sitters" and in the "sere and yellow leaf."

but in 2014, Richardson was moved to the top of the list following research by Rugby School.

Early life and career

Richardson was born in 1849 in Newcastle. After attending Rugby School he studied at Trinity Hall, Cambridge. He graduated BA in 1871 and MA in 1876. In 1874, he was called to the Bar at Inner Temple. He had a successful career as a barrister, working both in the north east and in London where he lived in Campden Hill Square, Kensington. He married Anne Longstreth, an American woman from Philadelphia, in 1879. They did not have children. He joined the Savage Club in 1897 under the category of science, giving his address as the Oxford and Cambridge Club.

He served in the Northumberland Artillery Militia as a captain from 1875 to 1880, and despite his age returned to serve his country when war broke out in 1914.[34]

First World War

Richardson was made an honorary lieutenant-colonel in the Royal Artillery. He was assigned the vital role of general staff officer (agriculture) – there were a vast number of men and horses requiring to be fed, with a chain stretching from ploughing of fields to delivering food and hay to the Front. He would have been behind the lines, but in 1918, the Front was becoming much more fluid with the Germans' Operation Michael followed by the Allied counterattack. The fighting eventually drew close enough to where Richardson was stationed for him to come within range of German artillery. He received multiple shell wounds on 21 March 1918 at Villers-au-Flos, near Bapaume, and was taken to the Duchess of Westminster's Hospital at Le Touquet, where he died on 30 March 1918.

He is buried at Étaples,[35] where his gravestone includes the inscription 'God proved him and found him worthy'.

Yet here I am a Lieutenant in HM army having to salute three sons if I meet them out here, a Colonel and two Majors. I am 1st Line Transport Officer to this Battalion and we have been plumb in the centre of the picture during the last ten days and gained no end of "kudos" and also a very severe mauling.

I am so far extraordinarily fit and well, though, when I tell you that for four consecutive days I was either on my feet or in the saddle for twenty one hours, out of twenty four, you will see that there is a bit of work attached to the job.'

See Jasper Copping, 'The WWI soldier who went to war in his 60s', *The Daily Telegraph*, 26 January 2014. Richardson is also mentioned in Charles Douie, *Weary Road: The Recollections Of A Subaltern Of Infantry* (Naval and Military Press, new edn, 2009, originally published in 1929).

34 See Jasper Copping, 'The barrister killed in WW1 at the age of 68', *The Daily Telegraph*, 9 February 2014.

35 According to the Commonwealth Graves Commission, Étaples is the largest CWGC cemetery

Major Charles Scott-Gatty: indefatigable actor

Charles Scott-Gatty did not attain the fame of some others on the Savage memorial, but it is evident he was a most popular and respected member of his community in Hertfordshire in his short life, and remains appropriately commemorated there.

Early life and career

Charles Comyn Scott-Gatty was born in 1880, into a prosperous middle-class family of the day. He was the second son of Sir Alfred and Lady Scott-Gatty. His father became a KCVO[36] and was a prominent mason, being the Garter Principal King-of-Arms of Wendover Lodge, Welwyn, and was also known as the writer of popular songs.

Charles was educated at Rugby School, and thereafter pursued a career in the City of London, becoming a member of the Stock Exchange in 1904 and a partner in the firm of Grenfell and Co. In 1901, he joined the 10th Herts Volunteer Battalion (Bedfordshire Regiment) and was promoted to captain in 1906. He was very popular with his men,[37] and often took them to the theatre in London, but did not stint on discipline or order, being well-regarded for the high standard of drills and general efficiency.

In 1904, he married Muriel, a daughter of Colonel Charles Gathorne-Hardy and cousin of the late adjutant of the Hertfordshire Regiment. Together they wrote the words and music of several musical comedies and many successful songs together – following in the footsteps of Scott-Gatty's father. He joined the Savage Club in April 1914, under the category of music, following his brother, Alexander Scott-Gatty, who had joined in February 1910 under the category of drama.

Throughout those years, Scott-Gatty became well known in Hertford for a series of amateur theatrical events held each Christmas at the Hertford Corn Exchange. He began with 'Ali Baba' appearing as Mrs Baba, and later undertook the roles of actor, author, composer, manager and producer, often on the same production. His plays included 'Cinderella and Private Smith', 'The

---

in France, with 10,773 Commonwealth burials (35 unidentified) from the First World War, the earliest dating from May 1915. It lies about 27km south of Boulogne on the former site of a large military hospital complex used by the Allies during the First World War. The cemetery was designed by Brother Savage Sir Edwin Lutyens, with George Hartley Goldsmith as assistant architect.

36 The Royal Victorian Order is a dynastic order of knighthood established in 1896 by Queen Victoria. It recognises distinguished personal service to the monarch of the Commonwealth realms, members of the monarch's family, or to any viceroy or senior representative of the monarch.

37 See the Welwyn and District History Society website 'Welwyn in World War I', http://www.welwynww1.co.uk/scottgattybio.html.

Military Girl', and 'Claude Alread'. Each was a great success – 'The Military Girl' had to return the following year by popular demand. Muriel assisted him writing the plays, though he composed all the music himself. The popularity of the productions led to people coming from other districts than Hertfordshire and, on one occasion, a special matinee was held to allow leading members of the theatrical profession in London to attend, including Sir George Edwardes. A posthumous appreciation of Scott-Gatty's life said of the plays:[38]

> Major Scott-Gatty always took the leading part and his songs and sallies kept the large audiences in continual merriment. A very large number of performers were engaged on the plays and they all retain vivid recollections of the Major's wonderful powers of organisation, which resulted in the work of everyone from the call boy to the leading actor or actress always going with a smoothness not often seen in amateur theatricals. His genial personality both on and off endeared him to everyone with whom he came in contact. The whole of his theatrical work was undertaken for the purpose of raising funds for the Hertfordshire Regiment and in this way he obtained very considerable sums which served a most useful purpose in furthering the efficiency of the Regiment. He also did a great deal for the London hospitals by reproducing in the Metropolis some of the plays he staged at Hertford and in recognition of his praiseworthy efforts, the King conferred upon him the honour of being an Esquire of the Order of St. John of Jerusalem, an order specially reserved for people who do great service for the hospitals.

First World War

When the First World War started, he was recalled for service to his regiment, and was gazetted temporary major in October 1914. He was unable to go to the Front, due to ill health, but he was recorded as having 'worked indefatigably in raising additional battalions of his regiment.' He was moved to Stowlangtoft when he continued to throw himself into his work, leading to a complete breakdown. He recovered nonetheless, and returned to Hertford where he acted as adjutant to the 3rd Battalion. They moved to Windsor, where his unremitting work ethic led to a second breakdown. In December 1915, he was honourably discharged from the army and provided with a pension. Nevertheless, he continued to be unwell and died in July 1916, aged just 35.[39]

A local publication recorded some details about the funeral, a moving illustration of life in the Home Counties during wartime:

---

38 Ibid.
39 The Welwyn Local History website records his funeral as taking place in Welwyn on 27 July 1916: www.welwynww1.co.uk.

The funeral took place at Welwyn on Thursday, the deceased being accorded full military honours. The 3rd Battalion of the Hertfordshire Regt., who are at camp in Halton Park, near Tring were unable to send a firing party and Major A H Pulman DSO, Commandant of the NCO's School of Instruction at Hertford, kindly came to the rescue and bought two officers, Lieut. and Adjutant C J Blackburn-Maze and Lieut. W H Martin and a firing party of 50 men and also a bugler. The Hertfordshire Regt. supplied the bearers and a bugler. Colonel H Baker, Major C F Puller, and Capt. A. Crossman of the 3rd Battalion came over from Halton Park and Lieut.-Colonel H J Gripper and Capt. M. McMullen from headquarters at Hertford. Among other officers present was Lieut. Lionel Faulder-Phillips. The principal mourners were the widow Mrs. Scott-Gatty, Sir Alfred and Lady Scott-Gatty and a number of other relatives and friends. A large number of Welwyn residents were present and a few from Hertford including Mr R Braund, Mr E H Oram, the deceased co-adjutor in the plays above referred to and a few of the chorus girls. The body was bought down from London by motor hearse, the coffin being enshrouded in a Union Jack and the deceased officer's cap and sword were placed on the lid, together with a beautiful bunch of lilies.

The first part of the burial service was held at the Parish Church, being conducted by the Rector, the Rev. P M Wathen. The hymns, most impressively rendered were 'Thine for ever', 'On the Resurrection morning' and 'It is not death but sleep'. At the close the organist played 'O rest in the Lord', The internment afterwards took place in Welwyn Cemetery in the presence of a large congregation, the three volleys and 'The Last Post' being most effectively performed, the firing party being under the direction of Sergt. Major Wombwell. By request there were to be no flowers but a few floral tributes including those from the Savage Club, the Hertfordshire Regiment, the NCO's School of Instruction and Mrs Charles Leslie. Members of the Hertfordshire Motor Volunteers and other friends kindly motored some of the party over from Hertford.

Both Scott-Gatty and his father are commemorated in stained glass windows at St Mary's Church, Welwyn Hatfield.

Lance Corporal Lance Thackeray: pictorial humourist

Lance Thackeray was one of many talented Savage artists of his time, particularly remembered for his humorous postcards.

Early life and career

He was born Lot Thackeray in 1867 in Darlington, County Durham, the fourth child of ten. Both his parents were from Yorkshire, but they had followed his father's occupation as a porter in the nascent but rapidly-expanding world of Victorian railways. Initially Thackeray also worked as a railway clerk.

In 1885 his father died, leaving him to help care for his widowed mother and the younger children. Despite those extra obligations, he managed to attend the School of Art at Darlington in his spare time. The school had been established by two Quaker businessmen: Edward Pease, who had made his fortune on the railways, funded the school, while George Gordon Hoskins, an architect, designed the school building and headed the school at its outset. Hoskins also financed the original Mechanics' Institute in the town. Thackeray and other Darlington residents were most fortunate for the efforts of those two men, who as well as their religious beliefs were clearly imbued with classical Victorian outlooks on charity and education.

Thackeray excelled as a student. In 1885 he won certificates in the second grade, with a prize for perspective, while in 1888 he won the highest third grade prizes and was awarded the art class teachers' certificate. He soon gained paid commissions drawing pictures for books, a market which grew exponentially following the Education Act 1870. Before the end of the century, he had moved to London and was working professionally from his own studio. He intended to continue with his education in the capital, but quickly found enough work to sustain himself full-time. He started to use the name 'Lance' instead of 'Lot' from 1894. In 1899 he was elected a member of the Royal Society of British Artists.

In 1898, he became one of the founding members of the London Sketch Club, which we will see again in the chapter on Savage artists. He was a regular participant at its meetings in the early days, having belonged to its antecedent, the Langham Sketching Club, but his enthusiasm waned until finally in 1912 he resigned. His biographer offered two possible reasons for his loss of interest: first, that he might have disliked the growing respectability of the club and the consequent reduction of its original bohemian spirit; and secondly, and more prosaically, the fact that the club only met from October to May, whereas Thackeray from 1907 spent the winter months in the rather sunnier climes of Egypt.

There is a third possible reason, which is that Thackeray had joined the Savage Club in May 1903 and may have preferred spending his evenings at the Adelphi. He clearly enjoyed the Savage, appearing in various events including the Royal charity matinee in June 1907, the anniversary dinner in 1908, the ladies' night in June 1914 (for which the interesting-sounding guest of honour was the Ranee of Sarawak) and the 1916 dinner welcoming Louis Raemaekers. He drew the menu card for the 1907 and 1916 events. *The Times* said of the 1907 menu card that it was 'as usual, a masterpiece of pictorial humour. It was designed by Mr Lance Thackeray, who had cleverly depicted many well-known men as Red Indians.'

Thackeray was able to spend winters in Egypt because of the regular income he was then earning from the picture postcard publishers Raphael Tuck & Sons,[40] for whom he had been producing humorous cards since 1900. He later collected some of the cards in a book called *The Light Side of Egypt*. In total, he drew more than 950 postcard prints. He also produced numerous cartoons and other drawings for magazines and newspapers. Unlike many of his contemporary artists he did not do much work for books or commercial posters, since he was making enough money doing his other work.

While in Egypt, he became a close friend of Brother Savage Lord Kitchener, and also met TE Lawrence (Lawrence of Arabia), who had arrived in Cairo in 1914 and set up his office in the Savoy Hotel. (Although ostensibly there as an archaeologist, Lawrence was in fact taking part in a covert British military survey of the Negev Desert.)

First World War

When the Great War broke out, Thackeray went to Egypt again, but found that not only was it difficult to travel there, resentment towards the British occupation was increasing amongst the locals. Worse, his normal line of work was drying up, since fewer postcards were being purchased. He was also not immune to the general feeling of patriotism and a wish to be seen to be doing something for the cause. He donated one of his pictures to be sold for the war effort. Then, in November 1915, he volunteered for the Artists Rifles, even though he was in his mid-forties and hence could have sat the war out had he chosen.

After four weeks' training, Thackeray joined the mapping section as an instructor in the officers' training camp at Hare Hall, near Romford in Essex, where he served under Brother Savage William Lee Hankey.

Thackeray's work as a draughtsman was considered to be first rate, and he was quickly promoted to lance corporal. He became a popular member of his regiment, and gave away many sketches to his comrades. He contributed to an exhibition of the Artists Rifles' work in London in early 1916. In its review of the event, *The Times* paid particular tribute to his picture 'Thames at Moulsford'.[41]

The routine at Hare Hall was described by one of his contemporaries as:[42]

> At 6.30 physical drills until 7. Breakfast 7.45 consisting of porridge, boiled bacon, bread and margarine (if you are lucky) and marmalade (if there is any left). At 8:30 parades, which may be squad drill, platoon

---

40 Tom Askey, *Lance Thackeray: His Life and Art* (ShieldCrest, 2016), p 16.
41 *The Times*, 15 January 1916.
42 Letter from David Henry Taylor, an officer in the Kings Royal Rifle Corps, quoted in Askey, op cit, p 88.

drill, company drill, or forty other kind of drill. Lunch from 1 to 2 o'clock, Parade at 2, which may be trench digging, map reading and drawing. Dinner at 5pm. At 6 o'clock parade for a lecture until 7. We have to be in bed at 9.15. Lights out at 10.

Hare Hall was the most up-to-date and best-equipped barracks of the time, though Thackeray was billeted in one of the camp huts, the house itself being the preserve of officers.

Despite the quality of the facilities, Thackeray soon suffered from ill health. In early 1916, he collapsed while visiting a friend. He spent three days in hospital before being sent home to rest. Five weeks later, he was still unwell and was sent to the Queen's Canadian Hospital at Beachborough Park, near Folkestone. The diagnosis was that he was suffering from 'exposure and hard work that he had not been accustomed to' during his military service. In April 1916, he was transferred to the Shorncliffe Military Hospital in Kent. He developed colitis, from which he had also suffered in Egypt, and then developed anaemia as well.

In August 1916, he was discharged from the army as 'permanently unfit'. He died two days later, in the London and Brighton Medical and Surgical Nursing Home,[43] aged just 47. He is buried in the Extra-Mural Cemetery, Lewes Road on the outskirts of Brighton. One newspaper obituary recorded:[44]

> The genial presence of Lance Thackeray, the artist, who has just died at Brighton, will be missed in the London Bohemian clubs ... A Northerner by birth and training he went to London some twenty-four years ago, and was successful from the first. His black and white sketches delighted the readers of innumerable periodicals, and his coloured sporting pictures were to be seen on the walls of nearly every billiard room. His one-man exhibitions at the London galleries also showed him to be the possessor of a sense of romance and sympathy unsuspected in the facile artist of the sporting prints and comic postcards.

Thackeray never married and his sister was given administration of his personal effects. He was not given a Commonwealth War Grave, as he had died after being discharged from active service. But there is no doubt that he died due to the rigours of that service, and in those circumstances he was rightly honoured by the Savage Club on its memorial.

---

43 According to one source (D Cupleditch, *The London Sketch Club* (1994) (quoted in Askey, op cit, p 88)), Thackeray was 'seconded to Egypt with the Artists'. I am not sure when that could have been, because Thackeray was clearly in England in early 1916 when he fell unwell and it is improbable he would have been sent overseas given his poor health, his age, and the work he was doing in England. He could not have been there for long if he was sent there.

44 *Birmingham Gazette*, 14 August 1916.

At the time of writing, his grave in Lewes Road was in a poor state of repair, but it still bore the epitaph composed by his sister Lena:

> Oh, my beloved, Spring is here again—
> They wayward English Spring you loved so well!
> But you, alas, lie cold in yonder grave,
> And yet not you—you have gone on—
> But that which once I knew as you,
> The dear familiar form, the thoughtful eyes,
> The quick expanding smile—all
> All the dear loving, human you
> Ah my beloved in yon narrow grave
> Lies all that made life beautiful to me.

CHAPTER 6

Savage Men of Letters

Introduction

In this chapter we meet a selection of esteemed Savage authors whose work covered a range of fiction and non-fiction. It is the longest chapter by some margin, partly because of the sheer number of Savage authors who served in the war, but also because I wished to incorporate as much of their own words on the conflict as possible.

As well as their literary achievements, the Savage authors include two of the most notable Savage soldiers of the Great War: Harold Auten for his Victoria Cross-winning bravery, and BH Liddell Hart for his work on military strategy. We begin, though, with James Agate, a Savage author who was always rather unnecessarily self-effacing about his own wartime contribution.

James Agate: a critical effort

James Evershed Agate was a famous diarist and theatre critic, whose civilian life-style was far removed from military life and who was too old for frontline service in any event. Nevertheless, as a man of duty, he offered his services to his country in its hour of need, and went on to serve in a vital if unglamorous capacity. He was also responsible for a notable early memoir of the conflict.

Early life

Agate was born in 1877 in Pendleton, near Manchester. His father worked as a draper, but was a musical enthusiast and had friends connected to the stage. His mother had been educated in France and Germany and was an accomplished pianist. The young Agate therefore had much exposure to a high standard of music while growing up. It was clearly a cultural household: his sister studied acting under Sarah Bernhardt, a doyenne of the theatre who was known to the family.

Agate attended Giggleswick School and Manchester Grammar School. Although he excelled academically, he did not go on to university. Instead, he followed his father into the family drapery business, and stayed working there for 17 years. In his spare time he attended the theatre whenever possible. As well as enjoying watching performances, he developed an intellectual interest in the stage, and greatly admired George Bernard Shaw's theatre criticism in *The Saturday Review*.

In 1906, he sent a letter to a local paper which so impressed the editor he invited Agate to contribute a weekly column on the theatre, the start of Agate's long career as a journalist, critic and author.

Agate soon moved to the *Manchester Guardian* (as the *Guardian* was then known) and made a name for himself with his lack of deference even to the top actors of the day such as Herbert Beerbohm Tree. Famously, he called Lilian Braithwaite[1] 'the second most beautiful woman in London'; more famously she riposted 'I shall long cherish that, coming from our second-best theatre critic.'

First World War

In 1915, Agate volunteered for the Army Service Corps, even though he was by then 37. He was not put in a combat unit but instead in a rear echelon administrative capacity – a vital if less well-reported or respected role. He sent open letters about his experiences to the *Manchester Guardian*, which along with some other pieces of his were collected and published in book form in 1917, constituting one of the very first memoirs of the Great War – before it had even finished.[2] The book, entitled *L. of C. (Lines of Communication) Being the letters of a temporary officer in the army service corps*[3] has since been digitised and made available free online.

To begin with, his letters covered the vicissitudes familiar to soldiers across the ages, including the old enemy of boredom during basic training:[4]

> Soldiers, when they join, bargain for everything except boredom. Hardships one understands, and it is agreed that the other fellow will be up to whatever heroism is going. But to eat in a field, and sleep in a

---

1 Dame Florence Lilian Braithwaite DBE (1873–1948), known as Lilian Braithwaite. She was an English actress, primarily of the stage.
2 See James Harding, *Agate* (Methuen, 1986).
3 James Agate, (Jelland, Goodchild and Stewart, 1917). Digitised version: https://archive.org/stream/cihm_65397?ref=ol#page/n7/mode/2up.
4 Ibid, p 30.

field, and work in a field, and play in a field, and always the same silly field, day in and day out, makes a stiff call on the higher patriotism. For, *pace* Wordsworth, a field is a field when all is said in done, and a damp place at that. Of course, you must understand that to grumble is the amateur soldier's new-found privilege, and you are not to run away with any impression of serious discontent.

The letters also showed how he struggled to adjust to the necessarily regimented and anodyne way in which the army functioned:[5]

The fascination of life in the army! Of course it's fascinating, even if the beginning is a trifle humiliating. It is humiliating to find that you, a person of some cultivation in your own walk of life, have not yet mastered the art of ordering a pair of boots, paying for the week's groceries, or even writing a report on some infantile matter of business. Heedless of formula, ignorant of the existence of any set of rules governing official correspondence, you fall into the trap of writing your C.O. a civil note as from one gentleman to another.

Later in the book:[6]

Let me describe a Soldiers' concert on Salisbury Plain. You must realise, first of all, the cardinal difference between the hours of leisure of the civilian and the warrior in training. The civilian, though his job be as tedious as tallow-chandling, has yet a few evening hours in which he may seek out the excitement or interest for the sake of which he has endured the day. The soldier is denied all interest in his hours of ease, and is confronted from retreat to Reveille with intellectual vacancy. There is nothing for him to do, and the most ardent volunteer cannot fill the empty hours for weeks on end with a sense of the Heroic, however sublime, or a feeling for Adventure, however romantic. And surely Wordsworth monopolised for all time all the fun there is to be got out of the Sense of Duty.

The sardonic style continued throughout. As an officer he described his charges as 'cheerful old birds from the London Docks, averaging fifty years of age. They look down on soldiering and call me Boss, Guv'nor, or even Gaffer.' He described them all as 'equally willing, good-natured, devoid of guile and irreclaimable. In a word they are just human.'

Towards the end of the war, and noting again that he did not serve at the Front, Agate reflected on the nature of courage:[7]

"What's that rubbish you're always writing?" said Dunscombe to me one night. "Expect to make money out of it or what? Chuck us over

---

5   Ibid, pp 41–42.
6   Ibid, p 84.
7   Ibid, pp 274–76.

some of the stuff and let's have a look." I think I ought to say here that Dunscombe has done his twelve months in the trenches and wears the ribbon of the Military Cross.

"Lumme!" said he, after I had chucked him a few sheets. "It's plain you've never been within a thousand miles of the front. Thinking's no use at that sort of game; and if you were Shakespeare and Julius Caesar rolled into one it wouldn't help any. You can't tell beforehand what sort of a show you're going to be put up. It isn't the question of being a decent chap or being a blackguard. It's just how long it takes you, like vaccination. And by the way, that Noblesse oblige idea of yours is all bally rot."

"Well, but," I replied meekly, "it's what I can't help thinking down here."

"It's not what you think down here but what you'd do up there, my son, that 'ud be more to the point," Dunscome retorted. "Thinking's no sort of a way out of it. You'd just get into a hell of a funk same as everybody else. We all of us get the wind up, only some show it more than others. Even those artist fellows you talk so much hot-air about get through all right. In fact they damned well have to. The bravest chap I ever met used to cry himself to sleep every night. Sheer nerves! I've even seen a lawyer fellow—and you know what skunks they are—go over the top and fetch a chap in. But he said it wasn't to be taken as a precedent. In fact, you never can tell and it's no use jawin'. Let's talk about something else."

So we fell to discussing the last revue we had seen at the Palace. And we agreed that the show had been top-hole and the girls ripping ...

I would reiterate the importance of Agate's service, even though he never experienced the front line and tended to downplay the value of his own contribution. It was an astonishing effort by the British Army to deploy several hundred thousand men and tens of thousands of horses at a time overseas and to keep them supplied with food, feed, equipment and a strikingly efficient mail service over a four-year period, especially given the miniscule size of the pre-war army and the more primitive technology available for organisation and communication.[8]

Agate was fluent in French, which would obviously have been of use in his role. He devised a new system of accounting for hay purchases, which was so well received it was made into an official handbook.[9] In recognition of his war service, his name was engraved on the memorial at Chapel-en-le-Frith in Derbyshire.

8   In that regard due acknowledgement should be made to the War Office for its organisational skills, and in that context we should mention Brother Savage Lieutenant-Colonel Charles Forbes Buchan CBE (1869–1954), who was deputy assistant director at the War Office during the conflict.

9   For an indication of how important horses were to the Western Front, and hence the value of Agate's work, it is worth remembering the British shipped a greater weight of fodder than weapons to the continent during the conflict: see Hew Strachan, *The First World War* (Penguin, 2005). Once it was known that cavalry formed a large part of the BEF, the RSPCA was urged

In the first volume of his autobiography *Ego*, Agate touched only briefly on his wartime service, almost dismissing it out of hand. He concluded 'My war career was neither glorious nor inglorious; it was just nothing.' Of his appearance on the memorial he said dryly: 'Derbyshire folk do not "see" being robbed of patriotic merit because they do not happen to have been killed. They got the year wrong, but the intention was good.'[10] He mentioned his work on the feed manual, though continued in his modest vein with the remark 'Throughout the war I held the record of being the British officer farthest from gunfire!'

In 1917, during his service, Agate married a local French woman. The marriage did not last, and after the war his relationships were exclusively homosexual. He said of the marriage in the first volume of his diaries:[11]

> But after the war it was inhuman to expect a Provencal to endure the English fogs and, obviously, I could not accept a life of idleness under that monotonous, infernal sun ... Of the rest of my sex-life there will be no account in this book. This is unfashionable, but I cannot help it. Every autobiography that I read to-day tells me at what age its author first practised masturbation, what at school he learned from his mates, and what in later life he taught his mistress. I appreciate that in the case of world-figures like Cellini, Rousseau, Wagner, Pepys, these details may have interest. But I am not of that size, and have enough of Victorian fastidiousness to believe that unless a man is of such stature his sex-experiences should be kept to himself.

For all his protestations, to a modern audience the treatment of sex in Agate's lifetime – heterosexual, let alone homosexual – would seem ridiculously prudish in the present day. Even basic bodily functions were considered too *outré* for public discourse until the latter part of the twentieth century: in the mid-1940s the BBC panicked because its new radio programme *Women's Hour* threatened to discuss the menopause.[12]

Of course, Agate's other motivation in refusing to discuss his sex life was the social opprobrium he would have received if he had been fully open about his sexuality. Male homosexuality was still illegal at the time,[13] even if the army

---

to make sure that 'no unnecessary suffering was caused to horses on the battlefield', surely one of the most tragically doomed exhortations the Society has received in its history. See Pound, *The Lost Generation*, op cit, p 25.

10 Agate, *Ego: The autobiography of James Agate* (Hamish Hamilton, 1935), vol 1, p 77.

11 Ibid, p 80.

12 'History of the BBC – 1940s': see http://www.bbc.co.uk/timelines/z2c3b9q.

13 For an illustration of the frankly hysterical reaction the subject could induce at the time, an MP by the name of Noel Pemberton Billing undertook an extraordinarily aggressive homophobic campaign during the Great War, claiming that the Germans were blackmailing '47,000 highly placed British perverts' propagating 'evils which all decent men thought had perished in Sodom and Lesbia.' Unsurprisingly, Pemberton Billing was sued for libel. Among the witnesses who gave evidence on his behalf was Lord Alfred Douglas, the most famous of Oscar Wilde's former lovers, who as we see elsewhere in this book was not above a ridiculous conspiracy of

during wartime tended to take a sanguine view of homosexual acts by soldiers on duty.[14]

Post-war career

After the war, Agate's stature as a theatre critic rose considerably. He was able to obtain the same job Shaw had held on *The Saturday Review* (another predecessor in the role was Brother Savage Max Beerbohm). He joined the Savage Club in November 1924.

As the doyen of London theatre critics his favourable reviews were partially responsible for the early success of Brother Savage Peter Ustinov in the 1930s.

Throughout his life after the First World War, Agate wrote a series of detailed diaries that garnered much critical acclaim and are now considered of important historical value for chronicling London life at the time. They revealed a lifestyle which explained why, despite his remunerative jobs, he usually sailed close to the wind financially.

Agate's health declined during the Second World War, and he died in 1947. A number of his books adorn the shelves in the present-day Savage library. He also gave to the Club one of its most significant treasures: the two canes proudly displayed above the bar, one of which belonged to Charlie Chaplin and the other to George Robey.[15]

Herbert Asquith: answering his father's call

The Asquith family was one of Britain's most interesting twentieth century political clans. They will forever be associated with the Great War, since it was Herbert Henry 'HH' Asquith who took Britain into the war as prime minister, though he failed to see out the conflict, being replaced by Lloyd George in December 1916.

---

his own. (Douglas was presumably trying to dissociate himself from any homosexual imputation, as he had been ever since Wilde's scandal. See Wilson, *Trials and Tribulations* (Wildy, Simmonds & Hill, 2015), Ch 2.) Billing won the trial amid huge publicity, despite acting in person and despite his wife saying in evidence that the judge was on the blacklist – not the sort of tactic recommended in most litigation textbooks.

14 Only 161 courts martial for 'indecency' on active service were conducted. Since the war involved well over five million men on active duty over a four-year period, that number seems remarkably low. The number of prosecutions for cowardice and desertion was not especially high either, again given the number of men on the receiving end of artillery fire. In both cases I suspect the commanding officers wrote off what they would have considered immoral behaviour or a fall in operational standards here and there out of sympathy for men under horrendous strain and out of the need to keep as many in the line as possible – other nominal requirements such as height and age were often overlooked for the latter reason. See further Richard Holmes, *Tommy*, op cit, pp 598–99.

15 George Robey (1869–1954), music hall comedian, singer and actor. He had a few film appearances over the years, though was never considered a star of the screen.

HH was married twice, and had seven children.[16] Among them Violet is probably best known to present-day Savages, since one of the most oft-used rooms for Savage functions in the National Liberal Club is named after her. Our subject here is HH's second son, Herbert Dixon Asquith – often confused with his father since they had the same Christian name. In his lifetime, the family referred to him as 'Beb', and his younger brother Arthur as 'Oc'; we will do so as well.

Early life

Beb was born in 1881. He excelled academically from an early age, going up to Oxford where he became President of the Oxford Union. He followed his father's first career by becoming a barrister, and was called to the Bar in 1907.[17]

In 1910 he married Cynthia, daughter of the Earl of Wemyss, a member of the Scottish aristocracy.[18] Like Beb, she was a writer, though she also worked as a secretary – including, during the Great War, to Brother Savage JM Barrie. Beb and Cynthia went on to have three sons.

Beb started writing poetry before the war. One of his noteworthy pieces was 'The Volunteer', which told the story of a City clerk who escaped drudgery and died a hero's death in war, as he (the clerk) had previously fantasised:

> Here lies a clerk who half his life had spent
> Toiling at ledgers in a city grey,
> Thinking that so his days would drift away
> With no lance broken in life's tournament
> Yet ever 'twixt the books and his bright eyes
> The gleaming eagles of the legions came,
> And horsemen, charging under phantom skies,
> Went thundering past beneath the oriflamme.
>
> And now those waiting dreams are satisfied
> From twilight to the halls of dawn he went;
> His lance is broken; but he lies content
> With that high hour, in which he lived and died.
> And falling thus, he wants no recompense,
> Who found his battle in the last resort
> Nor needs he any hearse to bear him hence,
> Who goes to join the men of Agincourt.

---

16 In 1877 HH married Helen (1855–91), who bore him Raymond (1878–1916), Herbert (1881–1947), Arthur (1883–1939), Violet (1887–1969) and Cyril (1889–1954). In 1894, three years after Helen had died of typhus, he married Margot (1864–1945), with whom he had Elizabeth (1897–1945) and Anthony (1902–68).

17 Much more detail is set out in his autobiography, *Moments of Memory* (Hutchinson & Co, 1937).

18 Hugo Richard Charteris, 11th Earl of Wemyss and 7th Earl of March DL (1857–1937).

The work is often erroneously stated as a Great War poem, but it was in fact written in 1912. The obvious irony is that Beb was working as a barrister in the city when he wrote it – sweating over court briefs rather than 'toiling at ledgers in a city grey' – but soon found himself on a French battlefield of his own.

First World War

Beginnings

Upon the outbreak of war, Cynthia had just given birth to their second son, and the family were staying at her parents' stately home in Scotland. Her father, the earl, barked that any eligible male in his employment who did not volunteer would be sacked. Thus Beb's first wartime role involved employing his Oxford Union debating skills to try and convince Scottish estate workers of the merits of his own father's war. (The earl, incidentally, was no hypocrite – both his sons would go on to fight and die in the war.)

As for Beb's siblings, Raymond initially denounced the war as a 'bore' and set about enjoying a planned holiday whilst enlisting in a volunteer regiment which he judged unlikely to result in active service. Oc, who was unmarried, became the first of the brothers to enlist, soon joined by Cyril and Beb himself.

Initially, Beb, Oc and Cyril trained together at Tidworth on Salisbury Plain, undertaking an infantry course designed for former public school cadets. Beb recalled:[19]

> The tents were full, and we slept with our feet congregated around the pole and our heads near the canvas, like the spokes in a wheel. We were all supplied with uniforms, rifles, and bayonets, but owing to the sudden inrush of men there were inevitably certain deficiencies with which the authorities had found it impossible to cope on the spur of the moment. Though we were provided with rifles, there was a shortage of knives and spoons, and in the large central mess tent it was a new and queer sensation eating hot mutton in one's fingers, stirring tea with a pencil, or trying to learn the strangely elusive art of buttering bread with a fork.

Raymond, despite his early cynicism, later joined the Grenadier Guards and died at the Front.[20] Oc served with distinction under horrendous conditions at Gallipoli and in France, while Cyril received a commission as captain in the

---

19 *Moments of Memory*, op cit, p 203.
20 The effect on HH of losing a son should not be underestimated, though it is beyond our scope here. We have already seen how Kipling turned from one the most jingoistic to one of the most scathing anti-war poets following the death of his son Jack. The death of two stepsons had a shattering effect on the German General Eric Ludendorff, while in the Aftermath later in the book we will see how the British press baron Lord Rothermere was driven to extreme appeasement by not wanting a reprise of the conflict which claimed two of his sons.

16th Battalion (Queen's Westminster Rifles), London Regiment, and went to America in 1917 as part of the Ministry of Munitions delegation.[21]

After his introductory training, Beb took a commission in the Royal Artillery. His first visit to France was in late 1914, not with the army but instead in the company of Cynthia and Violet. Violet had organised the trip to investigate the work of the medical corps and the Red Cross with the wounded – a classic example of *noblesse oblige* undertaken by wealthy women in wars past. It was not possible at that stage for Beb's unit to be deployed since it was awaiting guns, Britain's small pre-war munitions industry struggling to cope with the soaring demand. The fact of going to war without sufficient weapons was something which grated severely on him and led to him railing against politicians including his father later in the war.

To begin with, Beb's unit was distributed between Ypres and Nieuport Bains, the latter being where the Western Front met the sea. He was soon fighting daily artillery duels with his German counterparts. He undertook his duties with verve, displaying the customary bravery of a public school-educated junior officer. In his later memoir, he wrote in matter-of-fact style of some of the horrors he saw:[22]

> It was rumoured that the putting green of a golf links had once formed a part of No Man's Land, but now it was far beyond recognition: the ground was scattered with large numbers of the dead, French and German, lying on that powdered and shell-pitted soil, on their faces or their backs, tangled on the barbs of the rusted wire, or tossed over the brink of a shell-hole, and here and there a rigid arm stretched upwards aimlessly to the sky.

Like so many others, he seemed outwardly to be inured to the daily toll of death and to find the twice-daily exchange of artillery fire – 'morning and evening hate', as his unit called it – somewhat monotonous: 'Each day was very like that which had gone before it, with a growing list of casualties among men and guns and a gradual attrition of the forces on each side.'[23] In June 1915, however, the monotony was shattered when he was hit in the face by shrapnel, causing the loss of several teeth as well as inflicting gashes across his face.

Because he was due to go on leave anyway, it was suggested he receive treatment in London rather than a local field hospital, and so he returned to Britain. Although he seemed outwardly normal, he did not come back to domestic bliss: there were various sources of tension between him and Cynthia and much more between him and his father, due to Beb's immense frustration with HH's failure to supply the army adequately from the outset. The author DH Lawrence wrote

---

21 Cyril would however go on to become a law lord – a member of the Appellate Committee of the House of Lords, then the highest court in the land.

22 *Moments of Memory* (Hutchinson & Co, 1937), p 218.

23 Ibid, p 221.

after meeting Beb 'the war is the only reality to him. All this here is unreal, this England, only the trenches are life to him. Cynthia is very unhappy – he is not even aware of her existence. He is spell bound by the fighting line.'[24] In fact, Beb was suffering shell shock.

Shell shock

It is worth diverting for a moment to consider the phenomenon of shell shock, something intimately associated with the Great War. It was not understood at all as a condition prior to 1914 and only imperfectly understood by the war's end.

One of the key differences between the Great War and all previous large-scale conflicts was the role of artillery. The range and power of the guns available had increased exponentially from earlier European conflicts. Thus, when soldiers apparently untouched by enemy ordinance started exhibiting terrible physical and psychological trauma – including such symptoms as blindness, facial ticks and uncontrollable diarrhoea – doctors assumed that their nervous systems had been physically damaged by shockwaves from explosions. Hence in 1917 the term 'shell shock' was coined, by a medical officer called Charles Myers. The condition was also called 'war neurosis' at the time – actually more accurate since it did not erroneously assume that soldiers were suffering an actual physical injury caused by explosions.[25]

Unfortunately, partly out of ignorance, partly out of the values of the time, and partly due to the desperate conditions of wartime, commanders were often inclined to the view that soldiers suffering without an obvious injury were simply shirking. In the years since the war, there have been many accusations that those executed for cowardice included men who had undiagnosed shell shock. We will return to that controversy in Chapter 9 in the context of AP Herbert's book *The Secret Battle*.

Despite the lack of sympathy among commanders, the evidence became undeniable that many soldiers were genuinely suffering from something they could not control. In 1917, the British Army determined that (a) war neurosis accounted for one-seventh of all personnel discharged for disabilities;

---

24 Quoted in Colin Clifford, *The Asquiths* (John Murray, 2002), p 298.

25 In the years since the war, the terms 'combat stress' and – famously in connection with American veterans of the Vietnam War – 'Post Traumatic Stress Disorder' (often shortened to 'PTSD') have also been used.

For further reading on the phenomenon, see Anthony Babington, *Shell Shock: A History of the Changing Attitudes to War Neuroses* (Leo Cooper, 1997); JMW Binneveld, *From Shell Shock to Combat Stress* (Amsterdam University Press, 1997); Joanna Bourke, *Dismembering the Male: Men's Bodies, Britain and the Great War* (Reaktion Books, 1996); Suzie Grogan, *Shell Shocked Britain: The First World War's Legacy for Britain's Mental Health* (Pen & Sword History, 2014) and Eric J Leed, *No Man's Land: Combat and Identity in World War One* (Cambridge University Press, 1979).

(b) 'emotional disorders' – symptoms with no physical injuries – were responsible for approximately one-third of all discharges; and (c) while the ratio of officers to men at the Front was 1:30, among patients in hospitals specialising in war neuroses, the ratio of officers to men was 1:6. The inevitable conclusion was that even the strongest and bravest of men had a breaking point. The much greater incidence of shell shock among junior officers was due to the fact that they were expected to lead every attack from the front, and were supposed to show a stiff upper lip at all times, even under the greatest duress.

The British Army realised that one way to limit the number of cases would be to restrict the amount of time troops spent under fire. They therefore implemented a system of rotation in which battalions would move back and forth along the complex network of trenches. In a typical month, assuming no set battle was under way, troops could end up spending little time in the firing line, while some of the month would be almost the equivalent of being on leave, since they would be behind even the reserve trenches, sometimes mixing with civilians. Not all armies followed suit – one factor, no doubt, why the British were the only army who fought the war's duration but never suffered a collapse of morale.

Nevertheless, by the war's conclusion, there had been about 80,000 recorded cases of shell shock among the British. References can be found in literature written soon after the conflict, such as the character of Septimus Smith in Virginia Woolf's *Mrs Dalloway* (which also ruminates on the poor treatment of the shell shocked and of the mentally ill generally at the time). Moreover, some of the most upsetting surviving footage from the era is of men in hospitals (and 'lunatic asylums' as mental health institutions were then bluntly called) displaying horrendous symptoms. One can never know how many more cases were undiagnosed. Kenneth Duffield, the Australian composer we will meet in the next chapter, told of a harrowing experience in a London theatre when he had to overpower an armed Canadian member of the audience who was threatening to kill members of the cast; he surmised that the man was a veteran who had been gassed and was suffering terrible psychological problems as a result.[26]

Beb's breakdown

Beb was not the only one of the family to suffer from mental illness – all of his children with his first wife, Helen, suffered depression at some time in their lives. Even the formidable Violet suffered an episode of prolonged insomnia, 'hysteria' and barbiturate overdose. His two children with his second wife Margot both became alcoholics.[27] It is therefore possible that Beb's mental health problems were not wholly derived from the war.

---

26   Kenneth Duffield, *Savages and Kings* (MacDonald & Co Ltd, 1945), pp 169–70.

27   See Jonathan Davidson MD, *Downing Street Blues: A History of Depression and Other Mental Afflictions in British Prime Ministers* (McFarland & Company, 2011), pp 108–09.

To try to deal with his demons, he became withdrawn from many social activities and wrote poetry in the solitude of his own room. A notable effort from the time was 'The Fallen Subaltern':[28]

> Who looked at danger with eyes of laughter,
> And on the charge his days ended well.
> One last salute; the bayonets clash and glisten;
> With arms reversed we go without a sound:
> One more has joined the men who lie and listen
> To us, who march upon their burial ground.

His leave was extended on doctor's orders, but the family could not understand his problems and the strain on Cynthia became immense – not least since she had various other male friends whose company was more engaging than Beb's, even if she was not physically unfaithful.

The war struck Cynthia harder still when her younger brother died at the Front. Her father, the earl, was reported as breaking down in tears, 'naively astonished' according to Cynthia. Beb on the other hand found some relief spending time with a family friend, Aubrey Herbert, son of the 4th Earl of Carnarvon, who had been serving in Gallipoli and was also on leave with signs of combat stress.

It seems the family never came any closer to understanding Beb's condition: they ascribed his evident strain and difficulties to his drinking – the cruel irony being that even if he had been resorting to the bottle, it was probably to try to deal with his shell shock.

At the end of 1915, a volume of Beb's poetry, *The Volunteer and Other Poems*, was published. It was not a jingoistic collection – instead, it contained lines such as 'Above the Saints a village Christ forlorn, Wounded again, looks down upon his fold'. The book sold well, which pleased Cynthia no end and also did much to revive Beb's spirits, but it was not enough to pay the bills of their upper middle class lifestyle, and Beb was not in a condition to return to working as a barrister. He did receive a small job from the attorney-general, FE Smith, but again it was insufficient to maintain Cynthia's lifestyle as the daughter of an earl.

In 1916, Beb and Cynthia suffered two crushing blows. First, Cynthia's eldest brother died in a Turkish ambush in Palestine, and then Beb's older brother, Raymond, died on the Somme. One can therefore imagine the family mood when Beb and Oc themselves returned to war, both being sent to the Western Front.

Oc's bravery was evident through the conflict: he was awarded a DSO in 1917 for gallantry in a night attack on the Ancre, was given two bars in the same year, and was promoted to brigadier-general. In total he was wounded four times, once

---

28 Quoted in Clifford, *The Asquiths*, op cit, p 299.

in Gallipoli and three times in France. His final wound was from a sniper's bullet hitting his leg, causing its amputation and the end of his war as he returned to Britain for good.

Redeployment

Beb was sent towards Arras at the start of 1917. His unit moved forward as the Germans withdrew to the Hindenburg Line. Once more he witnessed many ghastly scenes:[29]

> I had a few hours' sleep in the old front line, and the sky was whitening, but dawn had not yet come, when I went forward with my signaller; it was a slow business finding our way in the dusk through the shell-holes and tangled wire of the old No Man's Land, and when the twilight came it brought slowly to view the bodies of French soldiers lying in tattered uniforms among the rusted stakes. Some of them were little more than skeletons; they looked as though they had lain there for years and it was clear that in this part of the line there had been no truce for burial. After crossing the German front line we came to their communication trench, but we had been warned not to go into it, as the Germans had left behind them a large number of booby traps, and bombs had been discovered laid under the duck boards.

In April and May 1917 his unit took part in the Battle of Arras itself. The British attack began on 9 April with the greatest advance by any army on the Western Front since trench warfare had begun – showing how far British tactics had evolved since the Somme the previous year[30] – but the German line was still not broken and as the days passed the battle ground to yet another bloody stalemate in the war of attrition. In total the battle cost the British about 160,000 casualties and the Germans approximately 125,000.

In July Beb's unit fought at Passchendaele, in another iconic battle of the war.

---

29 *Moments of Memory*, op cit, p 281.
30 Instead of attacking with lines of infantry marching towards the enemy lines, by February 1917 the training manual divided platoons into a small headquarters each with four sections, one with two trained grenade-throwers and assistants, the second with a Lewis gunner and nine assistants carrying 30 drums of ammunition, the third section with a sniper, scout and nine riflemen, and the fourth section comprising nine men with four rifle-grenade launchers. The rifle and hand-grenade sections were to advance in front of the Lewis gun and rifle-grenade sections, in two waves or in artillery formation, which covered an area 100 yards wide and 50 yards deep, with the four sections in a diamond pattern, led by the rifle section. German defenders were to be suppressed by fire from the Lewis-gun and rifle-grenade sections, while the riflemen and hand-grenade sections moved forward, preferably by infiltrating round the flanks of the resistance, to overwhelm the defenders from the rear.

The tactics were further refined for the Arras attack, with measurable success, though they also encountered improved German defences.

He wrote of the quality of German defences and the gross discomfort of lice, two contrasting components of much Allied misery:[31]

> One afternoon when I was acting as FOO at an infantry post in a captured pill box, three direct hits were made on it by the German field guns: each of these impacts shook the roof above us with a dull crunching thud; as the structure vibrated, there were some ugly moments of suspense for those who were squatting inside, but none of the shells came through, and moments such as these were the rare occasions when we felt grateful for the efficiency of German engineers. One minor defect from our point of view was that the doorways of captured pill boxes were usually facing the enemy; another defect was that some of them were inhabited by lice: these creatures had been even more plentiful in the Hindenburg Line than they were in the Salient, and in capturing part of that fortress our troops had also taken many millions of unwelcome prisoners who had lately pastured on their enemies. I was told by a friend who had inspected one of these little animals at close quarters that it resembled "a small grey hippopotamus," but I never made the experiment of testing his description.

Even though the conditions were much worse than those which had caused his shell shock in 1915, it seems that the aforementioned policy of rotating frontline troops assisted greatly and he made it through the experience without suffering breakdown.

He returned to Britain on leave over Christmas 1917 and went back to France in January 1918. Soon, the German Operation Michael led to furious fighting. Beb was in a sector hit by poison gas. He suffered only a mild dose, but went for days without sleep or food as the Germans poured everything into their final effort. He wrote of—

> scenes of great grandeur: the German aeroplanes came on, dipping and swerving in front of the grey lines of infantry and firing with their machine guns at the advanced sections of the British field artillery ... and there was a continuous background of thunder which seemed to extend for many miles on either side of us beneath the low dun-coloured sky in which the smoke of battle was mingled with the remains of the mist.[32]

The British line held nevertheless, and Beb was removed from it in the summer of 1918 when he caught influenza. After he recovered, he was appointed to staff training in France, and remained in that capacity until the Armistice.

When the war ended, he briefly visited Spa, where the Germans had based their GHQ. He wrote of some 'embarrassment' meeting German soldiers, but courteous salutes were exchanged and each went about their business. On visiting German frontier towns he noted that although the buildings were intact, 'the

31 *Moments of Memory,* op cit, p 296.
32 Ibid, p 321.

signs of desolation were of a subtler kind ... they were plainly evident in the faces of the people.' He wrote with pleasure that the German children quickly discovered the generosity of the British soldiers, who frequently shared their rations. Like so many others involved in all capacities in the war, it seems that he was neither triumphalist nor despairing, but instead simply wished to resume whatever approximation of a normal life was possible.

Post-war career

Beb returned to Britain in Spring 1919, and continueded writing both prose and poetry. In the 1920s he travelled to the Greek Island of Skyros to visit a corner of a foreign field that was forever England – the grave of the poet Rupert Brooke. Brooke, a family friend, had died of illness on the way to Gallipoli in the company of Oc.[33] He wrote a poem about his fallen friend, which began:

> Here passed of old the fleet of Persia,
> Wine-red sails and flashing oars,
> Splintered by charging triremes of Hellas
> And broken on her sacred shores.
> Here came Youth and the ships of England
> Eastward across the wave;
> Here came Valour, and Hope, and Sorrow,
> To make a poet's grave.

Beb's best known poem was possibly 'War's Cataract':

> In this red havoc of the patient earth,
> Though higher yet the tide of battle rise,
> Now has the hero cast away disguise,
> And out of ruin splendour comes to birth.
> This is the field where Death and Honour meet,
> And all the lesser company are low:
> Pale Loveliness has left her mirror now
> And walks the Court of Pain with silent feet.
>
> From cliff to cliff war's cataract goes down,
> Hurling its booming waters to the shock;
> And, tossing high their manes of gleaming spray,
> The crested chargers leap from rock to rock,
> While over all, dark though the thunder frown,
> The rainbows climb above to meet the day.

---

33 Brooke had written to Margot Asquith from the voyage, just before reaching Gallipoli, 'Please thank Winston very much for arranging for us to take part in this most interesting of expeditions'; his flippant tone belied the fact that he was under no illusions of the dangers he faced. Colin Clifford (op cit, pp 252–3) wrote 'No convicted felon ever mounted the scaffold more certain of his fate than Rupert Brooke as the Grantully Castle steamed ... bound for Gallipoli'.

He joined the Savage Club in March 1927.

His autobiography *Moments of Memory*, upon which I have drawn frequently in this chapter, was published in 1937. It was an unflinching look at the war, as indicated by the quoted passages above, though unsurprisingly made no mention of his shell shock, as well as being generally stoic on the terrible losses that both his and Cynthia's families had experienced.

He died in 1947.

Harold Auten VC: Q-ship hero

Harold Auten was a Savage who obtained the highest of all military honours, the Victoria Cross. He was not, however, a career soldier who had spent his life hell-bent on seeing action. Instead, he was a merchant navy sailor and naval reservist, who answered his country's call in the most distinguished fashion when the time came.

Early life and First World War

Auten was born in Leatherhead, Surrey, in August 1891, the son of a retired naval paymaster. He went to the grammar school in Camberwell, London. In 1898, he left school at the age of 17 to begin his career at sea, being apprenticed to the P&O line. In 1910, he joined the Royal Naval Reserve (RNR) and by the time of the First World War had been promoted to sub-lieutenant.

During the war, he served on armed merchant vessels known as 'Q-ships' (the name deriving from their home port of Queenstown, Ireland). Their weapons were hidden so as to trick U-boats into surfacing, where they could be attacked with the Q-ship's guns.

The need for the utmost secrecy had some happy side effects: a commander was allowed to choose his own ship. He would then discretely pass a request to the Admiralty and Whitehall would take care of the purchase. By that means the normally slow Admiralty approval process would be circumvented and the commander would get exactly the ship he wanted.

Nevertheless, creating successful Q-ships was not simply a matter of hiding a few guns on a merchant vessel. Instead, they had to be sufficiently armed to defeat a U-boat and in all aspects – appearance, course and speed – had to give a plausible impression of a merchant vessel. Since many German sailors were familiar with British ports and merchant vessels from their peacetime service – some would even have served on British-flagged vessels – they would not be easily fooled. If a U-boat held any suspicion that a merchant vessel was armed, it would not risk surfacing to fire its gun, but would instead only raise a periscope and fire a torpedo. If so, given the problems with visibility when facing only a periscope, the Q-ship would be unable to respond with her guns, though some did carry depth charges.

A further problem for Q-ships was that their modifications would not include warship-style armour below. They could therefore not hope to survive a torpedo hit – especially if a torpedo detonated their magazines – albeit they carried cargoes of balsa, cork or wooden casks, so as to give them a better chance of staying afloat after being holed below the waterline.

One additional measure the Q-ships employed to fool U-boats was the use of a 'panic party': a group of men who would get into a lifeboat and pretend to abandon ship, in order to gull the U-boat into thinking the Q-ship was doomed.

From 1915, Auten served on *Zylpha*, a former collier. In April 1917, when aged just 26, he was given command of *Q.16*, also known as *Heather*. He was awarded the Distinguished Service Cross while serving on her. He then joined another modified collier, HMS *Stock Force*, and it was in that capacity he was awarded the Victoria Cross. His citation read:

> H.M.S. "Stock Force," under the command of Lieutenant Harold Auten, DSC., RNR., was torpedoed by an enemy submarine at 5 p.m. on the 30th July, 1918. The torpedo struck the ship abreast No. 1 hatch, entirely wrecking the fore part of the ship, including the bridge, and wounding three ratings. A tremendous shower of planks, unexploded shells, hatches and other debris followed the explosion, wounding the first lieutenant (Lieutenant E.J. Grey, RNR) and the navigating officer (Lieutenant L.E. Workman, RNR) and adding to the injuries of the foremost gun's crew and a number of other ratings. The ship settled down forward, flooding the foremost magazine and between decks to the depth of about three feet. "Panic party," in charge of Lieutenant Workman, RNR., immediately abandoned ship, and the wounded were removed to the lower deck, where the surgeon (Surgeon Probationer G.E. Strahan, RNVR), working up to his waist in water, attended to their injuries. The captain, two guns' crews and the engine-room staff remained at their posts.
>
> The submarine then came to the surface ahead of the ship half a mile distant, and remained there a quarter of an hour, apparently watching the ship for any doubtful movement.
>
> The "panic party" in the boat accordingly commenced to row back towards the ship in an endeavour to decoy the submarine within range of the hidden guns. The submarine followed, coming slowly down the port side of the "Stock Force," about three hundred yards away. Lieutenant Auten, however, withheld his fire until she was abeam, when both of his guns could bear. Fire was opened at 5.40 p.m.; the first shot carried away one of the periscopes, the second round hit the conning tower, blowing it away and throwing the occupant high into the air. The next round struck the submarine on the water-line, tearing her open and blowing out a number of the crew.

The enemy then subsided several feet into the water and her bows rose. She thus presented a large and immobile target into which the "Stock Force" poured shell after shell until the submarine sank by the stern, leaving a quantity of debris on the water. During the whole of the action one man (Officer's Steward, 2nd Class, R.J. Starling) remained pinned down under the foremost gun after the explosion of the torpedo, and remained there cheerfully and without complaint, although the ship was apparently sinking, until the end of the action.

The "Stock Force" was a vessel of 360 tons, and despite the severity of the shock sustained by the officers and men when she was torpedoed, and the fact that her bows were almost obliterated, she was kept afloat by the exertions of her ship's company until 9.25 p.m. She then sank with colours flying, and the officers and men were taken off by two torpedo boats and a trawler.

The action was cited as one of the finest examples of coolness, discipline and good organisation in the history of "Q" ships.

After the war, Auten wrote a book on Q-ships. It was the first on the subject[34] and a more colourful read than many a dry memoir. Here is a representative passage:

The ideal "Q" boat commander should combine in his own person something of the qualities of Horatius Cocles and a successful impresario. Captain Gordon Campbell seemed to be imbued with both these qualities. As an impresario he possessed a wonderful eye for detail. It is said of him that he caused one of his crew to dress as a girl and sit in a prominent position on the poop on a deck chair with a view to attracting the Hun to his ship. On another occasion one of his officers, whose duty it was to go off with the "panic party," constructed a parrot, which he fastened inside a cage. This he proposed taking with him into the boat, thus lending local colour to the "panic party."

Post-war career

Auten joined the Savage Club in July 1928.

He later moved to the United States and began working for the Rank Organisation. He remained in the RNR, though, and once again stepped forward to serve his country when the Second World War began. Throughout the conflict he worked for the RNR organising trans-Atlantic convoys, and was promoted to acting captain. He was recognised for his services by the British with the Royal Naval Reserve Officers Decoration, by the Americans with the Officer of the United States Legion of Merit 'for distinguished service to the Allied cause throughout the war', and by the Dutch by being made a Commander of the Order of Orange-Nassau 'for service to the Royal Netherlands Navy during the War'.

He died in the United States in 1964.

---

34 Harold Auten, *"Q" boat adventures: the exploits of the famous mystery ships* (H Jenkins, 1919).

B Granville Baker: seeing both sides

Like many a Savage past and present, B Granville Baker could have qualified in more than one category of membership, for he was both a talented artist and a successful author. As with James Agate and AP Herbert, he wrote a book about the Great War while it was still taking place. Uniquely among Savages of this book, however, he had actually served in the German Army which he found himself fighting against.

Early life

Bernard Granville Baker was born in Poona, India in 1870, the son of Montagu Bernard Baker, an East India company employee, and Harriet Fanny *née* Bangh. He was educated in Europe, first at Winchester College and later at the Military Academy at Dresden. It was the start of a most adventurous military career. He left the German Army to fight in the Second Boer War, serving with the 9th Royal Prussian Hussars, Imperial Yeomanry, a volunteer mounted force created in January 1900 in response to the early reverses of the war.[35] After South Africa he served with the 21st Hussars in India and Burma (Myanmar).

As well as his military adventures, Baker started writing and painting. He was evidently classically educated and a man of taste and distinction. In 1910, for example, he published a book recording a trip around Istanbul studying the ancient walls and other Roman remnants. The introduction to the book began:[36]

> ROMANCE and the history of walled cities are inseparable. Who has not felt this to be so at the sight of hoary ruins lichen-clad and ivy-mantled, that proudly rear their battered crests despite the ravages of time and man's destructive instincts. It is within walled cities that the life of civilized man began: the walls guarded him against barbarian foes, behind their shelter he found the security necessary to his cultural development, in their defence he showed his finest qualities. And such a city—and such a history is that of Ancient Byzantium, the City of Constantine, the Castle of Cæsar.'

He followed up with another book, *The Passing of the Turkish Empire in Europe*, in 1913,[37] in which he pondered:[38]

> As I write this the sound of firing is borne on the westerly wind into the City of Constantine, Tsarigrad, Stamboul.

---

35 The Imperial Yeomanry was recruited from the middle classes and traditional yeomanry sources at the start, but loosened its requirements as it went on. The existing yeomanry regiments contributed only a small proportion of the total Imperial Yeomanry establishment. The Imperial Yeomanry was disbanded in 1908.

36 Captain B Granville Baker, *The Walls of Constantinople* (John Milne, 1910). The book was digitised and free online at the time of writing.

37 Seeley, Service & Co, 1913. The book was digitised and free online at the time of writing.

38 Ibid, p 10.

I was mightily drawn to revisit this ancient city now in these days of darkness, so I hurried out overland, crossing Germany, Poland, Roumania, till I landed on the banks of the Golden Horn. When I had passed I noted a feeling of deep anxiety, to account for which the present troubles of Turkey are insufficient; there seemed to me an undercurrent of unrest such as perchance preceded the "Völkerwanderung" of some fifteen centuries ago. I came here to record as best I can the doings of these days in Constantinople, the capital of a vanishing Empire, and while I went about the city, revisiting places I have seen bathed in summer sunshine, now gloomy under a lowering sky, as I noted the many signs of "Sturm und Drang," I was filled with grave forebodings; here where a mighty Empire is tottering to its fall under pressure of the vanguard of a "Völkerwanderung" I pondered whether another world-wide Empire were as secure as that of the Ottoman was till recently supposed to be.

First World War

Upon the outbreak of the First World War, Baker soon wrote and released a book entitled *The German army from within. By a British officer who has served in it.*[39] It set down his thoughts on the German Army based on his time in Dresden with it, noting that he was now bound to serve against it in combat. In the introduction, he asserted that he would exaggerate nothing and spare the reader nothing. In his first chapter, though, he made clear where his opinions lay:[40]

> From the official reports of atrocities committed by my late comrades-in-arms in Belgian towns and villages, one might draw the conclusion that the German soldier, officer and man, is badly afflicted with the Sadic temperament. This, however, would be unjust. I think a truer explanation is that the common sensibilities of the German, the peasant and the cultivated man, are blunter than those of any other civilised race, and what is horror to us is mere horseplay to him.

> It must be admitted, however, that there are, in every line of the German Army, numbers of men who would seem to be disciples of that Marquis who made a philosophy of luxurious cruelty.

He also noted that his regiment wished him well when he left to fight the Boers, though the German Army was by no means universally behind Britain in that conflict. Overall, though, he clearly threw his weight behind the propaganda stance of the British of the time, writing in his conclusion:[41]

> The conduct of the War by our enemies has not surprised me ... A great injustice has for many years been done to Spain, in that the Spaniard

---

39 Hodder and Stoughton, 1914. The book was digitised and free online at the time of writing.
40 Ibid, p 26.
41 Ibid, pp 180–81.

has been regarded universally as the most cruel of men. But he must retire from that unenviable notoriety now to make room for the Prussian butcher. Even allowing for the stress and strain of warfare, and the lust of battle that fires a man's blood at such times, and leads him to commit atrocities that he would never conceive at other times, the Prussians have always gone beyond all limits. Everybody knows that soldiers of all nations, in the excitement of victory, allow themselves to be carried away in the frenzy of the moment, and do more or less deplorable things. But the modern Huns have made a philosophy and cult of these outrages. Their excesses were not the excesses of war. They were largely temperamental, and largely designed by cold precept ...

Yes, Prussianism must go, and with it that gorgeous monster, the German Army. I cannot say that I shall view its passing without a twinge of regret; for, having been even a tiny part of that machine, I shall feel that part of myself is going too. And there is something infinitely saddening in the death of a monster, even a blood-thirsty monster.

This monster is so enormous that the mind can hardly conceive it as a whole. None but a German mind, cold, ordered, clear, and pitiless, could have planned it, built it, and have kept a firm grasp on every hair-spring and lever of it.

Baker went on to command the 13th Battalion of the Yorkshire Regiment (the 'Green Howards') from July 1916 to February 1918. The battalion had been raised in Richmond in 1915 as a 'Bantam Battalion' as it accepted men who did not meet the height and chest requirements of the regular army. But it was sent into the vanguard of trench warfare, beginning with the Battle of the Somme, already underway when it arrived in France. It took part in the final major engagement, the Battle of the Ancre, in November 1916, which gave a much better result for the British in terms of comparative casualties with the Germans than the Somme campaign as a whole.

In 1917, the 13th Battalion fought in several battles forming part of the German retreat to the Hindenburg Line. In one of those encounters, on 2 April 1917, Baker was wounded in a heavy German bombardment near Gouzeaucourt Wood, but was able to resume his duties.

In early 1918, the 13th Battalion suffered severe casualties resisting Operation Michael. By May they had been reduced to cadre strength.

Baker himself was awarded the DSO on 7 June 1918.[42] He reached the rank of lieutenant-colonel, a mark of the eminent service he had given throughout the war.

---

42 *Edinburgh Gazette* 7 June 1918, p 1897.

Post-war career

Baker retired from active duty in 1919, and resumed his successful painting and writing career. In recognition of his talents, he was elected a Fellow of the Royal Geographical Society, the Royal Historical Society and, in April 1938, a member of the Savage Club.[43] He also served as a Justice of the Peace.

Among his better known paintings were a number depicting the Napoleonic Wars, including *The 12ᵗʰ Light Dragoons at Salamanca, July 22ⁿᵈ 1812*; *Advance of the French at Barossa*; *Sir John Moore at Corunna, January 16ᵗʰ 1809*; *The Flight of King Joseph Bonaparte from Vittoria, June 21ˢᵗ 1813*; and *Waterloo, June 18ᵗʰ 1815: The Whole Line Will Advance*.

In 1897 he married Lorina, daughter of Rev AO Hartley. She died in 1942 without issue. Baker himself died in 1957.

Rupert Stanley Gwatkin-Williams: far-flung seas and feral sheep

Rupert Stanley Gwatkin-Williams was another Savage sailor. He is noteworthy for serving in two theatres of the war which appear much less often in factual or fictional works on the Great War than the Western Front.

Early life and career

He was born Rupert Stanley Williams in 1875. He joined the Royal Navy as a teenager, training on board HMS *Britannia*, from which he passed out in 1890. *Britannia* was the name given to the British Royal Navy's ships used for the preliminary education of naval officers from 1859 to 1905. Williams trained on the second iteration of the ship, a three-decker previously called *Prince of Wales*. Other future Savages to train on *Britannia* around the same time included Prince George (later George V), son of Edward VII. George's assignment was intended as a vote of confidence in the system after a bullying scandal, though he recorded that it was still a fairly gruelling environment:[44]

> It never did me any good to be a Prince. The *Britannia* was a pretty tough place, and so far from our benefiting, the other cadets made a point of taking it out of us, on the grounds that they would never be able to do it later on. There was a lot of fighting among the cadets, and the rule was if challenged you had to accept. So they used to make me go up and challenge the bigger cadets. I was awfully small then, and I'd get a hiding time and again. But one day I was landed one on the

---

43 I cannot be a hundred per cent sure because the handwriting in the candidate's book (it is entry 384 in the relevant volume) is unclear – the '8' might be a '6', but on balance I think it is an '8'.

44 Quoted in Admiral Sir Dudley De Chair, *The Sea is Strong* (George G Harrap & Co Ltd, 1961), p17.

nose that made me bleed. It was the best blow I ever had, as the doctor forbade me to fight any more.

After passing out from *Britannia*, Williams was appointed a midshipman on the armoured cruiser HMS *Imperieuse* in 1891 on the China Station. He was present at the taking of the Taku forts and served throughout the Boxer campaign, being promoted to lieutenant in 1896 and commander in December 1907.

In 1903 he married Evelyn, daughter of GL Gwatkin, and thereafter was known as Gwatkin-Williams. They had two sons and a daughter.

In 1908, he assumed command of HMS *Seal*, one of 24 'B-class' destroyers, known as a '30 knotter'. The following year, however, life took a turn for the worse as he was court-martialled for not reporting the grounding of *Seal* and for false and misleading entries in the ship's log. He was severely reprimanded and dismissed from the ship. He left the Royal Navy in 1912.[45]

First World War

Upon the outbreak of war, he wrote to the Admiralty, helpfully explaining that he had learned Portuguese and was prepared to offer his services as an interpreter. The offer was noted, but instead he was given the more conventional role of command of the armed boarding steamer HMS *Tara*.[46] She was the former TSS *Hibernia*, a twin-screw steamer passenger vessel which had been operated by the London and North Western Railway.

Tara's first duty was to patrol the North Channel, the strait between north-eastern Northern Ireland and south-western Scotland. For a time she found herself the only vessel armed with guns on the west coast of England. To begin with the crew thought themselves effectively sitting out the war, as it seemed a long way from any of the fighting, but German mines and submarines soon disabused them of that notion. On one occasion, they saw a small coasting steamer with her engines stopped, and assumed she was acting on the orders of a U-boat, it then being the custom (not always observed) for U-boats to give merchant seamen the chance to abandon ship before sinking their vessel:[47]

> At full speed we zigzagged towards her, with the men at the guns, and, as we got closer, our suspicions were yet further confirmed by observing that she had got her boats out. A moment later and we could make out through our glasses objects which we decided were rafts, spars,

45 His obituary in *The Times*, 9 August, 1949 does not mention his dismissal from the *Seal*, but it appears in his naval records at the National Archives. See http://discovery.nationalarchives.gov.uk.

46 A privately printed book on the *Tara* is Geraint S Griffith, *From Holyhead To Bir Hakkim (and back) the full story of HMS Tara* (2015).

47 RS Gwatkin-Williams, *Under the Black Ensign* (Hutchinson, 1st edn, 1922, reprinted by Forgotten Books, 2015), pp 23–24.

and smashed and overturned boats. Then suddenly we found ourselves traversing what I can only describe as a veritable forest of dead bodies —grim, stark, bearded men, each floating upright in his life-collar, yet all dead, the water washing in and out of their mouths as the commotion caused by our bow–wave reached them. No need now to call on the men for alertness; it was a lesson which the veriest dullard could understand. Quickly our own boats were in the water in order to help the small coasting steamer in the work of rescue, a work in which she had already engaged before the *Tara*'s arrival. Some twenty exhausted and half-frozen beings were in all picked up still alive. They were all that remained alive of the crew of the armed merchant cruiser *Bayano*, who had cleared from Liverpool the previous night with a company of some four hundred officers and men. She had been torpedoed during that darkest hour of the night which precedes the dawn by a submarine which remained unseen. She sank so quickly that the men were literally washed out of their hammocks into the icy element ...

Gwatkin-Williams wrote that death became so commonplace that sailors started to develop gallows humour as a survival mechanism. The sea lanes were littered with drifting corpses, which were seen so often that regular sailors such as minesweeper crewmen gave them pet names. Gwatkin-Williams himself had a narrow escape one morning when he awoke to find a trawler moored alongside with an unexploded mine attached to its stern. It transpired that the captain had intended to bring it home as a trophy to show off to his wife.

In 1915, *Tara* was redeployed to the Mediterranean. In November of the same year, she was sunk by a U-boat in Sollum Bay on the Egyptian coast. In a chivalrous gesture, the U-boat then rescued the crew and took them prisoner. Rather than being sent to Germany, the prisoners were handed over to the Senussi tribesmen, a religious sect found in Libya and Egypt who were fighting on the side of the Central Powers, having been cajoled into joining by the Ottomans.[48]

Gwatkin-Williams and his crew were taken by the Senussi to a desert oasis near Bir Hakeim, along with the crew of HMT *Moorina*, a horse transport which had also been sunk by enemy action. They were guarded by only a handful of tribesmen and some Ottoman soldiers, but were surrounded by an uncompromising desert. Although the guards were mostly civil in their actions towards the prisoners, provisions including food were inadequate. At times the British were fed little more than snails. Fearing starvation, Gwatkin-Williams attempted to

---

48 The Senussi crossed the Libyan-Egyptian border in November 1915 and fought a campaign along the Egyptian coast. The Grand Senussi Ahmed Sharif al-Senussi declared jihad on British forces The British withdrew but, using superior weapons and more developed tactics, defeated the Senussi in several engagements, culminating in the Battle of Agagia. They recaptured the coast in March 1916. In the interior, the 'Band of Oases' campaign continued until February 1917, after which a peace was negotiated. There was no further action in that theatre, save for desultory British patrols by aircraft and armoured cars.

escape. He wandered through the desert for two days before being recaptured when he stumbled across an Arab camp.

He was returned to the prison camp but, in an extraordinary turn of events, a letter he had written to a Turkish officer pleading about the desperate conditions at Bir Hakeim fell into the possession of the Duke of Westminster, who was in the region commanding an armoured car brigade. The duke, a major in the Cheshire Yeomanry, had designed the fighting vehicles himself based on the legendary Rolls-Royce Silver Ghost, the original 'best car in the world'. The cars had proven not to be of much use in the mud of the Western Front, but came into their own in the open deserts of North Africa. At the time he discovered Gwatkin-Williams' letter, the duke's brigade formed part of the Western Frontier Force under General William Peyton. The brigade had won a major victory over the Senussi at the Action of Agagia in February 1916.

The duke swiftly put together a land armada to lead a rescue mission. It consisted of nine armoured cars, three armed but unarmoured cars, and a further 28 cars and ambulances. The personnel included a guide who had been to Bir Hakeim three decades earlier as a child. The duke estimated the distance to the camp to be 70 miles, but it proved to be much further. Despite being low on fuel, the duke's men pressed on until finally finding the prisoners on 14 March 1916, by which time they had travelled 115 miles.

Gwatkin-Williams thought the prisoners would only have survived a few more days had not deliverance appeared out of the sun in the form of the duke's posse. The Senussi attempted to flee, but were swiftly cut down. The prisoners did not agree with the general slaughter, but after the surviving guards were rounded up, they did approve of the jailor responsible for the snail diet, a cleric nicknamed 'Holy Joe', being hanged.[49]

Gwatkin-Williams was admitted to hospital in Alexandria, suffering from 'slight neurasthenia' as well as being grossly underweight as a result of his imprisonment. He recovered quickly, though, and in April 1916 asked if he might be offered to the Portuguese Navy for service. Again, the Admiralty declined his somewhat unusual request. Instead, he returned to sea, being given command of HMS *Intrepid*, a second-class cruiser of the *Apollo* class.

Intrepid was part of the Arctic or 'White Sea'[50] squadron, based at Yukanskie, on a headland of the Murmansk Coast. It was not a glamorous posting, trying to keep the northern doorway at Archangel open to enable supplies to be sent to Russia. Gwatkin-Williams felt that the posting was consistently overlooked

---

49 The duke received the DSO for his exploits. He was subsequently promoted to colonel and, in May 1917, was named honorary colonel of the regiment.

50 'White Sea' refers to a southern inlet of the Barents Sea located on the northwest coast of Russia; it is one of the four seas named after a colour, along with the Black Sea, the Red Sea and the Yellow Sea.

by the Admiralty. Letters were sent to the wrong place, the Admiralty confusing his address at times with places in Japan and America. Yet the theatre was by no means insignificant, with hundreds of ships supplying Russia as they would do again in the better known Arctic convoys of the Second World War.[51]

> Through damage caused by stranding and collision, through fog and faulty navigation, through stress of tempest, ice, mine, submarine and treachery, not to mention the ordinary defects to hull and machinery inseparable from the navigation of a ship at sea, this vast allied merchant fleet was continually in need of the most urgent repairs. Neither at Arkhangel nor anywhere else within a thousand mils could such repairs be made good on that desolate coast line—it was only due to the presence there of the *Intrepid, Iphigenia* and other vessels of the British Arctic Squadron that these ships were able to be patched up sufficiently to face the return journey home.

To supplant the rather grim food on which they were subsisting, Gwatkin-Williams asked for some mountain sheep to be supplied; when they arrived they were found to be genuine feral sheep who took some skilful hunting to find once they had been let loose. The Admiralty then threw in a farcical bureaucratic insult by demanding that the sheep be shorn before being eaten, and the wool sent back to Britain. The men in the Arctic did not comply.

Among the various hardships, Gwatkin-Williams singled out the Arctic mosquito as the worst, describing it as being to the tropical mosquito as a hungry lion was to an unenterprising lamb. Even the Northern Lights provided little distraction; he found them disappointing, and thought them 'not to be compared for scenic effect with the search-lights playing on the clouds in London on a "Zep." night.' Moreover, aside from the constant danger of mines and submarines, the handling of munitions led to a colossal explosion in Archangel one day in which some 30,000 tons of munitions exploded. In Gwatkin-Williams' estimation, it had to have caused the death of several thousands, although the Russian authorities admitted only 130. He consoled himself with the fact that during 1916 the British had managed to ship approximately 750,000 tons of munitions to Russia so that the amount lost was only some 4 per cent of the total.

Gwatkin-Williams' efforts did not go unrewarded: in June 1917 the senior naval officer, White Sea, reported that he had acted with great judgement in dealing with a submarine raid on shipping, and in June 1918, he was appointed CMG for his services on board *Intrepid*.

By the start of 1918, *Intrepid* was obsolete,[52] and the Russian Revolution had led to the cessation of the Arctic convoys anyway. Gwatkin-Williams was sent

---

51 Gwatkin-Williams, *Under the Black Ensign*, op cit, p 51.
52 *Intrepid* was converted for use as a block ship along with five other *Apollo* class cruisers. She was expended in April 1918 in the raid on Zeebrugge.

instead to command the armed merchant cruiser HMS *Edinburgh Castle*, undertaking the much less gruelling task of escorting transatlantic ships bringing the rapidly-expanding United States' Army to Europe. He was still in command of *Edinburgh Castle* when the war ended.

Post-war career

In January 1919, Gwatkin-Williams was elected to the Savage Club under the category of literature, giving *Edinburgh Castle* as his address. He left the ship in February and was placed on the Retired List in March.

Once again showing lateral thinking and optimism in equal measure, he asked if he might be appointed as vice-consul at New York or elsewhere in the United States, but he was no more successful than he had been with his Portuguese-flavoured requests during the war.

Instead, he started writing books about his wartime adventures. In 1921, he published an account of his Egyptian travails, *Prisoners of the Red Desert, Being a Full and True History of the Men of the Tara*.[53] In 1922, he followed it up with a record of his other wartime naval experiences, *Under the Black Ensign*.[54]

In 1920 he married for the second time, to Florence Cross. They had one son, who was lost at sea in 1944, and a daughter, who survived him.

Gwatkin-Williams died in 1949.

Sir BH Liddell Hart: man of military letters and strategy

Brother Savage Captain BH Liddell Hart was one of the best known and most influential military writers and theorists of the twentieth century. He was not without controversy, having taken a few opportunities over the years to enhance his career at the expense of the truth, but he left behind many compelling and challenging works.

Early life and First World War

Basil Henry Liddell Hart was born in France in October 1895, to British parents. He was educated at St Paul's School in London and Corpus Christi College, Cambridge. When the First World War began he volunteered and was commissioned into the King's Own Yorkshire Light Infantry. He was deployed to the Western Front where, in 1915, he suffered serious concussion from a shell burst not long after going to the Front. It was sufficiently serious for him to be sent back to Britain.

---

53 Thornton Butterworth Ltd, 1921.
54 Hutchinson, 1st edn, 1922. The title was a riff on the Royal Navy's white ensign, referring to the filthy conditions and dilapidated vessels which characterised service in the White Sea.

After recovering from his injuries he was promoted to captain and returned to France in time to participate in the Battle of the Somme. His battalion was almost wiped out on the first day. Liddell Hart himself was hit three times in action but not seriously hurt until he was subjected to a severe gas attack a few weeks into the battle. Once again he was sent back to Britain, where he spent the rest of the conflict training new units. In that capacity, he wrote a number of short publications on infantry drill and training. His work was picked up by General Sir Ivor Maxse, a veteran of Hamel and Amiens. The two men began corresponding, and Liddell Hart started to develop a reputation as a military theorist.

Post-war writing

After the war, Liddell Hart transferred to the Royal Army Educational Corps, where he wrote a new edition of the *Infantry Training Manual*. In 1921 and 1922, he suffered heart attacks which were presumed to be caused by the long-term effects of the poison gas he had inhaled on the Western Front. His health combined with the winding down of the armed forces in peacetime precluded him from advancing further in his army career. He was placed on half pay from 1924.

In the same year, he began working as a lawn tennis correspondent and assistant military correspondent for the *Morning Post*. Evidently his tennis pieces were well received, as a collection of them was published as a book.[55] But it was as a military writer that he gained lasting fame his first step being in 1925 when he became military correspondent of *The Daily Telegraph*.

In February 1926 he joined the Savage Club under the category of literature, styling his name 'Hart, Capt. B. H. Liddell' and giving his address as the Junior Naval and Military Club, Piccadilly – the old 'In and Out'.

In 1927 he retired from the army to work full time as a journalist and writer. He moved from *The Telegraph* to *The Times* in 1935 and stayed there until 1939.

From the mid-1920s, he wrote a series of histories of major military figures, in which he advanced his ideas that the frontal assault was a strategy that was bound to fail at great cost to life. In doing so he became a severe critic of Haig and Robertson, arguing that their failure to appreciate his theory about the frontal assault had been responsible for the appalling losses on the Western Front. In his book *The Real War, 1914–18*, published in 1930, he argued that the British generals had also failed to appreciate modern weapons:[56]

> Even when the machine gun had obviously gained a dominance of the battlefield. General Headquarters in France resisted its growth from the puny pre-war scale of two in each battalion. One army commander, Haig, declared that it was 'a much overrated weapon' and that this scale

---

55 Liddell Hart, *The Lawn Tennis Masters Unveiled* (Arrowsmith, 1926).
56 Liddell Hart, *The Real War 1914–1918* (Faber and Faber, 1930, Wildside Press, 2012 reprint).

was 'more than sufficient'. Even Kitchener laid down that four were a maximum and any in excess a luxury—until the Ministry of Munitions came to the rescue of the machine-gun advocates and boldly multiplied the scale of provision by sixteen. It was due also to Mr. Lloyd George that the Stokes gun, a quick-firing light mortar, had the chance to surmount the official barrier and develop into the outstanding and ubiquitous trench weapon of the war. And later, the Ministry of Munitions succoured the tank when it was repeatedly threatened by the suffocating embrace of the War Office.

As to wider strategy, Liddell Hart contended that Britain should never have intervened directly on the Continent in the first place. Instead, it should have confined its contribution to sea warfare, with the army fighting in a minimal capacity away from the principal front. In that respect he was no fan of Robertson, writing of a proposed Franco-British thrust against Austria which was rejected by the commanders of both countries, despite support from Lloyd George:[57]

> An offensive towards Vienna would have had formidable difficulties to overcome, especially from the mountainous country; but in judging the objections to it the historian is compelled to note that the Franco-British strategists showed no signs of recognising a fundamental truth of strategy—that a concentration at one place is unlikely to succeed unless an adequate distraction to the enemy's counter-concentration is provided elsewhere. In their justifiable conviction that the main effort of France and Britain must be made on the Western Front, they seem to have dismissed too lightly the possibility of helping Italy to create a distraction to their own benefit. Yet, with Russia palpably flagging, the need to develop some fresh channel of pressure had become more urgent. When Robertson dogmatically asserted that the first lesson of history was to concentrate all available force in the main theatre, and that 'any departure from this rule has invariably proved to be disastrous', he exposed his own ignorance of history. Lloyd George might well have reminded him of the effective way in which the Italian theatre had been used by Eugene, with Marlborough's support, as a lever against France in the War of the Spanish Succession; and by Napoleon Bonaparte, as a lever against Austria in the War of the First Coalition. It was a reflection on modern strategists that, with superior facilities, they treated as insuperable the obstacles of nature which their ancestors had repeatedly overcome.

Later historians have criticised Liddell Hart for factual inaccuracies on his accounts of the Western Front battles. Some have even impugned Liddell Hart's own combat record. Richard Holmes wrote that Liddell Hart's 'evergreen rank veiled about six weeks' service at the Front followed by a longer stint in the Army Educational Corps',[58] while Gordon Corrigan sneered:[59]

---

57 Liddell Hart, *A History of the First World War* (Pan Macmillan, 2014 edn).
58 Holmes, *Tommy*, op cit, pp xx–xxi.
59 Corrigan, *Mud, Blood and Poppycock*, op cit. Corrigan's source for his slights against Liddell Hart's service record was Alex Danchev, *Alchemist of War: The Life of Basil Liddell Hart*,

Liddell Hart became the leading exponent of the study of the Great War, and anyone who expressed a view contrary to his was unlikely to be widely published or listened to. Unfortunately Liddell Hart had a personal axe to grind. He was evacuated from the battle area on three occasions during the war: once with a fever, once when concussed by an exploding shell, and finally in July 1916 when he incurred flesh wounds and suffered the effects of gas. On the second and third occasions he was sent back to England to recover, and after his second evacuation he did not return to the front. It does now appear that the injuries from his third experience of battle were more psychological than physical. One cannot blame him for that, but having been found wanting in physical courage—at least in his own mind if not those of others—he sought ways to explain why it is not courage but intellect that wins wars.

I do not think it especially fair to malign Liddell Hart's service record – he fought and was seriously wounded on the Western Front, two credentials missing from most who have written on the Great War. But his ideas about the war were not always original and not always practicable. A naval-based strategy was precisely what Britain had planned for most of the century after Waterloo. In 1914, however, it was not an option: had Britain not contributed a substantial land army, Germany would have defeated France by 1916 or, at the latest, 1917. On the other hand, Liddell Hart's general theory of indirect strategy, aimed at dislocating the enemy and reducing his means of resistance, with the emphasis on the need for mobility and surprise, contained much that was intellectually sound.

Later work

Liddell Hart is noteworthy for two later aspects of his work: famously, his ideas which contributed to the development of modern armoured warfare, and infamously, his extraordinary self-serving attack on the author Richard Aldington.

His work on armoured warfare was formulated through the inter-war years. After the Second World War, several German generals, including Heinz Guderian, credited him with having invented the tactics they had adopted for the Blitzkreig assaults. Some controversy emerged later when it appeared that Liddell Hart had leant on the German generals, or their surviving families, to give him credit in order to boost his own career.[60]

(Weidenfeld & Nicholson, 1998).

60 Liddell Hart had contact with Rommel's widow and other family, and may have prevailed upon them to boost his career as a *quid pro quo* for Liddell Hart promoting the idea of Rommel as a 'good German', fighting a fair fight and disdaining Nazism. Britain and America were trying to build up the West German armed forces as a bulwark against the Soviets. In order to quell public fears about the rise of German militarism, they had to rehabilitate the Wehrmacht to some extent, by arguing that it was not wholly composed of fanatical Nazis. The myth of Rommel was created to serve that end (the reality is that Rommel ran with hares and hunted with hounds – he did not rock the Nazi boat when climbing through the ranks of the German Army, but hedged his bets should the Von Stauffenberg plot to assassinate Hitler succeed). The

The clash with Aldington arose out of Liddell Hart's part in the creation of one of the First World War's most enduring characters, Lawrence of Arabia. Liddell Hart had written a biography of Lawrence back in the 1930s, with the assistance of Lawrence himself. It had been a substantial contribution towards creating the public image of Lawrence as the dashing Great War hero. Others followed on the same path, including Robert Graves (author of the classic Great War memoir *Goodbye To All That* as well as notable books such as *I, Claudius*). They built up the legend of Lawrence as having routed the Turks through his daring bravery, understanding of the Arabs, and strategic and tactical genius.

By the 1950s, that legend was firmly established. It was therefore to Liddell Hart's great discomfort when he learned that Aldington, a fellow Great War veteran,[61] was writing a new book intended as a 'warts and all' re-examination of Lawrence's life. Liddell Hart realised that if Aldington undertook rigorous research with an objective mind, he would soon discover that Liddell Hart and others had exaggerated Lawrence's achievements and suppressed aspects of his personal life.

Liddell Hart's strategy was to orchestrate an almost obsessive campaign against Aldington. He roped in Graves and Eric Kennington, who had illustrated Lawrence's *Seven Pillars of Wisdom*, and the three of them set about discrediting Aldington as a person. They petitioned publishers, the prime minister and even Queen Elizabeth II.

Undeterred – though he was badly affected by their vicious assault – Aldington went on to publish his book in 1955, entitled *Lawrence of Arabia: A Biographical Enquiry*.[62] Among other things, the book contained claims that Lawrence was illegitimate[63] and was homosexual, two things that would not attract comment

---

other German whom Liddell Hart certainly influenced was Heinz Guderian, the father of Blitz warfare: the German language edition of Guderian's memoirs had contained a passing mention of Liddell Hart; the English language edition, published after contact between the two men, paid an effusive tribute to Liddell Hart. In truth the work of JFC Fuller, mentioned in the entry on Field Marshal Byng in Chapter 4, was more influential on the Germans than Liddell Hart. Fuller was invited to Germany before the war and continued to complain afterwards that Britain had been fighting on the wrong side. His fascist support discredited him in Britain and hence gave the field of military history to Liddell Hart.

61 Richard Aldington (1892–1962) was commissioned as a second lieutenant in the Royal Sussex Regiment in 1917. He was wounded while serving on the Western Front and is often said to have suffered post-traumatic stress disorder. He published a number of poems and also the anti-war novel *Death of a Hero* (published in 1929, based on an earlier manuscript). Aldington's anti-war views as expressed in the book would have signalled to Liddell Hart and others that he would not be writing a hagiography of Lawrence.

62 My edition was published by Praeger in 1976.

63 The issue of Lawrence's sexuality has remained contentious. The historian Antony Copley argued in his book *A Memoir: Historian and Homosexual: Search for a Post-War Identity* (Upfront Publishing, 2016) pp 190–191 that 'Lawrence may have identified with outcast illegitimate boys and sought masochistic punishment following his humiliation at Deraa, but he was not gay. Rather he was an ascetic and celibate.'

or interest in the twenty-first century but which were both still deemed shameful in the 1950s. Aldington went on to denounce Lawrence as a charlatan, a pervert and an 'impudent mythomaniac'. He dismissed Lawrence's military achievements, ridiculed his literary style and for good measure also disputed his knowledge of medieval French poetry.

Aldington's book was highly controversial – not least because of the efforts of Liddell Hart and the others (whom Aldington termed 'the Lawrence Bureau' as a joke on Lawrence's 'Arab Bureau'). In later years, though, it has been accepted that Lawrence embellished his own story,[64] and therefore Aldington deserved at least some credit for his efforts, although one later reviewer wrote that '[r]eading Aldington's book is a bit like standing under a waterfall of venom'.[65] Some of Aldington's material was drawn upon for the legendary 1962 David Lean film *Lawrence of Arabia*, though the film was not as critical of his overall character. Liddell Hart attacked the film publicly and engaged in correspondence with one of the screenwriters, Robert Bolt.

Despite the furore concerning Aldington, Liddell Hart continued to work as an historian and was knighted in 1966. Among other things, he was dubious about nuclear deterrence and instead emphasised the need for conventional forces.

He died in 1970. In his will he donated his papers to King's College London, which later established the Basil Liddell Hart School of Military History. It now forms one of Britain's most important academic centres for the subject.

Basil and Lewis Hastings: chalk and cheese

The brothers Basil and Lewis Hastings formed quite contrasting characters. Basil was a slightly-built author, journalist and playwright, a typical man of letters of his day. Lewis was a soldier-adventurer, a physically robust sort who travelled the world perpetually in search of action and derring-do.

Basil's influence on the Savage Club went somewhat further, since he was

---

64 At the turn of the century, the author and television presenter Clarissa Dickson Wright wrote a book in which she mentioned Lawrence's estate refused permission to use some material 'but that may be because I inadvertently sent my introduction which describes his life as one of the great Boy's Own adventures of the 20th century, despite the fact that he was an alcoholic, a runt and a homosexual in the days when that was still illegal. He was a patient of my father's so I was talking from an informed position.' See Clarissa Dickson Wright, *Food: what we eat and how we eat* (Ebury Press, 2000). See also Fred Crawford, *Richard Aldington and Lawrence of Arabia: A Cautionary Tale* (Southern Illinois, 1998) and Michael Asher, *Lawrence the Uncrowned King of Arabia* (Viking, 1998).

65 Robert Irwin, 'Top Grumpy's Top Hate', *London Review of Books*, vol 21, no 4, 18 February 1999, pp 25–26.

the father of Mac Hastings, a redoubtable Savage for many years. He was also the grandfather of Sir Max Hastings, a Fleet Street grandee and one of Britain's best-selling military historians, whose work I have frequently drawn upon in this book.

Early life

Lewis was born in 1880 and Basil in 1881 in London, the second and third eldest of eleven children (the eldest being a daughter, Ethel).[66] The family lived comfortably enough by the standards of the day, although not without difficulties: in 1898, Lewis and Basil were attending Stonyhurst College in Lancashire when the former – who was in his final year – was accused of homosexual conduct. Lewis furiously denied the charge, pitting him firmly against his father, who took the view that the Jesuit teachers could not tell a lie. Lewis left home and worked his passage to South Africa, which was in the middle of the Second Boer War. A few years later, in 1903, a double tragedy occurred when their father died from a heart attack and their sister Ethel died of tuberculosis.

By the later date, Basil had left Stonyhurst and attended King's College London for a short duration (probably leaving because of lack of money) before starting work as a clerk in the War Office in 1902. He stayed there until the end of the decade, by which time his energies were directed towards freelance journalism. His writing covered a range of subjects and often took the form of light verse.

He also found time to engage in Catholic charities around his home in Denmark Hill, South London. In 1908 he married a local girl, Wilhelmina White They had two children, the future Brother Savage Douglas Edward Macdonald 'Mac' Hastings (b 1909) and Beryl Ursula Hastings (b 1911).

In 1910, he became assistant editor of *The Bystander*, a popular magazine of the time. The following year he wrote a comic play, *The New Sin*, which became remarkably successful, bringing both recognition and financial security. Basil even travelled to New York (on the RMS *Lusitania*, as it happened) in order to attend the opening night on Broadway. It was to be the high point of his success in the genre, however, since his subsequent plays did not meet with anything like the same commercial or critical acclaim, even when working with the legendary Joseph Conrad.

Lewis, meanwhile, was acting like a character out of Conrad's *Heart of*

---

66 His early years, spent in the Victorian and Edwardian middle classes, were described in his autobiography *Memoirs of a Child*, and more recently by his journalist grandson Max Hastings, *Did You Really Shoot the Television?* (Harper Press, 2010, Kindle edn).

Darkness, or perhaps someone invented by one of the two Savage 'boys-own' authors George Henty and Edgar Wallace.[67] In South Africa he had started out working as a hunter selling meat to the mining community, before serving for a time in the Cape Mounted Police. While the bookish Basil stopped growing at five foot seven (not particularly short by the standards of the day), Lewis grew well over six foot and was solidly athletic to boot. He also had some literary ability, as reflected by a verse composed during his time as a mounted policeman. It began:

> When I was out in Africa amaking of my pile
> I met a sort of auxiliary bloke got up in reg'lar style;
> He was sitting over a Kaffir pot concocting a sort of stew
> 'And so,' says I, 'excuse me please, but who the deuce are you?'
> Says he, 'I'm His Majesty's half-and-half, policeman
> and soldier too.'
> They can handle a sword or carbine, a lance or billiard cue.
> And what they learned of botany was never learned at school.
> They can follow the spoor of a cattle thief from the bleating
> of a ewe.
> Though they're only blooming hermaphrodites, policemen
> and soldiers, too.

All in all, Lewis was utterly at home in the wilds of Africa, leading the heady life of a big-game hunter. He once wrote 'To be nineteen years old, to wake before sunrise with Halley's Comet overhead, a rifle by one's side, and a whole perfect day before one on the plains, that was surely very near the crown of life. It was so cold at early morning that the frost crackled beneath our feet and the rifle barrel seemed to burn one's fingers.' Flying aircraft before the Great War had to have taken serious bravery, so to no great surprise Lewis took to it with zeal when he had the chance. He was also enthralled by the local African cultures, even if his views on black Africans would be as dated to modern eyes as his embracing of big-game hunting (which even he himself came to regret in later years). Not long before the Great War, he began to be involved in the maelstrom of South African politics, helping in suppressing a miners' strike, during the course of which a rioter died at Lewis' hand, when he cracked the rioter's head with a rifle butt.

---

67 We have already met Wallace as the reporter who gained the great scoop at the end of the Boer War. He joined the Savage Club in February 1905, Lord Kitchener's name unsurprisingly not appearing on his candidate page.

First World War

Basil

At the outset of hostilities, Basil was deemed too infirm to serve, and so continued with his writing career. The relative failure of his later plays was outweighed by the great success he enjoyed writing comic revues, a genre enormously popular during wartime – clearly, both troops on leave and the anxious families of those still at the Front were looking for escapism, not worthy drama. The most notable revue he produced was written in conjunction with the cartoonist Bruce Bairnsfather, who had served at the Front with the Royal Warwickshire Regiment as a second lieutenant until suffering shell shock during the Second Battle of Ypres in 1915. Back in Britain, Bairnsfather started drawing a series of cartoons set in the trenches featuring 'Old Bill', a walrus-moustachioed soldier barking cantankerous observations.[68] They were featured in *The Bystander*.[69] Bairnsfather and Hastings collaborated on a scene for the revue *Flying Colours*, entitled *Bairnsfatherland, or The Johnson 'Ole*. The play had a running joke about a general who had fallen into a hole, with a lower ranked character stressing over whether he should 'let him drift or fish 'im out'. The theme was a variation of a joke in Bairnsfather's most famous cartoon of the war, which depicted two desperate Tommies sheltering in a trench hole with another soldier and growling at him 'Well, if yer knows of a better 'ole, go to it'. In 1916, that cartoon was also turned into a play, called *The Better 'Ole*, though without Hastings' input.

It is noteworthy that, despite the almost paranoid censorship Kitchener was imposing upon news from the Front, the censor in Britain when reviewing *Bairnsfatherland* simply recorded that 'The authorship is a guarantee of lifelikeness and ... takes away any possible offence there could be in treating trench life lightly', and hence permitted the revue to proceed.

By 1917, demands for manpower at the Front meant that the physical requirements for new recruits had steadily been reduced, making it possible for even the comparatively feeble Basil finally to be accepted into service. He was made a corporal in the King's Royal Rifle Corps. He was, however, only rated 'B2' medically, meaning he could not serve on the very frontline: anyone in the B categories was deemed to be 'Free from serious organic diseases, able to stand service on lines of communication in France, or in garrisons in the tropics', while B2 meant they were considered 'Able to walk 5 miles, see and hear sufficiently for ordinary purposes.'

Rather than be assigned garrison duties, however, Basil was transferred to the Royal Flying Corps, where he spent his time creating a weekly newspaper

---

68 A modern reader might call the cartoons 'Blimpish', but they were before Blimp's time and may have in fact influenced David Low with his most famous creation.

69 See Gordon Williams, *British Theatre in the Great War: A Revaluation* (Bloomsbury, 2003).

for flight trainees, *Roosters and Fledglings*. He reached the rank of lieutenant in the newly-created Royal Air Force. Because of his B2 rating, he was specifically forbidden to fly except if required (for some unspecified reason) for discharging his normal duties.

Lewis

As in most other aspects of life, Lewis had a very different experience to Basil during wartime. If the role of rugged big-game hunter could have been invented for Lewis, so might be said of the war itself, such was the alacrity with which he took His Majesty's Shilling. Upon the outbreak of war, he signed up with the imperial British troops to fight against the Germans in South West Africa. Alongside him were some hardened Boer veterans whose commander had prepared his men for battle, then cabled General Botha to ask which side they were on.

If the British had struggled in the Boer War as fish out of water, the luckless German soldiers deployed in South West Africa were even more out of place. Worse for them, unlike the British in 1899, they were outnumbered and facing an enemy just as well-equipped with modern weaponry. The result was a predictable rout, with the Germans surrendering in July 1915. One almost has the impression Lewis could have defeated them single-handedly.

Upon the German defeat, Lewis promptly sailed to Britain and took a commission in the Royal Field Artillery. He served on the Western Front for the rest of the war, reaching the rank of major and being awarded the Military Cross.

Unlike most veterans, Lewis enthusiastically discussed the war at any opportunity. He began immediately upon the war's end, when he was sent to France to buck up the morale of soldiers about to try to return to civilian life (it had been noticed by his superiors that he was a good public speaker). He was confronted at one gathering with having murdered the man in South Africa during the riot. Lewis casually replied 'I didn't murder him. I broke my rifle stock over his head.'[70]

Nearly half a century later, when his great-nephew Max was working on the BBC's landmark television series *The Great War*, Lewis wrote him a letter warning him not to overdo the 'horrors of the trenches' or the generals-as-donkeys thesis, stating forcefully that conditions in the Napoleonic wars were just as bad as on the Somme and that the 1918 victories were the greatest achievements in the history of the British Army. It was a view that became something close to the received academic theory which we discussed earlier in the context of the Great War generals. And yet by the 1960s Lewis was becoming less jingoistic about

---

70 Ibid, p 34.

the war. Even when serving during the war he had noted the rows of dead at the Somme, not and in any blasé sense.

Two other Hastings brothers also served on the Western Front, with much less evident enthusiasm than Lewis. One of them, Aubery, was killed in October 1915 at Loos, having unsuccessfully sought Basil's help in transferring to the Royal Flying Corps (seemingly unaware that pilots had a higher mortality rate than soldiers in the trenches).

Post-war careers

Basil resumed his full-time writing career after the war. He wrote a play, *A Certain Liveliness*, which opened in 1919 but soon closed. He then released a dramatisation of Joseph Conrad's novel *Victory*, on which he had been working for three years in collaboration with Conrad himself.[71] It was not a critical success either, though it at least produced some income. A farce called *Hanky-Panky John* followed in 1921 but again was only a modest success. Then, in 1923, his adaptation of another novel, ASM Hutchinson's *If Winter Comes*, failed on both sides of the Atlantic.

Things sadly went from bad to worse, as in 1926 he was diagnosed with bowel cancer and soon found himself unable to write. He died in 1928, leaving his widow and two children penniless.

Lewis, on the other hand, lived on much longer. In 1920 he made the economically sound move of marrying a Scottish heiress, whom he had met whilst he was recuperating from a gas attack on the Western Front. She was divorced, which was a scandalous state of affairs at the time, but it did not deter Lewis, possibly because he had gone one worse in the form of bigamy: he had apparently married a woman in South Africa before the Great War and not bothered to secure a divorce.

Lewis and his wife had two children, but he then set off for Southern Africa again, shamelessly using her income to enjoy his lifestyle, turning up at home whenever he felt like it, and generally outliving everyone else in every sense. Even the prospect of another war with Germany did not strike any fear in him. He took the time in the 1930s to travel to Nazi Germany to see it for himself, and to buy a copy of *Mein Kampf*.

During the Second World War, Lewis (who had fooled the RAF into giving him a parachute jump though he was more than twenty years older than regulations allowed) worked as a commentator for the BBC. In the spring of 1945 he followed the troops into Germany and found himself in conversation with a fellow Great War veteran, the nonagenarian Field Marshal August von

---

71 See Martin Ray (ed), *Joseph Conrad: Interviews and Recollections* (University of Iowa Press, 1990), p 224.

Mackenson. It was all very gentlemanly until Lewis brought up the subject of the recently-liberated Belsen concentration camp, which unsurprisingly silenced the previously loquacious old German officer. Subsequently Lewis walked alone into Bremen Town Hall, waving a German walking stick at the local soldiers. 'Lewis had twenty years to live, but nothing was ever quite as good again. Peace brought the introduction of a permanent close season on Germans, and the old hunter was too long in the tooth to return to his beloved bush.'[72]

Coda: The Hastings Clan, the Great War and the Savage Club

Basil joined the Savage Club in June 1916. He was on good terms with many of the other Savage literati of the day, including Edgar Wallace, Hilaire Belloc, JM Barrie and James Agate, and clearly was an enthusiastic member of the Club:[73]

> In that clubbable age, he loved the Savage, whose members were almost all writers, painters, actors, music hall stars. He was a regular performer, sometimes producer, at the club's smoking concerts. Poems were recited, songs sung, turns rehearsed by some of the great comics of the day, including George Robey and Wee Georgie Wood ... Though Basil was a Londoner by upbringing and instincts, he professed a devotion for rural life, which caused him to rent a country cottage, tend his vegetable garden, and enthuse about the superiority of Sussex pubs to London ones. He organised a regular Savage 'Country Members' Night', at which his friends dressed in yokels' smocks and sang jolly rustic songs. Keenly gregarious, Basil was never happier than when chattering in the club bar with a cluster of theatrical friends.

Lewis, for his part, 'blew into London at irregular intervals, towering over the bar of the Savage Club as he captivated Mac with his tales of shooting elephant and lion, of camps in the bush under the stars'[74] ('Mac', as noted, being Basil's son.) He did not actually join the Club until February 1941 but clearly turned up before then as a guest of Basil and Mac in turn.

Like his father, Mac came to love the Savage Club, which he joined in October 1936:

> He lived upon a principle that was the antithesis of Groucho Marx's. Any club that would admit Mac became, in his eyes, the cynosure of exclusivity and excellence. He shared Basil's enthusiasm for the Savage, then in Carlton House Terrace, with its matey and—from a less roseate perspective than his own—somewhat *passe* congregation of writers, artists, actors and publishers.

---

72 Max Hastings, *Did You Really Shoot the Television?*, op cit, p 108.
73 Ibid pp 53–54.
74 Ibid, p 63. Incidentally Lewis's son Stephen had never got on with him, mostly due to Lewis's protracted absences from the family home, but he won the MC and served with the embryonic SAS.

Mac was unable to continue his formal education after Basil's death, even though various family friends including Edgar Wallace offered financial support. He declined their offers, feeling that it was incumbent on himself to support his mother. He found work first as a clerk at Scotland Yard and later in the publicity department of a catering company. During the latter role, he started writing freelance journalism and eventually was successful enough to leave his day job and concentrate on writing full time.

In 1939, he started working for *Picture Post*. The publication aimed for location reporting and live-action photography. Max recalled:[75]

> Father's appearances were most readily identified with the presents he brought home from far-flung places: an authentic cowboy outfit from America; model soldiers which he showed me how to array into a British fighting square; toy guns of many shapes and sizes; smelly Bedouin robes from Jordan; the mounted hoof of a bison he had shot in India; a Norwegian model of the balsa raft Kon-Tiki, in which Thor Heyerdahl had recently crossed the Pacific, and which Father himself constructed with extraordinary dexterity from a kit of logs and string. For the most part, however, he was more frequently observed going than coming: to shoots and fishing expeditions, assignments abroad, his beloved Savage Club.

Mac's taste for adventure – heavily influenced by Lewis – meant that when the Second World War broke out he went looking for action near the Front. Initially he was embedded in torpedo boats to Channel convoys. He went ashore with the Normandy invasion in 1944, where he gained a reputation for being courageous and foolhardy, something echoed decades later by Max's famous stunt in becoming the first man into Port Stanley at the end of the Falklands War.

After the war, Mac edited *The Strand Magazine* until it folded in 1950, whereupon he resumed working freelance. One of his more notable projects was working (with Brother Savage John Worsley) on the *Eagle* magazine. Most of his conributions were in the guise of the globetrotting 'Eagle Special Correspondent'.[76]

He appears in numerous places in Bradshaw's centenary book, as both the subject and the teller of anecdotes. In one of the latter he wrote:[77]

> Willie Richardson, our Adelphi librarian, was a diminutive little man who used to pass his time scribbling obscure paragraphs for obscure papers in the library; nobody quite knew what it was in aid of. But the habit exasperated James Agate into protesting that he made a noise like two mice mating in a waste-paper basket.

Mac died in 1982.

---

75 Ibid, p 127.

76 See also *Drumbeat* (No 138 – Summer 2017), which reported a Savage lunch on 10 May 2017 celebrating the *Eagle* and explaining how it came into being.

77 Bradshaw, op cit, p 86. See also pp 71, 109, 111, 123, 141, 148–9.

Gilbert Jessop: 'The Croucher'

As well as the pantheon of writers, artists, scientists and entertainers we see throughout this book, the Savage Club of the first half of the twentieth century contained several luminaries from the world of cricket. Charles W Alcock was an immensely important early sporting organiser, responsible for the first cricket test to be played in England, and serving as secretary of Surrey County Cricket Club from 1872 until 1907. He also edited the *Cricket* newspaper for nearly 25 years, and edited *James Lillywhite's Cricketers' Annual* (an early rival to the cricketing bible *Wisden Cricketer's Almanack* from 1872 to 1900). If anything, he was even more influential in early football.[78] CB Fry was arguably the finest all-rounder of his generation. Neville Cardus and RC Robertson-Glasgow were two of the greatest cricket writers of any generation.[79] Later, the South African Bob Crisp had a decent if not exceptional cricket career, but due to his off-field activities (including bravery bordering on lunacy when commanding tanks in the Second World War), he was described in his obituary by *Wisden* as 'the most remarkable man ever to play test cricket.'[80] Even Lewis Hastings would have had to take a bow to some of Crisp's life adventures.

Joining them as a Savage member was Gilbert Jessop, whose name still survives as a byword for a big-hitting batsman.[81]

Early life

Gilbert Laird Jessop was born Cheltenham in 1874, the eleventh child of Dr Henry Jessop, a local surgeon. There was no particular tradition of cricket in the family, though Dr Jessop was renowned as an all-round sportsman who was a skilled billiards player and shot. Gilbert took up cricket at Cheltenham Grammar School and soon excelled, but had to leave school in 1890 when his father died. He was forced to work in a school instead of studying in it: in those days, schools sometimes took on a form of apprentice teacher, who functioned somewhat like teaching assistants do nowadays. By the age of 20, his county cricket career had begun, joining WG Grace at Gloucestershire.

---

78 Perhaps most notably of all, Alcock came up with the idea of the FA Cup. He was also heavily involved in the formation of Wanderers FC, a highly influential early club, and organised the first ever football international, and coming up with the idea of the FA Cup, as well was playing to international level. Wanderers were an enormously influential early club. Alcock played for England against Scotland in March 1875, scoring a goal in a 2–2 draw.

He joined the Savage Club in May 1888, giving his address as the Oval, Kennington – the site of the 1880 test and still the home of Surrey Cricket today.

79 Robertson-Glasgow joined on 18 March 1934 and Cardus on 13 December 1934.

80 *Wisden* 1995. Crisp joined the Club in October 1945.

81 Alcock died in 1907, Cardus's eyesight kept him out of the Great War, Robertson-Glasgow was too young (only just, being born in 1901), while CB Fry spent the conflict running Hamble Naval College and was thus exempt from serving at the Front.

He attended Cambridge in the late 1890s but left without a degree, though his cricketing prowess had been fully on display. In 1899 he played his first test match, and went on to become one of the most memorable players of his time. *Wisden* later summarised his career:

> There have been batsmen who hit the ball even harder than Jessop, notably C. I. Thornton and the two Australians, George Bonnor and Jack Lyons, but no one who did so more often or who, in match after match, scored as rapidly. Where Jessop surpassed all other hitters was in the allround nature of his scoring. At his best, he could make runs from any ball, however good it might be. Although only 5ft 7ins in height, he bent low as he shaped to play, a method which earned him the sobriquet of The Croucher. Extraordinarily quick on his feet, he was ready to hit firm-footed if the ball were pitched well up and equally, when it was of shorter length, to dash down the pitch and drive. When executing leg-side strokes, he almost lay down and swept round with the bat practically horizontal, putting great power behind the ball as, thanks to strong, supple wrists, he also did when bringing off the square cut. Lightness of foot allied to wonderful sight made it possible for him to run out to the fastest bowlers of his time—Richardson and Mold— and at the peak of his form pull or straight-drive them with almost unerring certainty. No one ever approached him in this particular feat; indeed, nobody else could have attempted it with reasonable hope of success.

Upon the centenary of his birth, *The Cricketer* magazine published an article celebrating his phenomenal cricketing gifts:[82]

> His Test match appearances covered the years 1899 to 1912, but the selectors found him a problem; some were ready to regard him as an automatic choice, others regarded him as too much of a gamble. His greatest day was at The Oval on August 13, 1902, when England wanted 263 to beat Australia on a bad wicket. They lost three for 10, and five wickets were down for 48 when Jessop went in. Defeat seemed inevitable, but he scored 104 out of 139 in 77 minutes, and in the end England won by one wicket. An article in the recent Cricketer winter annual has supported by analysis the general feeling that this was the greatest innings ever played in Test cricket. His hundred remains the fastest in Anglo-Australian Test cricket—some 16 minutes faster than anyone else.

In Jessop's day, cricket in England was ruthlessly class-divided between gentleman amateurs and working professionals, the former supposedly playing for fun and the latter to earn a crust. In reality, the best-known gentleman amateur in history, WG Grace, made a fortune out of the game, shamelessly calling the money he made 'expenses' rather than income. Grace's problem was that he did

---

82 Gerald Brodribb, 'The Legend of Gilbert Jessop', *The Cricketer*, May 1974, http://www.es-pncricinfo.com/cricketer/content/story/134791.html.

not have the private income of the archetypal amateur. Jessop did not either, so had to make a living on the side. He did so by way of freelance journalism, beginning in 1897 with a piece for *The National Review* on cricket. There was some controversy over whether a gentleman amateur ought to be doing such things, and there was a separate controversy over whether ex-players made better correspondents than professional journalists – the latter question has been debated many times in many sports in the century that has passed since Jessop's playing career.[83]

Despite those mutterings, Jessop enjoyed measurable success as a journalist and author. By the end of 1903, he had written two books on cricket and had become a regular contributor to the *Daily Mail* – so regular that his biographer later reflected he may as well have been on the staff.[84] As well as cricket he wrote about many other sports, and wrote the odd short story and other ephemera. He was thus able to join the Savage Club in January 1905 under the category of literature. At some point he resigned or otherwise had his membership lapse, for the candidate books record him re-joining in June 1919.

Jessop was rightly proud of the fact that, unlike more than a few player-journalists (then as now), he actually wrote the columns appearing under his name. There was one interesting Savage-related exception. In 1904, he was sent to cover an all-in wrestling match at the Royal Albert Hall, for which the *Mail* had set aside a full column on the front page. Unfortunately the 'bout' only lasted a couple of minutes, since one of the 'competitors' broke his wrist. Jessop called someone to his house who was soon to be a fellow Brother Savage – Edgar Wallace – and, properly in the spirit of future Savagery, asked for a favour and gave him a bottle of whisky by way of thanks in advance. The piece was duly submitted and was considered a great success – no surprise given Wallace's pedigree as a prolific writer of 'boys' own' adventure stories and the future creator of King Kong.

First World War

When the war began, Jessop was aged over 40, but he joined up without hesitation. In December 1914, he was commissioned as a captain in the 14th Manchester Regiment. He was not sent to France with the BEF, but instead remained in England, where among other things he took part in various morale-boosting cricket matches organised by the army. On one notable occasion he scored 94 against a team including SF Barnes, statistically one of the greatest bowlers in

---

83 Cricket fans should read the extremely amusing commentary in *Wisden* 1996 (John Wisden and Co) in the 'Editor's Notes' and in the section 'Cricket and the Media'.
84 Gerald Brodribb, *The Croucher: A biography of Gilbert Jessop* (London Magazine edn, 1974).

history.[85] He also took part in a recruiting campaign along with another great cricketer of his era, Archie MacLaren.[86]

Jessop's sporting prowess was noted during a training exercise on throwing hand grenades – his went far further than anyone else's, and he did not expose himself above the parapet when throwing. By early 1916, however, as the British Army in France prepared for the great attack near the Somme River, Jessop was suffering severe back pain. He had been transferred to the Lincolnshire Regiment, but seems to have remained unfit for active service, and was sent to a medical clinic in Bath, Somerset. At the end of May, he underwent treatment described as 'Radiant Heat, Dousing with total immersion for 30 minutes at temperature of 201–300 degrees', which took place in a closed container. To modern readers the treatment sounded bad enough if it went to plan: instead, disastrously, the catch on the lid had slipped and Jessop was unable to escape as the attendant had left the room. When he was finally rescued, he had suffered serious heart damage, and was never to play a serious game of cricket again.[87]

Jessop returned to service with the Lincolnshire Regiment, but could only undertake limited duties and was invalided out of the army altogether in November 1917. He moved to Clevedon in Somerset, and was permitted to continue wearing his army uniform – an important measure given the hostility that was shown to apparently able-bodied men not at the Front. In June 1918, however, he suffered a serious heart attack as part of the continuing fallout from the appalling accident at Bath.

Post-war career

For the rest of the war and for some years after, he continued his work as a journalist while moving the family around different places in Britain. There was a slight upswing in the family fortunes not long after his heart attack, as his wife gained an inheritance. The money would have come in handy for his re-election to the Savage Club in June 1919.

In 1924 he became Secretary of Edgware Golf Club. He held the post until 1936, when the club grounds were sold for housing development. Jessop would not have been impressed, since he had campaigned hard in his role as a sportsman and journalist for towns and cities to have playing fields, having noticed how much fitter and stronger children from the countryside were in his time.

---

85 In Barnes' benefit match, Jessop belted him all around the park, prompting the taciturn Staffordshire bowler to growl – in a combination of WG Grace and Fred Trueman – 'Hey, Croucher, this is my ruddy benefit, not thine'.

86 During the First World War, MacLaren joined the Royal Army Service Corps as a lieutenant and worked in the Manchester area recruiting men into the army. He was promoted to captain before leaving the army on health grounds.

87 Gerald Brodribb, op cit, p 180.

After the closure of the golf club, Jessop and his wife moved to the Vicarage of Fordington St George, Dorchester, Dorset, to live with their son, also called Gilbert Jessop. He saw out the rest of his days there, dying in 1955 at the age of 80.

Sir Compton Mackenzie: nationalist, writer, raconteur, spy

Sir Compton Mackenzie was a prolific English-born Scottish writer, who wrote extensive works of fiction, biography and history as well as being well-known as a cultural critic and raconteur. He was a devoted Scottish nationalist and one of the founders of the Scottish National Party. During the First World War, he was embroiled in the field of espionage. All in all, one imagines his rich and varied experiences, along with his obvious erudition would have made him an ideal Savage.

Early life

Edward Montague Compton Mackenzie was born in County Durham in 1883. His parents were actors and theatre company managers, evidently well connected in that regard since his sister, Fay Compton, starred in many of Brother Savage JM Barrie's plays including *Peter Pan*.

Mackenzie attended St Paul's School in London and Magdalen College, Oxford, graduating from the latter with a degree in modern history. As a teenager he served in the Territorial Army in the 1st (Hertfordshire) Volunteer Battalion, The Bedfordshire Regiment, a line infantry regiment.

Soon after leaving university, Mackenzie began his remarkable career as a writer. His most notable early work was the two-part novel *Sinister Street*, published in 1914. The journalist and author Allan Massie said of Mackenzie's pre-war oeuvre:[88]

> *Sinister Street* is the masterpiece of Compton Mackenzie's first period, as an English, rather than Scottish, novelist. It offers not only a wonderfully vivid evocation of late Victorian and Edwardian England but a disturbing account of the hero Michael Fane's personal development.
>
> Mackenzie's own disposition was sunny, but in this novel there is an awareness of the attraction of evil and the dark side of life which he would seldom recapture in his later work. It was this and the exploration of adolescent sexuality which cause the book to be banned by circulating libraries, the young Cyril Connolly to be beaten for having it in his possession at Eton, and Edmund Wilson, who shared his friend Scott Fitzgerald's admiration for Mackenzie to declare that "the 'motif of utter foulness' is one of the most uncanny things in the book; you feel that you are not walking on solid ground, that it may give way at any moment and let you into the sewer" ...

---

88 Allan Massie, 'On Compton Mackenzie', https://www.faber.co.uk/blog/on-compton-mackenzie/.

Yet it is a book of glowing light as well as dark shades. The Oxford section is entrancing—as fine as Evelyn Waugh's portrait of Oxford in *Brideshead Revisited*. Max Beerbohm thought "There is no book on Oxford like it. It gives you the actual Oxford experience. What Mackenzie has miraculously done is to make you feel what each term was like".

Ford Madox Ford considered that the novel was "possibly a work of real genius", and it persuaded Henry James that Mackenzie was "very much the greatest talent of the new generation". He praised its "modernity" and, though there are some lush passages that now seem somewhat dated, that judgement was acute. *Sinister Street* is more than a period piece. Almost a hundred years after its first publication, it retains the "modernity" of all great novels. That is to say, its essence is not dated, but vividly alive.

In 1905, he married Faith Stone, who was to inspire some of his later work. From 1913 until 1920, the couple had a home on the Italian island of Capri at Villa Solitaria. The island appealed to the bohemian set of the day, since it had a liberal attitude in general and towards in sexuality in particular – something Faith took advantage of when she had an affair with the Italian concert pianist Renata Borgatti. A frequent visitor to the island who became friends with Mackenzie was his future Brother Savage, W Somerset Maugham, whom we will meet again shortly. Maugham reported one of his friends on the island expressing relief that there weren't any foreigners about – a strange wish from someone who had presumably deliberately travelled abroad.

Mackenzie and Faith returned to Britain in July 1914, partly due to the worsening European situation, but primarily because Mackenzie was hoping to volunteer for service against Ulster.[89]

First World War

When the war broke out, Mackenzie was not physically robust enough to serve on the frontline and was told that the army had no use for any married subalterns aged 31 anyway. Instead, he finished his novel *Sinister Street* and returned to Italy, somewhat depressed at being unable to serve. He was greatly relieved to feel he had been able to contribute in some fashion when he wrote an article for the Commission for Relief in Belgium. The piece was so well-received he was sent various letters of thanks from members of the Commission, most notably from Herbert Hoover – the future President of the United States.

Having been told that he would stand a better chance of serving in warmer climes, Mackenzie finally managed to acquire a posting with Sir Ian Hamilton's

89 Compton Mackenzie, *Gallipoli Memories* (Doubleday, Doran & Co, 1930), p 1. At the time of writing, the book had been digitised and placed online: https://archive.org/details/gallipolimemorie00comp.

'Mediterranean Expedition' – the invasion of Gallipoli – and was given a commission in the Royal Marines. One of his first duties, performed on board the ship to Cape Helles, was to censor letters home written by the soldiers. He vividly recalled one written on several sheets of toilet paper which concluded 'No more bloody armies for me. The next bloody army I join is the Salvation bloody army and don't you forget it.'[90]

Upon arrival in the theatre, when he was presented to Hamilton, the latter complained to him 'Lord Kitchener is a great genius, but like every great genius he has blind spots'. At that point Mackenzie felt Istanbul would never be taken.[91]

As the Gallipoli expedition slid to failure, Mackenzie moved into working for British Intelligence, and stayed in the Mediterranean region after the Turkish victory. Throughout 1916, he built up a network in neutral Greece. He was clearly talented at the work, but found himself getting caught up in Greek domestic politics. He supported 'Venizelism', the political movement and party named after the politician Eleftherios Venizelos. The movement was based on Greek nationalism and liberal democracy. It was also pro-West and anti-Communist. Venizelos ruled Greece from 1910 until the end of 1916, when an episode known as the 'Noemvriana' split Greece between Venizelos, who wanted Greece to join the war on the side of the Allies, while the pro-German King Constantine I wanted Greece to remain neutral, which effectively sided with the Central Powers.[92] Mackenzie was then forced to leave Greece, as was King Constantine and his son, Crown Prince George. George later became George II of Greece and, in 1942, as HM George of the Hellenes, was made a life member of the Savage Club.

In 1917, Mackenzie established the Aegean Intelligence Service, and was even offered the Presidency of the Republic of Cerigo when it enjoyed a short stint as an independent state before being re-absorbed into Greece as the civil war

---

90 *Gallipoli Memories*, op cit, p 31.

91 Ibid, p 45. Mackenzie also quoted Churchill's own view that a mental barrier descended upon those engaged in the Gallipoli campaign and prevented success as surely as the Turkish bullets.

92 Venizelos allowed the landing of Allied forces in Thessaloniki, whilst the King's actions enabled the German-Bulgarian forces to take over a Macedonian fort. Civil war loomed, with Venizelos' followers establishing a provisional state in Northern Greece in August 1916, with support from the Allied (Entente) powers, aiming to retake lost territory in Macedonia. Greece was effectively split in two.

After intense diplomatic negotiations and an armed confrontation in Athens, involving Allied troops facing off against royalists, Constantine I abdicated in June 1917, replaced by his second son Alexander.

Venizelos returned to Athens and led a newly unified Greece into war on the side of the Entente powers. Greece thus ended on the winning side, and obtained new territory by the Treaty of Sèvres. However, the whole episode would have severe repercussions in Greece for the next two decades. It contributed to Greece's defeat in the Greco-Turkish War, the collapse of the Second Hellenic Republic and the establishment of the undemocratic Metaxas regime.

played out. Mackenzie's unexpected offer mirrored a later story about his Brother Savage CB Fry, who was supposedly offered the throne of Albania in the 1920s. Both Mackenzie and Fry declined the chance to become statesmen.

In September 1917, with the Allies having prevailed in Greece, Mackenzie was recalled to the country, but had made too many enemies within the service to be able to play a role for the rest of the war. He had, however, clearly impressed a number of influential individuals, since after the war he was awarded an OBE, the French *Légion d'honneur*, the Serbian Order of the White Eagle and the Greek Order of the Redeemer.

Post-war career

Mackenzie resumed his writing career after the war. In 1920, he and Faith left Capri and moved to the Channel Islands, where Mackenzie was the Tenant of Herm and Jethou until 1923.

In 1928, he was one of the co-founders of the Scottish National Party, along with Hugh MacDiarmid, RB Cunninghame Graham and John MacCormick.

Mackenzie joined the Savage Club in January 1930. In the same decade, he started to put his money where his Scottish mouth was: in 1931, for example, he succeeded Stanley Baldwin as Rector of Glasgow University, defeating Oswald Mosley in the campaign for the post. He also built a house on Barra, in the Scottish Isles, where he found much creative solitude.

The most interesting of his post-war activities for our purposes were the memoirs of his war service and the imbroglio in which they landed him with the British government. His *Turkish Memories*, covering the Gallipoli campaign was uncontroversial, but *Greek Memories*, published in 1932, his account of his time in intelligence in Greece, enraged Whitehall. In 1933, he was prosecuted under the Official Secrets Act, charged with having quoted from secret documents and having identified a number of heads of station.[93] Among other things, the book set out the relationship between the Secret Service, the War Office and the Foreign Office, and how the structure had been reorganised in 1917 to co-ordinate with the Director of Military Intelligence's Department. The book also explained how many heads of station abroad worked under the secret cover of passport control officers through British legations, and how agents communicated with each other using a 'dictionary code'.

Mackenzie fired some shots by way of defence. Among the individuals whom the prosecution claimed had been wrongly identified in the book included a Captain Christmas and a Major CE Heathcote-Smith. Mackenzie pointed out that Christmas had died in 1922 while Heathcote-Smith, who was still alive, had

---

93 The case was something of an early precursor to the notorious 1980s book *Spycatcher* by Peter Wright.

already published the fact of his membership of the intelligence services in his entry in *Who's Who*.

The prosecution offered an agreement (what American, but not English, lawyers of the day would have called a 'plea bargain') in which Mackenzie would plead guilty and receive a fine of £500 with £500 costs. The attorney general, Sir Thomas Inskip, who was prosecuting, then annoyed the trial judge so much that both the fine and the costs order were reduced to £100 apiece. Nevertheless, even that reduced amount was a harsh financial blow, since Mackenzie's own (unrecoverable) defence costs amounted to more than £1,000.

To try to recoup some of the financial burden, Mackenzie asked Whitehall if the offending passages might be identified so they could be redacted and the book then published. Whitehall refused, but Mackenzie did go on to release an amended version in 1939. The original was kept in the British Library and was eventually published in 2011, containing a copy of the Secret Intelligence Service memo identifying the offending passages.

Mackenzie was evidently undeterred by his legal vicissitudes, since in 1933 he published the novel *Water on the Brain*, which took many more digs at the Secret Service. It also revealed a few quirks, such as the fact that the chief of the Service always wrote in green ink. It seems that the Service was more chastened than Mackenzie by the previous court action, since they did not attempt to stop the publication or otherwise censor *Water on the Brain*.

When not annoying his former masters, Mackenzie was a prolific novelist. His most lasting works, thanks to their screen adaptations, are probably *Monarch of the Glen* (1941) and *Whisky Galore* (1947). *Whisky Galore* was turned into a feature film in 1949 and again in 2016. The story was a fictional take on real events in 1941 when a cargo vessel bound for the United States with 28,000 cases of whisky ran aground on the island of Eriskay, an island visible from Mackenzie's Barra home. *Monarch of the Glen* was made into a successful television series between 2000 and 2005, although the programme toned down the book's Scottish nationalism.

Aside from his writing, Mackenzie was also rather prolific in the marital stakes, being married three times. Faith died after they had been together more than half a century. In 1962, after her death, he married Christina MacSween, but she died in 1963. Finally, in 1965 he married Christina's sister, Lilian MacSween.

Mackenzie was knighted in 1952. In the same year he suffered defeat in a very different court case from his memoirs action, when the Court of Appeal ruled[94] that money from the sale of the copyright of his books constituted income rather than a capital receipt as he had argued.

---

94 *Mackenzie v Arnold (HM Inspector of Taxes)* (1952) 33 TC 363.

He died in 1972, and was interred at Eoligarry on Barra. His biographer Gavin Williams wrote of him that—

> Although Mackenzie's output of novels (including delightful books for children), essays, criticism, history, biography, autobiography, and travel writing was prolific—a total of 113 published titles—it can truly be said that if he had never written a word he would still have been a celebrity. He had a personality as exhibitory and colourful as his writing, and remained throughout his life a gregarious man with a brilliant sense of comedy. Flamboyant, a raconteur and mimic, he was no less memorable as the formidable scourge of politicians, bureaucrats, and governments, and the passionate defender of the ostracised, the shunned, and the wronged.

W Somerset Maugham: storyteller and spy

Undoubtedly the master of the short story, William Somerset Maugham has to rank as one of the best-known of all Savage authors. Like most people from the period one detects outmoded standards, attitudes and values in his life and work, but the quality of his writing and storytelling has never dated and many of his books are still in print.

Early life

Maugham was born in the British Embassy in Paris, in 1874. The slightly unusual venue was because Maugham's father, Robert Ormond Maugham, worked as a legal adviser for the embassy, and was anxious to ensure his son was a British citizen – not least because anyone born on French soil was eligible for French conscription.

His mother died of tuberculosis in January 1882, just after Maugham's eighth birthday. Maugham never recovered from her loss, and kept a photograph of her by his bedside for the rest of his life. The family losses continued two years later when his father died of cancer.

Maugham was sent to Britain to be brought up by his uncle, but he did not have a happy childhood. He attended The King's School in Canterbury, but struggled at first, given that French was his first language and he was physically weak. Once he turned 16, he had had enough and persuaded his uncle to allow him to travel and study at Heidelberg University in Germany. Whilst there he wrote his first book, a biography of the opera composer Giacomo Meyerbeer.

Upon returning to Britain, he declined to follow older family members into the law, and instead studied medicine for five years at St Thomas's Hospital in Lambeth. Later in life he claimed to have learned much from his time as a medical student which he was able to incorporate into his fiction. Throughout his medical course he wrote in his spare time, and in 1897 published his first novel, *Liza of Lambeth*, drawing on the lives of the residents in a nearby slum.

The novel was such a success that he left medicine to become a full-time writer. It was to be another decade before he repeated the same commercial success, though, with his play *Lady Frederick* (1907). In 1908, he published *The Magician*, which was inspired by the famous (or infamous) occult leader of the time, Aleister Crowley, who would later influence a much younger Savage author, Dennis Wheatley. Crowley was annoyed by the book and accused Maugham of plagiarism. Perhaps reflecting the general ridiculousness of Crowley and his work, the accusation did not affect Maugham very much personally or professionally.

By the outbreak of the Great War, Maugham was very well established as a writer, with ten plays and ten novels to his name.

First World War

Maugham was anxious to join the war effort, but was too old for frontline service. Instead, he became one of the British Red Cross's 'Literary Ambulance Drivers', a group of 24 well-known authors including Ernest Hemingway who happened to be able to drive (by no means a universal skill in 1914). He described his service in his memoir *The Summing Up*:[95]

> I had a friend who was a cabinet minister and I wrote and asked him to help me to do something, whereupon I was invited to present myself at the War Office; but fearing that I should be set to clerical work in England and anxious to get out to France at once I joined a unit of ambulance cars. Though I do not think I was less patriotic than another my patriotism was mingled with the excitement the new experience offered me and I began keeping a note-book the moment I landed in France. I kept it till the work got heavy and then at the end of the day I was too tired to do anything but go to bed. I enjoyed the new life I was thrown into and the lack of responsibility. It was a pleasure to me who had never been ordered about since I was at school to be told to do this and that and when it was done to feel that my time was my own. As a writer I had never felt that; I had felt on the contrary that I had not a minute to lose. Now with a clear conscience I wasted long hours at estaminets in idle chatter. I liked meeting a host of people, and, though writing no longer, I treasured their peculiarities in my memory. I was never in any particular danger. I was anxious to see how I should feel when exposed to it; I have never thought myself very courageous nor did I think there was any necessity for me to be so. The only occasion upon which I might have examined myself was when in the Grande Place at Ypres a shell blew up a wall against which I had been standing just as I had moved over to get a view of the ruined Cloth Makers Hall from the other side; but I was too much surprised to observe my state of mind.

He continued writing and proof-reading during periods of quiet at the Front,

95 Published by William Heinemann Ltd, 1938. Quotes are from pp 53ff.

and in 1915 published the novel *Of Human Bondage*, which became possibly his best-known work. (For some random trivia, a 1934 film production of the book formed an important early role for Bette Davis.)

After spending some time in England promoting the novel, Maugham wanted to re-join the war effort. Rather than return to his ambulance unit, he joined British Intelligence, a role considered more suited to someone of his intellect, as indeed it had been for Compton Mackenzie. In September 1915, Maugham was sent to Switzerland to join the British effort aimed at disrupting the work of the 'Berlin Committee', a group of Indian nationalists formed in Germany the previous year.

Maugham was modest in his memoir when recalling his cloak and dagger career. He described with more relish how he went to America and the South Pacific once his work in Switzerland concluded:

> Later on I joined the Intelligence Department where it looked as though I could be more useful than in somewhat inadequately driving an ambulance. The work appealed both to my sense of romance and my sense of the ridiculous. The methods I was instructed to use in order to foil persons who were following me; the secret interviews with agents in unlikely places; the conveying of messages in a mysterious fashion; the reports smuggled over a frontier; it was all doubtless very necessary but so reminiscent of what was then known as the shilling shocker that for me it took most of its reality away from the war and I could not but look upon it as little more than material that might one day be of use to me. But it was so hackneyed that I doubted whether I should ever be able to profit by it. After a year in Switzerland my work there came to an end. It had entailed a good deal of exposure, the winter was bitter and I had to take journeys across the Lake of Geneva in all weathers. I was in very poor health. There seemed nothing much for me to do at the moment, so I went to America where two of my plays were about to be produced. I wanted to recover my peace of mind shattered through my own foolishness and vanity by occurrences upon which I need not dwell and so made up my mind to go to the South Seas.

His voyage to the South Pacific was predictably memorable:

> Now I entered a new world, and all the instinct in me of a novelist went out with exhilaration to absorb the novelty. It was not only the beauty of the islands that took me, Herman Melville and Pierre Loti had prepared me for that, and though it is a different beauty it is not a greater beauty than that of Greece or Southern Italy; nor was it their ramshackle, slightly adventurous, easy life; what excited me was to meet one person after another who was new to me. I was like a naturalist who comes into a country where the fauna are of an unimaginable variety. Some I recognized; they were old types that I had read of and they gave me just the same feeling of delighted surprise that I had once in the Malayan Archipelago when I saw sitting on the branch of a tree a bird that I had

never seen before but in a zoo. For the first moment I thought it must have escaped from a cage. Others were strange to me and they thrilled me as Wallace was thrilled when he came upon a new species. I found them easy to get on with. They were of all sorts; indeed, the variety would have been bewildering but that my powers of observation were by now well trained and I found it possible without conscious effort to pigeon-hole each one in my awareness. Few of them had culture. They had learnt life in a different school from mine and had come to different conclusions. They led it on a different plane; I could not, with my sense of humour, go on thinking mine a higher one. It was different. Their lives too formed themselves to the discerning eye into a pattern that had order and finally coherence.

Upon his return to Britain, Maugham was sent by British Intelligence to Petrograd to try to stave off the Russian Revolution,[96] but apart from the quixotic nature of the assignment his health was beginning to fail:

> I was diffident of accepting the post, which seemed to demand capacities that I did not think I possessed; but there seemed to be no one more competent available at the moment and my being a writer was very good 'cover' for what I was asked to do. I was not very well. I still knew enough medicine to guess the meaning of the hæmorrhages I was having. An X-ray photograph showed clearly that I had tuberculosis of the lungs. But I could not miss the opportunity of spending certainly a considerable time in the country of Tolstoi, Dostoievski and Chekov; I had a notion that in the intervals of the work I was being sent to do I could get something for myself that would be of value; so I set my foot hard on the loud pedal of patriotism and persuaded the physician I consulted that under the tragic circumstances of the moment I was taking no undue risk. I set off in high spirits with unlimited money at my disposal and four devoted Czechs to act as liaison officers between me and Professor Masaryk who had under his control in various parts of Russia something like sixty thousand of his compatriots. I was exhilarated by the responsibility of my position. I went as a private agent, who could be disavowed if necessary, with instructions to get in touch with parties hostile to the government and devise a scheme that would keep Russia in the war and prevent the Bolsheviks, supported by the Central Powers, from seizing power. It is not necessary for me to

---

96 Petrograd (St Petersburg) had been the Russian capital since 1732. In March 1917, during the 'February Revolution', Tsar Nicholas II abdicated, ending the Romanov dynasty. A provisional government took over, but on 7 November 7, 1917 (OS October 25), the Bolsheviks, led by Vladimir Lenin, stormed the Winter Palace in an event known thereafter as the October Revolution. They swept the provisional government aside and assumed all power. Their seat of government remained in Petrograd, but the city came under threat after Germany invaded the Western Estonian archipelago.. The Bolsheviks therefore moved the capital to Moscow in early 1918, where it remains today, although they also made peace with the Germans by the Treaty of Brest-Litovsk in March.

The Russian Civil War continued nevertheless, with the Western Allies making a failed attempt to support the White Russians against the Bolsheviks, as we will return to with Brother Savage Raymond Massey.

inform the reader that in this I failed lamentably and I do not ask him
to believe me when I state that it seems to me at least possible that if
I had been sent six months before I might quite well have succeeded.
Three months after my arrival in Petrograd the crash came and put an
end to all my plans.

I returned to England. I had had some interesting experiences and
had got to know fairly well one of the most extraordinary men I have
ever met. This was Boris Savinkov, the terrorist who had assassinated
Trepov and the Grand Duke Sergius. But I came away disillusioned.
The endless talk when action was needed, the vacillations, the apathy
when apathy could only result in destruction, the high-flown protestations, the insincerity and half–heartedness that I found everywhere
sickened me with Russia and the Russians. I also came back very ill
indeed, for in the position I was in I could not profit by the abundant
supplies that made it possible for the embassies to serve their countries on a full stomach and I was (like the Russians themselves) reduced
to a meagre diet. (When I arrived in Stockholm, where I had a day to
wait for the destroyer that was to take me across the North Sea, I went
into a confectioner's, bought a pound of chocolates and ate them in
the street.) A scheme to send me to Rumania in connection with some
Polish intrigue, the details of which I now forget, fell through. I was
not sorry, for I was coughing my head off and constant fever made my
nights very uncomfortable. I went to see the most eminent specialist I
could find in London. He packed me off to a sanatorium in the North
of Scotland, Davos and St. Moritz at that time being inconvenient to go
to, and for the next two years I led an invalid life.

Maugham was still recovering when the war ended.

The other significant event in Maugham's life during the Great War was his
marriage to Syrie Wellcome. Wellcome had been married to a successful businessman, Henry Wellcome[97] – ironically, a fellow member of the Savage Club,
rendering Maugham's actions far from brotherly. In 1915, Syrie and Maugham
had a daughter, Mary Elizabeth Maugham. Henry Wellcome brought an action
for divorce on the ground of adultery, naming Maugham as co-respondent. He
was granted a decree absolute in May 1917. Thereafter, Syrie and Maugham
married and changed Mary's surname to Maugham (incidentally, she was always
called 'Liza'). Syrie became a successful interior decorator, but the marriage did
not last. After they separated, Maugham only had same-sex relationships. He
lived with Gerald Haxton until the latter's death in 1944. He then lived with
Alan Searle until his own death in 1965.

---

97 Henry Wellcome (1853–1936) was an American British pharmaceutical entrepreneur. He
founded the pharmaceutical company Burroughs Wellcome & Company in 1880, which went
on to be one of the four companies which merged to form GlaxoSmithKline. He also left
considerable sums in his will for charity, which were used to establish the Wellcome Trust, one
of the world's largest medical charities.

Post-war career

Once his health recovered, Maugham resumed his lucrative writing career. His play *The Letter* enjoyed much success in London in the mid-1920s, and was made into a film twice. The first was in 1929 with Jeanne Eagels in the lead, and the second was in 1940 starring Bette Davis, who was nominated for an Oscar for her performance.

In 1926, his marriage having failed, Maugham moved to the French Riviera. His writing career continued to go from strength to strength, encompassing plays, short stories, novels, essays and travel books. He became especially well-known for his short stories.

During the Second World War, he moved to America to avoid the risk of internment by Nazis or their Vichy flunkies. He worked on film adaptations of his own stories in Hollywood, and made supportive speeches for the war effort at the behest of the British government. In 1944, he moved to England, where he stayed until the end of the war, and then returned to his villa in France.

He was made an honorary life member of the Savage Club in 1955. Apart from his travels – including a return to Britain in 1957 to attend the Savage Club's centennial dinner – he lived in France for the rest of his life. He retained friends from the Savage, including the artist Sir Gerald Kelly, whom he used as the model for various characters in his books; Kelly for his part painted Maugham on no fewer than 18 occasions.

In 1962, Maugham sold a collection of paintings, some of which had already been assigned to Liza by deed. Liza sued him and won the then-enormous award of £230,000. Maugham's response was to claim that she was not his biological daughter, and to adopt Searle for the purposes of making him his heir. He publicly attacked Syrie, who had died by then, claiming that Liza had been born out of wedlock – a scandalous accusation at the time. His thoroughly ungentlemanly actions gained him much opprobrium in society.

Liza successfully contested the change in Maugham's will, but when Maugham died in 1965, Searle still inherited a very substantial amount: £50,000 in cash, together with the contents of the French villa, Maugham's manuscripts and his revenue from copyrights for 30 years.[98]

HC McNeile: the man behind Bulldog Drummond

Herman Cyril 'HC' 'Sapper' McNeile MC was a Great War veteran responsible for a well-known literary character, Bulldog Drummond, who like many others considered in this book has been the subject of adverse historical revisionism.

---

98 Liza died in 1998. She was married twice and had two children with each husband. One of her grandchildren is the autistic savant pianist, Derek Paravicini.

Early life and First World War

McNeile was born in 1888. He was normally known as Cyril McNeile in person, less formally 'Mac' to his friends, and wrote under the name 'HC McNeile' or the pseudonym 'Sapper'. He went to Cheltenham College and then the Royal Military Academy, Woolwich, following which he was commissioned into the Royal Engineers as a second lieutenant in July 1907. Further training followed at the Royal School of Military Engineering before he was posted briefly to Aldershot. In June 1910, he was promoted to lieutenant, and then spent three years serving with the 3rd Field Troop in Canterbury. In January 1914, he was posted to Malta and promoted to the rank of captain.

Upon the outbreak of war, McNeile was recalled to England. He was sent to France as part of the BEF in November 1914. Most of his war record has since been lost,[99] but it is known he served with a number of Royal Engineer units on the Western Front and that he fought in the First and Second Battles of Ypres, the Somme and in the Hundred Days Offensive of 1918. He suffered at least one gas attack.

In 1916, he was awarded the Military Cross in 1916 and was twice mentioned in despatches. He was ultimately promoted to the rank of acting lieutenant-colonel and commanded a battalion of the Middlesex Regiment. When the war ended, he was convalescing after suffering a leg injury.

Whilst serving in the trenches, to alleviate the boredom, he started writing short stories. Many were published in the *Daily Mail*. Since serving officers were not permitted to publish under their own name whilst on duty, the stories were credited to 'Sapper', a *nom de plume* contrived by Lord Northcliffe in reference to McNeile's posting with the Royal Engineers. McNeile was so prolific an author that his wartime efforts amounted to over 80 collected and uncollected stories. They sold well and Northcliffe was sufficiently impressed to want McNeile to work as a war correspondent, but the army refused to release him from active duty.

Post-war career

After the war, McNeile moved onto the reserve officer list. He was confirmed in the rank of major in 1919. In 1920, he published the first story about his most famous literary creation, Bulldog Drummond. Drummond had appeared in an earlier short story as a police detective, but not in his familiar form as 'a demobil-ised officer who found peace dull' after the Great War.

---

99 About two-thirds of First World War service records were destroyed by German incendiary bombs which hit a warehouse of the National Archives. The surviving records are referred to as the 'Burnt Documents'.

Drummond was a gentleman with a private income, who placed an advertisement in *The Times* offering to assist anyone in trouble, as a means of dealing with his post-war ennui. He normally ended up trying to foil the scheme of some black-hearted foreign fiend, using the skills of stealth and hand-to-hand combat he had fashioned in the trenches.

The early Drummond novels gave rise to controversy, on two related grounds. The first was the blatant xenophobia in the stories. The second was that the ethos of Drummond appeared rather sympathetic to fascism, if not an outright personification of the philosophy.

The first point we have already encountered in respect of other authors of the age. Was McNeile any worse than his contemporaries such as Agatha Christie, Hergé or Hugo Lofting?[100] It seems unlikely: a better explanation is simply that McNeile wrote in a more florid style, being partial to the double-adjective throughout his books, not just when being disobliging about foreigners.

As for McNeile being a fascist sympathiser, in his case I suspect it is more a case of later critics retrospectively classifying his views in a form with which modern readers are familiar. Drummond was more of a public school/junior officer bully with innately conservative values concerning duty, respect, order and authority, rather than a proto-Mussolini.

Either way, the books were best-sellers and the character of Drummond was a major influence on WE Johns' Biggles and Ian Fleming's James Bond. Drummond appeared on both stage and screen as well, and continued to be a success up to McNeile's death in 1937.

McNeile had joined the Savage Club only a year before, being nominated in April and elected in June 1936. He died from throat cancer, often assumed to be a legacy of the gas attacks in the trenches. His friend Brother Savage Lieutenant-Colonel Gerard Fairlie, upon whom the Drummond character had been partially based,[101] and later the author Henry Reymond continued with the Drummond novels.

---

100 Lofting created his famous Dr Doolittle character when serving in the trenches in the First World War, in letters written to his children.

101 Francis Gerard Luis Fairlie (1899–1983), Scottish author and scriptwriter. He went to Sandhurst in 1917 and served in the Scots Guards from 1918–1924. He was an army boxing champion and a member of the British bobsleigh team in the 1924 Winter Olympics. 'Gerald had all the qualifications: a sort of Walter Mitty character, but for real. He could survive a couple of rounds on the British Amateur Golf Championship and ride a point-to-point': Victor Saville and Roy Moseley, *Victor Saville in his own words* (SIU Press, 2000), p 177.
Incidentally, Fairlie appeared on Arnold Ridley's episode of the television programme *This is Your Life* (1976).

Victor Odlum: media magnate, military man

One of a number of eminent Savage Canadians of the Great War era,[102] Brigadier-General Victor Odlum led a long life of adventure and controversy as a soldier, journalist, businessman and diplomat.

Early life and First World War

Victor Wentworth Odlum was born in 1880 in Cobourg, Ontario. His father, Edward Odlum (1850–1935), was a historian and supporter of the largely defunct movement known as British Israelism.[103]

In the Second Boer War, Odlum served with The Royal Canadian Regiment, but he left the army upon his return and started working as a journalist. He began as a reporter, but by the age of just 25 was editor of the paper *Vancouver World*.

When the First World War began, Odlum immediately stepped forward to serve. He was commissioned as a major in the 7th Battalion of the First Canadian Division of the Canadian Expeditionary Force, second-in-command to Lieutenant-Colonel William Hart-McHarg.

The Canadian forces moved to the front line in April 1915. They arrived in time to be the subject of a grim historical milestone – the first gas attack of the war, at the start of the Second Battle of Ypres. The attack occurred at sunset on 22 April 1915. Odlum distinguished himself with tremendous bravery during the battle. He and Hart-McHarg were surprised by small arms fire from hidden Germans, and were forced to take cover in a shell-hole. Hart-McHarg had been badly wounded, so Odlum, with no regard to his personal safety, ran up a hill under heavy fire to seek medical help. Despite his efforts, Hart-McHarg died of wounds, and Odlum assumed command of the 7th Battalion.

The 7th Batallion was soon transferred to the 3rd Brigade under Brigadier-General Richard Turner. They were moved to St Julien, where once again they came under very heavy attack. His men started to run low on ammunition and were suffering serious casualties. Calls for assistance went unheeded so Odlum put together an ammunition party – including his brother Joseph – and sent them to reinforce the frontline. Tragically, the party was hit by shellfire and several of its members, including Joseph, were killed in full view of Odlum's command post.

One can scarcely begin to imagine the strain Odlum had to have been under

---

102 For space reasons I have not discussed at length all of the Canadian Savages, though one of their number, Captain Harwood Steele MC, wrote an early history of the Canadian contribution, *The Canadians in France 1915–1918* (EP Dutton & Co, 1919). Steele joined the Savage Club in March 1927 under literature.

103 British Israelism (also called Anglo-Israelism) held that the British were genetically, racially, and linguistically the direct descendants of the Ten Lost Tribes of ancient Israel.

at that point, but he ordered a withdrawal and conducted it with great professionalism.

His superlative abilities under fire led to regular promotions, but despite his advancing rank he continued to visit the front lines and personally take part in attacks, suffering wounds on three occasions.

As well as the men under him, Odlum took care of his commanding officer, General Arthur Currie, by dipping into his own pocket (as did a fellow officer and future Brother Savage, David Watson[104]) to help Currie repay regimental funds he had 'borrowed' before the war, and thus Currie escaped an embezzlement charge.

He finished the war with the rank of brigadier-general.

Post-war career

Odlum joined the Savage Club in March 1919, under the category of literature, but he soon returned to Vancouver. In 1923, he established the investment firm Odlum Brown with his fellow veteran Colonel Albert 'Buster' Brown. Odlum and other 7th Battalion veterans also built a memorial tablet in Christ Church, Vancouver, for Hart-McHarg.

From 1924 until 1928 he served as a state politician. He also re-entered journalism by purchasing the Vancouver *Daily Star*. Rather less impressively, his paper participated in the 'yellow journalism' of the time, the most famous exponent of which was probably his American contemporary William Randolph Hearst. The disreputable stories run by Odlum included stirring hatred against the nascent Chinese immigrant population, communists and unionists. He eventually closed the *Star* rather than concede ground to the union over wages.

His pugilistic style evidently did not put off the establishment, however, since he served on the board of the Canadian Broadcasting Corporation from its beginning in 1936 until the start of the Second World War. Once war broke out, he used his connections to obtain a commission as a major-general in command of the 2nd Canadian Infantry Division.

By that stage, however, Odlum was out of touch with modern warfare and

---

104 Major General Sir David Watson, KCB CMG (1869–1922) was, like Odlum, a Canadian journalist, newspaper owner, and senior military officer. He enlisted as a young man with the rank of private, but by 1912 had been raised to lieutenant-colonel. In 1914, he volunteered for the Canadian Expeditionary Force and was soon given command of the 2nd Battalion, CEF. In 1915 he was promoted to brigadier-general and took command of 5th Brigade, 2nd Canadian Division. He was promoted to major-general and took command of the 4th Canadian Division upon its formation in 1916. Watson fought in most of the major Canadian battles of the war, including Second Ypres, the Somme, Vimy Ridge, Passchendaele, Amiens, Second Arras, and Cambrai.

After the war, he joined the Savage Club in March 1919, though returned to Canada to work in newspapers.

he was soon removed from command and appointed High Commissioner to Australia (though his son served during the conflict). He stayed in the diplomatic service until 1952, serving in China and Turkey as well as Australia.

He died in 1971.

Reginald Pound: half a century a Savage

Reginald Pound was one of the Savage Club's most prolific authors and longest-standing members.

Early life and First World War

He was born in Whatlington, East Sussex, in 1894, the son of a grocer. In 1911, he was recorded working as an auctioneer's clerk. When the First World War began, he joined the 5th Battalion of the Royal Sussex Regiment as a private. He was later commissioned as a lieutenant in the Shropshire Light Infantry.[105] Pound was sent to France in mid-February 1915. Like Agate and a number of other officers, he sent back to Britain a number of articles and commentaries which formed his first publications on the conflict.

Post-war career

Pound married Cicely Margaret Dawes in 1916 and they went on to have seven children.

After being demobilised, he worked as a freelance writer for some years. In the mid-1920s the editor of the *Daily Express* invited him to become the first literary editor of the paper. He transformed the leader page into a platform from which well-known public figures could sound off on issues of the day. The feature was then copied by every other major newspaper.

In the 1930s Pound joined the *Daily Mail*. During the Second World War, he worked for the Ministry for Information, the BBC and, from 1942, was editor of *The Strand Magazine*. One of his notable achievements in that role was to publish colour reproductions of some of Winston Churchill's paintings. He was in the Savage Club the day that it was hit by a bomb during the Blitz, and wrote a brilliant account of the event, later reproduced in full in Percy Bradshaw's centenary book of the Club.

After the war, in 1946, he left *The Strand Magazine* and was replaced by Brother Savage Macdonald Hastings. The magazine lasted until 1950; Hastings was the final editor.

From the early 1950s, Pound became a prolific biographer. His first work was

---

105 There is a good website dedicated to the history of the regiment: http://www.shropshire regimentalmuseum.co.uk.

on Arnold Bennett, for which he won the WH Heinemann Foundation Award. His second, an official biography of Lord Northcliffe, published in 1959, was perhaps his best-regarded. Other subjects included Henry Selfridge, the department store magnate; the artist Sir Alfred Munnings, a noted destroyer captain; Admiral Lord Mountevans; Eric Gillies, a great surgeon; Brother Savage Robert Falcon Scott of the Antarctic and Brother Savage AP Herbert. He was elected a Fellow of the Royal Society of Literature in 1953.

The lost generation

For our purposes, Pound's most interesting book was his 1963 First World War study called *The Lost Generation*. The title has long been a popular phrase to encapsulate the sheer scale of the losses in the conflict. Approximately 750,000 British lost their lives with a further 200,000 Empire soldiers – more than any other conflict in British history. By way of comparison, British casualties in the Second World War totalled 442,000, and that included many more civilians killed by the Blitz.

One factor which further concentrated the sense of loss for some was that the army famously created the 'Pals' Battalions', the units composed of people who worked, lived or sometimes played together in the same occupation, village or sports team. The reasoning was that they would fight better with their friends and colleagues than with strangers. The terrible downside was that some entire villages, companies or other groups lost all or nearly all their young men, sometimes at a stroke if there was a large-scale failed assault. Just to add a surreal touch, those villages who had escaped wholly unscathed felt a weight of shame that they had not contributed to the general sacrifice – another indication of a changing perspective on the world, since it is hard to imagine present generations feeling such regret.

In that light, it might seem that the Savage Club was fortunate to have such an apparently short casualty list: only 9 dead out of 147 who served in one capacity or another. And yet it is not so surprising, because the number of casualties has to be set against the sheer scale of the war. Nearly 90 per cent of those who served in the British Army in the trenches came back alive. Proportionately the casualty rate was almost half that of the English Civil War,[106] though the population was much smaller in the seventeenth century. Even in more recent wars,

---

106 The respective figures are 2 per cent of the population in the First World War and about 4 per cent of the population of England and Wales, and considerably more than that in Scotland and Ireland, in the Civil War. See 'Viewpoint: 10 big myths about World War One debunked', *BBC Magazine*, 25 February 2014, http://www.bbc.co.uk/news/magazine-25776836.

See also the BBC guide 'How did so many soldiers survive the trenches?' which points out that the average battalion spent only about five days of each month in the front line, http://www.bbc.co.uk/guides/z3kgjxs.

though, the death rate in the Crimean War was proportionately higher than the First World War.

One might also compare the toll of British dead with that of their chief ally France and their chief opponent Germany. France's total casualties were approximately double those of Britain, even though the two countries' populations were about the same, and proportionately Germany's losses were nearly double those of Britain. Also, France suffered in a way Britain did not, since a large part of her territory was occupied for much of the conflict. If the tales of German brutality towards civilians were exaggerated by wartime propaganda, most historians have since agreed that the Germans were not benevolent occupiers.

In those circumstances, some[107] have argued that the phrase 'Lost Generation' is hyperbole. To expand further, the number of males aged 20–40 (the age group which did the bulk of the fighting) per thousand of the population in Britain dropped between 1911 and 1921 from 155 to 141: a significant loss, 'but not sufficient to destroy a generation – if one defines a generation in mass terms as a group of people of roughly similar age bound together by a common historical experience and a common fate.'[108]

First-hand accounts

So much is all grist to the mill of First World War debates. But the value of Pound's book goes much beyond statistics and grand sweeps. It contains many graphic descriptions of the combat and portraits of young individuals whose lives were ended tragically early by the war. Here, for example, is Pound's description of the first poison gas attack by the Germans, which we have just seen while discussing Victor Odlum. Drawing upon an account written by a territorial of Queen Victoria's Rifles (QVR), Pound wrote:[109]

> The QVRs, a London battalion, had just come out of the fighting for Hill 60. Utterly weary, they were resting in a meadow near the Poeringhe-Ypres road. Many of the men dropped their kits and fell instantly asleep. "suddenly down the road from the Yser Canal came

---

107 See for example Robert Wohl, *The Generation of 1914* (Harvard University Press, 1979) and Gordon Corrigan, *Mud, Blood and Poppycock,* op cit.

108 Wohl, op cit, p 113.

109 Pound, op cit, pp 130–31. The quote is from Anthony M Hossack in *Everyman in War* (Dent, 1930). The gas in the attack was chlorine, used against two French colonial divisions. They had tried to use tear gas earlier in the war, without success. They did use xylyl bromide on the Eastern Front in January 1915, with limited success because of the cold, though the Russians did report casualties. The Western Front attack described by Pound formed the only German offensive of 1915, referred to as the Second Battle of Ypres. The attack did not result in any significant gain for the Germans, but it prompted all sides to begin developing poison gas. In total, over 100,000 tons of chemical weapons agents were used in the conflict, causing 500,000 injuries and killing nearly 30,000. After the war, the Geneva Protocol of 1925 banned the use of chemical weapons in war but not their development or stockpiling.

a galloping team of horses, the riders goading on their mounts in a frenzied way; then another and another, till the road became a seething mass with a pall of dust over all. Plainly something terrible was happening. What was it?"

Officers, including some of the Staff, were astounded. While more horses and shouting men filled the road, "over the fields streamed mobs of infantry, the dusky warriors of French Africa; away went their rifles, equipment, even their tunics that they might run faster. One man came stumbling through our lines. An officer of ours held him up with levelled revolver. 'What's the matter, you bloody lot of cowards? says he. The Zouave was frothing at the mouth, his eyes started from their sockets, and he fell writhing at the officer's feet." On the northerly breeze was borne a sickly odour that was followed by throat irritation and smarting eyes. Men going home on leave had dreadful tales to tell of the slow asphyxiation of their comrades.

"There was no difficulty in finding them," wrote an officer who visited a field hospital the next day. "The noise of the poor devils trying to get their breath was sufficient direction. Twenty of the worst cases were on mattresses, all more or less in a sitting posture, propped against the walls. Faces, arms, hands, were a shiny grey–black. With mouths open and lead-glazed eyes, they were all swaying backwards and forwards trying to get breath, struggling, struggling for life. There was nothing that could be done except to give them salt and water emetics. The gas fills up the lungs and bronchial tubes with froth, which finally suffocates the victim. It is like slow drowning, taking sometimes two days."

No one who saw (as the present writer did) those first victims, many of them the finest specimens of young Canadian manhood from Winnipeg, can ever forget it.

The use of poison gas and the response in the form of gas masks of increasing sophistication forms another enduring image of the Great War. That first attack caused 1,200 dead and 3,000 wounded. In total, approximately 20,000 deaths and 500,000 wounded on the Western Front were caused by poison gas, comprising 186,000 British and Empire troops, 130,000 French, 107,000 Germans and 76,000 Americans – horrific figures, but for some grim contextualisation, they amounted only to about 3.4 per cent of the total Western Front casualties, and may be compared with 500,000 Russian gas casualties on the Eastern Front. 'Yet its significance did not lie only in the number of casualties; all sides invoked the use of gas to accuse the enemy of using inhumane weapons. In particular, it epitomised a qualitatively new mobilisation of the tools of war, and a changed perception of war itself. In the contemporary picture of the war, with its iconic images of soldiers in the trenches, the wearing of gas masks already symbolised how every conceivable weapon was being used to attack the bodies of enemy soldiers. Any conventional notion of fair play in positional warfare, involving fixed, transparent rules and a modicum of trust as in the Christmas Truce of

1914, went by the board in the face of these new implements of battle.'[110] The strongest indication of how badly all sides had to have been shaken by the horrors of gas is that the Western protagonists did not use it on each other in the Second World War, for fear of reprisals.

A great Savage

Away from the horrors of war, Pound was an enthusiastic member of the Savage Club for more than half a century, having been elected in September 1924. He was in the chair for the Club's ninety-ninth anniversary dinner. Of the Club he once said:

> Each of us has his own private chapel of memory, hung with the banners of Savage Club friendships. Old familiar faces, voices, mannerisms, come crowding back. We raise our glasses to our Club and let us gratefully remember those who can no longer hear the beat of our famous drum.

Pound died in 1991.

Alec Waugh: prisoner and poet

A member of the well-known Waugh writing dynasty, Alec Waugh was a successful author in the mid-twentieth century and doubly notable in the present context as a prisoner of war and war poet.

Early life and First World War

Alexander Ragan 'Alec' Waugh was born in 1898. He was the elder brother of Evelyn Waugh and the son of Arthur Waugh, who was also an author, critic and publisher. Alec Waugh went to Sherborne School in Dorset, which he later recorded in a semi-autobiographical novel, *The Loom of Youth* (1917), a book inspired by Arnold Lunn's *The Harrovians*. Waugh's book was highly controversial because it contained references, albeit somewhat veiled, to homosexuality.[111]

There has since been controversy over whether Waugh was dismissed by the school's old boys' club, The Old Shirburnian Society, because of the book or whether he had resigned. Whichever was the case, the controversy did not harm Waugh since the book was a best-seller.

Waugh was too young when the conflict began in 1914, but he signed up when he became of age and was commissioned in the Dorset Regiment in May 1917. He saw action on the Western Front at Passchendaele. In March 1918, he was

---

110 Figures and quotation both from Jörn Leonhard, *Pandora's Box: A History of the First World War* (Belknap Press, 2018), pp 265–66.
111 At the time of writing, the book was free online on Project Gutenberg.

captured by the Germans near Arras, and spent the remaining months of the war as a prisoner of war. He was first held in Karlsruhe and later the Mainz Citadel.

Waugh wrote of his experiences soon after being freed, in his book *The Prisoners of Mainz*, published in 1919. The book opened with a description of the gas masks British soldiers had to wear, and a gas attack taking place as part of the German Operation Michael:[112]

> The small box respirator, like the thirty-nine articles of the Faith, should be taken on trust; one is quite prepared to believe in its efficiency. Countless Bass instructors have extolled it, countless memos from Division have confirmed their panegyrics; and with these credentials one carries it on one's chest in a perfect faith; but one has no wish to put its merits to the test. No one if he can help it wishes to have his face surrounded by elastic and india-rubber, and his nose clamped viciously by bent iron; and for that reason my chief memory of March 21st was the prolonged discomfort of a gas mask.
>
> For from the moment that the barrage opened at 5 am, the air was full of the insidious smell of gas. Masks were clapped on, and thus hooded the machine-gunners fumbled desperately in search of stoppages; it was an uncomfortable morning.

Waugh then described how his company had to move in advance of the expected German assault. They settled down in their new location with a substantial delivery of mail to read, telling themselves that the impending action might not involve them, but their peace was short-lived. He recorded the following events from 27–28 May 1918:[113]

> My sleep did not last long. Within an hour Evans was shouting in my ear.
>
> "Hell of a strafe upstairs. I think they're coming over."
>
> And indeed there was a strafe. Verey lights were going up all along the front. Three dumps were hit in as many minutes, from the right came the continual crump of "minnies." Luckily we were in the shelter between the barrage on the eighteen-pounders and the barrage on the front lines. The only shells that came disconcertingly close were those from our own heavies that was dropping short, like a man out of breath.
>
> At seven o'clock the Germans came over, and by twelve we were being escorted to Berlin.

Waugh was soon interrogated, though not in an arduous fashion, and it quickly emerged that his interrogator knew much more than the average British squaddie about the structure of the British Army: 'Any one possessing a quarter of

---

112 Alec Waugh, *The Prisoners of Mainz* (Chapman and Hall, 1919), p 1.
113 Ibid, pp 15ff.

his knowledge could have had a staff appointment for the asking.' There was no brutal interrogation of the type one always reads about from Second World War prisoners, with jack-booted Gestapo officers promising ways of making them talk. Instead, the main concern of the Germans questioning Waugh seemed to be to impress upon the British that Germany, not the Allies, was fighting a just war, and that the anti-German propaganda was wrong.

Waugh's group soon marched to Vitry and thence to Douai, where they began to suffer from boredom, exhaustion and, above all, hunger. The Germans installed what have to have been very primitive listening devices in prisoners' rooms, though Waugh brushed it aside by saying the only conversations began with unsavoury epithets preceding the word 'Boche'.

Their next stop was Marchiennes, where conditions were still harsh, though they were lucky to have a guard from Alsace, who much preferred English and French company to that of Prussians and managed to obtain more food for them. At the prisoner distribution in Karlsruhe, their next destination, they discovered more inept guards, reflecting the fact that the more capable soldiers were more likely to be deployed to the Front. They also found the local population to be curious about them, rather than hateful, and to be thoroughly weary of the war.

After a week at Karslruhe, Waugh was moved to Mainz, where he would remain until the end of the war:

> The routine of the camp was very simple. At eight o'clock in the morning breakfast, consisting of coffee, was brought to the rooms. At half-past nine there was a roll-call. At twelve midday there was lunch in the mess-rooms; at three in the afternoon coffee was brought round to the rooms; at six there was supper in the mess-rooms. At nine the doors of the block were closed; at nine-thirty there was an evening roll-call; at eleven lights went out.

Once again Waugh managed to obtain some books, but could not escape the overriding problem of hunger: 'It is hard not to make the first two months a mere chronicle of sauerkraut'. He did not believe the Germans were deliberately withholding food; instead, they simply had no more to give. By that stage of the war the blockade was beginning to tell, and thus Waugh's belief was most probably correct. 'The psychology of semi-starvation would make an interesting study' he wrote, 'and it would bring out very clearly the irrefutable truth that the only way to get any peace for the mind is by throwing sops to the physical appetites'. The men tried progressively more desperate ways of getting more food. They received money from Britain, but a profiteering German intermediary left it much less valuable once it had been converted into marks.

By May 1918 Waugh and his fellow prisoners assumed they would be in for the long haul, envisaging a stay of two years. They started to turn their mind to civvie street, reasoning that whatever happened their soldiering days were finished. An effort to provide education in the camp met with much initial enthusiasm, which dwindled swiftly 'for really people do not want to be taught things' wrote Waugh with a degree of ennui, even if he himself kept trying to study as best he could. Sporting activities were also less of a diversion that one might have expected: injuries from playing football on the hard ground could not be treated since there was no medicine, the hockey sticks were soon broken, and tennis could not be played until equipment arrived from England, but even then there was precious little to go around and a game for four players at most at a time was not going to occupy 600 prisoners.

Two newspapers were found in the camp, one amusingly entitled the *Anti-Northcliffe Times*, which Waugh never saw, and another called *Continental Times* – a Berlin-printed propaganda rag which the prisoners easily saw through. Its efforts were the same as those of the Germans with whom Waugh interacted in person – to paint Germans as the victims of Russian brutality, and to blame everyone else for starting the war.

Waugh also found the Germans much better disposed to the British than the French. That general sentiment continued once the war finished and he was waiting around to be repatriated. The German civilians did not understand why the blockade was not lifted instantly, nor why they had to suffer in other respects since they did not consider themselves responsible for the war.

Post-war career

Following the Armistice, Waugh returned to England but went on to spend much of his life overseas, as a full-time novelist. The fact that his second wife, an Australian woman, Joan Chirnside, was very well-off also helped facilitate his lifestyle. His travels seem to be the reason for leaving and rejoining the Savage Club; he joined initially in January 1920,[114] and was re-elected in December 1936 after a period of absence.

Waugh did not enjoy the same critical or commercial success as Evelyn, or their nephew Auberon – who once remarked waspishly that Alec 'wrote many books, each worse than the last'. But his 1955 novel *Island in the Sun* was a best-seller. Not only that, but he was paid a then-record sum for the film rights. The resultant 1957 film of the same name was notable for starring Harry Belafonte, who also sang the well-known theme tune, and for inspiring the creation of Island Records, an important company in the history of reggae music.

Waugh also enjoyed much success with his 1973 novel, *A Fatal Gift*. Of particular interest to Savages would be his books on alcohol: 1959's *In Praise of Wine*

---

114 I think there is an error in the candidates' book: it states that he was nominated in December 1919 and elected in January 1919 – the latter I presume should be January 1920.

& Certain Noble Spirits and the 1968 work *Wines and Spirits*. Being an oenophile would have been a great asset to his membership of the Club. But more important for our purposes are his poems of the Great War, which are reminiscent of the style of Wilfred Owen. His best-known was 'Cannon Fodder', the opening lines of which read:

> Is it seven days you've been lying there
> Out in the cold,
> Feeling the damp, chill circlet of flesh
> Loosen its hold
> On muscles and sinews and bones,
> Feeling them slip
> One from the other to hang, limp on the stones?
> Seven days. The lice must be busy in your hair,
> And by now the worms will have had their share
> Of eyelid and lip.
> Poor, lonely thing; is death really a sleep?

Waugh died in 1981.

Dennis Wheatley: almost a gentleman

Dennis Wheatley was one of the most successful authors in Britain, or indeed globally, from the 1930s to the 1960s. Among other things, his character 'Gregory Sallust' provided another inspiration for Ian Fleming's Bond. As a young man, Wheatley served on the Western Front, almost but not quite living the part of the raffish young officer to which he aspired and who would appear in various guises in many of his novels.

Early life and early war

Dennis Yeats Wheatley was born in 1897, the son of a wine merchant. He attended Dulwich College – which he hated, and from which he was expelled for allegedly forming a 'secret society'. He then enrolled as a British merchant navy officer cadet on the training ship HMS *Worcester*, which functioned as a sort of nautical public school, complete with the bullying and beatings one associates with Roald Dahl stories of a similar era. Wheatley later called it 'a pretty savage jungle', which was not a complimentary nod to his future club's conviviality.

He was aged 17 when the First World War began, and was earning some money in the family wine business. Two of his friends were members of the Territorial Westminster Dragoons. Wheatley tried to join them, but failed the riding test. In all probability that saved his life, since the regiment went on to be almost annihilated at Gallipoli in 1915.

Through his father's connections, he was commissioned in the City of London Territorial Royal Field Artillery as a second lieutenant. Wheatley had been trying to enlist in the ranks, but his elevation to the officer class was of substantial social significance at the time; as recorded in the *London Gazette* it made him a 'temporary gentleman'.

He remained in England for the first three years of the war. In his memoirs, he recalled how he had a rather hedonistic time on the Home Front. He kept a diary of his female conquests, most of whom, according to his biographer, would have been prostitutes.[115] He enjoyed the popular music of the time, such as the ditty 'She Was Poor But She Was Honest', later made famous by Brother Savage Billy Bennett.

Wheatley tried and failed to be accepted for the Royal Flying Corps due to being colour blind – possibly another lucky escape given the dangers of flying at the time. He also annoyed a brigadier-general who then attempted to have him promoted to staff captain in charge of trench mortars on the frontline. That was yet another exceptionally dangerous job even by the standards of wartime, but the plan failed since Wheatley was diagnosed with pneumonia.

Upon Wheatley's recovery in early 1917, his battalion was sent to France, but he remained in England. He was assigned to the 6th Reserve Brigade at Biscot Camp, near Luton, joining a number of invalided or convalescent soldiers. While there, Wheatley made friends with a soldier named George Tombe. Tombe was a would-be gentleman, and clearly something of a rogue, in which capacity he provided Wheatley with inspiration both for his personal life and for some of his later literary characters.

To the Front

Finally, on 8 August 1917, Wheatley was sent to France. Initially, behind the lines, he continued to lead a similar lifestyle to his time in England, making use of the local prostitutes at Le Havre. He soon experienced the blunt horror of the reality of war, though, when he was moved closer to the front line. En route, he saw countless shattered vehicles and carts on the supply road – supply routes being one of the prime targets for enemy artillery.

Wheatley was never sent over the top as a frontline infantryman, nor was he even placed on garrison duties in a frontline trench, but he came close enough to enemy lines to come under shell fire. He saw the grim results of artillery and was given the gruesome ancillary task of putting down wounded horses.

By a stroke of fortune, his time in danger did not last long as he was reassigned to the IV Corps ammunition dump at Ytres, a ruined village on the Somme. His

---

115 Phil Baker, *The Devil is a Gentleman: the life and times of Dennis Wheatley* (Dedalus, 2011, Kindle edn).

role there was to supervise the placement and camouflaging of the unloaded ammunition. It gave him enough time to start his first novel.

He then moved around to various other ammunition dumps and was able to watch the opening phases of the Battle of Cambrai in November 1917, though once again he took no part in the actual fighting and continued instead to work on ammunition supply.

His comparative luxury was shattered in early 1918, as the German Operation Michael crashed towards his position. He managed to retreat and to organise men under his command sufficiently well for them to escape danger. Finally, in April 1918, with the Germans renewing their attack near his position, Wheatley contracted bronchitis and was sent home, reaching England on 15 May 1918.

Years later, Wheatley ascribed his bronchial suffering to the effects of the Germans' poison gas. That claim, however, was simply false. He never mentioned gas in any of his contemporaneous writing. Nor was he recorded as having the full panoply of symptoms associated with gas – certainly nothing resembling the horrifying description from Reginald Pound we saw earlier.

Wheatley's biographer concluded:[116]

> Wheatley's army career had not been glorious, but he had done his duty; no less, if no more. He was well-liked by the men, seemingly because he was cheerful and humane. In later years he became President of the Old Comrades Association, where he was able to meet the men socially and get a better sense of what they thought of him. Far from seeing him as a monocle ubermensch, it seemed they regarded young Lieutenant Wheatley as a kind of mascot.

Post-war career

In 1919, Wheatley took over running the family's wine business, but trade fell away during the Great Depression and Wheatley began working as an author. His book *The Forbidden Territory*, published in 1933, was a great success. As well as adventure stories and thrillers, Wheatley also had much success writing occult stories, and met the notorious 'black magic' Svengali Aleister Crowley, a faintly ridiculous character notorious for his 'work' in the supernatural (and for being a double agent during the First World War) who, as we saw earlier, had some inter-actions with Somerset Maugham.

Unlike some writers, most notably among Savages probably Henry Williamson and Sapper McNeile, Wheatley did not use the Great War extensively in his fiction, though he did make the occasional reference. In his best known novel, *The Devil Rides Out* (1934), for example, a character explains:

---

116 Baker, op cit.

"War, Plague, Famine and Death. We all know what happened last time those four terrible entities were unleashed to cloud the brains of statesmen and rulers."

"You're referring to the Great War I take it," Rex said soberly.

"Of course, and every adept knows that it started because one of the most terrible Satanists who ever lived found one of the secret gateways through which to release the four horsemen."

"I thought the Germans got a bit above themselves," Rex hazarded, "although it seems that lots of other folks were pretty well as much to blame."

"You fool!" De Richleau suddenly swung upon him. "Germany did not make the War. It came out of Russia. It was Russia who instigated the murder at Sarajevo, Russia who backed Serbia to resist Austria's demands, Russia who mobilised first and Russia who invaded Germany. The monk Rasputin was the Evil genius behind it all. He was the greatest Black Magician that the world has known for centuries. It was he who found one of the gateways through which to let forth the four horsemen that they might wallow in blood and destruction – and I know the Talisman of Set to be another. Europe is ripe now for any trouble and if they are loosened again, it will be final Armageddon. [...] We've got to kill Mocata before he can secure the Talisman and prevent his plunging the world into another war.

Therein some might suspect a German apologist, but the consensus of Wheatley enthusiasts and critics alike seems to be that the passage was more anti-Russian than pro-German. Although his works are redolent of the values of the day, they cannot plausibly be described as fascist or even proto-fascist.

As well as his writing, Wheatley invented a number of board games in the 1930s – a popular form of entertainment in his time.

He joined the Savage Club in August 1936.

During the Second World War Wheatley served in the London Controlling Section, which coordinated strategic military deception and cover plans. As a well-known author, he was engaged by the War Office, for whom he wrote numerous papers including planning for D-Day. He was awarded the US Bronze Star for his role in the war effort.

After the war Wheatley continued as a successful author, introducing the Sallust series and a different series on espionage, the 'Julian Day'. He worked the occult into his more conventional series on occasion, and was considered something of an authority on black magic and Satanism.

Wheatley died in 1977.

Henry Williamson: a literary genius lost

Henry Williamson's life amounts to one of the saddest stories in this book. He survived the First World War physically, but psychologically he was tortured by it for the remaining 59 years of his life. He was undoubtedly a great author, but one whose reputation suffered for the terrible choices he made in his political life. I would classify him as more of a tragic villain than an out-and-out villain, though that qualification seems not to have rescued his good name among the reading public – something which raises an interesting artistic and moral question of general application.

Early years and First World War

Henry William Williamson was born in London in 1895. He grew up in Ladywell, Kent, now part of south-east London but then still a semi-rural area, and developed a love of nature early in life. In January 1914, he joined the London Rifle Brigade as a territorial. At the outbreak of war, he was deployed to the Ypres salient, where he participated in the Christmas Truce of 1914. He described the truce in a letter to his mother written on Boxing Day 1914, when he was aged just 19:

> I am writing from the trenches. It is 11 o'clock in the morning. Beside me is a coke fire, opposite me a 'dug-out' (wet) with straw in it. The ground is sloppy in the actual trench, but frozen elsewhere. In my mouth is a pipe presented by the Princess Mary. In the pipe is tobacco. Of course, you say.

> But wait. In the pipe is German tobacco. Haha, you say, from a prisoner or found in a captured trench.

> Oh dear, no!

> From a German soldier. Yes a live German soldier from his own trench. Yesterday the British & Germans met and shook hands in the Ground between the trenches, and exchanged souvenirs, and shook hands. Yes, all day Xmas day, & as I write. Marvellous, isn't it? Yes.

> This is only for about a mile or two on either side of us (so far as we know). It happened thuswise.

> On Xmas eve both armies sang carols and cheered & there was very little firing. The Germans (in some places 80 yds away) called to our men to come and fetch a cigar & our men told them to come to us. This went on for some time, neither fully trusting the other, until, after much promising to 'play the game' a bold Tommy crept out & stood between the trenches, & immediately a Saxon came to meet him. They shook hands & laughed and then 16 Germans came out.

Thus the ice was broken. Our men are speaking to them now.

They are landsturmers or landwehr, I think, & Saxons & Bavarians (no Prussians). Many are gentle looking men in goatee beards & spectacles, and some are very big and arrogant looking. I have some cigarettes which I shall keep, and a cigar I have smoked.

We had a burial service in the afternoon, over the dead Germans who perished in the 'last attack that was repulsed' against us. The Germans put 'For Fatherland and Freedom' on the cross.

They obviously think their cause is a just one.

In 1964, he was one of the veterans interviewed by the BBC for the fiftieth anniversary of the war. He again recalled the truce: [117]

We crept out, trying to avoid our boots ringing on the frozen ground, and expecting any moment to fall flat with the machine guns opening up. And nothing happened. And within two hours we were walking about and laughing and talking, and there was nothing from the German side.

And then about 11 o'clock I saw a Christmas tree going up on the German trenches. And there was a light. And we stood still and we watched this and we talked, and then a German voice began to sing a song—*Heilige Nacht* [the German version of *Silent Night*].

And after that, somebody, 'come over, Tommy, come over'. And we still thought it was a trap, but some of us went over at once, and they came to this barbed wire fence between us which was five strands wire ... hung with empty bully beef tins to make a rattle if they came. And very soon we were exchanging gifts.

Unlike some others interviewed at the same time, his accounts closely tallied not only with known facts but with his own accounts which had been written during the war.[118]

The truce in Williamson's sector continued for four days. He noticed that the Germans wrote on wooden crosses for their graves 'Für Vaterland und Freiheit' – 'For Fatherland and Freedom', and that they referred to God on their engravings for unknown dead.

Williamson described the site as 'a tremendous shock. One began to think that these chaps, who were like ourselves, whom we liked and who felt about the war as we did.' He asked them how they could be fighting for freedom, since they had started the war and it was the English who were fighting for freedom,

---

117 Jasper Copping, 'Tarka author tells of 1914 Christmas Truce', *Daily Telegraph*, 9 March 2014. http://www.telegraph.co.uk/history/world-war-one/10685149/Tarka-author-tells-of-1914-Christmas-truce.html.

118 Detlef Siebert, 'I Was There: The Great War Interviews', BBC Blog 14 March 2014, http://www.bbc.co.uk/blogs/tv/entries/80a43bad-458d-3e19-8a3d-3aa2d92abe9d.

and why they thought God was on their side when He was clearly backing the English. The Germans dismissed his questions and said they should not quarrel at Christmas.

In January 1915, Williamson was sent back to England after suffering trench foot and dysentery. Upon recovering, he was commissioned as a second lieutenant with the 10th (Service) Battalion of the Bedfordshire Regiment. He again suffered ill health in May 1916, when he was forced to spend time in hospital with anaemia, but eventually recovered and in February 1917 was able to return to the Western Front.

In June 1917, he suffered a gas attack and had to return to England for convalescence. He was classed unfit for active service, and though he tried to find a way back to the Front, he never managed to do so before the war ended.

When the war ended, he wrote in his diary:[119]

> HW was a soldier 2¼ months later; in France 5¼ months later
>
> And Finish, Finish, Finish, the hope and illusion of youth,
>
> For ever, and for ever, and for ever.

In his 1964 interview, he told the BBC of his feelings about the Armistice:

> No more verey lights[120] going up with their greenish wavering flare. No lilies of the dead, in the light. No flash of howitzers on the horizon. No downward droning of the shells. No machine guns. No patrols going out. Just nothing. Silence.

Williamson's writings on the war were extensive. His first book was *The Wet Flanders Plain*, written in 1929 following his return to the battlefield. Here is a representative passage:[121]

> We come to wire that is uncut, and beyond we see grey coal-scuttle helmets bobbing about, and the steam of over-heated machine-guns wafting away in the fountainous black smoke of howitzer shells; and the loud crackling of the machine-guns changes to a screeching as of steam being blown off by a hundred engines; and soon no one is left standing. And an hour later our guns are 'back on the first objective', and Kitchener's Army, with all its hopes and beliefs, has found its grave on those northern slopes of the Somme battlefield.

---

119 'Henry Williamson and the First World War', Henry Williamson Society Website. The site is an extensive and invaluable resource, https://www.henrywilliamson.co.uk/hw-and-the-first-world-war.

120 Flares fired from a form of pistol.

121 Henry Williamson, 'I Believe in the Men Who Died', *Daily Express*, 17 September 1928. Williamson's biographer, his daughter-in-law Anne Williamson, considered that essay to be Williamson's most important work on the First World War.

A year drifts by, and I am standing on a duckboard by a flooded and foul beek in the Salient, listening in the flare-pallid rainy darkness to the cries of tens of thousands of wounded men lost in the morasses of third Ypres. To seek them is to drown with them ... The living are still toiling on, homeless and without horizons, doing dreadful things under heaven that none want to do, through the long wet days and the longer nights, the weeks, the months, of a bare, sodden winter out of doors.

The survivors are worn out; some of them, tested beyond breaking point, put the muzzles of their rifles in their mouths, in the darkness of the terrible nights, and pull the trigger.

Those at home, sitting in armchairs and talking proudly of patriotism and heroism, will never realise the bitter contempt and scorn the soldiers have for these and other abstractions; the soldiers feel they have been betrayed by the high-sounding phrases that heralded the war, for they know that the enemy soldiers are the same men as themselves, suffering and disillusioned in exactly the same way ...

And in the stupendous roar and light-blast of the final barrage that broke the Hindenburg line I see only one thing, which grows radiant before my eyes until it fills all my world: the sight of a Saxon boy half crushed under a shattered tank, moaning 'Mutter, mutter, mutter', out of ghastly grey lips. A British soldier, wounded in the leg, and sitting nearby, hears the words, and, dragging himself to the dying boy, takes his cold hand and says: 'All right, son, it's all right. Mother's here with you.'

The bells cease, and I descend again to the world of the living, and move among men who did not go through the fire, and who think the old thoughts, and who seem not to care that it will happen again unless all believe in the sacrifice of the men who died. For it was a sacrifice, and we did believe, in a dull sort of way, that out of our loss would come a better world for our children.

In 1930 he wrote *The Patriot's Progress*, a fictional story of an ordinary soldier named John Bullock which drew heavily on his own experiences. His most significant *roman à clef* on the war was his series of novels known as *A Chronicle of Ancient Sunlight*, the fourth to eighth volumes of which concerned the years 1914–1918.

There is no doubt that Williamson experienced the full panoply of horrors of the Western Front, and that that experience – particularly when combined with the tiny snapshot of humanity which the Christmas Truce provided – led him desperately not to want another war with Germany. His friend and Brother Savage Reginald Pound once said of him:[122]

The truth about H. W., or at least a good part of the truth about him, is that he was a war victim and should in fairness be judged as such. For

---

122 Reginald Pound, *Running Commentary* (Rockliffe, 1946).

him the war was a crucifixion of the spirit which marked him for life.

He came out of it expecting a better world, an England that would prove worthy of the men who had saved her. He expected that all men had been purged by war as he had been. He expected that life itself had been refined by it. He expected too much.

Inter-war years

In the 1920s, Williamson began work on his most famous novel, *Tarka the Otter: His Joyful Water-Life and Death in the Country of the Two Rivers*. The book, which took several years to research, told the story of an otter in the West Country. It was no genial anthropomorphic tale with a Disneyesque happy ending; instead it comprised a factual account of otters' lives with an unstinting description of the violence inherent in otter hunting, which was still legal at the time.[123]

The book was first published in 1927 and has never been out of print. It was highly influential in a number of respects. Its prose style was cited with reverence by both Ted Hughes and Roger Deakin, and Hughes befriended Williamson later as well. Its depiction of, and attitude to, the countryside and nature were praised by the pioneering environmentalist Rachel Carson and the nature writers Kenneth Allsop and Denys Watkins-Pitchford. Another fan was TE Lawrence (Lawrence of Arabia), who developed a friendship with Williamson after reading the book, albeit one conducted mainly via correspondence as they only met in person twice. Lawrence's fatal motorcycle accident occurred during an excursion to send a telegram to Williamson.

Williamson joined the Savage Club in mid-1928 under the category of literature.

Despite his critical acclaim and publishing success, Williamson remained tormented by his time in the trenches. He was utterly determined that Britain should never again go to war against Germany. We will return to Williamson's experience in this regard in the Aftermath, along with those other Savages who decided to take a more morally sound stance against the rising evils in the 1930s.

Coda: Artists and their art

Williamson's fascist liaisons undoubtedly condemned much of his work to a much smaller readership than would otherwise have been the case. Judged purely on literary merit and for their historical verisimilitude, his First World War

---

123 For an entirely random coincidence, AK Harvey-James's daughter Olive wrote in her memoirs about being invited to join a party attending the Devon Otter Hunt Ball in Barnstaple in 1922. 'Oblivious to the poor otters, it sounded to me like a dream come true' she recorded, but her grandmother overruled her on the ground she was too young. See Olive Ordish, *Jill of All Trades* (1990).

memoirs seem fit to rank in the same league as Robert Graves' *Goodbye to All That* or Siegfried Sassoon's 'Sherston trilogy', and overall Williamson's *Chronicle of Ancient Sunlight* series deserves comparison with Anthony Powell's *A Dance to the Music of Time* or Ford Madox Ford's *Parade's End*.

Therein lies an interesting ethical and artistic question: should the interpretation or appraisal of a work of art be affected by one's knowledge of the artist's political views or otherwise with his or her character? If so, should it depend upon whether the artwork in question had some conceivable political angle or not, or whether it can be seen as purely abstract or otherwise unrelated to politics? Should it make a difference if the author is still alive and the events in question therefore within living memory?

The well-known author Will Self addressed the point directly in a piece about Williamson's book *Dandelion Days*. Self explained that the book had been highly influential on him in his childhood. He explained what happened when he went looking for more books by Williamson:[124]

> I remember being taken enough by *Dandelion Days*—which I had found lurking on my parents' cluttered bookshelves—to look into the other books of Williamson's *The Flax of Dream* tetralogy, of which it's the second. But before I could read them some intelligence reached me about their author that, for the precocious ideologue that I was, effectively banished him and all his works to the outer limits. Williamson—who was extremely well-known as the author of *Tarka the Otter*—was a Hitler apologist rather than an appeaser, who joined Mosley's British Union of Fascists in 1937, and who—so far as we can tell—remained fairly unrepentant about his fascism until his death in 1977.
>
> Nowadays I hope I have a rather more nuanced view of the relationship between works of art and their creator; indeed, some of my favourite artworks—Wagner's *Tristan und Isolde*, Céline's *Voyage* au bout de la nuit—have a proto-fascist provenance; but when I first read *Dandelion Days* I was still as idealistic as Willie Maddison, and the revelation stung me quite as much as his rejection by the flaxen-haired—and distinctly wooden—Elsie hurt him.

As a starting point, it seems wrong to judge art on the basis of the artist's political views. For some, politics is everything and everything is politics; to others, that sort of approach is crashingly dull. I doubt anyone listening to Wagner nowadays would be inclined to start oppressing Jews because of the Ring Cycle. Moreover, it is a truism that people with abysmal views or other unappealing traits might have other more redemptive sides to their character, and indeed contrasting someone's dark side with their art makes often for an interesting critique.

It is true that knowledge of the artist might inform or put an interesting – or,

124 Will Self, 'Henry Williamson's soft-touch depiction of male adolescent sexuality left a lasting impression', *The Guardian*, 15 August 2013.

as with Williamson, disturbing – slant on the artwork, but it is surely possible to enjoy a piece of music, a bottle of wine or a novel without concerning oneself with the creator's political or personal life. If it were otherwise, much great art would have to be re-evaluated in a tedious and pointless fashion. Perhaps it is different if the artist is still alive, and promoting his or her work might advance some dubious cause,[125] but in the case of someone like Williamson, who has been dead for over 40 years and whose political ideas have been dead for much longer, it seems unnecessary to judge his work according to his politics.

That, however, has to be a debate for another day. Instead, let us turn to the great Savage entertainers of the Great War era.

---

125 For example, at the time of writing, the Australian entertainer and artist Rolf Harris was still alive, and serving a jail term for sexual offences. His paintings had come down drastically in value since his conviction. No doubt people did not want to promote his reputation or enhance his wealth by paying large sums for his work; either way, of course, it is obviously up to the buying public what they wish to pay for art and on what basis.

Another example would be the actor Kevin Spacey, who found himself ostracised by Hollywood after sexual allegations were made, even though unlike Harris, Spacey had not been charged, let alone convicted of anything.

A third example might be Lewis Carroll. A twenty-first century television documentary alleged that photographic evidence had been found which heightened the historic suspicion that his relationship with the Liddell girls had been improper. With a century and a half since *Alice in Wonderland* and *Through the Looking Glass* were written, though, the books' reputation seemed (correctly) not to be affected by anything that the Rev Charles Dodgson might or might not have done all those years ago.

Savage Entertainers

Introduction

If the category of literature comprises an illustrious collection of twentieth century names, that of the Savage musicians and actors of the same period is arguably even more impressive. As with other fields, the Savage entertainers spanned quite a range within the broad definition of their genre: the likes of Bud Flanagan, Chesney Allen and Billy Bennett were masters of music hall comic ditties and cheap gags, while at the more rarefied end of things Basil Cameron and Harold Williams excelled at symphony orchestras and opera respectively.

We start with a musical technological pioneer still warmly remembered in the Savage Club today.

Joseph Batten: 'a good Savage'

Joseph 'Joe' Batten was an important figure in the early history of the gramophone, and a most enthusiastic member of the Savage Club.

Early life

Batten was born in London in 1885. At the time his uncle owned a factory in the East End making artificial flowers, and his father worked as the manager. Batten later wrote of his childhood:[1]

> In my memories Mother remains an exemplar to me of the period. Loving, patient and cheerful, she worked every day from early until

---

1 Joseph Batten, *Joe Batten's Book: The Story of Sound Recording* (Rockliff Publishing Corp; 1ˢᵗ edn, 1956, Kindle edn).

late, dividing her time between factory and home. In those days people did work hard and I believe were happier and more contented than this generation. No doubt the factory girls Father employed, who worked the long hours of the then six-day week, would now be pitied as victims of sweated labour and of the capitalistic system. It is not easy for me to visualise Father as a bloated capitalist. When on the occasions I went in search of Mother in the factory, I entered into a buzz of conversation, of cheerfulness and laughter. If our girls sweated they seemed happy enough.

He was interested in music from a very early age. He took piano lessons from an apparently inept tutor, but made up for it himself by obsessively reading musical scores borrowed from the library in Shoreditch and by attending as many concerts as he could. As a result he managed to become a proficient pianist while still a child. At the age of 12 he started playing as an accompanist to his father, who was then singing professionally to supplement the family income because artificial flowers had dropped in fashion and his usual business was therefore struggling.

In 1900, Batten started on the path that was to make his name and career, when he went into a dingy office in Holborn which was displaying the nameplate 'The Musiphone Company Recording Room' (the term 'studio' for such facilities was not then in use). He was soon working full-time playing the piano to accompany singers of the day in the rudimentary recording facility. By 1906, the year he became married, he had managed to more than double his fees for the work. He also began working for the Neophone Recording Company, at the same time as landing various other musical commissions, so was able to live comfortably for the next few years.

In mid-1914, however, his father died and Batten found himself looking after not just his own two children, but his mother and six brothers and sisters as well. Three of his siblings were still at school (his mother had obviously given birth to him while she was very young).

Wartime service

In 1916, Batten received his call-up papers, being conscripted into the Honourable Artillery Company (HAC). At the start of the war, the HAC mobilised two infantry battalions and five artillery batteries. Various of its units saw action in France and Flanders, but it also maintained two reserve batteries in England.[2] Batten was assigned to one of those batteries and hence did not serve overseas during the conflict. He may well have been deliberately kept in England to continue his gramophone work, which was recognised as an important morale

---

2   See https://www.hac.org.uk/home/about-the-hac/history/world-war-1/.

booster for both soldiers overseas and their families back home. Years later he recalled:[3]

> Far from the industry being set back by the war, the reverse was the case. Both in the trenches and in English homes, the gramophone now had a tremendous boom; soon I was involved in a variety of rush recordings bearing such titles as "The Landing of the Troops in France", and more particularly "Tipperary" as a song, "Tipperary" as a march, "Tipperary" paired with "God Save the King", and "Tipperary" treated as a descriptive sketch. "Tipperary" had been published a year or so previously, and had, before the war, passed into the limbo of songs forgotten. So it seemed. But a Tommy in the Northumberland Fusiliers remembered it, he sang it on a route march, its lilting tune was recalled by the marching soldiers, who made the solo into a chorus. So the song came to life, a soldiers' song marched along the cobbled Flemish roads, spreading to Gallipoli and the remote parts of what was then an Empire. Why? Because it was one of the few great march tunes, worthy, martial and stirring enough to rank with such companions as "John Brown's Body" and the "Marseillaise".
>
> Next we plunged into recordings of "National Anthems of the Allies", "Regimental Marches of the British Army", and "War Song Medleys" of such popular tunes as "Here We are again", "Belgium put the Kibosh on the Kaiser", "Keep the Home Fires Burning ("Till the Boys Come Home)", "Good-by-ee", and then we turned again to "Tipperary". It is a curious reflection that whilst the popular of the First World War are still remembered and sung, those of the second have already been forgotten. The songs of the South African War of over fifty years ago are better known today than those of the 1940 vintage.
>
> Meanwhile, in the midst of all these activities I was now a full-fledged private of the HAC: moreover, my extensive knowledge of horses derived from witnessing feats of horsemanship at the various London circuses had resulted in my becoming Driver Batten of Reserve Battery, RHA. Fortunately, I was able to get all the leave I required to continue with my recording work of conducting, accompanying and orchestrating, all this being carried out within a very short distance of HAC Headquarters. Perhaps the light-hearted view of my Army duties was possible due to the fact that I had become prominent in working for the Soldiers' Entertainment Fund, forerunner of ENSA, and assisting in shows given two or three times a week at camps widespread over the length and breadth of England, and this certainly kept my name off the periodical lists of drafts for overseas posted in battery orders. I must admit that, unlike the majority of men at that time, eager to get into the trenches (and such is human nature, once there, as eager to get out again), the prospect filled me with anxiety and dismay. I had two families dependent on me, and how I was to manage, if I was drafted and reduced to little more than my soldier's pay I could not imagine.

Even though he stayed in England, Batten did not wholly avoid the danger of

---

3   Batten, op cit, pp 36–37.

war. He was at the British Polyphon Company, next to the HAC parade ground, when an air raid took place and a bomb hit just by the dugout where he was sheltering. Fortunately it was a dud and he was unharmed.

Batten befriended Brother Savage George Baker[4] during the conflict and the two put on many HAC shows. One such performance satirised the officers of the HAC once too often, and Batten was sent to the reserve depot at Leeds to deprive him of his enjoyment. He soon started arranging shows there instead, and despite the earlier jape was eventually demobbed with papers stating that he had been 'honest, sober and industrious'.

Post-war career

After the war, Batten joined the Edison Bell Company as the house conductor for its 'Velvet Face' label, the name deriving from its supposedly quiet surfaces. He continued with his successful career in the recording industry, conducting, playing and advising. He joined the Savage Club in 1923, and quickly became one of its most enthusiastic members. Club membership also helped facilitate his career: in 1927, he moved to the Colombia recording company after a lunch with one of its employees, Arthur Brooks, at the Club, and began working permanently as its music adviser.

In his memoirs he stated that in the Savage Club he had 'found friends that no man could hope to better.' Of the house dinners, held on Saturdays in those days, he said they were one of 'the notable amenities of the Club. Rich in membership of professional singers, musicians, actors and artists, rich also in amateur talent, these after dinner entertainments attained an atmosphere far different to those post-prandial affairs of interminable speeches.'

Throughout his career, Batten worked with countless famous musicians, many of them Savages of the day, producing innumerable recordings across the classical canon. He even entertained Laurel and Hardy at the Savage Club. One individual he singled out was Brother Savage Stanley J Rubenstein, for 'the valuable work he accomplishes as Hon Solicitor to the Savage Club.'[5]

In 1943, Batten became a life member of the Club. He died in 1955, but remains fondly membered by the Savages. He appeared in numerous places in Bradshaw's centenary history, where among other things it was recorded that a 'Savage Parade' organised by the Entertainments Committee under the chair-

---

4   George Baker (1885–1976), a baritone singer who recorded thousands of gramophone records over half a century, beginning in 1909. He was renowned for his work in Gilbert and Sullivan operas. He joined the Club in February 1915, having been nominated in December 1914. For many years he served as honorary secretary to and trustee of the Club, and became a life member in 1937.

5   Stanley Jack Rubenstein joined the Club in February 1931, under the category of literature; Basil Cameron and Reginald Pound were among his supporters.

manship of Batten in 1933 'was a brilliant success'[6] and that he had received the formal thanks of the Club in 1937 for the 'inspiration and achievement of his unforgettable contribution of Old Savage voices recorded at the Farewell Dinner'.

In more recent times, Batten was profiled by Brother Savage Alan Williams in *Drumbeat*, No 139, Autumn 2017. Williams noted that Sir Henry Wood had attested that 'no man in the history of our musical art did more for its advancement than he'.

Batten wanted his epitaph to read: 'He loved the Club – he was a good Savage.' On all available evidence, he was certainly that.

Billy Bennett: almost a hero

Brother Savage Billy Bennett was one of the most famous comedians of his day. On the face of it, he also had one of the most distinguished records of all Savages in the Great War. In recent years, however, there has been some controversy over his wartime achievements, making him an intriguing subject for a very different reason.

Early life and First World War

Bennett was born William Robertson Russell Bennett in 1887. His father was a music hall comedian, and although the younger Bennett joined the army initially, he resigned in order to pursue a career on stage. When the First World War began, he immediately re-enlisted by joining the 16th Lancers (the same regiment Brother Savage Sir William Robertson had joined as a private many years earlier). The 16th Lancers was a highly-esteemed unit. By the start of the First World War, they had amassed more battle honours than any other British cavalry regiment. They were also notable for being the first regiment to use the lance in combat, and on the Western Front they would become the last British cavalry regiment to do so. They were deployed to France as part of the British Expeditionary Force in 1914 and served throughout the conflict.

Bennett later reflected upon his wartime experiences in the following passage in the sleevenotes to one of his compilation albums, issued many years afterwards:[7]

> As a boy I was trained as an acrobat, but I took such a dislike to the business that I ran away from home and joined the Army, enlisting in the 16th Lancers. I, however, found cavalry soldiering much harder than acrobating, but had to stay in the Army, so my father said, "to teach me a lesson." In course of time, my father bought me out of the

6 Bradshaw, op cit, p 94, 101.
7 This information was shared with me by a private individual who owned the album.

Army and I went back to the professional life to try something not so hard—that is to say, in sketches, comic singing, etc. Just as war broke out I was making a little progress, but, as I was a trained soldier, I thought it was my duty to rejoin my old regiment, and served with it in several campaigns on the Western Front—Ypres, Loos, Somme, Arras, Perrone, Cambrai, and several other minor engagements. And I think I served in almost every capacity that was possible in the Army—shoeing-smith, cook, batman, policeman, officer's valet, signaller.

The medals

The notes also recorded that he was awarded the Distinguished Conduct Medal (the DCM was only one below the Victoria Cross, and therefore superior to the Distinguished Service Order, with which it is sometimes confused), the Military Medal and the Belgian *Croix de Guerre*. Those medals also appeared in a number of his obituaries upon his death in 1942. They amounted to a very fine record in the conflict indeed.

Or at least they would have done, but unfortunately there is substantial reason to doubt that he was actually awarded them. I have been unable to find any citations in the *London Gazette*, despite several efforts including trying different variations of his name. In the *Gazette* for 1917, two W Bennetts are recorded as receiving the Military Medal, '7959 Sgt. W. Bennett, M.G. Corps' and '55169 Pte. W. Bennett, R.W. Fus'. But Billy Bennett's numbers were 5273 16th Lancers and 41590 MGC (Cav), as confirmed by his card on the website ancestry.co.uk. That medal card records that Bennett was only awarded the 'trio' of Victory, British and Star medals – a far cry from the MM or DCM.

He joined the Savage Club in February 1931. No mention of his medals appears on his candidate's page. A number of others with significant achievements such as the MM did put it on theirs, but we cannot be sure that they all would have done, or that it would have been expected, especially more than a decade after the war's end and with Bennett having established himself a world away from military matters in the field of light entertainment. Once again, therefore, the evidence does not conclusively prove he did not win the medals – but nor does it provide any support for his claim.

I have failed to find any references to the medals in newspaper articles on Bennett published during his lifetime.[8] Moreover, the regimental history of the

8   I am grateful to Brother Savage Andrew Riddoch, author of *When the Whistle Blows: The Story of the Footballers' Battalion in the Great War* (Haynes Publishers, 2008), for his assistance in researching Bennett's war record.

16th Lancers has a list of medal winners and Bennett's name is not among them.[9] If he did win them, it would therefore have to have been during his time with the Machine Gun Corps.

None of the prestigious medals were mentioned in his profile in a well-researched 1979 book by Brother Savage Eric Midwinter,[10] who stated only that Bennett 'had been an entertainer in the army during the 1914–18 war'.

The online Great War Forum – not an official source, but nonetheless home to many boffins – has run several comment threads on Bennett,[11] and each time none of the members has been able to substantiate Bennett's record. There was even some doubt in the sleeve notes quoted above, which contained a subtle caveat noting 'If this account of his war service be true, Billy was a lucky man to have survived that horrific war.'

It would be surprising – though not unprecedented – if Bennett had lied about winning the claimed medals. If anyone had found out in Bennett's lifetime he would have been disgraced, to put it mildly. Many of his former colleagues would have survived the war, and presumably they would have been incensed had they discovered Bennett lying about his achievements.

No doubt there have been Walter Mitty types since time immemorial. Perhaps Bennett made the claim over a few beers with friends and then found himself in a situation akin to Macbeth, having gone too far down the wrong path to pull back from the lie. Or perhaps a publicist or promoter made the claim on his behalf, and Bennett did not feel able to correct the record without damaging his name.

On the other hand, the records might have been lost. If so, maybe the reason for his heroism not being mentioned more often was that Bennett, in common with most veterans, did not like recalling the war. Alternatively, he could have used that normal reticence to avoid answering any probing questions about a false claim, and relied upon everyone assuming it was wrong to ask an old soldier to relive unpleasant memories.

I would hope that someone might come forward with definitive proof of him being awarded the medals. For now, however, the conclusion has to be that he was never awarded them, though there is no doubt he saw active service during the conflict and deserves respect accordingly.

---

9   Colonel Henry Graham, *History of the Sixteenth, the Queen's Light Dragoons (Lancers) 1912 to 1925* (privately published, 1926), p 117.

10   Eric Midwinter, *Make 'em laugh: Famous Comedians and their Worlds* (Allen & Unwin, 1979). I had the honour of being able to discuss Bennett with Eric one evening in the Club.

11   http://1914-1918.invisionzone.com/forums/topic/2226-billy-bennett-comedian/.
     http://1914-1918.invisionzone.com/forums/topic/2226-billy-bennett-comedian/.
     http://1914-1918.invisionzone.com/forums/topic/237582-comedian-billy-bennetts-wartime-service/.

Post-war career

There is also no doubt about the success of Bennett's post-war career as an entertainer. It began in 1919 on the stage, where his act consisted of sending up the dramatic monologues popular at the time. He also sang comic songs. In 1928 he made his film debut in a short picture *Almost a Gentleman*, filmed in the DeForest Phonofilm sound-on-film system. From 1930, he appeared regularly on radio as well. Eric Midwinter called Bennett 'the most attractive comedian straddling the end of the music hall and the beginning of the mixed bag of variety, radio, records, cinema and television.'[12]

One of Bennett's better-known songs was *My Mother Doesn't Know I'm On The Stage*, in which the lyrics explained that he was content for his mother to think of him as a bigamist, a thief, a murderer – but not as an actor. They included the verse:

> Sometimes she sees the powder on my clothing
> And then it's such a nuisance to explain.
> If she thought it was powder she'd go crazy
> So, of course, I have to tell her it's cocaine.

James Agate wrote of Bennett:

> Nobody who saw him is ever likely to forget that rubicund, unaesthetic countenance, that black, plastered quiff, that sergeant-major's moustache, that dreadful dinner-jacket, that well-used dickey and seedy collar, the too-short trousers, the hob-nailed boots, the red silk handkerchief tucked into the waistcoat, the continual perspiration which was the outward and visible sign of a mind struggling for expression - these things will not be forgotten.

Bennett died in 1942. He has been cited as an influence on many later performers including the likes of George Formby, Tommy Cooper and Eric Morecambe. Whatever he did or did not achieve during the Great War, we can celebrate his work on stage. And we can also note with satisfaction the fact that Bennett proposed another famous actor and singer, Bud Flanagan, as a member of the Savage Club in 1939.

Midwinter's conclusion was:[13]

> Billy Bennett acted as a second string relay sprinter, accepting the baton of popular comedy from music hall and handing it over to variety. He made his own success by compounding fantasy and earthiness for

---

12 Midwinter, *Make 'Em Laugh*, op cit, p 19.
13 Ibid. My thanks also to Eric for discussing Bennett's case with me in the Club while this book was being written.

a public whose mood was tuned to something like that bizarre mix of escapist notions and downright rawness; he helped usher in a half century of comic performers who spoke, rather than sang, of humorous happenings. He accomplished this in years of troubled minds and consciences, when foundations, good or ill, were laid, and the social dimension was brittle and nervy at the top and disillusioned and acrid at the bottom. Possibly the Einsteinian paradox of his own couplet is not an unfair epitaph of the time:

> Think of what we have done in the future—
> Shall we do our duty in the past?

Basil Cameron: conducting with authority

Basil Cameron CBE is normally remembered as another Savage high achiever in the field of music, in his case as a conductor. During the First World War, as with most people in Britain thought – rightly or wrongly – to have some connection with Germany (in his case a Germanic surname) he swiftly became the target of baseless accusations, and was forced to change his name. Thereafter, he went on to serve at the Western Front and thus rebut his critics in the most forceful fashion.

Early life

Cameron was born in 1884 in Reading, Berkshire, the son of German immigrants. On his birth certificate his name was recorded as Basil George Cameron Hindenberg.

His early family history is an example of the grim mortality rate of the Victorian and early Edwardian periods: his parents' first three children all died aged less than three months. Their only two children to survive infancy were Basil and their daughter Gertrude, who was a year older. In 1887, only three years after Basil's birth, his mother died aged just 32. His father moved the family to Tiverton in Devon, where he remarried and had two more children. In 1893, yet further tragedy struck when Gertrude died.

Despite all of those cruel family setbacks, Basil was able to begin studying music at a very young age, encouraged by his father, who was a piano tuner and part-time music teacher. At just seven years of age, he made his debut on the stage with the Tiverton Amateur Dramatic Society, playing the midshipman in Gilbert and Sullivan's *HMS Pinafore*. By the age of eight, he was learning the violin. The family then relocated to Yorkshire. Basil continued with his musical education, being singled out by his teachers as highly promising with the violin, as well as learning from Tertius Noble, the organist and choirmaster at York Minster. From 1902–1906, he studied at the Berlin Hochschule für Musik, where he was taught the violin by the Hungarian virtuoso Joseph Joachim, conducting by Robert Hausmann, the famous cellist of the Joachim Quartet, and composition by the composer Max Bruch. It had to have been one of the finest classical musical educations available anywhere in the world at the time.

Upon returning to England, Basil played as a violinist in the Queen's Hall Orchestra for five years. In 1912, he began his conducting career with the Torquay Municipal Orchestra. They put on festivals of Wagner and Richard Strauss, which attracted much critical acclaim – well exceeding that expected of a small provincial orchestra.

First World War

When war broke out in 1914, Basil's German surname quickly became a liability, just as Battenberg was for the soon-to-be Mountbatten family and Saxe-Coburg-Gotha for the royals. He decided to adopt his middle name of Cameron, and thereafter became Basil Cameron.[14] The Torquay Orchestra then placed an advertisement in *The Times*, *The Daily Telegraph*, the *Morning Post*, the *Torquay Directory* and the *Torquay Times*, from 12–16 December 1914, stating 'MR BASIL HINDENBERG (Conductor of the Torquay Municipal Orchestra) being of ENGLISH BIRTH, has decided to adopt his baptismal name of CAMERON and hereby gives notice that in future he wishes to be known and addressed as BASIL CAMERON).'

The fact of him changing his name was even debated in the House of Commons, with the Home Secretary, Herbert Samuel, being asked 'why this was allowed', when there was a policy that 'Germans who are naturalised should not change their names'. Samuel replied that Cameron was a natural-born British subject, and the son of a natural-born British subject.[15] It was but one more example of the wartime anti-German paranoia.

As if there was any doubt about his allegiance, Cameron enlisted in the British Army in November 1915. After officer cadet training, he received a commission as a second lieutenant with the 13th London Regiment (Kensingtons), effective from 30 May 1917.[16]

---

14 Note that some sources have said that he had only used 'Hindenberg' as a musical *nom de guerre* to secure work before the war. For example, the music historian Eric David Mackerness wrote that 'Up to the First World War even so distinguished a musician as Basil Cameron thought fit to adopt for professional purposes the name of Basil Hindenburg (sic)' (in *A Social History of English Music*, Routledge, 1964, 2007 edn, p 208). This is not correct, as confirmed by his birth certificate. See also Samuel Hynes, *A War Imagined: The First World War and English Culture* (Random House, 1990), who mentions Cameron's change of name.

15 I am very grateful to Mr Andy Murray, Hermitage, Berkshire for supplying me with details of Cameron's birth certificate, the advertisement from the newspapers and an item drawing attention to the House of Commons' questions.

16 *The London Gazette*, 15 June 1917, p 5949.

The 13th was originally a unit of the Territorial Force, with headquarters at Iverna Gardens, Kensington. When war broke out, they were serving with the 4th London Brigade, 2nd London Division. They went to France in November and saw action at Neuve Chapelle and Auberts. In 1915, they were transferred to a composite unit with other London battalions, but regained their own identity in August of that year. In 1916 they fought on the Somme, where they were involved in the diversionary attack at Gommecourt on 1 July.

Cameron joined them in France in June 1917, just after receiving his commission. He fought in the Battle of Langemark in August and, under the overall command of Brother Savage Julian Byng, the Battle of Cambrai in November. In 1918, he fought in the March retreat and the subsequent British counter-advance through Albert. He was wounded towards the end of the war (being recorded in the 16 September daily casualty list in *The Times*) and returned to England.

On 30 November 1918, less than a month after the war had ended, he was promoted to lieutenant.[17] He relinquished his commission on 30 September 1921.[18]

One of his fellow veterans later recalled:[19]

> I first saw him in a hut behind the lines—it was, I think, in 1917. The hut was being used as a dressing-room by the theatrical troupe of the 56th Division. The curtain had just been rung down, and the make-up and the motley were being removed. At the first glance the presence of an inconspicuous second lieutenant in such a place attracted no attention, for in that region the green-room was a fashionable place of call, and it was no uncommon thing for young officers to visit the prima donna behind the scenes in search of peace-time illusions. Suddenly I heard a sound that did call for attention. It was the opening of Bach's Chaconne, played by fingers that had evidently learnt their discipline in a thorough school. On looking up I saw that our visitor had borrowed one of our violins and was seeking peace-time illusions in a way of his own. I walked across and was introduced to Mr. Basil Cameron of the 13th London Regiment (Kensingtons). He had come to pay a call on the two principal violinists of our orchestra, who were, it appeared, old professional acquaintances of his (for the last few years they have been a popular turn on the music-halls). From that evening until his final departure for England Mr Cameron kept up a close, if broken, friendship with the party. Whenever the Kensingtons were out of the line and billeted within easy distance of the divisional troupe, we could look forward to a visit from our quiet-mannered officer-friend, whom we welcomed both from his amiability and for the opportunity

---

17 *The London Gazette*, 10 February 1919, p 2066.

18 *The London Gazette*, 21 November 1921, p 9239.

19 William McNaught, 'Mr. Basil Cameron', *The Musical Times*, vol 72 (1060), 1 June 1931, pp 497–500. McNaught (1883–1953) was a music editor, critic and adjudicator. He edited the *Musical Times* from 1944 until his death. His father had been the founder of the *School Music Review* and the editor of *The Musical Times* from 1910–1918.

he brought us—those who were interested—for a little talk on musical shop. Occasionally we gave him a desk in the orchestra and a part to play from ... One can readily believe Mr. Cameron when he says that nothing more effectively banished war's alarms than an evening spent in doing his bit in the theatre band. We, on our side, appreciated the honour of having a real Queen's Hall man to help us. There was an element of risk that added to the fun, for this levelling of ranks, even in the brotherhood of art, was against the law, and it was necessary to conceal the visitor from exalted and prying eyes. In fact, there was a time when, threatened by King's Regulations and a certain high officer, Mr. Cameron was rescued from an awkward situation only by the activity of neighbouring Germans.

Once again, we see the class divisions in action, as reflected in the officers being precluded from fraternising with the ranks, even if they both happened to be virtuoso violin players. Hence, once again we can see how far-sighted the Savage Club of the day was, allowing all ranks of the armed forces to join so long as they were deemed clubbable sorts who would enrich the intellectual and social life of the Club.

Post-war career

Cameron resumed his musical career after the conflict. He joined the Savage Club in May 1923. Among his supporters was Norman O'Neill, a well-known composer of the day.[20]

In 1924, he became director of the Harrogate Orchestra, which had a very high reputation at the time. It used to perform daily, with a symphony concert on Wednesday evenings. Upon the summer season finishing, the orchestra would move to the South of England and refashion themselves as the Hastings Municipal Orchestra. In that latter guise, and with Cameron conducting, they made recordings in 1929 for the new Decca Record Company. The orchestra did not simply play existing classics but introduced many new composers, including work by Eric Coates, who later composed the theme for Brother Savage Roy Plomley's 'Desert Island Discs' radio programme and, in 1955, one of Britain's most famous film soundtracks, *The Dam Busters*. From 1928 onwards Cameron also acted as an occasional guest conductor, most notably for the London Symphony Orchestra.

By the end of the 1920s, however, the Great Depression started to bite and the Harrogate Orchestra disbanded at the end of the 1930 season. Cameron went to

---

20 Norman Houston O'Neill (1875–1934). He specialised mostly in works for the theatre. Like Joseph Batten, he was a pioneer in gramophone recording: in 1910, he became the first British composer to conduct his own orchestral music on record, when he directed the Columbia Graphophone Company's house ensemble in a suite taken from his 'Blue Bird' music. Elsewhere, his work was praised by Sir Edward Elgar.

He was treasurer of the Royal Philharmonic Society from 1918 until his death and taught at the Royal Academy of Music, a measure of his stature in classical music circles of the day.

America, where from 1930 until 1932 he acted as joint music director with the San Francisco Symphony. He enjoyed much critical and commercial success in that role, but his next move, to the Seattle Symphony, was not a success, due to creative differences with other members. As a result he returned to England in 1938, where he remained for the rest of his career.

During the Second World War, he was too old for military service. In 1940, he joined the conducting staff of the Proms as an associate conductor to Sir Henry Wood, and assumed greater responsibility after Wood's death. Along with Malcolm Sargent, he was responsible for the bulk of the programming. For just one of other his career highlights, in 1950 he appeared at a Royal Albert Hall Promenade Concert directing the soprano Elisabeth Schwarzkopf in a performance of a rare Franz Liszt arrangement of Schubert's 'Der Hirt auf em Felsen'.[21]

He was appointed a Commander of the Order of the British Empire (CBE) in 1957 and, in 1966, was made an honorary life member of the Savage Club. He died in 1975. Of some of his recordings a music critic opined:[22]

> [Brother Savage Sir Henry] Wood admired Cameron greatly: "a practical and professional musician with a real grip over the orchestra". Wood also considered Cameron to be a "shy and sensitive man, but his music is right". Seemingly indefatigable, Cameron conducted Proms night after night—invariably these were long programmes—sharing each season with Sir Malcolm Sargent and covering a vast repertoire, from core to light, and he was no stranger to conducting premieres or leading such complexities as The Rite of Spring on the minimum of rehearsals. Cameron retired from the Proms at the age of 80 in 1964 and was to live another eleven years. It wasn't solely the Proms for Cameron for he enjoyed international engagements and visited the recording studio ...
>
> Shy he might have been but he obviously got orchestras to play for him with commitment and excellent ensemble; there's no lack of engagement or combustibility, the music served whole without interference and with keen observation and identification. Within the British hierarchy of conductors, Cameron belongs in the Boult/Handley axis. He, like them, has his own way of doing things; the music comes first with all of them.

Sir Lewis Casson: a pacifist who went to war

Lewis Casson was an actor-manager who enjoyed great success with the stage over many years. He was also well known as the husband of Sybil Thorndike –

---

21 See Erik Eriksson, 'Basil Cameron – Artist Biography', AllMusic website, https://www. allmusic.com/artist/basil-cameron-mn0001647907/biography.

22 Colin Anderson, 'Basil Cameron – The Quiet Maestro', Classical Source, http://classicalsource. com/db_control/db_cd_review.php?id=835.

they were one of the first married couples to be given a knighthood and a dame-hood each in their own right. Casson served in the Great War with distinction, despite having vehemently opposed it at the outset and being old enough to avoid the initial conscription rules.

Early life

Casson was born in Cheshire in 1875, the son of a bank manager and amateur organ-builder. His early life was in Wales, but in 1891 the family moved to London so his father could build organs full-time.

Casson was always interested in acting and appeared in many amateur productions, though initially he did not pursue a career on stage. Instead, he worked in different roles including assisting his father in the organ business. The business was not a success to begin with, so Casson trained as a teacher for a while before joining his father's second attempt at organ making from 1900. The business prospered more the second time around and Casson stayed for the next four years.

From quite an early age Casson had also been interested in politics. He developed strong socialist ideas, initially inspired by Robert Blatchford, and later the likes of William Morris and HG Wells. His part-time acting led him to appearing at the Royal Court Theatre. The company started putting on modern plays as well, and Casson appeared in several written by George Bernard Shaw. He became friends with Shaw, whose left-leaning views were well-known, providing an immediate common interest with Casson. Some of Shaw's plays were nakedly political statements, such as *Widowers' Houses*, a criticism of slum landlords.

During one of his performances Casson was seen on stage by Sybil Thorndike, who wrote to her brother afterwards saying she thought she had seen someone she could marry. They were introduced shortly afterwards and grew close. They married in 1908 and their son John was born the following year. At the start of their marriage, Sybil was not interested in politics or Casson's socialist views, but became more involved after Casson introduced her to the Suffragette movement, which he strongly supported.

First World War

Initially, Casson opposed the First World War on the ground that it was an imperialist war. Instead, he backed its opponents, including Labour politicians such as Keir Hardie and Ramsay MacDonald. Sybil hated the idea of the war as she had had many German friends and colleagues over the years. Others in their circles, however, including Casson's brother and Sybil's two brothers, did sign up, and eventually Casson decided to join them in the hope that at the end of the conflict substantial social change would be introduced. By that time, he was much older than most frontline infantry, being 39, but he nevertheless joined the Army Service Corps. Sybil was appalled but was unable to talk him out of it.

At first, Casson was assigned home duties, working in the cook-house and as a driver, but he was sent to the Western Front in January 1915 where he fought in the Battle of Loos. He survived, but his brother William and a friend, Harold Chapin, were both killed.

The army hierarchy noticed that Casson had studied chemistry and so, in 1916, he was given a commission in the Royal Engineers (Special Brigade) and set to work on developing poison gas. He was promoted to captain and placed in charge of a company assigned to prepare and place cylinders along the frontline during the Somme Offensive.

Another blow to the family occurred in August 1917, when Sybil's younger brother Frank died of his wounds. Her father was devastated, and died himself a few months later. Casson meanwhile was wounded in his shoulder while trying to lay phosgene cylinders in Arras. The wound constituted a 'Blighty' so he was returned to England, where he was awarded the Military Cross.

In January 1918, he returned to the Western Front, by then with the rank of major, and again worked with poison gas. He devised a more efficient system for the delivery of gas ordinance, and was sent to Washington to share his expertise with the Americans, a mission also undertaken by a Savage scientist, Captain Noel Heaton.[23]

Post-war career

After the war, Casson suffered some depression, but managed to resume a successful career in the theatre as a director and promoter. He found success with the horror genre, which rankled with the Lord Chamberlain, the theatre censor of the day. He also directed Sybil in various productions including the George Bernard Shaw play *Saint Joan*, which Shaw had written specifically for her. The play provided much relief to the straitened family finances: the couple had been scraping a living for a while, with Sybil playing some roles in horror plays of the day at small theatres.[24]

Casson continued to involve himself in politics, supporting the General Strike

---

23 Heaton, who joined the Club in March 1919, was recorded as a member of the British war mission instructing Americans in the use of poison gas in *Popular Science Monthly*, August 1918, p 260.

24 Of one such role, Louise in De Lorde and Binet's *Un crime dans une maison de fous* ('Crime in a Madhouse', though Christopher Holland's translation was 'The Old Women'), her character was threatened by two insane women preparing her for the arrival of a terrible witch. Sybil's brother Russell recalled that 'Sybil's terror of them was soul-shuddering, and when I came on as the old lady maniac with the bodkin, I longed to shout a brotherly warning so that Sybil could jump over the footlights and take refuge in the Savage Club, and thus save her eyes from being gouged out.'

as well as the Labour Party, and acting in a play about the Tolpuddle Martyrs.[25] In early 1939, he led a tour of the Old Vic around the Mediterranean, controversially visiting Italy under Benito Mussolini. Casson was unrepentant, stating that given world tensions it was particularly important not to let political differences interfere with the ordinary human relations between nations.

During the Second World War, Casson joined the Air Raids Precaution Service in Chelsea. One of his sons joined the Royal Navy but his daughter and his other son, along with Sybil, took a pacifist stance and declined to participate. In 1939 the Council for the Encouragement of Music and the Arts (CEMA) was formed in order to promote amateur and professional arts through the country. Casson worked as its Advisor on Professional Theatre. Continuing with his socialist endeavours, he also played an important part in the creation of the Actors' Association, which later merged with the Stage Guild to form the British Actors' Equity Association. Casson acted as president of Equity between 1941 and 1945.

He was knighted in June 1945.

After the war, he continued with his successful theatre career, winding down from the age of 75, when he and Sybil moved to Kent, but he still made the odd appearance up to his death in 1969.

Kenneth Duffield: from the outback to the frontline

The Australian contribution to the First World War was remarkable for a small population of a fledgling nation. From fewer than five million people in total, 416,809 men enlisted, of whom more than 60,000 were killed and 156,000 wounded, gassed, or taken prisoner.[26] One of their number to serve and survive was the composer Kenneth Duffield. He has perhaps not been as well remembered as he might have been – an article in the magazine *Fine Music* in February 2017[27] described him as a 'forgotten composer' – but he was nevertheless a great success in his day. He was also a most enthusiastic member of the Savage Club, serving on the Club committee as well as being a regular attendee.

---

25 The Tolpuddle Martyrs were a group of six Dorset agricultural labourers who were convicted in 1834 of swearing a secret oath as members of the Friendly Society of Agricultural Labourers, an early form of trade union. They were sentenced to penal transportation to Australia, and became a totem for the nascent trade union movement.

26 As an aside, one interesting example of the esteem in which Australia evidently held Britain at the time was the construction of the Australian High Commission during the war – a magnificent building in central London which cost a fortune and remains arguably the most impressive of all high commissions or embassies in Britain.

27 Stephen Pleskun, 'Forgotten Australian Composers – Kenneth Duffield', *Fine Music*, p 8.

Early life

Kenneth Launcelot Duffield was born in South Australia in 1885. His father owned a large sheep station in South Australia called Koonoona. The family was well known in the region since Duffield's grandfather, the Hon W Duffield, had been a foundation member of the South Australian parliament.

Duffield clearly retained fond memories of his childhood, writing of 'interminable drives when we used to jog along in the two-horsed wagonette that had been hired to take us kids to the theatre or to some gay children's party – and that sleepy drive back'; recalling how he used to watch Stoddart, Brother Savage Gilbert Jessop and Ranji play cricket at the Adelaide Oval, and remembering how he would travel the vast internal distances of Australia to watch the Melbourne Cup or to see Sydney Harbour.

He was educated at St Peter's College, Adelaide, and then at Cambridge University in Britain, sailing there with his father in 1903. He graduated from Cambridge with a BA in 1906. Whilst there, he was a producer with the well-known Footlights Club, and it was in that capacity that he became the first person to set lyrics by PG Wodehouse to music.

After graduating from Cambridge he returned to Koonoona for several years, before coming back to Britain in 1913, fired with an ambition to succeed in the West End, only to find Europe plunge into catastrophe the following year.

First World War

Duffield enlisted upon the outbreak of war and initially served with the North Devon Hussars. As an Australian bushman, he had the odd cultural clash with the class-conscious English officers in the regiment:[28]

> When it came to this fox-hunting jargon, I was nonplussed, because we don't hunt foxes in Australia. We follow the scent of a kerosene rag, and don't shout "Gone away", "Yoiks", or anything of that sort.
>
> One of my jobs, having a fictitious reputation as an Australian rough-rider, was to take the "rawness" off the officers' charters, a painfully suggestive process for man and beast, and I felt a bit sore one morning when our Galloping Major suggested I should "Try a spot of buck-jumpin', old fellah", with which he levered me up on to the back of the most vicious-looking mare I have ever thrown a leg across.
>
> She was a high-withered brute, standing about seventeen hands it seemed, and as soon as I was on we were "off" to a neck-dislocating leap – and then I was off. I did not take a very good view of the performance, either mine or the mare's, or that of the giggling young subalterns who had shouted, "Ride him, cowboy", "Yoicks", "Good show, Aussie", and the like.

---

28 Kenneth Duffield, *Savages and Kings* op cit, p 67.

However, I soon got used to their "Poona-isms", and they were kind and decent on the whole, particularly when I kept their mounts glossy and fit, and in the Mess when I regaled them with some pianoforte selections from a music manual I had sent to London for, called *Hauntin' Huntin' Ballads.*

Although our training was perfunctory, monotonous and medieval, I suppose it was adequate. We all galloped about a good deal and sabred imaginary Cossacks with impossible swords. One morning when we were doing even less than usual, the Colonel, Lord Clinton, dapper, dignified, and, in his own magnificent home at Bicton, a delightful host, sent for me and told me he was "detailin' me for a spot of spy-catchin'".

It turned out that the British had discerned that U-boats were somehow being resupplied off the Devonian coast, but they could not find the hidden facility. Duffield, drawing upon his bush experience, had spotted unusual tracks, and so took with him one night a party of a dozen or so of the hardest men of the unit. They moved as quietly as they could manage, silencing the tyres of the harnesses by winding plaited straw around them – an innovation for which he would later be mentioned in despatches on the Somme. They placed armed guards in wait along the way, and eventually a car came speeding towards them. The driver did indeed turn out to be a German engaged in the U-boat resupply ('not a bad type as Germans go' Duffield later wrote, 'I forced him, as our Yankee Allies say, to "give me the woiks"'). They found the hidden pipes which had been lowered through a blow-hole and into a storage tank in a cave which was hidden at high tide.

Thereafter Duffield was sent to the Western Front, where he fought on the Somme. He took part in the attack on Pozières, in which he was lightly wounded by poison gas. Whilst in Arras refitting after the battle, he had an enjoyable evening with a most arresting *mademoiselle* who turned out to be the daughter of Raymond Poincaré, President of the French Republic. He also befriended the famous British flying ace, Captain Albert Ball, and was taken on a terrifying flight over the trenches by a senior officer. Another notable comrade of his in the trenches was the author AA Milne, and in one battle the two men found themselves taking cover in the same shell-hole.[29]

As well as serving with unquestioned bravery, Duffield made use of his musical skills entertaining the troops with a somewhat damaged French piano, which was moved about with his unit in a cart.

By the end of the war, Duffield had reached the rank of captain in the Royal Warwick Regiment, but he was seriously wounded just before the Armistice.

Duffield thus had a most interesting time during the war. Yet he chose to write about it sparingly in his autobiography, *Savages and Kings*, writing in some detail about the diverting incidents with the U-boat refuelling in Devon and the people

---

29 Ibid, p 97.

he met at various points in France, rather than the horrors of the Front, which he certainly experienced. Perhaps he shared the same reticence as so many other veterans of the Great War to speak about it generally or indeed to discuss his own experiences. Moreover, since his autobiography was published in 1945, he might also have assumed his audience would not wish to relive another terrible war. He did write about his experiences in the Blitz in the Second World War, which many of his readers would have shared.

Post-war career

While convalescing after the war, Duffield returned to his interest in the theatre. He wrote the music for *Puss! Puss!*, *Pot Luck*, *A to Z* and *Snap*, each of which was an immediate success. Among his popular songs were 'When a Girl's in Love', 'If We Were Married', 'The Long, Long Way', 'Sing It Again', 'Aurora Borealis', 'Caravan Days', and 'My Alco-Holiday'.

In 1922, however, his father died, and he returned to South Australia to manage the family property, though he retained an interest in the theatre in Australia and put on performances of several of his productions. He achieved much success, though was amused by the response to a ropey opening night to his *Pot Luck*, writing 'One Press notice consisted of two lines which read: "Mr Kenneth Duffield invited us to the Theatre Royal to take Pot Luck. We took it."[30] Five years later, he came back to the London stage and once again produced a string of successes, including *Jack of Diamonds*, *Little Miss Gruno*, *After Dark*, and *When Spring Comes Round*.

During the Second World War, he lived for a time at the Savage Club until he fell ill, which in the event was most fortuitous as he it meant he was not in the Club when it was bombed. He worked on a launch on the Thames, following the lead of his great friend Brother Savage AP Herbert, whom we shall meet later as a Savage man of law. Writing just as the war in Europe was ending, looking back over the Blitz, he was full of admiration for the locals, not to say the RAF, and confidently wrote 'London will rise again'.[31]

In 1948 Duffield retired to Adelaide, though he visited London again later in life. He died in 1958.

Bud Flanagan: from teenage private to *Dad's Army*

One of the most recognisable and enduring features of *Dad's Army* was the theme tune. *Who Do You Think You Are Kidding, Mr Hitler?* was a pitch-perfect pastiche of wartime songs, played over a cartoon depiction of the British retreat of 1940. The song was performed in such an accurate fashion that many over the years

---

30 Ibid, p 137.
31 Ibid, p 167.

have mistaken it for a genuine wartime song – chiefly because it was sung by one of the best-known wartime voices, Bud Flanagan. Two decades before his morale-boosting work in the Second World War, Flanagan had fought on the Western Front.

Early life

Flanagan was born Chaim Reuben Weintrop in 1896 in Whitechapel, East London, the son of Polish Jews who had married in Radom, Poland. They had had to flee to Łódź on their wedding day to avoid a pogrom. They tried to emigrate to New York but a con-man sold them a ticket to London instead. After Flanagan was born the registrar wrote down 'Winthrop' rather than 'Weintrop' because, Flanagan later assumed, he was impatient with foreigners who were trying to pronounce their names in English and failing.

Flanagan went to school in Petticoat Lane. By the age of 10 he was working as call-boy at the Cambridge Music Hall. In 1908, he made his debut in a talent contest at the London Music Hall in Shoreditch, performing conjuring tricks as 'Fargo, the Boy Wizard'.

He went on to have a very adventurous adolescence, getting work on a ship as a teenager and travelling to America. There he worked various odd jobs before joining a vaudeville show which toured across the country. He also worked for a show which even toured New Zealand, Australia and South Africa before returning to America.

First World War

Being based in America, Flanagan might have evaded serving in the war, but he clearly felt a debt to the country which had given his parents sanctuary. In 1915, he decided to return to Britain and sign up. He enlisted as 'Robert' Winthrop of the Royal Field Artillery.

It was a harsh introduction, as he recalled in his autobiography:[32]

> I was soon knocked into shape with drilling, marching, rifle drill and horse riding. The riding master was a tyrant. His long whip would rap your knuckles if you didn't hold the reins in the proper manner. I dismounted one day and threatened to punch him on the nose if he didn't cut it out. That finished it! "Fall in, two men." I was put under arrest, marched to the C.O. and charged with insubordination.
>
> The C.O., looking severe, started to question me. "I've come all the way from America to enlist and have never been on a horse in my life before," I said hotly. "I don't like being whipped." The C.O. read me a little lecture but dismissed the charge. I had made my first enemy. For weeks afterwards, that riding master watched me and in the end

---

32 Bud Flanagan, *My Crazy Life* (Frederick Muller Ltd, 1961).

I'd have been better off to have kept my big mouth shut and taken my medicine.

Flanagan was then sent to the Western Front. In Belgium he reached the front-line:

> We shifted about up and down the line between Lavantie and Ypres, where I had my first real taste of war. We were at Zonnebeke every night, and I had to take ammunition up to Passchendaele Ridge, a really hot spot. To get there we went through the crossroads at Zonnebeke, up through the ghost town of Ypres, then in single file to the duck-board track and so to Passchendaele. How the Germans strafed that mile or two! Some well-meaning bloke had nailed a poster to the stump of a tree. It read: "You are now nearer to God than you will ever be," and every night as we went past that sign we cursed the guy who put it there, but no one else would pull it down.

Not long afterwards he met Chesney Allen for the first time, who was serving in the Royal West Kents in Flanders:

> The village, or what was left of it, was Poperinghe, which boasted a couple of frowsty estaminets. I wandered into one of them for egg and chips. The place was crowded, but one table for four had only three at it, so I sat down, gave my order, and started a conversation with a spruce-looking soldier. He was in the Royal West Kents and had been a legitimate actor in peacetime. His name was Chesney Allen. I told him I was a comedian, and after a few beers we said goodnight. He went his way, and I went mine. We did not meet again until after the War.

Flanagan auditioned successfully for a concert party and was soon spending time entertaining troops rather than running the gauntlet of shells. In that capacity he met a corporal with whom, in contrast to Chesney Allen, he shared immediate enmity: 'We simply hated each other'; the corporal doubtless exhibited some of the anti-Semitic behaviour rife in Western society at the time. Worse, the corporal was promoted to sergeant and soon had Flanagan charged with 'silent contempt', or as Flanagan put it, 'dumb insolence'.

Flanagan saw action at Vimy Ridge in the bitterly cold Easter of 1917, which he described as 'hell, but nothing to what the sergeant cooked up for me. Everything dangerous or unpleasant that had to be done was handed to me.' Finally, Flanagan was transferred to another unit:[33]

> When I was packed, the sergeant-major came up to me and growled, "You'll be back". "Never," I said. "And I'll never forget you. When this war is over, I shall always remember you. I shall use your name on the stage, you horrible bastard." Those were my farewell words, as I took leave of Sergeant-Major Flanagan.

---

33 Ibid, p 72.

Though he had at last escaped one form of torment, Flanagan encountered another when he was gassed at Vandelle Wood in March 1918, as the German Operation Michael hammered the British lines. He was temporarily blinded and only began to regain his sight in hospital back behind the lines in Deauville. He was fit and able to resume singing after three weeks, but had a lingering itching in his fingers which lasted the rest of his life. Once again he got on the wrong side of a sergeant major, when one charged him with insubordination following a series of impersonations during a stage act. The commanding officer robustly dismissed the charge, saying that as a doctor he could prescribe medicine but not laughter, and that laughter was invaluable to the wounded. He also praised the accuracy of Flanagan's parodies.

Post-war career

After being demobbed, Flanagan formed a comedy double act, 'Flanagan and Roy', but gained lasting fame in a different double act with Chesney Allen. 'Flanagan and Allen' began in the mid-1920s,[34] performing a classic music hall combination of sketches and songs. They joined several other double acts and formed a new show called 'The Crazy Gang'. The group enjoyed much success, appearing at the London Palladium and the other leading venues of the day. They were clear forerunners of *The Goon Show* – as acknowledged in the early days of the Goons (which, incidentally, starred a future Savage Club member, Harry Secombe), which BBC mandarins had intended to call 'The Junior Crazy Gang' until their lack of imagination was thankfully overruled.

In 1925 Flanagan married Anne ('Curly'), the daughter of the Irish comedian Johnny Quinn (known as 'The Singing Clown'). The following year their son Buddy was born who was to tragically die young from leukaemia in 1956.

Shortly after the Second World War began, Flanagan joined the Savage Club, being nominated in November and elected in December 1939, in the category of drama. He was proposed by Billy Bennett.[35]

Flanagan had very fond memories of his membership of the Club:[36]

---

34 I have seen different dates on which they met and began performing after the war (1924 and 1926); I believe it to have been the earlier date – see http://voices-of-variety.com/chesney-allen/ although it is not of much importance.

35 One of his seconders was an expatriate New Zealander, John Batten, who was a successful actor in Britain at the time, and also notable for being the brother of the pioneering aviatrix Jean Batten (whose statue stands outside the international terminal of Auckland Airport today). The other was Jack Hylton. Note also one of those signing Flanagan's candidate's page was the actor Bernard Lee, who would find fame in roles including M in the early Bond films.

36 Ibid, p 134. Flanagan seems to have been slightly confused about when he became a member. The passage in his autobiography suggests that it was some time in the late 1920s or early 1930s, but the candidate book records it was 1939. Perhaps Flanagan (who was writing in about 1960) had been as a guest many times before joining and conflated that with his membership.

Ches and I also became members of the Savage Club, the premises of which are in Carlton House Terrace a few hundred yards from Buckingham Palace. Our Brother Savages were men famed in the Arts and I was thrilled to lunch there and listen to so much wit and wisdom. It was a refreshing change from the hurly-burly of show business.

Throughout the Second World War, Flanagan and Allen grew in stature as they recorded many popular songs ridiculing the Germans, such as 'We're Going to Hang Out the Washing on the Siegfried Line', and 'Run Rabbit Run',[37] the latter written by Brother Savage Noel Gay, although their most famous number was the more sentimental 'Underneath the Arches', written by Flanagan himself as a paean to the time in his youth spent on his uppers.

Allen retired in 1945. Flanagan continued as a solo performer until the early 1960s, by which time popular music had moved on from his style. He invested some of his accumulated wealth in betting shops and was able to live comfortably. He came out of retirement in the late 1960s when Jimmy Perry, co-writer of *Dad's Army*, managed to persuade him to record the theme song, *Who Do You Think You Are Kidding, Mr Hitler?* Flanagan did so with the backing of the band of the Coldstream Guards. All the other music in the show was genuinely from the 1940s, and included a number of Flanagan's own songs.

Flanagan died in 1968, less than a year after singing the *Dad's Army* theme. He left money in his will to start a charity to promote cancer research, in memory of his son. The Bud Flanagan Leukaemia Fund's first act as a registered charity was to establish the Bud Flanagan Ward at the Royal Marsden Hospital, Surrey. At the time of writing, the charity was still operating.[38]

Chesney Allen: from the cavalry to the Crazy Gang

Flanagan's legendary stage partner, William Ernest 'Chesney' Allen was born in 1893, into very different circumstances. His father was a prosperous builder. Allen, like Lord Denning, showed that a degree of social mobility existed at the time by entering the law. In Allen's case, though, he swiftly abandoned it to become an actor whilst he was still a teenager. He appeared in a wide variety of roles in 'stock', or what would now be called 'rep'. He worked six days a week appearing in dramas before moving on to farce and music hall, later reflecting 'If you're doing drama you're improving your timing all the time, and this training helped me to get the laughs when I went into comedy. You have to have perfect timing to get the best out of a gag.'

---

37 Flanagan used to change the lyrics of 'Run Rabbit Run' to include well-known Nazis as a way of taunting them.

38 See its website: http://www.bflf.org.uk/.

First World War

During the First World War, Allen enlisted in the cavalry, in the 9th Lancers. He formed part of the mounted escort to the 14th Army Corps Commander, General Lieutenant Earl Cavan. He was also assigned to be escort to the Prince of Wales – the future Edward VIII – and later said 'I don't care what they say about the Prince of Wales – he was a very brave man. They had to stop him going to the Front Line eventually. Any man with two stripes on his arm was given orders to prevent him going to the Front Line at all costs, because he was too valuable to lose.' As with some others in this book, I wonder if Edward might have been surprised to find Allen later joined one of his clubs.

After a time, Allen transferred to the infantry and joined the 10th Battalion Royal West Kents as a sergeant. The battalion was part of Kitchener's new armies. They were raised at Maidstone in May 1915 by Lord Harris, Vice-Lieutenant of Kent. After training they deployed to France in May 1916 and saw action at Flers-Courcelette and Transoy Ridges as part of the Battle of the Somme. In 1917, they fought at Messines, Pilkem Ridge, Menin Road and the operations on the Flanders coast, before being sent to Italy in November where they took the front line near the River Piave. In February 1918 they returned to France, where they went on to suffer very heavy casualties resisting the German Operation Michael.

General Sir Horace Smith-Dorrien,[39] a senior commander of the BEF before being removed by his old adversary Sir John French, had the highest praise for the regiment, stating 'I am perfectly certain there is no other Battalion that has made such a name for itself as The Royal West Kents. Everyone is talking about you. They say: Give them a job, they will do it; they never leave the trenches!'

Allen himself was gassed twice during the war. After the first occasion he spent time in Britain recovering before returning to France. We have already seen how he met Bud Flanagan in the midst of the conflict, without either man attributing any significance to the meeting at the time.

His second gas attack took place in March 1918, while he was with a gun team at the Front. Temporarily blinded, he was taken to hospital in Deauville. He was

---

39 General Sir Horace Smith-Dorrien (1858–1930), a career soldier who had served in Africa during the nineteenth century, where he survived the British defeat at Isandlwana. He also distinguished himself in the Second Boer War. In the early days of the First World War, he commanded II Corps at the Battle of Mons (the first major engagement of the BEF) and led a strong rearguard action at the Battle of Le Cateau. Sir John French, an old adversary, removed him after he requested permission to retreat from the Ypres Salient to a more easily defended position – a sound enough request in principle since a salient could be fired upon from three directions.

The news of his sacking from the Western Front was broken to Smith-Dorrien by Sir William Robertson, who is supposed to have said 'Orace, yer for 'ome', dropping his aitches as normal, although Robertson might instead have said 'Orace, yer thrown', a cavalry metaphor.

demobbed in February 1919. 'War turned him into the kind of tragic-comic hero who found humour in adversity and solace in the company of the lowly, the poor and the scared,' wrote Maureen Owen, the Crazy Gang's biographer.

Post-war career

After the war he went back into the theatre. He began by playing straight roles, but soon turned to comedy. After learning from a double act that they were getting rather better paid than he was, he turned to that form, and began working with Bud Flanagan in the mid-1920s. Another writer described their partnership thus:[40]

> Of all the double acts of the earlier variety period, none is remembered more lovingly than that of Flanagan and Allen. It differed curiously from the others, namely in the absence on stage of any deep antagonism between the two partners. Any disagreements they shared were fleeting, superficial, a pretext for single gags and nothing deeper. Whereas in other acts rivalry informs the whole atmosphere, the essential ethos of Bud and Ches was one of pure and simple comradeship. That they had first met in the First World War and were to reach the peak of their career together just before the Second would appear to have had some influence on this aspect of their style. That they saw themselves as buddies in a troubled world where both had experienced the difficulties of succeeding single-handed is clear from Ches's background. The traditional double act of the halls was a crystallisation of the double plot, high life and low life, expounded by literary critic William Empson in his pastoral theory. On the top level there is the well dressed socially secure straight man, on the lower the layabout, the labourer as funny man, guaranteed to put his superior in some ludicrous situation before the night is out. And yet while Ches and Bud fitted visibly into those two roles, there was never any question that they were now anything but socially equal. However debonair Ches may have appeared, however much his early social background differed from Bud's, you knew that he had since been tempered by the same straits and misfortunes as Bud himself.

Throughout the Second World War, he and Flanagan kept up their morale-boosting performances. In December 1939, with the war but a few months old, he joined the Savage Club for some well-deserved escapism. He was proposed by Billy Bennett and seconded by Jack Hylton and Joe Batten – quite a line-up of Savage entertainers.

Allen largely retired from performing after the Second World War, but continued working as the director of a theatrical and variety agency, and managed the Crazy Gang for a time. He performed in two more films with Flanagan,[41] and

---

40 John Fisher, *Funny Way to Be a Hero* (Preface, 2013), p 62.
41 *Dunkirk* (1958, directed by Leslie Norman), a straight film about the evacuation of the British and French troops in 1940, in which Flanagan and Allen appeared as themselves in a minor

made other guest appearances here and there, including the 1980 Royal Variety Performance. He died in 1982, at the age of 88.

Stanley Holloway: 'I don't care to ponder on it'

Stanley Holloway OBE enjoyed one of the longest and most successful careers on stage and screen of all twentieth century Savages. Perhaps his most enduring work was his turn as Alfred Doolittle in *My Fair Lady*, but it came after decades of success as a singer, comic and actor on stage and screen.

Early life

Stanley Augustus Holloway was born in Manor Park, Essex, in 1890. His father was a lawyer's clerk, and his mother a housekeeper and dressmaker. The name 'Stanley' was chosen after the famous Victorian explorer Henry Morton Stanley. He was the second child of the family after his older sister Millie. Their father walked out in 1905, however, and was never seen nor heard from again.

Holloway left school aged just 14, in order to work as a clerk in a boot polish factory, but he had been at school long enough to join the choir, which inspired him to try and find other opportunities to sing or act. While working at the factory he performed part-time as 'Master Stanley Holloway – The Wonderful Boy Soprano'. In 1905, he started working at Billingsgate Fish Market as a clerk. He lasted two years before joining the London Rifle Brigade as an infantryman.

His career on stage started in 1910, when he joined a concert party known by the now-unacceptable but then unremarkable name of *The White Coons Show*. The show was the brainchild of Will C Pepper, whose son Harry S Pepper followed him into showbusiness and would later work with Holloway as well.

In 1913 Holloway joined a different concert party *Nicely, Thanks*, run by the comedian Leslie Henson. Henson became a significant influence on the young Holloway as well as a personal friend. Later the same year, Holloway studied singing in Italy, but returned to the British stage after only six months.

First World War

When the First World War began, Holloway was on tour in America. He tried to return to England, but had to remain for six weeks to fulfil his contract with the touring promoters. When he did make it back, he joined the Connaught Rangers[42] after bumping into a member of the unit while wandering around

---

role; and *Life is a Circus* (1960, directed by Val Guest), about a failing circus whose employees find Aladdin's lamp and try and use it to save the show.

42 The Rangers (known as 'The Devil's Own') were an Irish line infantry regiment of the British Army formed by the amalgamation of the 88th Regiment of Foot and the 94th Regiment of Foot in July 1881. It was one of eight Irish regiments raised largely in Ireland. The 2nd Battalion's

Clacton in Essex wondering how to sign up. He was commissioned as a second lieutenant,[43] due to his earlier training as a private in the London Rifle Brigade. He later reflected: 'if they signed me up as an officer, however junior, the war must have been going stickily.'

To begin with, Holloway was stationed in Ireland, and was there during the Easter Rising of 1916, but did not take part in much fighting. 'I didn't fancy being shot down in Ireland, having the silly, romantic idea that it would be more exciting in France' he later wrote. 'But the fracas turned out to be an anti-climax. Nothing happened. The enemy didn't show up so we all marched back again to barracks.'

He then went to France and served on the Western Front. One of his comrades there was Michael O'Leary of the Irish Guards, who later won the Victoria Cross.[44] The two became friends and were in touch for many years afterwards, including when O'Leary was working as a concierge in London near the West End; Holloway, having better values than the snobbery then prevalent, would take the time to speak to O'Leary whenever he saw him.

Like many of his fellow veterans, Holloway was not keen to relive his wartime experiences. In his autobiography the war occupied only slightly more than three pages out of 343, and less than a single page on his time fighting in France. He gave a few perfunctory details as set out above and then clearly ran out of patience trying to recall those grim years:[45]

> I am afraid this is not a great heroic saga. I had a few vicissitudes, including one occasion when I helped to bring down an enemy plane and capture the crew (though that wasn't too tough, for the poor chaps were only too pleased to be alive and captured) but World War One is so many years ago I don't care to ponder on it. I am just grateful that I was still fit and well when I was demobilised.

For the later war years, Holloway's entertaining skills were put to use in morale-boosting shows across the Western Front. He met well-known actors of the day in France including Edmund Gwenn, Basil Hallam (a matinee star

marching song 'It's a long way to Tipperary' became one of the iconic tunes of the war.

43 The *London Gazette*, 8 December 1915, p 12297, records him being commissioned as a subaltern. In his autobiography, *Wiv a Little Bit O' Luck* (as told to Dick Richards) (Leslie Frewin, 1967), p 58 he stated he was a second lieutenant.

44 O'Leary's citation for his VC read: 'For conspicuous bravery at Cuinchy on the 1st February, 1915. When forming one of the storming party which advanced against the enemy's barricades he rushed to the front and himself killed five Germans who were holding the first barricade, after which he attacked a second barricade, about 60 yards further on, which he captured, after killing three of the enemy and making prisoners of two more. Lance Corporal O'Leary thus practically captured the enemy's position by himself and prevented the attacking party from being fired upon.'

45 Holloway, op cit, p 60.

killed in action), Godfrey Tearle, Vernon Castle and Eric Blore. Following the Armistice, Holloway and the actor Leslie Henson toured with a show written during the war by Blore.

Post-war career

Holloway resigned his commission in May 1919. He returned to London and continued with his West End career. His film career began in 1921 in the silent comedy *The Rotter*, and in 1923 he began performing on the radio with the fledgling BBC. The following year he made his first gramophone record. He joined the Savage Club in October 1924, left for a time and was re-elected in October 1936.

By the time of the Second World War, he was a well-established star. He helped make wartime propaganda films, including *The Way Ahead* (1944), a significant film co-written by Brother Savage Peter Ustinov and directed by the genius Brother Savage Carol Reed[46] (who would go on to make one of the finest British films of all, *The Third Man*).

After the war, he appeared in a number of Ealing comedies, including the classics *Passport to Pimlico* (1949), *The Lavender Hill Mob* (1951) and *The Titfield Thunderbolt* (1953). But it was his role as Alfred P Doolittle on stage and screen in *My Fair Lady* which secured for him lasting fame and, as he delightedly explained, the ability to choose his own roles thereafter. As much as those films were better known in Britain than America, Holloway did enjoy some success in Hollywood, and there befriended some stars of the day including Graucho Marx, of whom he wrote:[47]

> We usually dine with him from time to time when he is here or we are in New York or Hollywood. The last time we went to the Hillcrest Golf Club. This was built by the Jewish people because the other big Hollywood golf club won't have Jewish people as members or anybody connected with showbusiness, so the Jews built their own club and a very handsome place it is, too. This, I quickly add, is not the club from which Groucho is alleged to have resigned in one of my favourite stories about him. Remember it?

> He is said to have resigned from a certain club on the valid grounds that 'I have no wish to be a member of a club that would condescend to have me as a member!'

Note the uncritical reporting of the discrimination, albeit it was plain from

---

46 Reed was already a Savage, having joined in October 1940, though Ustinov did not join until after the war.

47 Stanley Holloway, *Wiv a Little Bit O' Luck*, ghost written by Dick Richards (Leslie Frewin, 1967), p 151. One such club offered to waive its no-Jews rule for Marx provided he abstained from using the swimming pool. Marx, married to a non-Jewish woman, asked 'My daughter's only half Jewish, can she wade in up to her knees?'

Holloway's friendship with Marx that he was no anti-Semite himself. Again, though, the incident shows how progressive the Savage Club was compared with other institutions of the day, since there were many Jewish Savages, including Herbert Lightstone and Bud Flanagan. (There was some good-natured banter on occasion: when Jack Hassall became annoyed at the noise from a group of Jewish members he called out 'Silence in the Ghetto!'[48] Also, when Mark Hambourg was being disturbed during a bridge game at the Club by the chatter of some German-Jewish refugees in the Club, he heard one ask 'Is there much anti-Semitism in this country?', and immediately retorted 'No, only among the Jews!'[49]).

Holloway continued performing into his eighties, including at the Royal Variety Performance at the London Palladium in 1980 at the age of 89. He died in 1982.

He was remembered by Eric Midwinter in *Drumbeat* in 2017:[50]

> Has Britain ever boasted of a more versatile performer than Stanley Holloway? I was privileged to prepare his notice for the Dictionary of National Biography, an arduous task of crushing his manifold successes, inclusive of 60 film appearances, into the wordage allowed. He was closely connected with the Savage Club. The famous "Pukka Sahib" sketch, was tried out at a Savage Club dinner before inclusion in the 1940 Saville Theatre revue Up and Doing. Stanley Holloway attempted to recite Milton Hayes' "The Green Eye of the Little Yellow God" while, from an adjacent box, Leslie Henson and Cyril Richard, as colonel and major respectively, forced him into various amendments based on their Indian Army experience. However, it is as one of the nation's three best monologists (take a bow Gracie Fields and Brother Savage Billy Bennett) that I wish to consider him.
>
> It was Leslie Henson and Gracie Fields who suggested that he should include monologues in his variety act which initially consisted just of bracing baritone songs like "the Sergeant major's on Parade". In 1929 he varied this diet with the recital of "Sam Small", the private in Wellington's army who resolutely refused to pick up his musket. In 1932 at the Northern Rugby League Annual Dinner in Newcastle he first introduced "the Lion and Albert" to enduring fame. In all there were 34 monologues, the majority of them penned by Brother Savage Marriott Edgar, a half brother of Edgar Wallace (Edgar was a family surname but the Wallace is not the reason Albert's lion is so called).
>
> Having served with the Yorkshire regiment the Green Howards in World War I, Stanley Holloway, himself a Londoner, adopted a Yorkshire accent for the monologues. It did not work too well. Stage Yorkshire tends to be brusque, knowing and dominant. These tales required a more mordant, sombre tone. The South Lancashire speech

---

48 Bradshaw, op cit, p 72.

49 The story was told by George W Bishop, *My Betters* (Heinemann, 1957), p 86. Bishop was a theatre critic and redoubtable Savage for many years.

50 No. 137, Spring 2017.

pattern of the Mersey valley or, industrially, the lines of the Worsley to Runcorn Bridgewater Canal and the Manchester Ship Canal, served the purpose admirably. Quietly ruminative, warily resigned, flatly unemotional. its timbre captured the character of the verse sublimely.

The monologues fall into three main genres. There are Sam Small's martial ventures; there are reports of the Ramsbottom family of which Albert was the scion and after whom eight monologues are named; and there are the history lessons such as "the Battle of Hastings" or "the Burghers of Calais" and including the occasional biblical epic, for instance, "Three Ha'pence a Foot". What a feast of droll humour.

Stanley Holloway's favourite stanza was the last four lines of 'Magna Charter' which still has a present day resonance:

And it's through that there Magna Charter
As were signed by the barons of old
That in England today we can do what we like
As long as we do what we're told!

Raymond Massey: a statesmanlike actor

Raymond Massey was a successful actor for many decades. He was another Canadian Savage, even if he became best known for playing American characters on screen. Most importantly for our purposes, he was a Great War veteran as well, who served not only on the Western Front but in the largely forgotten – though bloody and historically significant – theatre of the Russian Civil War.

Early life and First World War

Massey was born in Toronto in 1896. His father was Chester Daniel Massey, the owner of the successful Massey-Harris Tractor Company, which eventually became the Massey Ferguson company. (The company had been founded as a farm-implements manufacturing concern by Raymond Massey's great-grandfather Daniel Massey.[51])

Raymond Massey attended secondary school for a short time at Upper Canada College before transferring to Appleby College in Oakville, Ontario. He went on to study at the University of Toronto, where he was an active member of the Kappa Alpha Society, the progenitor of the modern fraternity system in North America.

During the First World War, he enlisted with the Canadian Army on 8 November 1915, in Ontario, when aged 19.[52] He underwent officer training in artillery before being sent to Europe and to the Western Front. In 1916, he

---

51 Daniel Massey (1798–1856), a blacksmith in what became Newcastle, Ontario. He started an agricultural implements business in 1847.
52 http://www.canadiangreatwarproject.com.

was wounded twice and suffered shell-shock, spending four months in hospital. Thereafter he returned to Canada, where he worked as an army instructor for American officers at Yale University.

Allied intervention in the Russian Civil War

In 1918, Massey went on a rather interesting engagement to Siberia as part of the Allied intervention in the Russian Civil War, one aspect of the First World War that usually receives little attention in Anglo or American works on the conflict, although it has been claimed to have shaped much of later Russo-Western relations (for the worse).

The intervention came about when the Tsar abdicated. German troops invaded Russia and advanced on Petrograd, the then-capital of Russia, in early 1918. In late February, Bolshevik Russia switched sides and supported the German position, signing the Treaty of Brest-Litovsk. The Allies turned against the new regime and stared supporting the 'White Russians', a loose group of disparate interests united only by their opposition to communism.

As well as the immediate concern of not wanting Russia to supply Germany, the Western Allies feared (i) a possible Russo-German military alliance, (ii) the Bolsheviks defaulting on Imperial Russia's substantial foreign loans and – a fear that was to dominate much of the twentieth century's geo-politics – (iii) the possibility that communist revolutionary ideas would spread.

The problem for the Allies was that the Western Front was as bloody as ever and stretching the European powers to the limit. They therefore turned to the United States, who, in July 1918, against the advice of the United States Department of War, agreed to send 5,000 US Army troops to the campaign. They became known as the 'American North Russia Expeditionary Force' and were sent to Archangel. A further 8,000 soldiers, designated the 'American Expeditionary Force Siberia', went to Vladivostok. The Canadian government agreed to lead a British Empire force and sent troops including Massey. The largest contributor was Japan, who sent approximately 70,000 troops.

The specific goals of the Allied intervention were ostensibly (i) to assist the Czechoslovak Legion (some 30,000 troops formerly under Russian command who were against the Bolsheviks), (ii) to secure supplies of munitions and armaments in Russian ports, and (iii) to re-establish the Eastern Front. The Japanese also wished to set up a buffer state in Siberia.

In the event, the campaign was a complete failure. The Red Army defeated the White Army in 1919 in Ukraine and Siberia in 1919. The remainder of the White forces were defeated in Crimea in late 1920.[53]

---

53 Smaller skirmishes continued for two more years. By 1923, the Red Army controlled all of the newly- created Soviet Union, though there was still some armed national resistance in Central

The Western Allies – jaded from the First World War anyway – withdrew in 1920. Japanese forces stayed on in Siberia until 1922 and in Sakhalin until 1925, but left having not secured any buffer zone for Japan. All in all, the quixotic intervention by the Allies was not a great start to relations between the Soviet Union and the West.

Massey's own part in that ill-conceived adventure was confined to serving in Siberia in 1918. Whilst there he debuted on stage, in front of American troops, and it was during those performances that he said 'the bug bit me' and he became set on a career in the theatre.

Post-war career

After the war Massey attended Balliol College, Oxford for a time, before returning to Canada. He worked in the family farm-implement business for a time, but managed to persuade his family – strict Methodists – to allow him to continue acting. Permission was given by his father on the condition that he would not rehearse on the Sabbath.

Massey returned to England to pursue a professional career on the West End stage. There were no doubt more opportunities in London than in Canada, and he was also far enough away from his father to avoid the stricture about rehearsals. Initially, Massey had some problems in that the English perceived his speech as too American, just as Americans were later to consider it too English. Nevertheless, he appeared in the West End regularly throughout the 1920s, enabling him to qualify as a Savage in the category of drama. He was proposed for Club membership by Reginald Berkeley, seconded by Norman O'Neill and Aubrey Hammond, and elected in May 1927.

He first appeared on film in *High Treason* (1928). In 1936, he starred in *Things to Come*, a film notable for being an adaptation by HG Wells of his own novel *The Shape of Things to Come* (1933). He went on to appear in films including *The Scarlet Pimpernel*, *The Prisoner of Zenda*, *Reap the Wild Wind*, *Mourning Becomes Electra*, *Arsenic and Old Lace*, *East of Eden* and *Seven Angry Men*.

One of his interesting support roles came just after the Second World War, when he played Abraham Farlan, the American Revolutionary War character in Powell and Pressburger's classic film *A Matter of Life and Death* (retitled *Stairway to Heaven* in America), starring David Niven and Kim Hunter. The film, nowadays acclaimed as a classic,[54] was a thinly-veiled propaganda piece aimed at enhancing Anglo-American relations after the war, at a time of some fear in

---

Asia until as late as 1934.

54 See for example the review by Roger Ebert: https://www.rogerebert.com/reviews/stairway-to-heaven-a-matter-of-life-and-death-1995.

Britain about its diminishing status in the world, the end of the Empire and the rise of America as a superpower.[55]

Massey's other roles included playing the abolitionist John Brown in two films, and Abraham Lincoln in *Abe Lincoln in Illinois* (1940), for which he was nominated for an Academy Award. He had earlier played the role of Lincoln on stage, and ended up playing Lincoln so many times in different productions that he joked about being typecast as a president. One wag said Massey was so obsessive about his preparation for Lincoln that he would not be satisfied until someone assassinated him.

Late in his career, in the 1960s, he performed a regular role on the well-known television series *Dr. Kildare*.

By the 1970s, Massey had grown tired of the direction of the stage. According to his obituary in *The New York Times*:

> He was offended, though, by what he considered excessive vulgarity in the theatre in the 1970's. "To me," he said, "the theatre should be enchantment, make-believe, let's pretend. Today it's sex, obscenity and squalor."

> Although he wrote two books about his career, "When I Was Young" and "A Hundred Different Lives," he did not enliven them, as was the fashion in such books, with malicious gossip, scandal or sexual episodes.

Massey also had some interesting relatives. His brother, Vincent Massey, was the first Canadian-born governor general of Canada, appointed in the aftermath of the King–Byng affair. Reputedly, the Marquess of Salisbury said of him: 'Fine chap, Vincent, but he does make one feel a bit of a savage' – sadly, not a reference to the Club, but instead a nod to the fact that Massey had perfected upper class British airs rather better than the British themselves.

He was married three times: to Margery Fremantle from 1921 to 1929 (divorce), with one child, architect Geoffrey Massey; to Adrianne Allen from 1929 to 1939 (divorce), with two children, the actors Anna Massey and Daniel Massey, and to Dorothy Whitney from 1939 until her death in 1982. His estrangement and divorce from Adrianne Allen was the inspiration for Ruth Gordon and Garson Kanin's script for the film *Adam's Rib* (1949), starring Katharine Hepburn and Spencer Tracy. As in the film, Massey and Allen married their respective lawyers in real life (who were the then-married legal team of Dorothy Whitney and William Dwight Whitney).

---

55 The Savage Club, meanwhile, was doing its bit for building post-war Anglo-American relations when in 1951 it appointed the United States' Ambassador to Britain, Walter S Gifford (1885–1966), an honorary life member of the Club. Gifford had worked in telecommunications for many years and during the Great War had been a junior statistician helping to marshal America's incomparable industrial resources for the war effort.

Massey died in 1983, coincidentally on the same day as his former co-star David Niven. As well as two stars on the Hollywood Walk of Fame (one for television and one for film), he is remembered in a Canadian cocktail, the Raymond Massey, which consists of rye, ginger syrup, and champagne.

John Mackenzie Rogan: the leader of the band

Lieutenant-Colonel John Mackenzie Rogan, CVO, was a leading figure in military bands for many years in the nineteenth and early twentieth century, and an important person in the history of music generally. Like some other distinguished Savages we meet in these pages, he managed to rise up through the ranks of the armed forces in spite of the more rigid class system of his day.

Early life

Rogan was born in 1855 in the Isle of Wight. He joined the army as a 'boy soldier' in 1867 as 'No. 1832 Boy John M Rogan' with the 2nd Battalion (North Devon) Regiment of Foot. As he explained in his autobiography:[56]

> To tell the truth, Her Majesty's Forces might have had to rub along without the four-feet-seven of John Rogan, only that the boy's father had told the boy so many soldier stories of adventure in the Peninsula, the Mediterranean Islands, and other fascinating places, that John, eager to see the world, thought he could not do better than go soldiering too.
>
> My great-grandfather fought under Marlborough, my grandfather was a soldier, my father joined the British Army in the year before Waterloo, my step-brother was a soldier and served in the Crimea and the Indian Mutiny, and so also was my eldest brother. To carry on the line, I may add parenthetically that my younger son joined His Majesty's Forces in the second week of the Great War. He was wounded at the Battle of the Somme, was afterwards transferred to the Indian Army, and served in India, Egypt and Palestine.

He served with the regiment in South Africa and in India, as well as domestic postings. In January 1880, having reached the rank of drum-major, he was sent to the Royal Military School of Music at Kneller Hall in South West London to qualify as a bandmaster. He excelled at Kneller Hall and was appointed acting sergeant major of the establishment.

In May 1882, he was appointed bandmaster of the 2nd Queen's, then serving at Peshawar. He found the band to be under strength, primarily due to discharges,

---

56 John Mackenzie Rogan, *Fifty Years of Army Music* (Methuen & Co Ltd, 1926), p 2. Note that his surname is occasionally spelt Mackenzie-Rogan, but in his autobiography he said that 'Mackenzie' was his second Christian name. Also, one sees a capital 'k' in his name in some sources, but not in his autobiography, hence not here either.

and set about enlisting new members whom he then trained himself to a high standard. As well as his evident musical talent, he was a talented cricketer, playing for the regimental XI, and he was an above average shot, even by the high standards of marksmanship of his day.

In 1895 he moved to the Coldstream Guards, the oldest extant regiment in the British Army,[57] which also had an interesting musical history. As explained by the regimental website:

> [The Coldstream Guards had] in addition to a Corps of Drums, a band of eight musicians as early as 1742. By 1768 the Coldstream Guards had what was described as "a fine Band of Musik", comprised of civilians who were hired by the month. Their only military duty was to march the guard from St James' Park to the Palace and back.
>
> An inherent conflict between musical and military roles was exposed in 1783, when Lord Cathcart, an officer of the Regiment asked the Band to play during an aquatic excursion to Greenwich; the musicians refused on the grounds that such an engagement was "incompatible with their several respectable and private engagements". The officers petitioned their Colonel-in-Chief, the Duke of York, then in Hannover for leave to have a band that they could command at all times. The Duke enlisted twelve German musicians—two oboes, four clarinets, two bassoons, one trumpet, two horns and a serpent—and sent them to London. They were led by Music-Master Eley, remembered today for his slow march, 'Duke of York'. Reporting on the change, *The Times* of 20 May 1785 spared a thought for the dismissed musicians:
>
> > In all probability we never shall hear a regimental band equal to that which is dismissed, they have for many years been a treat to those persons who have attended the courtyard at St James's, and we sincerely hope, after so long and faithful service, they will at least be entitled to half pay for the remainder of their lives.
>
> Mr Eley was succeeded in turn by John Weyrauch in 1800 and by James Denman in 1815. By this time the band had been augmented by flutes, key bugles and trombones and now numbered 20 performers. With this combination, the Coldstream Guards were ordered to Paris during the occupation following Waterloo.
>
> For several years, the Coldstream Band in keeping with those of other regiments, had three black musicians playing tambourines and a 'Jingling Johnny'. The practice was discontinued in 1837.

---

57 One of the best-known regiments in military history, the Coldstream Guards claim a double distinction in the British Army. First, they are the oldest regiment in continuous existence. Secondly, they are the sole representative by direct descent of Cromwell's New Model Army, the first regular army in Britain.

The regiment was raised in 1650 by General George Monck (sometimes spelt Monk) and transferred to the new standards in 1661 in a ceremony that consisted of laying down its arms and taking them up again in the service of the King. Charles II conferred the titles of Duke of Albemarle and Lord General upon Monck.

Rogan flourished in the role. He became the first bandmaster in the history of the Brigade of Guards to be granted a substantive commission, being promoted to the rank of second lieutenant in 1904. By 1900 the size of the band had grown to 51 musicians and during the years before the First World War the band reached new heights of excellence in concert. They made pioneering (for an army band) visits to Canada, France and Russia, and also appeared in the new medium of gramophone, with their first recording taking place in a London hotel in 1898.

A particularly notable moment in his career occurred when he introduced Tchaikovsky's *1812 Overture* to Britain, having brought it back from St Petersburg in 1896. Brother Savage Sir Henry Wood recalled in his autobiography:[58]

> Mackenzie Rogan, Conductor of the Coldstream Guards' Band, met me one day in the street.
>
> "Do you know Tchaikovsky's overture 1812?" he asked.
>
> "No," I said. "Never heard it."
>
> "It's fine; just been published. Would you like to hear it?"
>
> Naturally I said I would, whereupon Rogan invited me to go down one morning to a public house near Victoria station where he was rehearsing. I seem to think my father went with me; at all events, I was sufficiently taken with what was only a military band arrangement to perform the work at the Promenade concerts; but I took good care, of course, to obtain the original version.

Wood played the piece regularly at the Proms, and Rogan played it throughout the land with the Coldstream Guards, so that it soon became one of the most recognisable pieces in the entire classical canon.

In all, Rogan served for 20 years as the senior director of music of the Brigade of Guards. Among other things, he was responsible for the massed bands of the brigade at the funeral of Queen Victoria and the coronation of George V. He was also a talented composer himself. His most notable work was a march entitled 'Bond of Friendship' which he dedicated to the Coldstream Guards. It is still performed today.

Once again we return to the theme of patriotism of a bygone age, since Rogan was absolutely thrilled to preside over the music of a state occasion. One music historian noted:[59]

> He was a man who genuinely believed that what he did as a musician for the state and his sovereign was important to their purpose and welfare: it was a patriotic act. The type of excellence after which he

---

58 Sir Henry Wood, op cit, pp 91–92.

59 Trever Herbert and Helen Barlow, *Music and the British Military in the Long Nineteenth Century* (Oxford University Press, 2013), p 217.

encouraged his musicians to strive was part of a larger endeavour to mark and celebrate the greatness of Britain and its empire, and the increasing proximity of the monarch to such events made this purpose all the more lucid and authentic.

The list of medals and awards he collected over the years was remarkable. They included the Commander of the Royal Victorian Order, Officer (Knight) of the Order of the Crown of Belgium, Cavaliere of the Order of the Crown of Italy and Officer of the Black Star of Benin (France); with service medals comprising the Silver Medal Queen Victoria's Jubilee, Silver Medal Royal Victorian Order, Long Service Medal, Burma Medal and two clasps (1885–87 and 1887–1889), Victory Medal, General Services Medal and Coronation Medal (1911).

In October 1904 he was elected Honorary Member of the Royal Academy of Music, and in 1907 he received an honorary doctorate in music from the University of Toronto.

First World War

On 4 August 1914, Rogan was with the Coldstream Guards Band at the annual fete and flower show at Stourbridge, and he was told that a declaration of war would be made at 11pm. He explained: 'There and then I addressed the many thousands gathered round the band-stand and appealed to the young men to enlist and go forward to fight for their King and Country. All joined in singing "Rule Britannia" and "God Save the King." It was an impressive scene.'[60]

Thereafter the bands of the Brigade of Guards played daily for troops heading to the Front. From the middle of August, Rogan continued with a pre-planned tour of the country, using each concert as an opportunity to appeal for volunteers. He also headed the executive committee of the Fund for National Bands for the New Army, set up by *The Daily Telegraph*. As he later wrote:[61]

> "Music hath charms to soothe the savage beast" and also, if I may be allowed to put it so—to make the crowd invest! Music performed many services in the Great War, and having already seen something of its magic in other spheres I was not at all surprised when I was invited to play to the people of the City of London, so that they might be charmed into opening their pockets and putting their savings and their earnings into the great War Loan.

The Guards themselves were quickly expanded by the formation of the Welsh Guards in February 1915, soon after which the City of Cardiff stated that it 'wished to have the honour and privilege of presenting a Band to the Regiment of Welsh Guards' and thus purchased its first set of instruments. The band was

---

60 Rogan, op cit, p 182.
61 Ibid, p 185.

created later that year with Brother Savage Major Andrew Harris MVO (a life member of the Savage Club from 1918) appointed as the bandmaster. Its first public appearance was at the King's Guard Mounting on St David's Day 1916 and took part in a Grand Welsh Patriotic Meeting held at the London Opera House that evening. It came under the aegis of Rogan as with all the guards' bands. The band leader, pianist, composer and impresario Jack Hylton (1892–1965), who became a life member of the Savage Club in 1931, was musical director of the band of the 20th Hussars and the Director of the Army Entertainment Division during the War. He thus fell under the command of Rogan, as did Captain FW Wood MVO (1864–1944[62]), the head of the Band of the Scots Guards from 1900 until 1929 and a Savage Club member from January 1936.[63]

Rogan's performances met with much critical success. On 16 July 1915, for example, *The Times* reported:

> The Duchess of Albany and Princess Victoria of Schleswig-Holstein were present at an "At Home" in aid of the funds of the Professional Classes War Relief Council, held at 13, Prince's-gate, Kensington, yesterday afternoon, the house being lent by Mr J. P. Morgan.
>
> The band of the Coldstream Guards, under Captain Mackenzie Rogan, played in the gardens, and other attractions included a "witch's corner," a camp concert, illustrated war stories by Miss S. MacNaughtam, and Maori songs and dances. Tea was served on the terrace and in the gardens.

In early 1915, the Coldstream Guards Band volunteered to go to the Front. The War Office did not respond until the autumn, when it resolved to send out all the bands of the Brigade of Guards in turn for spells of three months' duty with the Guards Division. Rogan made three tours in total. The first was from January to May 1916 in France and Flanders. He wrote:[64]

> I shall never forget the first time we went to meet a battalion coming out of the line. We took them by surprise a couple of miles from La Gorgue and they happened to be our own 3rd Battalion, commanded by Colonel John Campbell, DSO, who later on won the VC. They, good chaps, were tramping along, each man carrying his seventy or eighty pounds of kit, and many of them bent over with the weight of it. But, at the first tap of the big drum the difference in those self-same men was wonderful to see, and when the band began to play there were cheers you might have heard miles away. I saw tears trickling down Colonel

---

62 I have seen different dates for his death, including as early as 1932, which is obviously incorrect since he joined the Savage Club after that date. I believe it to have been either 1944 or 1954.

63 Under Wood the Scots Guards' Band recorded extensively (around 350 sides) for Columbia and its associated Rena and Regal labels from about 1910 to 1916. Wood was decorated by King George V with the Royal Victorian Order in 1928.

64 Rogan, op cit.

Campbell's face. It was a wondrous and very affecting experience. We
played them for five miles or so, then returned to La Gorgue.

On tour he met his fellow Savages the Prince of Wales, Lord Kitchener and
Prince Arthur of Connaught, the last of whom reminded him that the previous occasion they had met had been rather different – it had been the Prince's
wedding. Showing yet again the catholic membership of the Savages of the time,
he also met a fellow member from a somewhat lower status in both the army
and society of the day: 'I came across a Brother Savage – Lieutenant THG Bird,
gunner and Irishman. We took wine and cigars together and he reminded me
that I should not be in the chair at the house dinner that St Patrick's Day, as I had
been in other years.'[65] As it happened, he instead gave a concert dedicated to the
Irish Guards on St Patrick's Day 1916, and accompanied them for a few miles as
they moved towards the line that evening. Rogan experienced air bombardment
and was close enough to the Front to come within range of German artillery, as
well as continually hearing deafening artillery bombardments further away.

In May 1917 Rogan began his second tour of Continental Europe with the
Guards' Band. They were given a rousing send-off by thousands gathered at
Folkestone, and played before 30,000 people on arrival in Paris. They continued
to play to rapturous applause across France, one particularly memorable occasion being performing for 6,000 female workers at the Citroën munitions factory
– and being allowed to fraternise with them afterwards. Clearly knowing their
audiences, they regularly played the 'Marseillaise'.

The year 1917 also marked Rogan's fiftieth year in the army. As a measure of
his esteem in the music industry of the time, a concert to mark the achievement
was planned and held at Queen's Hall in January 1918. A special ticket-selling
committee was formed by Lady Randolph Churchill – mother of Winston – and
Lady Maud Warrender.[66] The event was a great success, *The Times* reporting the
following day:

> The Band of the Coldstream Guards gave a concert at Queen's Hall
> yesterday on the occasion of the military and musical jubilee of Major
> Mackenzie Rogan, MVO, in which Sir Thomas Beecham, Sir Alexander
> Mackenzie, Sir F. Cowen, Mr E German, and Mr A Fagge took part
> as conductors. Mme Vandervelde recited in Elgar's "Carillon," Miss
> Muriel Foster sang two of Elgar's "Sea Pictures," Miss Margaret
> Cooper, "The Green Hills of Somerset," at the piano, and Mr Thorpe
> Bates, "Ho, Jolly Jenkin"; Miss Carrie Tubb, who was to have sung, was

---

65 Ibid, p 193.
66 *The Times*, 12 January 1918. See also the description in pp 201–2 of Rogan, op cit. I was slightly
    thrown when first reading Rogan's book as he did not make clear that the concert was in 1918,
    but I have double checked the dates in *The Times* and, although 1917 was his fiftieth year, the
    concert was definitely held in January of the following year.

unfortunately unable to reach the hall.

A collection of interesting Indian melodies arranged by Major Rogan, Miss Foster's beautiful singing of "Where Corals lie" and "The Swimmer," conducted by Mr Fagge, and the spirited playing of the band in Sullivan's "Macbeth" under Sir Thomas Beecham, were the chief objects of musical interest.

The presentation, consisting of an address, a grandfather clock, and a cheque, was made by Sir Alexander Mackenzie in an excellent speech laying weight on "our friend's talent for friendship," his long services, and the growth of English music during that period, and expressing his conviction that military bands had had much to do with this. He believed that English military bands, of which Major Rogan was the senior officer, were now as good as any in the world. Major Rogan made a suitable reply.

They were often transported around France by former London omnibuses; quite a luxury for the time, one imagines.

In 1918, he travelled again to France, stopping at Berle-au-Bois, Lagnicourt, Cambrai and elsewhere. He also led the Guards' Bands on a tour of Italy. *The Times* reported a highly successful performance in Rome:[67]

> The Allied concert last night at the Augusteo was a brilliant success. The triumph of the evening was won by the massed bands of the Guards, under Major Mackenzie Rogan. They had intended to play music, but the promoting committee insisted on "Tipperary," with which we are now identified for better or for worse. So, after the three old English dances from Nell Gwynn, they played, not only "Tipperary," but "Tipperary" with humorous variations, in which the part of the low comedian was taken by the bassoons. Various other instruments played pranks, the bandsmen sang and whistled, and it was all very jovial. The "humouresque," as it was called, gained a rapturous encore, and Major Rogan brought the audience to their feet with a volley of applause when the 250 bandsmen crashed out the opening bars of Garibaldi's Hymn. Another encore was demanded, and "Rule Britannia" was received with equal enthusiasm. The audience still clamoured for more, but it was now nearly midnight, and the Guardsmen, who looked very magnificent in their scarlet and gold and vast bearskins, filed off the platform, with the audience still cheering.

The Guards' Bands continued playing to domestic audiences. In June 1918, *The Times* reported under the disarming headline of 'Music as Propaganda':

> The summer season of open-air concerts arranged by Vickers (Limited) for the recreation of their munitions workers in North Kent, has started with a visit to Dartford of the band of the Coldstream Guards, under the direction of Major Mackenzie Rogan, who has a firm belief in the

---

67 *The Times*, 25 February 1918.

propaganda value of music, not only as performed by British bands in Allied countries, but for keeping up the buoyancy of people at home.

Support for his belief was forthcoming on Wednesday night when, remembering a previous Guards' concert, people asked for his setting of "The Hymn of Hate," and also for a speech. Major Rogan gave a little account of the recent visit of the band to Italy and said that we might shortly have an Italian military band giving performances in London.

In recognition of his unstinting efforts during wartime and the great reception his bands received everywhere they played, Rogan was awarded the French Black Star 4th Class and the Italian Order of the Crown 5th Class.

Post-war career

After the war, he continued touring Europe, leading bands in performances in Paris and Rome in 1919. In March 1920, he was promoted to lieutenant colonel[68] – the first time in the history of the British Army that a musician had attained that rank – but he retired from the army later that same year.

In his retirement, he continued his musical interests by becoming Honorary Director of Music for the British Legion. He also took part in the arrangements for the Armistice Night music festival at the Albert Hall, and was in the crowd at the Royal Academy as a form of reciprocation when Sir Alexander Mackenzie, who had presented him with the gifts and address at his fiftieth anniversary army concert, received the Beethoven Medal of the Royal Philharmonic Society (note that Beethoven correctly transcended any lingering anti-German sentiment).[69]

He died in 1930.

Coda: Rogan and the Savage Club

Rogan was elected to the Savage Club in 1899. He chaired his first house dinner in 1911, the year of George V's Coronation. He devoted a chapter of his autobiography[70] to his membership of the Club. Here are some representative extracts:

> Of all the clubs in existence, for those who seek refuge from the sins and sinners of this wicked world, the Savage Club is the most famous. These Savages are the most civil and civilised of all the races of humanity ...

> Royalty has shown that it thinks well of us. George V, as Prince of Wales, was one of us for many years and the Prince of Wales was our guest in 1909 and the Duke of Connaught in 1906. I recall great nights

---

68 *The Times*, 11 March 1920.
69 *The Times*, 11 December 1922.
70 Rogan, *Fifty Years of Army Music*, op cit.

with members of the Scott and Shackleton Polar expeditions as well as Lord Kitchener and Lord Roberts. Many eminent Savages have taken the Chair over the years including Lord Alverstone the Lord Chief Justice of England.

The 1909 dinner took place in February of that year at the Hotel Cecil, Adelphi Terrace being too small for the event. Rogan referred to the 'beautiful souvenir' of a silver cigar and cigarette case which the Prince of Wales presented to the Club after the dinner, inscribed: 'To my Brother Savages'. That 'beautiful souvenir' is still proudly displayed in the Clubroom, and a photograph of the dinner is framed and on the wall opposite the bar.

Rogan is another who is still fondly remembered by the Club today – Alan Williams wrote a piece on him for *Drumbeat*, Winter 2018.

Arnold Ridley: Lance Corporal Ridley to Private Godfrey

> If you've ever tried to keep awake when you haven't had any sleep for days, it's not a question of allowing yourself to go to sleep. I can remember lying in a sunken road behind Gueudecourt. The trenches were full of water and I can remember getting out of the trench and lying on the parapet with the bullets flying around because sleep was such a necessity and death only meant sleep.
>
> *Arnold Ridley*

He was the ultimate non-soldier: one of the key characters in *Dad's Army* was the completely unwarlike Private Godfrey, well into his dotage and congenitally incapable of hurting a fly. Early in the series it was revealed Godfrey had been a conscientious objector during the First World War. He received the contempt of his commander, Captain Mainwaring, upon the revelation. He redeemed himself in the same episode, first by saving Mainwaring's life and then when it was discovered he had in fact been a medical orderly and had won the Military Medal for saving lives under fire on the Western Front. Thereafter Godfrey assumed his familiar position as the platoon's medical orderly.

There was much irony in the casting of the role of Godfrey, because the actor portraying him, Brother Savage Arnold Ridley, had in fact been an extremely brave soldier on the front line during the First World War, and had volunteered again during Second World War.[71]

---

71 A rather dull pedant might point out that the character Godfrey would have been too old to have been called up in the First World War so would not have needed to have been a conscientious objector: assuming him to have roughly corresponded to Ridley's actual age at the time of filming, he would have been well over the age conscripted in 1916.

Early life and First World War

William Arnold Ridley was born in 1896 in Bath, Somerset, the son of a gym instructor who also ran a boot and shoe shop. Later in life, Ridley enjoyed saying that he inherited his father's love of sports and his mother's inability to play any of them.

He trained as a student teacher and made an early start as an actor before the First World War broke out. Aged 18, he volunteered immediately. Initially he was rejected due to a foot injury, but in 1915 he managed to enlist in the Somerset Light Infantry. He had only been on the frontline for two days when he was wounded by shrapnel. After recovering in the base hospital at Étaples, he returned to the trenches, where he was shot in the leg and then sent back to England.[72]

He recovered sufficiently to return to France and participate in the Battle of the Somme where he went over the top in September 1916. He later recounted:[73]

> We were told that there was a pocket of resistance left over and that two advances had left this pocket and we were told that we would attack. We would get a five minute barrage, which we got, but Jerry and the German machine guns were firing, saying "we know you are coming over, come on, where are you?" Although the plans had gone wrong, the whistles blew and we went over the top just the same. At that time I was a bomber and we got down to the first trench ...
>
> I went round one of the traverses and someone hit me on the head with a rifle butt. I was wearing a tin hat, fortunately, but it didn't do me much good. A chap came at me with a bayonet, aiming for a very critical part naturally and I managed to push it down, I got a bayonet wound in the groin. After that I was still very dizzy, from this blow on the head presumably. I remember wrestling with another German and the next thing I saw, it appeared to me that my left hand had gone. After that, I was unconscious ...
>
> I always remember my disappointment the next morning when I found that my hand was still on because I thought, well, if I lost my hand I'm all right, I shall live, they can't send me out without a hand again. I was 20 then, it's not altogether a right thought for a young man to hope that he's been maimed for life.

He was asked by a surgeon if his hand wound had been self-inflicted.

> I was still suffering from shell shock, blue with cold and in consider-

72 See John Simpkin, 'Arnold Ridley', *Spartacus Educational*, September 1997 (updated August 2014).

73 Arnold Ridley, *The Train and Other Ghosts* (1970). And see Nigel Blundell, 'Dad's Army's Godfrey "tried to strangle his son" when he had a flashback to the horrors of the Somme', *Daily Mail*, 20 September 2008. http://www.dailymail.co.uk/tvshowbiz/article-1058810/Dads-Armys-Godfrey-tried-strangle-son-flashback-horrors-Somme.html#ixzz4sZTbUmNE.

able pain. "Yes sir," I replied. "My battalion is famous for self-inflicted wounds, and just to make sure, I cracked my skull with a rifle butt as well and ran a bayonet into my groin."

In total he was to have 17 operations on his hand to try to save it. He was discharged with the rank of lance corporal on medical grounds, suffering blackouts and shell shock. He would continue to suffer from both for the rest of his life. According to his son, Nicholas Ridley:

> He had bad feet—"twisted like a tramp's", he'd say—caused by conditions in the trenches. He had terrible headaches and he'd awake from sleep drenched in sweat.
>
> He lost all his teeth. He lost the use of three fingers in his left hand. And he had shrapnel coming out of his back for years. As for the psychological damage, he used to say: "The mental suffering was far in excess of the physical."
>
> He was angry and bitter for some time after the First World War and the horrors of trench warfare stayed with him all his life.
>
> But a mark of his great courage was that he found a way to deal with an awful lot of it. He survived, both mentally and morally, because he was a thoroughly kind, gentle, decent man.

Nicholas also recalled the extent of the suffering the family witnessed:

> He needed his afternoon sleep and I remember, as a child of five or six, waking him up suddenly. He instantly had his hands round my throat. It was a most appalling moment for both of us.
>
> We could never wake him suddenly because he'd go straight into "trench mode", even in his 80s.
>
> We would have to knock on the sitting room door first and warn him that we were coming in. The involuntary reactions were still there.

Post-war career

Between the wars, Ridley wrote the play *The Ghost Train*, which had a very successful run with two revivals and was made into a film on numerous occasions. Unfortunately, he sold the rights early on and thereby deprived himself of what would have been a lucrative source of income for the rest of his life. He also lost money trying to establish a film company. He was clearly a man of some integrity, though: instead of accepting bankruptcy, he suffered penury for years working to pay off his creditors.

He joined the Savage Club in March 1934, under the category of drama. At the time he was living in Bath, so joined as a country member.

When the Second World War broke out, he was over 40 and could probably have sat out the conflict. Instead, he volunteered and crossed the Channel with the British Expeditionary Force. His role was a 'conducting officer' supervising journalists on the frontline. Immediately on arrival in France he suffered terrible shell- hock as the memories of his previous experiences returned with a vengeance. After the Allied defences were cut in two by the Germans, he managed to escape on the last British ship leaving Boulogne. It was dive-bombed for 17 hours, but managed to return to Britain unscathed. Once again Ridley was discharged on medical grounds.

Back in England he joined the Home Guard. The war had one further horror in store for him, though, since his house in Caterham in Surrey was hit by one of the first V1 'buzzbombs' fired at Britain, and Ridley, who was outside at the time, was knocked unconscious by the blast.

After the war, he continued with his acting and writing career. He wrote or co-wrote 28 plays, and performed on the radio soap *The Archers* and the television soap *Crossroads*, but he acquired neither riches nor fame until *Dad's Army*. *Dad's Army* ran on television from 1968 to 1977 and was also made into a radio series, stage play and feature film.

He was not dismayed that Godfrey was a conscientious objector; instead, he felt it right they were recognised, and did not judge them harshly. He wrote: 'I knew one man who was very badly treated as a Conscientious Objector because he wouldn't submit to a medical examination. Had he submitted, he would have been grade 99 and they would never have had him. He was half-blind and weedy but he just wouldn't on principle.'[74]

The character of Godfrey, like many others on the show, was written with genuflections towards the class system as it would have obtained during the war. In one episode, it was explained that Godfrey had not married Mrs Prentice, his former lover, because of the class differences between them. From time to time Godfrey also turned up overdressed for some platoon functions, indicating he was from a higher class than the others (save perhaps Sgt Wilson, whose superior social status to Mainwaring was a central source of the humour in the programme).

On 7 January 1972, Ridley chaired a Savage house dinner at the height of his *Dad's Army* fame. He also appeared on Brother Savage Roy Plomley's radio programme *Desert Island Discs* and on the long-running television programme *This Is Your Life*.[75] In the former, he was clear about the long-term effects of both wars, referring to the First World War as 'those dismal days', though he added

---

74 Ridley, *The Train and Other Ghosts*, op cit.
75 In the programme, broadcast in 1976 and available online at the time of writing, it was noted that he had been bayoneted twice and that his left arm had been operated on 17 times.

'You know, memory is a strange thing. After a lapse of time, even the most miserable set of circumstances, roses seem to grow round them a little bit.' There were no roses for his Second World War memories, which he refused to discuss, saying 'To recount events, I would have to relive them. I am too afraid.'

He was over 80 before *Dad's Army* finished. During the 1970s, he added to his workload by managing the Leas Pavilion in Folkestone – it was only in his very final years that he ceased performing.

He was awarded the OBE in the early 1980s. It would not have impressed him to win it for a comedy acting performance given he never received anything for his military service. He died in 1984, aged 88.

Many years after his death, Ridley is another Savage entertainer who remains proudly remembered by the Club. On 19 September 2017, for example, the Savarail group held a member event, chaired by Michael Purton, for a special screening of the 1941 Gainsborough film of *The Ghost Train*.

Jack Warner: the Western Front to Dock Green

Another in the pantheon of great Savage thespians was Jack Warner, for a long time one of Britain's most recognisable television actors due to his role as Dixon of Dock Green.

Early life and First World War

Warner's real name was Horace John Waters. He was born in 1896 in the East End of London, and attended Coopers' Company's Grammar School for Boys in Mile End. After leaving school he began studying the new science of automobile engineering, but left after a year to work at the repair facilities of FW Berwick and Company in Balham. In 1913, the firm sent Warner to work as a mechanic in Paris. He drove completed chassis to the coast from where they were shipped to England. During the course of the work he picked up conversational French.

His skills with motor vehicles meant that during the First World War he served in France as a driver in the Royal Flying Corps. He described his service in these words:[76]

> I was attached to the French Army as an interpreter and driver at the time when the Germans were driving towards Paris in 1914. Everyone, however, was convinced that the war would be over by Christmas that year, but it was not to be, and in 1915 it became painfully apparent that a long and bitter struggle was inevitable. I decided to return to London

---

76 Jack Warner, *Evening All: The Autobiography of Jack Warner* (WH Allen, 1975, 1979 edn), pp 25–26.

and join the Royal Flying Corps, as a driver. Flying was out until later because when I was medically examined the doctors discovered the secret I was trying to conceal – that I was colour blind.

This peculiar disability has always caused minor problems. Many times I have lost snooker matches because I have not been able to distinguish the colours of the balls. Sometimes people ask me what colours I can actually identify. It is a difficult question to answer. What I do know is that when I stand on green grass wearing a suit of a particular shade of brown, the suit and the grass merge into one.

My younger brother Bill did become a pilot but my aeronautics were confined to the observer's seat during flights with some very rash and daring young men in their flying machines. I well recall a trip over Arras one misty day when we missed a church spire by, I am sure, no more than a couple of feet.

I had been posted to an operational Royal Flying Corps squadron as a driver and had to ferry wireless operators to and from the lines. I think I can claim to be the only driver during hostilities who got his Crossley tender balanced upon the edge of one of the second line trenches, at a place called Monchy-le-Preux, which many old soldiers will remember.

I ended up like that on a night of heaving shelling when I lost my way, and I didn't realise what a precarious position I had reached until the whole area was illuminated by flares.

At the time I was a flight-sergeant and engaged on a special mission which entailed going up to the front line at all hours to salvage engines from aeroplanes which had been shot down. We were always on call and one night I had just got my head down when with two or three other chaps I was summoned to the C.O. for a special briefing. We were shown a map and ordered to the front just beyond Arras to drag one of our aero-engines back to the lines. It was a hazardous operation in thick fog and, ironically, it was only German flares which actually enabled us to reach the engine we wanted. It was no picnic and we were very relieved when our mission was accomplished.

On another night I had a corporal in my squad who annoyed me by constantly wandering around seemingly unaware that he was likely to get his head blown off at any moment. His behaviour prompted me to shout, 'Why don't you sit down and die nicely?' In the tenseness of the night, some of the lads found humour in my remark and it became a bit of a catch phrase. I didn't mean it to be funny and it was no joke for the corporal because he was killed soon after while I was on leave.

Warner was awarded the RAF Meritorious Service Medal. He also took part in some amateur dramatics during the war as part of a concert party – his first experience in writing entertainment material – and he was encouraged by the reaction from the troops. He stayed on in the army of occupation for some time after the Armistice, and suffered badly from Spanish flu.

Post-war career

After recovering and being demobbed, he returned to working in the motor trade in England, and raced at Brooklands (a far more dangerous hobby than motor racing in the twenty-first century). He did not become a full-time entertainer until his thirties, when he appeared in music hall and radio. The radio show *Garrison Theatre* (1939) established him as a star. According to *The A to Z of British Radio*, 'With no formal training, Warner's great gift was sincerity, a quality heard and understood by the radio microphone, which established him as a major British star with an affectionate following.'[77]

In the Second World War, he was too old to serve at the Front, but continued his acting career. He made his film debut in *The Dummy Talks*. In May 1940, he joined the Savage Club under drama.

After the war he appeared in several more films including the successful *Holiday Camp* (1947), which developed into a series of films with three more made from 1948 to 1949. The following year, he played PC George Dixon in *The Blue Lamp* (1950), the most successful film of the year.

He continued to act in other films, including *Albert R.N.* in 1953, about a brilliant creation of Brother Savage John Worsley. In 1955 *Dixon of Dock Green* began, reprising Warner's role from *The Blue Lamp*, though in the film version the character had died at the end. The series lasted until 1976, even though after a few years Warner was older than the normal police retirement age. The series looks dated in every respect to twenty-first century eyes, not the least in the crimes with which Dixon was concerned. *Private Eye* once ran a spoof updated version, where in his 'Evenin' all' monologue Dixon mused about having to sort out some crack dens, anti-social behaviour and Yardie gangster murders. But some might suggest the contrast reflected worse on twenty-first century Britain than it did on the idealised twentieth century world of Dixon.

While the series was running, Warner still continued to act in films from time to time, his final one being *Dominique* in 1978.

He died in 1981, aged 85. As a mark of the respect his character of Dixon had gained among the real police, officers from Paddington Green Police Station bore the coffin at his funeral.

---

77 Seán Street, *The A to Z of British Radio* (Scarecrow Press Inc, 1999).

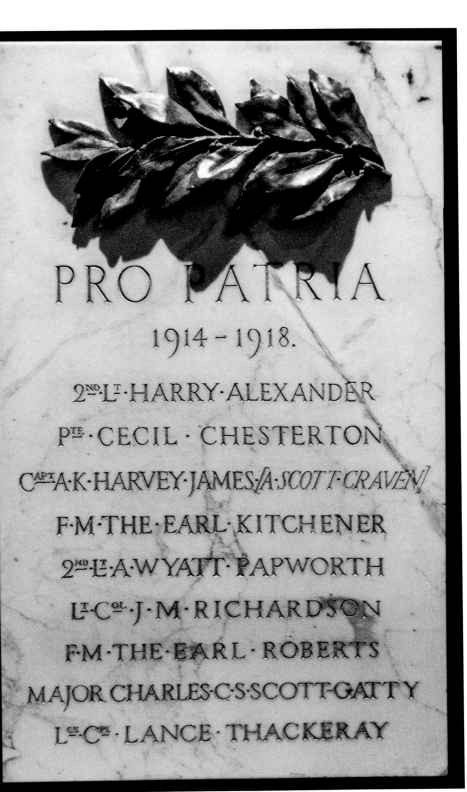

PRO PATRIA

1914 – 1918.

2ND LT HARRY ALEXANDER

PTE CECIL CHESTERTON

CAPT A.K.HARVEY JAMES [A.SCOTT CRAVEN]

F.M THE EARL KITCHENER

2ND LT A.WYATT PAPWORTH

LT COL J.M RICHARDSON

F.M THE EARL ROBERTS

MAJOR CHARLES C.S.SCOTT-GATTY

LCE CPL LANCE THACKERAY

The Savage Club War Memorial by Albert Toft.

Savage Generals.
Clockwise from top
left:
Earl Kitchener,
Sir William
Robertson,
Earl Roberts (centre),
Earl Jellicoe,
Viscount Byng.

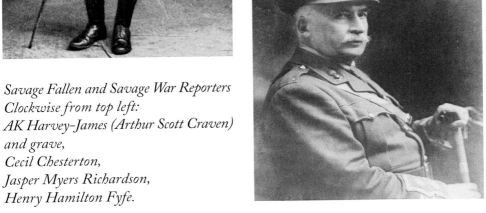

Savage Fallen and Savage War Reporters
Clockwise from top left:
AK Harvey-James (Arthur Scott Craven)
and grave,
Cecil Chesterton,
Jasper Myers Richardson,
Henry Hamilton Fyfe.

Jasper Myers Richardson's grave, Étaples, framed by Sir Edwin Lutyens' monument

Savage Club—Candidates' Book.

318

Savage Men of Letters. Herbert Asquith (top left), Sir Basil Liddell Hart (top right),
Candidate book entry for Henry Williamson (above).

Stanley Holloway's candidate page (below), Arnold Ridley (bottom left),
CRW Nevinson (bottom right).

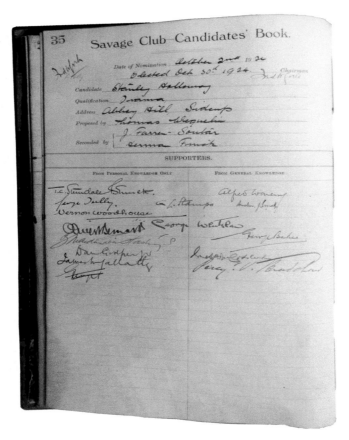

Alfred Leete's famous image of Kitchener.

Bert Thomas's legendary Arf a Mo' Kaiser!' cartoon.

CRW Nevinson's La Mitrailleuse.

CRW Nevinson's The Doctor.

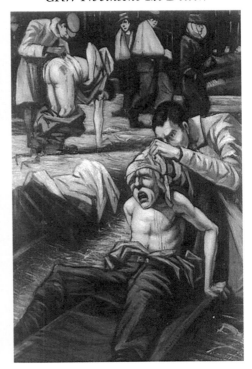

Sir AP Herbert

Lord Moulton

*Below and right:
Norman Holbrook VC
and his candidate page.*

Above: four Kings of England, four Savages. Edward VII (far right), his son George, Prince of Wales, later George V (far left), and grandsons Edward, later Edward VIII (rear), and Albert, later George VI (foreground), c 1908.

Above: the Adelphi, home of the Savage Club during the Great War, photographed c 1935. The degradation of the once-grand walls is evident.

Above: the Adelphi, c 1935. Sadly much of the memorabilia on the walls has gone missing over the years.

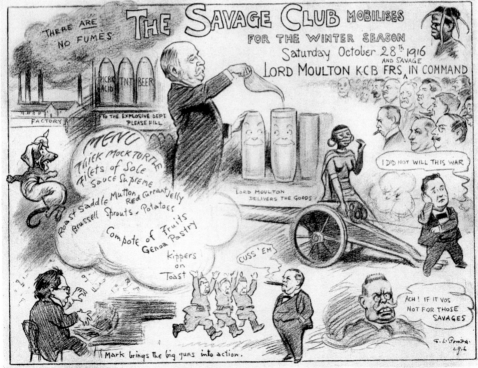

Two wartime menus.

British soldiers in action at Loos.

Canadian soldiers advance on Vimy Ridge, 1917.

A Royal Aircraft Factory FE2b.

Sir Edwin Lutyens' monuments: Thiepval Monument at the Somme (below),
the Cenotaph (bottom left), two views of Étaples (bottom right).

Top: Lance Thackeray's grave, Brighton.
For the inscription, see p 136.
Left: Harry Alexander's grave, Arras
Road Cemetery, Roclincourt, Pas de
Calais.
Above: Harry Alexander.

Grave of Charles CS Scott-Gatty in Welwyn Cemetery, Hertfordshire. The inscription has faded considerably but as best I can make out it states: 'Born 5th October 1880/ Died 24th July 1916/ I saw the river which must be passed order to reach the kingdom of heaven and the name of that river was suffering./ And I saw the boat which takes so many souls across the river and the name of that boat was love.'

Detail of the portrait of Sir Winston Churchill, by Ernest Townsend, on display in the National Liberal Club foyer. The painting shows Churchill in a Privy Councillor's uniform as First Lord of the Admiralty, although by the time the sittings had started in late 1915 Churchill had been forced out of that office by the Gallipoli disaster and was seeking to redeem his reputation by serving in the trenches on the Western Front.

CHAPTER 8

Savage Artists

Introduction

The Great War was extensively photographed, and there were a number of short silent films made during its course as well. Some of the photographs and moving images have become truly iconic, such as the pictures of devastated countryside in No Man's Land, or the footage of the soldier on the Somme carrying one of his wounded comrades on his back and looking hauntingly at the camera. Equally, however, some of the most memorable imagery of the conflict appears in cartoons, drawings and paintings of the period, and a number of the best wartime artists were members of the Savage Club. For example, the famous picture of Lord Kitchener commanding his fellow subjects 'Your Country Needs You' was drawn by Brother Savage Alfred Leete. In the years since, it has become arguably the most widely known of all wartime posters, though, as we will see, there are arguments that it was not at all well-known during the conflict itself and owes its reputation to later re-imagined history. Instead, during the years 1914–18 themselves, the most famous image was probably Bert Thomas's 'Arf a Mo', Kaiser!' cartoon. We will discuss both pictures in more detail later in this chapter, but it is sufficient for now to note that since Leete and Thomas were both Savages, the Club's claim to wartime artistic fame remains assured either way.

We have already met Lance Thackeray as one of the Savage fallen. His artistic colleagues at the Club included John Hassall,[1] Dudley Hardy, Walter Churcher,

---

1   John Hassall RI (1868–1948), joined the Savage Club in June 1906. He was proposed by the painter Edward John Gregory RA, PPRBSA (1850–1909). His seconders were Yeend King and the artist W Douglas Almond (1866–1916). Hassall's most famous works were the 'Jolly Fisherman' advertisement for Skegness, commissioned by the Great Northern Railways, and the 'Kodak girl' used by the photographic company from 1910 until the 1970s.

Alexander MacLean, Phil May, George Parlby, Harry Rountree and Starr Wood. Most Savage artists of the time were also members of the London Sketch Club.[2]

After the war broke out, many of the artists who volunteered naturally chose to serve in the Artists Rifles, a regiment dating back to the 38th Middlesex Rifle Volunteer Corps, created in May 1860 in response to a feared invasion by Napoleon III. Its first commanders were the painters Henry Wyndham Phillips and Frederic Leighton, and they were joined over the years by the likes of Ford Madox Brown, John Everett Millais, John William Waterhouse and Dante Gabriel Rossetti. The regimental badge was designed by WC Wyon, an original member of the unit. By the time of the First World War, the Artists Rifles formed one of 28 volunteer battalions in the London and Middlesex areas. They were combined to form the new London Regiment.

During the war, the Artists Rifles formed an Officers' Training Corps. It produced a total of 10,256 officers, who went on to serve in many regiments across the army. Our first Savage in this section, however, Cecil Aldin, did not go to the Front, but instead performed a vital role on the Home Front as well as creating another of the conflict's great works of art.

Cecil Aldin: master of the war horse

Cecil Aldin painted one of the classic images of the Great War, *A Land Girl Ploughing*, a picture of a lone woman in charge of two substantial horses pulling a plough against a broad rural landscape. The painting reflected Aldin's great attachment to animals and to the countryside, and the unstinting contribution he had made to preparing horses for the war effort. Like so many others, though, he paid a terrible price during the conflict as his teenage son was killed on active duty.

Early life

Cecil Charles Windsor Aldin was born in 1870 in Slough, the son of a builder and amateur artist. He attended Eastbourne College and Solihull Grammar School. He went on to study at Albert Joseph Moore's studio in Kensington, London, but did not enjoy the experience and left after only a month to study animal anatomy at the National Art Training School in South Kensington.

Aldin then attended a summer school run by William Frank Calderon at Midhurst, Sussex. Unfortunately, he contracted rheumatic fever, but had progressed enough to sell his first drawing to *The Building News*, published in September 1890. The next year he sold a picture of a dog to *The Graphic*, and in 1892 started selling pictures regularly to the *Illustrated London News*. The income

---

2   Bradshaw, op cit, p 70.

was sufficient for him to rent a studio in Chelsea. He often drew the animals in the London Zoological Gardens, and on the strength of those pictures was commissioned by *The Pall Mall Budget* in 1894 to illustrate the serialisation of stories from Rudyard Kipling's *The Second Jungle Book*.[3]

Aldin married his wife Marguerite (Rita) in 1895, and they had two children, Dudley (born 1897) and Gwen (born 1899).

His career continued to flourish as a book and magazine illustrator. While staying with Walter Dendy Sadler at Chiddingstone, he came into contact with many other artists of the day, including John Hassell and Lance Thackeray. Together they formed the London Sketch Club. At Thackeray's nomination, Aldin also joined the Savage Club in May 1908.

Aldin also joined the Chelsea Arts Club, but his love of the countryside soon took him away from London to Henley (his address in the Savage candidates' book was 'Southfields, Henley-Upon-Thames'), and in 1910 he became Master of the South Berkshire Hunt. He lived at Kennelgates, the farmhouse which was the headquarters of the hunt.

First World War

At 44, Aldin was too old for frontline service. Due to his expertise with horses as a Master of Foxhounds, he was commissioned with the rank of captain and given a vital role as remount purchasing officer in charge of an army remount depot. The depot was a facility to prepare horses for military use. There was an insatiable demand from the army for horses throughout the war, as we noted in the previous chapter when discussing James Agate. Vehicles of the day were in short supply, and were often incapable of dealing with the bucolic French roads, let alone the mud at the Front. They were also of a very rudimentary design and usually unreliable. For the great majority of logistical work, therefore, the army was still dependent upon horses (this was no indicator of a Luddite tendency among the British: the same applied to all armies of the time and the German Army was still heavily reliant upon horses for logistical support as late as the Second World War). The British also retained active cavalry units throughout the Great War, though stories of brave men on horseback making suicidal charges at machine guns and artillery are usually gross exaggerations. Instead, once trench warfare set in, cavalry was mostly used for reconnaissance and moving troops into position.

Aldin established a number of remount depots around Berkshire, including several run exclusively by women, which had become a necessity given that most able-bodied men were being sent to the Front and those who remained often had no experience or ability with horses. As with many other areas of life during the

---

3   Roy Heron, *Cecil Aldin: The Story of a Sporting Artist* (Webb & Bower, 1981).

war, the men of Aldin's generation were surprised when they discovered women were able to do traditional male roles with alacrity. Aldin later wrote:[4]

> It is almost unbelievable to recall that ten girls, in many cases slight little things, would cheerfully walk to a railway station a mile or two away on a winter's afternoon, halter and detrain from cattle-trucks forty or fifty gun-horses or L.D2s that they had never seen before, and bring them safely into the depot four or five tied abreast, each file led by one small girl. Yet this I have seen happen fifty times. Many of my staff were so small that they found it impossible to groom without having buckets or boxes to stand on. At one time I had a large number of mules in the depots. In my home stables, a large barn accommodated forty animals stabled between hanging bails. Some of the worst mules were put here under specially selected girl grooms, who had asked to be allowed to have the bad animals under their charge. One day my head woman at one of the other depots told me that one of her "grooms" had asked if she could be moved to where the bad mules were stabled. She mentioned that the girl was quite good with horses but was a tiny, pale-faced little thing and did not look over-strong although she never seemed to tire. I had a look at her, and thinking it might be asking for trouble with so fragile a little girl shook my head. Before I left the depot she came up to me, begged to be allowed to come, and finally persuaded me to give her permission to do so on trial. That girl turned out to be the best stablewoman I knew during those remount days and one who seemed to have more control over wicked or kicking animals than any other man or woman in the depot.

Aldin usually had more than 300 horses on his property and was responsible for up to 200 more around the country. At one stage during the war he had to travel 60 miles on his daily inspection round.[5] His arduous labours continued despite the shattering news in 1916 of the death of his son Dudley on the Western Front.[6]

After the war, Aldin's work establishing the ladies' remount depots led the Women's Work Sub-Committee of the newly-created Imperial War Museum to try to purchase two of his wartime paintings, including *A Land Girl Ploughing*. Aldin considered that *A Land Girl Ploughing* was not up to standard because of the materials he had had to use for its composition, and insisted upon redoing it on location. A former member of the Women's Land Army attended as the

---

4   Cecil Aldin, *Time I Was Dead* (Eyre & Spottiswoode Ltd, 1934), p 169.
5   Ibid, p 167.
6   John Fairley, *Horses of the Great War: The Story in Art* (Pen & Sword, 2015), p 122 stated that Dudley died in Flanders in 1916, while Wikipedia at the time of writing stated that he died at Vimy Ridge in 1917. In fact Dudley died in France on 15 May 1916, aged 19, while serving with the 105th Field Coy of the Royal Engineers. See https://livesofthefirstworldwar.org/lifestory/641669 and the Project Purley Journal, http://www.project-purley.eu/J0095.pdf. Note that the latter erroneously states that Dudley was working on the British trench system near Verdun – the British were not based in that sector and did not participate in the eponymous battle.

model for the plough girl, bringing her old uniform and otherwise lending her experience to ensure that all details of the picture were accurate. The resultant painting received much critical acclaim[7] and remains not just a fine work of art but a record of a vital if less glamorous component of the war effort.

Post-war career

Aldin remained severely affected by Dudley's death. He commissioned a brass memorial to be placed in St Mary's Church, where it remains today. When he visited Dudley's grave in Ecoivres Military Cemetery Mont-St-Eloi, Pas de Calais, France, he obtained a lamp from the ruined local abbey and hung it in the chancel of St Mary's as well.

In spite of his ongoing grief, he continued with his artistic work, and also organised many pony and dog shows. In 1923, he published a short series of illustrated books, *Old Manor Houses* and *Old Inns*.

In 1930, suffering from arthritis, he moved to live in Mallorca, where he hoped the climate would ease his condition. He kept working as an illustrator until, in January 1935, he suffered a heart attack on board a ship on the way to England. He was rushed to hospital in London after the ship docked, but died shortly afterwards.

Oliver Bernard: hidden talent

Oliver Bernard was an influential artist and designer, who lived through one of the Great War's seminal moments, the sinking of the *Lusitania*. He also had some interesting family and Savage connections.

Early life

Bernard was born in 1881 in Camberwell, South London. His father, Charles Bernard, was a theatre manager and his mother, Annie Allen, was an actress. Charles died in 1894, leaving behind Annie, Oliver and a younger brother. The two boys were sent to the care of a woman who, as it happened, was an aunt of the very young Stanley Holloway. Over half a century later Holloway recalled:[8]

> ... I think [Bernard's] story is one of the remarkable ones in showbusiness. I'd met Oliver when I was very young—he was a few years older than I—and after his father died he and his brother were brought up by an aunt of mine. The younger boy was put into an orphanage, thanks to the kindness of the Actors' Benevolent Society, but young Oliver was a bit of a problem.
>
> He didn't seem to know what he wanted to do and used to lounge

---

7   Gill Clarke, *The Women's Land Army: A Portrait* (Sansom & Company, 2008).
8   Holloway, *Wiv a Bit O' Luck*, op cit, pp 74–75.

around the house endlessly. Worse, he was badly deaf in one ear. What to do with Oliver? It happened that my mother had relations who ran a scenic artist's studio up in Liverpool. It shows what a bit of luck will do, for Mr Le Maitre agreed to take on Oliver as a junior apprentice and it was to be the turning point of his life.

Not immediately though. He soon got bored with his very humble job [a sort of theatrical dogsbody], which mostly seemed to consist of pushing a truck of paint around. But one day he found himself at Liverpool docks, saw the big ships and felt the lure of adventure. Anyway, he hopped it and we didn't hear of him for a long time. Suddenly Oliver wrote to my uncle from a London address ... Rowton House, a tuppenny dosshouse.

My uncle met him, gave him a meal and asked him what he wanted to do with his life. 'I want to be a scenic artist!' said Olly, and produced some sketches to prove that he knew something of what it was all about. So my uncle got him a job with a London scenic artist, Walter Hann. Again it was a very menial job, mainly sizing up backcloths, but this time Oliver Bernard knew where he was going and he had the initiative to prove it. One day Walter Hann was called to the phone and, in his absence, Oliver cheekily finished off a designing job that the boss was doing for a theatre. Instead of getting fired Olly was promoted, for Hann was so impressed with the promise that the lad showed.

From then on young Oliver went from strength to strength.

Even while financially straitened, Bernard was able to continue his own education by reading the likes of John Locke and John Ruskin in his spare time, and working on drawing and painting.

He soon began to prosper as a set designer, working in London, New York and Boston, and undertook a theatrical tour of Australia. He was nominated for membership of the Savage Club in November 1913 under the category of art, giving his address as the Covent Garden Theatre. By then, he held the post of resident scenic artist for the Grand Opera Syndicate Ltd, managers and lessees of the Royal Opera House.

A few months before the Great War broke out, Bernard went to Berlin to attend a production at the then-new opera house in Charlottenburg. At one point in the trip he was surrounded by German men on the train, who gleefully told him 'Germany will soon show your Mr Churchill how to trim his navy.'

First World War – *Lusitania*

Bernard volunteered upon the outbreak of war, but was rejected for active service due to partial deafness. He stayed working in the theatre but became impatient because of his inability to serve. He was also losing interest in the direction the London theatre was taking. In November 1914, therefore, he returned to America and his Savage application was withdrawn.

Upon learning that the armed forces were loosening requirements in order to gain more recruits, he decided to return to the United Kingdom and try again. His Savage membership was revived and he was elected on 12 February 1915.[9] He did, however, stay in America slightly longer so that he could finish a commission to design theatrical sets for the Boston millionaire William Lindsey.

Lindsey persuaded Bernard to take his daughter Leslie and son-in-law Stewart Mason under his wing. Leslie and Stewart had been married on 21 April 1915, and they were set to begin their honeymoon by sailing to Britain at the same time as Bernard. All three of them joined the same vessel, scheduled to leave New York on 1 May 1915. It was a fateful voyage, because the vessel was none other than the RMS *Lusitania*.

By the time of the *Lusitania's* departure from the United States, the U-boat menace had become a significant factor in the naval war. Germany had declared the seas around the United Kingdom a war zone, and the German embassy in the United States had placed advertisements in American newspapers warning civilians of the dangers of making the crossing. Bernard himself saw one such advertisement before he sailed.

Nevertheless, Germany had not formally declared unrestricted submarine warfare. Instead, it was at least nominally abiding by the international 'Prize Rules' or 'Cruiser Rules'. The rules provided that unarmed merchant vessels were not to be attacked without warning. Instead, submarines were to surface, search the vessel, then place crews in 'a place of safety' (not lifeboats, except under restricted circumstances) before attacking the ship, unless the ship showed a 'persistent refusal to stop … or active resistance to visit or search'.

The problem for the Germans was the British practice of 'Q-ships', such as those brilliantly commanded by Brother Savage Harold Auten, in which merchant vessels were secretly armed to entice unsuspecting U-boats to the surface where they would be vulnerable to the Q-ships' superior gunnery. The *Lusitania* herself had been fitted with six-inch gun mounts but the guns were never installed.

The first few days of the voyage passed without incident, with Bernard's chief complaint being the inherent snobbery of the upper middle classes with whom he was forced to share the confined spaces on the ship. On the first night he came to dinner and found that a 'supercilious steward' had given his table to someone else. He barked at the offending official 'Perhaps you could tell me why the genius of the engineers that built this ship should be depreciated because you think some passengers are more important than others?' He took a particular dislike to the extremely wealthy first class passenger Alfred Vanderbilt. More seriously,

---

9   The dates in the candidate book are unambiguous, so I would infer that Bernard confirmed his wish to rejoin by letter or telegram, or made an earlier return trip since he was elected before the *Lusitania* sailed.

he was unimpressed by the lifeboat drills and told a fellow passenger who asked a fatuous question about which lifeboat he would prefer 'I would prefer a raft'.

By the afternoon of 7 May, the *Lusitania* was off the southern coast of Ireland and hence within Germany's declared war zone. Bernard was walking around on deck, as was his habit both for exercise and to avoid socialising. Pausing at one point, he saw a ripple on the water, which a fellow passenger recognised as a torpedo. Bernard was too stunned to reply. He held on to the railing as the torpedo struck, after which the ship soon began to list. He tried to help the Masons, but was unable to locate Stewart, and in the event the couple both died despite Bernard's frantic efforts to find them. In the course of moving about the ship he noticed Vanderbilt and his valet calmly handing out lifebelts and showing passengers to the lifeboats, exuding the same gentlemanly calm with which Benjamin Guggenheim and his valet had famously met their end on the *Titanic*.[10] Vanderbilt, like Guggenheim, went down with the ship, having given his lifebelt to a female passenger who was holding a baby.

As he climbed onto the funnel deck, Bernard noticed a stoker covered with soot and blood across his face, the crown open 'like a bloody sponge pudding.' He then saw a naked man swimming away from the ship. By that stage Bernard would have believed himself in extreme peril, since he was unable to swim. He started taking off his own clothes in preparation for going into the water, and later said he had mused: 'Death is close. How insignificant everything seems in retrospect. All one's struggles, hopes and achievements will be wiped out in seconds. What a fuss I've made about my life. It has amounted to nothing. When I'm dead everybody will say "How sad," and go on fussing until they come to their own silly end.'

When he declared his inability to swim, one of the crew pushed a swivel chair over and told him to hold on to it. 'I'm no good at waterwheels either' was his gallows-humour reply. Eventually, he made it on to one of the last lifeboats to leave the ship. Only 18 minutes had elapsed between the torpedo striking and the ship going down. Bernard then spent four hours in the lifeboat before being rescued by a trawler. Throughout the sinking and its aftermath he deplored the lack of efficiency of the crew.

Once he arrived in London, he was commissioned by *The London Illustrated News* to draw sketches of the sinking. He was and remained happy to discuss the circumstances of the sinking, unlike many other survivors, but nevertheless was not called to give evidence to Lord Mersey's inquiry. One possible reason was that Bernard maintained, in his sketches and elsewhere, that only one torpedo had struck the ship, whereas the official line was that two had done so (officialdom

---

10 As it happened, early reports of the sinking of the *Titanic* assumed Vanderbuilt had been on board, but he was not. See Steven H Gittelman and Emily Gittelman, *Alfred Gwynne Vanderbilt: The Unlikely Hero of the Lusitania* (Hamilton Books, 2013), p 167.

presumably thought that it would make for better propaganda about murderous Germans).

In total, 1,198 passengers and crew died in the sinking, with 761 survivors. Because the *Lusitania* was a non-military vessel and the Germans had not issued a warning, the British immediately decried the action as a war crime, in contravention of the Prize Rules. In America, public opinion was outraged since 128 American civilians had been among those killed, and the episode has been credited as a major step towards bringing the United States into the war.

The Germans maintained that the *Lusitania* was correctly treated as a legitimate military target because she had been carrying hundreds of tons of war munitions in violation of the Prize Rules. The British government adamantly denied that the *Lusitania* had any munitions, and continued to do so until 1982, when it quietly warned prospective salvage operators not to go near the wreck because of the dangers of explosives it might contain.

First World War

In 1916, Bernard was commissioned into the Royal Engineers as a camouflage officer, a nascent role eminently suited to those with artistic talent. A year earlier the French Army had become the first to create a dedicated camouflage unit (the word 'camouflage' derived from a French verb meaning 'to make up for the stage' – precisely Bernard's peacetime occupation). The role of camouflage artists was to try to conceal objects such as guns and vehicles. Tanks were painted with the equivalent of nautical 'dazzle camouflage' known as 'disruptive pattern', though it soon became pointless as the mud of the Western Front would cover the paint.

The British Army camouflage section was known as the Special Works Park RE (Royal Engineers). Its first commanding officer was Lieutenant-Colonel Francis Wyatt. Bernard professed himself 'elated and profoundly grateful' at being able to serve at the Front as an officer.[11] He was sent to France as part of a group including Walter Russell ARA, the painter Roland Harker (who joined the Savage Club in 1934 and became a life member in 1936) and FW Holmes, the last of those being someone recommended by Bernard himself because they had worked at the theatre 20 years earlier when Bernard was just starting his working life.[12]

Though not required to go over the top with the infantry, Bernard had to work on the frontline, exposed to enemy machine guns. He also regularly came under shellfire; the 'evening hate' as he described it, using the same term as Beb Asquith. One of his roles was to construct observation posts disguised as trees, placed in No Man's Land where there were no natural surveillance points. The artist had to get

---

11 Oliver P Bernard, *Cock Sparrow* (Jonathan Cape, 1936).
12 Roland's brother Joseph Harker (a life member of the Savage Club from 1936), another theatre designer in his day job, also worked on camouflage during the Great War.

close enough to sketch the area. A suitable tree would be identified, and a team behind the lines would construct a replica, then replace the real tree at night in which an observer would hide – all exceptionally dangerous work. One of Bernard's trees was known as 'The Cow' and was preserved by the Imperial War Museum after the war.

Much of Bernard's work was in the Ypres salient – a notorious part of the line which saw some of the heaviest fighting – and involved working all night then reconnoitring during the day, serving with both the British and Canadian forces. He was not always impressed with what he saw, dividing his 'military clients' into three categories:[13]

> ... those who believed in any effort to make things a little more diffi-
> cult for the enemy by means of camouflage; those who made things
> difficult for everybody but the enemy by misplaced belief in camou-
> flage; and those who regarded any form of concealment as a breach
> of the King's Regulations. The type of be-ribboned sahib who insisted
> that gallant soldiers should keep their heads up and die like gentle-
> men at Spion Kop and Magersfontein now exercised some authority in
> Flanders. Such gentlemen were readily accommodated by much more
> accomplished opponents than Boer farmers, magnificently trained and
> perfectly equipped opponents who designed the most scientific means
> for protecting and concealing themselves in and behind their own lines
> throughout the western front; furthermore, those opponents thought
> it no disgrace to imitate the best methods of camouflage discovered in
> the French and British lines; they also copied some of the worst and
> discarded examples of so-called camouflage.

He was also unimpressed by many of the brass hats whom he encountered, decry-ing the army's promotions based on seniority.

Eventually, after nine months on the Western Front, he was shot in the leg just below the kneecap and returned to Britain. He recovered, however, and returned to duties, serving not just on the Western Front but in Italy as well. For his services, he was awarded both the Military Cross and OBE.

Post-war career

In 1919, Bernard continued his theatrical work, including designing sets for his Brother Savage Sir Thomas Beecham's Ring Cycle at Covent Garden. In the 1920s, he developed a strong interest in interior decoration. He undertook some consulting work for the British government, among other things renovating the lighting and stage management at the Admiralty Theatre in 1924 and acting as a consultant to the British contribution to the *Exposition Internationale des Arts Décoratifs et Industriels Modernes* in Paris in 1925.

---

13 Ibid, p 255.

A second significant client of Bernard was the restaurant chain and food retailer J Lyons and Co. Bernard became their consultant artistic director, in which capacity he designed the interiors for their Oxford Street, Coventry Street and Strand Corner Houses, along with the Cumberland Hotel. The latter opened in 1934. In the same year, Bernard remodelled the interiors of the Regent Palace Hotel, including the basement bars, restaurants, and the ground-floor coffee room, known today as the 'Titanic Room'. He also created the Art Deco illuminated entrance canopy and staircase of the Strand Palace Hotel (later dismantled but kept by the Victoria & Albert Museum in London).

A third major venture of Bernard's was in helping found PEL (Practical Equipment Ltd) in 1931. He also designed their iconic 'SP 4' office chair and other now familiar items of office furniture.

On top of all that, he designed the Supermarine factory in Southampton and the IMCO building in Dublin.

In 1939, he died suddenly from peritonitis.[14]

Coda: Family life

Bernard had such an interesting family life that it deserves its own coda here.

Bernard was married twice. His first marriage from 1911 to 1924, was to the singer Muriel Theresa Lightfoot and was without issue. His second marriage, from 1924 until Bernard's death, was to the opera singer Dora Hodges, whose stage name was Fedora Roselli. They were married from 1924 until Bernard's death and had two daughters and three sons.

The sons were the poet and translator Oliver (1925–2013), the photographer and art critic Bruce (1928–2000), and the journalist and incorrigible old soak Jeffrey (1932–1997). All three boys went to independent schools despite their mother struggling with finances after their father's death. Jeffrey was probably the best known of the three, since he was immortalised by the byline 'Jeffrey Bernard is unwell' every time he failed to file his copy for his *Spectator* column 'Low Life'.

When Oliver, the oldest and longest-lived, died in 2013, the journalist Christopher Howse reflected in *The Daily Telegraph*:[15]

> The drunkest man in the Coach and Horses,[16] Soho, said to me, with an intonation of wisdom: "Don't mess with those Bernards." That was 30

---

14 Despite all his successes, he left considerable debts behind for his young family. For more on his work, see Charlotte Benton, *Art Deco 1910–1939* (V&A Publications, 2003) and Irena Murray and Julian Osley (eds), *Le Corbusier and Britain: An Anthology* (Routledge, 2009).

In 2012, the Irish artist Gavin Murphy released a film on Bernard's IMCO building and a book, *On Seeing Only Totally New Things* (Royal Hibernian Academy) on Bernard's life and work.

15 6 June 2013.

16 A legendary Soho watering hole for hacks of the day.

years ago, but already it was too late.

The three brothers were, to be sure, dangerous. I spent more time with Jeffrey Bernard, mostly in the Coach, than Boswell did with Johnson. Boswell just remembered more. Jeffrey, the youngest, died first, in the same week as Diana, Princess of Wales, and Mother Teresa.

If Jeffrey resented living in the shadow of his talented brothers, in an extreme act of passive-aggression he outshone them. The Byronic Jeffrey became the star in his own drama, literally when Keith Waterhouse made a hit play of his downhill struggle, *Jeffrey Bernard is Unwell*, with Peter O'Toole impersonating his unending bare-knuckle fight with alcohol, which he lost on points.

Bruce, the middle brother, regarded drinking, I think, as a human duty, just as he found virtue in having no fixed abode. He disapproved of my giving up drink, but would make elaborate arrangements, not in an entirely satirical way, for proper afternoon tea, with cucumber sandwiches.

It says something about Bruce Bernard, a historian of pictures who photographed Lucian Freud at work and was painted by him, that his way of doing things became a model. When he made tea, he put into the pot a lot of tea, then poured it out straight away. When he drank in a pub he knew whose right it was to be bought a drink in a round and whose duty it was to buy one. These unspoken little Soho laws became known as "Bruce's Rules", amusing in a way, but deadly if broken.

An abiding property of Soho was to exclude, partly for survival: to repel bores who might otherwise suck the life out of the dangerous edge of existence in the Coach, the French, the Caves de France, the Colony, and, for the desperate, the Kismet, an afternoon drinking club nicknamed "The Iron Lung" and "Death in the Afternoon". (Of that underground den, a visitor once asked: "What's that peculiar smell?" The reply was: "Failure.")

Bruce, when he died in 2000, was not killed by drink, just by cancer like anyone else. And now Oliver, the eldest, is dead. Born in 1925, he knew Soho precociously in the Forties (the days of Julian Maclaren-Ross and, just passing through, Dylan Thomas[17]). He knew it familiarly in each decade after, but familiarity did not breed contempt. Not for everybody, at least.

Oliver survived into his late eighties because he did not join the repertory company staging every night (with frequent matinees) the tragi-comedy of Soho life, than which nothing could be funnier.

It wasn't that every remark was lapidary. "Get out! You can't paint. You've got nothing to offer," is not wit. But said by the monstrous-nosed Ian Board, proprietor of the Colony Room Club, while belabouring Francis Bacon about the shoulders with an umbrella on the steep bend of a dark staircase, it acquired dramatic energy.

---

17 Dylan Thomas, the famous Welsh poet, was also a member of the Savage Club.

Will Dyson: 'the artillery of art'

Will Dyson was an Australian artist who held the distinction of being his country's official war artist on the Western Front.

Early life

Dyson was born at Alfredton, now in Ballarat, Victoria, in 1880, into a working class family. His father was George Dyson, who was working as a hawker at the time but later worked as a mining engineer. His mother was Jane, *née* Mayall.

Dyson attended state schools at Ballarat and South Melbourne. There was clearly artistic ability in the family since one of his brothers, Ambrose Dyson (1876–1913), was a prolific and successful popular illustrator. Dyson soon followed him, having a drawing published by the newspaper *The Bulletin* before he turned 21. Thereafter, he moved to South Australia to work for the *Adelaide Critic* as a black and white artist.

In 1902, Dyson returned to Melbourne, where he worked for publications including *The Bulletin* and *Melbourne Punch*. In 1910, he married Ruby Lindsay, who was also from a well-known artistic family. They moved to London, where Dyson worked for the *Weekly Despatch* as well as contributing coloured cartoons to *Vanity Fair* (which he signed 'Emu') and black and white cartoons to the *Daily Herald*. He continued to receive critical praise and in 1914 he published a collection of his work, entitled *Cartoons*. According to the *Australian Dictionary of Biography*:[18]

> His work, published full newspaper size, was sensational. A convinced socialist, with a humanist outlook generated in his youth when the conflict between labour and capital was emerging as the dominating theme in Australian politics, Dyson hacked into the pomposity and humbug of pre-war England, championing the working man boldly and without reserve. 'In British cartooning Before Dyson', his friend Vance Palmer wrote, 'the working man had been depicted as a pathetic figure, a depressed person lacking any human dignity. Will Dyson drew him young, militant, an image of hope with fist up-raised'. He at no time called for bloody revolution, but he was stronger in his demands for social justice than most progressive intellectuals of his day, fighting the slum landlords, courts, Labour renegades, the press, exploitation, and Tory reaction in all forms. His cartoons were graphically dramatic, and in tone bitter, attacking unemployment, hunger and suffering.

18 Vane Lindesay, 'Dyson, William Henry (Will) (1880–1938)', *Australian Dictionary of Biography*, Volume 8, (MUP), 1981.

First World War

In 1915, Dyson became Australia's official artist on the Western Front. He showed a determination to experience the conditions for himself by going to the frontlines, and was wounded twice in 1917. Exhibitions of his war cartoons were held in London during the war, and in November 1918, he published the best of his drawings in a book, *Australia at War: A Winter Record made by Will Dyson on the Somme and at Ypres during the Campaigns of 1916 and 1917*.[19] It contained an introduction by GK Chesterton.

Dyson's author's note, dated 'May, 1918', and thus written whilst the fate of the war still hung in the balance, stated:

> This selection of drawings, made during the winters at Ypres and on the Somme reflects more the misery and the depression of the material conditions of these campaigns than it does any of their exaltations or their cheerfulnesses.
>
> Here and now – here on the new Somme and now when Spring is about us in a land upon which War has not had time to fully wreak his wicked will—these two latter qualities are dominant. In the spirit of Dernacourt and of Villa-Brettoneur the selection made from my drawings may seem to overstress this winter note. They are not primarily cheerful—but it is open to doubt whether we are behaving generously in demanding that the soldier who is saving the world for us should provide us with a fund of light entertainment while doing it.
>
> The truth is that War has many moods and nothing more is hoped than the selection made from my drawings and my notes may record something of the one of its moods to which I was temperamentally most attuned during those bad seasons on the Somme and at Ypres.

In his introduction, Chesterton wrote of the power of Dyson's work and finished with the following paragraph:

> We are fighting against a living slime, like that mud of Flanders which men loathe more than wounds and death. And indeed the two spirits of the war might be conceived as meeting in the flats of the Flemish coast under the emblems of the two elements; the strange slow strength of the inland swamp and the force and freedom of the sea. Against such elemental emptiness of bare lands and bleak waters Dyson has moved and showed his comrades moving; and his stroke is here none the less militant because he is now using only the artillery of art, which fights not with fire but with light.

---

19 Published by Cecil Palmer & Hayward. At the time of writing, it had been digitised and published online.

Post-war career

In March 1919, Dyson was widowed. In 1920 he published a selection of his wife's work as *The Drawings of Ruby Lind* along with a short book of poems in her memory.

Not long after her death, he drew a cartoon for the *Daily Herald* entitled 'Peace and Future Cannon Fodder'. It showed the prime ministers of Britain, Italy and France (David Lloyd George, Vittorio Orlando and Georges Clemenceau) along with President Woodrow Wilson, after a meeting at Versailles to discuss the Peace Treaty. Clemenceau, identified by his nickname 'The Tiger', was saying to the others 'Curious! I seem to hear a child weeping!', whilst behind a pillar was a child in tears with the label '1940 Class'. The prescience of the cartoon meant it later attained near-legendary status.

Dyson was devastated by his wife's early death. It was said that:[20]

> The fire and sting went out of him from this time on. His utter grief was evident in his *Poems: In Memory of a Wife* (London, 1919). The next blow to his fortunes came in 1922 when the *Daily Herald* was taken over by the Trades Union Council: Dyson resigned, to become, in effect, unemployed for the next two years. For he was staunchly independent and would not work for a direct organ of a political party.'

In 1925, Dyson accepted an offer to return to Australia and work for the *Melbourne Herald* and *Punch*. He stayed for five years though he did not get on with the editor, Keith Murdoch. Thereafter, he returned to London, holding a successful exhibition in New York on the way. In Britain he again worked for the *Daily Herald*, and continued producing cartoons until just before his death.

Perhaps due to their common membership of the Savage Club, he became interested in the Social Credit theory of Major CH Douglas. Reflecting his displeasure with the capitalist system, and the Great Depression, in 1933 he published another book, *Artist Among the Bankers*.

He died in 1938. His final cartoon was published on the day of his death. It showed two vultures watching aeroplanes in the Spanish Civil War, with one muttering to the other 'Once *we* were the most loathsome things that flew!'

His obituary in the *Sydney Morning Herald* stated:[21]

> [According to Lionel Lindsay, artist and critic] his caricatures of public men were intellectualised, being not merely the portraiture, slightly exaggerated, which had so long passed here for caricature. They had a psychological reach, and revealed the mind and general character—

---

20 Vane Lindesay, op cit.
21 'Will Dyson: Death of Famous Cartoonist', *The Sydney Morning Herald*, 24 January 1938, p 14, https://trove.nla.gov.au/newspaper/article/17438500.

all that stayed below the surface—yet were wonderful in their grip of exterior characteristics. He was not properly appreciated in Australia. In Europe, his qualities were esteemed by Bernard Shaw, H. G. Wells, and G. K. Chesterton, who wrote a panegyric on his war cartoons, Mr. Lindsay added ... As a war artist and cartoonist, Will Dyson took his place with Raemakers and Forain he continued. His greatness lay in his ability to illustrate ideas and drive them right home.

He was a great humanist, who hated to see useless suffering of the poor. During the war he worked in the zone of fire, and was twice wounded. To make his studies he devised a tray with a celluloid top, and hung it about his shoulders. Through it he could see his paper, and work, even in the pouring rain.

He paid a noble tribute to the A.I.F. in the splendid series of lithographs which he made of their suffering and endurance. The organised exhibition of these drawings was opened by the Queen, and the £2,000 for which they were sold was presented to war charities. "An original artist, a great wit, a greater humanist has left us," said Mr. Lindsay.

Mr. Kerwin Maegraith, the cartoonist, who knew Mr. Dyson in London, said last night that the work of the artist was sometimes infinitely delicate in line, but was always dramatic in intensity. He said that Mr. Dyson never recovered fully from the death of his wife, to whom he was greatly attached.

"Some of Mr. Dyson's addresses to the Chelsea Arts Club, and on Sunday nights at the Savage Club, were gems of stinging satire and brilliant wit," Mr. Maegraith said. "He could have been a statesman if he had not been a great artist.'

Alfred Leete: 'Your Country Needs You'

'One of the quieter wits of the Savage Club' is how Reginald Pound described Alfred Leete. And yet, Leete created one of the most memorable images of the war, for it was Leete who was responsible for the legendary picture of Lord Kitchener, finger outstretched, with the ringing declaration: 'Your Country Needs You'.[22]

Early life and First World War

Leete was born in 1882, in Northampton, the son of a farmer. The family moved to Weston-super-Mare when he was still a child, since his father's health declined and prevented him from continuing as a farmer.[23] Leete left school aged 12 and worked as an office boy in a surveyor's office in Bristol, before starting work as a draughtsman in a furniture company and a lithographer – two occupations eminently suited to someone with artistic talent.

---

22 Martyn Thatcher and Anthony Quinn, *Kitchener wants You: the Man, the Poster and the Legacy* (Uniform, 2016).

23 Mark Bryant, 'Poster Boy: Alfred Leete', *History Today*, vol 59. issue 7, July 2009.

Leete's drawing ability was apparent early on, and he had his first cartoon published when he was just 16. He went on to be published in *The Pall Mall Gazette*, *The Bystander*, *London Opinion*, *The Sketch* and *Punch*. In 1905, he became a full-time illustrator. As well as cartoons, he drew posters and advertisements.

When the First World War began, he joined the Artists Rifles. During the conflict he produced several pro-war pictures, such as one entitled 'Get Out and Get Under' depicting the German fleet as a cowering daschund with a British bulldog emerging over the horizon, and the illustrations for books with fairly self-explanatory titles such as the 1916 works *All the Rumours* and *Bosch Book*. He also drew a strip called 'Schmidt the Spy' playing on one common wartime fear for the weekly magazine *London Opinion*. It was so successful it was made into a silent film that year.

Your country needs you

His picture of Kitchener first appeared as the cover for the 5 September 1914 issue of the *London Opinion*. A week later, the magazine said readers would be able to buy postcards of the image, and later on it was released by the magazine as a poster.

Leete's picture differed from official posters of the time, in that the latter only comprised text and were usually stated in the name of the King, not Kitchener or any other non-Royal. Other magazines, however, had used similar sorts of imagery to Leete's on their covers: the Northcliffe paper *Weekly Dispatch*, for example, had a dramatic picture of a wounded soldier next to a fallen comrade, imploring people to join him by the heading 'Will they *never* come?'

Exactly how ubiquitous Leete's poster was during the war years – as opposed to later fame due to the numerous pastiches and imitations – has been the subject of some debate. Reginald Pound, writing in 1963, stated that '[w]ithin a few hours of its appearance on the bookstalls later that week, the War Office secured the right to reproduce it in poster form. Soon it was displayed on every hoarding in the land. It was the prototype recruiting poster and has since served as a documentary recruiting poster in many histories of the First World War.'[24] The Imperial War Museum, however, published an article in 1997 which asserted that the poster was little known during the war years, and only gained fame because the museum itself used the picture in its artwork some time after the conflict.[25] The author James Taylor in a 2013 book *Your Country Needs You: The Secret History of the Propaganda Poster*[26] echoed that finding and argued:[27]

24 Pound, *The Lost Generation*, op cit, p 25.
25 Thatcher and Quinn, op cit, pp 108–110.
26 Saraband, 2013.
27 Jasper Copping, '"Your Country Needs You" – The myth about the First World War poster that "never existed"', *Daily Telegraph*, 2 August 2013.

> There has been a mass, collective misrecollection. The image's influ-
> ence now is absolutely out of all kilter with the reality of its initial
> impact. It has taken on a new kind of life. It is such a good image and
> saying that it was later seized upon. Some many historians and books
> have used it and kept repeating how influential it was, that people have
> come to accept it.

It would not be the only example of an image becoming wrongly thought of as
ubiquitous in a particular time. There is a notorious photograph of the infamous
phrase 'No Irish, No Blacks, No Dogs' that was supposedly displayed regularly
outside small hotels and bed & breakfast establishments in the 1960s. It has been
reproduced many times by various forms of media including *The Guardian* newspaper.[28] In fact, there is not much evidence of such photographs in the national
archives, nor were they mentioned in parliament in the 1960s race relations
debates. One source suggested that the photograph was created in the 1980s for
an exhibition, and thus was not a genuine example from the earlier period.[29]

Martyn Thatcher and Anthony Quinn, however, in a book published in 2016[30]
disputed Taylor's scepticism about Leete's poster and pointed out that it appeared
in the background of some wartime photographs, as well as being copied overseas, most notably by James Montgomery Flagg in the United States in 1917.[31]

In his memoir published in 1936, Oliver Bernard recalled his impressions of
London when he came back injured in 1917: 'A poster of Kitchener flashed by.
Oh yes, your country needs you all ...'[32] It is improbable he was referring to a
different poster. Could Bernard – and Reginald Pound – have both had a false
memory induced by the Imperial War Museum's work in the 1920s? It is possible,
though it would seem less so in the case of Bernard since he was writing in the
1930s and thus much closer to the time than Pound.

If nothing else, the sales of the *London Opinion* were extensive (between

---

28 Alan Travis, 'Right to rent scheme to be extended nationwide from February', *The Guardian*, 20
    October 2015.
29 Letter by John Draper to *The Guardian*, 21 October 2015, and see the responses on 28 October
    2015, one an assertion by Dr Tony Murray of London Metropolitan University that the pho-
    tograph was genuine, even if its provenance was uncertain, and one from Professor Steve Bruce
    of the University of Aberdeen stating that he had tried and failed to find one when researching
    a book in the 1990s. Doctor Murray claimed in aid 'oral testimony' of Irish and Caribbean
    immigrants, just as has been proffered in support of the Leete image being ubiquitous in war-
    time. Whilst I do not doubt that there was discrimination against both immigrant groups in
    the 1960s, that does not mean that the particular poster was genuine. One should also recall
    that the great West Indian cricketer Learie Constantine successfully sued a hotel during the
    war for turning him away (at the behest of bigoted American servicemen) (see my book *Trials
    & Tribulations*, Ch 42), so British institutions of earlier generations were not as prejudiced as
    some might believe.
30 Thatcher and Quinn, op cit.
31 Ibid. Pound makes the same point about American appropriation of the image.
32 Bernard, *Cock Sparrow*, op cit, p 265.

100,000 and 300,000), so Leete's image would have been well-known for that reason at least. Whatever its audience at the time, though, there is no doubting the power of the image or how it has endured when the circumstances giving rise to its creation have long vanished.

Post-war career

After the war, Leete continued with his successful career, drafting advertising posters for such commercial entities as Bovril, Ronuck Polish, Pratt's Petrol, Hector Powe, Connolly Leater, Rowntree's Chocolate and William Younger.

He died in 1933.

Sir Edwin Lutyens: architectural genius

Of all the Commonwealth Great War memorials, the most significant is the Cenotaph on Whitehall, a monolithic structure of Portland stone with the simple inscription 'The Glorious Dead'. It has formed the centre of the Remembrance Day commemorations in Britain for nearly a century. Its designer was the great Savage architect, Sir Edwin Lutyens, one of the best known architects of the late nineteenth and early twentieth centuries – or, for that matter, *any* century. As well as the Cenotaph, his work ranged from English country houses to the design of the heart of an entire city, New Delhi in India, often called 'Lutyens Delhi' because so much of it was his brainchild. There is no possibility of doing justice to his life in the space available here, so instead we will attempt a short sketch with the emphasis on the Cenotaph.

Early life

Lutyens was born in 1869 in London, the tenth of 13 children, though he spent his childhood in Thursley, Surrey. He studied architecture at South Kensington School of Art, London from 1885 to 1887, and then entered practice. Evidently he was successful from the beginning, for he started working for himself after just one year, starting with a commission for a private house in Farnham, Surrey. In the course of designing the house he met the garden designer and horticulturalist Gertrude Jekyll, with whom he would undertake many commissions for country houses in the following years. Partly thanks to publicity in the new publication *Country Life*, Lutyens' reputation flourished before the end of the century. Most of his work to that point was in the Arts and Crafts style, but in the twentieth century he switched to more conventional designs.

His work in Delhi began after it was decided in 1911 to make Delhi the new capital of India. Among the highlights of his work on the city was the Viceroy's Palace, now known as Rashtrapati Bhavan. An area of about 26 square kilometres became known as the 'Lutyens' Bungalow Zone', and it remains among the most expensive real estate in India in the present day.

First World War

Lutyens' status as one of the country's leading architects was reflected in his appointment as one of three principal architects for the Imperial War Graves Commission, which later became the Commonwealth War Graves Commission. He was responsible for a number of monuments including the War Memorial Gardens in Dublin, the Tower Hill memorial, the momument at the Commonwealth War Grave at Étaples and the magnificent Memorial to the Missing of the Somme at Thiepval. The Thiepval monument displays no fewer than 72,337 names of the dead from the most costly action in the history of the British Army. The collective achievement of the Commission, in providing a monument to every single British soldier who fell in action, was described by Rudyard Kipling (the Commission's literary advisor) as 'The biggest single bit of work since any of the pharaohs—and they only worked in their own country.'[33]

The Cenotaph was originally intended to be a temporary structure to serve as the centrepiece of the Allied Victory Parade in 1919. Lloyd George had the idea for a low, empty platform, but Lutyens instead designed a taller, classical structure, reflecting the fact that the word 'Cenotaph' was Greek in origin, meaning 'empty tomb'.

Upon its unveiling, the Cenotaph was spontaneously covered in wreaths to the dead, given by members of the public. The feeling was so resounding that it was decided that the Cenotaph should become a permanent structure. The resulting stone construction was unveiled in 1920. It was intended to retain exactly the same shape as the earlier wooden structure, though in the event Lutyens refined the design slightly. The words 'The Glorious Dead' appear below the wreaths on each end, along with the dates of the Great War in Roman numerals.

The stone version of the Cenotaph was unveiled by George V on Armistice Day in 1920, the same day that the Unknown Warrior was brought to Westminster Abbey.[34] The funeral procession of the Unknown Warrior passed the Cenotaph, where George V placed a wreath on the Unknown Warrior's gun-carriage before carrying out the unveiling. He also placed a card on the

---

33 See David Crane, *Empires of the Dead: How One Man's Vision Led to the Creation of WWI's War Graves* (Harper Collins, 2013). Crane's book is on Sir Fabian Ware (1869–1949), who in response to his perceived indifference of the military to the fate of soldiers after they died in action, Ware established the Graves Registration Unit within the Red Cross.

34 The Unknown Warrior was selected to represent those whose bodies were never recovered. He was selected by a method designed to ensure his identity would never be known.

carriage which read 'In proud memory of those Warriors who died unknown in the Great War. Unknown, and yet well-known; as dying, and behold they live. George RI November 11th 1920.' The carriage then proceeded to the Abbey, where the pallbearers included Lord Byng.

The Cenotaph remains the place of the annual National Service of Remembrance held at 11am on Remembrance Sunday, the nearest Sunday to 11 November. It is also where the Anzac Day ceremony is held on 25 April, and the Combined Irish Regiments Association commemoration each June, which remembers the war dead of the Irish regiments that were disbanded on 12 June 1922 (the parade taking place on the Sunday following the Queen's Birthday Parade). In July, the Belgian Parade is held on the Sunday preceding the Belgian National Day of 21 July. Belgium remains the only nation permitted to parade its troops in uniform and carrying arms in Central London. Finally, the War Widows' Association of Great Britain Annual Service of Remembrance is held at the Cenotaph on the day before Remembrance Sunday.

As a mark of the status which it still holds in British society, various controversies in the twenty-first century took place, such as when a student protestor, Charlie Gilmour (son of the Pink Floyd guitarist David Gilmour) was jailed for a violent protest which the judge noted with fury included climbing up the Cenotaph's side. Gilmour claimed not to have known what the structure was, even though he was studying history at Cambridge University. Later, the BBC television programme *Top Gear* attracted criticism when they filmed a stunt driver performing various manoeuvres within sight of the Cenotaph. Both incidents, ostensibly trivial, showed that public sentiment for the monument remained undiminished, though I suspect the men of the *Wipers Times* would have fashioned an amusing response on both occasions.

Post-war career

Lutyens' career continued successfully after the Great War. As well as the extensive work in Delhi, he undertook projects as disparate as the refurbishment of Lindisfarne Castle, the construction of the Midland Bank in Manchester, and a small country house in Kent known as The Salutation, made for the Farrer family. The last of those received great critical acclaim and was among the first twentieth century buildings to receive Grade I listing.

Lutyens became an honorary life member of the Savage Club in 1942, in addition to the many other honours and distinctions he had accumulated, which included the Order of Merit, the Order of the Indian Empire (Knight Commander) and President of the Royal Academy of Arts.

He died in 1944.

CRW Nevinson: paint and prejudice

> I wish to be thoroughly disassociated from every "new" or "advanced"
> movement; every form of "ist," "ism," "post," "neo," "academic" or
> "unacademic." Also I refuse to use the same technical method to
> express such contradictory forms as a rock or a woman.
>
> *CRW Nevinson*

Christopher Richard Wynne Nevinson ARA, usually called CRW Nevinson and
occasionally Richard Nevinson, became one of the most famous of all British
war artists during the Great War. In the first years of the conflict he produced
some arresting works, combining the then-*avant-garde* styles of futurism[35] and
cubism[36] to fashion a unique method of depicting the horrors of the Front. No
less an authority than Walter Sickert rated Nevinson's *La Mitrailleuse* as 'the
most authoritative and concentrated utterance on the war in the history of painting.'[37] Nevinson was appointed an official war artist in 1917, but in retrospect it
seems he had already reached his peak by that stage. He turned to painting in a
more conventional style, which attracted less critical acclaim, and arguably his life
after the war was never as happy or fulfilling as his talent had once promised.[38]

---

35 According to the Tate Gallery website, Futurism was 'an Italian art movement of the
early twentieth century that aimed to capture in art the dynamism and energy of the modern
world. Futurism was launched by the Italian poet Filippo Tommaso Marinetti in 1909. On 20
February he published his Manifesto of Futurism on the front page of the Paris newspaper
Le Figaro.
Among modernist movements futurism was exceptionally vehement in its denunciation of
the past. This was because in Italy the weight of past culture was felt as particularly oppressive.
In the Manifesto, Marinetti asserted that 'we will free Italy from her innumerable museums
which cover her like countless cemeteries'. What the futurists proposed instead was an art
that celebrated the modern world of industry and technology', see https://www.tate.org.uk/art/
art-terms/f/futurism.

36 Again according to the Tate Gallery website, Cubism was 'a revolutionary new approach to
representing reality invented in around 1907–08 by artists Pablo Picasso and Georges Braque.
They brought different views of subjects (usually objects or figures) together in the same picture, resulting in paintings that appear fragmented and abstracted. Cubism was one of the
most influential styles of the twentieth century. It is generally agreed to have begun around
1907 with Picasso's celebrated painting Demoiselles D'Avignon which included elements of
cubist style. The name 'cubism' seems to have derived from a comment made by the critic Louis
Vauxcelles who, on seeing some of Georges Braque's paintings exhibited in Paris in 1908, described them as reducing everything to 'geometric outlines, to cubes', see https://www.tate.org.
uk/art/art-terms/c/cubism.

37 Quoted in EA Carmean Jr, 'War and Death in the Age of the Machine: A dose of trench warfare's reality', *Wall Street Journal*, 25 July 2014.

38 For more information on Nevinson's work, see Jonathan Black, *CRW Nevinson: The Complete
Prints* (Lund Humphries, 2014); Michael JK Walsh (ed), *A Dilemma of English Modernism:
Visual and Verbal Politics in the Life and Work of C R W Nevinson (1889–1946)* (University of
Delaware Press, 2007) and Sue Malvern, *Modern Art, Britain, and the Great War: Witnessing,*

Early life

Nevinson was born in Hampstead in 1889, one of two children to the war correspondent and journalist Henry Nevinson and the suffragette author Margaret Nevinson. They were able to provide Nevinson with a first-rate education, sending him to Shrewsbury and Uppingham schools, though he was not enamoured with the latter. His artistic talent was evident from an early age, and after leaving school he attended the St John's Wood School of Art followed by the Slade School of Art at University College, London (UCL).

At UCL he studied with the likes of Dora Carrington, Mark Gertler, Paul Nash and Stanley Spencer. Nevinson and Gertler became close friends and formed a group calling themselves the 'Neo-Primitives', dedicating themselves to following the art of the early Renaissance. The friendship did not last, though, since they became love rivals for Carrington. Nevinson had worse luck when he was told by the UCL's Professor of Drawing, Henry Tonks, to forget about having an artistic career. Nevinson never forgot the slight and continued to express animus towards Tonks decades later.

In 1912 and 1913 Nevinson studied on the Continent, attending the *Academie Julian* in Paris and the *Cercle Russe* in Geneva. Whilst in Paris he shared a studio with Amedeo Modigliani, and developed his interest in cubism, meeting Picasso in person as well as the Italian futurists Marinetti and Gino Severini.

Upon his return to London, Nevinson made friends with the radical writer and artist Wyndham Lewis, and joined Lewis' 'Rebel Art Centre', a short-lived movement whose other members included Ezra Pound. Nevinson was involved in the creation of still another movement, the 'London Group', and published various newspaper articles propounding a manifesto for English futurism called 'Vital English Art', rubbishing most of contemporary art (using the erudite insult *passéiste filth*) and proclaiming futurism as the way forward in the age of technology. It caused a rift between Nevinson and Lewis since Nevinson had attached the name of the Rebel Arts Centre to the manifesto without asking Lewis.

First World War

Nevinson's family was muted when war was declared. He recalled:[39]

> Our household in London took the outbreak of war with the utmost calm. There was no hysterical talk, no wild ideas about God, cricket and democracy. My father had been for years a war correspondent, and my mother had always expected the Germans to make another attack on France. I regarded myself as having no patriotism, although I preferred

---

Testimony and Remembrance (The Paul Mellon Centre for Studies in British Art) (Yale University Press, 2003).

39 CRW Nevinson, *Paint and Prejudice* (Teeling Press, 2013, Kindle edn).

> the English. This state of mind and this preference I put down entirely to my travels abroad. A man who lives and works in a foreign country begins to understand its people, and surely understanding is the enemy of all such folly as patriotism and insularity. Preference, on the other hand, is quite another matter. The longer I live and the more I travel, the more strongly do I believe that he British are the best and the only "grown-up" nation.

He added that 'Brass bands, union jacks, and even "Kitchener Wants YOU" had no power to move me.'[40]

Despite that underwhelming response, Nevinson himself was anxious to serve. He knew he would never pass a medical examination for the infantry due to his poor physical condition, which was partly caused by rheumatism. Instead, he learned some mechanical skills which enabled him to find a role driving ambulances (through his father's contacts) for the Red Cross. He went to France in November 1914 and was assigned to help French wounded housed at a disused goods shed near Dunkirk rail station known as 'The Shambles'. The station contained some 3,000 French wounded who had suffered appalling neglect since being removed from the Front. In amongst them were a few wounded German prisoners. Nevinson robustly defended the practice of Red Cross doctors of attending to the sick according to need, with no regard to nationality. He had the support of a cockney cook, who reasoned about foreigners: 'They're all bastards, so wot's the odds?'[41] Nevinson later painted two pictures of his time at The Shambles, *The Doctor* and *La Patrie*. When the latter was displayed in London in 1916, a critic wrote 'La Patrie will stand, to the astonishment and shame of our descendants, as an example of what civilized man did in the first quarter of the 20th Century.'[42]

As well as The Shambles, Nevinson worked at a dressing-station in Ypres, which was closer to the Front. It was regularly shelled and at times threatened by the German advance. Despite their theoretically non-combatant status, the British Red Cross men took what weapons they had and prepared to make a stand when they thought the Germans were coming. In the event they did not have to engage in combat, though a shell once passed through Nevinson's ambulance. Among his anecdotes from the time was one concerning the conviction of some French soldiers that the German advance had halted at Reims because the soldiers had drunk themselves into a stupor on champagne. Nevinson's physical problems meant that he struggled to control the vehicles of the day. In January

---

40 Ibid. The Kitchener mention was presumably a reference to Leete's poster, and thus constitutes another straw in the argument about how widely known it was during the conflict.
41 Ibid.
42 'Oil Painting – La Patrie', Birmingham Museums and Art Galleries website, http://www.bmagic.org.uk/objects/1988P104.

1915, he was deemed unfit for service and returned to Britain (as he put it, 'I crocked up and was sent home').

He was no longer at the Front, but it was by no means the end of his war service. In March 1915, he had four pictures included in the Second Exhibition of the London Group, among which his *Returning to the Trenches* was one of the best-reviewed pictures of the whole exhibition. He then enlisted as a private in the Royal Army Medical Corps and spent the rest of 1915 working at the 3rd London General Hospital in Wandsworth, a specialist centre for the treatment of shell shock and severe facial injuries. He had no medical qualifications, and hence worked as an orderly and a labourer, rather to his chagrin, though he received no sympathy from his colleagues. Occasionally he was assigned to help to care for those suffering shell shock or other mental conditions, which he later called the worst job of his life. As a private he also suffered condescension and class prejudice from the nursing staff, art critics and life in general.

Despite his lowly army rank, his paintings continued to attract much praise, especially *La Patrie, The Road to Ypres* and *The First Bombardment of Ypres,* all of which were displayed in 1915. Much to his contempt, though, *The Times* described the pictures as 'not a bit like cricket', which he scornfully described as

> ... an interesting comment on England in 1915, when war was still considered a sport which received the support of the clerics because it brought out the finest forms of self-sacrifice, Christian virtues, and all the other nonsense. I had painted what I had seen, without a thought for exhibition. To me the soldier was going to be dominated by the machine. Nobody thinks otherwise today, but because I was the first man to express this feeling on canvas I was treated as though I had committed a crime. The public, however, as usual, showed more intelligence than the intelligentsia, and I was also well treated by the general Press.

The other significant event in his life in 1915 was his marriage in November to Kathleen Knowlman; they had one child who died in infancy while Nevinson was overseas.

By January 1916, his rheumatic fever was so bad he had to withdraw from active duty again. In March 1916, he exhibited his legendary *La Mitrailleuse* (he had painted it during his honeymoon at the end of 1915), which as noted was rated by Walter Sickert as the greatest of all war paintings. The Tate Gallery, where the painting is now housed, has the following description:[43]

> Nevinson aligned himself with the Italian futurists who celebrated and embraced the violence and mechanised speed of the modern age. But his experience as an ambulance driver in the First World War changed his view. In his paintings of the Front, the soldiers are reduced to a

---

43 See https://www.tate.org.uk/art/artworks/nevinson-la-mitrailleuse-n03177.

series of angular planes and grey colouring. Here, they appear almost like machines themselves, losing their individuality, even their humanity, as they seem to fuse with the machine gun which gives this painting its title.

The extremely positive reception of *La Mitrailleuse*[44] led to the Leicester Galleries offering Nevinson his own exhibition. It was held in October 1916, with a preface by General Sir Ian Hamilton, who as we have seen commanded the failed Gallipoli campaign. The exhibition was another critical and commercial success for Nevinson, attended by many luminaries from politics, the arts and the military,[45] with all of the paintings being sold.

Nevinson's health was still poor, but he was frightened by the prospect of discharged men being re-evaluated for service (given the pressure the army was under at the time). He went to apply for a commission, but instead was offered a role in early 1917 as an official war artist for the Bureau of Information, the only problem being there were no funds to pay him. In mid-1917, he spent a month as an official artist at the Western Front, coming under enemy fire on several occasions, including when a passenger with the Royal Flying Corps. His apparent disregard for danger led to an official reprimand and a return to London (though he claimed that his offence had been to go to Passchendaele, where he was not permitted, except that no one was permitted to tell him so).

Upon his return to London, he created six lithographs on the subject of building aircraft for the War Propaganda Bureau portfolio of pictures, 'Britain's Efforts and Ideals'. He then set to work creating paintings from the sketches he had made at the front, using a much more realistic style than his earlier futurist/cubist works. It was to the dismay of the art advisers from the Department of Information, who found the works boring. For their part, the War Office censors found three of the paintings objectionable, and although Nevinson agreed to the minor changes of one painting, he held his ground with the other two. One

---

44 The source for the picture might not simply have been Nevinson's own experiences at the Front. The author Ben Jones argued that the picture was clearly inspired by a double-page spread in the *Sphere* titled 'The Steel Helmet in Actual Use in the Trenches: The Disappearance of the Old French Cap', dated 20 November 20 1915 – precisely when the time in which Nevinson was composing *La Mitrailleuse*. See Ben Jones, 'Denying the "foe-to-graphic": C. R. W. Nevinson and photography' in Walsh, op cit, p 142. Jones went on to note that Sickert often used newspaper photographs as the source for inspiration for his own work, but Nevinson would have been incensed at any suggestion he had done so (not that it took much to inflame his temper, it would seem).

See also James Fox, *British Art and the First World War, 1914–1924 (Studies in the Social and Cultural History of Modern Warfare)* (Cambridge University Press, 2015).

45 Including Ramsay MacDonald, Winston Churchill, Bernard Shaw and Joseph Conrad. Afterwards the publicity led to him meeting and forming friendships with the Sitwell family of intellectuals – Osbert, Sache and Edith – three people who had the unusual distinction of unalloyed praise in Nevinson's memoirs.

of them, *A Group of Soldiers*, offended the censors because it depicted 'the type of man represented … not worthy of the British Army', but was eventually passed for display. The other impugned work was *Paths of Glory*, which showed two fallen British soldiers in a field of mud and barbed wire. Nevinson was so incensed by the attempt at censorship that he displayed the picture in 1918 with a brown strip of paper across the painting, with the word 'Censored' written on it. He thereby added to official indignation since he had used the word 'Censored' without permission – in other words, he was censured for saying 'censored' about a painting the authorities wished to censor.

In 1918, Nevinson was engaged by the British War Memorials Committee to produce a single large artwork for the proposed Hall of Remembrance, though in the event the hall was never constructed. He was also offered an honorary commission as a second lieutenant, but declined on the ground that it might prejudice his medical exemption from combat duties. The lack of a commission made life more difficult when he visited the Western Front, since he had to be accompanied by an army minder who, to his fury, tried to restrict his movements. His later trips to the Front did however result in the painting *The Harvest of Battle*, his largest ever single work. The painting was first displayed in April 1919, with some journalists claiming that it was being partly withheld from the public on the ground it was too gruesome. It was kept in a side gallery at the Imperial War Museum war paintings exhibition at Burlington House in December 1919, enraging Nevinson (an entirely predictable reaction). His resultant vitriol raised difficulties for his future dealings with the museum and various others who presumably could not be bothered with his temper.[46]

Post-war career

In March 1919, before his fulminations over the Burlington House exhibition, Nevinson had visited New York, where his pictures were well received. A second exhibition there in October 1920 failed to draw the same acclaim, however, leading to yet more Nevinson remonstrations. Just before that exhibition he had designed a poster in Britain for a production by Viola Tree of *The Unknown* by Somerset Maughan, showing bombs exploding around a crucifix. It was banned from display on the London Underground, but Nevinson, rebarbative in the face of authority as usual, distributed the poster outside the theatre and attracted much publicity accordingly.

His career continued its variable path in the 1930s. On the one hand, his cityscapes of London, Paris and New York were well-regarded, and he placed himself on the right side of history by creating an anti-fascist painting, *The Twentieth*

---

46 See also Paul Gough, *A Terrible Beauty: British Artists in the First World War* (Sansom and Company, 2010) and David Boyd Haycock, *A Crisis of Brilliance: Five Young British Artists and the Great War* (Old Street Publishing, 2009).

Century. On the other hand, his large historical allegories were thought inferior to his Great War paintings, leading him to fall out with the famous critic Kenneth Clark, who was Director of the National Gallery at the time.

In 1937 he published a memoir, *Paint and Prejudice*.[47] It remains an entertaining read, and I have quoted from it several times already, but it is also a work which needs to be approached with caution;[48] Nevinson's confrontational nature was accompanied by a tendency to exaggerate some of his experiences. The book sought to play up his wartime activities, when in truth he spent much less time at the Western Front than so many others.

Despite all his life's controversies, it seems clear that he remained appropriately highly regarded for his artistic work, since he was awarded the Chevalier of the *Légion d'honneur* in 1938 and made an Associate of the Royal Academy in 1939.

During the Second World War, Nevinson worked as a stretcher-bearer in London, and suffered personally as both his studio and family home were hit by bombs. He was left out of the War Artists' Advisory Committee, in part no doubt because it was chaired by Clark. The committee also rejected three paintings he submitted, though it did eventually purchase his Blitz paintings *Anti-aircraft Defences* and *The Fire of London*.

Nevinson had better relations with the RAF, who commissioned a painting of airmen preparing for the Dieppe raid in 1942 (a raid that turned out to be a disaster, as we will see later when discussing Brother Savage Lord Mountbatten). The RAF also permitted him to fly in aircraft as preparation for his paintings of the air war. One such piece, entitled *The Battlefields of Britain*, was presented to Churchill as a gift to the nation and was hung in Downing Street, where it remains today.

Not long after presenting *The Battlefields of Britain*, Nevinson suffered a stroke, leaving his right hand paralysed and his speech impaired. Showing considerable stoicism, he learned to paint with his left hand, and had three pictures shown at the Royal Academy in the summer of 1946, but his always frail health was failing completely, and he died in October of the same year.

The Savage Club

Nevinson joined the Savage Club in August 1924. He had worried that his reputation for confrontation might prevent him being thought a clubbable chap, but he was admitted nonetheless (one of his seconders being Basil Cameron, the great conductor discussed in Chapter 7) and went on to embrace the Club most enthusiastically, as he later described in *Paint and Prejudice*:

---

47 *Paint and Prejudice*, op cit.
48 Paul Gough, *A Terrible Beauty: British Artists in the First World War* (Sansom & Co, 2010), in particular Chapter 3: 'C.R.W. Nevison: a painter with prejudice'.

My membership in the Savage was an entirely new experience for me. No longer did I feel the outcast among the set I had been brought up with—demi-socialists who wrote for unimportant little reviews; painting people who exhibited in obscure places; men and women who for the most part had been too superior to take any active part in the affairs of the day, who were proud of saing they never had anything to do with the War because their objections to a German policeman were no stronger than their objections to an English one. These people had a vague love for Russia simply because they knew nothing about it, and an avowed detestation of England simply because they were English. Yet they professed to be international. It was a class which could be summed up as Fabian Shavians, vaguely connected with political economy and the *New Statesman*. They hated the realism of the French, but praised any art, no matter how bad, as long as it came from Paris. They wrote about English bad taste in French magazines, often accusing the English of failings which were common to all nations and thus demonstrating their insularity. Most of them had allowances from their fathers. They seldom worked; they used the arts as a refuge for their laziness, taste as a hedge to screen their inferiority as craftsmen, and economics as an excuse for their incapacity to meet creditors. They were intensely envious of anyone capable of earning his living. No wonder the trade unionists despise the intelligentsia of the Labour Party. Nearly all are without scruple and rely on their superior education to grab power from an ignorant democracy, which they despise and misunderstand even more than "the ruling classes."

These people now faded into the distance as far as I was concerned. In the Savage Club I was able to mix with numbers of great doctors, eminent scientists, actors, writers, musicians, artists—sensible, hard-working men, all busy at their arts or professions, all men of the world, and generally speaking all possessed of X-ray eyes and capable of stripping a high-brow of all poses, affectations, and pretentions. There is no other collection of men in the world to compare with it. There are field-marshals and fiddlers, mummers and millionaires, and when they enter those dignified doors in Carlton House Terrace they leave all differences behind them and meet their fellow members on common ground. I found myself in an atmosphere I loved. It reminded me somewhat of the early art days before the War, when tolerance and artistic camaraderie were accepted facts among practising artists ...

Sometimes the Savage reminds me of my early life, when journalists used to come to my father's house and discuss the news which did not appear in the papers. Here men come from every sort of queer place and speak authoritatively on every subject.

As a final Savage coda, Nevinson also recorded in *Paint and Prejudice* that when he needed expensive medical care (in those pre-NHS days), he was finally able to obtain it when a Brother Savage doctor (unnamed, but perhaps one of the eminent surgeons we will meet in Chapter 10 or Appendix III) performed the operation for a pittance.

EH Shepard: the man who drew Winnie-the-Pooh

Ernest Howard (EH) Shepard will forever be famous for his drawings for AA Milne's *Winnie-the-Pooh* and Kenneth Grahame's *Wind in the Willows*. Long before he contributed such marvellous work in the genial world of children's illustrations, Shepard – like Milne – served with distinction in the unmitigated horror of the Great War.

Early life

Shepard was born in London in 1879 to a prosperous middle-class family. His father was an architect and his mother the daughter of the well-known painter William Lee, who had also been co-founder of *Punch* magazine. In 1889, the family was devastated when his mother died. Nevertheless, he was still able to attend the prestigious St Paul's School, where his artistic talent was soon noticed.

In 1897, he won a scholarship enabling him to attend the Royal Academy Schools with three years' free tuition. He prospered as a student, winning a Landseer scholarship in 1899 and a British Institute prize in 1900, and also having two pictures accepted for the Royal Academy Summer Exhibition. It was unfortunately against the background of further family suffering, since his father's finances and health both declined. In 1902 his father died and Shepard, along with his older brother Cyril and his younger sister Ethel, had to move to rented lodgings.

Shepard nevertheless continued to advance his career as an illustrator, having his work published in editions of famous books including *Aesop's Fables* and *David Copperfield*. In 1904, he married, and two children were born before the end of the decade. In 1905 he and his wife left London and moved to Sussex, which was to become the county of the Hundred Acre Wood. In 1906, he was published in *Punch* for the first time.

First World War

After the outbreak of the First World War, Shepard did not move to enlist immediately; in those initial stages, married men were not among those exhorted by Kitchener to sign up, and there was still a hope among the general public that the war would be over by Christmas. By spring 1915, though, the war was progressing far worse than expected, and Shepard applied successfully for a commission with the Royal Artillery. He spent four months training at Weymouth and Lydd before being commissioned in December 1915. He was assigned to the 105th Siege Battery when it was formed at the start of 1916.

The 105th went to France and first saw action in front of Mont-St-Eloi on 10 June 1916 as part of the lead up to the Battle of the Somme. Shepard's brother,

Cyril, was serving as a second lieutenant with the 9ᵗʰ Devonshire Regiment. Cyril wrote to Shepard in early June 1916 joking 'if you happen to be behind us be careful of the angle for I don't want to be crumpled by your ruddy guns.' Tragically, Cyril was killed on the first day of the Somme, though Shepard did not find out until he received a letter from Ethel some time later.

Shepard himself was engaged throughout the battle, with the artillery in constant demand. He was nevertheless able to continue his work as an illustrator (and, almost bizarrely, received chasing letters from his editor in the middle of the battle; the editor apparently not reading the London papers of the time, or perhaps adhering to the adage 'don't ask, don't get'). He also sent regular letters home, such as the following from Bronfay Farm, dated 13 July 1916:[49]

> Having fixed a candle stump into the siege lamp to do duty in place of my torch (which has given out), I feel equal to facing the dark outside and perhaps dodging some of the pools, the largest of which is immediately outside our "front door". It is wretchedly draughty in here, so bad that Richards and I have put on our "warms", but then we had to build the place in a day. It is only six feet square and six feet high, just a hole in the ground with logs laid across and the excavated earth thrown on top—"splinter-proof" we call it.
>
> The rain has found us out already, but there are a few dry spots ...
>
> We are going on with this all night—ie, bursts of intense fire at frequent and irregular intervals—and I hope it is causing as much inconvenience to the Boche communications as it is to our own domestic arrangements. The men are absolutely top-hole,[50] working like Trojans in spite of every disadvantage—guns to which they are not accustomed (French 120mm long) and which they hate. The thing sheds a few nuts and bolts at each round. Our gun-pits are deep in sticky mud. Fortunately the Boche has left us entirely alone up to the present. I went across to the 1/1 Lowland Brigade, R.G. A., just now (beyond the 75s on our left); they have a brazier going behind their guns and were brewing hot tea. Their 4.7's are simply wallowing in the mud ...
>
> Time is getting on, 2.10am, and I have put the men on fuzing shell; we shall want a lot presently. I nearly put my foot in it now. We were hard at it getting the rounds off in salvos "in succession from the right" (our own patent), and I was squidging across to No. 2 gun when I collided with two strangers. I had used the necessary bad language before my light revealed General East, commanding the Heavy Artillery of the corps, and Andrews, his brigade major. The general was thoroughly amused, and stayed talking to me for ten minutes, telling me what was going on, etc. He climbed into No. 1 pit, and discussed the French method of laying; he was awfully nice.

---

49 See James Campbell, *Shepard's War: EH Shepard, the Man Who Drew Winnie-the-Pooh* (Michael O'Mara, 2015, Kindle edn).

50 'Top hole' was clearly a superlative then in general parlance; Dennis Wheatley, among others, used it in his letters home as well.

> It is almost light and we have been at "gunfire" and are now down to an ordinary rate. It is a dull grey morning, but there is a wide yellow streak across the sky to the south-east. I am sitting on top of the dugout and feel as I used to after a dance, in the dim ages.

Shepard stayed at the Western Front until having some leave at the start of 1917. On 16 February 1917, he was promoted to acting captain. The 105th Siege Battery fought in the Battle of Arras, which took place in April and May 1917, during which time Shepard served as an acting major, but then returned to his rank of acting captain.

In July 1917, he was made substantive lieutenant. The 105th Siege Battery went into action in the same month during the Third Battle of Ypres (Passchendaele). The battle lasted from July until December 1917. The bleak weather turned the landscape into a desolate sea of mud which formed some of the most arresting scenes of the Great War, and Shepard drew several classic examples. For his actions in the battle, he was awarded the Military Cross. His citation in the *London Gazette* stated:

> For conspicuous gallantry and devotion to duty. As forward Observation Officer he continued to observe and send back valuable information, in spite of heavy shell and machine gun fire. His courage and coolness were conspicuous.

It had been intended for the 105th Siege Battery to be sent on home leave after the Passchendaele Offensive, but the Italians had suffered a disastrous reverse at Caporetto, losing much of their own artillery pieces. The 105th was included among British reinforcements rushed to the sector to try to prevent an Italian collapse.

Pulling large siege weapons through the roads of 1914 with horse-drawn carriages cannot have been an easy experience, but after a journey of five days through France, the 105th arrived in Italy. It went into action in early December on the Montello Hill, near the Piave River. The winter conditions limited the amount of fighting. Shepard was given some leave in early 1918 but returned to Italy in February to help prepare for the expected Austrian Offensive. In May, however, he went back to England and attended a gunnery course, after which he was granted home leave. He was also presented with his Military Cross and promoted to major.

His leave ran out on 24 June and he left once more for Italy. The Austrian Offensive had begun on 15 June, but was already faltering by the time Shepard arrived. Over the next few months the Austrian Army ceased to function effectively and, after the heavy defeat at Vittorio Veneto in late October, threw in the towel, slightly before the general Armistice. The 105th Battery was engaged in action at Vittorio Veneto and Shepard drew some moving pictures of the scenes of Austrian prisoners and other wartime imagery.

After the end of hostilities, Shepard was not demobbed immediately, but stayed in Italy trying to arrange prisoner exchanges and the disposal of all the weaponry, including captured Austrian equipment. Shepard managed some sightseeing as his duties lightened, on one notable occasion meeting Ernest Hemingway, whom he called 'an awfully good sort'.

Post-war career

In February 1921, Shepard joined the Savage Club, and later the same year joined the staff of *Punch*. The latter was a fateful move as the deputy editor was his fellow Great War veteran AA Milne. A fellow staff member, EV Lucas, recommended Shepard to Milne for the children's books Milne was writing. Initially Milne did not think Shepard's style was suitable for *Winnie-the-Pooh*, but asked him to illustrate another of his books, *When We Were Very Young*. When he saw Shepard's work, he then demanded Shepard also illustrate *Winnie-the-Pooh*. He was so pleased with Shepard's contribution that he arranged for Shepard to receive some of the royalties.

The model for Pooh Bear was not in fact the toy owned by Christopher Milne, but Shepard's son's toy 'Growler'. Growler would therefore be worth a fortune today, as are the other toys and all of Shepard's original drawings, but sadly he met a grim fate: after being passed down to Shepard's granddaughter, he was eaten by a neighbour's dog.

Shepard also did the drawings for another children's classic, Kenneth Grahame's *Wind in the Willows*, for an edition first published in 1931. He was not the first to do so – the book was originally published in 1908 – but many consider his drawings to be the best and most recognisable. Grahame declared himself pleased with the early sketches, but died before the finished edition was published.

During the Second World War, Shepard was too old to serve, but suffered inconsolable tragedy when his son died in action.

Shepard was promoted to lead cartoonist of *Punch* in 1945. One of his 1947 cartoons, a joke on petrol rationing entitled 'Gunpowder Plan', is framed on the Savage wall today. He stayed with *Punch* until 1954, when he was evicted without much ceremony by the incoming editor, Malcolm Muggeridge.[51]

Shepard wrote two autobiographies: *Drawn from Memory* (1957) and *Drawn*

---

51 Interestingly, during the Second World War, AA Milne had been one of the critics of Brother Savage PG Wodehouse for his broadcasts on Nazi radio, while Muggeridge was sent to France after the liberation of Paris to interview Wodehouse for MI5, in order to determine whether he should be charged with treason.

From Life (1961). In 1972, he donated his personal collection of papers and illustrations to the University of Surrey. He was made an OBE in 1972.

He died in 1976. He received many fulsome tributes. Milne, who predeceased him, had already inscribed a copy of *Winnie-the-Pooh* with the following:

> When I am gone,
> Let Shepard decorate my tomb,
> And put (if there is room)
> Two pictures on the stone:
> Piglet from page a hundred and eleven,
> And Pooh and Piglet walking (157) ...
> And Peter, thinking that they are my own,
> Will welcome me to Heaven.

Nearly 40 years after Shepard's death, a trunk was found containing an extensive collection of his drawings from the war, along with various military effects. The drawings were used as the basis of a new book, which reproduced them along with a detailed narrative of Shepard's time during the war.[52] As to how such a priceless treasure could have remained hidden for the rest of Shepard's life and decades beyond, the most plausible explanation seems to me that Shepard, in common with so many of his comrades, chose not to dwell on the war and would not actively speak about it. He had served with distinction, as his Military Cross and promotions make clear, and he had escaped any serious injury. But he had lost his older brother, and had seen the deaths of many others (to say nothing of the death of his son in the Second World War). Those of us born in easier times can only imagine how much of a toll that had to have taken upon him.

Sidney Strube: 'Little Man', big success

Sidney Strube was a quiet man who created a character called the 'Little Man', but there was nothing silent or diminutive about his phenomenal success as a cartoonist. Among many accolades, he had the honour of being the subject of a poem 'Strube' by AP Herbert, which began:

> A Rose by any other name
> Would smell as rosy; all the same
> It is important—yes, it is,
> To know how STRUBE pronounces his,
> For instance, does he rhyme with "Tube"
> I cannot tell you. (Nor can STRUBE.)
> For many a wife informs her hubby
> "The only man I love is STRUBE."

---

52 Campbell, *Shepard's War*, op cit.

> While there are those who rudely dub
> This brilliant little fellow STRUBE ...
>
> No doubt you think the simplest plan
> Would be to ask the little man.
> Well you are wrong, for when I pounced
> And said, "Hi! How are you pronounced?"
> He took his horsewhip from the shelf
> And said, "I do not know myself."
> So we must leave it, I suppose—
> The only thing that no one knows.

Pace Herbert's inimitable wit, I am given to understand the name was pronounced 'Stroobee'.

Early life

Strube was born in London in December 1891. His father, Conrad Frederick Strube, was a German immigrant who came to Britain as a young man to work improving drainage in the Fens in East Anglia and Cambridgeshire. By the time Sidney was born, Conrad and his English wife ran the Coach and Horses pub in Old Compton Street London (later named the Cambridgeshire).[53] In 1894, they sent Sidney to live with his maternal grandparents in the fresher air of Cambridge, where they had a farm. Sidney attended the village school and soon showed a talent for drawing.

At the age of 11, Sidney returned to his parents' house in London, and attended the Licensed Victualler's School in Holborn. He won several prizes there, but in 1907, aged just 15, left school to become an apprentice furniture designer in London. Due to the repetitive nature and limited creative scope, he found the work tedious, and did not enjoy a second draughtsman's job either. The following year he began working for an advertising agency in Fleet Street. He lasted two years in the role, but still found it unsatisfying for his creative instincts. The turning point came in 1910 when he enrolled, aged 19, in John Hassall's School of Art in Kensington.

To begin with, Strube envisaged a career as a poster artist, but during his time at the school was inspired by a general election cartoon in the *Daily Express*. With Hassall's encouragement, he successfully submitted caricatures to the *Conservative & Unionist* magazine. His first political cartoon published in a newspaper was on the 'Zeppelin Scare' – the fear (not unrealistic, as events proved) growing that German Zeppelins would attack British cities in the event of war

53 Timothy S Benson, *Strube: The World's Most Popular Cartoonist* (The Political Cartoon Society, 2004). See also: https://www.cartoons.ac.uk/cartoonist-biographies/s-t/SidneyConradStrube. html.

– which the *Evening Times* reproduced after Strube's flatmate had fished it out of the wastepaper basket and sent in without Strube knowing. The cartoon even caused ructions in Westminster, which of course did great things for Strube's profile and career. He was published regularly thereafter and secured an exclusive contract with the *Daily Express* in 1912. His work was so popular that, in December 1913, the *Daily Express* issued an album of his cartoons. In the spring of 1914, he signed a contract with the paper under which he was to be paid £15 per week (over £1,500 in today's currency, according to the Bank of England's inflation calculator).

First World War

When war broke out, Strube was on holiday – an indication that the British public and even the British press did not think British participation in a European war was inevitable. Upon his return, he was told by his editor at the *Daily Express* that humorous cartoons were inappropriate during wartime. Worse, he was also told that due to the consequent reduced demand for his work, for the duration of hostilities he would be on £15 per month instead of per week, despite his contract.

He might have sued for breach of contract, but instead Strube accepted his lot and started drawing dour cartoons. Soon, though, it was realised that humour, far from being inappropriate, formed a necessary relief during wartime, and Strube's cartoons resumed a lighter touch.[54] His work received the praise of Lord Kitchener, who called him a genius, and said 'in this time of stress and sorrow his sense of humour and power of conveying it are invaluable.'

At the suggestion of his editor, Strube drew a calendar for 1915 taking the mickey out of 'Kaiser Bill' and his misfortunes. It sold out quickly and proved popular amongst the troops, leading to the paper printing a warning on the calendar not to send it to troops at the Front since 'the Germans have been known to kill prisoners on whom they have found caricatures of the Kaiser.'

By mid-1915, the war had been going badly for the British, with the Western Front at stalemate and the Gallipoli campaign failing. The supply of volunteers was running dry, leading the authorities to place as much pressure as they could on men yet to enlist. Any refusenik of eligible age was denounced as a shirker and a coward. (The tactics were insufficient as conscription was introduced in 1916.) Strube decided to volunteer. His decision had an immediate tragic family consequence: his father was appalled at the thought of his son fighting the land of his

---

54 Somewhat bizarrely in the circumstances, the *Daily Express* started reproducing German cartoons, and continued doing so until December 1916 when its new owner Lord Beaverbrook stopped it.

birth, but was unable to talk him out of it. Strube signed up on 29 October 1915 and his father, devastated, died two weeks later.

Although his editor had done him a poor turn by unilaterally slashing his wage by three-quarters, he then did a volte-face of sorts by promising Strube he would continue to pay the £15 per month even while Strube was in the army, a magnanimous offer that Strube greatly appreciated.

Appropriately, Strube had enlisted with the Artists Rifles. He undertook basic training and was then posted to the 2ⁿᵈ Battalion at Hare Hall, where other Savages including Lance Thackeray and William Lee Hankey also served. Strube's role there was that of a PT instructor. On occasion he would fill a bayonet practice dummy with red paint, which terrified the new recruits when they stabbed it. It was also at Hare Hall that Strube picked up an affectation of calling everyone 'George', following the lead of a corporal who could not be bothered learning the names of new recruits, so instructed them all to respond to being called 'George'. Strube would later do the same in correspondence with friends.

Though he did not receive a commission, and reached only the rank of sergeant at Hare Hall, Strube was well-known and popular in the camp. He was regularly asked by his superiors to design posters and programmes for army concerts, and draw menus just like the Savage Club tradition.

In October 1916, a year after enlisting, Strube went to the Officers Training Camp in St Omer, France, where he stayed for another year. Then, in November 1917, he went to the Front with 1ˢᵗ Battalion, 28ᵗʰ London Regiment (part of the 63ʳᵈ Royal Naval Division) and joined the Battle of Passchendaele (usually called Third Ypres).

Passchendaele was a battle fought in atrocious conditions, where the improved British assault tactics and initial success achieved by detonating huge mines under the German lines, all came to nothing due to the weather turning the battlefield into a sea of mud. Strube's battalion went over the top in the worst of those conditions and were cut to pieces. The journalist Philip Gibbs described the situation:[55]

> It is idle for me to try to describe this ground over which the London men and the Artists had to attack. Nothing that I can write will convey remotely the look of such ground and the horror of it. Unless one has seen vast fields of barren earth, blasted for miles by shell-fire, pitted by deep craters so close that they are like holes in a sieve, and so deep that the tallest men can drown in them when they are filled with water, as they are now filled, imagination cannot conceive the picture of this slough of despond. The London men had to wade and haul out one leg after the other from deep sucking bog as though in glue, and sank

---

55 Philip Gibbs, *From Bapaume to Passchendaele*, quoted in S Stagoll Higham, *Artists' Rifles. Regimental Roll of Honour and War Record 1914-1919* (Howlett & Son, 1922, Reprint by Naval & Military Press, 2002, Digital version by Andrews UK Ltd, 2012), pp xxiv ff.

above their waists. A rescue party led by a Sergeant-Major could not haul out men, breast high in the bog, until they had surrounded them with duck-boards and fastened ropes to them. Our barrage went ahead, the enemy's barrage came down, and from the German blockhouses came a chattering fire of machine guns, and in the great stretch of swamp they struggled.

And not far away from them, but invisible in their own trouble among the pits, the Artists Rifles, Bedfords, and Shropshires were trying to get forward to other blockhouses on the way to the rising ground beyond the Paddebeeke. The Artists and their comrades were more severely tried by shell-fire than the Londons. No doubt the enemy had been standing at his guns through the night ready to fire at the first streak of dawn, which might bring an English attack. A light went up and instantly there roared a great sweep of fire from heavy batteries and field guns: 4.2's and 5.9's fell densely and in depth and this bombardment did not slacken for hours. It was a tragic time for our men, struggling in the slime with their feet dragged down. They suffered but did not retreat: no man turned back but either fell under the shell-fire or went on ...

Strube himself was literally trapped in No Man's Land during that assault, since he and some colleagues sank to their waists in the freezing mud and could not move for three days. They were eventually rescued by men who brought ropes and duck-boards – but not before a sniper killed one of Strube's party. The rest hobbled back in bare feet, their shoes having stayed trapped in the mud.

Gibbs also wrote on another occasion of the attack:[56]

The London Regiment and the Royal Fusiliers fought this battle, and not far from them were the Artists Rifles—the dear old 'Artists,' who, in the old volunteer days, looked so dandy in their grey and silver across the lawns of Wimbledon. They suffered yesterday in hellish fire, and made heavy sacrifices to prove their quality. It was a fight against the elements, in league with the German explosives, and it was a frightful combination for the boys of London and the clean-shaven fellows of the Naval Brigade.

Strube's battalion was due to go over the top again as soon as the weather cleared, but he became unwell. He was diagnosed with trench fever and was sent to hospital and, in February 1918, returned to Britain to recover at the Colchester Military Hospital. Whilst there he was diagnosed with an irregular heartbeat. At the time it was blamed on the trench fever, though his biographer concluded that it was hereditary.[57]

As with EH Shepard, Strube had continued drawing even – or perhaps especially – when under the awful conditions of the Western Front. His sketchpad was left in Flanders as he had been too unwell to take it with him to the hospital. He

56 In a letter, quoted in S Stagoll Higham, op cit.
57 Benson, op cit.

did, however, manage to keep a Colman's mustard tin containing what he called his 'Flanders mud', with which he used to draw sketches. (One such sketch had been sent to the *Daily Express* editorial department, who greatly valued the fact it had had been made with liquid mud.) The staff at Colchester threw it away thinking it was 'in a filthy disgusting state' but retrieved it at Strube's request, much to his relief.

In June 1918, Strube was retired from his battalion and returned to the OTC (Officers' Training Corps) at Hare Hall to resume his old role as an instructor. He held that position until the end of the war. He spent a month recuperating before rejoining the *Daily Express*, although he was not officially demobbed until January 1919.

Post-war career

Strube's return to the *Daily Express* was marked by a major headline 'Strube Comes Back', and a particular welcome from the owner, Lord Beaverbrook, who understood the power and value of the cartoonist. Strube's career as a political cartoonist brought much success throughout the decade. One of his best-known creations was the 'Little Man', a depiction of an everyman facing life's travails with a degree of optimism, caution and realism. As Strube himself put it, the Little Man was supposed to represent the man in the street, 'trying to keep his ear to the ground, his nose to the grindstone, his eye to the future and his chin up – all at the same time.'

He joined the Savage Club in December 1924.

The University of Kent described his style thus:[58]

> An admirer of Partridge, Frank Reynolds and Low, Strube worked on Whatman board with indian ink, after sketching preliminary outlines in pencil. In 1927 one journalist described Strube's working on the roughs, his face "set and solemn": "When he is sorting out his ideas he takes a piece of drawing board and his pencil begins to dance over it, making little rough scrawls which resolve themselves into Mr Baldwin's pipe, Mr Ramsay MacDonald's moustache, a tall stove-pipe hat to which becomes added the face of Sir William Joynson Hicks." He only smiled when the rough was complete, and he began transferring it to Bristol board.
>
> Strube was fond of allegorical characters, and in 1942 a writer described calling at his office in the *Daily Express* building to find him standing in front of the large mirror: "He balanced a drawing-board on his left arm, a pencil was in his right hand, his trousers were rolled up over his knees. "I'm Mars," he explained, "working against time. Got to be wired to Glasgow and Manchester in half an hour." A fastidious worker, his motto was "Never let it go until you are satisfied—and never be satisfied!"

---

58 https://www.cartoons.ac.uk/cartoonist-biographies/s-t/SidneyConradStrube.html.

Strube never allowed malice to enter his cartoons, and was known familiarly as "George", from his habit of addressing others by this name—although his son really was called George.

By 1931, Strube was the highest paid man in Fleet Street, earning the then-enormous sum of £10,000 per year (again using the Bank of England inflation calculator, about £625,000). Although Strube did not court publicity, and was not promoted as a person by his paper, he was shown in waxwork form by Madame Tussauds in 1934 along with his fellow cartoonists David Low and Percy Fearon.

Percy Bradshaw, a fellow member of both the Savage and the Sketch Clubs, recalled:[59]

> 'George' Strube was beloved by everybody at the Club for his complete modesty. He had, as most of us know, a fantastic record of success as cartoonist of the *Daily Express*—a responsibility which rested on his broad shoulders for nearly thirty years. I frequently joined him in the Express office, where he did his work. There were no tiger skin rugs or decorative accessories in George's 'studio', and he was very frequently interrupted by the telephone at his elbow. But he got through his job with unfailing regularity and continually increasing popularity. His 'Little Man' did a great deal to cheer up the nation during the war. At the beginning of every new year he used to take the chair at a house dinner. He did scores of menu designs for his Brother Savages; he was feted, wined, dined and written about, but if you dared to suggest he was anything out of the ordinary, he would promptly cut you short with 'Oh! Chuck it, George!' His Christian name was Sidney, but he called everybody George, including his wife and every other woman. He said it made life simpler, and, anyhow, he never could remember names. But we remember his; and the Club was very sad when our dear George died in March 1956.

In the Second World War, Strube created some patriotic images and slogans about saving, making do and mending and similar themes, while also producing some advertisements. His popularity was sustained during and after the conflict, though he was fired from the *Daily Express* in 1948 after a disagreement with the editor, Arthur Christiansen.

Strube nevertheless found work as a freelancer for other papers, and continued working until shortly before his death in 1956.

Bert Thomas: 'Arf a Mo' Kaiser!'

If the most famous picture from the First World War remains (or has become) Leete's image of Kitchener, there are others which are not far behind, and which were probably better known during the conflict itself. One of those was the 'Arf a Mo' Kaiser!' picture drawn by Brother Savage Bert Thomas.

59 Bradshaw, op cit, pp 134–35.

Early life

Thomas was born in Newport in 1883. His father, Job Thomas, who was 65 years' old when Bert was born, worked as a monumental sculptor. Among other things, he had helped decorate the Houses of Parliament. The younger Thomas initially followed his father into the same trade, starting as an apprentice in 1897 at the age of 14 with an engraver in Swansea. His work mostly consisted of engraving names on doorplates and monograms on cutlery.

In his spare time, Thomas started drawing cartoons, and managed to sell some to magazines as early as his teenage years, beginning with a publication called *Pick-Me-Up*, and later selling them to the likes of the *Swansea Daily Leader* and the *Daily Post*. At the age of just 17, one of his drawings was published in *The Strand Magazine* after it was seen by the magazine's founder, Sir George Newnes, MP.

In 1900 Thomas was paid £5 (about £563 in 2018 currency) by a music hall comedian, Albert Chevalier, to design a poster. It was so well-received that Chevalier managed to persuade Thomas to move to London. The move was not a success, and Thomas soon came back to Swansea. In 1902, however, he tried again in London with better luck, landing a job in an advertising agency with Chevalier's help.

Thomas went through his workload effortlessly, and started drawing humorous illustrations in his spare time. He sold a number on a freelance basis and, in 1905, started regular work for *Punch*. In 1909, he started contributing to *London Opinion* as well. Four years later, he exhibited at the Society for Humorous Art and received a positive review in *The Times*.

First World War

Arguably the greatest moment in Thomas's career came in the first few months of the war, with his 'Arf a Mo', Kaiser!' cartoon, with the caption appearing with a grinning Tommy lighting his pipe. Apparently it only took Thomas ten minutes to draw. It was printed in the *Weekly Dispatch* on 11 November 1914, as part of the paper's tobacco-for-troops fund – a fund which ultimately raised a quarter of a million pounds for the war effort (£26.5m in 2018).

Thomas joined the Savage Club in March 1916, having been nominated the previous month. In the same year, he enlisted in the Artists Rifles as a private. Subsequently, though, making the best use of his talents, he served as an official war artist for the National Savings Campaign.

In 1918 he drew a giant poster – the largest in Britain – as part of an appeal for War Bonds, which was hung over the façade of the National Gallery. The poster comprised an oil painting approximately 75 feet long which depicted Sir Francis Drake facing the Spanish Armada.

Thomas created similar posters for the Royal Exchange in London, and also for public buildings in Cardiff and Glasgow. In June 1918, he was awarded an MBE for his contributions to the war effort.

Post-war career

After the war, Thomas produced a full-page series of red-and-black cartoons for *The Sketch*, and was a freelance illustrator for the 'Cockney Spirit in the War' letters column which ran in the London Evening News from 1929, a collection being published in 1930.

He was certainly an active member of the Savage Club. Among other things, he sponsored Percy Bradshaw's membership application. He later contributed anecdotes to Bradshaw's centenary publication on the Club: as well as recounting the story of Percy Gibbon's ill-judged contretemps with another member, he also recalled the time a soon-to-be-ex member tried to bring his wife in disguised as a man.

In 1936 he joined the staff of the *Evening News* to illustrate a new series of readers' letters under the title 'Arf a Mo' Stories'. He also contributed to a wide range of other publications including the *Radio Times*. During the Second World War, he once again produced memorable posters, including the series 'Is Your Journey Really Necessary?', drawn in 1942 for the Railway Executive Committee.

He died in 1966.

CHAPTER 9

Savage Men of Law

Introduction

The presence of only three lawyers in this book might come as something of a surprise to modern Savages, given that the profession is well-represented in the Club in the twenty-first century. In fact, law was not a category of membership until 1956. (I am unable to substantiate the rumour that it was added because in difficult financial times lawyers could be relied upon to pay their membership fees and keep the bar in business.)

Having said that, many esteemed lawyers found other ways of joining the Club. Lord Moulton obtained membership through his formidable scientific achievements, while Lord Denning led a remarkably long life and joined as late as 1968. AP Herbert is included in this category due to his brilliant legal writings, though he joined under the category of literature and was notable for his political career as well. All three men made important contributions to the war effort in different ways, from the teenage soldier Denning to the septuagenarian Moulton.

It is not the place here to discuss the legal profession of the day,[1] though I cannot resist adding an anecdote from Brother Savage Herbert 'Beb' Asquith, who we met as a Savage man of letters. Beb, who followed his father to the Bar, remembered as a child going to a restaurant for the first time in his life as a

---

1   For some other random Savage legal trivia, Brother Savage Somerset Maugham's grandfather, Robert Maugham, was a prominent lawyer and co-founder of the Law Society of England and Wales. An enjoyable memoir of a Savage barrister of nineteenth and early twentieth century is Ernest Bowen-Rowlands, *Seventy-Two Years at the Bar* (Macmillan and Co, 1924).

guest of the barrister Richard Haldane,[2] an important influence in his father's life and career. Beb recalled:[3]

> Haldane was a magnificent and generous host, lavish to his guests, and very courteous to children, treating them as though they were his contemporaries. He had not followed Gilbert's advice for obtaining a practice at the Bar by marrying 'a rich attorney's elderly ugly daughter'; but he told me that he had once performed a feat, perhaps more arduous even than this, by patiently drinking glass after glass of a solicitor's port wine in spite of the fact that it was badly corked, without betraying the tragedy or shewing any sign of emotion. After this supreme act of stoicism the solicitor sent him an important brief, perhaps as a compensation for his sufferings; this brief was followed by others, and so a connection was formed, of which in those early years he stood very greatly in need.

Since I no longer work in the profession I am unable to verify if either tactic remains advisable.

Lord Denning: the people's judge

Lord Denning was without doubt the best known English judge of the twentieth century, and probably the only judge in modern times to have truly resonated with the public. He was famous for his defence of the powerless against the powerful, be it an indigent plaintiff suing a large corporation or an honest citizen being leaned on by the state. He was and remains a favourite among law students for his inimitable prose – always concise and to the point – and for never allowing desiccated precedent to stand in the way of what he saw as justice (or 'short sentences and simplistic reasoning' according to an uncharitable former law professor of mine). A famous joke in legal circles in the 1960s was that students used to write to him and ask him not to change the law again before their exams.

Denning was the author of the official report into the Profumo Affair of

---

2   Richard Burton Haldane (1856–1928) was a barrister and liberal politician who enticed his friend HH Asquith into politics. Haldane served as secretary of state for war from 1906 to 1912, following which he became Lord Chancellor. He undertook substantial reorganisation of the army into an expeditionary force: infantry battalions were integrated into divisions, each almost self-contained with its own artillery, engineers, and support. Haldane's successor, Jack Seely, resigned in March 1914 following the Curragh incident. Asquith took over the office himself, though he drew upon Haldane's advice and assistance and delegated various tasks to him.

    On the eve of the First World War, Haldane convinced Asquith to appoint Kitchener as secretary of state for war instead. After the war broke out, Haldane was falsely accused of pro-German sympathies. Asquith refused his resignation in September 1914, but he had to go in May 1915.

3   Herbert Asquith, *Moments of Memory* (Hutchinson & Co, 1937), p 27.

the 1960s, said to be the 'raciest blue book ever written', albeit not against much competition. More significantly for our purposes, he was both a member of the Savage Club and a Great War veteran.

Early life

Alfred Thompson 'Tom' Denning was born in 1899 in Whitchurch, Hampshire, the son of a local draper. The family story – recorded by Denning in a book written in his early eighties[4] – was remarkable in itself. Denning was one of six children, five of whom were boys. The eldest son, Jack, was killed in 1916 near Gueudecourt on the Somme. Gordon Denning fought in the Battle of Jutland but died of tuberculosis later in the war. ('They were the best of us' Denning later said of his deceased brothers.) Reginald Denning became a lieutenant-general in the British Army, while Norman Denning became a vice-admiral and served as director of naval intelligence and deputy chief of the defence staff (intelligence). All in all, it was quite a collective achievement for the children of a draper in Whitchurch.

Denning was recognised as a brilliant scholar from his early days in school – so much so that he had to learn mathematics himself, since he soon surpassed the local teachers' knowledge. In 1916, he went up to Oxford to study mathematics.

The First World War – signing up

At the outset of war, Denning was too young to enlist, though years later he recalled the general sentiment:[5]

> On the outbreak of war all the young men flocked to the colours. None stopped to inquire the need for it. Everyone accepted that we were right to go to war. We were to defend Belgium—whose neutrality we had guaranteed. We had given our promise—on 'a scrap of paper'—and must honour it. The Germans made scorn of it. Their despatch to our Foreign Office said:
>
> > Just for a word—"neutrality", a word which in wartime has so often been disregarded, just for a scrap of paper—Great Britain is going to make war.
>
> There was no conscription at the beginning. Volunteers came forward in thousands.

He attempted to sign up himself at the first opportunity, in August 1917, upon reaching the age of eighteen-and-a-half. By that stage his two older brothers were both dead, but Denning was spurred on rather than deterred by their loss. 'We were not allowed to go to France until we were 19' he later wrote. 'But we

---

4   Lord Denning, *The Family Story* (Butterworths, 1981).
5   Ibid, p 43.

were all anxious to join as soon as we could. No hesitation—not even on my part in spite of the grievous loss the family had already borne. All the keener because of it.'[6]

It is worth pausing to reflect upon Denning's enthusiasm for the war. He was typical of millions across the country who volunteered with alacrity in spite – or even because – of losing friends and relatives in the cause. Modern readers might find that hard to understand, but there seem to me several reasons why.

First, in a much more homogenous, monocultural society, the population was more likely to respond to a national crisis in a united fashion.

Secondly, modern media has left potential soldiers in no doubt about what they might expect to see during wartime, whereas there was a degree of ignorance in 1914 (not that Denning could have been unaware of the perils by 1917).

Thirdly, the majority of the population in Britain now are much better off materially than in the First World War, when the promise of three square meals a day was a good inducement to patriotism for many living in the squalid industrial towns of the time (again, less relevant in Denning's case, since although not from a wealthy background he did not live in poverty).

Fourthly, patriotism, jingoism and imperialism were concepts that were embraced, rather than disdained, a century ago. People of Denning's generation were brought up to be chivalrous to ladies, honour God and the King, salute the flag, revere the British Empire, and uphold the rule of law. Schoolchildren were taught to shoulder the white man's burden, keep a stiff upper lip, play the man, and observe the tradition of service.[7]

Finally, and most importantly, in 1914 the rights of individuals were accompanied by a very different concept of the rights and duties of nations. In particular, the notion of a country acting with 'honour' was highly valued; it formed 'a fundamental political and international currency in diplomatic affairs.'[8] Hence, as we noted in the Chapter 3 when discussing Sir Basil Clarke, the Belgian nation stood firm against Germany even though to do so was virtually an act of national suicide given the disparity in the two countries' respective resources.

Of the German threat to Belgium, the British Foreign Secretary, Sir Edward Grey, told the House of Commons that he—

---

6   Ibid, p 71.
7   Early in 2018, during the course of researching this book, I visited the National Army Museum in Chelsea, London. It is clear those responsible for the museum did not share Denning's values: the museum offers countless apologia for the days of Empire and seems anxious to disdain and disown any sense of patriotism.
8   Heather Jones, 'A Prince in the Trenches? Edward VIII and the First World War' in Heidi Mehrkens and Frank Lorenz Müller (eds), *Sons and Heirs: Succession and Political Culture in Nineteenth-Century Europe* (Palgrave Macmillan, 2016), Ch 14, p 230.

would like the House to approach this crisis in which we are now, from the point of view of British interests, British honour, and British obligations ... if, in a crisis like this, we run away from those obligations of honour and interest as regards the Belgian Treaty, I doubt whether, whatever material force we might have at the end, it would be of very much value in face of the respect that we should have lost. [9]

'National honour' was also one of the reasons that all nations were prepared to accept the appalling casualties at the beginning of the war. It arguably contributed to the strategy on the Western Front, in that the generals felt they had licence to mount attacks even if they knew in advance that would be very costly, since the cause was just (albeit had they the means or imagination to pursue a more economical strategy they would have done).

By 1916, the rate of volunteers had slowed such that the British government introduced conscription for the first time in its history. By 1918, the shattering cost of the war in blood and treasure had created far greater cynicism across Europe about the notions of national honour and whether Horace's line '*Dulce et decorum est pro patria mori*' ('It is a sweet and beautiful thing to die for one's country') was still valid – as it had been used at the foot of each one of Denning's letters to his brothers serving during the war[10] – or had instead become 'the old lie' as Wilfred Owen memorably put it. For Denning, however, the values that had impelled him to sign up never faded. Nor did they in the case of his brother Reginald, who wrote many decades after the war's end:[11]

> From the declaration of war in 1914 and until after I was wounded, it was with a proud and gay heart, because I considered myself privileged to be able to do something for the country in a time of dire need. The King and parliament had declared that the country was in danger and that was quite sufficient for hundreds of thousands like myself. I was all eagerness to get to the Front. Even after being wounded, I retained a keen desire to return to the Front and to the fighting there ... Convalescent at Hythe, I remember the wishfulness with which I saw ships leaving Folkestone with troops bound for the front ...
>
> In 1918 I was gratified to be ordered to France where I arrived in time to meet the last big German offensive.

For all Denning's enthusiasm, he was initially ruled unfit on the ground of a systolic heart murmur. He believed the doctor had invented the diagnosis

---

9   Heather Jones, op cit, p 229.
10 Ibid, p 49.
11 Ibid, p 51. Lieutenant-General Sir Reginald Francis Stewart Denning KCVO, KBE, CB, MC (1894–1990) was badly wounded on the Western Front in 1915 by a bullet which passed through his shoulder and hit his head. He recovered and went on to have a long career as a staff officer and administrator.

because he was tired of sending young men off to die – since Denning lived to the age of 100, his suspicion had some credence.

Denning appealed the decision successfully and enlisted as a cadet in the Hampshire Regiment. He retained (some say exaggerated) his Hampshire burr all his life, even in the cloistered environs of the Court of Appeal, where anything other than received pronunciation was rare at the Bar in his time and almost unknown on the bench (in both respects, not much has changed).

Denning applied to join the Royal Engineers, because he thought his mathematical background would be useful. He was sent to the Officers' Training Corps near Newark and was commissioned as a second lieutenant in November 1917. 'What I liked most was the horses' he later mused.

The First World War – to the Front

Because of his young age, Denning was not supposed to be deployed to France, but in early 1918 the Germans launched Operation Michael and severely threatened the Allied lines. By March they were within striking distance of Amiens and Paris. The next month Haig issued his order for every position to be held to the last man, and Denning's unit was rushed to France to try to prevent the Germans breaking through. He joined the 151st Field Company of the Royal Engineers, attached to the 38th Welsh Division. They were placed on the frontline opposite the town of Albert, which was then in German hands.

Denning was under near-continuous shellfire for several months:[12]

> In trench and bivouacs. Never knowing where the next shell would fall. There was a cartoon by Bruce Bairnsfather which caught the mood exactly—the man looking over the top of a shell-hole, saying "If you knows of a better 'ole, go to it". Night after night we made a reconnaissance—creeping close up to the enemy. It was a dangerous task. The River Ancre was flooded to a width of 200 to 300 yards and there were no bridges. The enemy held the other side in force.

Then the tide turned, and the British began the 'Hundred Days' Offensive that would lead to the Armistice. At an early stage in the British attack, in late August 1918, Denning's unit spent days building a bridge, only for the Germans to bomb it and force them to start again. During that period they went 48 hours without sleep. His work on the bridge was mentioned in the regimental history as having enabled an attack to be launched which resulted in the capture of Thiepval, with 634 prisoners and 143 machine guns being taken.[13]

As the advance continued, Denning was required to create access across the Canal du Nord. All the bridges had been destroyed and the valley was smothered

---

12 Ibid, p 73.
13 *History of the 38th Welsh Division*, quoted in Denning, ibid, p 74.

in poison gas. Denning's unit therefore had to establish pontoons across the canal. They did so under shellfire, whilst wearing gas masks. 'At one point one of my men pulled off his mask and said, "The gas is coming through my mask." About half-a-dozen others pulled theirs off too. We went on without them—and completed the job.' Denning then continued:[14]

> There were other crossings made too—over the rivers Selle and Sambre—and there was heaving fighting all the way. I can still see the line of infantry advancing under heavy fire—first one falling and then another—with us following close behind them. I can still see the battle-field strewn with hundreds of our best officers and men—lying dead—shot down as they went forward. I can still see the dead horses lying in piles beside the roads; and dead Germans black in the face. Such is war.

In November 1918, he fell ill with influenza, and was in hospital when the Armistice was signed. 'There was little rejoicing in our ward', he recalled, 'Too many were ill. There was relief. That was all.' But for the rest of his life Denning remained proud of his service. He gave it fairly cursory treatment during his *Desert Island Discs* interview with Brother Savage Roy Plomley, but in his family memoir he spent more time explaining his experiences, and summed up his feelings by quoting from Shakespeare's *Henry V*, Act IV, Sc 3, in which the legendary phrase 'We few, we happy few, we band of brothers' appears.[15]

Post-war life and career

Upon being demobbed in February 1919, Denning returned to Oxford and continued to study mathematics. He graduated in 1920 with a first in Mathematical Greats, and began teaching mathematics and geography (reading up on the latter the night before, since he had not studied it at university) at Winchester College. He did not enjoy the work, however, and decided instead on a career in the law.

Denning won a scholarship to study law at Oxford, returning to his old college of Magdalen. He completed his legal studies in a very short period of time and was called to the Bar in November 1921. He progressed to King's Counsel in 1938 – an unusual achievement for someone under the age of 40 – then, in 1944, was appointed a High Court judge in the Probate, Divorce and Admiralty Division (known to lawyers of the day as 'wills, wives and wrecks').

Within five years of his first judicial appointment, Denning reached the Court of Appeal – again, in an unusually short time. In 1957, he reached what was then the apogee of the bench when he was elevated to the House of Lords.[16] Denning

---

14 Denning, ibid, p 75.
15 Ibid.
16 In those days, 'House of Lords' was legal shorthand for the Appellate Committee of the House of Lords, not the entire House of Lords. Judges appointed to it were known as 'Lords of Appeal in Ordinary' although, confusingly, they were also members of the full House of Lords. The

did not enjoy the Lords, however, partly because his much more conservative judicial brethren stymied his attempts at reaching what he saw as the just result. In 1962, therefore, he stepped down from the Lords to head the Court of Appeal (a position known as 'Master of the Rolls' (MR)), the role in which he achieved lasting fame.[17]

By the end of the 1970s, he had built up a considerable reputation with the public and with the profession, sometimes controversially, but he was universally respected for his intellect and the clarity of his reasoning. Also, his personal integrity was never in doubt.

In some respects he was seen as a pioneering radical, with his loose adherence to precedent and propensity to find justice for the historically powerless. In other respects, though, Denning reflected his age, such as with his obstinate inability to comprehend the Sex Discrimination Act.[18] Further, in those days, there was no compulsory retirement age for judges, and Denning was fond of saying he had 'all the Christian virtues save resignation'. He continued sitting until he was aged 82, and only retired when he offended modern opinion by making an unfortunate comment about multi-racial juries in one of his books.[19]

---

convention was that they never voted or spoke on party lines, though after retiring from the bench they would often contribute, usually on the technical points of draft legislation. There was no suggestion that the Appellate Committee was not independent of government, but the reforming New Labour government of 1997–2010 did away with it anyway and created a new Supreme Court, something I thought involved a lot of time and money to answer a question no-one was asking. See Wilson, 'The new (as opposed to the existing) Supreme Court', *A(nother) Lawyer Writes*, 24 February 2010, http://timesandotherthings.blogspot.co.uk/2010/02/new-as-opposed-to-existing-supreme.html.

17 Although the Court of Appeal was lower in the judicial hierarchy, it gave Denning more opportunities to change the law since it heard many more cases. Moreover, Denning as MR could decide which cases he sat on and which judges accompanied him. In the House of Lords, at least five and sometimes seven judges would sit on appeals, meaning Denning would have to persuade at least two others to agree with him. In the Court of Appeal, by contrast, only three judges per appeal was the norm and so Denning only had to persuade one other (and then hope that the losing party did not appeal to the House of Lords, which most would not).

18 In the case of *Peake v Automotive Products Ltd* [1977] IRLR 365, Lord Denning and his colleagues on the Court of Appeal upheld a practice allowing women to leave a factory five minutes earlier than men, contrary to the obvious words of the Act, which precluded discrimination against either sex in the workplace. The court's reasoning was that the practice represented 'chivalry and administrative convenience' – an invention of their own since no such defence was envisaged under the Act. In the High Court (below the Court of Appeal) Mr Justice Phillips had said that instinctive feelings based on the 'women and children first' philosophy 'are likely to be the product of ingrained social attitudes, assumed to be permanent but rendered obsolete by changing values and current legislation'. Unfortunately, by overturning Mr Justice Phillips' obviously correct decision, Lord Denning and his colleagues had shown precisely those obsolete attitudes.

19 Most wished him well in his retirement, perhaps most eloquently the barrister, journalist and author Fenton Bresler, who said 'the ordinary people of this country have lost a spokesman'. One correspondent to *The Guardian*, however, referring to an unpopular case about bus fares which Denning had sat on and the various minorities he was supposed to have offended during his career, said that he wished Denning would spend his dotage 'trapped at a bus-stop every

In seeing how Denning eventually fell foul of the *zeitgeist*, we should not be smug about our supposedly superior values, since there is no doubt that attitudes will change again – and again. Perhaps a few decades from now veganism will win the day, and the current generation will be retrospectively condemned as murderers and slave owners for its treatment of animals.

Or perhaps later generations will wonder why we think it at best *risqué* and at worst perverted to pay money to watch two strangers have sex in public, let alone cheer them on[20] and write an intellectual description afterwards, yet we consider it a noble and civilised pastime to watch two men don gloves and try to inflict permanent brain damage on each other in a boxing ring.

As LP Hartley put it in *The Go-Between*, the past is a foreign country. Today's social convention is always a candidate for tomorrow's criminal offence, and vice versa. And perhaps the difference between fundamentalists and liberals is that the latter understand that point but the former do not. Or, to put it another way, a liberal is someone who is prepared to admit he or she might be wrong. Ultimately, like everyone privileged to lead a long life, Denning became the embodiment of the cliché *autres tempes, autres mores*.

He died in 1999, aged 100 – a truly remarkable life almost exactly spanning the entire twentieth century.

Sir AP Herbert: uncommon talent

Sir Alan 'AP' Herbert remains one of the Savage's most distinguished authors, best known for his 'Uncommon Law' series of 'misleading cases' – fictional accounts of court cases occasionally ridiculous but so cleverly crafted and argued that they have found their way into real-life legal discussions. He also had a fine record in the Great War and wrote two publications during the conflict which remain of great value.

Early life

Alan Patrick Herbert was born in Ashtead in Surrey, in 1890. His father was a civil servant who worked in the India Office, while his mother (Beatrice Herbert, *née* Selwyn) was the daughter of Lord Justice Selwyn, a member of the Court of Appeal in the nineteenth century.

Herbert attended Winchester College, where he won a prize presented by the

---

night in outer Ealing, without the money to pay for a taxi, in the stimulating company of blacks, gays, trade unionists and women.' Iris Freeman, *Lord Denning: A Life* (Hutchinson, 1993), p 396.

20 Unlike centuries past: Charles II was 'in the crowd' watching William of Orange consummate his marriage, and then there was the well-known pornographic imagery of Pompeii, for two random historical examples about different attitudes to sex in public.

prime minister, HH Asquith, and was also awarded a scholarship to New College, Oxford. At Oxford he started studying classics but changed to law, going on to obtain a first in jurisprudence in 1914. His roommate at New College was the future Viscount Monckton. Herbert was also good friends with Duff Cooper and Harold Macmillan.

His ability as a writer of humorous prose was evident very early on, being published in *Punch* in 1910 when he was just 20 years of age.

First World War

When the First World War started, he enlisted as an ordinary seaman in the Royal Naval Volunteer Reserve. He suffered a shattering blow in the first few weeks of the war when his brother, Owen Herbert, was killed in the retreat from Mons in late 1914. Herbert returned to Oxford in Autumn 1914 to sit the exam for All Souls, but was unsuccessful. He later claimed he only sat the exam 'for a lark' and enjoyed writing answers in light verse laced with humour, not to the amusement of the joyless clergy who held the whip hand over the Oxford of the day.[21]

In early 1915, Herbert was promoted to sub-lieutenant and was assigned to Hawke Battalion of the recently formed Royal Naval Division. The division was a brainchild of Churchill, who decided the best use of the excess volunteers to the navy was to form an infantry division, reasoning correctly that the demand for boots on the ground would never be sated (and also reasoning that it would give him more soldiers to command. Asquith remarked to his wife 'Winston … evidently means to run a war of his own'[22] – which in a sense he did, first deploying the Naval Division to his ill-fated Antwerp operation and then to his even more ill-fated Gallipoli invasion).

Herbert was sent to Gallipoli. He was given charge of a platoon comprising Tynesiders, whose dialect was almost incomprehensible to him, along with two Northumbrian men, who were incomprehensible to him and the Tynesiders, reflecting the Babelesque linguistic diversity of the British Isles in the days before modern telecommunications. Herbert resolved to include lectures based upon his classical education as the men headed towards Turkey, which they seemed to find of interest though few had encountered the subject before.

Upon arrival at Gallipoli, his unit went into action immediately at the Third Battle of Krithia.[23] Through his time there, he sent a number of letters home.

---

21 Reginald Pound, *AP Herbert: a biography* (Michael Joseph, 1976), pp 40–42.

22 Colin Clifford, *The Asquiths*, op cit, p 234. As noted, Asquith's third son, Arthur, served in the division at Gallipoli.

23 The battles of Krithia during the Gallipoli expedition involved three separate Allied attempts to capture a high point on the Alçı Tepe peninsular, which they had assumed they would take at the start of the campaign in April 1915. Each attempt ended in failure, as did the

Unfortunately all were lost, though his biographers, including Brother Savage Reginald Pound, have agreed that Herbert's own experiences were reflected in his book *The Secret Battle*.[24] The following extract gives some flavour:

> ... in those hill-trenches of Gallipoli the Turk and the Gentile fought with each other all day with rifle and bomb, and in the evening crept out and stabbed each other in the dark. There was no release from the strain of watching and listening and taking thought. The Turk was always on the higher ground; he knew every inch of all those valleys and vineyards and scrub-strewn slopes; and he had an uncanny accuracy of aim. Moreover, many of his men had the devotion of fanatics, which inspired them to lie out behind our lines, with stores of food enough to last out their ammunition, certain only of their own ultimate destruction, but content to lie there and pick off the infidels till they too died. They were very brave men. But the Turkish snipers were not confined to the madmen who were caught disguised as trees in the broad daylight and fought their way into the picture papers. Every trench was full of snipers, less theatrical but no less effective. And in the night they crept out with inimitable stealth and lay close in to our lines, killing our sentries, and chipping away our crumbling parapets ...
>
> The fire seemed to come from all angles; and units bitterly accused their neighbours of killing their men when it seemed impossible that any Turk could have fired the shot.
>
> For a little, then, this sniping was thoroughly on the men's nerves.

Herbert survived the fighting, but was taken ill in July 1915 and returned to England.

After a time recovering, he was passed 'fit for light duty', and seconded to the Naval Intelligence Division at Whitehall. In June 1916, he was passed fully fit for duty again and rejoined Hawke Battalion on the Western Front at its base in Abbeville. The battalion fought in the Somme and suffered very heavy casualties at Beaucourt, from which Herbert was one of only two officers to emerge unhurt. In 1917, he suffered a 'Blighty' during an attack on Gavrelle, near Arras and returned to England. Whilst convalescing he wrote *The Secret Battle*, and became a member of the Savage Club (having been nominated in October 1917, he was elected in April 1918).

The Secret Battle was an unflinching narrative of a soldier, Harry Penrose, convicted of cowardice and executed. Penrose's trial and punishment are normally assumed to have been inspired by Herbert's colleague in the Royal Naval Division, Edwin Dyett, who also served at Beaucourt and was broken by the experience, resulting in his court martial and execution. Herbert probably did not know

---

campaign as a whole.
24 Pound, op cit, p 45.

Dyett personally, since they served in different battalions, but would certainly have known of his death. One would have expected word to have spread quickly, since Dyett was one of only two officers in the entire war who were executed for cowardice.[25] Yet it also seems Herbert was writing as much about himself as about Dyett. Dyett had only recently joined the division, whereas the character of Penrose followed a similar path to Herbert: he was an Oxford man who enlisted in the ranks, took a commission and served at both Gallipoli and on the Western Front. In the story, Penrose's supply of courage – immense at the beginning of the war – eventually ran dry, leading to his execution.

Dyett's story became a source of public debate even during the war itself. It was taken up by the journalist Horatio Bottomley, editor of the popular publication *John Bull*, not because of the fact of execution per se, but because of what Bottomley considered to be a failure of natural justice in the court martial procedure. There were echoes of the long-dead Admiral Byng's case, in so far as it was suspected Dyett was killed *pour encourager les autres*. Dyett's case was debated in the House of Commons in early 1918, just as the Germans were shooting their final bolt in the form of Operation Michael – a good example of the importance of freedom of speech in the darkest of times.

Nonetheless, Herbert was careful to try to confine the message of the book. On the final page, he had the narrator state:[26]

> This book is not an attack on any person, on the death penalty, or on anything else, though if it makes people think about these things, so much the better. I think I believe in the death penalty—I do not know. But I did not believe in Harry being shot.
>
> That is the gist of it; that my friend Harry was shot for cowardice—and he was one of the bravest men I ever knew.

Herbert's fellow Savage and fellow Great War veteran, Field Marshal Montgomery, thought *The Secret Battle* was the best book written about front-line combat.[27] Lloyd George found it 'engrossing', while Churchill, according

---

25 Three officers were executed in the conflict, but only two for cowardice. The other (Patterson) was executed for murder.

26 Herbert, *The Secret Battle: A tragedy of the First World War* (Frontline Books, 2009, Kindle edn).

27 Unfortunately, I fear that Monty did not heed one of the book's chief lessons. 'Courage' as defined by the example of Penrose was finite and years of continuous fighting ran it dry. In the Second World War, when Monty returned from the Mediterranean theatre to prepare for D-Day, he insisted on bringing some of his seasoned units with him, including the 7th Armoured Division, the 'Desert Rats', and sending them among the first units ashore on 6 June 1944. That caused great resentment among the division, who knew that most of those in British Army uniform had never set foot overseas or fired a shot in anger, while their members had been away for up to five years and engaged in some brutal close quarter battle. They also showed signs of combat stress during the Normandy campaign.

to Herbert, ordered changes to the courts martial procedure (in his capacity of ninister of war) after reading it.[28]

Churchill also wrote a foreword to a 1927 edition of the book, declaring it to be 'a monument of the agony, not of one but of millions, standing impassive in marble to give its message to all wayfarers who pass it. It speaks to the uninformed, to the unimaginative, to the headstrong, and to the short-memoried folk who need a word of warning on their path'[29] – words that could describe all the authentic Great War writing.[30]

As well as his superb novel, Herbert also wrote his own Great War poem, 'Beaucourt Revisited', to set down his feelings about the sacrifice of that terrible battle. The first three verses give a representative taste of the poem's power:

> I wandered up to Beaucourt; I took the river track,
> And saw the lines we lived in before the Boche went back;
> But Peace was now in Pottage, the front was far ahead,
> The front had journeyed Eastward, and only left the dead.

> And I thought, How long we lay there, and watched across
> the wire,
> While the guns roared round the valley, and set the skies afire!
> But now there are homes in Hamel and tents in the Vale of
> Hell,
> And a camp at Suicide Corner, where half a regiment fell.

> The new troops follow after, and tread the land we won,
> To them 'tis so much hillside re-wrested from the Hun; We
> only walk with reverence this sullen mile of mud;
> The shell-holes hold our history, and half of them our blood.

In spite of the searing tone of his book and poem, Herbert was not one of those rendered wholly disillusioned by the war. He remained 'mainly persuaded' it had been a just cause, and he was not impressed by Joan Littlewood's *Oh, What a*

---

28 Michèle Barrett, 'Shell Shocked', *The Guardian*, 19 April 2003.

29 Herbert, *The Secret Battle*, op cit.

30 The Great War historian Malcolm Brown, in his introduction to *The Secret Battle*, explored the Churchill connection further. He pointed out that the death penalty for military crimes was abolished in 1929, after a campaign led by Ernest Thurtle, a Labout MP who had been seriously wounded during the Battle of Cambrai in 1917. Thereafter, capital offences in the army only existed for the same crimes as would be capital offences for civilians. During the Second World War, as Britain suffered serious defeats first in France and then in North Africa, the respective senior commanders Lord Gort and Sir Claude Auchinleck, floated the idea of reintroducing capital punishment for cowardice, but Churchill quashed it. Aside from anything else, it would have signalled to the world that Britain had a serious problem with discipline and morale, though one suspects Churchill, as the author of that moving foreword to Herbert's book a few years earlier, might have had other considerations as well.

Lovely War! or the other pacifist denunciations of the 1960s; instead, he sneered at those he called 'anaemic belittlers of our past.' Decades after the war's conclusion, he told the Oxford University Conservative Association:[31]

> I am one of the too-fortunate survivors of that lost generation of 1914, who suffered our Schools in June of that year, and heard our fate in July. For a week or two of that brilliant summer we strutted the world, boasting about our degrees or explaining them away, and in either case considering ourselves lords of life—and then in August, or maybe September, discovered ourselves, with some astonishment, recruits or combatants in a war that was to save civilisation and be the last war of all. Yes, though we were thrilled by the bugles and the drums, and though we delighted in our flags and uniforms, we did believe that.

Hence, just as with Lord Denning, neither losing a sibling nor experiencing all the horrors of battle himself – and we should note that Herbert served for much longer than Denning, and on two fronts – Herbert never lost faith in the values he had signed up to defend, nor the sense of honour for which he believed the war was being fought.

Post-war career

Herbert was called to the Bar by Inner Temple in 1919. He joined chambers in London, but never actually practised. Instead he turned to writing full-time. Despite its formidable critical acclaim, *The Secret Battle* had not been a best-seller. Churchill, in his foreword to the 1927 edition, felt that the book had been 'a little swept aside by the revulsion of the public mind from anything to do with the awful period just ended.'

Herbert therefore resumed writing the humorous material which brought him more commercial success. In 1924, he joined the permanent staff of *Punch* – making him a contemporary at the magazine of Brother Savage EH Shepard – but continued writing books published elsewhere as well.

His most important and enduring works were arguably his 'Uncommon Law' series of spoof legal cases.[32] They were so well-constructed that they were occasionally mistaken for real cases. They usually featured a tireless and inventive litigant called Albert Haddock, trying to right some real or imagined wrong. Perhaps the best known was *Board of Inland Revenue v Haddock*, in which Haddock paid his tax bill with a cheque written on the side of a cow – something taught to me as a true story when I was in primary school in New Zealand in the 1980s.

As well as a lucrative source of income, Herbert often used the stories as a way

---

31 Pound, op cit, p 40.
32 See for example AP Herbert, *Uncommon Law* (Independent Publishers Group, 2001).

of highlighting some arcane or absurd law here and there. He used the work in his law-reforming work as an MP: his parliamentary career began in 1935 and he held office until 1950.

During the Second World War, he enrolled his boat *Water Gipsy* in the River Emergency Service. His crew included Brother Savage Magnus Pyke, who later became famous as a science presenter on television. Herbert was the only non-commissioned officer in the Commons during the war, passing up the opportunity for a commission and declining an offer to sit in Churchill's war cabinet.[33] He was knighted in 1945.

He continued with his writing career after the Second World War, and was made a Companion of Honour in 1970 for 'services to literature'.

In Bradshaw's centenary book on the Savage Club, Herbert was described thus:[34]

> AP Herbert has always been a popular Savage. His tousled hair, his spectacles, his pipe and 'pint' fit perfectly into our restful lounge or the livelier atmosphere of our North-West Room. He never gives a hint that he may be a person of some importance. He was, in his Oxford days, uncertain whether his future would be in law or literature, but early successes in *Punch*, followed by books and lyrics, pointed the way to a long series of comic operas which he eventually wrote, though he seemed happier when he was doing half a dozen different jobs simultaneously, including organising the campaign for his election as an MP for Oxford University, in 1937. His first speech in the House surprised even such an experienced statesman as Winston Churchill, who stopped him in the Lobby afterwards to protest. "Call that a maiden speech? It was a brazen hussy of a speech—the most painted harlot of a speech ever presented to a modest Parliament."

It seems there was no hyperbole in his publisher's blurb: 'There is more than a touch of the universal man about Alan Herbert—a great Englishman. Outspoken patriot, spirited denouncer of injustice, Bumbledom and humbug, tenacious defender of a good cause, he never loses his sense of fun—a *very* English attribute.'[35]

He died on 11 November 1971, the fifty-third anniversary of the Armistice.[36]

Coda: shot at dawn

Amidst all the illustrious guests and new members of the Savage Club throughout the twentieth century were some who applied and were rejected. One was the slightly sad character of Frank Percy Crozier (1879–1937), who had a long and

---

33 Note that Herbert would have resigned his commission at the end of the First World War and would not have been entitled to have it back automatically.

34 Bradshaw, op cit, p 134. Clearly Herbert was an enthusiastic Savage for many years: among his other activities, he presided over the ladies' night dinner in May 1933.

35 Quoted in Malcolm Brown's introduction to *The Secret Battle*, op cit.

36 Many years later he was profiled in *Drumbeat*, Spring 2018.

distinguished military career, during the course of which he had to preside over executions in the First World War.

Crozier had earlier served in the Second Boer War. In the First World War, he commanded the 9th (Service) Battalion of the 107th (Ulster) Brigade in the Battle of the Somme, and the 119th (Welsh) Brigade at the Battle of Cambrai under General Byng. He reached the rank of brigadier-general and was awarded the CMG and DSO.

After the war, he became dismayed by the British conduct in Ireland and then gave up war altogether, becoming a pacifist. He had to resign his army post and struggled to make a living writing 'factual' books. I suspect he represented another example of Herbert's Harry Penrose, in that he was a man of whom one too many cheques were drawn on his bravery account. Whether that was the case or not, there was a distressing parallel with Herbert's book, since Crozier had presided over a firing squad during the Great War.

The victim of the firing squad was one James Crozier. He was not related to Frank, but there was a crushingly ironic connection between the two all the same, since the young Crozier had signed up when very young[37] and Frank had promised his mother he would 'watch out for' his namesake.

The execution took place in February 1916. Frank Crozier recorded the event in the following matter-of-fact style:[38]

> Now, in peace-time, I and the rest of us would have been very upset indeed at having to shoot a colleague, comrade, call him what you will, at dawn on the morrow. We would not, in ordinary circumstances, have slept. Now the men don't like it, but they have to put up with it. They face their ordeal magnificently. I supervise the preliminary arrangements myself. We put the prisoner in a comfortable warm place. A few yards away we drive in a post, in a back garden, such as exists with any villa residence. I send for a certain junior officer and show him all. "You will be in charge of the firing-party," I say; "the men will be cold, nervous and excited, they may miss their mark. You are to have your revolver ready loaded and cocked; if the medical officer tells you life is not extinct you are to walk up to the victim, place the muzzle of the revolver to his heart and press the trigger. Do you understand?" "Yes, sir," comes the quick reply. "Right," I add, "dine with me at my mess tonight." I want to keep this young fellow engaged under my own supervision until late at night, so as to minimize the chance of his flying to the bottle for support. As for Crocker,[39] he leaves this earth, in so far as knowing anything of his surroundings is concerned, by midnight, for I arrange that enough spirituous liquor is left behind him to sink a ship. In the morning, at dawn, the snow being on the ground, the

---

37 His exact age is not clear: the sources range from 16 to 21.

38 Brigadier-General FP Crozier, 'A Firing Squad At Dawn', in his *A Brass Hat in No Man's Land* (Jonathan Cape & Harrison Smith, 1930), pp 83–86.

39 'Crocker' is a pseudonym Crozier was using for the victim.

battalion forms up on the public road. Inside that little garden on the other side of the wall, not ten yards from the centre of the line, the victim is carried to the stake. He is far too drunk to walk. He is out of view save from myself, as I stand on a mound near the wall. As he is produced I see he is practically lifeless and quite unconscious. He has already been bound with ropes. There are hooks on the post; we always do things thoroughly in the Rifles. He is hooked on like dead meat in a butcher's shop. His eyes are bandaged—not that it really matters, for he is already blind. The men of the firing-party pick up their rifles, one of which is unloaded, on a given sign. On another sign they come to the "Present" and, on the lowering of a handkerchief by the officer, they fire—a volley rings out—a nervous ragged volley it is true, yet a volley. Before the fatal shots are fired I had called the battalion to attention. There is a pause, I wait. I see the medical officer examining the victim. He makes a sign, the subaltern strides forward, a single shot rings out. Life is now extinct. We march back to breakfast while the men of a certain company pay the last tribute at the graveside of an unfortunate comrade. This is war.

Crozier tried to stop James's family from discovering how their son had died. He attempted to pass off his death as 'killed in action', but nevertheless the truth leaked out, even if the details were not officially made public at the time. Some weeks after the event, one of Crozier's officers was asked by a civilian about the shooting while he was on leave. The civilian inferred that the execution had brought shame on both the battalion and the city of Belfast. Crozier's colleague retorted that James Crozier had 'tried and failed. He died for such as you! Isn't it time you had a shot at dying for your country?'[40]

Elsewhere in his book Frank Crozier said of trench raids 'As we require only one prisoner on each occasion, and as more are a nuisance, all other enemy soldiers encountered must be put to death.'[41]

By the time the book was written, Crozier had become a committed pacifist, and therefore some caution has to be exercised about the veracity of his claims – he may have exaggerated what he saw, though he could hardly have described a trench raid, let alone an execution, in anything other than horrific terms. Assuming his account broadly accurate, therefore, one can understand why he had abandoned his brutal military professionalism.

40 Crozier, op cit. See also Stephen Walker, *Forgotten Soldiers: The Irishmen Shot At Dawn* (Gill Books, 2008).
41 Of his methods in the trench raids, Crozier explained:

> What are our weapons? The pistol, the rifle, the bullet, the bayonet, knuckle-dusters, hook knives with which to rip up, daggers for the heart, butchers' knives for the throat, the bomb for random work, once the prisoner has been extracted and bags of aminal thrown into the dugouts, served up with time fuses, to blow whole companies to smithereens. Tear gas bombs to cause temporary blindness, egg bombs charged with deadly poison to pulverise the lungs and stop the breathing complete the outfit. We moderns are extraordinarily unkind to each other in war—and in peace!

The banning of capital punishment for cowardice, and the failure to revive it during the Second World War did not quite end the story, however. In the mid-2000s, a campaign which had been brewing for some years to pardon those executed during the Great War reached its apogee with judicial review proceedings begun by the daughter of one of the condemned, Harry Farr. I did not agree with the campaign, for all the sympathy we might have with individual cases. On 11 April 2006 I had the following letter published in *The Times*:

> Trevor Harvey is right to infer that we should not attempt to pass judgment on events in our distant past such as the execution of Private Harry Farr for cowardice during the First World War. Already the case has taken up valuable judicial resources, as indeed have other recent reviews of long ago cases such as Derek Bentley, Ruth Ellis and James Hanratty. In all of these cases judicial proceedings only came about because of the accident that each of the deceased had living relatives. We should not expend public resources on cases which turn on that happenstance.
>
> Debating whether the likes of Private Farr suffered shell-shock is a matter of interest for medical historians but we should hesitate long and hard before presupposing to pass judgment on events as far removed as the Great War. It is fashionable to dismiss the generals of the day as 'donkeys' and to rail against the supposed brutality of shooting for deserters. But it should also be recalled that of all the armies which were involved in the war from the outset, only the British did not suffer a severe collapse of morale at any point as well, of course, as emerging victorious.

I remain of the same view, which was also set out a greater length in my first book.[42] We should not be investigating past injustices when the victims and the convicted person are long since dead and the circumstances under which the offence arose have long since vanished – even accepting that we might consider some of those shot at dawn to have been killed unjustly, either because of sympathy to their predicament or the inadequacy of their courts martial. Reviewing ageing cases would be an expensive use of scarce judicial and other public resources, which should instead be spent on solving present-day crimes. The judicial system is always under heavy strain: it is not unusual, for example, for a person charged with murder to be remanded in custody for many months awaiting trial. Some of those currently serving life imprisonment think they have a case to be reviewed; their cases should logically have priority. Moreover, with no witnesses left alive and all records a century old, the chances of accurately reviewing cases from the Great War have to be correspondingly low.

Parliament eventually enacted s 359 of the Armed Forces Act 2006, which

---

42 James Wilson, *Cases, Causes and Controversies: Fifty Tales from the Law* (Wildy, Simmonds & Hill, 2012), Ch 9.

provided that anyone executed during the Great War for offences such as cowardice[43] would be 'taken to be pardoned', but it added that no individual soldier's conviction or sentence was overturned and no surviving relatives or anyone else was to be given compensation. It was a classic British compromise – offering a general pardon but stopping short of exonerating individual cases.

Lord Moulton: the ultimate Savage polymath

On 18 May 1911, a lunch for some of the Great and the Good was held in London at 28 Queen Anne's Gate. The guest of honour was none other than the German Kaiser Wilhelm II, invited by Richard Haldane, then secretary of state for war. The Kaiser was seated next to Lord Moulton, member of the Savage Club and also a member of the Appellate Committee of the House of Lords, then the most senior court in the land. After they had eaten, the Kaiser took Haldane aside and, gesturing to Moulton, asked: 'Who is this man? You say he is a judge, but he seems to know everything.' Haldane did not demur; he was of the opinion Moulton had 'perhaps the most rapid intelligence with which I ever came in contact.'

Just over three years later, Moulton and Haldane on the one hand, and the Kaiser on the other, were otherwise occupied in trying to annihilate each other's countrymen. Moulton's intelligence was put to very good use indeed in the British war effort.

Before the First World War: scientist, lawyer, politician, judge

John Fletcher Moulton was born in Shropshire in 1844, the third son of a prominent cleric. He was educated at Kingswood School, a Methodist independent day and boarding school in Somerset, and came first in the Oxford-Cambridge local examination. He spent three years at University College London, then went to St John's College, Cambridge, on a scholarship, where he had to abandon his Methodism in favour of Anglican tenets. In 1868, he was Senior Wrangler in the Mathematical Tripos with the highest score on record, and won the Smith's prize. He was elected to a fellowship at Christ's College, but left to read law in London. He was called to the Bar in 1874.[44]

---

43 Note that other Great War executions took place for offences such as murder, which were sometimes muddled in with those for cowardice.

44 See William Van der Kloot, 'Lord Justice of Appeal John Fletcher Moulton and explosives production in World War I: "the mathematical mind triumphant"', *Notes and Records: The Royal Society Journal of the History of Science* (2014) vol 68, 171–186.

Pedant's corner: Moulton by the time of the First World War was a Lord of Appeal in Ordinary (a member of the Appellate Committee of the House of Lords), and thus should be referred to as Lord Moulton, not Lord Justice of Appeal – that refers to judges in the Court of Appeal, one below on the judicial hierarchy. Lord Denning was an exception as he did not lose his title of 'Lord' when he stepped down from the House of Lords; neither did Lord Neuberger when

As well as a full-time legal practice, he worked closely with the scientist William Spottiswoode, who became President of the Royal Society in 1878. They collaborated on experiments on the conduction of electricity through tubes. Moulton was elected a Fellow of the Royal Society in 1880 on the basis of their published results. He was possibly unique in being both a Queen's Counsel[45] and an FRS. Later he was also made a Fellow of the Royal Astronomical Society (FRAS).

His scientific expertise led him into patent work litigation. He appeared in a number of important scientific cases which would stand him in good stead later in life, including a major case on dyestuffs, and another in which he was lead counsel for the Nobel Explosives Company Ltd, which alleged the British government had committed patent infringement by manufacturing cordite. In the latter case, one of the two scientists who stood accused of the infringement was Brother Savage Sir Frederick Abel (1827–1902),[46] ordnance chemist at the chemical establishment of the Royal Arsenal at Woolwich. The case went to the House of Lords. Working on his brief gave Moulton very detailed knowledge of cutting-edge military explosives.[47]

In another significant case, Moulton earned a small fortune acting as counsel for the newly-constituted Water Board in connection with the acquisition of the water undertakings in London. It was later said that only a trained mathematician could have mastered the complex figures involved in the case.

In 1883, Moulton served on the International Commission on Electrical Units that met in Paris, and was made a member of the *Légion d'honneur*.

He joined the Savage Club, under the category of science, in July 1890.

He was elected a Liberal MP for Clapham (1885–86), South Hackney (1894–95) and the Launceston division of Cornwall (1898–1906). While in parliament he supported Gladstone's efforts to achieve Irish Home Rule, though he was mostly remembered as a parliamentarian for his work in his specialist area of patent law reform.

His time in politics ended in 1906 when he was made a Lord Justice of

---

he did the same thing in protest at the rushed and unnecessary creation of the Supreme Court in the twenty-first century. Outside court, Lord Justices of Appeal are normally only referred to as 'Sir', and that is how Lord Denning's successor as MR, Sir John Donaldson, was known.

45 'Queen's Counsel' or 'QC' for short is a rank bestowed upon senior barristers. In Moulton's day, they were appointed by the Lord Chancellor in an entirely opaque procedure, usually said to be determined in White's or the Garrick or in the splendid dining halls of the Inns of Court.

46 He was nominated for Savage membership in February 1887, though the date he was elected is not easy to read (I think it either February 1887 or 1888).

47 The case (*Nobel's Explosives Co Ltd v Anderson* [1895] 12 RPC 164 (HL)) was also of considerable significance in the development of patent law: see Seymour Mauskopf 'Nobel's Explosives Co Ltd v Anderson (1894)' in Jose Bellido (ed), *Landmark Cases in Intellectual Property Law* (Bloomsbury, 2017).

Appeal. He was also made a Privy Councillor in the same year. Unfortunately, 1906 involved a less enjoyable experience for Moulton as he ended up in court in the capacity of litigant rather than barrister or judge.

The background to the case was Moulton's marriage in 1875 to a widow who had two sons and two daughters, and a very substantial private income, said to have been between £2,000 and £3,000 (at the time, many workers could expect to earn much less than a pound a day). All was well until she died in July 1888. In her will, Moulton was made sole trustee of her estate. The will provided for a fund, to be paid in equal shares to all the children except the eldest son, who was otherwise provided for and had left home some years earlier. Each share amounted to about £620 a year.

In 1901, Moulton remarried, by which time the elder daughter had also married – in her case to the author Kenneth Grahame, who wrote the children's classic *The Wind in the Willows*. In 1902 the elder daughter asked for an account of the income to which she and her sister were entitled under their mother's will, and after a time she and her sister sued Moulton for the money.

Moulton's defence was that there had been an agreement made soon after the mother's death by which the whole family was to live together, and both daughters' contribution to the expenses would be their share of the revenue from the trust. No such agreement had been formally recorded, however, and the daughters disputed its existence.

The judge ordered the account and inquiry which the daughters demanded, but also held the moneys proved to have been expended by Moulton for their benefit, and directed that a reasonable allowance should be made out of the daughters' income for their maintenance in Moulton's house since their mother's death. The daughters successfully appealed to the Court of Appeal.

It was expected that Moulton would appeal in turn to the House of Lords, but in the end he decided against it, since the negative publicity for him as a newly-appointed judge of the Court of Appeal would have outweighed anything he might have gained from winning the case. Unfortunately, he gained some negative publicity anyway, when a monthly magazine wrote a distorted review of the case. Moulton successfully sued for libel.

The regrettable affair did not affect his career as a judge, however, and in 1912 he was promoted to the Appellate Committee of the House of Lords.

First World War

At the outbreak of war, Britain had only a basic organic chemical industry – nothing like as large as that of Germany. That posed all manner of problems, since Britain had been relying upon German imports of medicines, dyestuffs and other supplies. One immediate manifestation was the struggle to equip the new armies with uniforms.[48] More critical to the war effort, however, was the supply of chemicals for use in munitions – without which no war could be fought.

Up to 1914, cordite, gunpowder and picric acid (used in high explosives until it was replaced in late 1914 by trinitrotoluene (TNT)) were supplied by the national ordnance factories at Woolwich and Waltham Abbey, with any extra required bought in from private companies on an ad hoc basis. It was obvious that demand for all three chemicals would increase exponentially during the war. Haldane, by then Lord Chancellor, was appointed as chair of a committee on the supply of chemical products. At the first meeting of the committee, they co-opted Moulton on the basis that he had undertaken very significant research into the chemical industry for the patent cases in which he had been instructed. Moulton was 70 years old at the time.

In November 1914, the committee established an advisory committee on explosives and appointed Moulton as chair. The scale of the task was immense: during the two-and-a-half years of the Second Boer War, the British had fired 273,000 shells; between 15 August 1914 and 15 February 1915 the BEF fired a million,[49] just one example of the incredible logistical challenge the unprecedented scale of the First World War presented.[50]

Moulton threw himself into his work, swiftly recruiting many leading chemists not just from Britain but from around the Empire. At the munitions headquarters in London, he had a staff of approximately 700 under him. It was said he worked a ten-hour day and took fewer than ten days' holiday during the entire war. He spent his weekends travelling the country inspecting munitions plants and looking for suitable sites for new ones. Early on, he realised that he would never be able to obtain enough picric acid and TNT from the raw materials available. He therefore urged the immediate adoption of mixed explosives, and arranged experiments with the mixing of TNT and ammonium nitrate until

---

48 By 1913, Germany was exporting more than 20 times the volume of dyes coming from Britain. To begin with, the British secretly continued importing the dye used in making khaki uniforms from Germany, but that soon ran dry. Early recruits to the new British armies were given replacement uniforms, including 500,000 suits of blue serge uniforms from Post Office stocks, and some 500,000 greatcoats purchased from trade. Greatcoats were too large and heavy for use in combat and were replaced by a lighter form of sports coat which soon became known as 'trench coats'; the name stuck. The new uniforms were dubbed 'Kitchener blue' since blue was the colour of the Post Office uniforms. See Jane Tynan, *British Army Uniform and the First World War: Men in Khaki* (AIAA, 2013).

49 Holmes, *The Western Front*, op cit, p 54. For another illustrative statistic, in the Battle of Neuve Chapelle alone more shells were fired in 35 minutes than had been fired in 18 months of the Second Boer War: see Pound, op cit, p 99.

50 For a few other examples, existing barracks at the start of the war provided for no more than 175,000 troops, which was exceeded within a fortnight of the war's beginning. The Fortifications and Works Branch of the War Office built 300 new rifle ranges, often to the annoyance of local residents in classic British NIMBY fashion.

amatol was produced that would be equal or superior to the single substances.[51] He met with various objections from other committee members, but managed to prevail and obtained full authority to make any form and kind of explosive that could be produced in the country.

Overall, he had conspicuous success: under his leadership, production increased more than twenty-fold and more explosives were produced than there were shells to hold them. When asked to advise how much would be needed, he had replied that there was no limit, since he knew demand would far exceed any contemplated peacetime production and any excess could be used by Britain's allies.

Moulton carried out his orders to produce poison gas, though he was an opponent of its use, considering it not to be a 'civilised form of war'.

He was made a KCB (Knight Commander of the Bath) in 1915 and GBE (Knight Grand Cross of the Most Excellent Order of the British Empire) in 1917. More colourfully, he was the recipient of the last ever Order of the White Eagle bestowed by the Tsar of Russia before the 1917 Revolution.

Post-war career

After the war, he was asked to consolidate the British organic chemical plants into a cartel on the German model, the government fearing that the Germans would soon dominate the production of dyestuffs again. He was also asked to oversee the construction of new facilities. Moulton agreed but only served for a year before returning to the law.

He died in 1921. His obituary in *The Times* suggested he might have spread his abilities too thinly:

> Lord Moulton was a man of striking and even extraordinary ability yet it can hardly be said that he was, or would ever have become, a great Judge. In the first place he was not primarily a lawyer, and among his varied tastes and acquirements law did not, perhaps, hold the first place. In mathematics or physical science he might have made a European reputation, or if he had reached the Bench at an earlier age he might have taken a foremost rank among Judges.

---

51 The reason Moulton sought to use amatol was because TNT is made from toluene, and toluene was used in the dye (and other) industries and therefore in very short supply. Amatol is a physical mixture of ammonium nitrate (very cheap, and used as a fertiliser) which is dried (as it absorbs water from the atmosphere), then powdered and then mixed with toluene. Amatol consists of 80:20 ammonium nitrate:TNT. Hence it is much cheaper and extends the use of available toluene.

The TNT in amatol is toxic and can be absorbed through the skin, causing irritation and bright yellow staining, hence the nickname 'canaries' for the women workers. At the Woolwich Arsenal, about 100 workers died from the hazard until respirators, protective grease and uniforms were required. Three explosions at the Barnbow factory in Leeds killed 40 workers, most of whom were women. See William J Reader, *Imperial Chemical Industries: A History: The Forerunners, 1870–1926*, vol 1 (Oxford University Press, 1970).

It was, however, much more complimentary about his time in the House of Lords, stating that he brought 'a store of scientific and judicial experience and learning which greatly strengthened that tribunal', and acknowledged his vital war work with explosives.

Near the end of Moulton's life, Haldane had said of his one-time lunching companion:

> I choose my words carefully when I say that I greatly doubt whether it would have been possible for the war to have been brought to a successful conclusion when it was, but for the part Lord Moulton took in it. I hope the country will not soon forget the extraordinary work of this most remarkable man.

The Savage Club did not forget him: almost a century after his death, Moulton was profiled in *Drumbeat*,[52] in which Brother Savage Alan Williams wrote:

> As to the Savage Club, Aaron Watson's book on the Club at page 308 shows the menu for the 42nd Anniversary Dinner of the Club on 9 December 1899 at the Hotel Cecil. He is described on that menu as J Fletcher Moulton QC, MP, FRS.[53] He also appears on the menu of the Founders Dinner of 1895, Henry Irving in the Chair, giving the toast to the visitors. A print of that menu appears in *Drumbeat* number 136. You will recall that the most fascinating thing about that menu was the presence of Sir Edward Clarke QC, MP and Edward Carson QC, MP, who that very year had been the opposing Counsel in the trials of Oscar Wilde.[54]
>
> He was regarded as a man of great charm and geniality with wide interests. He was said to be an excellent talker and good listener. The very epitome of a Savage Club Member!

---

52 No 138 – Summer 2017.
53 Moulton also chaired a house dinner on 25 March 1911.
54 I wrote about Wilde's trials in *Trials & Tribulations*, Ch 2.

CHAPTER 10

Savage Men of Science

Introduction

Science has always advanced especially rapidly during wartime, one of the ironies of humanity's most destructive activity. The Great War was no exception. Perhaps the greatest irony was that one of its most horrific inventions, mustard gas, later played a role in the development of chemotherapy.

Elsewhere in the conflict, aeroplanes, barely more than a decade old when the war began, reached a far greater capability by 1918, with nascent aircraft carriers on naval architects' drawing boards. Tanks had been invented and used in combat. Sound-ranging and sonar had become crucial devices on the battlefield and at sea, and myriad other inventions had come as by-products of efforts to inflict greater slaughter.

We will see in this section and in Appendix III some of the brave and skilful work of the surgeons of the Great War. Having the finest quality medical care for troops in the field is almost taken for granted in modern times, but it was by no means always the case. The Royal Army Medical Corps (RAMC) had only been created in 1898 after years of campaigning by the British Medical Association, aided by the efforts of famous Victorians such as Florence Nightingale. It was not as though there was no awareness of the problems, but not for the first or last time in British history there was no appetite for novel forms of increasing expenditure on the armed forces in peacetime. The problem was compounded by the rigid British class system of the day, which deemed army medical officers for much of the nineteenth century an inferior species compared with their fellow officers dedicated to killing. Doctors were paid less than regular officers and otherwise treated shabbily, even if some won the Victoria Cross for their efforts.[1] Hence they were not well-placed to compel reform, and the better doctors were dissuaded from joining the military.

Another famous Victorian, Sir Frederick Treves – known for his care of the 'Elephant Man' Joseph Merrick – went to South Africa during the Boer War as a consulting surgeon. In public he spoke highly of the medical care of the troops, but in private he could see the system was still shambolic. He kept his counsel until the war ended, whereupon he added his voice to those calling for further reform and investment for the RAMC. In 1901 there was a Royal Commission on South African Hospitals which led to substantial reform including the creation in 1905 of the Field Ambulance.

The reforming secretary of state for the army, Richard Haldane, whom we have already met in various contexts in this book, made an important contribution to the reform of army medical care. He assisted the development of the RAMC and the improvement of the education of regular officers in sanitation and other health matters.[2]

> The cumulative effect of these various advances in preventive medicine was a dramatic reduction in losses from disease. The death rate had fallen from twenty per thousand in 1898 to eight per thousand in 1907; likewise, the number of discharges due to invaliding had fallen to eight per thousand in 1907, from nineteen per thousand in 1898. This trend towards improved army health continued throughout the pre-war years. In 1912, Sir WL Gubbins, the DGAMS, pointed out that the result of these health improvements was "equivalent to an annual addition of 6,164 men to its fighting strength".

By 1914, the British Army could finally be said to have a modern medical corps. It was still not prepared for the cataclysm of war, however, since during the retreat from Mons, it found itself overwhelmed by the amount of casualties and the general disarray. A senior officer, Colonel Arthur Lee, reported to Kitchener that the RAMC staff were 'undoubtedly overworked and overstrained. There were probably not enough Medical Officers in the first place, and many had been killed or wounded.'[3]

In 1915, the War Office, acutely aware of the reverses of the early phase of the war, set its mind to the necessary expansion of the RAMC. Among other things, it withdrew 2,000 doctors from private practice, and successfully appealed to help from the Dominions, each of which had excellent medical professions. In 1916, when conscription was introduced, doctors were not among the exempt profes-

---

1   Ian Whitehead, *Doctors in the Great War* (Leo Cooper, 1999, reprinted by Pen & Sword, 2013, Kindle edn), Ch 1, n 9.
2   Whitehead, op cit.
3   Whitehead, op cit.

sions. Yet the scale of the war effort was such that demand on the doctors in the field never lessened throughout virtually the entire conflict, even though ultimately more than half of the nation's doctors served.[4]

We begin this chapter away from the medical sphere, however, and instead with a Savage physicist who was responsible for one of the most important technological advances.

Sir William Bragg: father of sonar

Sir William Bragg was a British physicist, chemist and mathematician, who in peacetime made outstanding contributions in the fields of telegraphy and X-rays, and during the war worked on the development of sonar.

Early life

William Henry Bragg was born at Westward near Wigton, Cumberland, in 1862. His father, Robert John Bragg, was a merchant navy officer and farmer, while his mother Mary was the daughter of a clergyman. Mary died when he was just seven, and thereafter he was raised by his uncle in Leicestershire.

Bragg attended Market Harborough Grammar School, followed by King William's College on the Isle of Man. Evidently an outstanding student, he won a scholarship to study at Trinity College, Cambridge, from which he graduated in 1884 as Third Wrangler, and in 1885 he was awarded first class honours in the Mathematical Tripos.

In 1885, aged just 23, he was appointed to a chair at the University of Adelaide, and began working there the following year. At the time, Adelaide had fewer than a hundred full-time students in all subjects. Bragg therefore devoted time and energy to developing the university as an institution as well as his own teaching and research.

In addition to his intellectual gifts, Bragg was a talented sportsman, playing tennis, golf and lacrosse, and he helped promote lacrosse in South Australia. He also served as secretary to the Adelaide University Chess Association.

In 1889 he married Gwendoline Todd, a watercolour painter. Their first son, William Lawrence (known as Lawrence), was born the following year. In 1893 they had a second son, Robert, and in 1907 a daughter, Gwendoline.

Bragg had started his intellectual career in mathematics but moved to physics, especially after meeting the New Zealander Ernest Rutherford in 1895. Rutherford visited Adelaide on his way from New Zealand to Cambridge, where he would achieve lasting fame in atomic physics. He and Bragg became lifelong friends.

---

4 Whitehead, op cit.

Bragg's areas of expertise in physics included X-rays and wireless telegraphy. In September 1897, he gave the first recorded public demonstration of the working of wireless telegraphy in Australia. In 1904, when touring New Zealand, he gave an address in Dunedin on 'Some Recent Advances in the Theory of the Ionization of Gases' followed by more research in the same area that was so well respected he was made a fellow of the Royal Society of London.

Bragg returned to England permanently at the end of 1908 and took up the Cavendish Chair of Physics at the University of Leeds from 1909. He continued his work on X-rays, developing the first X-ray spectrometer. His son Lawrence followed him in the field, studying at Cambridge University. Together father and son founded the new science of X-ray crystallography, the analysis of crystal structure using X-ray diffraction.

First World War

Bragg himself was too old for frontline service, though he was anxious to lend his scientific expertise to the war effort, and both his sons joined up early in the war.

In 1915 the family experienced triumph and tragedy. Bragg was appointed Quain Professor of Physics at the University of London, and in July finally managed to obtain a post directly concerned with the war when he was assigned to the Admiralty Board of Invention and Research in July. The crowning triumph was in November, when he and Lawrence were jointly awarded the Nobel Prize in recognition of their work on X-rays – the only time in history that a parent and child won jointly (other parents and children have won independently). The tragedy came in September, however, when Robert was killed at Gallipoli.

Lawrence went on to make a critical contribution to the war effort with his work on sound ranging, for which he was awarded the Military Cross. He was part of a group who devised hot wire sound ranging, which solved the problem caused by the fact that microphones of the day could not pick up the low frequency sounds of heavy guns.

William, meanwhile, had begun working for the Admiralty in the hydrophone research centre in Scotland, trying to counter the U-boat threat. He was appointed director of the centre in July 1916. Under his supervision, an improved directional hydrophone was developed. Later in 1916 the centre moved to Harwich and took on more staff. They built upon the work of the French physicist Paul Langevin, who had made major advances in echolocation. Langevin's work involved generating intense sound pulses with quartz sheets oscillated at high frequency, which were then used as microphones to listen for echoes. Quartz was usable when vacuum tubes became available at the end of 1917 to amplify the faint signals. Bragg's team made sonar practicable by using mosaics of small quartz pieces rather than slices from a large crystal.

In January 1918, Bragg became the head of scientific research in the Admiralty's anti-submarine division. By the end of the war, Royal Naval vessels were equipped with sonar manned by trained listeners, still the standard method of submarine-hunting today.

Post-war career

After the war Bragg returned to London and continued his work on crystal analysis. In 1923 he became Fullerian Professor of Chemistry at the Royal Institution and director of the Davy Faraday Research Laboratory. He oversaw the Institution's rebuilding and expansion from 1929–30. In 1935 he was elected President of the Royal Society, and in 1936, he became an honorary life member of the Savage Club.

Bragg used his position as President of the Royal Society to agitate for better scientific development by the military, seeking to avoid a repeat of the frustration he had felt at the beginning of the Great War. The society appointed members as consultants to the government, compiled a register of qualified men, and recommended a committee on science to advise the committee on imperial defence. To begin with, their recommendation was refused, but the outbreak of the Second World War changed the government's mind, and in 1940 a scientific advisory committee to the war cabinet was created.

Bragg died in 1942.

Sir Philip Brocklehurst: explorer, guardsman, gentleman

Sir Philip Lee Brocklehurst Bt was another model Corinthian of his day – a member of the upper classes who displayed immense physical courage and a taste for adventure throughout his life.

Early life

He was born at Swythamley Park, Staffordshire, in 1887. His father was Philip Lancaster Brocklehurst, who had become a baronet in 1903. The family money came from his grandfather, John Brocklehurst, who had a silk-weaving business in Macclesfield and was an MP. Philip Lancaster was created a baronet in 1903 and Philip Lee succeeded to it the following year.

He followed the well-trodden path of the wealthy of the day by attending Eton and Cambridge. His sporting prowess was evident during his university days: he represented Cambridge at boxing in 1905, 1906 and 1907 as a lightweight against Oxford, and obtained a half blue. In 1904, he also joined the Territorial Army in the Derbyshire Yeomanry.

Brocklehurst eventually left Cambridge without a degree, but it was there that he met and befriended his future Brother Savage, the legendary explorer Ernest Shackleton. From 1907 to 1909 Brocklehurst took part in Shackleton's first attempt at reaching the South Pole, known as the Nimrod expedition. Brocklehurst's role was ostensibly as assistant geologist, though his place had actually been secured by his family making a substantial donation to the cost of the adventure.[5] He joined the expedition late, having travelled via Australia where he took time to watch an Ashes test in Sydney during late 1907 (Australia won), before meeting up with Shackleton's men in Christchurch, New Zealand.

Although it was unsuccessful, the expedition reached much further south than any other journey to that point, and was a record convergence on either Pole. It also achieved the first ascent of Mount Erebus, Antarctica's second-highest volcano. Brocklehurst took part in the ascent as a member of the support group, but did not reach the top as he suffered frostbite.

Perhaps the most frightening episode of the expedition occurred in January 1909, when the ice on which the men were camping broke off and floated along the coast. The men faced the twin danger of the open sea and death by orca (nowadays, orca attacks on humans are known to be extremely rare, but one doubts that that knowledge was available to Brocklehurst, or would have provided much comfort even if it had been). With no means of steering or propelling their ice floe, and with swimming in Antarctic waters meaning certain death, the men were entirely at nature's mercy, but they had the great good fortune the next day of the floe drifting close enough to shore for them to jump across. 'The killer whales were all around the foot of the glacier, great ugly brutes deprived of their unusual breakfast' noted an understandably unsympathetic Brocklehurst in his diary.

After the expedition returned to England, Brocklehurst and the other members were recognised with a Polar Medal.[6]

Brocklehurst had two more significant events before the Great War. First, in July 1909, he joined the Savage Club under the category of science. Then, in 1913, he married Gwladys Murray. Ernest Shackleton was the best man.

First World War

At the beginning of the war, Brocklehurst had been intending to join another of Shackleton's expeditions to Antarctica – that which was to secure the latter's lasting fame – but instead decided to head to the Western Front. Although he was still a member of the Derbyshire Yeomanry, he immediately transferred to the senior regiment of the British Army, the Life Guards.[7]

5　The Brocklehurst family donated £2,000 of the total expedition cost of £30,000.
6　*London Gazette*, 28 November 1909, p 8665.
7　The Life Guards together with the Blues and Royals form the Household Cavalry.

Brocklehurst was assigned to 1st Life Guards, who were soon deployed to Belgium. He was wounded in the First Battle of Ypres. Two entries from the regimental diary of the 7th Cavalry Brigade describe the action:[8]

> 16th Oct 1914. Friday.
>
> The 3rd Cavalry Division marched to Ypres, 7th Cavalry Brigade leading to take up a line from ST JULIAN to POELCAPPELLE STATION. On arrival of the Brigade at WIELTJE the 1st Life Guards were sent to reconnoitre the FOREST de HOUTHULST. Meanwhile intelligence was received from inhabitants that 400 or more Germans were in OOSTNIEWKERKE.
>
> 13:15. The GOC determined to verify this report. Lt Sir P BROCKLEHURST 1st Life Guards was sent down the road from WESTROOSEBEKE towards HOOGLEDE with a patrol.
>
> 15:10. He was fired at short range by a hostile Maxim placed about a mile NE of WESTROOSEBEKE. The GOC then sent two Squadrons 2nd Life Guards to work round South of the road and afterwards sent the third under Colonel FERGUSON. These troops made some progress against German s occupying farm houses South of the Road.
>
> 16:00. The Royal Horse Guards were then sent up the road towards HOOGLEDE. It was now getting dark and as the evidence pointed to the fact that the enemy was holding a line running NW to SE about one mile SW of OOSTNIEWKERKE and had considerable strength behind him the GOC decided that no more could be done that day and troops retired to billets, 1st Life Guards in WESTROOSEBEKE and the remainder of the Brigade with K Battery RHA in PASSCHENDAELE.
>
> Casualties:
>
> 1 Officer (Lt Sir R DUFF 2nd Life Guards)
>
> 5 men wounded ...
>
>
> 19th Oct 1914. Monday.
>
> 09:00. The 6th Cavalry Brigade being due at the same time at ST PIETERS the whole Division acting on the left flank of the 7th Division in its advance East.
>
> 10:30. The Advanced Guard of the Brigade reached the crossroads and immediately became engaged with the head of the column of a strong hostile force. The Advanced Guard was able to advance. They took up a position 200 yards East of the road but were soon outflanked and had to retire to a position on the road.

There were a few other Yeomanry Officers with prior regular service who transferred back into the Cavalry. I assume Brocklehurst was technically in the reserve of officers as well as being a commissioned officer in the Territorials.

8   In the present day there is a memorial to the action at Zandvoordeplaats 58, Zonnebeke, Belgium.

Hostile guns immediately got the range of the road the Brigadier decided to retire to a stronger position one mile West of the road covered by the fire of the guns. This position was held by 1st Life Guards North of the road and 2nd Life Guards South of the road for some hours under the shell and rifle fire of the enemy. Sir PHILIP BROCKLEHURST and four men of the 1st Life Guards were wounded here and Capt ASHTON PALMER and a number of men of the 2nd Life Guards were killed in an attempt to retake the line of the main road which was still very strongly held.

12:30. Both flanks were nearly turned by the enemy and the Brigade retired to high ground East of MOORSLEDE. The enemy did not pursue but shelled the position heavily.

15:00. The 6th Cavalry Brigade were seen retiring on our right flank.

16:00. Orders were received from the Division for the Brigade to hold on to the position. Went back to billets to ZONNEBEKE, the Royal Horse Guards rejoined the Brigade before the final retirement. The casualties during the day were heavy. In addition to the above mentioned Officers, Capt NEILL the Brigade Major and Lt R HAMILTON the Interpreter were wounded. 60 Other Ranks killed, wounded or missing. The latter were principally from Capt ASHTON'S Squadron 2nd Life Guards.

The Life Guards' own regimental diary recorded for the same days:

16th Oct 1914. Friday. GROOTE VIERSTRAAT.

Marched at 07:40 (A Squadron Advanced Guard to Brigade) via YPRES to POELCAPELLE STATION.

Patrols under Lt Hon G WARD and Lt Sir P BROCKLEHURST sent out from POELCAPELLE to STADEN, one by East and one by West. One by East under Sir P BROCKLEHURST met the enemy on outskirts of STADEN came under close fire of machine guns and lost one man killed (Tpr HENLEY).

15:00. POELCAPELLE STATION. With reference to BM 3 16th attached messages received from Advanced Guard. No engagement with enemy ensued.

Brigade billeted at PASSCHENDAELE at 21:30 ...

19th Oct 1914. Monday. NORTH OF POINT 29.

06:00. Brigade marched in accordance with BM 2 to 11th kilometre stone on ROULERS—MENIN road. On arrival there is became heavily engaged with hostile infantry and artillery. Maintained position for three hours and then retired on MOORSLEDE. Heavy casualties in 2nd Life Guards Regiment. Lost Lt Sir P BROCKLEHURST wounded and one man killed and 4 wounded. 6th Cavalry Brigade practically not engaged. 7th Division also forced to retire in front of superior numbers. French Cavalry Division acted on our left.

Brocklehurst's injury consisted of a bullet wound through the shoulder. It constituted a 'Blighty' and he was therefore returned to England, where he spent time recuperating at Mrs Claude Watney's Hospital for officers in London.[9] He had only been in Belgium for 11 days.

After a period of light duties, he re-joined his regiment in February 1915 and was posted to the Signal Squadron.[10] In 1917, he was recorded as being assistant superintendent of the Physical Training Corps in Aldershot, which might imply that his adventurous war was over. In fact, in 1918 he transferred to the Egyptian Army.

Post-war career

The reorganised Egyptian Army had been formally raised in 1883. It was initially composed of 6,000 men, forming eight battalions expected to serve for four years in the army, and then four each in the police and the reserves. British officers seconded to the Egyptian Army were given a commission of one or two ranks above their own.[11]

Brocklehurst served in one of the Sudanese battalions, which were generally considered the best units in the Egyptian Army. They were recruited from Southern Sudan and the Nuba Mountains, and in the early days of the new Egyptian Army included many veterans of earlier conflicts. Brocklehurst ended up serving for two years as 'bimbashi' in command of a post at Kereinik on the extreme western frontier, 200 miles from El Fasher.

After returning to Britain, he gave an account of a trip to Lake Chad to the Royal Geographical Society, in 1922. The speech led him to be considered for the Mount Everest expedition with Mallory and Irvine, but was ruled out because of his earlier frostbite injury. Nonetheless, he retained an interest in exploration and stayed in contact with Shackleton and other members of the British Antarctic

---

9   I assume it was the same Mrs Claude Watney who was listed in a 1903 motoring guide with the following description: 'Mrs. Claude Watney is one of the most tastefully gowned and attractive among London society motoring women. Her beautiful 24-horse Panhard, "Frou-Frou I" served to rouse Mrs. Watney's motoring enthusiasm to the point of buying a fio-horse Mercedes, "Frou-Frou III" which she intends to enter for all racing events. Mrs. Watney has recently bought "Frou-Frou II," a lovely 15-horse Pi, most tastefully upholstered in cream, and painted in electric blue, with a pretty canopy and bowed glass dust screen.' See https://www.gracesguide.co.uk/1903_Motorists.

10 TNA WO339/11493.

11 Egyptian ranks (as well as the drill) were in Turkish. They were: sirdar (commander-in-chief), farik (lieutenant-general), and lewa (major-general) which were all called pasha; miralai (colonel), kaimkan (lieutenant-colonel) both being called bey; bimbashi (major), yuzbashi (captain), mulazim awal (first lieutenant) and mulazim tani (second lieutenant) all of which were called effendi. In keeping with the way the British Empire tended to run things, it was soon the case that all British officers were bimbashi or above while few Egyptian officers were ever above the rank of yuzbashi.

Expedition throughout the 1920s. He undertook another brave adventure, though in warmer climes, when he took the first car journey across the Sahara Desert in the 1930s.

He retained his army links as well, serving with the 24th (The Derbyshire Yeomanry) Armoured Car Company, Royal Tank Corp (Territorial Army) from 1925 to 1932. In the final year he was gazetted major and brevet lieutenant-colonel in the Territorial Army reserve of officers.

Away from exploring and military matters, he participated in football and hunting.

He died in 1975.

Douglas Derry: doctor and Egyptologist

One of many fine Savage surgeons of his day, Douglas Derry gained fame after the war as the first medically qualified person to investigate the body of King Tutankhamun.

Early life

Douglas Erith Derry was born in 1875, one of 14 children of an accountant who was also a devout Plymouth Brother. He endured a strict upbringing, and went on to succeed in life through his own formidable intelligence and resolve. As with all his siblings, he received a sound education, and was imbued with the values of the brotherhood, even though none of the children remained within its order. Due to financial considerations, he left school in his mid-teens and went to work for a tea company. Even at that early stage, he had decided upon a medical career, and so purchased textbooks which he read in his spare time.

At the age of 18, Derry left for Southern Africa, where his brother-in-law owned property near Bulawayo in Rhodesia, to help work on the land. It was a tough journey since railways at the time only reached as far as Pretoria, and life was not much easier when he reached his destination, given the frontier nature of the settlement at the time. Nonetheless, he retained his determination to become a doctor, and by the late 1890s had saved and borrowed enough to return to Britain, where he enrolled at Edinburgh University. He graduated in 1903, and stayed in Edinburgh working as a demonstrator in anatomy.

Soon after graduating, Derry married Margaret Ramsay and in 1906 their first child, Duncan, was born. They went on to have two more sons, Hugh and John, and a daughter, Helen. It seems that Derry's taste for adventure was undiluted by fatherhood, since he moved the family to Egypt not long after Duncan's birth to take up a post as assistant professor in anatomy at Cairo University.

First World War

When the Great War began, he moved the family back to Britain, basing them in London while he himself joined the Royal Army Medical Corps (RAMC). He obviously set himself up for some appropriate rest and recreation during the conflict, since in 1914 he became a life member of the Savage Club.

Throughout the conflict Derry served with 101st Field Ambulance. The field ambulance was a mobile frontline medical unit, usually under the command of a division. RAMC officers and men did not carry weapons or ammunition. The ambulances usually had special responsibility for the care of casualties of one of the brigades of the division. They would establish and maintain a series of points along the casualty evacuation chain, from the bearer relay posts found up to 600 yards behind the regimental aid posts in the frontline, taking casualties rearwards through an advanced dressing station (ADS) to the main dressing station (MDS), as part of the process of moving the wounded progressively behind the lines, the process so well described by Brother Savage Basil Clarke. Field ambulances also provided a walking wounded collecting station, as well as various rest areas and local sick rooms. They would usually establish one ADS per brigade, and one MDS for the division.

In theory, a field ambulance comprised 10 officers and 224 men, divided into three sections, which in turn were divided into stretcher bearer and tented subsections; and their capacity was supposed to be 150 casualties. In reality, they sometimes made do with fewer staff and many battles produced far more than 150 casualties for each unit.

The 101st assembled at Clipstone camp near Mansfield in Nottinghamshire in July 1915. It was sent to France in November of the same year as part of 33rd Division. Initially it was stationed near Morbecque, and for most of its time on the Western Front stayed in a small area of France and Flanders, apart from one posting to the Belgian coast.

Major battles in which the 101st served included the Somme in 1916 and Arras in 1917. In November 1917, Derry won the Military Cross for his actions on the Western Front. His citation read:

> For conspicuous gallantry and devotion to duty. While he was posting stretcher bearers the locality was very heavily shelled, and many men were wounded, but he succeeded in dressing and removing them all under heavy fire. Later, in a small dressing station, when the shelters were hit and damaged by shell fire, he showed a splendid example to all by his coolness and resource.

The 101st also saw action on the Hindenburg Line, the operations on the Flanders coast and in Third Ypres.

Derry was demobbed in early 1919, having performed with much credit in a vital role throughout the war.

Post-war career

After the war, Derry took his family (save the older sons, Duncan and Hugh, who were in boarding school) back to Cairo and took up his old post at the university. Margaret fell ill and so the younger children, John and Helen, were sent back to Britain to be cared for by an aunt. (Margaret did not die until some years later, but never saw her young children again as she did not properly recover from her illness).

He travelled extensively throughout Egypt. The most significant work he undertook there was in November 1925, when he became the first medically qualified individual to undertake an autopsy on King Tutankhamun:[12]

> The mummy was intact, although not in as good a condition as was hoped. Few royal mummies survive today which have not at some time or other been rifled by robbers, who have torn the wrappings and left the corpses damaged and exposed to the atmosphere.
>
> The first problems soon became apparent as the magnificent gold death mask which covered Tutankhamun's head, shoulders and part of his chest was stuck to the bottom of the coffin in which they had rested for so long. This was due to unguents which had been poured over the mummy after it had been placed in the coffin, which with the passing of time had dried to a stony hardness.
>
> The linen bandages were in a fragile condition and crumbled at the slightest touch. It proved impossible to unwrap the mummy layer by layer as had been hoped. They had to cut the bandages.
>
> Enclosed in the many layers of wrappings were a vast number of personal and mystical ornaments. The King lay with his arms across his body, each covered from the elbow to the wrist with bracelets of gold, silver and semi-precious stones. It was not until the greater part of the bandages had been removed, that Tutankhamun's remains could be lifted from the coffin.
>
> The bandages that covered the head of the King seemed to be in a better state of preservation. The removal of the final bandage from the King's face was a delicate operation, as the danger of damaging the King's features was uppermost in Dr Derry's mind.
>
> The face of the young pharaoh, whose reign had ended over 3,000 years earlier, was then revealed. A serene, refined and cultured face, it had

12 Michael Ridley, 'Tutankhamun: So who was the golden boy?', *The Independent*, 24 January 2005. The diary of Howard Carter, who discovered Tutankhamun, had been digitised and placed on-line at the time of writing at http://www.griffith.ox.ac.uk/discoveringtut/journals-and-diaries/season-4/journal.html.

well formed features and lips clearly marked. His skin was brittle and cracked. His eyes were partly open and had in no way been interfered with, except to be covered with fabric impregnated with resin.

Dr Derry concluded that Tutankhamun would have been between 18 and 20 when he died. But there was no visible clue as to whether or not he had met his death naturally.

Later work on the body included X-rays in 1968, which suggested Tutankhamun might have been killed by a severe blow to the head. The idea was disputed, since the wound showed some signs of healing, but that might have taken place while Tutankhamun was in a coma.

The school of medicine at which Derry taught eventually became the Faculty of Medicine of the newly-formed Egyptian University. During the time he taught there, the number of undergraduates increased from 600 to 3,600.[13] After the Second World War, however, the English were less welcome in Egypt. One of his students injured him with a revolver, and he was dismissed from his chair without ceremony in January 1952, for political reasons. He returned to Britain, but suffered tragedy later the same year when his son John, a test pilot, was killed at the Farnborough Air Show in one of Britain's worst peacetime air accidents.[14]

Derry lived until 1961, and was reputedly active and alert right to the end of his life.

Arthur Edmunds: surgeon rear-admiral

Arthur Edmunds was another Savage to escape poverty through his own talents and industry, going from a straitened background to some eminence in both medicine and the armed forces.

Early life

Edmunds was born in London in 1874, the fourth child and third son of Joseph Edmunds and Ann Stroud Swift. Joseph Edmunds worked as a 'manufacturing dry-salter', a term no longer in use but which was in common parlance from the early eighteenth century to the early twentieth century. It referred to a person who traded in chemical products, including glue, varnish, dye and colourings. Dry-salters also supplied salt or chemicals for preserving food and sometimes

13 'Derry, Douglas Erith (1874–1961)', *Plarr's Lives of the Fellows Online*, Royal College of Surgeons.
14 The total killed was 31, including 29 spectators. In a remarkable display of the stiff upper lip of that generation, the crash site was cordoned off and the airshow continued. See James Hamilton-Patterson, *Empire of the Clouds: When Britain's Aircraft Ruled the World* (Faber & Faber, 2010).

sold the finished product. It was not a role which brought riches to the Edmunds family, however, and Arthur was compelled to leave school and work in the family business. Nevertheless, he had shown sufficient promise at school for his schoolmaster to persuade him to study at night school to continue his education. He managed to gain entrance into King's College, London, and never looked back: he obtained scholarships to maintain him in his studies, and won the University Exhibition in Zoology in 1883 and the University Scholarship in Physiology in 1895, before graduating with a BSc.[15]

Thereafter, he entered King's College Hospital medical school, and again obtained financial help by winning a succession of scholarships and prizes, including the Exhibition and Gold Medal in Physiology and first class honours in materia medica in 1898. He also earned money by coaching, or tutoring as it would be called in modern university parlance. He qualified MRCS, LRCP in 1900. The following year he became an MBBS (London) and a Fellow of the Royal College of Surgeons.

Having qualified as a doctor, he was appointed as house surgeon at King's in 1901 and steadily progressed up the medical hierarchy. He lived in chambers in Lincoln's Inn Fields with another surgeon, Archibald Reid, and worked closely with Sir William Watson Cheyne (a Scottish surgeon who pioneered the use of antiseptic surgical methods), to whom he was house surgeon and private assistant. It was said of his work at that time[16]

> Edmunds acquired consummate skill and speed in cutting and staining pathological specimens for Cheyne. From him he adopted the strictest Listerian antiseptic practice, for Cheyne had been Lister's assistant. Edmunds always used a strong cleansing mixture before operation, distrusting the attempts of later surgeons to obtain absolute asepsis. He liked simple instruments, did without needle-holders, and used sharp hooks instead of forceps for holding the tissues. He made his own instruments in a workshop at the top of his house, 57 Queen Anne Street. Edmunds devised a successful operation for hypospadias and several delicate plastic operations.

In 1911 he married Maud Dampier. They did not have children.

Throughout his career, he was a prolific medical author.[17] By 1913, he had reached the level of assistant surgeon, and was in that role the following year when the First World War began.

---

15 See his obituary in the *British Medical Journal* December 15, 1945, p 866.

16 From the biographical entry on *Plarr's Lives of the Fellows Online*.

17 In 1911 he co-authored with TP Legge the second edition of Watson Cheyne and Burghard's *Manual of Surgical Treatment* in five volumes. As well as numerous papers on scientific and surgical subjects, he published in 1908 *Glandular Enlargement and Other Diseases of the Lymphatic System*.

First World War and Savage Club

Edmunds served throughout the conflict as a consulting surgeon to the Royal Navy. Among other things, he was deployed to Gallipoli, from where his reports contributed to the debate on antiseptics in which Alexander Fleming also participated. Edmunds wrote to Sir William who was serving as temporary surgeon general, RN. Edmunds argued 'most men have been so impressed by their teachers with the dangers of antiseptics that they are timid of using any'. He reported success with a particular technique, but warned 'even when cleaned they pass through such a number of hands that they are pretty certain to go wrong.'[18]

Edmunds attained the rank of surgeon rear-admiral, and was created a Companion of the Order of the Bath (CB) in 1918.[19] He joined the Savage Club in the middle of the conflict, being nominated in November 1916 and elected in December 1916. His proposer was, unsurprisingly, another eminent surgeon, Dr Walter D'Este Emery.[20] More curiously, one of his seconders was John Mackenzie Rogan, whom we met earlier as one of the Savage entertainers – an intriguing connection therefore existed between the armed forces' most distinguished band leader and one of its most distinguished surgeons.

One can imagine Edmunds as an interesting and formidable debater over a glass or two at the Savage bar of the day. The surgeons' biographical register *Plarr's Lives of the Fellows* described him as 'a bearded man, of outspoken sincerity and honesty. He did not care for sports and abhorred blood-sports',[21] qualities which doubtless would have led to him crossing intellectual swords with the Savages of his time, when country sports were much more widely-supported than in the twenty-first century.

Post-war career

After the war, he returned to working for King's. In 1934 he reached the retirement age for surgeons, and moved to Bramley Cottage, Charing, Kent. He continued with his hobbies of metal-working and painting. He also grew orchids

---

18 Ana Carden-Coyne, *The Politics of Wounds: Military Patients and Medical Power in the First World War* (Oxford University Press, 2014), p 126.

19 The Order of the Bath is the fourth-most senior of the British Orders of Chivalry, after The Most Noble Order of the Garter, The Most Ancient and Most Noble Order of the Thistle, and The Most Illustrious Order of St Patrick (dormant). Members belong to either the Civil or Military Division. The three classes of membership are Knight Grand Cross (GCB) or Dame Grand Cross (GCB); Knight Commander (KCB) or Dame Commander (DCB); and Companion (CB).

20 See Emery's obituary in the *British Medical Journal*, 30 June 1923, pp 1116–1117, which recorded he was an outstanding medical scholar and practitioner: 'Philosophical and profound, he was also a clear and concise teacher … his labours at King's College Hospital were almost more than one man could accomplish … [he was] an accomplished, an inquiring, and a loveable companion.'

21 Biographical entry on *Plarr's Lives of the Fellows Online*.

and roses. When the Second World War broke out, however, he stepped forward to serve his country once more, at the age of 66, volunteering to work as a surgeon at Cuckfield Hospital, Sussex, under the Emergency Medical Service.

He died in November 1945, not long after the war's conclusion.

Sir Alexander Fleming: the Savage who changed the course of medical history

One of the Savage Club's most prized possessions hangs discreetly on the wall near the side of the bar, in the alcove to the left as one enters the room. Alexander Fleming's Nobel Prize medal for medicine is proudly framed, accompanied by an appropriate inscription. The works of the combined Savage literary, musical and stage stars have entertained the lives of millions over the years. Fleming's work, on the other hand, undoubtedly *saved* the lives of millions. Some of the groundwork for his discovery of penicillin took place during the Great War, in which he served in the Royal Medical Corps for the entire duration. He further refined his work between the wars, though the full significance was not realised until after the Second World War had broken out.

Early life

Fleming was born in Ayrshire, Scotland, in 1881, the third of four children to local farmers. He attended Loudoun Moor School and Darvel School, before winning a two-year scholarship to Kilmarnock Academy. He then went to London to study at the Royal Polytechnic Institute. Upon finishing, he worked as a clerk for a shipping company in London. He did not enjoy the work, and as means of escape he joined the army upon the outbreak of the Second Boer War in 1899. He enlisted as a private and stayed in that rank throughout his time there.

In 1901, he received an inheritance from an uncle, which enabled him to leave the army and study medicine, on the advice of his older brother, who was already a doctor. In spite of having had no education since leaving school, Fleming prepared thoroughly for his entrance exam and achieved the highest score in the country. He began his studies at St Mary's Hospital in Paddington where he quickly excelled. He stayed in touch with the army by enlisting as a private in the London Scottish Regiment of the Volunteer Force, and he also joined the rifle club at the medical school. He qualified with an MBBS degree with distinction in 1906.

His membership of the rifle club led to a fateful twist: the captain wanted Fleming to stay on at St Mary's after qualifying so he could remain in the club. He suggested Fleming work at the inoculation department. Fleming did so where he met another outstanding practitioner, Almroth Wright. He obtained a BSc with a Gold Medal in Bacteriology in 1908, and stayed at St Mary's as a lecturer. Among other things, he and Wright worked on developing an anti-typhoid vaccine.

First World War

When the First World War began, Fleming and Wright both joined the Royal Army Medical Corps and were sent to work at the hospital in Boulogne. Septicaemia, tetanus and gangrene were rife amongst the wounded sent to him from the Western Front. Fleming determined that the problem was the amount of dead tissue around the wound, which provided the breeding ground for malign microbes. He argued in *The Lancet* in September 1915 that it was imperative to remove as much dead tissue as possible from wounds.

His research also showed that the traditional treatment of infected wounds with antiseptics was failing to prevent gangrene and other problems among war casualties – and in fact doing more harm than good. The reason was that scraps of underclothing and other dirty objects were driven by the force of an explosion deeply into the patient's tissues, where antiseptics were unable to reach. (Fleming ingeniously used his glass-blowing skills to create an experiment to prove the theory.) Fleming and Wright therefore set about finding a way of assisting the natural resources of the body. They demonstrated that a high concentration of saline solution would assist, but the Royal Army Medical Corps was slow to accept their findings, and throughout the conflict antiseptics were still used in the traditional fashion even where they harmed the patient.

Post-war career

After the war, Fleming returned to St Mary's, and in 1921 was made assistant director of the inoculation department. He made the first recorded discovery of lysozyme, an enzyme present in many bodily secretions including tears, saliva, skin, hair and nails as well as mucus. The problem was that the enzyme only seemed effective against small counts of harmless bacteria, and therefore had little therapeutic potential.

In 1928 he became Professor of Bacteriology at the University of London, and it was there that he made his legendary discovery. On 3 September 1928, he was clearing out some old dishes in which he grew his cultures. He noticed that on one of the mouldy dishes, the microbes had apparently been dissolved by the mould. He took a small sample of the mould and determined that it was from the penicillin family. His assistant pointed out that that was the same method by which he had discovered lysozyme. Thus, from that idle failure to wash out his petrie dishes, Fleming was able to make one of the greatest discoveries in medical history.

Fleming published his research in 1929, in the *British Journal of Experimental Pathology*, though the reception was muted. He continued working on the idea but struggled in cultivating penicillium and isolating the antibiotic agent. As a result he started to doubt the practical use of penicillin in treating infection, especially as he thought it would not last long enough in the human body to work effectively. One problem with his clinical tests was the use of penicillin as a surface antiseptic, which did not indicate how it would work as a tablet.

Fleming persevered through the 1930s, and he kept trying to find a chemist who might be able to refine useable quantities. By 1940, he had ended his own research, but shortly afterwards two other doctors, Howard Florey and Ernst Chain, at the Radcliffe Infirmary in Oxford, managed to isolate and concentrate penicillin. After Pearl Harbour and the consequent entry of the United States into the war, they received funding from both the British and American governments and were able to begin mass production. By 1944, enough had been produced to treat all the wounded in the Normandy campaign following the D-Day invasion.

Fleming, Florey and Chain won the Nobel Prize for Medicine in 1945. Fleming discounted his own efforts, referring to his reputation as the 'Fleming Myth', and instead directed attention to the work of Florey and Chain for transforming his discovery into a useable drug. His later biographers have debated why there was such a gap between his initial discovery and the eventual use of penicillin,[22] but there seems no doubt that without Fleming there would have been nothing for Florey and Chain to build upon.[23]

Fleming also worked during the conflict with another future Savage, the Canadian Earl Judson King (1901–1962). The two men were engaged in organising the pathological services in one of the London sectors of the emergency medical services.[24]

In 1946, Fleming was made an honorary life member of the Savage Club. He died in March 1955. In 1957, his widow, Lady Fleming, donated to the Club the replica Nobel Prize medal and the notes Fleming made on the occasion of

---

22 See for example Gwyn McFarlane, *Alexander Fleming: The Man and the Myth* (Harvard University Press, 1984), who argues that Fleming was essentially a bacteriologist, not a clinician, and had not explored the possible uses of penicillin in vivo (by, say, testing on animals), because he was following too narrow a view of experimentation which he had learned from Wright.

23 See for example Kevin Brown, *Penicillin man: Alexander Fleming and the antibiotic revolution* (History Press, 2005).

24 King also became involved in research on antimalarial drugs and served on various committees connected with the war effort. In 1945, he was sent to India, with the equivalent status of a brigadier, to advise the Indian command on chemical pathology. He returned to Britain in 1946. In 1950 he became a consultant in chemical pathology to the army. He was elected to the Savage Club on 19 October 1950. For more on his life, see his obituary in *Biochem Journal* (1963) 89, 401.

his speech when being made an honourable life member. Both can now be seen framed on the wall to the left of the bar, a prized possession of the Club indeed.

Colonel Lawrence Whitaker Harrison: 'Father of the Venereal Diseases Services'

Yet another notable Savage medical practitioner was Lawrence Whitaker Harrison.[25] His name may not have been as well known amongst the general public as that of Fleming, but his contribution to the welfare of the troops would have been appreciated at least as much. For, owing to his medical speciality, he became known as the 'Father of the Venereal Diseases Services' and thus alleviated a form of suffering that has affected soldiers for as long as there have been soldiers.

Early life

Harrison was born in 1876 in Haslingden, in Lancashire. His father, Jonathan Harrison, was a general practitioner and a Justice of the Peace. Harrison was educated at Manchester Grammar School and then the University of Glasgow, from which he graduated MB, B Ch in 1897. According to his page on the University website:[26]

> His passage through medical school was orderly and smooth. Each year he gained at least one Merit, almost always a Second Class except for Clinical Surgery, where he took a First Class Certificate in the session 1896–1897. It was an enviable undergraduate record and when he graduated, on 22nd July 1897, it was with good first-time passes in all his professional exams and a score that put him closer to the top than the middle of his year.

At the time, those suffering from venereal diseases could find themselves turned away from hospitals, so it was not axiomatic that medical students would encounter real-life cases. In his capacity as a student, Harrison was only shown one syphilis case surreptitiously by an assistant surgeon. However, he also served as a private in the Volunteer Medical Staff Corps while still a student and during that time he visited the Royal Victoria Hospital in Netley, where he witnessed a number of soldiers whose faces were literally rotting away with tertiary syphilis.

---

25 I have drawn substantially upon a much more detailed study of Harrison's life and career: Ambrose King, 'The life and times of Colonel Harrison', First Harrison Lecture, 1974, published in *British Journal of Venereal Diseases* (1974) 50, 391, http://sti.bmj.com/content/sextrans/50/6/391.full.pdf. See also Obituary: *The College Courant*, vol 17, no 33 (1964) 68; Obituary *British Journal of Venereal Diseases* 1964, 40, 228; and Philippa Levine, 'Lawrence Whitaker (1876–1964)', *Oxford Dictionary of National Biography* (Oxford University Press, 2004).

26 'Lieutenant Colonel Lawrence Whitaker Harrison', on the University of Glasgow website, https://www.universitystory.gla.ac.uk/ww1-biography/?id=167.

Two years after graduation, Whitaker joined the Army Medical Services. He served in the Boer War as a medical officer from 1899 to 1902, spending most of the time with units in the field. He was mentioned in despatches for his work in South Africa.

In 1903, he was posted to India, and it was there that he first developed his intellectual interest in the study of venereal diseases, when he was placed in charge of a cantonment hospital (cantonments were permanent British military garrisons) at an Indian military station. Soldiers and prostitutes alike were found with various cases of venereal disease, but the medical officer responsible for them seemed to have little or no interest, boasting that he completed his rounds before his cigarette burned out. Harrison experimented with different forms of treatment and eventually met with success when, using money subscribed by British units, he rented a small room at the end of the prostitute quarter in the local bazaar and instructed the matron of the cantonment hospital to disinfect the women daily.

In 1904, Whitaker was granted six months' leave. He returned to Britain and married the following year; he and his wife went on to have four children. They went back to India in 1905, where they stayed until returning to England in 1908. Harrison then worked in military medicine at Millbank. The next year he started work as a pathologist at Rochester Row Military Hospital, which had been converted into a hospital for research and instruction in the venereal diseases, operating as an offshoot of the Millbank Hospital and the Royal Army Medical College. Its commanding officer was Colonel FJ Lambkin, like Harrison a pioneer in the treatment of venereal disease. The two men experimented in the use of the drug salvarson to treat syphilis. Harrison made a modification to the Wassermann test (an antibody test for syphilis, named after the bacteriologist August Paul von Wassermann). He was promoted to the rank of major in 1911.

First World War

At the outset of the First World War, Harrison was sent to the Western Front and placed in charge of a hospital at Le Havre. Venereal diseases were an obvious problem from the beginning, the more so since the army was very short of salvarson, as it was made in Germany. As a biographer of Harrison put it:[27]

> On the outbreak of war in 1914 Harrison was swept away from all activities concerned with V.D. to join the British Expeditionary Force in France. He seems to have regarded this as a welcome break and at this point in his career he hoped he would never again have anything to do with the subject. But circumstances were to prove too much for him.

The British Expeditionary Force went to France in 1914 with no

---

27 Ambrose King, op cit, pp 393–94.

special provision for the treatment of V.D. There was no arsenoben-zol, no mercury, and not a single irrigating apparatus for the treatment of gonorrhoea. The sole anti-venereal measure was a leaflet signed by Lord Kitchener, the Secretary of State for War, exhorting the troops to sexual continence. When patients with V.D. began to report at medical units, senior officers raved about unpatriotic conduct and some advo-cated letting the adjectival patients rot. However, as numbers increased, it became clear that something more was required. It was then decided that a whole stationary hospital, containing 250 beds, should be allot-ted to this task. The choice of hospital seems to have been determined by the fact that the Commanding Officer was unpopular with his supe-riors. There seems no other valid reason for he knew nothing about V.D. and had no specially trained staff. Things became chaotic and the hospital became little more than a rest station before repatriation to the United Kingdom. Thus V.D. became a passport for home which was militarily unsound. So they had to call on Harrison, no doubt still reluctant but as ever determined to give of his best. He took over the hospital in January, 1915, when it contained about a thousand patients. No arsenical treatment had been given and there were still no Medical Officers in the hospital who knew anything useful about the treatment of V.D. The hospital was situated outside Le Havre on a site which seemed to the new C.O. the muddiest in France. Anyone who stepped off one of its few paths would be lucky to return to solid earth without losing his gumboots. So, in spite of constant changes of staff, continual admonitions from the "high-ups" that there was a war on, and repeated curses by the General Officer Commanding Lines of Communication for keeping a hospital of this kind eating up his rations, Harrison set about bringing order out of chaos.

By the spring of 1916, the hospital had more than 3,000 beds. Its work was so successful that there were only five deaths among 16,000 cases of syphilis treated up to the end of the war.

Later in 1916, Harrison returned to London to serve as adviser to the War Office on venereal diseases. Reflecting his seniority and the importance of his work, he was promoted to the rank of colonel. In 1917, he was appointed Honorary Physician to the King.

Post-war career

After the war he worked as lecturer in venereal diseases at the University of Edinburgh and later became director of venereal diseases at St Thomas's London. He was widely published in the field and worked as an adviser to the Ministry of Health.

He was elected to the Savage Club in July 1924.

In 1946 he retired from working for the Ministry of Health and was awarded the Companion of the Order of the Bath (CB). He died in 1964.

Commander Norman Holbrook VC: a naval VC from a family of heroes

The second of our Savage Victoria Cross winners, Commander Norman Holbrook was the first submariner to be awarded the VC and his was also the first naval VC gazetted in the First World War, although there had been an earlier nomination.

His father Arthur and two of his brothers were also notable Savages, though we have space only to consider Norman's exploits in any detail.

Early life and First World War

Norman Douglas Holbrook was born in 1888 in Southsea, Hampshire. He was the fourth son of Brother Savage Colonel (later Sir) Arthur Richard Holbrook and Amelia Mary *née* Parks. The family ultimately comprised six boys and four girls. Colonel Holbrook was evidently a driven and successful individual: along with his military interests (which began at the age of 10, when he joined the third Volunteer Battalion of the Hampshire Regiment as a drummer-boy), he was the proprietor of the *Portsmouth Times*, founder of the *Southern Daily Mail* and owner of Holbrook Printers. He also served at different times as a deputy lord lieutenant and an MP.

Norman Holbrook attended Portsmouth Grammar School. In 1903, he passed the entrance exam for the officer training establishment at Britannia Royal Naval College, and in January 1905 was appointed midshipman. In 1911 he served on the submarine depot ship HMS *Bonaventure*. Before the war he served on the boats[28] HMS *F3*, *V4* and *E41* before assuming command of HMS *B11* at the end of 1913.

He was still commanding *B11*, with the rank of lieutenant, when the Great War began. *B11* was an elderly vessel by the standards of submarines, having been launched in 1905. Famously, Admiral Sir Arthur Wilson, then controller of the navy, when shown the first British submarine (*Holland*, launched in 1901) had barked that submarines were 'underhand, unfair and damned un-English.'[29] *B11*'s underwater capabilities were limited: she was able to make only 6½ knots. On the surface she could manage 12 knots with her petrol engine, but at the expense of producing bad fumes for the 11-man crew.

B11 was serving in the Mediterranean. Once Turkey joined the war in October 1914, British and French vessels moved to control the Dardanelles, the strategically important narrow strait which connected the Sea of Marmara with the Aegean and Mediterranean Seas (and also allowed passage to the Black Sea via the Bosphorus), and which formed part of the continental boundary between

---

28 Pedants' corner: submarines are the only vessels in the Royal Navy called 'boats'.

29 There are variations on the quote, another being 'undersea, underhanded and un-British', but I believe he did make a comment to that effect rather than the entire quote being apocryphal.

Europe and Asia. In early November 1914, British surface ships shelled the fort at Seddülbahir (Sed el Bahr). The Turks tried to counter the Allied presence by the use of mines; the British, in turn, sent the submarines including *B11* to attack the minelayers and their escorts. It was in carrying out that mission that Holbrook won the VC.

Although the Turkish vessels' location was known to the submariners, there were formidable obstacles to moving within striking distance. The strong currents in the strait would run their batteries down quickly and hence restrict their already modest underwater range. If they surfaced to recharge batteries, they would be targets for Turkish warships and shore batteries. Further, the mixture of salt and fresh water at different depths in the straits upset the submarine's 'trim', the balance between water and air in her ballast tanks which kept her submerged. On top of all that, the straits had been heavily mined from just below Kepez Point to above Çannakale. A submarine could negotiate minefields if fitted with equipment for pushing aside the mooring ropes that anchored the mines to the sea bed, but 'B class' vessels had not been designed with the equipment, necessitating a quick improvised retrofitting of *B11*.

With no illusions about the scale of the task ahead of her, *B11* started on her way up the Dardanelles at 3.30 am on 13 December 1914. For the first five hours of the outbound voyage, she rose to periscope depth periodically to fix her position. For the final hour, she had to remain completely submerged as she was entering the most dangerous part of her mission.

As soon as he considered *B11* to be clear of the mines, Holbrook returned to periscope depth, where he spotted exactly the sort of target for which he had hoped, the Turkish ironclad *Mesûdiye*. Holbrook manoeuvred *B11* into the channel, watching the current, and closed to a range of less than one kilometre before firing a single torpedo. He scored a direct hit, but Turkish reprisals were immediate. The *Mesûdiye* managed to fire a broadside in his direction before she listed and sank. Much more dangerous for Holbrook was the plethora of other defences which had now been alerted to his presence. *B11's* compass had been damaged, leaving it to Holbrook's own wits to navigate her back through the minefield. In the enforced haste, *B11* struck the sea floor, but had to press on at top speed because of the certain death awaiting at the surface in the form of Turkish warships. At 10.20 am, she rose to periscope depth and managed to navigate into the main channel, but still had a long return journey through the minefield ahead of her, and one requiring regular surfacing to periscope depth to fix her position in the absence of a working compass. Throughout the return voyage Holbrook stayed calm under extreme pressure, and successfully brought his vessel back to the safety west of Cape Helles.

Holbrook was immediately declared a hero, and was given the nickname 'Five

Rows of Mines'. He was nominated for the Victoria Cross, and the award was gazetted on 22 December 1914, with the following statement:[30]

> His Majesty the KING has been graciously pleased to approve of the grant of the Victoria Cross to Lieutenant Norman Douglas Holbrook, Royal Navy, for the conspicuous act of bravery specified below—
>
> For most conspicuous bravery on the 13th December, when in command of the Submarine B. 11, he entered the Dardanelles, and, notwithstanding the very difficult current, dived his vessel under five rows of mines and torpedoed the Turkish battleship "Messudiyeh," which was guarding the mine-field.
>
> Lieutenant Holbrook succeeded in bringing the B. 11 safely back, although assailed by gun-fire and torpedo boats, having been submerged on one occasion for nine hours.

As well as destroying an enemy vessel, Holbrook and his crew had shown that a submarine could successfully negotiate the Dardanelles, demonstrating a serious problem for the Turks.

There was no denying Holbrook's heroism or the success of his individual mission, but so far as the wider campaign in the region was concerned, his raid was a false dawn. In February and March 1915, the British and French launched more attacks along the Dardanelles, but the operation failed when three battleships were sunk and seven more badly damaged by mines, three of them never returning to service. The Royal Navy had reasoned that the lost vessels were obsolete and therefore expendable. But it was clearly apparent that seapower alone would not secure the Dardanelles. The Allies were therefore compelled to use land forces, leading to the failed Gallipoli campaign we have covered elsewhere in this book.

Holbrook, for his part, continued to serve on submarines for the rest of the war. In May 1915, he was the first to spot an enemy vessel in the Gulf of Smyrna, but had to retreat as he lost the element of surprise before he could fire a torpedo.

In August 1915, he was wounded when trying to negotiate with Senussi tribesman on the Egyptian coast – the same theatre in which Brother Savage Rupert Gwatkin-Williams had one of his memorable wartime adventures. He was sent back to Britain to recover, and in October he was presented with his Victoria Cross by George V at Buckingham Palace.

In April 1916, the French awarded him the *Légion d'honneur*. In July 1916, the crew of *B11* were given £3,500 by a navy prize court in July 1916, of which Holbrook received £601 10s 2d. Most remarkably of all, the Australian town of Germanton, faced with having to rename itself due to the rampant anti-

---

German hysteria we have seen in other contexts, chose to name itself 'Holbrook', in honour of the Victoria Cross-winning hero. Holbrook visited the town several times later in life.

Holbrook went on to command the new vessel *F3*, then later *V4*, the mine-laying *E41* and finally, in 1918, the new submarine design *J2*. He was promoted to lieutenant-commander.

Post-war career

Holbrook married Viva Dixon, a widow, in 1919; they had one son. He retired from the navy in 1920. In February 1927, he joined the Savage Club under the category of science. The following year he was promoted to commander on the retired list.

Upon leaving the navy, he worked in the family printing business with evident success, as he and his family were able to buy a mansion in Surrey. During the Second World War, the house was used as a base first for the American High Command and later as accommodation for the Dutch Royal Family. Holbrook himself served as an officer in the Admiralty Trade Division, where his duties included interviewing survivors of ships lost by enemy action. He suffered tragedy, however, as his son was killed in action while serving in Italy.

After the Second World War, Holbrook continued working in the printing business, before moving to a farm in West Sussex. His wife died in 1952, and he re-married the following year to an Austrian woman, Gundula Felder. At the time of writing, Frau Holbrook was still alive, aged 103, and possibly the only surviving Great War widow as well as the oldest Savage Rosemary.[31]

He died in 1976, just before he would have turned 88. The Holbrook family retained its links with the eponymous Australian town, as it was given all of Norman's medals[32] by Gundula. In 2004, the medals were placed under the care of Greater Hume Shire Council, who, in December 2009, agreed to loan them to the Australian War Memorial, Canberra. The town of Holbrook retains a copy of Holbrook's VC and also a model of the *B2* submarine. Elsewhere, in Gallipoli, a gun survives on rudimentary display which was salvaged from the *Mesûdiye*, while in Britain, two monuments to Holbrook's VC actions were unveiled in 2014, a plaque in Portsmouth Grammar School and a commemorative paving stone in Palmerston Road, Southsea.

---

31 See the letter from Mr Philip Harris to *The Times*, 6 August 2018. See also 'Family meet to honour VC submariner', *Mail Online*, 13 December 2014.

32 In total: the VC, the 1914 Star, British War Medal 1914–20, Victory Medal 1914–19 with Mentioned in Despatches oak leaf, Defence Medal, War Medal 1939–45, George VI Coronation Medal 1937, Elizabeth II Coronation Medal 1953, and the Knight of the *Légion d'honneur*.

Coda: An impressive family

Like the Denning family, the Holbrooks made a remarkable contribution to the nation during the First World War. In total, five of the six brothers served, three in the army and two in the navy. Between them they were awarded a VC, DSO, MC and CBE. Colonel Holbrook, their father, commanded Royal Army Service Corps units in the Salisbury Plain training area, for which he received a knighthood.

Aside from Norman, the most notable son for our purposes was Leonard (b 1882), who became a Savage in March 1927, nominated by his father.

Leonard had joined the navy in 1896 and had been awarded the MVO as a midshipman of HMS *Majestic* for serving with the guard of honour at Windsor during Queen Victoria's funeral. At the start of the First World War, he was serving as a gunnery officer aboard HMS *Devonshire*. He was promoted commander on 31 December 1914. Thereafter he served successively as Flag Commander (a form of naval *aide-de-camp*) to Vice-Admirals Sir Martyn Jerram, Sir Herbert Heath and Sir Dudley de Chair in the Grand Fleet.

After the war, Leonard stayed in the navy. At the end of 1927 – the year he joined the Savage Club – he was given command of the light cruiser HMS *Calliope*. Twelve months later he commanded the light cruiser HMS *Birmingham*. In 1929 he was seconded temporarily to the Royal Australian Navy as second naval member of the Commonwealth Naval Board – thus forging another link between the Holbrook family and Australia. Leonard became commodore, first class in command of HM Australian Squadron, and served on the heavy cruiser HMAS *Canberra*. In October 1932 he was promoted to the rank of rear-admiral and went on to serve as *aide-de-camp* to his former Brother Savage George V.

He died in 1974, aged 92.

In October 1945, a third Holbrook brother, Lieutenant-Colonel NW Holbrook, joined the Club under the category of science. He was nominated by his father and seconded by Leonard and Norman.

Herbert Lightstone: decorated soldier-surgeon

Herbert Lightstone was a fascinating Savage of his day, a Jewish Canadian who saw action across the globe as a decorated soldier in different conflicts as well becoming as a physician of note.

Early life and First World War

Lightstone was born 'Hyman Lightstone' in 1878. He was clearly keen on adventure at an early age, serving in 1898 in the Spanish-American War with the

American Red Cross in Cuba. He then joined the Canadian Army and fought in the Second Boer War with the Canadian Field Artillery.

In 1901, he obtained his first medical qualification, later adding an MD from the prestigious McGill University. Thereafter, he worked as medical superintendent of the Women's Hospital, Montreal, and demonstrator of anatomy at Bishop's College, before emigrating to the United Kingdom.

In Britain, Lightstone became a registrar at the London Throat Hospital, working as an ear, nose and throat specialist.

During the First World War, he served in different posts, all with distinction. He was promoted to captain in April 1915 and was awarded the Military Cross in January 1916[33] and the Distinguished Service Order (DSO) in June 1917.[34] He was also mentioned in despatches six times.[35] One of his posts was medical officer to the headquarters of IV Army, a new army formed in February 1916 under the command of General Sir Henry Rawlinson to carry out the main British contribution to the forthcoming Battle of the Somme – thus placing Lightstone in arguably the most challenging position for a medical officer in the history of the British Army.

Tragically, the medical preparations for the famous assault on 1 July 1916 proved to be as deficient as the general army preparations. It was estimated that than casualties on that day would be 10,000, and the number of hospitals, bandages and other facilities and equipment were established on that assumption; they were in the event 57,000, and thus the RAMC was desperately overstretched. There can be no real dispute that many of those who died of wounds might have been saved had a more accurate assessment of the casualty figures been made – assuming that the leaders had pressed on with the assault in those circumstances (which they might have done). The historian Penny Starns wrote:[36]

> Casualty clearance stations were soon overwhelmed. A basic triage system assessed the injured upon arrival, and many men were simply put to one side to die; others, unable to access medical assistance, died where they fell. Those who were fortunate enough to reach first-aid posts and advanced dressing stations were quickly treated with rudimentary dressings. As many of the injured as possible were placed on hospital trains and shipped back to England. Casualty numbers were so high that only the most seriously wounded could be kept in France.

---

33 *London Gazette*, 11 January 1916, p 579.

34 *London Gazette*, 4 June 1917, p 5471.

35 Two examples could be found in the online version of 'The despatches of Lord French: Mons, the Marne, the Aisne, Flanders, Neuve Chapelle, the second battle of Ypres, Loos, Hohenzollern redoubt, and a complete list of the officers and men mentioned'. See: https://archive.org/stream/despatchesoflord00fren/despatchesoflord00fren_djvu.txt.

36 Penny Starns, *Sisters of The Somme: True Stories from a First World War Field Hospital* (The History Press, 2016, Kindle edn).

By 3pm on 1 July news of the appallingly high casualty figures gradually filtered through to Sloggett [Director General of the Medical Services], and he called the rail transport office at Amiens to urgently order more hospital trains. By this time base hospitals were overrun with wounded. Every conceivable mode of transport had been commandeered to shift wounded men away from the battlefield toward some semblance of care, and medical personnel worked around the clock to help the injured.

First-hand testimony was recorded by the diaries of a medical professional serving at the Front, Sister Edith Appleton:[37]

3 July

Our much-longed-for advance has begun after many days of heavy bombardment, and we launched an attack at 7:30 on Saturday morning. They went over in waves, the second one so many minutes after the first, and so on. Where one man from the first wave was wiped out, so was the second, which gave the Germans time to adjust their machine-guns to receive the rest. After the second wave they began to make headway and had them fairly on the run. We took the front-line trenches for a distance of 25 miles and actually took the four front lines, but had to retire to the first because they had the range of the other three and started shelling them. We had a couple of trainloads of wounded down—1,100 in all, including 153 officers (very dirty), and the London Scottish kilts were a sight to behold. I don't know how many we took in the annexes, I remembered up to 140, then lost count. The first lot were all fed and more or less washed, but not all dressed, when the second lot came at 6pm. At 9:30 we sent off 360 from the whole hospital, then at 2am more were to go—then at 7pm the next train of wounded is expected.

4 July

Wounded! Hundreds upon hundreds on stretchers, being carried, walking—all covered from head to foot in well-caked mud. The rush and buzz of ambulances and motor-buses is the only thing I can remember of yesterday outside my wards. Inside it took us longer than the whole day to anything like cope with the work of changing, feeding and dressing the wounds of our share of them. We had horribly bad wounds in numbers—some crawling with maggots, some stinking and tense with gangrene. One poor lad had both eyes shot through and there they were, all smashed and mixed up with the eyelashes. He was quite calm, and very tired. He said, "Shall I need an operation? I can't see anything." Poor boy, he never will. Three men died in the train and two only just reached hospital before they went west too. Three were completely dumb. They say we are serving the division that has acted as a "draw" to save the other divisions. If any are left, they deserve all honour.

---

37 Ruth Cowen, *A Nurse at the Front: The First World War Diaries of Sister Edith Appleton* (Simon & Schuster, 2012, Kindle edn).

It is not difficult to imagine the strain that Lightstone would have found himself under trying to deal with such a desperate situation unfolding across the Front and involving so many men.

Lightstone's wartime achievements were noted in the *British Jewry Book of Honour, 1914–1920*, which was free online at the time of writing. It seems, though, that he was on the receiving end of the anti-Semitism that was all too prevalent in Britain at the time, because he felt compelled during the war to change his first name from Hyman to Herbert (the change is recorded in the *London Gazette* for April 1918, the notice stating that Lightstone had changed it on 21 November 1917[38]).

Post-war career

In 1919 Lightstone joined the medical staff of the Ministry of Pensions. He was promoted to director of medical services in 1932 and deputy director-general a year later. He became a member of the Savage Club in July 1940.

He died in 1942. In his obituaries, one can detect the qualities not just of a respected surgeon and a fine soldier, as Lightstone undoubtedly was, but also an ideal member of the Savage Club. For example, in Lightstone's obituary in the *British Medical Journal* it was said:[39]

> From the end of the world war, 1914–18, to the present one Dr Lightstone, after an Army career of exceptional distinction, served with the Ministry of Pensions Medical Department practically from its inception until a few days ago. Not long after joining the Ministry in 1919, at the very beginning of a cycle of the Ministry's most strenuous years, he was appointed Headquarters Medical Inspector, a post, especially at that stage of formation of the Medical Division, which called for a rather rare combination of qualities. Loyal, indefatigable, no matter how arduous the journey or the job, imperturbable but inspiring others, Dr Lightstone more than fulfilled the requirements of his post. His subsequent advancement to Director-General could only seem natural and to be expected of a man of his measure, by those who knew him even in those early days.
>
> He was a man of wide horizons: a spacious mind with many and diverse interests—art, music, and sport—but essentially he was a man of action. Careful to arrive at the truth, when that was attained his words were brief, uncompromising, and to the point, and his actions swift and strong. But he also had in large measure that "understanding of the heart" for which Solomon prayed, and doubtless received, "to discern judgment." And so a very brave soldier, a strong and faithful civil servant, and a great friend has gone from us, and surely, as he passed, "all the trumpets sounded on the other side."

38 *London Gazette*, 26 April 1918, p 5102.
39 *British Medical Journal*, 28 February 1942, p 311.

Ronald Norrish: from prisoner of war to Nobel Prize

The third Savage Nobel Prize winner, Ronald Norrish FRS, gained the award for chemistry in 1967. Unlike Bragg and Fleming, he was young enough to serve at the Front during the Great War.

Early life and First World War

Ronald George Wreyford Norrish was born in Cambridge in 1897. He attended The Perse School and then Emmanuel College at Cambridge University, studying chemistry.

During the First World War, he was commissioned in the Royal Field Artillery in 1916 as a second lieutenant. He was captured in March 1918 and spent the rest of the war as a prisoner in Germany, first at Rastatt, Germany, and later at Graudenz in Poland.

We have already discussed the experience of prisoners of war (POWs) in the First World War in the context of Alec Waugh. It is worth expanding on the subject as it is not an aspect of the war which most general histories dwell upon, nor has the experience of POWs in the Great War been glorified in the same way as those in the Second World War, familiar from films such as *The Great Escape*.[40]

The most remarkable aspect of First World War POWs is the sheer number: more than 7 million in total, of whom about 2.4 million were held by Germany. The demands of such huge numbers made it difficult for all of the countries to keep to the promises of humane treatment for POWs which most of them (with the notable exception of the Ottoman Empire) had agreed in the Hague Conventions of 1899 and 1907. Often sanitation and water supplies were inadequate. Over time, since the general German population was struggling for food as the Allied blockade took effect, many POWs in that country suffered severe malnutrition as well.

There were basic library facilities at some camps, but for most prisoners the chief source of relief on all fronts was the delivery of mail and the Red Cross packages. By the end of the war, roughly 9 million food parcels and 800,000 clothing parcels had been sent to British prisoners abroad. Families were able to send food and other luxuries, with various restrictions on what the parcels might contain.[41]

---

40 There were escape attempts in the Great War, see for example Jacqueline Cook, *The Real Great Escape: the story of the First World War's most daring breakout* (Vintage, 2013). Two films were made between the wars on POWs. The celebrated French director Jean Renoir made *La Grande Illusion* in 1937, a film about as realistic as *Hogan's Heroes*, showing nothing of the malnutrition and general mistreatment in the camps. The following year Maurice Elvey directed *Who Goes Next?*, a film little known at the time or since.

41 Robert Jackson, *The Prisoners 1914–18* (Routledge, 1989); Oliver Wilkinson, *British Prisoners of War in First World War Germany* (Cambridge University Press, 2017).

The American Red Cross wrote a report on German POW camps, published in 1919.[42] Of the first camp at which Norrish was held, Rastatt, it stated:

> In the prison camp of Rastatt American prisoners started a newspaper known as the "Barbed Wireless," a delicious bit of satire on the conditions under which they lived.
>
> The officers were quartered in many instances in hotels, schools, barracks, and chateaux taken over for the purpose. They were allowed cooks and orderlies to look after their comfort and were permitted in most camps to take walks outside the prison upon giving their word not to attempt to escape.
>
> The conditions described above were general and there were many exceptions as to living accommodations and privileges. These were largely affected by the commandant of the camp, who could usually make conditions good or bad at will.

Norrish was later held at Graudenz. An eye witness account by Lieutenant Arthur Hollis RFC, who was captured on 26 March 1918, recalled[43]

> Graudenz, in West Prussia—a huge garrison town, on the east bank of the Vistula, about half-way between Danzig and Warsaw and quite close to the Polish frontier. It formed a part of some huge new German barracks and was very well built. There are 600 British officers imprisoned there and 800 British NCOs and me to look after them. As the camp had only been opened a fortnight, everything was more or less in a state of chaos. The buildings consisted of two huge blocks; each block had cellars, ground floor, 1st and 2nd floor, and right at the top some arrest cells for prisoners, and rooms for the British orderlies. The rooms varied in size and contained beds. Each bed had a sheet, two blankets and a pillow, a mattress in three sections supported by four bed boards. There was also a wooden stool for each officer, a cupboard for every two or three officers and an electric light and a stove. There were 300 officers in each of these blocks and they were very crowded. There was also a separate building containing kitchens, mess rooms, and shower baths and I must admit that in all the camps of which I had experience the baths were good. There was also a smaller building which ultimately became a parcel store. There was a piece of barrack square about 110 yds x 80 yds on which roll calls were held twice daily and which formed the only ground for exercise. Completely surrounding the camp was a foursquare barbed wire fence of terrific strength, about 12 ft high, and the barbed wire so thick that you could only just put your arm through it; on the top of each post in the fence was a barbed wire cage; ten feet outside this fence was a new high brick wall, ten to fifteen feet; with 4 ft of barbed wire on the top leaning inwards. Every 50 yds or so inside the inner fence was a German sentry with a

42 Carl P Dennett, *Prisoners of the Great War; Authoritative Statement of Conditions in the Prison Camps of Germany* (Houghton Mifflin, 1919).
43 From Anne Warin (ed), *Dear Girl, I Escaped: Experiences of the Great War, 1914–18* (Redcliffe Press Ltd, 1989), pp 38–40.

loaded rifle, and outside each of the outer walls was one or more similar sentries pacing up and down. These guards were strictly mounted and watched, and were on duty night and day. Every 50 yds along the fence and at intervals on the barrack square were huge electric arc lamps which were during all night and made the whole place, especially the ground all round the outside walls, as light as day.

The Red Cross in Britain maintained records of British soldiers held in Germany as best they could, and at the time of writing Norrish's record could be found online.[44] It recorded his representative as being a 'Mr E. Mellish Clark, Cambs. & Isle of Ely Prisoners of War Help Committee, County Hall, Hobson St, Cambridge.'

As with Waugh, Norrish was captured in the final year of the conflict, and therefore would not have suffered for as long as many others, though he was held at the time when Germany was facing a severe shortage of food.

Post-war career

Norrish was repatriated in 1919. He returned to Emmanuel College, first as a student and after 1925 as a Fellow. He became head of the physical chemistry department at Cambridge, although during his lifetime Cambridge also had a separate department of chemistry (organic, theoretical and inorganic chemistry). In 1924, his PhD thesis was completed on radiation and chemical reactivity. His supervisor was Sir Eric Rideal, another outstanding scientist of the twentieth century.

Norrish's principal area of research was photochemistry using continuous light sources. He was elected a Fellow of the Royal Society (FRS) in 1936. In 1967, he was awarded the Nobel Prize in Chemistry, along with Manfred Eigen and George Porter, for the study of extremely fast chemical reactions. He had a notable student in Rosalind Franklin, who together with Watson and Crick was one of the discoverers of the structure of DNA.

His gruelling wartime service – being a POW was no picnic, and he had of course known the horrors of the Front before being captured – along with his phenomenal academic achievements perhaps masked the fact that, as with Lightstone, Norrish was fully imbued by the sort of spirit one would expect of a member of the Savage Club. One writer explained:[45]

> Not only had he been a brilliant academic but also an alcoholic and martinet whose former students still told stories of his outland-ish behaviour and often hilarious feats. There were fewer and fewer

---

44 ICRC, 1914-1918 Prisoners of the First World War Historical Archives, https://grandeguerre. icrc.org/en/File/Search/#/3/2/224/0/British%20and%20Commonwealth/Military/norrish.

45 Maxine Handy, *Wishing-well and Other Fantasies* (Lulu.com, 2010), pp 142–3.

colourful characters left in academia, that wonderful side of university life was sadly in decline ...

[M]eeting him for lunch in The Spread Eagle pub was even more unwise. The legendary Professor had his very own corner chair, which he loved to use for impromptu lunchtime meetings which often extended into closing time. DD turned up promptly to discuss a problem in reaction kinetics, only to leave many hours later in a state of complete drunkenness. In contrast, Professor Norrish could consume large quantities of alcohol without any apparent ill effect or impairment of his intellectual faculties.

Norrish died in 1978. His profile on Emmanuel College's website notes:[46]

Norrish was a man of immense energy, who worked hard and relaxed hard and expected other people to do the same. He enjoyed meeting people from other countries and walks of life, and this temperament found full play both in the extensive travels for which his scientific reputation gave him opportunities, and in the reciprocal entertainment of visitors to Cambridge—entertainment always warm and memorable, if sometimes overwhelming. He lived for much of his life in Park Terrace, adjacent to the grounds of the College, to which his lifelong devotion was marked by two characteristic bequests—one for the College library, the other for the purchase of silver wine-stoups and for gratuities for the College staff.

---

46 http://www.emma.cam.ac.uk/about/history/famous//?id=12.

CHAPTER 11

Savage Politicians

Introduction

'Politician' is not and has never been a category of membership of the Savage, and so each of the men in this section qualified under another category. Once again they show the diverse range of interests common to the Savage, not just in terms of their artistic endeavours, but also in their politics, for members of the time included representatives of each of the three main parties of the day – Labour, Liberal and Conservative – as well radical thinkers such as Major CH Douglas.

Oliver Baldwin, 2nd Earl of Bewdley: the apple that fell far from the tree

Oliver Baldwin was the son of the Conservative prime minister Stanley Baldwin, but one who very boldly did not follow his father's political predilections. He did not, it is fair to say, enjoy a particularly distinguished political career beyond the notable fact of deviating from his father's allegiances, but he served bravely during the First World War and led an interesting life which doubtless would have provided many engaging stories at the Savage bar of the day.

Early life and First World War

Oliver Ridsdale Baldwin was born in 1899 at Astley Hall, Worcestershire, the first son of Stanley and Lucy Baldwin. As with so many sons of the establishment then and now, Oliver was sent to Eton, but he despised what he saw as the snobbery and cruelty of the school and the old fashioned values it represented, and it formed the first stage in developing his non-conservative political views.

When the First World War broke out, he assumed it would be over before he was old enough to join up – reflecting the general feeling that it would be 'all over by Christmas'. His view was sharply changed in October 1915, however, when he learned from his mother of the presumed death of his cousin – one John Kipling, son of the famous author Rudyard Kipling. Baldwin was fired with a determination to avenge the younger Kipling's death.

At 16 years old he was still too young to enlist, though he was physically large for his age and soon passed six foot in height. Rudyard Kipling wrote to Baldwin's father, asking him to support Oliver's wish to enlist at the soonest opportunity. Kipling elsewhere tried to pull strings as he had for John – evidently, he had not then developed the strong anti-war feelings he would later express in his verse 'Common Form'.

In the meantime, Baldwin went up to Cambridge. He joined the cadet force, somewhat ironically as his rooms were owned by a conscientious objector and there was much anti-war literature about. Much of the pacifist sentiment at Cambridge at the time was encouraged by one of its better known intellectuals, Bertrand Russell. Nevertheless, Baldwin was not converted and continued with his adamantine determination to serve. He passed out at the second attempt, in June 1917, and followed John Kipling into the Irish Guards.

Initially, Baldwin stayed in Britain, training with the Guards, though he managed one taste of the war whilst there as he was in Chelsea Barracks when a Zeppelin bomb landed on the Embankment.

In 1918, he was finally sent to France, reaching the Front in June not long before the Allied victory push began. His letters home to his father were quite candid about his experiences. In one he wrote half-jokingly 'It's about time I got wounded; it seems to be the best way of getting home these days.' Two letters from October 1918 give a representative sample of his experience:

> Darling Father,
>
> At 5:15a.m. on the 27th of September when you were asleep, your son 2nd in command for the day of the 1st Guards Light Trench Mortar Battery was crouching in a 3 foot trench with the Irish Guards, smoking one of his grandfather's cigars, waiting for "zero" & under-going a slight German barrage. At 5:20am ("zero") a noise like six trains rushing through a narrow tunnel, coal being thrown downstairs, pots & pans being upset etc, rent the air. In other words our barrage of 9.2", 6" and 4.2" howitzers, 60 and 18 pounder, machine gun & every gun on our sector tore "No man's land" & the canal bank to pieces – & we (as they say in the paper) "went over the top." How we got through the wire & the German barrage of "Minnies" I cannot tell, but we leapt into our first trench for a pause. This trench was receiving direct hits-one in the next bay to me & one on the parados wherein all went dark & I thought I was finished; but only covered with dirt. I thought it was time to get out so I led the battery to the canal.

Darling Father,

Just finished my fourth "show": in other words I've been in every attack since the advance began. In the last show (20th) I had the honour and the appalling worry of commanding the Coy in the attack. I must say this last show was the worst as far as nerves are concerned & towards the end I'm afraid my nerves were completely "dissed". There can be no greater strain in the world than commanding a coy. in the attack & on top of that we had to hold the line for two days after, which meant digging in little posts & not daring to stir by day. I've never been so badly shelled before & I don't want to be again. I suppose it was an honour but I'd rather do without …

According to his biographer, Baldwin in later life became less enthused about war, seeing it as a job to be done rather than a matter for glorification.[1] On the Western Front, though, there was no doubting his bravery or commitment.

Post-war career

Arguably, Baldwin had a more interesting military career after the war. In the immediate aftermath he joined the Comrades of the Great War, a forerunner of the British Legion, in the hope that the group might be able to initiate social change. (There is also the possibility that he had suffered mild shell shock.) He then left Britain and served for a short time as British vice-consul in Boulogne, before going travelling in North Africa. He declined any support from his father and instead paid his way by working as a journalist and travel writer.

In 1920, thanks to the contacts he made in Egypt, he found a somewhat unlikely role as an infantry instructor in Armenia, which had recently gained independence from the Ottoman Empire. Not long after he arrived in Yerevan, however, the democratic government collapsed and he was imprisoned by Bolshevik-backed revolutionaries. He was freed two months later when democracy was restored, and set off for Britain, but was arrested by Turkish authorities who, angered by his support for Armenian independence, accused him of spying for the Soviet Union. He was held for five months in Turkish prisons. He later wrote a book of his experiences, entitled *Six Prisons and Two Revolutions*.

Upon his return to Britain, Baldwin was briefly engaged to be married, but after the relationship ended accepted his homosexuality and started living with his partner Jonnie Boyle. The two lived in Oxfordshire in what Baldwin's biographer referred to as a life of 'gentle, amicable, animal-loving primitive homosexual socialism.'[2] His family seemed to accept the situation and, to the extent that his colleagues knew, it did not seem to stall his career either. One wonders

---

1   Christopher J Walker, *Oliver Baldwin: A Life of Dissent* (Arcadia Books, 2003).
2   Ibid.

though how much strain having to live a public lie placed on Baldwin, as with James Agate.

In 1924, Baldwin stood unsuccessfully for the seat of Dudley for the Labour Party. His father was by then leader of the Conservative Party and prime minister, so naturally Oliver's Labour affiliation was the subject of significant press interest. Oliver was elected to Dudley in 1929, so joined his father in the Commons on the opposite side. Despite their political differences, the two always remained close, and Baldwin never attacked his father personally when discussing politics in public.

Early in 1931, Baldwin resigned from the Labour Party and was briefly associated with Oswald Mosley's New Party, but soon left him and rejoined Labour. When MacDonald formed the national government, Stanley Baldwin and the Conservatives joined it; most Labour members, including Oliver Baldwin, did not.

The 1931 general election resulted in a landslide win for the national government and a disaster for Labour. Baldwin was among the casualties, losing his seat to a Conservative. He therefore returned to journalism. In that field he deserves recognition as an anti-fascist, even though – or, perhaps, especially because – he was often published in the Rothermere papers which were sympathetic towards Germany. In 1934, the *Daily Herald* published an article by him entitled 'No Fascism for British Youth'. He joined the Savage Club in March 1931 under the category of literature, one of his seconders being AP Herbert. As well as his journalism, he wrote various books about Armenia and politics, and also a novel called *The Coming of Assia* which had a Christian-socialist theme.

In 1937 Stanley Baldwin retired from politics and became Earl Baldwin of Bewdley. Oliver therefore acquired the courtesy title Viscount Corvedale, though it did not entitle him to sit in the House of Lords. Percy Bradshaw had a memory dating from what must have been soon after Stanley Baldwin's retirement:[3]

> Another of my happier memories is of an entertainment given by a group of Brother Savages, in which I was included, at the home of the Rt. Hon. the Earl Baldwin of Bewdley, a former Prime Minister. During his premiership the then Mr Baldwin had often expressed a wish to attend a Savage house-dinner, but this was impossible until he resigned the cares of office. It was then that his son, our Brother Savage Oliver, persuaded us to take a Savage entertainment to his father. Among the party were George Baker, Sterndale-Bennett, Mark Hambourg, Flotsam & Jetsam, Parry Jones, Joe Batten and myself. I was afraid that my turn, in which I masqueraded as an old explorer, Colonel Livingstone-Stanley, would shock the Countess Baldwin and the other ladies. I am happy to remember that it did not.

---

3   Bradshaw, op cit, p 103.

When the Second World War broke out, Oliver volunteered and served in the Intelligence Corps in the Near East and North Africa, reaching the rank of major. His duties included running a loudspeaker unit broadcasting propaganda to try to win over doubtful enemy soldiers on the battlefields in Eritrea.

After the war, he was elected again for Labour as part of the Attlee government. In 1947 he was ennobled by Attlee, but before he could take his seat his father died so he automatically became a member of the Lords as the second Earl Baldwin. Had his father lived, then father and son would, uniquely, have opposed each other in both Houses of Parliament.

In February 1948, Baldwin was appointed governor and commander-in-chief of the Leeward Islands. He was recalled in 1950, though, with some complaints about his left wing views not being acceptable – he had dared to support multi-racial inclusiveness. There were also mutterings about the private activities in the household which Baldwin had set up with two male friends, one working as butler and the other as private secretary. Whatever the reason for his recall, however, it meant that he was able to chair a Savage Club dinner on 6 March 1954.

He died in 1958.

Reginald Berkeley: a life of many parts

Reginald Berkeley was born in England, lived in Fiji and New Zealand, died in Hollywood, and achieved distinction as a soldier, politician and screenwriter. It can be no surprise such a well-travelled and erudite man found a convivial home in the Savage Club.

Early life and First World War

Reginald Cheyne Berkeley was born in London in 1890. His father moved him to Fiji where he was working as a lawyer, and then to Auckland, New Zealand, where he studied at Auckland University before being admitted to the New Zealand Bar in 1912. He served as a lieutenant in the New Zealand Territorial Army from 1911 to 1913, and full-time in the army as a captain in the Rifle Brigade during the First World War.

The Rifle Brigade was one of five regiments having four regular battalions before the war. It had two special reserve battalions – in which Berkeley served – but, as with the Guards, the Irish Regiments and the King's Royal Rifle Corps, it had no territorial battalions. In terms of social cachet the Rifle Brigade was quite high up in the British Army of the day, just below the Guards Regiments.[4]

4　The Rifle Brigade began in Napoleonic times, when in January 1800 an elite and 'Experimental Corps of Riflemen' was raised by Colonel Coote Manningham and Lieutenant-Colonel the Hon William Stewart. It took recruits from a variety of other regiments to train them as

Berkeley was in D Company of the 11th Battalion, which was sent to the Western Front. The high point of his service was being awarded the Military Cross for his actions on 3 September 1916 during the Battle of Guillemont, forming a later part of the Battle of the Somme. He himself described the action in the first volume of the brigade's official history, though relegating his own part to a footnote:[5]

> The attack of the Eleventh Battalion was made by "A" and "B" Companies (Captain E. R. Donner and 2nd Lieutenant A. M. Hepburn) supported respectively by "C" (2nd Lieutenant CAC Murdoch) and "D" Captain M L Cope, MC[6]). The Tenth was led by "C" and "D" followed by "A" and "B". After their brief rest at the Craters both Battalions were in magnificent spirits; the assembly was carried out without a casualty or hitch of any kind; and they breakfasted in their trenches next morning full of heart for their first battle and taut with curiosity and expectation.

> Zero came; they left their trenches behind a magnificent barrage and fell on the Germans in the first sunken road. The flame projector and the mine had both failed, but so swift were the Riflemen behind the barrage that, almost as soon as it had passed on, the strong point had been entered and the garrison killed. The fury of the fighting in the first sunken road may be judged from the fact that one hundred and fifty German dead were afterwards counted in it. Captain Donner and 2nd Lieutenant Hepburn of the Eleventh Battalion and Lieutenant F. D. Byng of the Tenth all lost their lives at the head of their men; the support companies of both Battalions swarmed forward to assemble in the captured position and the 6th Bn. Oxfordshire and Bucks Light Infantry passed through with mechanical precision and flung themselves into the first divisional objective, the Guiellemont-Hardecourt road, which they captured after killing eighty of the enemy.

> It was now the turn of the remaining companies of the two Rifle Brigade battalions and one company of the 10th Bn. 60th to take the lead again. In the act of leaving the sunken road Captain Cope, who had lined up his men with the strictness of a ceremonial, was severely wounded[7]

'sharpshooters, scouts and skirmishers'. Note that at the time the conventional infantry tactics involved massed squares of men firing from near point-blank range at each other.

During the Great War, the 1st to the 4th, 7th to 13th and the 16th battalions all fought on the Western Front, though the 4th was sent to Salonika in November 1915 where it remained for the rest of the conflict.

In 1948, the regiment was merged with the King's Royal Rifle Corps to form The Green Jackets, and after more mergers became known as the Royal Green Jackets. In 2007, they were joined with the Devonshire and Dorset Light Infantry, The Light Infantry and The Royal Gloucestershire, Berkshire and Wiltshire Light Infantry to become The Rifles.

5   Captain Reginald Berkeley and Brigadier-General William W Seymour, *History of the Rifle Brigade in the War of 1914–1918* (Naval and Military Press reprint, 2003), vol 1, p 188. I have broken up the quote into separate paragraphs; the original all runs together.

6   The footnote in the original records that he was the grandson of Sir William Cope, the historian of the regiment.

7   He writes a footnote at this point stating '2nd Lieut. RC Berkeley then took over "D" Company,

by the enemy barrage which had just begun to fall in the old German front line. But the companies swept on through the Oxfordshire and Bucks Light Infantry and poured into the objective beyond. By now the enemy's resistance was flagging. Fifty-two were killed in the Wedge Wood switch; but the Germans began to surrender freely.

The Riflemen were armed with phosphorous bombs for clearing dug-outs, of which there were a great number. The choice for the occupants was to come out with a good face or be smoked out like a wasps' nest. At one dug-out, however, there was a show of resistance; and resistance of an unpleasant kind. Two men emerged and surrendered, and then instead of a third man a bomb came through the entrance. It happened that the explosion further disabled an already wounded man. There was a cry of "Bombing our wounded!" Half a dozen Riflemen rushed forward and, before the smoke had cleared away, a shower of hand grenades into the dug-out had turned it into a charnel house of dead and dying. Forty-two bodies were taken from it afterwards for burial.

By now the enemy was fairly on the run. The Oxfordshire and Bucks Light Infantry came up, passed through to the next objective, where they were joined by the Rifle Brigade; and at 2pm with the two Rifle Brigade battalions still on the right, the line went forward to the Gincy-Wedge Wood road which was reached if anything a little in advance of the time-table—for the artillery was still barraging immediately beyond it; and one or two shorts caused casualties. Here "C" company (2nd Lieutenant Murdoch) of the Eleventh Battalion, which had lost direction by following the Guillemont-Wedge Wood switch-line down into the Wedge Wood valley, reappeared marching up the road under its officer, and driving before it a large number of German prisoners captured in the dug-outs that lined the western face of the road.

The haul of prisoners taken by the Eleventh Battalion was considerable. Receipts were in its possession for one hundred and fifty out of the divisional total of five hundred, and that figure should be accepted as a minimum.

His citation stated 'For conspicuous gallantry in action. When his company commander was wounded, he led the company with great dash to its final objective, and later displayed great determination in consolidating the captured line.'[8] His account of the action is particularly interesting as it shows how the army had learned from the first-day disaster just two months earlier: the soldiers in Berkeley's account rushed their objectives under a creeping barrage, instead of walking slowly across No Man's Land after the cessation of the preparatory artillery fire.

Another change by the end of 1916 was the abandonment of any feelings of empathy that might have been felt with their Saxon foe:

leading it to the final objective, where he was wounded but remained at duty. He was awarded the MC.'

8 *Supplement to the London Gazette*, 14 November 1916, p 11046.

Christmas Day 1914 had been a truce; and there were efforts to renew it in 1915. Christmas 1916, however, passed in the line like any other day. The enemy, dispirited and alarmed at the inroads made by the battle of the Somme, was in no mood for a fraternization that might still further have undermined the moral of his troops. For it cannot be denied that the British offensive had shaken that moral severely. The British, on the other hand, had no feeling but disfavour for the nation whose submarine atrocities had been so boastfully carried out. The First Battalion spent the day in support at Priez Farm on the Rancourt-Combles road. "It was only remarkable for the extra amount of work done improving the very bad accommodation there; and the blowing up of one of our bomb stores by a German shell."

Post-war career

After the war, Berkeley was admitted as a barrister in England and Wales and co-wrote the aforementioned history of the Rifle Brigade.[9]

In 1919, he joined the League of Nations Union as editor of pamphlets, then worked as the rather archaic-sounding 'director of propaganda'. He left the League when he was elected as the MP for Nottingham Central in the 1922 election, as a member of the Liberal Party. In his maiden speech he concentrated on foreign policy, and made some perceptive remarks that resonate all the more with the benefit of hindsight:[10]

> I envy anyone who can look at the present situation on the Continent without the deepest misgiving. Wherever one looks one sees the same sight, either a nation in ruin or a nation being dragged down to ruin. The position of the Continental exchanges seems to go from bad to worse. Everything seems to point to the necessity for serious international co-operation to relieve this state of affairs. The Hon. Member for Clitheroe (Captain Brass) who moved the Address said that the apparent bankruptcy on the Continent was only what he called a monetary bankruptcy. I cannot let that pass. It seems to me to go far deeper than that. It seems to me to be a bankruptcy of hope and endeavour. Wherever one looks there is a kind of fixed and awful despair seizing upon the Central European peoples. Some countries are in such a pitiable economic state that they do not seem to be able to nerve themselves to check this terrible downward tendency. What I would impress most on the House is that that kind of despair is the half-brother, if not the full brother, of international violence. That is the kind of atmosphere in which thoughts of war flourish. That is the first danger in the international situation to-day, which I am anxious to point out.
>
> There is also another danger. At the moment, unless I have misread the statements of policy made from time to time on behalf of the Government, we seem to be basing our foreign policy on what I would

---

9   Berkeley and Seymour, op cit.
10 *Hansard*, HC Debates, 24 November 1922, vol 159, cc185–224.

call a group system, understandings between what we used to call the principal Allies during the War, especially the friendly Powers of France and Italy. Those friendships and understandings are all very well, so far as they go. So far as they go I am all for them, but I do not want them to be exclusive. History surely tells us that foreign policy based purely on the group system is sure to be met by a counter group. I would ask the House to consider whether a counter group is not at this very moment in the process of formation. During the Genoa Conference, which was a great effort on the part of the late Government, for which they must receive a great deal of thanks even though it failed, an understanding, some people believe, a military understanding—and there are good grounds for the belief—was entered into between Germany and Russia. Later than that, during the Near Eastern crisis, it seemed that there was some similar understanding between Russia and the Angora Government—at least there was reciprocity between them. If we continue to base our foreign policy upon the group system and on an exclusive alliance with the principal Allied Powers, that group will most assuredly be met by a Russo-Turko-German entente. That is the second danger in the existing situation.

This is not a criticism in any way of the Lausanne Conference. That is a temporary Conference called to meet a particular state of affairs. It may well achieve its purpose, and I am sure that everyone on this side of the House hopes that it will. But what I am criticising is the revival of the group system, which was the basis of our foreign policy before the War, and which, it seems to me, did not do so well for itself as to make it a very desirable basis for our foreign policy in the future.

He was re-elected to parliament in 1923, but did not stand for the 1924 general election. He stood unsuccessfully in 1929, 1930 and 1931 – his lack of success reflecting the decline of the Liberal Party.

By that stage, he had made a name for himself with his stage plays, including *French Leave* (1920, made into a film twice), *The Lady With The Lamp* (1929, based on the life of Florence Nightingale), and *The Man I Killed* (1931, also made into a film), and his screenplays, including *Dreyfus* (1931), *Cavalcade* (1933), *The World Moves On* (1934), *Carolina* (1934) and *Nurse Edith Cavell* (made into a film in 1939, after his death). While living in Beverly Hills, however, he died from pneumonia in 1935, at the age of just 44.

Berkeley married twice: Gwendoline Cock in 1914, and Clara Hildegarde Digby in 1926. One of his sons, Henry Robert, was killed aged 21 in March 1944 while serving with the Royal Canadian Naval Volunteer Reserve on board MTB *417*, and is buried in Coxyde Military Cemetery, Belgium. Another, Humphrey Berkeley, became a politician and was notable for crossing the floor many times and, more substantively, for his work in bringing about homosexual law reform in the 1960s.[11]

---

11 Berkeley raised the issue in the Commons, and eventually the Law Reform Bill made it through

Major CH Douglas: engineering a new way

Among the different political movements that came and went across the Anglosphere in the twentieth century, one interesting idea was known as 'Social Credit'. The movement has essentially disappeared now but for a time enjoyed moderate success, the apogee being probably forming the government of the state of Alberta in Canada and creating a minor party in New Zealand which had two long-serving MPs. The ideas were all generated by Brother Savage Major CH Douglas, who held an important engineering role in the Great War.

Early life and First World War

Clifford Hugh Douglas was born in 1879, in either Edgeley or Manchester. Not many details of his early life survive. It is presumed that he undertook an apprenticeship before going on to work for different companies in the field of electrical engineering, and it is recorded that he taught at Stockport Grammar School for a time. At the age of 31, he went up to Cambridge to study engineering, but only lasted four terms and did not earn a degree.

Over the next few years he travelled abroad, including to America, although again surviving details are comparatively sketchy. It is, however, certain that he served as assistant superintendent of the Royal Aircraft Factory, Farnborough (the Factory), during the First World War, during which he held a temporary commission as captain in the Royal Flying Corps.

The Factory had started life a decade before the war began when it became the new home of the Army Balloon Factory, developing the then-new technology of dirigibles. It soon began experimenting with aircraft. In 1909, it changed hands from the army to at least nominal civilian control. In 1912, it changed its name to the Royal Aircraft Factory and used the initials RAF.

The first new designer was Geoffrey de Havilland, who subsequently founded his own company and went on to make some of the most legendary British aircraft in history.[12] While at the Factory, de Havilland designed the BE 2,[13]

---

the Lords in part thanks to its support by Lord Arran, who otherwise was known for his work on behalf of badgers. When asked why he had greater difficulty with the latter, he replied 'not many badgers in the House of Lords'.

12 Including the Gypsy Moth, Tiger Moth, Mosquito and Comet.

13 Until approximately 1913, British aircraft types were known by the layout of the plane, using French terminology. Hence 'SE' stood for 'Santos Experimental' and referred to an aircraft with a tail-first layout; BE (Blériot Experimental) referred to a propeller-first layout, also known as a 'tractor'; and FE (Farman Experimental), with the propeller behind the pilot, also called a 'pusher', which had the advantage of allowing the pilot unrestricted vision out the front and an unobstructed machine gun, but which was discarded when it was shown that the tractor layout gave better performance. After 1913, English abbreviations were used, based on the intended role of the aircraft, hence AE (Armed or Armoured Experimental), CE (Coastal Experimental), FE (Fighting Experimental), NE (Night Experimental), RE (Reconnaissance

a sturdy biplane of which some 3,500 were made, and which served in various capacities throughout the First World War.

Despite the success of the BE 2, the Factory was not without its critics throughout the conflict, prominent among them being Noel Pemberton Billing, the homophobic MP mentioned in Chapter 6, in the context of the Savage man of letters James Agate. Billing was an aviation pioneer, founding the company that became Supermarine (years later, the manufacturer of the Spitfire).[14] He complained bitterly that the Factory was merely 'tinkering with science' instead of facing up to the scale of the Fokker threat.[15] He was joined in his attack by CG Grey, founder of the magazine *The Aeroplane*, who had been criticising the Factory from as far back as the days when it produced balloons.

The two men were mainly exercised by the fact that a government body was competing with private industry, and they alleged favouritism on the part of the Royal Flying Corps towards the Factory.[16] The fact that managers at the Factory such as Douglas held temporary commissions in the RFC would have given them some ammunition in their campaign.

There seems little doubt that both Grey and Pemberton Billing exaggerated their criticism, but then again, they had a point in that the Factory's designs were uncompetitive for long periods of the war. The Airco DH 2, the first British aircraft to match the early Fokker threat, was designed independently by de Havilland, while probably the best British plane of the whole conflict, the Sopwith Camel, was also designed by an independent company.

One of the more notable aircraft designed and built at the Factory was the RE 8, a two-seat biplane reconnaissance and bomber aircraft, which, as noted in Chapter 7, was popularly known as the 'Harry Tate'. The RE 8 was also produced

---

Experimental) and SE (Scout Experimental).

14 He sold his share in the Supermarine company in 1914. The company then passed through various forms of ownership over the decades until finally forming part of BAE Systems. At the time of writing, the company had a short biography of Pemberton Billing on its website, which did not mention his riotous court case. The other Savage Supermarine connection was the fact that the Savage artist Oliver Bernard designed a notable building for the company, https://www.baesystems.com/en/heritage/pemberton-billing.

15 In April 1915, the Germans had developed the Fokker Eindecker (monoplane), the first purpose-built German air-to-air fighter, and the first aircraft to be fitted with a synchronisation gear, enabling the pilot to fire a machine gun through the arc of the propeller. The aircraft arrived at the Western Front in numbers from July 1915 and gave Germany the balance of power in the air war from then until early 1916, a period of time known as the 'Fokker Scourge'. It should be noted that Fokker may not have been responsible or solely responsible for all the innovations for which he was subsequently credited, though he was certainly a pivotal person in the development of the synchronising device. That said, early examples of the device caused serious problems: both Oswald Boelcke and Max Immelmann survived their propellers being shot off and even engines pulled out of their mountings.

16 See also Lieutenant-Colonel Eric Ash, *Sir Frederick Sykes and the Air Revolution 1912–1918* (Frank Cass, 1999), p 34.

by Austin Motors, Daimler, Standard Motors, Siddeley-Deasy and the Coventry Ordnance Works. It replaced the rather feeble BE 2, and more than 4,000 were produced, but it never shook off a reputation for being dangerous to fly. Even though it stayed in use as a reconnaissance and artillery observation aircraft from mid-1917 to the end of the war, and saw service not only at the Western Front but also in Italy, Russia, Palestine and Mesopotamia, it was painfully obsolete by the war's end.

In 1918, with the formation of the Royal Air Force, the Factory changed its name to the 'Royal Aircraft Establishment' (RAE) to avoid confusion with its initials. By that stage it had largely abandoned manufacturing and was instead a research centre.

In the course of his work with the Factory, Douglas made what he thought was an alarming discovery. He calculated that the total cost of goods produced each week exceeded the sums paid to the workers by way of salary, wages or other compensation, a statistic that ran counter to classical (Ricardian) economics of the day, which held that costs were simultaneously distributed as purchasing power. Douglas investigated further, obtaining data from over a hundred large businesses, and saw the pattern repeated in almost every case barring companies which went insolvent. His conclusion was that workers were not being paid enough to buy back what they had made, and he set about trying to devise a system to right what he thought was an evident wrong.

Post-war career

Just after the war finished, Douglas published his findings in the magazine *English Review*. He argued that the country was 'living under a system of accountancy which renders the delivery of the nation's goods and services to itself a technical impossibility,'[17] and that the system was organised on that basis to maximise profit for those with economic power by creating unnecessary scarcity.

He joined the Savage Club in December 1921, under the category of literature. Curiously, his address in the candidates' book was given as 8 Fig Tree Court, The Temple, London. I have not found any reference to him ever becoming a barrister.[18]

Douglas further developed his ideas in two books published in 1920: *Economic Democracy* and *Credit-Power and Democracy*, with a third book, *Social Credit*, published in 1924. He continued to seek a method of bringing purchasing power

17 CH Douglas, 'The Delusion of Super-Production', *English Review*, December 1918.
18 The Temple houses two of London's 'Inns of Court' (Middle and Inner Temple) and consists of barristers' chambers, dining halls and flats. Ordinarily its accommodation is used by barristers who are members of one of the Inns. Fig Tree Court itself was destroyed by enemy action in 1940. Having said that, Professor FG Parsons FRCS also gave The Temple as his address, so it was clearly not unknown at the time for non-barristers to obtain accommodation there.

in line with production. He offered two solutions: first, a national dividend to distribute money (debt-free credit) equally to all citizens, over and above their earnings, to bring purchasing power in line with prices; and second, a price adjustment mechanism, which he called the 'just price', to preclude inflation.

According to Douglas, the just price would lead to a reduction in retail prices by a percentage reflecting the physical efficiency of the production system. He argued that the cost of production was consumption – the physical cost of production comprised the total resources used in the production process. As the physical efficiency of production increased, the just price mechanism would reduce the price of products for the consumer.

Douglas's ideas never gained much traction in Britain, but did rather better in the dominions. They formed the basis of the Canadian Social Credit movement, which won power in Alberta in 1935. In Australia, the Douglas Credit Party was formed, though it did not last long. In New Zealand, the Social Credit Political League lasted much longer and had MPs as late as the 1980s.

Douglas spent the remaining years of his life travelling the world promoting his theories. He was referred to in various notable publications of his time, including Keynes's *General Theory of Employment, Interest, and Money* (1936), the work of the poet Ezra Pound and books by the science fiction writer Robert Heinlein. He died in 1952.

Ian Fraser, Baron Fraser of Lonsdale: in bounden duty and service

Ian Fraser, Lord Fraser of Lonsdale, was another of the great humanitarians of the twentieth century, thanks to his formidably stoic response to the tragedy he suffered on the Western Front in 1916. Among his many life awards, he was made an honorary life member of the Savage Club.

Early life and First World War

Fraser was born in 1897 in Eastbourne, England. He spent his early years in South Africa where his father was a successful businessman. He was sent back to England for his education, and attended St Cyprian's School, Eastbourne, and Marlborough College.

Following the outbreak of war, he went to Sandhurst and was later commissioned as a captain in the King's Shropshire Light Infantry. After a year with a reserve battalion he was sent to France in 1916. On 23 July 1916, during the Battle of the Somme, he was hit in the head by a German bullet. He was sent back to England and, when his bandages were removed in hospital, it was discovered that he had been completely blinded. The bullet had entered the edge of his right eyebrow, traversed the front of his face behind his nose, and then exited through his left cheek bone.

Over half a century later, in the final year of his life, Fraser reflected that he had managed to avoid regret for his blindness, with one exception:[19]

> I have, in fact, always had one regret and that is that my War Service was so brief—only a few weeks.[20]
>
> Having gone to Sandhurst when I was just 17 and spent a year there, probably one of the happiest years of my life, and then, still being too young to go to the War, having spent nearly another year with my reserve battalion in Pembroke Dock and the beautiful countryside surrounding it, I felt I was a useful young officer and that a wise army would have sent me to some quiet War in Mesopotamia or some other place like that. If they had done this, after a year or two I would have been of infinite (sic) more value because I would have had some experience and they would not have wasted my young life.
>
> There were three boys of my age who went with me from Sandhurst to fight in France. We all belonged to the Kings Shropshire Light Infantry though none of us ever served with that Regiment as on our arrival in France in the early months of 1916, we were sent to the First/Fourth Gloucesters who were short of Subalterns.
>
> Incidentally, I led my Platoon over the top of our trenches to attack the German Lines and so did my friends. Each of us were wearing an Officer's Jacket with a shirt and tie, whereas the N.C.O.'s and Privates wore tunics which buttoned right up to the neck. Thus it was easy for the Germans with a telescopic lens to pick out the Officers and shoot them one after the other and this they did. Of course, we did the same thing to them, but we learned much too late. Very soon after the Somme Battle, Officers wore ordinary tunics and webbing equipment so that they could not be so easily distinguished.

Post-war career

Sir Arthur Pearson, the Chairman of St Dunstan's (now Blind Veterans UK), the independent charity for blind servicemen and women, wrote Fraser a letter explaining how he had gone blind in middle life and how he had tried to make the best of it. He invited Fraser to go to St Dunstan's, which Fraser accepted. (The letter had been delivered to Fraser by Irene 'Chips' Mace, whom Fraser later married.) He also gave Fraser a braille watch. Fraser later said:[21]

---

19 The extract is from a manuscript which Fraser had begun writing in 1974 but had completed only 28 pages by his death. The papers went undiscovered for many years after his death, but are now online, https://www.blindveterans.org.uk/articles/battle-of-the-somme-and-sir-ian-frasers-memoir/.

20 The word is garbled in his manuscript: it could be 'years' but since he was injured so soon on the Western Front, and was referring specifically to war rather than his army service in general, I assume he meant 'weeks'.

21 'Battle of the Somme and Sir Ian Fraser's memoir', Blind Veterans UK, https://www.blind

I held the watch in my hand and felt the face with my thumb. For the first time since I was wounded I was able to tell the time.

The value of the watch to me far exceeded its usefulness. That in itself was considerable, for you to tend to want to know the time often when you are in permanent darkness, and have no means of distinguishing even night from day. Of course, in hospital, one could always ask. But that was the whole point. With this watch I did not have to ask anyone. I would never have to ask again. I was able to do it myself.

In 1921, Pearson died and Fraser took over as chairman of St Dunstan's. He was only 24, but went on to perform the role with distinction for 52 years. In 1922, he received the CBE (Commander of the Most Excellent Order of the British Empire). In the same year he entered politics as a member of the London County Council.

In 1924, he became MP for St Pancras North, as a member of the Conservative Party. He lost the seat in 1929 but regained it in 1931.

In 1934, he received a knighthood for his work in developing St Dunstan's, and in 1936 he was appointed a governor of the BBC. At the time governors were not permitted to be MPs, so Fraser resigned his seat in parliament.

When the Second World War began, Fraser wrote a book entitled *Whereas I was Blind* in anticipation of other soldiers being blinded in combat. In 1940, an Act of Parliament was introduced which allowed certain people to be MPs and hold office in the BBC in the public interest during the war. Fraser was therefore able to stand for parliament again. He was elected for Lonsdale in 1940 and held the seat until 1958.

Fraser also held several seats on commercial companies, following on from his father's successful business career. He was made an honorary life member of the Savage Club in 1948.[22]

In 1953 he was made a Companion of Honour. In 1958, he became Baron Fraser of Lonsdale, the first ever life peer, created under the Macmillan government's Life Peerages Act 1958.

He died in 1974, aged 77. Lord Redcliffe-Maud said at the service of Thanksgiving held in Westminster Abbey:

> I will lift up mine eyes unto the hills. Therefore, indeed we would if we have eyes to lift. However, the achievement of Ian Fraser's life can be summed up like this; he lifted up the loss of his eyes, in bounden duty

---

veterans.org.uk/articles/battle-of-the-somme-and-sir-ian-frasers-memoir/.

22 There had been an earlier instance of a notable blind individual being granted honorary life membership: in 1942, the actor Esmond Knight was granted that status. He had been blinded while serving on board HMS *Prince of Wales* when she engaged the German battleship *Bismarck* in the ill-fated Battle of the Denmark Strait in 1941, in which HMS *Hood* was sunk within minutes of the battle starting. He recovered some sight in one eye after two years.

and service, day by day for nearly 60 years of his 77 years of life. That living sacrifice was accepted and made creative of great good. It has put new heart into tens of thousands of the sightless (and the sighted) that came within its influence, and nothing will stop the good work now. It would never be the same if Lord Fraser had not lived and learnt the mystery of the road of Suffering.

In 1976, a memorial plaque was placed in the West Cloister of Westminster Abbey, with the following inscription:

IAN FRASER Baron Fraser of Lonsdale CH.CBE 1897–1974 Blinded in the Battle of the Somme in 1916, for half a century he served his country in both Houses of Parliament, championed the cause of ex-service men and women and inspired the blind of many nations by his leadership as Chairman of St Dunstan's.

CHAPTER 12

Royal Savages

Introduction

Despite its name, and its reputation for not putting on airs, the Savage Club has long had a link with royalty, going back to the very beginnings of the Club, and over the years has had the distinction of no fewer than four future kings of England chairing house dinners.

Monarchs are precluded by constitutional convention from joining clubs, while the monarch when the Savage Club began in 1857 was precluded by the Savage's own constitution anyway, given her gender. Nevertheless, in 1860, with the Club barely three years old, Queen Victoria attended a charity performance by theatrical Savages at the Lyceum Theatre. The show was put on to raise money for Savage widows and orphans. It returned the substantial sum of £364 and was considered such a success that Victoria asked if the players might do a repeat performance in Liverpool for the relief of the Lancashire unemployed. They did so, and raised £1,500 on that occasion.

On 11 July 1883, the Savage Club Entertainment and Costume Ball took place at the Royal Albert Hall – the first ever ball held at that venue. It was attended by the Prince and Princess of Wales (the future Edward VII and Queen Alexandra), and attendees enjoyed a champagne supper with 'a midnight performance of the Buffalo Dance by club members dressed in Native American costumes.'[1]

In June 1907, a charity matinee was put on by the Savage Club at His Majesty's

---

1   Liz Harper, 'Having a Ball at the Royal Albert Hall', Albert Hall website, 3 December 2013, https://www.royalalberthall.com/about-the-hall/news/2013/december/having-a-ball-at-the-royal-albert-hall/.

Theatre in London, again before the Prince and Princess of Wales, in aid of The Lord Mayor's Crippled Children Fund.

The more formal link between Savages and the royal family began in 1882, when the Prince of Wales was elected an honorary life member on the occasion of the Club's twenty-fifth anniversary dinner.[2] He remained a member until his accession to the throne in 1901. His mother was not wholly taken with his membership, any more than she had been by his various other antics. Edward was a serial gambler and philanderer, both of which helped land him an unwanted role in the Royal Baccarat Scandal (sometimes called the 'Tranby Croft Affair' after the country house in which it took place, it was the leading society trial of its day[3]). He also belonged to White's and the Turf Club, both of which were rather less unacceptable to Victoria, given their establishment reputation.[4]

Subsequently Edward's son, the future George V, followed in his father's footsteps by becoming an honorary member while he was Prince of Wales from 1901 to 1910. In turn, two of his sons, Edward (from 1919 until 1936, when he became Edward VIII) and Bertie (from 1928 until becoming George VI later in 1936), were notable members. Later royal Savages included the Duke of Gloucester[5] (an honorary life member from 1944 until his death), Earl Mountbatten (from 1947 until his death in 1979), Prince Philip (from 1953)[6] and the present Duke of York, Prince Andrew (an honorary life member from 1999).

Among the Club's mementos of royal attendance over the years is a section of the former interior wall containing some royal graffiti – a more appropriately Savage reminder perhaps than the royal trinkets and paintings which are also found scattered around the Clubroom.

Returning to the much darker times of the First World War, the royal family's German antecedents and German name Saxe-Coburg-Gotha proved problematic as anti-German feeling rose. Eventually, in 1917, they changed their surname to Windsor. Meanwhile, George V and other members of the family made sure to visit the Front whenever they could, as we will now see.

---

2   His speech on the occasion was reproduced in Norgate and Wykes, op cit, pp 17–18. A portrait of him by Alfred Praca hung in the Savage entrance area at the time of writing; it was presented to the Club by Sir William P Treloar Bart.

3   See my book *Trials & Tribulations* (Wildy, Simmonds & Hill, 2015), Ch 1.

4   Christopher Hibbert, *Edward VII: The Last Victorian King* (Palgrave Macmillan, 2007), p 74.

5   Prince Henry, Duke of Gloucester (1900–1974), the third son of George V and Queen Mary.

6   At the time of writing Prince Philip had not been seen at the Savage bar for some years. Things were different in the Carlton House days of the Club, when Philip was apparently a semi-regular. I am told that a Club wit once announced loudly in his direction just before 11pm, 'Right, closing time – everyone back to your place old boy!' The Duke reputedly put his head in his hands and groaned 'She'd kill me.' But he was well enough disposed to the Club to ask them to represent him in a tiddly-winks competition against Cambridge University in 2008, a clear indication that he retained fond memories of his Savage days. See https://www.cam.ac.uk/news/royal-match-of-tiddlywinks.

Edward VIII: from the Western Front to abdication

Undoubtedly the most controversial member of the Royal Family in the twentieth century, Edward VIII's abdication and subsequent life are well enough known not to require a detailed exposition here. Less well known is the fact that Edward volunteered for duty the moment the First World War broke out and served creditably in the limited capacity he was permitted.

Early life and First World War

Edward Albert Christian George Andrew Patrick David Saxe-Coburg-Gotha, known to his family as 'David', was born in June 1894, the eldest son of the future George V[7] and Queen Mary.[8] Following the usual convention, he became Duke of Cornwall when his father ascended to the throne in 1910, and Prince of Wales later the same year upon his sixteenth birthday.

He served for a short time in the Royal Navy, including as midshipman for three months aboard the battleship HMS *Hindustan*, before going up to Oxford. He did not prosper academically, at least partially because of a lack of preparation, though he enjoyed learning to play polo. Eventually he left Oxford after only eight terms, without a degree.

After Oxford he returned to the military, and took a commission in the Grenadier Guards in June 1914. Upon the outbreak of war, he immediately expressed his desire to fight at the Front. He dismissed the risk of being killed, saying it did not matter as he had four brothers. Lord Kitchener forbade him from frontline action nevertheless, reasoning that it would be too great a propaganda coup for the Germans if Edward was captured.

The same dilemma has applied to later royals as well. Prince Andrew was able to serve as a helicopter pilot during the Falklands war. Perhaps there was little chance of him being captured in that capacity, but there was certainly a risk of him being killed, since he was based aboard HMS *Invincible*, one of the two aircraft carriers which formed the most highly prized targets for the Argentine Air Force. The government had some nerves about his deployment, but the Queen insisted he serve, reasoning it was unthinkable for a member of the royal family to shirk from the same danger all other members of the armed forces were undertaking in her name. Andrew went on to gain the respect of his colleagues for his diligent service in the conflict.[9]

---

7   George V at the time of his own birth was the second and eldest-surviving son of the Prince and Princess of Wales (later King Edward VII and Queen Alexandra).

8   Mary was the eldest child and only daughter of the Duke and Duchess of Teck.

9   The Sea Harrier pilot Nigel 'Sharkey' Ward wrote: 'His Royal Highness Prince Andrew was embarked as a helicopter pilot in Ralph's squadron, 820. When at sea or with his squadron ashore he was treated very much on merit as a pilot and junior officer. And there was no doubt that he was an excellent pilot and a very promising officer. To make life easy for everyone, he

In the twenty-first century, however, Prince Harry was prevented from going to Iraq whilst serving with the Blues and Royals. He did manage to serve for a time secretly in Afghanistan, but was withdrawn when news of his deployment was made public, on the basis that his presence there heightened the risk for those serving with him. He was able to return in a different capacity later.

It seems to me that there was some justification in each war for not wanting to hand the enemy a propaganda coup in the form of a dead or captured royal, but that should have been outweighed by the need for the royals to be seen taking the same risk as ordinary soldiers. That, certainly, was the view of Andrew and Harry themselves: Harry repeatedly expressed his great frustration at being withdrawn from the frontline.

Returning to Edward and the Great War, he tried hard to serve as best he could in the face of Kitchener's restriction, and visited the frontline regularly. In the spring of 1916, he spent six weeks in Egypt inspecting the defences at the Suez Canal, before returning to France, where he joined the staff of XIV Corps on the Somme where he served as a staff officer. Upon hearing of the Battle of Jutland, in which his brother participated, he wrote to his father's equerry saying 'I'm so glad old Bertie was in the fight as it will buck him up a lot; and it seems to have cured him of the slight return of his old complaint which was a d-d (sic) bore as I really hoped he was cured once and for all!!'[10] – the last part being an unkind reference to Albert's famous stutter.

In the King's Birthday Honours in June 1916, Edward was awarded the Military Cross, though he subsequently conceded 'I can't say I feel I have earned the MC at all, but that's nothing to do with me!'[11] He added that he was finding life near Ypres dull and monotonous. Later in life he rarely wore the MC.

It is indeed hard to see how Edward would have been able to fulfil the MC requirement of 'an act or acts of exemplary gallantry during active operations against the enemy on land' when he could not go over the top with his fellow guardsmen. That said, he was not free from danger during his visits to the Front. On one occasion, a German shell struck his car and killed the driver only minutes after the Edward had left it to inspect the troops. Moreover, the restriction on his service was not his fault and he seems to have done the best he could to contribute to the war effort. As seen in Chapter 7, he gained the respect of Chesney Allen, a private soldier during the war. And his actions outside wartime showed that

---

was content to be referred to as 'H' by fellow officers on board, and became very popular not only within 820 but also in 821.' See Commander 'Sharkey' Ward, DSC, AFC, NR, *Sea Harrier over the Falklands: A Maverick at War* (Leo Cooper, 1992, Kindle edn). Note that Ward was no establishment toady: his book was highly critical of senior naval officers, the entire RAF and various others who crossed his path.

10 Gordon Rayner, 'Edward VIII admitted he did not feel he had earned his Military Cross, letters reveal', *Daily Telegraph*, 30 March 2016.

11 Gordon Rayner, op cit.

he had physical courage and a taste for danger: he rode in steeplechases until he suffered a bad fall and his father forbade him to continue competing. He also learned to fly in an age when it was a far more dangerous activity than in the present.

By August of 1916, the Battle of the Somme was raging, and Edward wrote:[12]

> There's the hell of a battle going on here just now and this corps took Guillemont yesterday, tho it was only part of a huge battle in which 6 corps took park. Of course our casualties are fearful tho the Huns are not enjoying it at all and we got 400 prisoners (17 officers!!) all glad to be captured!!
>
> But [the Germans] are stout-hearted devils and no mistake every hard of ground has to be fought for!! But ours and the French shelling is more than they can stomach; it's the nearest approach to hell imaginable tho. They hat (sic) us up all night still!!

The XIV Corps fought at Ypres in 1917 and in November in Italy. In 1918 Edward returned to France.

Later years and controversy

After the war, he continued with the usual royal duties as Prince of Wales. As all readers will know, he became king upon the death of his father on 20 January 1936, but abdicated in December 1936 in order to marry the American divorcee Wallis Simpson. Thereafter he became the Duke of Windsor, where he encountered more controversy in various contexts, being labelled a Nazi appeaser and effectively exiled from the royals and consequently Britain as well. During the Second World War, he managed to escape from Europe and was sent out of sight and mind to Bermuda, where he served as governor, not wholly to his enjoyment.

Nowadays, with the stigma of divorce having mostly vanished, the chief source of controversy concerning his life is his appeasement. I would note that among his pronouncements on the subject, one can have a degree of sympathy for the speech he gave in May 1939 from the fields of Verdun, the scene of one of the worst of all First World War battles:[13]

> I am deeply conscious of the presence of the great company of the dead, and I am convinced that could they make their voices heard they would be with me in what I am about to say. I speak simply as a soldier of the Last War whose most earnest prayer it is that such cruel and destructive madness shall never again overtake mankind. There is no land whose people want war.

---

12 Letter dated 2 September 1916, held by the Imperial War Museum.
13 Verdun to the present day remains one of the best-preserved Great War battlefields; it would have been a shocking reminder of the war to any Western Front veteran in 1939 when the Duke visited.

It is, however, not the place here to deal with those matters or the rest of his life until his death in 1972. Whatever view one takes of his various controversies, we can say that Edward deserves credit for donning his country's uniform and doing as much as he was permitted during the Great War.

George VI: the man who would be king

George VI is remembered nowadays for unexpectedly ascending to the throne following Edward's abdication in 1936, for his calm leadership of the nation during the Second World War, and for being the father to Britain's longest-serving monarch, Elizabeth II. As a very young man, he served in the Royal Navy during the Great War and took part in the Battle of Jutland, before joining the Savage Club in his last relatively carefree years.

Early life

George was born Albert Frederick Arthur George Saxe-Coburg-Gotha at Sandringham on 14 December 1895, the second son of the future King George V and Queen Mary. His birthday was the thirty-fourth anniversary of the death of Prince Albert, his great-grandfather, and his Christian name of Albert was chosen as a tribute. He was soon nicknamed 'Bertie'.

From an early age, he developed a stammer and was not especially physically well, suffering chronic stomach problems and being forced to wear corrective splints for his knock knees. In 1909, aged just 13, he attended the Royal Naval College, Osborne, on the Isle of Wight. He did not excel in his studies but nevertheless went on to attend the naval college at Dartmouth.

In 1913, he served on the training ship HMS *Cumberland*, sailing in both the Atlantic and in the Mediterranean. He was promoted to the rating of midshipman and held that rank when the First World War broke out.

First World War

During the First World War, his most notable action was serving as a sub-lieutenant commanding the forward turret of HMS *Collingwood*, a St Vincent-class dreadnought.

Collingwood was armed with 5 twin 12-inch guns and 20 single 4-inch guns, meaning she was not in the first order of dreadnoughts of the day, which were armed with 15-inch guns. *Collingwood* was nevertheless included in Jellicoe's Grand Fleet during the Battle of Jutland and was the eighteenth ship from the head of the battle line.

In the main part of the battle, when the Grand Fleet met the High Seas Fleet and crossed its 'T', *Collingwood* fired eight salvos from her main guns at the crippled light cruiser SMS *Wiesbaden*, though it is not known how many hit. Her secondary armament then engaged the destroyer SMS *G42,* which was trying to assist *Wiesbaden,* but scored no hits. *Collingwood* later fired two salvoes of high explosive shells at the battlecruiser SMS *Derfflinger,* scoring one hit before visibility was lost. Finally, *Collingwood* fired at the German destroyer attack at around 7:20 pm in the battle, but scored no hits. She managed to dodge two torpedoes fired by German destroyers at the same point in the action. Along with the rest of the Grand Fleet, that was the end of her participation in the battle as the Germans slipped away. She had fired a total of 52 shells from her main armament and 35 from her secondary, 4-inch guns during the battle.

Albert was mentioned in despatches for his part in the battle. He wrote afterwards:[14]

> I am quite all right and feel very different now that I have seen a German ship filled with Germans and have seen it fired at with our guns.
>
> It was a great experience to have gone through and one not easily forgotten. How and why we were not hit or damaged beats me, as we were being fired at a good part of the time.
>
> The ship ahead of us was hit but it did not do any damage. We had torpedoes fired at us which we got out of the way of luckily. It seems to have resulted in a victory for us ... the Germans must have suffered very severely as our ships were hitting very nearly all the time.

His tone can be seen to be much more sober than Edward's letters of the same period, reflecting both their different personalities and the fact that Albert genuinely was on the naval frontline – the navy being unique amongst the three services given that high ranking officers have the same risks as the lowest ratings when on the same ships.

Albert did not see any further action during the war. He suffered from a duodenal ulcer, for which he had an operation in November 1917. At the beginning of 1918, he was appointed officer in charge of boys at the Royal Naval Air Service's training establishment at Cranwell. When the Royal Air Force was formed shortly afterwards, it assumed responsibility for Cranwell and Albert transferred to the new service. He was appointed officer commanding Number 4 Squadron of the Boys' Wing at Cranwell. He held the position until August 1918, when he joined the RAF's Cadet School at St Leonards-on-Sea. He undertook two weeks' training and assumed command of a squadron on the Cadet Wing, becoming the first member of the British royal family to qualify as a pilot.

He hoped to serve on the Western Front before the war's conclusion, when he was posted to General Trenchard's staff. In late October 1918, he went to

---

14 Gordon Rayner, 'Edward VIII admitted he did not feel he had earned his Military Cross, letters reveal', *Daily Telegraph,* 30 March 2016.

Autigny and he served on the staff of the RAF's Independent Air Force at its headquarters in Nancy, France, though did not reach the frontline.

At the war's end, he stayed on as a staff officer for two months, accompanying Belgium's King Albert I on his triumphal return to Brussels on 22 November.

Later years

In July 1919, Albert qualified as an RAF pilot and was promoted to squadron leader the next day, though he soon curtailed his military service. Later the same year he went to Cambridge for a year to study history, economics and civics. He was created Duke of York in June 1920 and then started to take on more royal duties.

In those days he was handicapped by his stammer, which exacerbated his natural shyness. He started courting Lady Elizabeth Bowes-Lyon, the youngest daughter of the Earl and Countess of Strathmore and Kinghorne, in the early 1920s. She rejected his marriage proposal in 1921 and 1922, but eventually agreed and the couple were married in April 1923. They went on to have two children, Elizabeth (later Elizabeth II) and Margaret.

His closing speech at the British Empire Exhibition at Wembley in October 1925 was a crushing embarrassment because of his stammer. Thereafter, he engaged the services of Lionel Logue, an Australian-born speech therapist – an arrangement later made famous by the film *The King's Speech*. Logue had first developed his technique helping his fellow Australians who were suffering from stuttering induced by shell shock from the First World War. His efforts paid off as Albert made a much more confident speech in Canberra, Australia, during a tour of the Empire in 1927.

Albert's involvement with the Savage Club began in 1928 when he was guest of honour at a house dinner. He was elected an honorary life member of the Club at the same time. He clearly enjoyed his experience, since he returned to preside over the seventy-seventh annual dinner in 1934; the menu can now be seen framed on the wall in the entrance to the Club, near the Great War Memorial. Interestingly, Logue was also a member of the Savage Club – yet another example of the Savage Club rising above artificial social barriers.

In 1936, Albert was thrust into permanent limelight when his brother abdicated and he had to assume the role of king as George VI. He also had to resign his Savage Club membership in accordance with the normal protocol, though the Savages delighted in his coronation, reflecting the much higher royal sentiment of the day. Percy Bradshaw recorded that '[t]he Savage Club played its part in the rejoicing by holding a Coronation Party, which gave our members and their friends an opportunity to witness the procession, from Carlton House Terrace, as it passed along the Mall. Three hundred seats were erected, and our visitors also saw our new home *en fete*.'[15]

During the Second World War, George VI and Elizabeth resolved to stay in London despite German bombing raids. They gained much public respect for doing so, especially after Buckingham Palace was bombed. They were also (theoretically) subjected to the same rationing as others for food and fuel.

By the 1950s, George's health was suffering badly from a combination of the stress of the war years and his own heavy smoking. He died in February 1952 from a coronary thrombosis.

Earl Mountbatten: from junior snottie to Admiral of the Fleet

Lord Louis 'Dickie' Mountbatten achieved many high ranks during a long career in the Royal Navy, and held a number of important commands during the Second World War. He served as the last Viceroy of India, as that country was torn asunder by the bloodshed of partition. He is also remembered for the fact he was murdered along with some of his family and an innocent child bystander by the IRA in 1979, in one of the most shocking days of the Troubles. Before all those events, he too served as a very young man in the Great War.

Early life and First World War

Mountbatten was born Prince Louis of Battenberg in 1900, another great-grand-son of Queen Victoria. It was she who suggested his nickname of 'Nicky', but to avoid confusion with Nicholas II of Russia, he was called 'Dickie' instead. His father, also called Prince Louis of Battenberg, was born in Austria in 1854 and lived his early years in Italy and Germany, but had come to England aged 14 and joined the Royal Navy. He worked his way up to rear-admiral, and in 1912 was made First Sea Lord.

The following year, Dickie followed in his father's footsteps by joining the Royal Naval College. He was too young for active service when war broke out in 1914, but one of the key events in his life took place that year, when his father was unceremoniously removed from his post as First Sea Lord, principally due to xenophobic bias against his surname of Battenberg. Mountbatten later wrote:[16]

> All this was a form of hysteria which gripped people at that time. They insulted German governesses; they wouldn't listen to German music; they would even kick daschunds in the streets; they saw spies under every bed.

---

15 Bradshaw, op cit, p 114.
16 John Terraine, *The Life and Times of Lord Mountbatten* (Bloomsbury, 1968).

And the Press played this hysteria up and made it worse. Lord Haldane, the great War Minister who had reformed the Army only a few years earlier, was accused of being pro-German, hounded out of public life.

My father was attacked because of our German name. One paper even carried an attack on my father on one page, and on another a glowing report of the first death in action of a member of the Royal Family—his nephew, Prince Maurice of Battenberg, killed at Ypres, fighting in the 60th, the King's Royal Rifle Corps.

My father came to the conclusion that these attacks on him were damaging to the Navy. On October 29th 1914 he resigned from his post as First Sea Lord, and the Government, under duress, accepted his resignation.

'Dickie' felt the slight against his father desperately keenly. It helped forge his determination to succeed in his naval career and ascend to the post of First Sea Lord himself, in order to restore the family honour. It also gave his family the sympathy of the First Lord of the Admiralty, Winston Churchill, which was to come in handy much later in life. And it doubtless played a part in the decision of all the royals to change their surnames in 1917, when Saxe-Coburg-Gotha became Windsor and the Battenbergs became the Mountbattens.

During the war, Mountbatten first served as a midshipman on HMS *Lion*, which had served as Beatty's flagship at Jutland, though he only joined the ship after the battle. He said of his time on board:

I joined the *Lion* less than seven weeks after the Battle of Jutland. She was still under repair in Rosyth dockyard, and she was in a pretty good mess. There was a gaping hole where the centre turret had been, and cordite fires had left their marks all over her.

But the spirit of the ship's company was sky-high.

I was terribly disappointed to have missed the battle; my brother, in the *New Zealand*, had been in the thick of it, and, of course, everybody was talking about it.

I was tremendously excited to be in Beatty's flagship. I was one of his most ardent hero-worshippers—and he certainly looked every inch a hero ...

We thought the *Lion* was the greatest ship in the world, with the bravest men and the finest admiral.

Mountbatten wrote those recollections in the 1960s. I wonder what he himself saw as the parallels between his own life and career and that of his former commander and hero Beatty. Both were reckless with often disastrous results in wartime, both nevertheless always found a way to blame others for setbacks and somehow claim credit for anything that looked like success, and both profited in career terms from their relationship with Winston Churchill. On shore, both were married to extremely wealthy women whose money enabled them to move in the social circles which they craved, and both of their marriages involved a great deal of adultery for all concerned. On the other hand, Jellicoe may have left a more lasting impression on Mountbatten, teaching him the need for the highest officers to understand naval technology, and imparting a sense of professionalism, attention to detail and an interest in the wellbeing of the lower decks.

All that was far in the future when Mountbatten – still Battenberg at that stage – was serving on the *Lion*. It seems life on board resembled that of the public schools of the day, with harsh privations and institutional bullying. Mountbatten explained:

> I had just turned sixteen when I joined as a midshipman. In some respects conditions were not very different from those of Nelson's days. The midshipmen slept in hammocks, which we slung wherever we could find a space—we had no proper quarters of our own. By the time I came along, all the best billets were taken. I had to sling my hammock under a police-light, which was never switched off; it was just a few inches above my face. I got used to sleeping with a handkerchief over my eyes.
>
> On Sunday mornings we were called at 4 am. We had to scrub out the Mess, polish the bright-work and get everything ship-shape. One of my jobs was to look after the leather settees; on one occasion, when I failed to have one of the seams sewn up, I was beaten.
>
> That was the traditional gun-room treatment of midshipmen—'snotties', as we were called. For instance, at meals, if the sub-lieutenant of the Mess stuck his fork into the beam above him all the junior snotties had to clear out; the last one got beaten. Or if the Sub said, "Breadcrumbs", all the junior snotties had to block their ears. If he then quietly said: "All right, Battenberg, *you* can listen" and you took your fingers out, showing that you *had* been listening, you got beaten.
>
> This happened the whole time; it was barbaric, I suppose, but we expected it. However, the whole thing got so bad that it had to be stopped by Admiral Beatty himself—so I was probably one of the last to go through it.
>
> But naval life in general was tough and tiring in those days. Take coaling, for instance, a chore which vanished many years ago. The *Lion* was a coal-burning ship. This meant that whenever we came in from a sweep we had to coal ship. That was an exhausting, filthy business, because the coal had to be dug out of the holds of the colliers, bagged, transported to the *Lion*, then re-distributed in her holds. The whole ship's company took part in this; no one was excused. It would take from ten to twelve hours and one became absolutely encrusted in coal-dust from head to foot. The junior snotties, I might add, only had small tin baths to wash it all off in afterwards; it hung about one for days.

When Mountbatten's brother George was transferred to the *Lion*, he himself was sent to the battleship HMS *Queen Elizabeth*, pursuant to the policy of brothers not serving on the same ship.[17] With not much fighting to be done, since the German High Seas Fleet was resolutely avoiding a reprise of Jutland, Mountbatten spent some time creating and editing a shipboard magazine. The magazine further raised his profile on board and in the service generally – already much higher than any other junior snottie, thanks to his father – although the consensus seems to be that he did not distinguish himself with his literary ability.

In July 1918, he paid a short visit to the Western Front, which struck home severely when he contrasted the scenes there with those in the navy. 'Now I was really able to understand about war on land – what the casualty lists really meant, and the horrors of the conditions in which those enormous numbers of men were fighting and dying.'[18] He also spent two months as a senior midshipman aboard the submarine *K6*, which fired his enthusiasm for the 'Silent Service', not least because he reasoned it was the only part of the navy actually fighting the otherwise absent Germans at sea. His father advised him to spend time on a small surface vessel before going permanently into submarines. Thus, in October 1918, just before the war's end, Mountbatten was made second-in-command of HMS *P31*, one of 44 of the 'P' Class small patrol vessels – an impressive achievement for someone still in his teens. He received solid endorsements from his commanding officers during the conflict.[19]

Later years

The rest of Mountbatten's life is much too complex to do it justice here. He briefly attended Cambridge, where he was undistinguished academically, and even 'suspected of Labour Party sympathies'. Otherwise, he ingratiated himself further in the establishment as he steadily climbed the ranks both of the Royal Navy and the royal family. His royal connections no doubt helped save him from the 'Geddes Axe'; the cutbacks in naval staff that followed wartime demobilisation.[20]

He reached the rank of captain between the wars. During the Second World War, he ascended the ranks in quite an extraordinary fashion, beginning as a destroyer captain, becoming chief of Combined Operations and ending as supreme Allied commander South East Asia Command (SEAC) with promotion to acting full admiral – despite the fact that (i) his reckless command led to

---

17 The United States had the same policy in the Second World War, but did not enforce it rigorously, meaning that the five Sullivan brothers famously all perished on board the light cruiser USS *Juneau* during the Guadalcanal campaign in 1942.
18 Adrian Smith, *Mountbatten: Apprentice War Lord 1900–1943*.
19 Philip Ziegler, *Mountbatten: The Official Biography* (HarperCollins, 1985; my copy was published by Book Club Associates), p 47.
20 The axe was wielded by Sir Eric Campbell Geddes, who, as we saw earlier, had dispensed with Jellicoe during the First World War.

his destroyers being torpedoed; (ii) at Combined Operations he presided over the Dieppe disaster;[21] and (iii) in the Far East the true military genius responsible for the great victories over Japan was General William Slim, arguably the finest British general of the war. But Mountbatten's royal connections, seemingly limitless ambition and energy, and excellent diplomatic skills secured him senior post after senior post.

After the war he would have preferred to resume his naval career, but was instead installed by the Attlee government as Viceroy of India, with the critical task of overseeing the transition to independence. The resulting partition of India was accompanied by much bloodshed when fanatical religious and tribal differences manifested themselves in the slaughter of those who found themselves on the 'wrong side' of the border.

Once again, Mountbatten applied his two-pronged if inherently contradictory strategy of first blaming everyone else and then asserting that the outcome had been, if not what one could call a 'success', then at least the best possible in difficult circumstances.[22] Ultimately, his reputation was saved by the fact that there were few hard facts about the scale of the post-partition slaughter back in Britain. He could also dismiss any criticism of his actions as counter-factual speculation.[23]

After returning from India, Mountbatten was able to restart his naval career, and he managed to achieve his ultimate ambition of securing his father's old role of First Sea Lord.

---

21 Dieppe was a cross-Channel raid in 1942 intended to seize and hold the town for a short while, to 'singe the Führer's moustache' (a riff on the old saying 'singeing the King of Spain's beard' from much earlier times). It was hoped to show the Russians that the British were harrying the Germans, and to act as a dress rehearsal for the eventual Allied invasion of France. In fact the Allies – British and Canadian – were shot to pieces and the RAF came off much worse than the Luftwaffe in the skies above. Much debate ensued at the time and since about responsibility; since Mountbatten was in charge as chief of Combined Operations, I do not know how he ever escaped full responsibility.

22 Among the casualties of the pro-Mountbatten narrative was Sir Cyril Radcliffe, who headed the commission drawing up the boundary. He was ridiculed for never having been east of Paris before taking the job. Yet Radcliffe himself was under no illusions. He asked for two years to undertake the task; he was given 40 days, Mountbatten not being prepared to countenance any delay. So Radcliffe did what he could in the time he had, and even then was subject to Mountbatten's meddling. It emerged many years after the event that Mountbatten had interfered with the commission to ensure that Ferozepur and Zira went to India, when they should have been part of Pakistan since they were largely Muslim. See the documentary *Secret Lives: Mountbatten* (Tim Shawcross (dir), 1995), in which Mountbatten's official biographer Philip Ziegler admitted that he would have to revise his opinion of Mountbatten (downwards) on the basis of his interference with the Radcliffe Commission.

23 One is left wondering, though, if there really was nothing Mountbatten could have done differently at the time to at least reduce the amount of death and destruction that followed. Certainly, Tory grandees of the day privately blamed Mountbatten: Eden thought him a 'congenital liar' and RAB Butler held him responsible for a million deaths. See Andrew Roberts, *Eminent Churchillians* (Weidenfeld & Nicolson, 2010, Kindle edn).

In his retirement, Mountbatten enjoyed honorary membership of the Savage Club and belonged to no fewer than 16 clubs in total. He was the guest of honour in the first house dinner of the 1950s, with Sidney Strube in the chair – there could be no more appropriately Savage combination than a former sergeant instructor chairing a dinner with the Admiral of the Fleet, with no-one batting an eyelid, since the erstwhile sergeant happened to be an artistic genius and thus the archetypal Savage. It also somewhat belied the rumour that every time Mountbatten shook hands with anyone his eyes were gazing around the room in to check whether there was anyone more important in attendance (although there is no doubting the scale of Mountbatten's ambition or the ruthlessness with which he pursued it).[24]

Mountbatten was murdered by the IRA in August 1979, who seemed unaware that he had actually expressed support for a unified Ireland and had generally opposed British colonialism wherever he found it. Ironically, the terrible nature of the event ensured that Mountbatten received the fulsome tributes and uncritical praise which he craved.[25]

Nearly a year elapsed after Mountbatten's death before Richard Ingrams, then-editor of *Private Eye*, published a less flattering portrait of Mountbatten in *The Spectator*.[26] Later authors, including Mountbatten's official biographer Philip Ziegler,[27] then started to uncover the extent to which Mountbatten had tried to manipulate the public record all his life.[28] As with Edward VIII, however, it is right to record that Mountbatten's service as a junior rank during the Great War has never been impugned.

---

24 Andrew Roberts, *Eminent Churchillians*, op cit.
25 See for example *The Spectator*, 1 September 1979, pp 3, 6 and 9, http://archive.spectator.co.uk/article/1st-september-1979/3/the-last-viceroy.
26 Richard Ingrams, 'The Old Sea Dog', *The Spectator*, 28 June 1980.
27 Ziegler, op cit.
28 See for example Andrew Roberts, *Eminent Churchillians*, op cit. Ziegler wrote that at times he became so annoyed by what he saw as Mountbatten's attempts to hoodwink historians with filleting the historical record that he found it necessary to put a note on his desk reminding himself that, whatever he had done, Mountbatten was still a 'great man'.

CHAPTER 13

Savage Future Generals

Introduction

In this section we look at the First World War service of three Savage Club members who went on to become very senior leaders during the Second World War. Each became among the best-known Allied leaders in that conflict and indeed had successful careers spanning more than half of the twentieth century.

As with the royal Savages, no attempt is made here to cover their life achievements in any depth. Each has been the subject of detailed biographies, and there are literally hundreds of books on their campaigns in the Second World War. Instead, our focus is on the distinguished service all three gave when they were much more junior soldiers during the Great War.

Field Marshal Bernard Montgomery: Monty – 'in defeat, unbeatable, in victory, unbearable'

Field Marshal Bernard Law Montgomery, known as 'Monty', remains the most famous British general of the Second World War. He played centre stage in what one might call the 'Churchillian narrative' of that conflict. Generations after 1945 were told of his pivotal role in reversing the early failures of the war by delivering victory over the 'Desert Fox' Rommel at El Alamein, then supervising the masterly Operation Overlord (D-Day) followed by the race to Berlin, with the admitted hiccup on the way of Operation Market Garden (aka 'A Bridge too Far').

In recent years historians have been more measured in their assessment of Monty's part in those battles and the overall victory. As with Mountbatten, his gift for self-promotion has acted against him in later years as it has tended to make biographers inherently sceptical about his claims. What has never been disputed is Monty's personal courage and the fact that he led quite an extraordinary life. And that personal courage was never more evident than on the Western Front from 1914–18.

Early life

Monty was born in Kennington, Surrey in 1887, the fourth of nine children. His father was a Church of Ireland minister, of Ulster-Scots background who was working as vicar of St Mark's Church in Kennington at the time. For financial reasons, his father accepted an Empire posting in 1889 to Tasmania and took the family with him. Monty later recalled how his father was away travelling much of the time (not easy, one assumes, in the rugged parts of rural Tasmania even now, let alone in the late nineteenth century), leaving the children in their mother's sole care. She administered a brutal regime of beatings to the children – one lasting effect was that Monty refused to allow her any contact with his own son later in life, and did not attend her funeral when she died in 1949.

The family spent some time in England in 1897, enough for Monty to attend The King's School in Canterbury for a term. They moved back to England permanently in 1901. Monty was sent to St Paul's School in London and then to Sandhurst.

His time at Sandhurst – and with it his military career – almost came to an ignominious end: during the ragging of an unpopular cadet he set fire to the tail of the victim's shirt as he was undressing, and singed the man's buttocks. Monty narrowly escaped expulsion for his part in the unpleasant jape. Nevertheless, he graduated in 1908 and was commissioned into the 1st Battalion of the Royal Warwickshire Regiment as a second lieutenant. He was posted to India later that year. In 1910, he was promoted to lieutenant, and in 1912 was made adjutant of his regiment at Shorncliffe in Kent.

First World War

When the First World War began, Monty went to France almost immediately as part of the British Expeditionary Force. At the time, the Royal Warwickshires formed part of the 10th Brigade of the 4th Division. As would be the case in 1940, the small BEF soon found itself on the run from a fast and brutal German thrust through the Allied lines, the key objective being to avoid encirclement.

Early in its 1914 retreat, the BEF became split into two main forces: I Corps under General Haig and II Corps under General Smith-Dorrien. The 4th Division was part of the latter. Smith-Dorrien demanded rest for his troops when they arrived at the town of Le Cateau; the Germans ensured it would not be a peaceful pause.

On 26 August, according to Sir John French's orders, II Corps were supposed to be under way again at 7am. Smith-Dorrien, however, believed his troops were too exhausted, and decided to stay and make a stand. There were three problems. First, troops too tired to retreat were not going to be in proper fighting condition. Second, they had chosen Le Cateau for shelter, not to dig in and form a defensive line. Third, they were severely outnumbered. 'Thus between the villages of Ligny and Haucourt, west of Le Cateau, dawn of 26 August 1914 marked for Monty the beginning of his education in the cock-ups of real warfare.'[1] The battle began with an artillery duel and ended with a reduced British force continuing its retreat.

In the grim score-sheet familiar to accounts of all major Great War battles, Le Cateau constituted a clear German victory, since they suffered 2,900 casualties as against more than 7,000 British and, moreover, the British had been forced to flee the battlefield.

Some historians have maintained that the 1914 withdrawal of which Le Cateau formed a part was the performance of a well-trained and disciplined army, and have painted the French Army of the same period unfavourably in comparison.[2] One of Monty's most significant biographers, Nigel Hamilton, was having none of it:[3]

> The performance of the British Army at Le Cateau was characterized by both lack of communication and, where contact was made with higher HQs, a constant countermanding of orders. The 5th Division's artillery brigadier felt that to conceal one's field guns "lacked gallantry"; most of them were hit by German gunfire or captured. Infantry battalions had few machine-guns, no training in modern continental warfare, and command by "umpiring": issuing orders/directives, and leaving others to carry them out. The result at Le Cateau was a massacre. The 4th Division was stretched across a five-mile front, with 15,000 unsupplied and unfed troops, without divisional artillery, signal companies, engineers, ammunition or cavalry. It was small wonder they were pulverized.

In October, Monty took part in an Allied counter-attack at Méteren, near the Belgian border at Bailleul. By that stage the German advance had slowed and the British were moving to try to outflank the Germans. The action is sometimes misleadingly called the 'Race to the Sea', whereas the intention of both sides was to hook around behind the other, rather than to establish the line of trenches to the North Sea, even if that was what actually resulted.

On 13 October, Monty's battalion went into action. Unfortunately, they had

---

1   Nigel Hamilton, *1914: The Days of Hope* (Penguin, new edn 2014).
2   See for example Lyn Macdonald, *1914: The Last Days of Hope*.
3   Hamilton, op cit, p 56.

no proper artillery bombardment preceding them, and more than a hundred men were cut down as they advanced towards the Germans. Monty himself was badly wounded when he was shot in the lung and in the knee. He was assumed to be dead and believed that he only survived because a dead soldier had fallen on top of him, whom he could not move. His actions earned him the Distinguished Service Order, the citation for which referred to his 'Conspicuous gallant leading … when he turned the enemy out of their trenches with the bayonet' before receiving his wounds.[4]

After five days recovering in a French hospital, he returned to England to continue his convalescence. He later conceded that the experience of battle had been psychologically shattering as much as physically; any idealism about war had been well and truly blown away.

Monty spent seven weeks in hospital, and was given three months' leave upon discharge. When he was able to return to uniform, it was as a staff officer, even though he had yet to attend staff college. He was promoted to the rank of brigade major and given charge of the 104th Brigade, part of Kitchener's new armies – a role to which he was eminently suited:[5]

> [I]n a New Army, with no regimental bores, no class or caste distinctions to maintain and full freedom to act on behalf of his brigadier general, Monty could test and develop his own skills in command, communication and, above all, training …
>
> In other words, the misfit outsider became, for a brief time in World War I, a model insider, as he would a generation later, once given an army to command: decorated for bravery, highly competent, uninterested in preserving the traditional army hierarchy and zealous in his determination in 1915 to turn a 5,000 strong brigade of civilian volunteers from the Lancashire area into effective soldiers.

Monty returned to France in early 1916, when he was assigned to the 33rd Division. The division took part in the Battle of Arras, in which, as we saw in Chapter 6, participants included Herbert 'Beb' Asquith.

Later in 1917, Monty became a general staff officer serving with IX Corps in the British Second Army under General Sir Herbert Plumer.[6] He finished the

---

4   *The London Gazette*, 1 December 1914, p 10188.

5   Hamilton, op cit, p 74.

6   Sir Herbert Plumer (1857–1932) was one of the most senior British officers during the Great War. His achievements included leading the Second Army to a major victory over the Germans in June 1917 at the Battle of Messines, which began with the famous mines exploding under the German lines after being placed there by the Royal Engineers' tunnelling experts, drawing upon the knowledge gained from building the London Underground. The noise of the explosions was heard in London.

After the war, he served as governor of Malta and later high commissioner of the British Mandate for Palestine.

war as general staff officer grade 1 with the temporary rank of lieutenant-colonel – all in all, a proud record indeed in the conflict.

Later career and Second World War

During the inter-war years Monty fought in the Irish Civil War. Like Roberts and Kitchener in South Africa, his approach was one of a professional soldier sent to win a conflict, not a politician seeking to mediate between factions or negotiate a compromise agreement. After the conflict, however, Monty took a realistic view of the ending:[7]

> I consider that Lloyd George was right in what he did [granting Eire independence], if we had gone on we could probably have squashed the rebellion as a temporary measure, but it would have broken out again like an ulcer the moment we removed the troops. I think the rebels would probably [have] refused battles, and hidden their arms etc. until we had gone.

In reaching that conclusion, Monty recognised exactly what would plague the Americans in Vietnam half a century later, and the British and Americans in Afghanistan and Iraq almost a century later.

He continued to rise through the ranks of the army in the inter-war years. When the Second World War began, he went to Belgium with the BEF, commanding the 3rd Infantry Division. In 1940, his division was commended for withdrawing to Dunkirk with order and discipline,[8] though Monty rubbished the wider Allied effort in that first phase of the war as a 'dog's breakfast'. One can imagine after his experience at Le Cateau it would have been exceptionally tedious for Monty to find himself involved in another swift rout by the Germans at the start of a continental war.

Nevertheless, as mentioned, he went on to become the best-known British general of the war, leading the Eighth Army to victory in the Western Desert and then commanding British forces from D-Day to Berlin. His leadership was characterised by outstanding organisational skills, an unflinching will, and superb oratory in front of his troops – the latter being a valuable commodity for soldiers whose morale had suffered terribly from a series of reverses at the hands of the Germans.

In the course of the war, however, Monty fell out with badly with the overall American commander (and future US president) Dwight D Eisenhower, as well as some British colleagues including Air Marshal Tedder. He avoided dismissal

---

7   William Sheehan, *British Voices: From the Irish War of Independence 1918–1921: the Words of British Servicemen who Were There* (Collins Press, 2005), pp 151–152.

8   See for example Walter Lord, *The Miracle of Dunkirk* (Viking Press, 1999) and Julian Thompson, *Dunkirk: Retreat to Victory* (Pan Macmillan, 2010).

because he had, in modern parlance, become 'too big to fail' – after El Alamein he had been hailed throughout the Allied countries as a conquering hero, Britain's answer to the 'Desert Fox' Rommel, and he received banner headlines as the commander of the successful D-Day invasion of 6 June 1944. At a social function with George VI in 1944, chief of the imperial general staff, Sir Alan Brooke, revealed that every time he met Monty he feared Monty was after his job. George replied: 'You should worry, when I meet him, I always think he's after mine.' Churchill himself said of Monty: 'In defeat, unbeatable, in victory, unbearable' and, after learning of Monty's habit of inviting defeated German generals to dine with him, groaned that no worse fate could befall an enemy officer. More seriously, the charge against Monty was that he was too egotistical for his own good,[9] that he took credit for the work of others in successful operations but lumped the blame elsewhere whenever anything went wrong, and that he persistently failed to take objectives (especially in Europe) for which he had demanded scarce resources and made extravagant predictions which he failed to make good.

Again, those controversies are for another time. I would simply observe that unreasonable times demand unreasonable men. No one ever won a military medal for being sensible and proportionate; medals have always been awarded to those who recklessly disregard their own safety. Nor have many wars been won by anyone acting in moderation. The ultimate verdict is that Monty finished on the winning side or, to use a cricketing analogy, his team had the runs on the board.

Unfortunately, it is more difficult to defend Monty's conduct after the Second World War. He advised Attlee to strip-mine Africa of her resources, reasoning that Africans were savages in the wrong sense, incapable of managing their own affairs.[10] Having insulted an entire continent, he then raised the bar even further with his memoirs, published in 1958,[11] in which he was disobliging about his enemies (the Italians), his fellow British generals (including Auchinleck) and his allies (the Americans). In response, an Italian officer challenged him to a duel, Auchinleck threatened a libel suit, and the President of the United States held a conference at Camp David to discuss how to destroy Monty's credibility.

---

9   A classic example of Monty's self-importance was when he won a bet with an American general, who had promised him a B-17 Flying Fortress if he managed to take an objective. Monty insisted the Americans pay up when he won, though they had thought it was a joke. Monty took it as far as Eisenhower, and enjoyed his chauffeured strategic bomber until the campaign shifted to Sicily, where the airfields were too short.

10 Colin Baxter, *Field Marshal Bernard Law Montgomery, 1887–1976: A Selected Bibliography* (Greenwood Press, 1999), pp 125, 129.

11 Viscount Montgomery, *The Memoirs of Field-Marshal the Viscount Montgomery of Alamein, KG* (World Publishing Company, 1958).

    Monty's papers for the Africa campaign can be found in Stephen Brooks, *Montgomery and the Eighth Army: a selection from the diaries, correspondence and other papers of Field Marshal the Viscount Montgomery of Alamein, August 1942 to December 1943* (Bodley Head for the Army Records Society, 1991).

Monty wrote favourable articles about apartheid South Africa and spoke badly of Jews (although he had worked well with Emanuel Shinwell when the latter was secretary of state for war).[12] To complete a trifecta of views that would offend modern readers, he opposed legalisation of homosexuality, though some later writers have suggested Monty was a repressed homosexual himself[13] like many a homophobe before and since.

He was able to express all those views because he had developed a media profile later in life. It was most unfortunate: there was no reason to solicit his opinion on race relations or sexual orientation, since he had no expertise, authority or originality on either subject. Instead, he was being wheeled out as a real-life Blimp or, closer to his time, the character of General Denson at the end of Lindsay Anderson's 1968 film *If...*, who ranted to the schoolchildren about the importance of old fashioned values before being gunned down by the rebellious lead characters. Even those wholly opposed to his views found sympathy for Monty himself for the unnecessary media humiliation.[14]

Monty was, therefore, yet another person who outlived his time. We should add, however, that he was not wrong about everything after the war. Notably, he correctly told the Americans their Vietnam adventure was folly, while during the twenty-fifth anniversary commemoration of Alamein in Egypt, he warned the locals they would not stand a chance in a war with Israel – as it proved in the Six Day War later the same year.

Monty died in 1976.

Coda: Monty and the Savage Club

Nestled away in the Savage library is a small volume, evidently well-struck in years, with a nondescript blank green hardcover binding. The book is entitled *El Alamein to the River Sangro* by Field Marshal Sir BL Montgomery. Inside the front cover is an arresting message:

> To: The Savage Club
> with due humility from the author.
> Montgomery of Alamein
> Field Marshal
> Berlin
> 28 – 2 – 46

---

12 Shinwell was the only person apart from Churchill who Monty permitted to smoke in his presence. Not that Shinwell got on with Churchill, as it happens. There is a story in which Shinwell asked Churchill for twopence so he could phone a friend from a House of Commons phone box. 'Here's fourpence', replied Churchill, 'Phone them all'. See Baxter, op cit, p 123.

13 See Nigel Hamilton, op cit, and the critical review by Michael Carver in *The Guardian*, 22 September 2001.

14 See Bernard Levin, *Taking Sides* (Jonathan Cape Ltd, 1979).

Here is one of those small nuggets which history buffs enjoy discovering as they pan through the archival streams and rivers. Having a personal dedication to the Savage Club from Britain's most famous Second World War general is intriguing enough. What makes it especially poignant, though, is the moment in time which the inscription encapsulates. The book did not arrive at the Savage Club in the form of a donation made by a retired field marshal clearing out his study. Rather, it was a personal gift to the Club when the war had been over less than a year and the grateful recipients were just starting to put their lives back together.

The book was presented on 2 March 1946, when Monty was the guest of honour at the Club and made an honorary life member. He also gave the Club one of his berets. He had previously lunched at the Club during wartime as a guest of his friend AP Herbert.

It seems Monty was not even supposed to give the book to anyone: inside the cover is the foreboding message:

> Published for private circulation in the British Army of the Rhine. NOT to be reproduced. Copyright reserved.

It is, therefore, a measure of the respect Monty must have felt for the Savages that he entrusted them with a copy of the book.

A second example of Monty's Savage sympathies came when, as an old man, he encountered the military historian Barrie Pitt.[15] The latter recorded their meeting in an unpublished manuscript. It seems that the ice was broken by Pitt wearing a Savage Club tie:

> "Ah! I see you're a member of my Club!" said the Field Marshal, pointing at my tie: and do you know, despite the fact that I doubt if he had set foot in Carlton House Terrace—or any of our subsequent addresses,—more than half a dozen times, he still managed to give the impression by the way he said "My Club!" that, if not actually a Founder Member, he was at least a popular and highly-respected Savage, and that my standing with him was increased by my own membership of an organisation which included himself. "Anyway," he said, turning to our mutual host Basil Liddell Hart, "what's he doing here and why have you invited him?"—this, I might point out, in Basil's own house! Basil then explained to him that I had written books on the First World War and was about to start one on the Second, and that I was interested to know the Field Marshal's opinion on the relative merits of the two groups of generals. "Right!" he said. "Come over to Bentley tomorrow

---

15 Barrie Pitt (1918–2006). Pitt was a respected author and military historian. He also served in the SAS, but used to enjoy telling different tales about his supposed wartime adventures. His obituary in *The Daily Telegraph* (28 April 2006) recorded 'A devotee of Wodehouse and Dick Francis and a keen member of the Savage Club, Pitt relished Guinness, had a penchant for brocade waistcoats and sported an eyeglass; he once appeared for lunch at a Somerset pub dressed in spats.' The manuscript of his account with Monty was offered for sale some time ago: see https://www.richardfordmanuscripts.co.uk/catalogue/18035.

morning and we'll talk about it. Can't stop now. Well Basil, give my love to Kathleen and stop bullying her! She's much too good for you!" and with a curt "Eleven o'clock, don't be late!" to me, he was off.

There can at least be no criticism of Monty's taste in clubs.

Field Marshal Harold Alexander: noblesse oblige personified

The Honourable Harold Rupert Leofric George Alexander was from a more aristocratic background than his future Second World War colleagues Monty and the future Arthur Tedder, the other subjects of this chapter. He was thoroughly suffused with the values of honour and duty expected of someone of his upbringing. As with many of those from the upper echelons of society who formed the more junior-ranking officers of the Great War, those values meant he had no hesitation in leading his men into battle even when it meant placing himself in extreme peril.

Early life and First World War

Alexander was born in 1891, the third son of the Earl and Countess of Caledon. Following a well-trodden path for younger sons of aristocracy, he went to Harrow and Sandhurst, and was granted a commission in the Irish Guards in 1911.

By the time of the First World War, he had reached the rank of lieutenant. Like Monty, he was sent to France as part of the British Expeditionary Force and participated in the retreat from Mons. He was badly wounded in the First Battle of Ypres and returned to England to recover in late 1914.

He was able to return to the Front in August 1915 as a major and commanding officer of the 1st Battalion, Irish Guards. He took part in the ill-fated attack at Loos, where he received the Military Cross for his bravery.

In Kipling's collected papers of the Irish Guards,[16] Alexander featured prominently. The following extract from 1915 shows a bit more of the mundane reality of life on the Western Front aside from the great battles:

> Bomb practice was taken up seriously while at La Gorgue, and the daily allowance of live bombs increased to sixty. Drums and fifes had been sent out from the Regimental Orderly Room, together with a few selected drummers from Warley. The Battalion promptly increased the number from its own ranks and formed a full corps of drums and fifes, which paraded for the first time on the 23rd November, when they

---

16　Rudyard Kipling (ed), *The Irish Guards in the Great War, edited and compiled from their diaries and papers* (Macmillan, 1923). It has been digitised and was free online at the time of writing. Quotations are from p 33 et seq, https://archive.org/stream/irishguardsofgre02rudy/irishguardsofgre02rudy_djvu.txt.

exchanged billets with the 1st Coldstream at Merville. The first tune played was the Regimental March and the second "Brian Boru," which goes notably to the drums. (In those days the Battalion was overwhelmingly Irish in composition.) Captain the Hon. H. R. Alexander, who had been in hospital with influenza for a week, re-joined on the 23rd as second in command.

Merville was a mixed, but not too uncomfortable, experience. The Battalion with the rest of the Guards Division was placed temporarily at the disposal of the Forty-fifth Division as a reserve, a position which meant neither being actually in the trenches nor out of them. They were beyond reach of rifle-fire and in a corner not usually attended to by artillery. There was a roof to the officers' mess, and some of the windows did not lack glass. They ate off tables with newspapers for cloth and enjoyed the luxury of chairs. The men lived more or less in trenches, but were allowed out, like well-watched poultry, at night or on misty mornings. All this was interspersed with squad drill, instruction, baths, and a Battalion concert; while, in view of possibilities that might develop, Captain Alexander and the four company commanders "reconnoitred certain routes from Merville to Neuve Chapelle." But every one knew at heart that there was nothing doing or to be done except to make oneself as comfortable as might be with all the blankets that one could steal, at night, and all the food one could compass by day. Leave was going on regularly. Captain and Adjutant J. S. N. FitzGerald left on the 26th for ten days and Lieutenant A. Pym took over his duties. When adjutants can afford to go on leave, life ought to be easy.

Then they shifted to Laventie in a full blizzard, relieving the 2nd Scots Guards in Brigade Reserve. Their own Brigade, the 2nd, was taking over from the 3rd Guards Brigade, and Captain Alexander, who not unnaturally caught a fresh attack of influenza later, spent the afternoon reconnoitring the trenches which he would have to occupy on the 28th. The No Man's Land to be held in front of them was marsh and ditch, impassable save when frozen. It carried no marks in the shape of hedges or stumps to guide men out or back on patrol, and its great depth—three hundred yards in places from wire to wire—made thorough ferreting most difficult. In this war, men with small-arms that carried twenty-eight hundred yards, hardly felt safe unless they were within half bow-shot of their enemy.

The Battalion's entry into their forlorn heritage was preceded by a small house-warming in the shape of an artillery bombardment on our side. This, they knew, by doleful experience, would provoke retaliation, and the relief was accordingly delayed till dark, which avoided all casualties. Their general orders were to look out for likely spots whence to launch "small enterprises" against the enemy. It meant patrols wandering out in rain and a thaw that had followed the stiff frost, and doing their best to keep direction by unassisted intellect and a compass. ("Ye'll understand that, in those days, once you was out on your belly in that muck, ye knew no more than a babe in a blanket. Dark, wet and windy it was, with big, steep, deep ditches waiting on ye every yard. All we took of it was a stiff neck, and all we heard was Jerry gruntin' in his pigstye!")

In 1916, the diaries recorded more memorable incidents:[17]

> While in Brigade Reserve for a couple of days No. 1 Company amused itself preparing a grim bait to entice German patrols into No Man's Land. Two dummies were fabricated to represent dead English soldiers. "One, designed to lie on its back, had a face modelled by Captain Alexander from putty and paint which for ghastliness rivalled anything in Madame Tussaud's. The frame-work of the bodies was wire, so they could be twisted into positions entirely natural."

> While they were being made, on the road outside Brigade Headquarters at Pont du Hem, a French girl came by and believing them to be genuine, fled shrieking down the street. They were taken up to the front line on stretchers, and it chanced that in one trench they had to give place to let a third stretcher pass. On it was a dead man, whom no art could touch.

> Next night, February 15, between moonset and dawn, the grisliest hour of the twenty-four, Lieutenant Pym took the twins out into No Man's Land, arranging them one on its face and the other on its back in such attitudes as are naturally assumed by the old warped dead. "Strapped between the shoulders of the former, for the greater production of German curiosity, was a cylinder sprouting india-rubber tubes. This was intended to resemble a flammenwerfer." Hand- and rifle-grenades were then hurled near the spot to encourage the theory (the Hun works best on a theory) that two British patrols had fought one another in error, and left the two corpses. At evening, the Lewis-gun party and a brace of bombers lay out beside the kill, but it was so wet and cold that they had to be called in, and no one was caught. And all this fancy-work, be it remembered, was carried out joyously and interestedly, as one might arrange for the conduct of private theatricals or the clearance of rat-infested barns.

Later in 1916, during the Battle of the Somme, Alexander was awarded the Distinguished Service Order for his actions on 15 September. His citation read:[18]

> For conspicuous gallantry in action. He was the life and soul of the attack, and throughout the day led forward not only his own men but men of all regiments. He held the trenches gained in spite of heavy machine gun fire.

After the hideous bloodshed of the Somme came a curious incident:

> A mystery turned up on the night of the 12th December in the shape of a wild-looking, apparently dumb, Hun prisoner, brought before Captain Young of the Support Company, who could make naught of him, till at last "noticing the likeness between his cap and that affected by Captain Alexander"[19] he hazarded "Russky." The prisoner at once awoke, and

---

17 Kipling, *The Irish Guards in the Great War, edited and compiled from their diaries and papers,* op cit.
18 'No. 29793', *The London Gazette* (Supplement), 20 October 1916, p 10169.
19 Kipling wrote in a footnote of his own at that point: 'This was pure prophecy. Captain, as he

by sign and word revealed himself as from Petrograd. Also he bolted one loaf of bread in two counted minutes. He had been captured at Kovel by the Huns, and brought over to be used by them to dig behind their front line. But how he had escaped across that wilderness that wild-eyed man never told.

Alexander continued to receive promotions during the war, rising to command the 2nd Battalion, Irish Guards in 1917. In the Third Battle of Ypres (usually known as 'Third Ypres'), he was slightly wounded at Bourlon Wood. The action was a disaster for his battalion, which suffered 320 casualties out of 400 men.

Throughout 1917 he continued to show his courage and cool, as related in the regimental diaries:

> Lieutenant Sassoon[20], 1 commanding No. 3, got his Lewis-gun to cover a flank attack on the machine-gun that was doing the damage, took it with seven German dead and five wounded prisoners, and so freed the advance for the Scots Guards and his own company. As the latter moved forward they caught it in the rear from another machine-gun which had been overlooked, or hidden itself in the cleaning-up of Hey Wood.
>
> Sassoon sent back a couple of sections to put this thing out of action (which they did) and pushed on No. 4 Company, which was getting much the same allowance from concrete emplacements covering machine-guns outside Artillery Wood. Captain Alexander launched an attack at these through a gap in our barrage, outflanked them and accounted for three machine-guns and fourteen Germans. There was some slight difficulty at this point in distinguishing between our barrage, which seemed to have halted, and the enemy's, which seemed to be lifting back. So Captain Alexander had to conduct his advance by a series of short rushes in and out of this double barrage, but somehow or other contrived to consolidate his position without undue delays. ("Consolidatin' positions at Boesinghe meant being able to lie down and get your breath while the rest of ye ran about the country hammerin' machine-gun posts an' damnin' our barrages.") Thus occupied, he sent back word to Captain Gunston that in the circumstances he waived his seniority and placed himself under the latter's command. "The pace was too good to inquire."

The following year, during the British defence against the German Operation Michael, Alexander took command of the 4th Guards Brigade and later resumed command of 2nd Battalion, Irish Guards again. Once more the battalion suffered terrible casualties.

---

was then, Alexander was credited with a taste for strange and Muscovitish headgear, which he possibly gratified later as a general commanding weird armies in Poland during the spasms of reconstruction that followed the Armistice.'

20 Note: this is Siegfried Sassoon, CBE, MC (1886–1967), the legendary Great War soldier, poet and author.

By the end of the war, Alexander had been promoted to acting lieutenant-colonel in command of a corps infantry school. Despite what the 2nd Battalion went through in the war, Kipling was complimentary about Alexander's command. Alexander could therefore look back and say with honesty that he had done his duty – and, for the men of his time, there could be no higher praise.

Later years and Second World War

In 1919, Alexander undertook one of the more interesting assignments of his career, when he commanded a unit of German Freikorps fighting the Bolsheviks in Latvia. He also served in India, commanding the Nowshera Brigade on the North West Frontier. In 1937 he was promoted to major-general, the youngest person in the British Army to hold the rank at the time.

At the start of the Second World War, Alexander was sent to command the 1st Division of the British Expeditionary Force in France. He was therefore involved in planning the defences which the Germans cut to pieces so ruthlessly the following year. As the net closed around the British, forcing them back to Dunkirk, the commander of the BEF, General Gort, gave Alexander the task of covering the retreat. It was a critical job which Alexander performed with distinction. He later wrote of the withdrawal that the men involved were 'patient, brave and obedient, and when finally ordered to embark they did so in perfectly disciplined groups, properly armed and equipped.'[21]

In truth, Alexander's words involved some exaggeration: other soldiers reported chaotic scenes, bemoaned the lack of organisation from the navy about getting the 'little ships' to ferry men from the beaches to the waiting larger vessels (which was their primary role, not to go back and forth across the Channel, a round trip of many hours at a time when every minute counted). Some 25 per cent of men did not even bring their rifles back, one indication of the extreme circumstances in which they found themselves. Yet the overall achievement – 338,226 men rescued, when Churchill and Gort had not anticipated much more than a tenth that number – was a remarkable success. Moreover, once again Alexander showed great stoicisim under the most severe duress: when the last BEF units left, just before midnight on 2 June on board the Channel ferry *St Helier,* Alexander and the naval commander, Captain William Tennant, went up and down the beach area on board a launch, with Alexander calling through a megaphone: 'Is anyone

---

21 It is not the place here to discuss Dunkirk at length. I would however note that many British accounts of the episode wrongly take an Anglo-centric approach in trying to understand why the German advance halted sufficiently to enable the British to escape. One vital reason thereby omitted is that the German focus was on defeating France, and the bulk of the French forces – far exceeding the BEF in number – was elsewhere. The Germans would therefore not have realised the significance of the BEF retreat across the Channel.

there?' When they found no-one, they themselves boarded a destroyer and left for England.[22]

Back home, Alexander assumed command of the defence of south-west England. He later served for a time in India, and took part in the retreat from the Japanese. In August 1942, he replaced Auchinleck as the Middle East commander-in-chief, while Monty simultaneously replaced Auchinleck at the head of the Eighth Army.

Alexander was gradually eclipsed by Monty, who was chosen ahead of him to command the D-Day invasion. Alexander remained in the Mediterranean theatre for the rest of the war, commanding the gruelling slog through Italy. His command also encompassed Greece, where the German retreat was followed by the start of a disastrous civil war.

On 29 April 1945, Alexander received the unconditional surrender of all German forces in Italy.

In 1946 he was ennobled as Viscount Alexander of Tunis and Errigal in the County of Donegal. He retired from the military and became yet another Savage to serve as a governor general, in his case (like Field Marshal Byng) of Canada.

Alexander returned to Britain in 1952 and took up the post of minister of defence in Churchill's government. Churchill had held the post himself during the war but did not feel up to it in his later premiership. Alexander was also raised in the peerage to an earl.

He retired from politics in 1954. In 1959, he was made an honorary life member of the Savage Club. From 1960 to 1965, he served as constable of the Tower of London, a traditional post for a long-serving member of the army. He died in 1969.

Marshal of the Royal Air Force Arthur Tedder: per ardua ad astra

We saw when discussing Monty how he developed a severe critic in his Brother Savage Air Marshal Tedder. One can but imagine what would have happened after the war if both had found themselves in the Savage Club at the same time, especially as Monty – a teetotaller – would have refused the normal social lubricant of a glass of gin or a martini. It is fair to say Monty won the post-war battle

---

22 Julian Thompson, 'Dunkirk: The Miracle of Deliverance', *Daily Telegraph*, 28 May 2010. And see his *Dunkirk: Retreat to Victory*, op cit. Note that that was not quite the end of the operation: the following night, 26,000 French troops were evacuated, the final vessel to leave being the destroyer HMS *Shikari*. Moreover, approximately 40,000 British soldiers were left behind further inland, defending the perimeter. For them there would be no exultant welcome back in Britain; instead, most would spend more than five years in captivity – assuming they survived the brutal route march which the Germans forced them to undertake first. See Sean Longden, *Dunkirk: The Men They Left Behind* (Constable, 2009).

of reputations. Yet Tedder had a distinguished career in both world wars, and deserves his own recognition accordingly.

Early life

Arthur Tedder was born in Scotland in 1890. His father was a diplomat and civil servant whose most notable achievement was holding the post of commissioner of the Board of Customs which created the first ever old age pension scheme.

The young Tedder was schooled in different parts of the British Isles, depending on where his father was stationed, before going to Cambridge. He graduated in 1912 with a lower second class honours degree in history. Initially he looked to follow his father into a career in diplomacy, though he also obtained a reserve commission in the Dorsetshire Regiment.

First World War

Tedder was living in Fiji when war broke out. He returned to Britain of his own volition and joined the regular army, but injured his knee during training, which rendered him unable to serve on the frontline, to his immense frustration. He did serve in France for a time behind the lines, before transferring to the Royal Flying Corps in January 1916, following a sustained campaign on his part.

Initially he was sent to Reading in Berkshire for ground instruction as a prospective pilot, then in March 1916 went to Norwich for flight training. He was surprised to be somewhat underwhelmed by his first flight, writing of 'the absolute lack of any special sensation. It was much nicer than on the ground and one got a splendid view of the countryside, but beyond that – well, it was not half as exciting as one's first motor drive.'[23]

He was soon promoted to captain and obtained his 'wings' by the middle of the year, before being sent to the Western Front as part of No 25 Squadron RFC. The squadron was equipped with the Bristol Scout C.[24] Tedder was soon promoted to flight commander. In those days, training was extraordinarily short: he undertook his first solo flight after less than two hours' experience in the air.

In June 1916, he qualified as an operational pilot and was sent to join 25 Squadron in Auchel. They were equipped with FE 2bs,[25] a bomber-reconnais-

---

23 Vincent Orange, *Tedder: Quietly in Command* (Routledge, 2004), pp 31–32.

24 The Bristol Scout was a single-seat rotary engine biplane originally designed as a racing air-craft. It was employed by the RFC as a 'scout', or reconnaissance type. It was one of the first single-seaters to be used as a fighter aircraft, although it did not have an effective forward-firing armament until the British managed to design a gun synchroniser in 1916, by which time the Scout was obsolete.

25 The designation 'FE 2' is confusing since the British used it for three superficially similar, but actually quite distinct, aircraft between 1911 and 1914. All were 'pusher' aircraft with the propeller behind the pilot, which enabled the use of forward facing machine guns and gave a better view, but which gave much inferior performance to a 'pulling' aircraft with the propeller

sance biplane which Tedder called 'a big heavy bus'. He enjoyed the camaraderie of the squadron, which included men from around the Empire, and was soon into action flying patrols. On only his second flight, his plane was hit by ground fire which cut one of the petrol pipes, but his luck prevailed and he made it back to ground without the machine catching fire. Six days later he was hit by fire from an enemy aircraft but again made it back to safety unharmed.

As well as the reconnaissance patrols, he undertook bombing raids on German supply lines. They inflicted minimal damage but did cause the Germans to expend resources trying to stop them, and they delayed German troop movements. Tedder's squadron also claimed the scalps of more than 30 enemy aircraft – all the more impressive since they were not flying specialised fighter aircraft – though caution is needed with that figure since it was often difficult to tell (or pilots deliberately exaggerated) whether a plane had been hit by ground fire or aircraft fire, or whether it had been damaged or destroyed if no-one saw it crash.

One of the claimed victims was the first great German ace, Max Immelmann. Showing the sort of chivalry that pilots were inclined to rather more than their comrades on the ground amidst the mud and squalor of the trenches, Tedder arranged for a wreath with a message of condolence to be dropped on a German aerodrome. The Germans sent a courteous acknowledgement in return, but their propagandists, not willing to allow the enemy a triumph, claimed that Immelmann's plane had crashed through mechanical failure.

A second bonus for the British from Immelmann's death was that the Kaiser insisted on grounding Germany's leading pilot of the time, Oswald Bolcke, because he feared for public morale if two aces were lost in short succession.

In October 1916, Tedder visited the Somme battlefield, expressing marvel at the cool efficiency of the enormous logistical operation behind the lines. He was horrified at seeing how whole villages had almost vanished, leaving only a pile of half-powdered brickwork or other random signs here and there.

As the war continued to rage, in the sky and on the ground, Tedder found himself in some furious large-scale air battles. Of one he wrote 'eleven of us against about 20 Huns … I wasn't flying level for two seconds on end, first up on one wing tip and then on the other … I must say that in a way I rather enjoyed it. Why no-one collided with a Hun or FE, I don't know.'[26]

In total, he recorded 323 combat hours in the FE 2b. At the end of 1916, he returned to England on leave. Without any forewarning, he was not returned to 25 Squadron, but was instead promoted to major and placed in command of 70 Squadron RFC. The squadron was equipped with the Sopwith 1½ Strutter, an

---

at the front. Tedder's FE 2b was from the last of the three types, a two-seater with the observer in the nose of the nacelle and the pilot sitting above and behind.

26 Orange, op cit, p 41.

aircraft notable for having the first synchronised machine gun and for being the first British aircraft with the propeller in front, 'pulling' the aircraft as opposed to the rear, 'pushing' it. It was however up against a superior German aircraft, the Albatross D III, which by spring 1917 equipped all German squadrons on the Western Front. The inequality of arms combined with the British policy of 'constant offensive' (unchallenged by Tedder) led to heavy casualties for 70 Squadron, which lost 18 aircraft and had three damaged in just two days over Cambrai in March 1917.

The carnage from that period would affect Tedder for the rest of his career. He began to suffer greatly from the attendant stress, not least because he insisted on writing all the letters of condolences to the parents of the dead men himself.

In May 1917 he was awarded the Italian Silver Medal for Military Valour. He expressed some embarrassment: 'I don't think I've ever seen an Italian, much less defended his hearth and home from the outrageous Hun.'[27]

In June 1917, he returned to England to command 67 Squadron at RAF Shawbury. He suffered the great frustration of seeing his old squadron finally equipped with a machine that could match the Germans, the famous Sopwith Camel.[28]

Tedder found the conditions at RAF Shawbury much more comfortable than the Western Front, but was disappointed to discover that the men under his command were an inferior lot to those he commanded under the pressure of war in France.

In 1918, Tedder was sent to Egypt at the request of an old patron of his, Brigadier-General Philip Herbert, who was head of Middle East Training Brigade. Tedder was not pleased to be given another assignment rather than going back to the Western Front, especially when the news of Operation Michael broke in March. Nevertheless, he followed orders and went on to take charge of the School of Navigation and Bomb Dropping and later the 38th Wing in Cairo.

He finished the war with the temporary rank of lieutenant-colonel. It has been said of Tedder that he 'did not have a particularly outstanding career in the First World War. He was certainly not a great ace, but he learned and grew and absorbed the emerging lessons of that terrible conflict.'[29] Certainly, Tedder's experience of command and organisation in wartime were to prove invaluable later in his career, when he ascended to the highest echelons of the RAF.

---

27 Orange, op cit, p 46.
28 Much of the Great War air imagery I grew up with consisted of the Sopwith Camel in duels with the Fokker Triplane. The Triplane was stronger, could climb faster and was more manoeuvrable in a dogfight. Crucially, though, the Camel was faster in level flight, so could choose when to fight. It was also much safer to land since visibility looking down was far superior.
29 Professor Williamson Murray, foreword to Orange, op cit.

Later career and Second World War

Among Tedder's assignments between the wars was a short deployment to Turkey in 1922–23 during the Chanak Crisis. In 1923 and 1924 he studied at staff college, and was promoted to wing commander. By the time of the Second World War he held the post of Director General for Research in the Air Ministry.

Tedder's department was soon moved to the new Ministry of Aircraft Production. The department was under the aegis of the minister of armaments, the Fleet Street grandee and former appeaser Lord Beaverbrook. He and Tedder did not get on, so Tedder was transferred to become deputy air officer commanding-in-chief, RAF Middle East Command, with the acting rank of air marshal. He assumed the highest command in the region in June 1941. He was, therefore, in a crucial role along with Alexander and Monty in the desert campaign.

Tedder was promoted to air chief marshal in July 1942. He played an important role in the victory at Second Alamein in October 1942.[30] In 1943, he served under Eisenhower in the Mediterranean, and oversaw the air operations in the invasion of Sicily and mainland Italy. As in the First World War, he was recognised by his allies, being awarded the American Legion of Merit and the Grand Cross of the Polish Order of Polonia Restituta.

He returned to Britain to assist Eisenhower in planning Operation Overlord, and was made deputy supreme commander in January 1944. He was to encounter severe problems with Monty in the Normandy capacity, despite all they had achieved together in the Mediterranean. One of his controversies concerned the question of how much damage should be inflicted on French infrastructure before the Allied invasion took place. Tedder's plan of trapping German forces by cutting off supply lines was correctly predicted to cause the large losses of French civilians, something Churchill and others wished to avoid.[31] In the event Tedder had his way and much damage was inflicted on German railways and other infrastructure, but at an appalling price: more than 15,000 Norman civilians were killed by Allied bombing before D-Day and another 20,000 perished in the two months following the landings. (In total, some 70,000 French civilians were killed by Allied bombs during the war – more than the number of British

---

30 It was the first time in the war to that point that Britain went into battle against the Germans with much superior forces. Tedder's resources in the air comprised more than 1,500 aircraft, with 1,200 of those based in Egypt and Palestine in support of a ground attack on Alamein. The Axis, by contrast, had only 350 serviceable aircraft. Churchill commended Tedder's conduct after the battle, and Tedder was made Knight Grand Cross of the Order of the Bath a month after it had concluded.

31 One is reminded of the Falklands War, when some Argentine commanders were court-martialled afterwards because they had surrendered without losing the ratio of troops specified in Argentine military doctrine. One wonders what they were supposed to do – hold a roll call mid-battle and then call a halt once the remaining number had been killed?

citizens killed by the Luftwaffe in Britain.[32]) There were also heavy casualties among the bomber crews themselves.

Tedder fell out with Monty for several reasons, including Monty's failure to take the town of Caen despite confident predictions. Monty's status as a celebrity general, however, meant he remained in post, even if Tedder would have preferred to remove him.[33]

Towards the end of the war, Tedder went to the Soviet Union to liaise with their commanders as they neared Berlin. He was in Germany in May 1945, where he signed the German surrender on behalf of Eisenhower. The Soviets granted him the Soviet Order of Kutuzov (1st Class), and before the end of 1945 he reached the rank of marshal of the Royal Air Force.

Tedder thus ended the war at the apex of the British armed forces, but there had been a terrible personal cost. His son died in France in 1940 and his first wife was killed in an aircraft crash in Egypt in January 1943.

In 1946, he became chief of the air staff and was ennobled as Baron Tedder of Glenguin. He was recognised by the Americans for his war service by being awarded the American Distinguished Service Medal. In the same year, he was made an honorary life member of the Savage Club.

As chief of air staff, Tedder was notably in overall command of the RAF during the Berlin Airlift in 1948.

He retired from the military in 1951. Thereafter, he spent much time in academia. He was also chairman of the Standard Motor Company from 1954 to 1960 and served as vice-chairman of the Board of Governors of the BBC.

On 5 December 1953, he chaired the Savage Club's ninety-sixth annual dinner, with Lord Horder as special guest.[34]

He died in 1967.

---

32 Antony Beevor, *D-Day: The Battle for Normandy* (Penguin, 2014, Kindle edn).

33 Not surprisingly, Monty's view of Tedder was not favourable either. He recorded in a note for his war diary that Tedder 'was completely ineffective; none of the Army Group Commanders would see him; and they growled at once if he ever appeared on the horizon.' See Nigel Hamilton, *Monty*, vol 3, op cit, p 529; also pp 645, 651, 652.

34 Thomas Jeeves Horder, 1st Baron Horder, GCVO (1871–1955), a leading physician of his day. During the Second World War, he sat upon various committees including one which advised the Ministry of Food. Interestingly, he was also opposed to many aspects of the NHS whilst it was being developed.

CHAPTER 14

Aftermath: The Savage Club 1919–1939

Club life between the wars

We come from dock and shipyard, we come from car and train,
We come from foreign countries to slope our arms again
And, forming fours by numbers or turning to the right,
We're learning all our drill again and 'tis a pretty sight.
Our names are all unspoken, our regiments forgotten,
For some of us were pretty bad and some of us were rotten
And some will misremember what once they learnt with pain
And hit a bloody Sergeant and go to clink again.

Brother Savage Edward Shanks, 'The Old Soldiers', 1915

Following the Armistice, the British armed forces were slowly demobilised over the next year or so, and all involved in what had been arguably the worst conflict in the history of the world to that point started to try to put their lives back together.

To help them adjust to civilian life, returning British serviceman were each given a protection certificate, a railway ticket to get home, a pay advance, a fortnight's ration book and a voucher for the return of his coat, with the option of a clothing allowance or a suit of (not very good quality) plain clothes.[1] Such was the lot of men who had served in some cases for four years and seen so many

---

1   In total 1,413,760 suits were issued, in dark blue, brown or grey, and they were denounced by the trade press as of poor quality, not fit for returning heroes. See Jane Tynan, *British Army Uniform and the First World War: Men in Khaki* (AIAA, 2013).

of their comrades killed or wounded in the most horrific fashion. The modest handout was some way short of 'a land fit for heroes' that had been promised by the prime minister, Lloyd George, and the resultant general discontent in the country culminated in the General Strike of 1926.[2]

For its part, the Savage Club did its best to carry on as normal, just as it had throughout the war years. In 1945, looking back at the inter-war period, Kenneth Duffield reflected on his time in the Club:[3]

"Boom! boom! boom!" protests the big bass native drum as Jack, the Irish hall-porter, viciously thwacks it, as though he were brandishing a shillelagh at Donnybrook Fair. "Zoom! zoom! zoom!" replies the echo, reverberating through the palatial hall and down the stately staircase.

The cacophony of animated voices in the "North-West Room" (The Bar) suddenly subsides, glasses are emptied, Savages and their guests file out into the handsome, broad corridor and so to the decorative dining room. The hush continues—more or less—as Tom Clark, our excellent Club steward, directs us to our seats, but soon the hubbub recommences.

We greet our *vis-à-vis* and next door neighbours as though they were long lost friends in spite of the fact (a) that we have recently jostled each other in the bar, and (b) that frequently we don't know their names or they ours until we surreptitiously refer to the name-cards on the table in front of us. It is characteristic of the Club that quite a number of us have for years called each other by our first names without knowing the surnames. The most popular and safest form of address is "Old man" or "Old boy".

Names or rank count for little in the Savage Club, so long as the individual is a congenial spirit, although, of course, his professional qualifications, achievements, and social status are most carefully considered before he is elected. Here, more than anywhere else I know, appearances are often deceptive. For instance, after a prolonged session in the bar with tow rubicund, farmer-like clubmates, one short, tubby, and cherubic, the other large and somewhat taciturn, we discover that the first is John Ireland, the famous composer, and the other Nathaniel Gubbins, the famous humourist, who "sits on the fence" with such laughter-provoking results every Sunday.

However, *revenons a nos moutons*: the meal is simple, homely and good, and we are hungry and happy. We exude bonhomie; we clink glasses with all and sundry, and we are beginning, perhaps, to feel a trifle mellow after a second glass of port when "Thump! Thump! Thump! Goes the Chairman's "gavel" (really a murderous-looking native knob-

---

2   Sir Henry Maximilian 'Max' Beerbohm (1872–1956), English essayist, parodist, and caricaturist under the signature 'Max', and a life member of the Savage Club from 1943, wrote an interesting piece showing the anxieties of the upper class about how to view the world and the rise of the labour movement after the war. See Beerbohm, 'Something Defeasible' in *The Owl*, 2 October 1919, p 33.

3   Kenneth Duffield, *Savages and Kings* (MacDonald & Co Ltd, 1945), pp 20–27.

kerrie), as it is cautiously banged on the table.

"Brother Savages and Guests," commands the Chairman, when the applause which greets his rising has died down, "I give you the toast of His Majesty the King" ... "The King!" we dutifully echo, as we drink the loyal toast ... "Brother Savages and Guests, you may smoke," allows the Chairman; and, the above traditional routine having been faithfully adhered to, another Savage Saturday "Night" has begun.

From time immemorial—anyhow, for eighty years or so—the above ceremony has taken place, stopping neither for wars nor their by-products, including blitzes.

Many Kings have come and gone since the Club was founded, and many have sat amongst us, having, as it were, left their crowns in the cloakroom. (En passant, I think it was the famous "tramp-author", Bart Kennedy, who first voiced the sentiment: "When you come into the Savage Club you hang up your ruddy halo in the hall.") A Royal Personage once remarked to us that he envied us our camaraderie and our Savage spirit as compared with the uneasy frailty of a Kingship ...

The much-battered and long-suffering top-table is again thumped with the knobkerrie, and after we have been unnecessarily reminded that a similar function will take place on the following Saturday with Brother Savage So-and-so in the Chair, Brother Savage Tommy Best (cheers) is commanded to sit at the piano and give us some digestive music. (Cheers.)

With glasses fully charged, and contentedly smoking our "Coronas" (that is to say, if one has been fortunate enough to have sold perhaps a picture, or maybe a book or a play), otherwise "Woodbines", we lean back to enjoy Tommy's faultless performance ...

At this point the worried Chairman (for it is a bit of a responsibility being in the Chair) is anxiously trying to catch the eye of the "Producer" or "Master of Ceremonies", whose onerous duties are so often and so ably carried out by Brother Savage Joe Batten. Where are the performers? There seems to be nobody present out of the inspiring list of "probables" so industriously compiled a fortnight ago.

George Baker, our able and popular Honorary Secretary, is absent, having been called away to do a broadcast; Mark Hambourg[4] has a guest and wants to enjoy his wine unmolested; "Flotsam" (BC Hilliam) has missed his train, but "Jetsam" (Malcolm McEachern) is there—and so are Tommy Handley, Gillie Potter, Will Kings and Charlie Clapham, so the comedy element will be OK ...

At the top table in a row sits the Chairman and other celebrities— maybe Royalty, or M Maisky,[5] or a Prime Minister perhaps, or the

---

4   Mark Hambourg, the great concert pianist. He is mentioned in despatches in Appendix III, as are Flotsam, Jetsam and Tommy Handley, whom Duffield also recalls above.

5   Ivan Maisky (1884–1975), Soviet Ambassador to Britain 1932–43. He famously attended a Savage Club house dinner during the Second World War (in 1941) with George Baker in the chair. Maisky was made an honorary life member at the dinner and later gave the Club a copy of his memoirs. What made the dinner especially poignant was the timing. At the moment the

> First Lord of the Admiralty, Barbirolli, Montgomery, or Evans of the "Broke"—who knows? Sometimes we entertain "angels unawares", inasmuch as frequently a member brings along a guest whose name and fame are world-wide, without announcing his identity.

As Duffield noted, the house dinners, usually with distinguished guests, continued as normal through the 1920s and 30s. Much Savage humour can be found on both the menus and in the accounts of the participants. In December 1920, for example, the Chinese ambassador appeared as a guest of honour. He drew considerable laughter with his almost Wodehousean observations about the trend then current for publishing memoirs:[6]

> I have nothing interesting to tell you, no anecdotes or secret history to extract from my diary. I note that the publication of biographies and diaries has become the fashion. I, too, wish to be in the swim. How interesting it must be to read the comments and praises, as the instalments appear, in the Western and Eastern hemispheres. It must be very pleasing to know how you read these; some amuse you, some abuse you, but all breathe a sigh of relief when the last instalment has appeared, not knowing what otherwise would come next. There is an old saying, "If you don't strike oil, you had better stop boring."

PG Wodehouse himself joined the Club in 1922. I wrote about his subsequent unfortunate experiences in the Second World War in *Drumbeat* in 2017.[7]

The Savage connections with royalty resumed soon after the war's end. The Prince of Wales, Prince Albert and Prince Henry attended the Savage Club Costume Ball at the Royal Albert Hall in June 1919. As we saw in Chapter 12, Prince Albert continued as an enthusiastic Savage until the abdication drama saw him unexpectedly assume the throne as George VI.

---

assembled company sat down the war situation on all fronts must have seemed desperate. The British and French had been vanquished on land in 1940, and while the RAF had seemingly seen off the threat of invasion, the chances of Britain actually defeating Germany by reinvading France would have been the stuff of fantasy. On the Eastern Front, Russia would have seemed close to collapse: they had lost some three million killed, wounded or captured in the opening few weeks in the summer of 1941, and by December the Germans were virtually at the gates of Moscow. If Russia were to fall, then Britain's war would surely be brought to a conclusion by a deal which would have left her at best a mere satellite off the coast of a German superpower stretching from the Atlantic to Vladivostok.

Yet within 24 hours the entire state of the war would change dramatically, for the date of the dinner was 6 December 1941. The next morning, Japan would bomb Pearl Harbour, bringing America into the war, and leading Hitler to make the fatal error of declaring war on America as well. No-one in the Savage Club being entertained by Baker and Maisky that night could have dared hope for that course of events. Instead, the desperate state of the war would have tested even the Savage bohemian atmosphere.

6   *The Times*, 13 December 1920, p 9. Incidentally, the Japanese ambassador and his wife were the guests at the ladies' dinner in May 1930, showing the cultural broad-mindedness of the Savages then as now.

7   *Drumbeat*, No 136, Winter 2017.

Despite having flourished during wartime, the Club started to struggle financially in the early 1920s. By 1924, it was in serious peril, being literally unable to pay the rent, and had to make a direct appeal for members' assistance. Fortunately, that help was forthcoming and the lease on the Adelphi was extended by another five years from 1925.[8]

As all members know from the marvellous letter framed on the Club's wall, the ranks of the Club were swelled by the addition of the great composer Sergei Rachmaninoff, who became an honorary life member in 1939. His works were celebrated in a house dinner menu for 17 October 1936. James Agate wrote of Rachmaninoff's visit to the Club in 1939:[9]

> As I was sitting at an angle of the table within four feet of the chair, I had plenty of opportunity to study in Rachmaninoff that visual magnificence which comes naturally to great men like Irving[10] and Chaliapin,[11] to whose type this major artist belongs. It is an extraordinary mask, at once gentle and farouche, noble melancholy and sardonic ... When the lean figure rose to leave, everybody in the room stood up. Apart from royalty, this has happened before at the Savage only in the cases of Irving and Lord Roberts.

Other notable guests of the Club in the interwar years included Sir Arthur Conan Doyle, the creator of Sherlock Holmes, who attended the sixty-eighth anniversary dinner in 1925 (having earlier, as we saw in the chapter on the Savage Club in wartime, used the Club as a setting in his novel *The Lost World*), Sir James Jeans, a distinguished mathematician and physicist,[12] who was the guest on 12 February 1938, and the thespian Sir John Martin-Harvey,[13] who came on 3 December 1938 – respectively, a great author, a great scientist and a great actor, thus showing the diversity of intellectual interests which the Savage Club has always represented.

In his speech to the Savages, Conan Doyle reflected upon the London literary scene in his early days, showing that the classic English 'fings ain't wot they used to be' mentality was just as prevalent 150 years ago as today. *The Times* reported:[14]

He well remembered the day when Kipling came into literature. The

---

8   See Bradshaw, op cit, p 79.
9   Quoted in Barrie Martyn, *Rachmaninoff: Composer, Pianist, Conductor* (Ashgate Publishing, 1990; Routledge edn 2016), p xxxix.
10 Sir Henry Irving (1838–1905), Victorian actor-manager, often said to have been one of the inspirations for Count Dracula, whose creator, Bram Stoker, was a fellow Savage. The Savage Club library is proud to own a book inscribed by Stoker to his friend John Hart, donated to the library by Brother Savage Arthur Phillips.
11 Feodore Ivanovich Chaliapin (1873–1938), Russian opera singer.
12 Sir James Hopwood Jeans OM FRS (1877–1946), physicist, astronomer and mathematician.
13 Sir John Martin-Harvey (1863–1944), leading stage actor of his day.
14 7 December 1925.

critics were deploring the fact that English literature was dead and that there was no sign of a literary crop springing out of the old soil. At that time he himself was practising in a small way as a doctor, and at a draper's close by there was an assistant whose name was H. G. Wells. There was also a raw-boned Irishman roaming about London. His name was Bernard Shaw. There was also a young man named Thomas Hardy, and a young journalist struggling for a living writing paragraphs in Nottingham, whose name was Barrie. So it was all along the line. These men were rising up, and if at the present time it was said that the soil was unfertile, they should never forget that in different guises and in different forms the old crop would always come out.

Savage authors of the day were joined in January 1933 by the notable novelist CS Forrester.

In the scientific field, we have already met three Savage Nobel Laureates, Sir Alexander Fleming, Professor Ronald Norrish and Sir William Bragg. Honorary Savage membership had been conferred in 1907 upon another Nobel Prize winner, the Norwegian explorer and diplomat Fridtjof Nansen (1861–1930), who deserves further comment in the post-war context.

Nansen had made his name before the war as a polar explorer, scientist and diplomat, and it was in the first of those capacities that he had been made a member of the Savage Club.[15] Norway was neutral during the Great War but Nansen had had to negotiate food and other supplies from the United States as the Norwegian economy had suffered so badly from the decline of international trade. After the war, his diplomatic skills and energy were directed to helping found the League of Nations and then conducting work on its behalf. That work included repatriating some 200,000 prisoners of war – the Soviet Union in particular had done little with those captured by Russia before 1917 – and assisting refugees displaced by the Russian Revolution and later the Armenian genocide (one of the Ottoman Empire's most heinous crimes). Nansen's efforts set a precedent for much of the later international work with refugees, and he was recognised with the award of the Nobel Peace Prize in 1922.

---

15 Nansen led the team that made the first crossing of the Greenland interior in 1888, traversing the island on cross-country skis. He set a record northern latitude of 86°14 during his North Pole expedition of 1893–96. Upon his return he retired from exploration, but his organisation and methods provided the template for many successful later explorers. Nansen then studied zoology and oceanography, and made substantial contributions to both disciplines.

He was a leading figure in the separation of Norway from Sweden. From 1906 to 1908 he served as the Norwegian representative in London, where he helped negotiate the Integrity Treaty that guaranteed Norway's independent status, and while there he was made the second-ever honorary Savage, the Prince of Wales being the first. He was followed by another great explorer Henry M Stanley, and the legendary humourist Mark Twain. Given that Robert Falcon Scott, Ernest Shackelton and the aforementioned Philip Brocklehurst also passed through the Savage doors (present-day Savages will note the Scott/Shackleton menu framed on the wall), it is fair to say few other venues in history could lay claim to be a better informal 'explorers club'.

At the other end of the scale of importance, Brother Savage Billy Bennett was having some success with his gentle send-up of the League of Nations and its constituent nations' stereotypes in his music hall song, 'The League of Nations', recordings of which still exist and were easily found online at the time of writing.

We have already seen how rich and varied the political membership of the Club was in the first half of the twentieth century. In February 1931 their mixture was varied further by the election of the Rt Hon Sir Richard A Squires, the prime minister of Newfoundland. At the time he joined, Squires was trying unsuccessfully to join Newfoundland to the Canadian Confederation and otherwise deal with the harsh effects of the Great Depression, rendering it slightly surprising that he found time to gain admission to a gentleman's club across the Atlantic.

Another interesting occurrence during the 1930s was the unsuccessful application for Savage membership on the part of Frank Percy Crozier, whom we met when discussing AP Herbert and those shot at dawn. Crozier was nominated by Basil Liddell Hart, at the behest of his friend Brother Savage CE Lawrence,[16] but for reasons now lost to history, his candidature was withdrawn before the qualifications committee met.[17] I wonder if it was related to his straitened financial circumstances, since he would have struggled to pay his membership fees or prop up his end of the bar. It seems unlikely he would have been rejected for his pacifism, since a notable Savage at the time was Cyril Joad, one of Britain's best-known anti-war campaigners.

For cricket followers, few Savage evenings in history would compete with 30 June 1934. Brother Savage Collin Brooks (1893–1959) recorded in his diary:[18]

> Saturday [30 June] was full of excitement—there was revolt in Germany —a strong attack by Hitler on his Steel Helmet malcontents. Such a day is interesting in a newspaper office even to a jaded old hand. I like

---

16 CE (Charles) Lawrence, author, playwright and editor of the literary *Cornhill Magazine*. Lawrence gave his address as the Savage Club when writing to *The Times*: in a letter published on 27 August 1924, contributing to a debate on whether London should have a motto, he argued that it need not be in Latin, and the simple word 'duty' would do, since it was 'surely the outstanding characteristic of London throughout'. Whether that is still the outstanding characteristic of London, I decline to comment.

17 Charles Messenger, *Broken Sword: The Tumultuous Life of General Frank Crozier 1897–1937* (Pen & Sword Books, 2013), p 190.

18 One trusts the Savages gave a better account of themselves than the official English team for the Ashes that year, who surrendered the urn they had won in such controversial circumstances in 1932/33. One fears not, since the two leading Australian bowlers, O'Reilly and Grimmet (both legendary spinners) might have put even more tweak on the cotton wool than the traditional ball. Worse for the Savages' prospects was the fact that the Australian batting line-up included one DG Bradman, who had famously honed his batting skills as a small boy in Bowral with the use of a stump hitting a golf ball repeatedly against a wall – doubtless good preparation for the use of a child's bat in the improvised circumstances of the match on the Club table.

the business of men being suddenly sent off in planes across half a continent—the telephone talks with Berlin and Rome—the attempt to keep pace with a running news story ... I left 'em hard at it at about 6:30 and went on to the Savage Club where the Australian Test team was being entertained at the Midsummer revel. The queerly assorted crush in the North West Room—a medley of men, with AP Herbert and Mark Hambourg in the thick of the melee—the jovial dinner—the concert afterwards with its retained bohemianism ... at one stage there was a match between some of the Australians and some of the English sporting journalists – the pitch the centre table, laboriously "rolled" with a wine bottle—the implements of a small boy's cricket set with stumps and a bat about a foot long and a ball of cotton wool—quite ridiculously puerile and ridiculously funny.

In 1936 the Club bade farewell to the Adelphi and moved to its new home in Carlton House Terrace, where it was to stay until 1963.[19] Pictures from the time show the Adelphi to have been in a poor state of repair, despite the splendour of its design.[20] Worse, the Club suffered terribly from cockroaches. Mark Hambourg recalled complaining that his bowl of soup contained some of the repulsive insects, only to have the waitress reply 'My oh my! Mr Hambourg, I did think I had taken them all out.'[21]

The Club marked the occasion of the change of premises with a dinner with CE Lawrence in the chair (he of the failed Frank Crozier nomination). Honorary life memberships were given to the brothers Joseph and Roland Harker for donating a mural painting to the new building, and to Guy Church for assisting with the move.[22]

AP Herbert's request for the new premises was for 'more lavatories and fewer Welsh tenors', while Mac Hastings was heard to remark upon seeing the new building with its spacious entrance 'This isn't a club. It's a bloody staircase.'[23]

Mark Hambourg felt some regret at the move:[24]

Everyone felt sad when we were forced to leave our old house in

---

19 The Club stayed in 1, Carlton House Terrace until 1963, when it moved to the National Liberal Club (NLC). It lasted two years there before going to 37 King St, Covent Garden, in 1965. In 1968 it moved to the Constitutional Club, at 86 St James's Street. In 1975 it moved to the Lansdowne Club in Berkeley Square, and finally returned to the NLC in 1990, where it remains at the time of writing.

20 There is a photo album of the Savage at the Adelphi still kept in the Club today, dedicated 'to Sir William Llewellyn GCVO, PRA, from the Savage Club, 16 November 1935.' It is normally found on the table by the entrance, where the current candidates' book is kept.

21 Bradshaw, op cit, p 106.

22 Bradshaw, op cit, p 101

23 Joe Batten, *Joe Batten's Book: The Story of Sound Recording* (Rockliff Publishing Corp, 1956, Kindle edn).

24 Hambourg, *The Eighth Octave* (Williams and Norgate, 1951), p 141.

Adelphi Terrace. It was uncomfortable, cramped for space, extremely dirty, but always romantic, with its view over the embankment, its beautiful Adams dining-room, and its literary surroundings, Bernard Shaw in one of the neighbouring houses, and Barrie in another. There was lamentation that we should never find a place like it in London. I was chairman at our last but one Saturday night concert there, and so I was allowed to make a speech in which I tried to assuage the general grief by suggesting that though it would indeed be difficult to replace the Adelphi atmosphere, that our committee were sure to succeed in finding us another desirable haven, which of course they did.

Some good news from the time of the move was that the Club's finances had become returned to good health, despite the tail end of the Great Depression, and thus members would or should have been most contented with Savage life once again. The problem was that events outside the Savage Club were starting to give grave cause for concern, something to which we will now turn.

Descent into darkness: the rise of fascism 1933–1945

The rise of Hitler and Nazism in the 1930s did not go unnoticed at the Savage Club.

To begin with, few in Europe suspected what Hitler was about. Characteristically, the Savages initially decided he should be a figure of fun. On 5 January 1935, a house dinner was held with Percy V Bradshaw (whose work as the editor of the centenary history of the Club I have drawn upon extensively in this book) in the chair. The menu for the dinner consisted of a cartoon picture of Hitler entitled, in mock-graffiti script, 'Heil Nazi Night', with the 'Savage Club' printed in a severe looking font and Bradshaw's name styled as 'Percy Von Bradshaw'.[25]

Whatever later readers might have made of it, the evening was only sending up what was then not much more than a curiosity. It was certainly not promoting a local branch of the National Socialists. For many years after the war the Club displayed the menu on the wall, but members grew tired of having to explain it to newcomers who drew the wrong conclusion devoid of any context, so they moved it to the archives. That seems a shame: laughter and mockery were vital tools against Nazism before, during and after the war, even if later generations have occasionally struggled with a humorous take on the Führer's fools (as evinced, for

---

25 The menu was reproduced in Matthew Norgate and Alan Wykes' 1976 collection of Savage stories and menus, *Not So Savage* (Jupiter Books, 1976), p 96. On page 95 they explain about the menu being a joke, since no-one knew what the 'V' in Bradshaw's initials meant, and no-one would have made a worse dictator than Bradshaw either.

example, by the needless furore over Prince Harry attending a fancy-dress party in a faux-Afrika Korps outfit in 2005).[26]

The faltering Savages

Unfortunately, some Savages did not go along with the joke and began to find common ground with the Nazi cause. Two Great War veterans in particular, Collin Brooks and Henry Williamson, acted in a fashion which from a modern perspective looks thoroughly shameful.

Collin Brooks

Earlier in this chapter we saw Collin Brooks record some fun with the Australian national cricket team. A few years beforehand, Brooks had been a wartime hero, spending time in the Tank Corp and Machine Gun Corp, both cutting-edge divisions in terms of the technology of the day. He fought on both the Western Front and in the Italian campaign. Near the end of the war, he was awarded the Military Cross. His citation read:[27]

> For conspicuous gallantry and devotion to duty during the attack across the Piave on 27 October 1918. This officer led his four guns forward under heavy shell and machine gun fire with the forward waves of the infantry. On arrival at the objective, by his skilful handling of his guns, he formed a defensive flank and in spite of heavy casualties he maintained his position. The coolness and energy of this officer was, throughout the action, a fine example to the men under him.

After the war Brooks became a full-time journalist. He rose to become editor of the *Financial News* in 1933. In that capacity he met the Fleet Street grandee Lord Rothermere, a man who had lost two sons during the war. The two men became very close over the next few years, with Brooks serving as a close advisor

---

26 Why anyone thought Harry was supporting the German regime is anyone's guess: the shop from which he hired the outfit had presumably hired it to many others without raising anyone's eyebrow; Prince Charles had earlier attended a performance of Mel Brooks' *The Producers*, while countless radio and television programmes and films had (correctly) sent up the Nazis and their ways from *The Goon Show* to *Dad's Army* to *Allo Allo*.

27 Brooks also made his own notes of the engagement:

> Have reached C. Fighera with two gun teams and am held by hostile MG [machine gun] with which we are dealing. Teams were considerably weakened by rifle & MG fire. Fording the river and further (MG) support on left boundary line is requested. No counter attacks have developed & local resistance is being rapidly overcome. Our line was badly broken by initial resistance and by natural features and lateral communication is poor." His next report states that nine men were wounded; this was followed by a report at 12:00 hrs: "At 11:00 I took over C. ARAGIOTTO and consolidated it into a double MG strongpoint firing W. and N. I am handing this over to No 2 Sec Select and am proceeding north.

and confidant as well as a friend (in a form partially restricted by the rigidity of the class system of the day).

Rothermere was an overt admirer and supporter of the Third Reich. He met Hitler in person and corresponded with him on a number of occasions over the following years.[28] He congratulated Hitler over Czechoslovakia and encouraged him to take Romania as an encore. As late as 1939, he was still writing sycophantic drivel, including a letter which began 'My Dear Führer, I have watched with understanding and interest the progress of your great and superhuman work in regenerating your country'.[29]

By dint of his close association with Rothermere, Brooks bears some vicarious responsibility for that hopeless saga. Moreover, some of his other diary entries over the 1930s were a good deal less appealing than his japes with Australian cricketers. On 7 June 1936, for example, he wrote:

> ... went to Bethnall Green for a Fascist rally, which I wrote up for the Daily Mail. ... it is lacking the real essence of the matter, which is that it was the anti-Jewish references that drew the cheers. These references the Mail took out because they thought their Jewish advertisers would be offended. This is the freedom of the Press, and this the power of the Jew. Here in little is the justification of Fascism.

On 12 January 1939:[30]

> ... He [a colleague] has taken into his home a young Jewish refugee of 19 and is to take in his younger brother. I refrained from asking if he had ever taken in a couple of young English unemployed.

He moderated his views once war broke out, though did not fully dissociate himself from the far right of the day.[31]

---

28 It is clear Rothermere's intention was not simply to avoid war. He owned the *Daily Mail*, reponsible for one of the most notorious headlines in British history ('Hurrah for the Blackshirts' it trumpeted on 15 January 1934). He consistently promoted Hitler to the British establishment. One of his papers wrote that Hitler had saved Germany from 'Israelites of international attachments' and declared the 'minor misdeeds of individual Nazis will be submerged by the immense benefits that the new regime is already bestowing upon Germany.'

29 His interactions with the Nazis included dealings with Princess Stephanie von Hohenlohe, a dubious woman who could have come straight from a Bond film. See Jim Wilson, *Nazi Princess: Hitler, Lord Rothermere and Princess Stephanie Von Hohenlohe* (The History Press, 2011). Rothermere paid her a retainer of £5,000 per year (an enormous sum at the time – Brooks' salary was a mere £2,000 per year, albeit bolstered by an £800 expense account). In 1939 she fled to the USA. A memo to President Roosevelt described her as a spy 'more dangerous than ten thousand men'.

30 In the same entry he goes on to report his friend telling him 'Hitler has now found himself a German girlfriend. Her name is Braun, she is the usual Teutonic broad hipped, blond type, and she likes swigging beer, but dares not swig when Hitler is present.'

31 On 23 May 1940 his diary read:

Henry Williamson

In the chapter on Savage Men of Letters we saw how Henry Williamson served throughout the Great War and then become a best-selling author. Sadly, he never recovered from the hellish experiences of the Western Front and in particular his shock during the Christmas Truce in 1914 upon discovering that the Germans were no different from himself. Like Brooks and Rothermere, that experience convinced him that anything was preferable to another war between Britain and Germany, and as with both of them he went further than simply supporting appeasement of German demands. He visited Germany in 1935 and returned full of praise for the new regime, in particular the Hitler Youth movement, and went on to join Oswald Mosley's British Union of Fascists. He also became a personal friend of the Mosleys. His son later wrote:[32]

> For my father [the Christmas Truce] was the most transcendent moment of his life. It crystallised his ideas of Brotherhood among men of which Beethoven had dreamed in his Ninth Symphony a century before. He thought: never again must such madness be allowed to happen. His mind was channelled and transfixed into ways in which he could help explain why that war must be the one to end all wars. For the rest of his life Father stuck to his light on the pole and raged, raged, against the dying of that light—a light of friendship and peace.

> Of course he was not waving but drowning in his hopeless cause. He thought the new German army would think like him since they too had been to the brink of extinction. Forgiveness, he thought, must work. Sometimes it does. The prime example is Nelson Mandela. That man's lack of revengeful thoughts and actions and his ability to refocus the opposition on to peace are a lesson to us all. But he understood the opposition. My father did not. His ideas were akin to a bull in a china shop trying to rearrange the ornaments.

Williamson offered to be a peace broker between Britain and Germany when

---

Great excitement in Great Smith Street – the British Fascists being rounded up by the police. Later in the day came the news that Captain Ramsay had been arrested which puzzled me. I took tea with him once and found him the conventional anti-Jew fanatic, tracing all our woes back to the Protocols of Zion, which most people, even anti-Semites, believe to be forged. A rather crazy man, was my summing-up of him.'

But Brooks also continued to edit the newspaper *Truth*, which was sympathetic to fascism. From 1944, his deputy on the paper was the notorious fascist sympathiser AK Chesterton (second cousin of GK and Cecil), another Military Cross winner from the First World War who was desperate to avoid a repeat of the conflict. Chesterton signed up nevertheless when the Second World War began, and served until 1943 when he was invalided out due to ill health. By then he had left any actual fascist party by then but was still prone to writing pro-fascist nonsense for Brooks under a pseudonym and commissioning sympathetic pieces from the reactionary wing of the Tory party. See D Renton, Fascism, *Anti-Fascism and Britain in the 1940s* (Palgrave Macmillan, 2000), pp 58–60.

32 Richard Williamson, 'Black earth and silence of peace in No Man's Land', Henry Williamson Society website, https://www.henrywilliamson.co.uk/hw–and–the–first–world–war/57–uncategorised/172–black–earth–and–silence–of–peace–in–no–man–s–land.

the war broke out. He was interred under Defence Regulation 18B as a Nazi sympathiser, but was released after only a week.

Even after the war, when there could no longer be any dispute about the fact of Nazi atrocities, Williamson was still expressing sympathetic views about fascism. In more recent times, editors of the website dedicated to his exceptional literary achievements have felt compelled to include a strongly worded message dissociating themselves from his political views and activities.[33]

His family have always denied that politics played a major part in his life and have maintained that his fascist dealings were born principally of a desire to avoid another war.[34] I do however have to take issue with the following statement found on the Williamson website at the time of writing:[35]

> By this time [1966] it was realised and recognised by many objective thinkers that Oswald Mosley's incarceration in prison without trial was in fact unfair and technically illegal—although such situations were covered by Defence Regulation 18B—and that in many ways Mosley had merely been ahead of his time, although a hothead in his methods. He was certainly no longer considered a political force or threat in any way.

It is true that Defence Regulation 18B as applied by the courts in the infamous case of *Liversidge v Anderson*[36] was unfair and contrary to basic justice as guaranteed by Magna Carta in the legendary passage that a 'freeman shall not be ... imprisoned ... unless by the judgement of his peers'. Regulation 18B allowed the Secretary of State to detain an individual with no recourse to the courts. In his famous dissenting judgment, long since part of legal folklore, Lord Atkin reminded everyone that the law is not silent during wartime, and that held that the court should read reg 18B as requiring a trial or at least judicial examination of the case for detention. Most lawyers nowadays side with Lord Atkin and there is little doubt that, fortified by the European Convention on Human Rights, the present-day courts would reach the same decision as him.

Nevertheless, that controversy says nothing about the individual cases of people detained under the regulation, and in particular whether they would have been detained anyway had the Home Secretary been answerable to the courts in the matter. Just because Mosley was detained under an unjust law does not redeem his character or his actions.

Further, at no stage of his life was Mosley 'ahead of his time'. He was a bigot

---

33 https://www.henrywilliamson.co.uk/57–uncategorised/55–fascism. At the time of writing, the Wikipedia page on Williamson contained various links to white supremacist organisations; I decline to provide the references.

34 Jasper Copping, 'Tarka author tells of 1914 Christmas Truce', *Daily Telegraph*, 9 March 2014.

35 https://www.henrywilliamson.co.uk/bibliography/a–lifes–work/a–solitary–war.

36 See my book *Trials and Tribulations* (Wildy, Simmonds & Hill, 2015), Ch 15.

who believed non-white races and Jews were inferior human beings. He was no longer considered a political force in 1966 because his ideas had long been discredited, not because he had mended his ways.

Some mitigation

The fact that Brooks and Williamson advocated appeasement is not sufficient of itself to condemn them. Appeasement was, after all, official government policy for most of the 1930s. For much of the time, there would have seemed little practical alternative, since the public would never have accepted a reprise of the Great War except under extreme circumstances. Also, Britain on her own was an empty threat to Germany. Lack of investment through the 1920s had left her forces in an unimpressive state; hence, if nothing else, appeasement bought Britain some time to rearm.

Obviously they were not the only ones impressed with Hitler either. Brother Savage CB Fry, the legendary former cricketer and all-round athlete, made almost toadying comments about the Nazi regime in his autobiography published in the late 1930s, and he even allowed the offending passages to remain in later editions of the book until well after the rest of the country knew what Hitler was about.[37] Then there were two royal Savages, Edward VIII and George VI, neither of whom (but especially the former) distinguished himself with his public or private stance towards Nazi Germany for most of the 1930s.[38]

Moreover, in his early letters to Rothermere, Hitler was careful not to disclose the extent of his ambition or his brutality. For example, in 1935 he wrote a letter containing the following passage:[39]

> I believe that a methodical, scientific examination of the European history of the last 300 years will show that 9/10ths of the blood sacrifices of the battlefields have been shed entirely in vain. That is to say, in vain measured by the natural interests of the participating nations.

Given what was to follow, that has to count as one of the most crushingly ironic statements in recorded history.

Further, it is easy for modern readers to insist from the far distance of the twenty-first century that those in Britain in the 1930s should have been more

---

37 CB Fry, *Life Worth Living* (Pavilion Library, 1939).

38 See for example Andrew Roberts, *Eminent Churchillians* (Weidenfeld & Nicolson, 2010, Kindle edn), Ch 1, which is an excoriating attack on the royal family and appeasement in the 1930s. For her part, in her old age, the Queen Mother recalled: 'The two people who have caused me most trouble in my life are Wallis Simpson and Adolf Hitler' (quoted in Craig Brown, *One on One* (Fourth Estate, 2011), p 329.

39 Letter of 3 May 1935 from Adolf Hitler to Lord Rothermere, quoted in NJ Crowson (ed), *Fleet Street, Press Barons and Politics: The Journals of Collin Brooks, 1932–1940* (Cambridge University Press, 1999), Appendix A.

confrontational. It would not have been obvious then that if there was war with Germany, Britain would prevail because the Germans would make the fatal strategic errors of fighting on two fronts and declaring war on the United States.

If there is a modern parallel to 1930s' appeasement, it might be the rise of the vile death cult ISIS in Iraq and Syria following the failed Anglo-American intervention in the former country in 2003. ISIS is at least as sadistic and twisted as the Nazis were, and has made a point of broadcasting its acts of savagery in high definition social media posts.[40] Life for anyone not on message in its territories (thankfully, it controls little remaining territory at the time of writing) has to be of unimaginable horror. Yet there has been no appetite for Western boots on the ground,[41] despite the sickening images and reports emanating from ISIS territory and despite the attacks on Western soil attributed to ISIS and its sympathisers.

The verdict

All of the mitigation notwithstanding, we cannot grant Brooks or Williamson (or, for that matter, Fry or Rothermere) a complete exoneration – or anything close. All of them continued their line of sympathy towards Hitler after Nazi abuse of Jews became incontrovertible, and after German territorial ambitions and contempt for international order were made clear. While they had fellow travellers – the 'guilty men' of the time[42] – there were contemporaries who knew full well what folly appeasement was. It is also not true that all Great War veterans were afraid of a reprise: the anti-appeasers Duff Cooper, Anthony Eden, Harold Macmillan, Roger Keyes and Louis Spears were all hardened veterans just as much as Brooks, but were not prepared to back down against the rise of German expansionism. We therefore have to conclude that Brooks and Williamson acted in a most deplorable fashion and brought lasting shame on themselves accordingly.

---

40 The barbaric antics of ISIS were, regrettably, not historically unprecedented. For a random Great War example of an equivalent atrocity, the Austro-Hungarians hanged an Austrian citizen, Cesare Battisti, in July 1916 after convicting him of treason. Many photographs were taken of his body surrounded by grinning individuals delighting in his death. See for example Jörn Leonhard, *Pandora's Box: A History of the First World War* (Belknap Press, 2018), pp 531–32.

41 Apart from special forces, whose deployments are always secret and therefore generally outside public debate.

42 One other interesting character in the very early days of British fascism was Admiral the Rt Hon Sir Edmund Fremantle, veteran serviceman who fought in the Maori Wars in New Zealand in the nineteenth century. He joined the first ever British fascist party in the 1920s, when he was well into his dotage. Fremantle was nominated for Savage membership in December 1912 (one of his seconders being Mostyn Pigott) but his candidature was withdrawn at his request.

The anti-appeasers

On a happier note, it is right to record that other Savages of the time were on the right side of history. Prominent among them were the great conductor Sir Thomas Beecham[43] and the great New Zealand cartoonist David Low.

By the 1930s, Beecham (who had joined the Savage Club in November 1916) had a towering international reputation as a conductor. When Dr Berta Geissmar, personal assistant to the famous German conductor Wilhelm Furtwängler, had to flee to Britain to escape persecution, since she was Jewish, Beecham hired her immediately as his secretary and took her with him when he toured Germany. Although she was terrified at the prospect of being abducted by the Nazis, no such attempt was made as she stayed close to Beecham.[44] During the tour, Beecham insulted Hitler on the radio at a concert in Berlin: one version of the anecdote started that when he saw Hitler applauding, Beecham turned to the orchestra and said, 'The old bugger seems to like it!',[45] while another had it that Beecham grumbled 'the old bugger's late' when Hitler did not turn up on time.[46]

Low, meanwhile, who joined the Savage Club in May 1924, used his inimitable character Colonel Blimp to satirise the power-crazed leaders who were gradually leading the world to Armageddon. Here are some of Blimp's lines from cartoons of the era:[47]

On the press barons' appeasement:

---

43 Sir Thomas Beecham (1879–1961). Among many life achievements, from 1906 to 1908 Beecham ran the New Symphony Orchestra, before leaving and being replaced by another eminent Savage conductor, Landon Ronald. Throughout the Great War, Beecham threw himself into trying to sustain live music in Britain, often working unpaid and donating money to musical institutions including the London Symphony Orchestra and the Royal Philharmonic Society. In 1915 he formed the Beecham Opera Company, composed mostly of British singers, and put on performances throughout the country. He was knighted in the New Year Honours in 1916.

Not long before the outbreak of war, his father, Joseph Beecham, had entered into an agreement to buy the Covent Garden estate from the Duke of Bedford and float a limited company to manage the estate commercially. The deal was held up by wartime, and in October 1916 Joseph Beecham died. After the war Beecham and his brother saw through a modified agreement which eventually led to the estate being included in a new company, Beecham Estates and Pills Ltd. The pressure of financing the deal kept Beecham away from music for three years, but he succeeded in raising the necessary funds.

Despite their common Club membership, Beecham did not always get on with Sir Henry Wood, or indeed other English conductors of the time, though he had much better relations with foreign conductors such as Wilhelm Furtwangler.

44 'Beecham as we knew him', *The Guardian*, 6 April 2001. The anecdotes were from Beecham's widow, still alive at the time, 40 years after his death.

45 Ibid.

46 John Lucas, *Thomas Beecham: An Obsession with Music* (Boydell Press, 2008), p 232.

47 David Low, *The Complete Colonel Blimp* (Bellew Publishing, 1991).

Gad, sir, Lord Rathermere is right. We must have a bigger Army to protect the Navy and a bigger Navy to protect the Army. Only then can we fight the French and the Italians and the Abyssinians and keep the war from spreading.

Gad, sir, Lord Blither is right. Baldwin must default on some more pacts and keep Lord Beaverbrook's promise to the British people.

Gad, sir, Lord Beaverbrook is right. This League of Nations is a big sham. Why, it's nearly all foreigners.

Gad, sir, Lord Beaverbrook is right. The only way to ensure peace is to give everybody plenty of arms and let them fight it out.

On the Abyssinia Crisis:

Gad, sir, the Worshipful Master is right. You can't expect a Dictator not to send reinforcements which he indignantly denies, to his troops which he has explained are not there. Dash it, it wouldn't be honourable.

Gad, sir, Lord Wallop is right. How can the black savages learn how to use poison gas unless they surrender to Italian civilization?

Gad, sir, the Archbishop is right. Now that Mussolini knows that we drink Italian blood like whisky, perhaps he will arrange to put a bit more soda in it.

On the Spanish Civil War:

Gad, sir, Lord Blast is right. Civilization demands the withdrawal of all Spanish troops from Spain, to let the foreigners settle it among themselves.

Gad sir, Lord Bunk is right. The only way Chamberlain can manage to keep a cool head is to keep raising his hat to Franco.

Gad sir, the Duce is right. It is very sinister that Moscow will give no undertaking to prevent the Spaniards from usurping Spain.

On the rise of Japanese aggression:

Gad, sir, Lord Poppycock is right. We can't declare a boycott of Japanese goods, because then how could Japan pay innocent business men for the raw materials to make their bombs.

On Stalin:

Who's next to be liberated from freedom, Sir?

Low's finest achievement in the 1930s was the fact he managed to annoy not just the appeasers in Britain but also those whom they were trying to appease.

His anti-Nazi cartoons led to the *Evening Standard* being banned in Germany. Even better, when Lord Halifax visited Berlin in 1937, Goebbels complained to him about Low's caricatures of Hitler (Low had drawn Hitler as a militant pigmy strutting across the page). Halifax, like a crawling school snitch, reported the remarks to Low, who commendably ignored them.[48] Interestingly, British newspaper columns also criticised the Nazis, but the Nazis did not try to silence them – thus demonstrating the power of the cartoon.

All of his efforts led to Low being put in the Nazi's infamous 'black book', *Sonderfahndungsliste GB* (Special Search List Great Britain), the list drawn up by the SS of prominent British residents to be arrested once the Germans had invaded. 'That's alright', said Low when the book was discovered in 1945, 'I had them on my list too.'

Blimp's critic Harold Nicolson was on there, as were Lord Beaverbrook and Neville Chamberlain – the latter two more surprisingly given they were appeasers whereas Nicolson and Low were not. Lytton Strachey was included despite having been dead for eight years. Philip Gibbs, the celebrated war reporter, was also included: he had worked briefly as a war correspondent for the *Daily Sketch* in 1939 and then moved to the Ministry of Information. Sybil Thorndike and Cyril Joad were on it despite their well-known pacifism. Kenneth Duffield was another Savage on the list.

The best riposte to the list came from the actress Rebecca West, who appeared in it along with her friend Noël Coward. When the list became public, with the assumption that the people on it would have been executed by the Gestapo, she wrote to Coward saying 'my dear – the people we should have been seen dead with!'

One other anti-appeaser we should mention was Lady Violet Bonham Carter, sister of Brother Savage Herbert 'Beb' Asquith (as already noted, her name adorns a room in the NLC which has hosted countless Savage functions over the years). She participated in a number of anti-fascist groups and came up with her own memorable aphorism when she derided Chamberlain for pursuing a policy of 'peace at any price that others can be forced to pay'.

Civilisation triumphs at the Savage Club

Finally, we can pay tribute to the Savage Club itself. In 1940, Henry Williamson arrived at the Club with Oswald Mosley as his guest. The Club denied entry to Mosley.

Williamson might have been labouring under illusions about Mosley and his ideas. To their great credit, his Brother Savages knew what Mosley was about and acted accordingly.

---

48 Low, op cit, Ch 21.

The eve of the war

In reaching the start of the Second World War, we have now come to an arbitrary stopping point. I say 'arbitrary' because I have always thought it wrong to separate the two world wars; they were not discrete events but were instead part of a disastrous continuum of world events, at least for the European theatre. Their origins lay with Napoleon's oppression of the German-speaking states and ended, so far as they have ended, with the fall of the Soviet Union. An alternative title might be 'The Wars of German Unification', certainly for the period 1870–1990.

One person who had not had a great time of it during the 1930s, but would shortly find his hour had arrived, was that most remarkable man, Sir Winston Churchill, whose portrait all modern Savages see en route to the Club. In Appendix II we will look at the history of that equally remarkable painting.

As a final word about the Club, I would draw readers' attention to the foreword to Joseph Batten's memoirs, written in the early 1950s, in which Sir Compton Mackenzie stated:

> A particularly attractive slice of this book is given to the Savage Club, and a devoted Savage has been able to convey in words much of what that has meant to him. There are not many clubs left that keep the authentic atmosphere of what a club once was. I suppose with a sigh that fifty years from now the club as we still know it will sound like a myth.

More than 50 years from then we can heave a bigger sigh of relief that Sir Compton was wrong with his prediction, and we can say with confidence that the Club today would be recognisable to any of the men written about in this book – as I hope it will be in another 50 years from now.

APPENDICES

Timeline of the Great War

1914	
June 28	Archduke Franz Ferdinand assassinated in Sarajevo
July 5	Kaiser Wilhelm II promises German support for Austria against Serbia
July 28	Austria declares war on Serbia
August 1	Germany declares war on Russia
August 3	Germany declares war on France and invades Belgium
August 4	Britain declares war on Germany
August 23	British retreat from Mons begins and Germany invades French territory
August 26	Russian Army defeated at Tannenburg and Masurian Lakes
August 27	'Battle of the Frontiers' in which France loses 27,000 killed in one day
September 6	Battle of the Marne begins
October 18	First Battle of Ypres
October 29	Turkey enters the war on Germany's side
1915	
January 19	First Zeppelin raid on Britain
February 19	British bombard Turkish forts in the Dardanelles
April 25	Allied troops land in Gallipoli
May 7	RMS *Lusitania* sunk by a German U-boat
May 23	Italy declares war on Germany and Austria
August 5	Germany captures Warsaw from Russia
September 25	Battle of Loos begins
December 18	Resignation of Sir John French takes effect
December 19	Allied evacuation of Gallipoli begins
1916	
January 27	Conscription begins in Britain
February 21	Battle of Verdun begins
April 29	British forces surrender to Turkish forces at Knut, Mesopotamia
May 31	Battle of Jutland
June 4	Brusilov Offensive begins

June 6	Death of Lord Kitchener
July 1	First day of the Battle of the Somme
August 10	End of the Brusilov Offensive
September 15	First use of tanks en masse, on the Somme
December 7	Lloyd George becomes British prime minister
1917	
February 1	Germany begins unrestricted submarine war
April 6	USA declares war on Germany
April 12	Canadians capture Vimy Ridge, under the command of Brother Savage Julian Byng
April 16	Start of French offensive on the Western Front
July 31	Third Battle of Ypres begins (Passchendaele)
October 24	Battle of Caporetto
November 20	British tanks achieve success at Cambrai under the command of Brother Savage Julian Byng
December 5	Armistice signed between Germany and Russia
December 9	Jerusalem captured by Britain from Turkey
1918	
March 3	Treaty of Brest-Litovsk signed between Germany and Russia
March 21	German 'Operation Michael' breaks through on the Somme
March 29	Marshal Foch appointed Allied Commander on the Western Front
April 9	German offensive in Flanders begins
July 15	Second Battle of the Marne begins
August 8	Battle of Amiens, start of the 'Hundred Days' Allied Offensive 'Black Day of the German Army' according to General Ludendorff
September 19	Turkish forces collapse at Megiddo
October 4	Germany asks for an Armistice
October 29	German Navy mutinies
October 30	Turkey makes peace with the Allies
November 3	Austria makes peace with the Allies
November 9	Kaiser Wilhelm II abdicates
November 11	Germany signs Armistice at 5am, and the guns fall silent as agreed at 11am
1919	
January 4	Peace conference begins at Paris
June 21	German fleet scuttled in Scapa Flow
June 28	Treaty of Versailles signed by Germany

APPENDIX II

The Churchill Portrait

For now the noise of hooves thundering across the veldt; the clamour of the hustings in a score of contests; the shots in Sidney Street, the angry guns of Gallipoli, Flanders, Coronel and the Falkland Islands; the sullen feet of marching men in Tonypandy; the urgent warnings of the Nazi threat; the whine of the sirens and the dawn bombardment of the Normandy beaches—all these now are silent. There is a stillness. And in that stillness, echoes and memories. To each whose life has been touched by Winston Churchill, to each his memory.

Harold Wilson, 1965 memorial speech to the House of Commons
upon the death of Sir Winston Churchill

Introduction

Every Savage member's journey to the Clubroom passes through the entrance to the National Liberal Club. As one reaches the staircase and turns right to head towards the Savage sanctuary, one glances naturally to the side and sees a stirring portrait of arguably the most famous person in British history, Sir Winston Leonard Spencer Churchill. The picture was painted in 1915 at the height of the First World War.

Fittingly, given the legendary life of its subject, the painting has an intriguing history as well. As the author Rosemary Hill put it in more poetic terms, the painting has undergone 'sympathetic sufferings with its subject on the scale of Dorian Gray's.'[1]

Somewhat surprisingly, Churchill's biographers have been unable to agree on all of the basic details of the painting. There is confusion over the uniform Churchill is depicted wearing: some assume it is of the office he had recently held, First Lord of the Admiralty, when it is in fact a Privy Councillor's uniform (there being no actual uniform associated with the role of First Lord since it was

---

1   Rosemary Hill, 'Churchill's Faces', *London Review of Books*, vol 39, no 7, 30 March 2017, p 18.

a civilian, not a military appointment).[2] Sir Martin Gilbert, author of one of the
most detailed multi-volume biographies, differed from other sources in a speech
in 1985 about the dates on which the painting was hung and when it had been
placed into storage.[3] Fortunately, a recent work by the art historian Jonathan
Black, *Winston Churchill in British Art*,[4] provides a much more comprehensive
story than what are really no more than anecdotes, footnotes and asides found in
the Churchill biographies.[5]

The artist

Ernest Townsend was born in 1880 in Derby. He enrolled at the Heatherly School
of Fine Art in London and then the Royal Academy, where he was taught by the
likes of John Singer Sargent. In 1904, he won the Royal Academy's Landseer
Scholarship for figure painting, and in 1905 he won the Academy's Creswick
prize.

He left London in 1907 and travelled in Europe before returning to Derby.
In 1910, a portrait of his was exhibited at the Royal Academy, which led to a
steady stream of portrait commissions which would sustain him for the rest of
his career. In total, Townsend exhibited 15 paintings at the Academy between
1910 and 1937. He also had the distinction of representing Great Britain in the
Olympic Games in Stockholm in 1912, in the now defunct category of painting.
Times change.

He was therefore an established artist, though still quite young, in 1915 when he
obtained the Churchill commission.

---

2   Roy Jenkins, *Churchill: A Biography* (Pan, 2001, Kindle edn). To explain the position: the
    Admiralty was the government department responsible for the command of the Royal Navy.
    The position of First Lord was a political post, established in the seventeenth century. From
    1806, it was always held by a civilian, as with Churchill, while the professional head of the
    navy was known as the First Sea Lord. There were major reforms in 1964, not relevant for our
    purposes.
3   Martin Gilbert MA, 'Spinning Top of Memories: Of Ungrand Places and Moments in Time',
    an address to The International Churchill Society, London, 17 September 1985. The text can be
    found on the Churchill Society website, http://www.winstonchurchill.org/resources/speeches/
    spinning-top-of-memories.
4   Bloomsbury, 2017, Kindle edn. One point of pedantry: Black assumes (at loc 696 of the Kindle
    edition) that Churchill was wearing an admiral's uniform rather than that of a Privy Councillor;
    I have been assured by NLC staff that Jenkins is correct and not Black, though I stand to be
    corrected if an authoritative primary source is drawn to my attention.
5   Various biographers do not even mention the portrait at all, including Piers Brendon, *Winston
    Churchill: a biography* (Harper & Row, 1984), Max Arthur, *Churchill: The Life: An authorised
    pictorial biography* (Cassell, 2015), Chris Wrigley, *Winston Churchill: A Biographical Companion*
    (ABC-CLIO, 2002) and Boris Johnson, *The Churchill Factor: How One Man Made History*
    (Hodder & Stoughton, 2014). The great value of Black's work is that he has researched the
    archives of the NLC Arts Committee.

The picture

Jenkins described the portrait as 'buoyant and verging on the glamorous', and Black also uses the latter adjective. It is certainly a resplendent image. I would suggest, though, that 'glamorous' is not quite the right word. Rather, the painting aims to convey the gravitas of the holder of one of the most important political or military positions, First Lord of the Admiralty – the highest civilian office overseeing the Royal Navy (irrespective of the precise detail of the uniform). That office was never more pivotal to the nation than when Churchill held it in 1915. The public anxiously awaited a second Trafalgar, in which it expected the British Grand Fleet would obliterate the German High Seas Fleet in one fell swoop and hopefully end the war at the same time. If, on the other hand, the Grand Fleet failed, then Britain would be out of the fight. Hence, as we saw in Chapter 4, Churchill himself memorably described the Commander of the Grand Fleet, Brother Savage John Jellicoe, as 'the only man who could lose the war in an afternoon'. The painting therefore captured Churchill at the peak of his career (as he would have assumed at the time) and a critical moment in the fortunes of the nation.

Churchill did not have the physical stature of Henry VIII, so perhaps the picture does not have the resounding impact as the classic Holbein portrait of Henry.[6] On the other hand, the picture does not rely on props, unlike, say, Van Dyke's famous depictions of Charles I. Van Dyke painted Charles on horseback, surrounded by Roman imagery, inferring a link to the most famous martial empire in history. That symbolism was intended to compensate for Charles's feeble physical stature.

Black's opinion is that in the painting 'Churchill emerges in the form of a late Pre-Raphaelite hero from fame and legend, the uniform of the First Lord of the Admiralty reminiscent of the elaborate armour worn by a knight as imagined by Burne-Jones, Waterhouse or Spencer Stanhope'. To my eyes, the portrait falls somewhere in between Holbein and Van Dyke's pictures: Churchill might not dominate the frame in the manner of Henry, but he still cuts a commanding dash, conveying resolve in his visage and military splendour in his regalia.

As ever, the final analysis is in the eye of the beholder. It is worth nothing, though, that it was never Churchill's favourite picture of himself – he preferred the portrait by William Orpen, painted in the summer of 1916.[7]

---

6 I refer to the famous image of Henry VIII by Hans Holbein the Younger, originally created in 1536–1537 as part of a mural showing the Tudor dynasty at the Palace of Whitehall. It was destroyed by fire in 1698, but remained famous due to the many copies.

7 That painting was commissioned by Lord Rothermere, founder of the *Daily Mail*, whom we

The donor

The next point in the history of the painting concerns the identity of the anonymous donor who paid for it. There was much precedent for the gift of a portrait in those days: Lloyd George, for example, had been presented with a portrait at the NLC at the end of January 1913, given to him by the Welsh members of the NLC 'and other Welsh friends, who desired in this manner to honour the Welsh Chancellor of the Exchequer, and express their appreciation of the eminent public services which their distinguished countryman has rendered.'[8] By contrast, the donor of the Churchill portrait was not even known to the NLC's Art Committee, beyond the fact that he was 'Liberal and admirer of Mr Churchill'. 'Liberal' in that context would have meant a member of both the party and the club.

We can infer that the donor would have been quite wealthy, since he was able to afford such a valuable gesture or gift. We can also assume he had particular reason to be grateful to Churchill in spring 1915, when Townsend was first approached for the commission (it was accepted by the club in July of that year). Black's preferred candidate is a dashing chap with the euphonious name of Baron Maurice De Forest (1879–1968), a well-heeled Liberal politician and close friend of Churchill.

De Forest led a most eventful life. He was a pioneering racing driver and aviator who once held the world land speed record.[9] His *outré* adventures also included the then-scandalous act of suing his wife for divorce, citing adultery (it was not so much the adultery which would have shocked the upper classes of the day as much as airing the dirty laundry in public by means of a trial). He lost the case and, as part of the fallout, had to resign from the Reform Club.[10] Churchill was so affronted by the latter action that he resigned from the Reform Club as well and offered Lloyd George's resignation too, despite not having asked

---

met earlier in the book in various contexts.

8   *The Times*, 1 February 1913.

9   De Forest competed in the legendary Gordon Bennett Cup for motor racing and, in 1909, offered a prize of £2,000 to the first Englishman who could fly across the English Channel in an English-built aeroplane. He would have been appalled when the Frenchman Louis Blériot beat them all to it later that year. He promptly doubled the prize, which was eventually won in December 1910 by Thomas Sopwith.

Sopwith, incidentally, was another extraordinary figure in the twentieth century. He founded first his own eponymous aircraft manufacturer, and then, after the war, one named after his chief engineer Harry Hawker. He was also a keen yachtsman who challenged for the America's Cup. A substantial private vessel he owned was later used as an armed escort during the Second World War and survives to the present day as the Royal Yacht of Norway, HNoMY *Norge*.

10 Black, op cit, p 29. For a contemporary account of the divorce trial, see 'Slander Actions in London High Life', *The New York Times*, 16 April 1911.

Lloyd George first. De Forest's friendship with Churchill went back some time: Churchill spent time on De Forest's yacht and stayed three times at De Forest's castle in Moravia, including during his honeymoon with Clementine in 1908.

When the Great War began, De Forest suffered unpleasant attention from the authorities because of his Austro-Hungarian title, even though he had been educated at Eton and Oxford, had been a naturalised British citizen since 1900, had served in the British Army and the British parliament,[11] and his title of baron had been authorised by Royal Licence.[12] With Churchill's help he staved off deportation and found his way into the RNAS Armoured Car Division instead. He promptly kitted out the division at his own expense with a fleet of Rolls-Royce armoured cars, akin to those with which the Duke of Westminster would later rescue Brother Savage Rupert Gwatkin-Williams in the North African desert, as we saw in Chapter 6. De Forest and Churchill parted their ways in later years as the former moved back to the Continent. He would occasionally run in to Churchill in the South of France, when the latter was staying at Lord Rothermere's house in the region.

All of those events support the idea of De Forest expressing his gratitude by funding a grand portrait of Churchill as First Lord of the Admiralty, and choosing the NLC as the home of the painting.[13] Unless something is unearthed in the De Forest family archives to confirm it, however, the conclusion will remain no more than informed speculation.

There is one other possible explanation: perhaps the donor, in a remarkable act of self-aggrandisement, was none other than Churchill himself. That would explain why 'the donor' was so anxious to avoid exposure, and also why he was happy for the portrait to be of Churchill in the prestigious role heading the Admiralty rather than the lesser position he held by the time the sittings began. For, by the time Townsend started work, the Dardanelles disaster had taken place and Churchill no longer held the post of First Lord of the Admiralty.

---

11 De Forest was commissioned into the militia as a second lieutenant in the Prince of Wales's Own Norfolk Artillery (Eastern Division) in 1900. He later became an honorary second lieutenant. He was elected to West Ham North in a by-election in 1911.

12 De Forest had been born in France, supposedly the son of an American circus performer. His parents died in 1882 and he and his brother were adopted by Baroness Clara de Hirsch, *née* Bischoffsheim, wife of banker and philanthropist Baron Maurice de Hirsch de Gereuth. De Forest inherited his adoptive father's title and residence in the Austrio-Hungarian Empire, and from his mother her estates in Rossitz-Eichhorn.

13 We should note that Churchill had begun his political career in 1900 as a Tory. He crossed to the Liberal Party in 1904 when the Tories, under the influence of Joseph Chamberlain (a former Liberal who had left in protest against the Irish Home Rule Bill), started to advocate protectionism.

The painting's progress

The sittings began in the second half of 1915. By November, one had been held with six more planned. Clearly Churchill's post-Gallipoli problems had not affected his standing with the NLC, since not only was the club happy for him still to be depicted as First Lord of the Admiralty, but the Art Committee also considered whether Townsend might be commissioned to paint a replica of the portrait as a gift to Churchill. In the event the prospective cost quashed the idea.

In December 1915, Townsend wrote to the NLC, promising that the painting was nearly finished. By then Churchill was serving voluntarily in the trenches in France with the rank of lieutenant-colonel,[14] though not with a division as he had hoped to command, only a battalion of the Royal Scots Fusiliers.[15]

The painting was finally finished in March 1916. Churchill returned to England on seven days' leave, with the official unveiling to be his only public engagement.[16] When he reached home, however, he learned that questions of the navy were to be debated in the House. He decided to skip the unveiling and head to the House of Commons to speak out against what he saw as a lack of initiative at sea and, while he was about it, to introduce his own policy for the air war. As had been inevitable all along, Churchill was re-entering politics.[17] Everything else, including the painting, would have to wait.

Townsend obtained permission from the NLC to display the portrait at the Royal Academy show in April and May. It finally arrived in the club in June, to be followed by six months of bickering over where it should be hung and whether an official unveiling should take place. Towards the end of the year, Churchill

---

14 Note that Black states that Churchill had the rank of major – he had done so when attached briefly to the 2nd Battalion Grenadier Guards.

15 Churchill later said 'Although an Englishman, it was in Scotland I found the three best things in my life: my wife, my constituency and my Regiment'. According to the Ministry of Defence (MOD) website, Churchill was popular with his troops, especially when ordering dry socks to aid comfort standing in the trenches, and there was no dispute over his physical courage as he made 36 forays into No Man's Land. See the MOD website archive, http://www.army.mod.uk/infantry/regiments/4598.aspx.

Having said that, his time in the trenches was ridiculed by the historian and former Gurkha officer Gordon Corrigan, who said 'To appoint an inexperienced outsider to command a battalion, and then to allow him to bring in a chum who was not even an infantryman as his second-in-command, was nothing short of disgraceful. It denied a professional officer of the regiment a command, and exposed the soldiers to the whims of a military dilettante.' Corrigan disputed that any noteworthy enemy action occurred during Churchill's brief time in the trenches, though he did not dispute Churchill's personal courage (Corrigan, *Blood, Sweat and Arrogance, and the myths of Churchill's War* (Phoenix, 2006), pp 22–23).

16 Martin Gilbert, *Churchill: A Life* (Pimlico, 2000), p 350.

17 Not that Churchill's mind was ever off greater things, even when stationed in the trenches. For example, he wrote to Lloyd George on 25 January 1916 about Lloyd George's position and the generally declining war situation, still arguing for an offensive away from the Western Front in spite of the failure of the Gallipoli campaign.

infuriated the pro-Asquith NLC by supporting Lloyd George when the two fell out. In response, the club decided in January 1917 to hang the picture somewhat out of the way in the committee room. It was also deemed 'inopportune' for a ceremony to accompany the move.

A rapprochement of sorts took place later in the same year, when Churchill was appointed to the key position of minister of munitions (on 18 July 1917). Once more an unveiling was considered, along with moving the painting to a much more prominent place in the dining room. Churchill himself, though, remained preoccupied with war business and so was never available for an official unveiling.

Following the Armistice, it was some time before the club reassumed its old premises, and it had to spend time and money refurbishing them. One imagines the Churchill painting was not high on the list of priorities. In December 1920, the party's internal strife manifested itself in the club when the Lloyd George portrait was removed. The Art Committee wanted to remove Churchill's as well, but it did not get around to it until after February 1921, when the painting was moved into 'a dry well-ventilated place', or the cellar as it was more usually known.

In 1922, the Liberal Party fell apart and the ruling coalition government collapsed. Churchill had to have an appendectomy during the resultant election campaign. In the event, he lost his Scottish seat, leading to his famous remark that he had left town 'without an office, without a seat, without a party and without an appendix.' Characteristically, he then switched horses and aligned himself with Asquith's faction of the party, pleasing the NLC so much that it retrieved his portrait and hung it in the smoking room.

It was not to last. Having failed to be elected as a Liberal in the December 1923 election, Churchill brazenly crossed the floor to the Tories. There were members of both parties who took a dim view of that sort of opportunism – Churchill himself conceded 'anyone can rat, but it takes a certain ingenuity to re-rat' – and the painting was banished to the cellar once again.

Difficult years

Churchill had a mostly unsuccessful time in frontline politics in the 1920s. The 1930s were even worse: he himself called them his 'wilderness years' as he fell from influence. He was further marginalised as one of the few voices opposing appeasement, and made himself more unpopular still by supporting Edward VIII's desire to marry Mrs Simpson. Boris Johnson, Churchill's most recent biographer at the time of writing, put Churchill's position at the beginning of 1937 in colourful words:[18]

---

18 Johnson, op cit.

He was by now sixty-two, and he looked obsolete, washed up, a great Edwardian sea creature flapping helplessly on the shingle and spouting empty nothings from his blowhole. Hardly anyone would have believed, at that point, that within three and a half years he would be Prime Minister.

As a result, hardly anyone would have believed that the painting would see daylight again. But then came Churchill's astonishing comeback, first to his old position as First Lord of the Admiralty, which prompted the famous signal to the Fleet 'Winston's back', and finally, at the age of 65, prime minister during Britain's darkest hour.[19]

Jellicoe once wrote that Churchill was unable to see his own limitations as a politician and a civilian. Few could disagree, but in 1940 those were precisely the qualities the country needed. Not many rational people would have argued in favour of Britain and her Empire continuing to fight on after the fall of France, when the Germans seemed unstoppable.

Hindsight, of course, tells us Churchill was right. It also tells us no other politician of the day could have had performed the same role and expected the same outcome.

Redemption

After Churchill had assumed the premiership, the NLC brought the painting out of storage in what Roy Jenkins called an 'ecumenical gesture'. It was placed in the now-familiar position by the staircase. Still another twist followed, as the painting was badly damaged in 1941 by the same bomb which caused such costly damage to the staircase.

Over the next two years, the painting was painstakingly restored (the staircase would take much longer). In July 1943, it was unveiled again – this time, at long last, in Churchill's presence. Others who joined him included Lady Bonham Carter and his favourite cartoonist, Brother Savage David Low.

Elsewhere, as the Blitz continued to rage, Ernest Townsend worked on another commission: creating designs to camouflage the Rolls-Royce aircraft engine factories in Derby. Those factories produced the Merlin engine of Spitfire, Hurricane and Lancaster fame, and were therefore critical to the war effort. Townsend's design made the buildings appear from the air to be nothing more

---

19 By sheer coincidence, at the precise time the decision was being made to replace Chamberlain with Churchill, the Germans were beginning their assault on the Western Front that was to rout the Allied forces and lead to the fall of France.

than an ordinary village. Sadly, he did not live to see Britain's eventual triumph, as he died in 1944.

Churchill said that when he became prime minister in 1940, all of his previous life experiences had seemed like mere preparation. Perhaps all the travails of the painting were also mere rehearsal for the justly proud position it holds today. We can certainly say that history lends the picture the sort of provenance that anything relating to Churchill deserves.

Mentioned in Despatches

As explained in the Introduction, there were many luminous Savages of the Great War era I would like to have included in this book, but who had to be left out for various reasons. Some did not serve in uniform during the war years or do anything of particular interest on the Home Front. Others did not have sufficient available information on their war record. Then there were those who were largely unknown in their civilian careers. Finally, there was the overarching consideration of wanting to keep the project within manageable boundaries. In this appendix, I have a few short notes on some other interesting Savages, rather like mentioning them in despatches. I do not doubt that there are still more men of interest lurking in the candidate books for future researchers to discover. I should also note that the books are thought to be incomplete; indeed, my source for some individuals' membership was the old lists of members (which included an In Memoriam section) printed occasionally over the years, some of which are now stored in the glass cabinet in the library.

Savage Generals

When the Great War broke out, Field Marshal **Lord Grenfell** (1841–1925) had been retired for six years, following a long and distinguished career taking in the 9th Xhosa War, the Anglo-Zulu War and the Anglo-Egyptian War. He served as commander-in-chief of the Egyptian Army and commanded the forces at the Battle of Suakin in December 1888 and at the Battle of Toski in August 1889 during the Mahdist War. After the declaration of war in 1914, he became responsible for raising the 16th (Service) Battalion, King's Royal Rifle Corps (Church Lads Brigade) in answer to Lord Kitchener's call for volunteers.

Brigadier-General **Sir Frederick Gordon Guggisberg** KCMG, DSO (1869–1930) was a Canadian-born British Army officer and British Empire colonial administrator. He wrote a number of books on military topics and Africa. Of all the men in this appendix, he is one I would have liked to have spent more time on, for he had a worthy record during the Great War. He joined the Savage Club in May 1910. In 1914 he was appointed director of public works in the Gold Coast, but he rejoined the army upon the outbreak of the First World War. From 1915 to 1916, he commanded the 94th Field Company, Royal Engineers. During the Battle of the Somme, he commanded the Royal Engineers in the 8th Division until November 1916, when he transferred to the 66th. From 1917 until 1918, he was brigadier-general commanding the 170th (2/1st North Lancashire) Brigade, and in 1918 commanded the 100th Brigade. He was mentioned in despatches five times, and was awarded the Distinguished Service Order in 1918.

We have already discussed the internal political strife Lord Kitchener encountered during his time at the War Office, the predecessor to the Ministry of Defence. Throughout his time there, he would at least have been able to call upon the dutiful service of Lieutenant-Colonel **Charles Forbes Buchan** CBE, OStJ (1869–1954), who joined the Savage Club in August 1918. When the Great War broke out, Buchan was a major in the Territorial Force Reserve. He served throughout the conflict and reached the rank of lieutenant-colonel as deputy assistant director at the War Office. He was mentioned in despatches and was made CBE in 1919 for valuable services rendered during the war.

In 1919, he left the War Office and went on to serve for years as honorary treasurer of the Navy League and a member of its executive committee. He was also honorary treasurer and secretary of the training ship *Stork*. In 1939 he was invested as an Officer of St John for his work with the Navy League.

Savage Men of Letters

Reginald Arkell (1882–1959) was a comic novelist and script writer who wrote many musical plays for the London theatre. In 1918, he became a life member of the Savage Club. His best known book was possibly *Old Herbaceous*, a comic novel about an aged gardener (he loved horticulture and it formed a theme or background in many of his books) while his best-known play was probably his adaptation of the spoof history *1066 and All That* by Sellar and Yeatman. During the Great War he served with the King's Own Yorkshire Light Infantry and The Norfolk Regiment. He was the composer of the following verse during the war, found among other places on a comic postcard:

> When the war will end!
> Actual evidence I have none;
> But my Aunt's Charwoman's Sister's son,
> Heard a Policeman on his beat,
> Say to a Housemaid in Downing Street,
> That he has a Brother who has a Friend,
> Who knows when the war is going to end!

William Berry, 1ˢᵗ Viscount Camrose DL (1879–1954), was a British newspaper publisher who established quite a dynasty during his lifetime. He was born in Wales, and worked in journalism from an early age. During the Great War, he made his fortune with the magazine *The War Illustrated*, which at its peak had a circulation of 750,000. It enabled him to purchase *The Sunday Times* in 1915 with his younger brother, Gomer Berry, 1ˢᵗ Viscount Kemsley. William served as editor-in-chief until 1937. In 1919 the brothers also purchased the *Financial Times*. William joined the Savage Club in May 1917.

After the war, the Berry brothers along with Sir Edward Iliffe established Allied Newspapers. They went on to purchase a substantial portfolio, including the *Daily Dispatch*, the *Manchester Evening Chronicle*, the *Sunday Chronicle*, the *Sunday News* and, in 1927, *The Daily Telegraph*. A decade later, in 1937, they bought the *Telegraph's* rival, *The Morning Post*.

Notably, after the Second World War, William Berry was one of the wealthy friends of Sir Winston Churchill who pitched in with £5,000 each to enable the Churchills to remain in Chartwell, with the proviso it was presented to the nation upon the death of the Churchills.

Reuben Kelf-Cohen (1895–1978), who joined the Savage Club in May 1936 and became a life member in the same year, served in the Royal Field Artillery during the Great War. In 1920 he joined the Board of Education, and taught at London University from 1924 to 1939. He worked as a senior civil servant during the Second World War, after which he wrote several books on nationalised industry.

Lewis Anselm da Costa Ricci (1886–1947) wrote naval short stories under the name 'Bartimus.'[1] Early in life he was blinded in one eye, which precluded him from serving aboard ships in the navy as he had wished. Instead, he worked for the navy in a desk job. During the Great War he was seconded to the Admiralty as secretary to Admiral CL Napier, and he also worked under Jellicoe. He wrote many stories during the conflict, drawing upon (declassified) information on operations and subjects such as Q-ships. He joined the Savage Club in April 1918. For a time between the wars he served on the royal yacht *Victoria and Albert*. During the Second World War, he worked for the Ministry of Information, until 1944 when he became press secretary to George VI. He held that post until shortly before his death in 1947.

Lieutenant **Norman Davey** (1888–1949) trained as an engineer but also worked as an author, and hence joined the Savage Club in August 1918 under the category of literature.

During the war, he was commissioned as a temporary second lieutenant, initially in the Royal Garrison Artillery and, from January 1915, the Royal

---

1   Bartimeus was the name of the blind beggar in *Mark 10:46–52*.

Engineers. In September 1915 he went to France with the Signal Service. He was later posted to Fifth Army Signals, and was mentioned in despatches in 1917. He returned to England in June 1918 due to ill health. At the war's end he was serving as a general staff officer, 3rd grade, under the assistant director of staff duties (education) at the War Office, with the rank of captain.

His work ranged from a well-received book on the gas turbine, published in 1914 (in the same year, he applied for a patent for the design), to short stories and novels.

In Chapter 6 we discussed Sir Compton Mackenzie and Somerset Maugham, who served in intelligence during the war. Joining them in that cloak and dagger field was the intriguing if less well known **Rowland Kenney** (1882–1961), a life member of the Savage Club from 1924. Kenney worked extensively in Norway during the war. His work was mostly forgotten by history until it became the subject of a 2016 PhD by Paul Buvarp. The abstract of Dr Buvarp's thesis stated:[2]

> Kenney was deeply involved in the development of propaganda policy and practice. In the First World War, his work in Norway resulted in thousands of pro-British articles appearing in the Norwegian press as well as the realignment of the Norwegian national news agency. In the interwar years, in spite of severe medical difficulties, Kenney continued to work within the field of propaganda, becoming instrumental in the establishment of the British Council. At the start of the Second World War, he returned again to Norway, but was forced to flee during the German invasion of April 1940. During the Second World War, Kenney became the Director of the Northern Section of the Foreign Division in the Ministry of Information where he continued to affect policy-creation and the development of propaganda. There is no doubt that Kenney was a key figure in this development. His professional network and his varied roles within the propaganda bureaucracy speak to his level of involvement, and his documented accomplishments even more so.

In the spy context one should also mention **Lawrence du Garde Peach** (1890–1974), **Herbert Claude Stanford** and **Ferdinand Tuohy**. All three served in the Intelligence Corps during the war and all three reached the rank of captain. Peach joined the Savage Club in November 1924, and was a successful author after the war, especially of Ladybird non-fiction history books for children.

Stanford won the Military Cross in 1918. He joined the Savage Club in January 1941.

Tuohy joined the Club in August 1918, just as the Allies were beginning their final victory push on the continent. After the war, he published a book called *The Secret Corps*.[3] A review in *The Spectator* of 26 June 1920 stated:

---

2 University of St Andrews, 2016, http://hdl.handle.net/10023/8647.
3 John Murray, 1920.

Captain Tuohy's "tale of 'intelligence' on all fronts" may be described as the complete manual for the writer of spy stories. He deals with all the methods of espionage and counter-espionage practised during the war, enlivening his exposition here and there with anecdotes. He explains incidentally the value of seemingly harmless military details to an alert enemy and thus justifies the censorship. He declares that our own system proved highly efficient and that our French Allies had, after February, 1916, to implore the assistance of our secret service in Germany as all their own agents had been captured. The British system was based on the principle that each agent should know and be known to his chief alone. It often happened that one agent would complain to headquarters against another agent whom he wrongly suspected of being an enemy spy. The author asserts that we had a secret agent on the staff of Prince Rupprecht throughout the war. "Intelligence," he thinks, was often hampered through the unwillingness of generals to profit by it. Captain Tuohy's book will be read with keen interest.

Captain **HM Raleigh** served with the Leicestershire Regiment during the War and joined the Savage Club in April 1937. He is not much known to history, except that he was the author of a delightful piece on his family's picture of an Egyptian earthenware statue of a hippopotamus, which led to the original statue becoming something of a semi-official symbol of the Metropolitan Museum of Modern Art in New York.

His article, simply entitled 'William', was first published in *Punch* and then reprinted in *The Metropolitan Museum of Art Bulletin*[4] at the request of the staff, who had been charmed by it. Many decades later, in reply to a reader asking why the blue hippopotamus had become so well-known at the museum, *The New York Times* explained:[5]

> A small hippopotamus of blue glazed earthenware, dating from around 1900 B.C., was unearthed in a tomb at Meir in Upper Egypt in May 1910. It was about eight inches long, and its glassy surface was decorated with lotus flowers, buds and leaves. Edward S. Harkness, a trustee, donated it to the museum in 1917.
>
> For a funerary object from the Egyptian Middle Kingdom, the blue hippo was pretty cute. Sensing its appeal, the museum, which had been selling retail goods since 1871, published a color print of the winsome beast. Fourteen years later, Capt. H.M. Raleigh, a British author, wrote a humorous article for Punch magazine describing the oracular powers of the hippo in his print, whom he called "William."
>
> "William is inscrutable, incomprehensible, yet with it all, the friendliest thing in the world," Mr. Raleigh wrote. The Met reprinted the article, and the name, as they say, stuck.

---

4 'William', published in *Punch*, 18 March 1931, and *The Metropolitan Museum of Art Bulletin* vol 26, no 6 (June 1931), pp 153–155.

5 Daniel B Schneiderdec, 'FYI' *The New York Times*, 29 December 2002.

"William and His Friends," a book of photos for children, was published in 1936, and the Met sold the first cast reproductions of the hippo in the 1950's. Today, about a dozen additional William-related items are sold in the gift shop, including neckties, tote bags, stuffed animals and, not surprisingly, tub toys. There is even a William Foundation, for donors who have remembered the Met in their wills. He was, after all, discovered in a tomb, a spokeswoman said.

Edward Richard Buxton Shanks (1892–1953) was a prolific and successful writer of his time. He was born in London and attended Cambridge University, graduating with a degree in history. Thereafter he worked as an editor. In December 1914, not long after the war began, he was made a second lieutenant in the Prince of Wales's Volunteers (South Lancashire Regiment).[6] His most notable wartime contribution was a series of propaganda verses known as *The Winter Soldier*, beginning with one entitled 'To be Sung to the Tune of High Germany':

> No more the English girls may go
> To follow with the drum
> But still they flock together
> To see the soldiers come;
> For horse and foot are marching by
> And the bold artillery:
> They're going to the cruel wars
> In Low Germany.

> They're marching down by lane and town
> And they are hot and dry
> But as they marched together
> I heard the soldiers cry:
> "O all of us, both horse and foot
> And the proud artillery,
> We're going to the merry wars
> In Low Germany."

In 1915, however, he was invalided out, and hence spent the rest of the war on the Home Front, undertaking administrative work. He continued writing, and in 1916 published a biography of Brother Savage Hilaire Belloc.[7]

After the war, Shanks was notable for being the first-ever recipient of the Hawthornden Prize,[8] in 1919, for his book *The Queen of China*. The prize was

---

6 *London Gazette*, 4 December 1914, p 10304.
7 Edward Shanks and C Creighton Mandell, *Hilaire Belloc, the man and his work* (1916).
8 The Hawthornden Prize is an annual British literary award established by Alice Warrender. The criteria is: authors under the age of 41, awarded on the quality of their 'imaginative literature' which can be written in either poetry or prose.

won in later years by Brother Savage Henry Williamson and also by other notable Great War veterans including Siegfried Sassoon and Robert Graves. Shanks joined the Savage Club in May 1924.

Major **James Thompson** DSO,[9] a Savage member from April 1920, evidently had an impressive military career, though left behind little of lasting interest in the category of literature under which he joined.

GM Trevelyan (1876–1962) was a leading British historian and academic in the first half of the twentieth century, even if the study of history has moved on since his time, leaving him much less widely read nowadays. He was a Fellow of Trinity College, Cambridge from 1898 to 1903, before spending the next two decades as a full-time author. In 1927 he returned to Cambridge as Regius Professor of History, and held the post until 1943. He also served as Master of Trinity College from 1940 to 1951.

During the Great War, his poor eyesight excluded him from frontline service, but he did command a British Red Cross ambulance unit on the Italian front from 1915 until the end of the war. He wrote to his father in May 1917:

> We are in the third day and night of the biggest battle we have had yet, and likely to be the most prolonged. It is a great pleasure to be in the fullness of activity and adventure day after day and night after night. Both in Gorizia and also in the high hills such scenes of beauty and romance as this big war in the mountains are wonderful indeed. It is a great life for me, rushing about from front to front and now and then to the base along this thirty miles of mountain battle. No one can have a pleasanter part in it.

After the war he published a book, *Scenes from Italy's War*,[10] recording his time there.

He was made a life member of the Savage Club in 1945.

Esmé Cecil Wingfield-Stratford (1882–1971) was a prolific man of letters. He epitomised the upper class values of his day, by using his ample spare time for athletic and scholarly pursuits.[11] He attended Eton and Cambridge, then the London School of Economics (LSE). In 1913, he published a two-volume work *History of British Patriotism*, bringing together the work he had done at the LSE

---

9   His middle initials are hard to make out in his entry in the candidates' book; they look like 'C. G.', but in O'Moore Creagh VC and E Humphris (eds), *The VC and DSO Volume III* (The Standard Art Book Company), p 69, the only entry that could correspond to him reads 'THOMPSON, JAMES GEORGE COULTHERED, Major, Royal Field Artillery. (Christian name Coulthered corrected to Ooultherd [London Gazette, 18 Feb. 1918)'.

10 Andesite Press, 2017.

11 His father, Brigadier-General Cecil Wingfield-Stratford, had been a soldier and sportsman who played cricket for MCC and one football international for England against Scotland. He played as outside-left for the Woolwich Academy and for Royal Engineers. As well as his England cap he also played in the replayed 1875 FA Cup Final for the Engineers, his team winning 2–0 at Kennington Oval.

and Cambridge, and was awarded a DScEcon by the University of London. In December 1913 he was nominated for membership of the Savage Club, with one of his seconders being Arthur Scott-Craven. He was not actually elected to the Club until December 1914. The candidate book does not disclose any reason for the unusual delay, so we are left to infer that some combination of his work ethic and world events conspired to keep his attention elsewhere. During the First World War he served in India, as a captain in the Royal West Kent Regiment, which spared him from the horrors of the Western Front.[12]

Arthur Winnington-Ingram (1858–1946) was Bishop of London from 1901–1939, and an honorary life member of the Savage Club from 1902. Upon the outbreak of the Great War, he came out so strongly in favour of the conflict – accepting stories of German atrocities without question, and preaching a torrent of anti-German sentiment – that even HH Asquith criticised his shallow jingoism. Nonetheless, Winnington-Ingram continued to throw himself into the cause, preaching at recruitment drives, encouraging younger clergymen to sign up, and visiting troops in Britain and abroad in France and Macedonia. In July 1916, for example, the *Illustrated War News* reported him holding a special confirmation service for the Grand Fleet at Scapa Flow, in the presence of Sir John Jellicoe. In recognition of his efforts he was mentioned in despatches and was awarded the Greek Grand Cross of the Order of the Redeemer and the Serbian Order of St Sava, 1st Class.

Away from the war he was a prolific author, mostly of religious books, and left quite a legacy in London since the 'billionaires' row', Bishop's Avenue in Hampstead, was named after him, as were Winnington Road, Ingram Avenue and Bishop Winnington-Ingram Primary School in Ruislip.

Savage Entertainers

John Ferguson (1890–1966), who performed under the stage name **AC Astor,** was a successful performer for many years in the now rare art of ventriloquism. Ferguson was born in Cumbria, though his act took him around the world, and some of his work survived on YouTube clips available at the time of writing. He served three years in the Great War as a 'soldier artiste' on the Western Front.[13] He joined the Savage Club in January 1930.

Sir Arnold Bax KCVO (1883–1953) was an English composer, poet,

---

12 His father, on the other hand, had retired in 1909 as a brigadier-general, but returned to active duty to have a most distinguished career on the Western Front. He fought at Loos and the Somme. In the latter he was in action on the first day, taking part in the attack on the Gommecourt salient. Wingfield-Stratford later served as Commander RE of the 46th Division. He was also mentioned in despatches four times and awarded the CMG in 1916 and CB in 1918.

13 John A. Ferguson, *'The Globe Trotting Ventriloquist' - A. C. Astor* (Cold Harbour Press, 2014).

and author, best known for his orchestral music, being the composer of seven symphonies. He also wrote popular songs, choral music, chamber pieces, and solo piano works. Although he was born in London, he was greatly interested in Irish culture and spent some time before the Great War in Dublin.

When war broke out he returned to England, but was ruled unfit for military service due to a heart complaint. Instead, he served for a time as a special constable. He wrote a substantial amount of music throughout the 1910s, and his profile rose considerably due in part to the absence of many other composers and musicians who were at the Front. The Easter Rising caused him much distress due to his connections with Ireland, leading him to compose the poem 'A Dublin Ballad' in 1916. It included the lines:

> And when the devil's made us wise
> Each in his own peculiar hell
> With desert hearts and drunken eyes
> We're free to sentimentalise
> By corners where the martyrs fell.

He also composed the orchestral 'In Memoriam' and the 'Elegiac Trio' for flute, viola, and harp, in reaction to the events in Dublin. Later in the 1910s he started turning to Nordic influences rather than Celtic. While the war was still ongoing, he started an affair with the pianist Harriet Cohen, and eventually left his wife and children to move in with her in a flat in Swiss Cottage, North London.

In the 1920s he started composing symphonies, and in 1942 was appointed Master of the King's Music. He was made a life member of the Savage Club in 1946. By then, the peak of his career had passed. For many years he was almost forgotten, though the search opportunities offered by the internet has led to a recent increase in his profile.

Noel Gay (1898–1954) (real name Reginald Moxon Armitage) was one of the most successful popular composers of his day – according to Sheridan Morley, he was the closest thing Britain came to an Irving Berlin. He is a great name to have in the annals of the Savage Club, and the club retains a framed tribute to him on the wall today, though his service in the Great War was somewhat perfunctory as he was unfit for active duty.

Gay was born in Yorkshire in 1898. His talent for music was obvious very early on: he deputised for the choirmaster at Wakefield Cathedral from the age of eight, and became honorary deputy organist at 12. At the age of 15 he won a scholarship to study at the Royal College of Music in London. Thereafter he went up to Cambridge University.

Records of his service in the First World War are sketchy. He signed up in Yorkshire in 1916, just after turning 18, giving his occupation as a student. The following year he was assigned to the Royal Fusiliers. He was demobbed at the beginning of 1919. His discharge papers showed that at the time he was assigned as a clerk in the pay office to the Royal Defence Corps (RDC), a unit comprising less able soldiers and given less arduous tasks such as home security, guarding prisoners or protecting installations. In Gay's case, he was medical category B3 (only suitable for sedentary work), having 'chronic discharge from the ears' and defective vision.

After the war, he began writing popular songs and adopted the name 'Noel Gay' as a *nom de plume*; he also occasionally used the name 'Stanley Hill' for more sentimental work. He developed a strong talent for short, catchy tunes. Perhaps most famously he wrote the music, though not the lyrics,[14] to *Me and My Girl*. He also wrote songs for the likes of The Crazy Gang, Flanagan and Allen, and George Formby. He joined the Savage Club in May 1936.

During the Second World War, he wrote a number of popular tunes such as 'Run Rabbit Run' – famously sung by Bud Flanagan. He did not enjoy as much success after the war, however, as his style of music became thought of as passé. His name lives on in the present, though, thanks to the business interests he started which still flourish under the direction of his family members: Gay created Noel Gay Music in 1938 as a business vehicle, which nowadays is part of the Noel Gay Organisation. It has divisions for television and theatre and remains one of the most significant British showbusiness agencies.

Mark Hambourg (1879–1960) was a Russian-British concert pianist, who was one of the most eminent musicians of his era and also one of the most eminent Savages: he joined the Club in 1904 and was a member for more than half a century.

He was born in Russia but his family fled to Britain in 1889 as refugees from the Tsarist regime. He was from a very musical family: his father, Michael Hambourg, was a pianist who had studied under Anton Rubinstein.

Although Hambourg was active as a musician throughout the Great War, disability precluded him from serving in uniform. When the war broke out, he took a friend to see the fleet at Dover:[15]

> It seemed as if the whole dock was crammed with men-of-war. I do not know how many there were, but to our astonished gaze not less than the whole British Fleet appeared to be present. Like hunting hounds they looked; devilish hounds! Straining at the leash, fuming to be off! Every funnel was belching forth black smoke, every keep just aching to dash across the Channel. The sky was dark and murky, a sinister

---

14 The lyrics were written by Brother Savage Douglas Furber, who also wrote the lyrics to 'The Lambeth Walk'. His other compositions included 'Limehouse Blues', written with composer Philip Braham.

15 Hambourg, *From Piano to Forte* (Cassell, 1931), p 227.

background to these panting dreadnoughts. We, however, felt cheered, sustained, enthusiastic. In the bottom of our souls we believed that those ships were just going to rush out of that harbour at the given signal "Off" and would never stop till they had dashed into the enemy ports, blown their navy to bits, and thus finished the war.

Hambourg was one of many (including, as we have seen, the Savages Basil Hindenberg/Cameron and Louis Battenberg/Mountbatten) who attracted opprobrium for having a German-sounding name. He fiercely protested that he was Russian-born, not German, and had been a naturalised British citizen for many years. He successfully sued the paper for libel[16] concerning his origins.

Hambourg travelled to America in late 1914 and returned in April 1915. He met some friends in New York who urged him to travel home with them, but Hambourg did not wish to wait another week for their ship. By that twist of fate he avoided joining them on board the *Lusitania*; none of his friends survived.

Back in England Hambourg toured extensively around the country, playing concerts and also playing special performances for the wounded. The air raids on London clearly caused great fear and concern to him. In his second memoir, *The Eighth Octave: Tones and Semi-tones Concerning Piano-playing, the Savage Club and Myself*,[17] he wrote:[18]

> When I looked out of the window of my house in Regent's Park and saw three German aeroplanes advancing down Albany Street I felt most uncomfortable. To think that it was not more than eight years ago that I had waited all day on the cliffs of Folkestone to see, what was then considered a miracle, the Frenchman De Bleriot, fly the Channel from the continent for the first time.

Hambourg was highly successful in his career, as measured by the fact that the Regent's Park home was in the prestigious Cumberland Terrace. He struggled to sell the house in the 1930s – reflecting the effects of the Great Depression – until a new neighbour, one Wallace Simpson, moved into the street 'and consequently there were pictures in all the illustrated papers advertising its architectural distinction.'[19] Thereafter Hambourg lived in St John's Wood.

In contrast with his reticence about the Great War, Hambourg was most effusive about his membership of the Savage Club. Percy Bradshaw's history of the Club contained many stories of him and his Brother Savage, Benno Moiseiwitsch, who was another great pianist of the age (one whom Rachmaninoff, no less,

---

16 It is sometimes said that the paper was the *Daily Mail*, but it was in fact the *London Mail*, which had ceased trading by the time Hambourg wrote his memoir.

17 Published by Williams & Norgate Ltd, 1951. He also wrote *How to Become a Pianist* (C Arthur Pearson, 1922).

18 Hambourg, *The Eighth Octave*, op cit, p 86.

19 Ibid, p 103.

called his 'spiritual heir').[20] In 1957, Moiseiwitsch selected the Club's Steinway grand piano, which was presented by Science members.

Clearly there was quite a bond between the two musicians. Dennis Castle recalled that Hambourg was once invited to play Beethoven in a film, and announced the role with delight. 'Very good' replied Moiseiwitsch, 'but who is to play the piano?' Bradshaw himself wrote that Hambourg 'has given such joy to his Brethren and to audiences all over the world.' He continued:[21]

> Becoming a Savage in 1904, he has performed hundreds of times at our house-dinners, spent long nights in our card rooms, played his highly individual brand of golf, and taken part in other sides of our Club activities. I see him very clearly sitting down to the club piano, arguing with himself as to what he will play. Having announced the item, he will play something else. 'It is very long', he may warn us, 'and you won't understand it. If you don't like it I will play something longer as an encore.' If it will add to his comfort, he will take off his coat before crashing out the opening chord. At poker one evening somebody asked, 'Where's Mark Hambourg?' He's playing at Newcastle,' was the reply. 'Strange,' observed Matthew Norgate, 'I can't hear anything!'

At the time of writing, a number of Hambourg's recordings could be found on YouTube, along with footage of him playing. Judging from that footage, his style might not have been to all tastes, but his technical mastery was beyond doubt.

Tommy Handley (1892–1949) was another enormously popular Savage of the Second World War, with his radio programme 'It's That Man Again' (often shortened to ITMA). During the First World War, Handley was just getting started in the field of light entertainment. On 11 November 1917 – exactly a year before the war's end – he began serving in a kite balloon section of the Royal Naval Air Service. His biographer Ted Kavanagh (who wrote the scripts for ITMA) wrote:[22]

> After the usual routine of "square bashing" and discipline, he was sent aloft in a new type of observation balloon to be used for artillery spotting. The thing did not rise quickly enough, and the officer in charge ordered a rather frightened AM2 Handley to throw out some of the sand ballast. The enthusiastic rookie, anxious to obey orders promptly, heaved a complete sack overboard. The balloon was little more than a hundred feet up at the time, and he had just time to see the numerous brass hats and experts who were watching the test dodge for cover as he was carried aloft at the rate of an express lift until the hawser jerked the crew almost out of the basket.

---

20 Benno Moiseiwitsch (1890–1963). See for example Percy Bradshaw, *Brother Savages and Guests: A History of the Savage Club 1857-1957* (WH Allen & Co Ltd, 1958), p 112. On p 113, there is a drawing of Hambourg by Bert Thomas.

21 Bradshaw, op cit, p 105.

22 Ted Kavanagh, *Tommy Handley* (Hodder and Stoughton, 1949), p 43.

Handley's sublime light entertainment skills were noticed quickly in the service, however, and he was then put to use in morale-boosting shows. A troupe he performed in over Christmas 1917 was given official status; one reflection of the different age was that a member performed under the name 'The Chocolate Coloured Coon'.[23] They performed on average three shows an evening in the London area. Venues ranged from the top of a tank used in recruitment drives to the slightly more palatial Chiswick Empire. In all, they performed approximately 1,000 shows in under a year. He joined the Savage Club in October 1927.

For successive generations of British children, **Derek McCulloch** OBE (1897–1967) was a central part of the entertainment in their lives. McCulloch was an avuncular BBC Radio presenter and producer, known as the voice of 'Uncle Mac' in *Children's Favourites* and *Children's Hour*, and 'Larry the Lamb' in *Toytown*. It is hard to think of a more genteel occupation in the world of broadcasting. To football historians he also holds the notable distinction of commentating on the first ever FA Cup Final to be broadcast on the radio.[24] In addition to those civilised vocations, however, McCulloch was also a seasoned veteran of the armed forces, and he experienced much suffering on the Western Front.

He was still at school when the First World War broke out. In 1915, aged just 17, he enlisted in the Public Schools Battalion of the 16th Middlesex Regiment, and went on to hold a commission in the Green Howards. He took part in the Battle of the Somme in 1916, where he was almost killed by a shell exploding nearby. He lay in No Man's Land for three days, badly injured, and eventually lost an eye from his wounds.

He otherwise recovered, however, and in 1917 joined the Royal Flying Corps (one historian noting with reference to McCulloch's eye injury that it was clearly 'the days before health and safety'),[25] albeit as an equipment officer rather than a pilot. He also served on HMS *Valiant*. On 19 September 1919, his RAF service record blandly recorded 'transferred to unemployed list'.[26]

He joined the BBC at a very early stage in the corporation, beginning in 1926 as an announcer. His time in children's entertainment began in earnest in 1931, when he joined *Children's Hour* as second-in-charge. Within two years he was first-in-charge of the programme and head of children's broadcasting.

In 1938, however, he suffered terrible physical injuries anew, when he lost a leg in a road accident, and was in constant pain for the rest of his life. Nevertheless,

23 GH Elliot (see Kavanagh, op cit, p 45).
24 It was for the 1927 final. McCulloch played the 'number two' man giving facts and figures, the chief commentator was George Allison, also a Great War veteran.
25 Roger Domeneghetti, *From The Back Page To The Front Room: Football's Journey Through The English Media* (Ockley Books Ltd, 2nd edn, 2017). See also Seán Street, *Historical Dictionary of British Radio* (Rowman & Littlefield, 2nd edn, 2015), p 217.
26 See https://search.livesofthefirstworldwar.org/record?id=gbm%2fair76%2f314%2f0%2f0553& parentid=gbm%2fair76%2f56332.

he continued with his immensely successful broadcasting career. By the time of the Second World War, *Children's Hour* attracted a regular audience of some 4 million listeners. McCulloch then found himself playing a very different role for the nation: keeping up the morale of all the evacuated children.

He was nominated for membership of the Savage Club in December 1946, but was not elected until June 1954, having withdrawn at his own request for the intervening years.

The Australian **Malcolm McEachern** (1883–1945) would later become the Jetsam of the popular duo 'Flotsam and Jetsam'. During the Great War he undertook morale-boosting tours of Australia with the legendary soprano Nellie Melba and others. He joined the Savage Club in March 1938 under the category of music. Flotsam was the Englishman **Bentley Collingwood Hilliam**, who joined much earlier, in May 1929, under the category of music as well.

Saville Esmé Percy (1887–1957), known as Esmé Percy, was a renowned actor in his day, who trained at the start of his career with Sarah Bernhardt. Thereafter he worked in repertory companies until the First World War. During the war, he put on over 150 morale-boosting shows for Allied troops. At its immediate conclusion, following the Armistice, he ran a theatre in Cologne, entertaining British troops by playing the role of Professor Henry Higgins in *My Fair Lady* – he was particularly renowned for acting in George Bernard Shaw productions.[27] He joined the Savage Club in July 1934. Later in life he traded on his French ancestry (and the absence of anything like modern sensibilities towards race) by playing various ethnic characters. In total he appeared in approximately 40 films, including an early Hitchcock, *Murder!* (1930).

Major **Frank Vernon** (1875–1940) was a producer, author and translator, born in Bombay. He worked in the West End before and after the Great War, often collaborating with JE Vedrenne. As well as his work in London, he produced plays in Paris. In January 1919, he joined the Savage Club under the category of drama. His death came in March 1940, during the Second World War, after he went to entertain troops in France.[28]

Sir Henry Wood (1869–1944) has been called 'the principal figure in the popularisation of orchestral music in England in his time'.[29] He was the founder of the legendary 'Proms', an annual series of promenade concerts which introduced much new music to British audiences and which are still held in the present day, well over a century after they began.

The origin of the Proms lay in the 1890s, when Wood was engaged by the

---

27 Colin Chambers (ed), *Continuum Companion to Twentieth Century Theatre* (Continuum, 2002), p 589.
28 Frank Vernon, *The Twentieth-Century Theatre* (Houghton Mifflin Co., 1924).
29 *Encyclopaedia Britannica*, https://www.britannica.com/biography/Henry-J-Wood.

impresario Robert Newman to conduct a series of promenade concerts which would play a mixture of classical and popular music, with tickets sold at a relatively low price. The concerts were popular from the outset, and Wood continued conducting them every year until his death in 1944.[30] He was knighted in 1911. Newman, meanwhile, was declared bankrupt in 1902 but the Proms were saved by Sir Edgar Speyer, who funded them thereafter.

He was nominated for Savage Club membership in January 1893, and elected soon after.[31] In 1936 he was made an honorary life member.

When the First World War began, Wood was too old for active service, but the question arose as to whether the Proms should continue (as we saw at different times earlier in the book, other puritanical sorts were trying to shut down various forms of entertainment. They succeeded in closing the Royal Opera House, among other things). A second question was whether, if they continued, what music might appropriate, given that classical music at the time was dominated by German composers and musical influences.

The Proms programme for 17 August 1917 announced the cancellation of that evening's Wagner performance, but also contained the following optimistic disclaimer:[32]

> The substitution of a mixed programme in place of a wholly Wagnerian one was not dictated by any narrow-minded intolerant policy, but was the result of outside pressure... The greatest examples of Music and Art are world possessions and unassailable even by the prejudices and passions of the hour.

Sadly that enlightened sentiment proved wishful thinking, as Basil Cameron soon discovered. The Proms had a further problem in that Sir Edgar Speyer suddenly found his Germanic origins made him unwelcome in Britain, despite the fact that he had been born in America and had been a British subject since 1892.

In spite of all those obstacles, the Proms did continue during the Great War, although in slightly reduced form. As the conflict went on the concerts had to be timed to avoid air raids. Wood was offered a position in America with the Boston Symphony Orchestra, which he regarded as the finest in the world at the time, but he remained in Britain out of a sense of patriotic duty.

Although Wood did resist the more extreme anti-German sentiment by continuing to perform works by Bach, Beethoven and Wagner, the Proms disdained

---

30 Initially the Proms were held in Queen's Hall, Langham Place. The building was destroyed by an enemy air raid during the Second World War and so the event switched to the Royal Albert Hall, where it continues to the present day.

31 The writing on the candidate page is smudged – I think it is meant to be May – but either way he was certainly elected in 1893.

32 Henry Wood, op cit, p 289. See also Hannah Nepil, 'The Proms and the First World War', *Financial Times*, 15 August 2014.

newer German composers and instead gave prominence to emerging British ones. The result was a great boon for British music. One of the more moving examples was the playing of George Butterworth's settings of AE Housman's poems from *A Shropshire Lad* at the Proms in September 1917, a year after Butterworth had died on the Somme. Nowadays Butterworth's pieces are often performed as a lament for the Great War dead.

A second consequence of wartime was the absence of many male singers, who were at the Front.[33] Not everyone was pleased with the resultant dominance of female soloists, and there were gripes about it being too dangerous for women to be out late and having to get home afterwards, or it being too inconvenient to have to provide extra changing facilities, or the perennial lament about women in wartime taking jobs from men when the latter returned home. On the other hand, as with other professions, women after the war could point to the manifest success of the female singers during the conflict to show that they should not be excluded from the stage.

Historians have credited Wood for making an important contribution towards public morale during the conflict.[34] In 2014, the Proms marked the centenary of the First World War by performing works by three composers who died during the conflict: George Butterworth and his fellow Englishman Frederick Kelly, and, appropriately in the light of the world moving on in the intervening century, the German Rudi Stephan.

Sir Edward Elgar (1857–1934) was also too old to serve in the war. He was appalled by the bloodshed which the casualty figures implied, but nevertheless tried to contribute to the war effort as he could. He was already known for 'Land of Hope and Glory', and added to it during the war with more patriotic compositions including 'Polonia' in honour of Poland and 'Carillon' for Belgium. He also set music to two great poets, Laurence Binyon and Rudyard Kipling. His work with the latter was called 'The Fringes of the Fleet' and met with great success, though Kipling later refused permission for it to be performed in theatres. Elgar was an honorary member of the Savage Club.[35]

Major **Leslie Faber** MC (1879–1929) was a stage actor during the first third of the twentieth century. A measure of his standing among his peers is that Michael Redgrave wrote 'some of you have never heard of Leslie Faber, who, it is true, was a popular, high-paid "star"-actor, but so complete an artist that he could

---

33 One exception was Brother Savage Norman Allin (1884–1973), a British bass singer of the early and mid-twentieth century, and later a teacher of voice, who performed during wartime Proms.

34 Ates Orga, *The Proms* (David & Charles, 1974), p 88.

35 Elgar's membership of the Club is mentioned by Richard Tames, *London: A Cultural History* (Oxford University Press, 2006), p 110 and in Christopher Hibbert, Ben Weinreb, John Keay, Julia Keay, *The London Encyclopaedia* (Macmillan, 3rd edn 2008, paperback 2010), p 822.

appear in *two* leading parts in the same play without the audience knowing of it.'[36] His *Times* obituary[37] stated:

> His career had been more smoothly successful than that of many of his calling; and he won his success by the trained and skilful use of his many gifts of appearance, manner and intelligence. He developed, as years went on, a kind of oddity, a hint of the sardonic, the mysterious, the uncanny, of anything out of the common which he wanted to convey; and this was serving him excellently well in the years when he could no longer rely on the charm of youth. Charm, however, he never lost; and even among the players of his day he was remarkable for the neatness and finish of his acting. He was neither sloppy nor histrionic, and always deft.

During the war he spent a period of time as a prisoner of war, although I have not traced his service record in detail. He joined the Savage Club in April 1920.

Count **John McCormack** was a highly successful singer in the first half of the twentieth century. In 1914 he became the first to record 'It's a Long Way to Tipperary', one of the songs most associated with the Great War.[38] He also recorded the 'Keep The Home Fires Burning' in 1917, though others had already released versions of the song.

McCormack was Irish, and supported Irish nationalism, though he became a naturalised American citizen during the conflict and evidently firmly supported the Allied cause, since he made a substantial financial contribution of $11,458 towards the American war effort – a small fortune for a private individual at the time. In 1928, he received the title of papal count from Pope Pius XI in recognition of his charity work and was often billed as 'Count John McCormack' thereafter. He joined the Savage Club in June 1939, on the eve of the Second World War, and died soon after its end, in September 1945.

I left out of the main text any mention of the **O'Donnell brothers (Rudolph,** (known as 'RP') and **Walton**), sublime musicians of their time, on the basis that they really belong in a book on the Second World War. During that conflict, RP

---

36 Sir Michael Redgrave, *The Actors' Ways and Means* (Taylor and Francis, 1995), p 19. Sir Michael narrated the famous BBC television series *The Great War* in 1964.

37 *The Times*, 6 August 1929, p 10.

38 The song was written in 1912 as an Irish music hall number. The *Daily Mail* war correspondent George Curnock heard the Irish regiment the Connaught Rangers singing it as they marched through Boulogne on 13 August 1914 on the way to the Front. He wrote about it in his report on 18 August 1914, and the song started to spread through the rest of the British Army. In October 1914, at a major fundraising concert for the Red Cross, attended by George V and Queen Mary, the great Italian-French singer Adelina Patti (1843–1919) came out of retirement for a final performance. She received great applause for singing *It's A Long way to Tipperary*. One other noteworthy fact is that the song was atypical for army marching songs to that point as it did not urge great deeds at the Front, but rather expressed longing for home; in that respect it set a pattern for popular songs of the Great War.

recruited and led an orchestra to tremendous critical acclaim.[39] He joined the Savage Club in March 1943, joining Walton, who had been elected in February 1935.

Another famous music hall star of the day, **Tom Clare** (1876–1946), did his best to maintain public morale at home during the Great War. Clare's ironically humorous songs included 'The Fine Old English Gentleman', a song taking the mickey out of modernity, the self-explanatory 'Who Bashed Bill Kaiser?', and the recruiting-drive ditty 'What did You do in the Great War, Daddy?' based on a 1915 Savile Lumley propaganda poster which attacked those profiteering at home instead of doing their duty at the Front. Clare performed in numerous charity concerts in aid of wounded soldiers. Before the war he had cut various recordings as early as 1906, the year he joined the Savage Club (in October).

Leslie Sarony (1897–1985) was a British entertainer, singer and songwriter. As with Arnold Ridley, he saw service in dreadful battles in the Great War, which stood in the starkest contrast with the rest of his life spent as a light entertainer. He began his stage career in 1911, aged 14, with the group Park Eton's Boys, so already had something of a name as an entertainer before the conflict began. The website Voices of Variety explained his war service:[40]

> When the First World War broke out soldiers in uniform used to call out insults to any young civilian men they saw in the street, implying that it was cowardice or lack of manliness that kept them out of the army. These were not challenges Sarony was prepared to tolerate and he tried to enlist but was turned down several times before he got in. "When I was in the First World War I was in The London Scottish and we went through France to Salonika. Incidentally, in France there was a very famous entertainment, an army show called The Barnstormers, and me and my pal joined it and we put on a smashing show but it only lasted for a fortnight because we were sent to Salonika and then I went down with dysentery."
>
> Sarony didn't seem to want to dwell on his war service when we chatted —and little wonder. His son, Peter Sarony, filled in a few details for me: "He was one of the fortunate few who survived the infamous WW1 Battle of Messines on Hallowe'en 31st October, 1914, where he was a member of 1st Battalion the London Scottish, which was the first territorial infantry battalion in action against the Germans. It was slaughter. They

---

39 Wing Commander Brother Savage RP O'Donnell managed to recruit much of the cream of London's orchestras for the RAF Symphony Orchestra. His players included Gareth Morris, Leonard Brain and Eddie Walker (woodwind), Dennis Brain, Harold Jackson and Norman del Mar (brass), and Harry Blech, Fred Grinke, Leonard Hirsch, David Martin, Jim Merrett and James Whitehead plus the Griller quartet (strings). They undertook a propaganda and morale-boosting tour of the United States in 1944, and played at the Potsdam Conference the following year.

40 http://voices-of-variety.com/leslie-sarony/.

had to hold the line, bayonets fixed, against the Germans as their rifles did not chamber the service ammunition provided!"

Not much to laugh at there, then, but there was an upside in the periods between marching, trying to sleep in mud-filled and rat-infested trenches and fighting for his life, sometimes in hand-to-hand combat with bayonets. "It was in the army that I found out that I could write songs," he said. "I'd always thought how marvelous it would be to write your own songs and right from the start I always tried to create songs with a silly idea behind them."

After the war, he appeared in many revues, pantomimes and musicals, before taking advantage of modern technology by moving into radio and records. In the Second World War, he recorded a version of 'We're Going to Hang out the Washing on the Siegfried Line'. Even in later life he stayed in the public eye. His song 'Jollity Farm' was recorded by the Bonzo Dog Doo-Dah Band in 1967, while he himself appeared on television throughout the 1970s and briefly in Monty Python's film *The Meaning of Life* in 1983.

Horace Stevens (1876–1950) was an excellent Australian bass singer. He began life as a dentist, initially apprenticed to his father. During the Great War he was made an honorary lieutenant (at 39 years old, he would not have been considered for front line infantry duties) and served on HMAT *Medic, A7*. He was invalided out in 1918 and went to Britain. After an impromptu performance, Brother Savage Henry Wood suggested he sing full time. Stevens followed the advice and soon received critical acclaim for his role in *Elijah*. He went on to have a successful career, as well as pursuing hobbies including rowing, marksmanship and tennis. In March 1924 he joined the Savage Club; he was also a member of the Melbourne Savages. It was once said of him that he was 'a magnificent singer but a ponderous bridge player' who frustrated Mark Hambourg to the point where Hambourg exclaimed 'My dear Horace, we all know you are the finest Elijah of our time but why in the name of Heaven do you have to play bridge like him!'[41]

Harry Tate (real name Ronald MacDonald Hutchison) (1872–1940) was a noted Cockney comedian and music hall star. He did not serve in the frontline during the Great War, but he had the distinction of a widely-used aircraft, the RE 8, named after him in the tradition of rhyming slang. Tate's name had already entered the vernacular to refer to anything clumsy and amateurish, due to his act as an awkward oaf who could not master various contraptions including a car

---

41 No less an authority than Sir Edward Elgar bestowed the accolade of the best Elijah of the day upon Stevens. The Hambourg anecdote came from George W Bishop, quoted in Bradshaw, op cit, p 107.

and an aeroplane.[42] Hence his name being assigned to the RE 8 was not entirely complimentary about the machine.

During the Second World War, his name was used by the Royal Navy to refer to the trawlers and drifters of the Royal Naval Patrol Service. In a classically British response, the RNPS adopted the name with pride and called themselves 'Harry Tate's Navy' thereafter. In time the name became less derisory and more a byword for courage.

Tate joined the Savage Club in March 1923. He was evidently well known and liked by his Brother Savages. Kenneth Duffield recalled a day at the races in 1935, in which the Club had hired a charabanc to drive a party of members to and from Epsom to watch the Derby:[43]

> When the time arrived for us to leave the downs—so-free—we found to our dismay that—owing to the prolonged Bacchanalian revels— our chauffeur had "died on us", and preferred to lie underneath the charabanc and sing, rather than take his place at the steering wheel, "because", he said (vide the Irishman who objected to pushing his wheelbarrow but preferred to turn his back and pull it), "he hated the sight of the damned thing" ...

> Volunteers were called for, and I, who had once driven a tank at Woolwich Arsenal (with disastrous results, I must add, because the shutter of the peep-hole had fallen and I blindly drove clean through a greengrocers' shop in High Street), was about to apply for the job, when Harry Tate forestalled me and volunteered to drive us "home". With a flourish of his famous moustachios and remarking that it was only "about ninety miles without the petrol, Pappa", he leapt into the driver's seat, and with a convulsive and discomforting jolt the jugger-naut leapt forward like a blood-hound unleashed.

> Harry drove like Jehu, so fast up hill and down dale that those of us who were awake did not realize what direction he was taking. We negotiated some rather never-racking corners, but repaired the moral damage at the next "local" and were always hoping that very shortly we would be coming in sight of Westminster and the Savage Club precincts.

> It was getting rather late and very dark when we pulled up in a pictur-esque but narrow lane in front of a charming, rose-clad villa. Our driver descended, and nonchalantly striking a match on the side of our car, made his way to the front door—and with a familiar, stentorian "Good-byee" was gone. Harry had driven us "home" all right; but it was *his* home—and about fifteen miles from the Savage Club. However, I took the wheel and we had all several drinks at Harry's expense when, at a very late hour, we got back to the club; and rumour hath it that the bill he received on our account amounted to exactly "one pound, nineteen shillings, and elevenpence, Pappa".

---

42 Away from the stage, Tate's lack of ability with the piano was recalled with detached amuse-ment by Mark Hambourg. See Hambourg, *The Eighth Octave*, op cit, p 145.

43 Kenneth Duffield, *Savages and Kings* (MacDonald & Co Ltd, 1945), pp 69–70.

Another Australian veteran of the Great War and the Savage Club was **Harold John Williams** (1893–1976), who went on to become a baritone singer of repute in both Britain and his home country. His singing talent was evident early on, when he sang as a boy soprano with the Waverley Methodist Church Choir and continued to do so as a baritone after his voice broke. Nevertheless, his singing took second place for some time behind his impressive sporting prowess. He played cricket for Waverley and rugby union for New South Wales, turning out for the latter against New Zealand just as both Australia and New Zealand were entering the First World War in August 1914.

Williams signed up with the Australian Imperial Force in July 1915, and travelled to Britain in May 1916 as a corporal in the 9th Field Ambulance. His singing provided much welcome distraction for the troops on the way over. Upon arrival in England, he spent some time training and was promoted to sergeant. He went to France in November 1916, hence missing most of the Battle of the Somme, though he did see action at Armentières. His singing came to the authorities' attention, and in January 1917, at the request of General Sir William Birdwood, he joined the Australian entertainment unit, 'Anzac Coves.' It was not the end of his active service, however, as he rejoined the 9th Field Ambulance in March 1917 and fought at Passchendaele and Messines. From December 1917 he was made regimental quartermaster sergeant.

While on leave in England in 1918, his singing voice was heard by several musicians who demanded he undertake formal lessons. In August 1918, he transferred to the 1st Australian Auxiliary Hospital, Harefield.

After the war, Williams studied in London whilst serving at the Australian Imperial Force headquarters. He was demobbed in in July 1919. Throughout the 1920s, his singing career went from strength to strength in England. He joined the Savage Club in October 1927. Among other things, Williams sang in every season of Sir Henry Wood's Promenade Concerts from 1921–51 in which he was in England. He worked with Sir Edward Elgar, sang at the coronation of King George VI in 1937, and was one of the soloists for whom Vaughan Williams wrote the 'Serenade to Music' in 1938.

Savage Artists

The cartoonist **George Belcher** (1875–1947) was a member of the Savage Club from April 1920. He left at some point and was re-elected in May 1934. During the Great War he drew humorous pictures for *Punch*.

Arthur Ferrier (1891–1973) was a Scottish artist, illustrator and cartoonist, who became a life member of the Club in 1924. During the Great War he created a number of paintings, some of which are now held by the Imperial War Museum.

David Ghilchik (1892–1972) was a painter who also worked as a cartoonist for *Punch* and the *Daily Sketch*. During the Great War he served as a truck driver on the Italian Front. After the war he participated in the now defunct Olympian sport of Art at the 1928 and 1932 Summer Olympics, representing Great Britain in the mixed painting, drawing and watercolour categories. He joined the Savage Club in May 1924.

BF (Bernard Finegan) Gribble RBC, SMA (1872–1962) was a noted naval artist, who painted many depictions of famous naval battles and incidents. His pictures were particularly renowned for their technical accuracy, the result of careful research and preparation on Gribble's part. He was educated at the College of St Francis Saviour, Bruges, Belgium; South Kensington Art School; and under his Brother Savage Albert Toft. As a measure of his reputation, his pictures were regularly exhibited at the Royal Academy and in the Paris Salon. Among the purchasers of his work before the war was Kaiser Wilhelm II, who was such a fan that George V summoned Gribble to a royal residence so the Kaiser could meet him.

During the Great War, Gribble served as the Official Maritime Painter to the Shipwrights' Company. At the end of the war he painted the arrival of American destroyers at Queenstown in Ireland. The picture was bought by none other than Franklin D Roosevelt, who later hung it in the Oval Office of the White House during his presidency.

Roosevelt also purchased Gribble's 'Surrender of the German Fleet to the Grand Fleet at Scapa Flow', which Gribble painted after witnessing the event first hand, in 1919.

As with many professional artists, Gribble worked as an illustrator, which provided him with a ready income from magazines, books, postcards and chocolate boxes.

After his death in 1962, his widow donated about 250 examples of his work to Poole Museum. Over half a century later, the museum held a Gribble exhibition as part of its Great War centenary commemorations.

Herbert James Gunn (1893–1964) was a successful portrait painter who depicted soldiers, academics, judges and others. His portrait of the blind composer Delius was the public's choice as 'picture of the year' at the Royal Academy in 1933, while he himself served as President of the Royal Society of Portrait Painters. During the Great War, he served in the Artists Rifles before being commissioned in the 10th Scottish Rifles. His most notable work during the war was the painting 'The Eve of the Battle of the Somme', a (deliberately) crushingly ironic depiction of British soldiers bathing in front of tents in an idyllic rural scene just before so many of them would be slaughtered on the infamous first day of the battle. He joined the Savage Club in August 1926.

Harold William Hailstone (1897–1982) was a cartoonist and illustrator. During the First World War he enlisted in the army, and then served as a trainee pilot in the Royal Flying Corps.

He became a successful artist between the wars, being published in the likes of the *Illustrated London News*, *Punch*, *The Sketch*, *Strand Magazine*, and *Tatler*, all familiar to many other Savage artists of the era.

As war threatened in Europe he once again offered his services to his country, joining the Royal Air Force in 1938. He stayed in the service for the duration of the war, being a flight lieutenant from 1940 and a war artist in 1944. Among his notable works was a sketch of the German commanders' surrender on Alderney in 1945.

He joined the Savage Club in May 1940. After the war, he worked as staff cartoonist for the *Daily Mirror*, before retiring to Kent.

William Lee Hankey (1869–1952) was another Savage who was too old for frontline service in the Great War, but volunteered all the same and went on to undertake vital work behind the lines. By the time the Great War began, he was an established artist: he had exhibited at the Royal Academy in 1896, and from 1902–1904 he was president of the London Sketch Club. He had then moved to Étaples, France, where he painted many bucolic scenes of Normandy and Brittany, becoming known as one of the most gifted of the figurative print-makers working in original drypoint at the time.

Being based in Étaples placed Lee Hankey in a dramatic position at the start of the war, because the town became the primary logistical hub for the British Expeditionary Force. It also took in a large number of refugees fleeing the German advance.[44] Lee Hankey captured the images of refugees in some arresting works, including a picture of a young mother carrying a child, both bearing the grim visage of fear and strain.

Lee Hankey joined the Artists Rifles at the beginning of 1915, and served in France until June of that year. Thereafter he was commissioned as a second lieutenant and served in the United Kingdom as an instructor, including his time at Hare Hall commanding Lance Thackeray.[45] In January 1918, he was promoted to acting captain (meaning he did not receive the pay or allowance of the rank). He retained that rank until being demobbed in January 1919.

---

44 After the war, the importance of the town was recognised when Étaples was awarded the *Croix de Guerre* by the French state, in recognition both of the difficulty of accommodating up to 80,000 men at a time and of the damage done by enemy bombing which the men's presence had attracted.

45 Newspaper archives depict him teaching field sketching on Hampstead Heath in February 1916, by which time he had reached the rank of lieutenant. The papers of the time also mention his well-received contribution to the OTC Art Exhibition in London. See for example the *Daily Mirror*, 1 February 1916.

After the war, Lee Hankey continued with his successful career. He joined the Savage Club in July 1935. The following year he was elected a member of the Royal Watercolour Society, and went on to serve as its acting president from 1947–50.[46]

Thomas Cecil Howitt (1889–1968) was one of the most notable Savage architects, who left behind a succession of impressive public buildings, especially in his home town of Nottingham. He completed his studies and began practising before the Great War, but signed up at the outset of the conflict. He was commissioned in the Leicestershire Regiment[47] and went on to serve on the Western Front with great distinction. As well as being awarded the Distinguished Service Order by the British,[48] he was awarded the French *Croix de Guerre*, and was made a *Croix de Chevalier* for his actions on the Battle of the Marne.[49] For his award of a DSO and bar, the *Gazette* recorded:[50]

> For conspicuous gallantry and devotion to duty when in command of his battalion during an enemy counter-attack. He displayed conspicuous ability in handling his battalion and in reorganising the defences of the front line. He went forward through a very heavy enemy barrage to make a personal reconnaissance, and his coolness and decision contributed very largely to the defence of the line.

The regimental history stated of the actions in 1917–18:[51]

> [I]n France and Flanders the Regiment had given a splendid account of itself. In a key battle at Polygon Wood near Ypres in October 1917, Lieutenant Colonel Philip Bent was awarded a posthumous VC when in command of 9th Battalion. In the last desperate attacks by the German armies launched in the spring of 1918, the "Tigers" fought with unsurpassed heroism. The sterling courage of the 110th Brigade in the defence of Epehy in March 1918 was a fine example of British grit. Exposed to the full blast of constant attacks delivered by three fresh German divisions, the stubborn soldiers of Leicestershire refused to budge, but met each attack with such devastating rifle and machine gun fire that, when night fell, the front of their position was marked by heaps of German dead. Only at one point did the enemy succeed

---

46 See further Martin Hardie, *The Etched Works of W. Lee-Hankey RE from 1904-1920* (LH Lefevre & Son, 1921) and Anthony J Lester, 'An English Impressionist', *Antique Dealer and Collector's Guide*, vol 42, pt 11, June 1989. He has been associated with the Newlyn School, an art colony based in or near Newlyn, a fishing village in Cornwall, from the 1880s until the early twentieth century, https://www.rountreetryon.com/artists/163-william-lee-hankey/biography/.

47 *Supplement to the London Gazette*, 16 November 1914, p 9383.

48 *Supplement to the Edinburgh Gazette*, 21 November 1917, p 2398; *Supplement to the London Gazette*, 19 November 1917, p 11950.

49 *Supplement to the London Gazette*, 22 November 1918, p 13726. The *Supplement to the Edinburgh Gazette*, 25 November 1918 records him as being awarded the *Croix de Chevalier*.

50 *Supplement to the Edinburgh Gazette*, 25 March 1918, p 1138.

51 See: https://www.royalleicestershireregiment.org.uk/history-of-the-regiment-2.

in piercing the line at Vancellette Farm, defended to the last man by the party of Leicester men who held it. Then in the summer came the final British and French advances against which the German defences availed nothing. Lieutenant John Barrett was awarded the VC while serving in the 1/5th Battalion at Pontruet in September. The enemy's prepared defences were in turn overwhelmed and the Regiment took a creditable share in the long advance which ended in victory.

In 1919, Howitt was demobbed with the rank of major. He joined the City Engineer's Department at Nottingham City Council, and designed Nottingham Council House, the city hall of Nottingham. The building's most striking feature was the 200ft high dome which, at the time of writing, still forms the centrepiece of the city's skyline. Among his other notable achievements were the headquarters of the Raleigh Cycle Company, which won the RIBA bronze medal in 1933. He also designed several churches, cinemas and university buildings in the Nottingham area.

He joined the Savage Club in May 1953.

Sir William Oliphant Hutchison LLD, PRSA (1889–1970) was a Scottish portrait and landscape painter. Among many distinctions, he was an honorary member of the Royal Academy, president of the Royal Scottish Academy and a member of the Royal Society of Arts.

Hutchison attended Kirkcaldy High School and Rugby School, before going on to the Edinburgh College of Art. He became a professional painter upon graduation, holding regular exhibitions in Edinburgh and elsewhere. During the Great War, he served with the Royal Garrison Artillery and was wounded on the Western Front.

He returned to Edinburgh after the conflict, and in 1921 moved to London. In August 1926 he joined the Savage Club. From 1933 to 1943 he served as a popular director of the Glasgow School of Art and, after the Second World War, served as president of the Royal Scottish Academy from 1950 to 1959. He was knighted in 1953.

David Jagger (1891–1958) was a successful English portrait painter. Early in life he studied at the Sheffield School of Art, winning prizes for his mural design and painting. Upon graduating he moved to London. To begin with, he worked for a commercial art studio and painted portraits in the evening, but his work was so well received he was able to establish his own professional portrait studio in Chelsea. During the Great War, he painted his brother (Charles Sargeant Jagger), who was serving as an officer. The painting was entitled *Portrait of an Army Officer* and received much critical acclaim.

After the Great War, in 1921, he married Katherine Gardiner. She had become his muse and appeared in many of his subsequent paintings. He continued to paint eminent individuals as well, most notably the founder of the Scout movement, (Lord) Robert Baden-Powell. The portrait was presented to Baden-Powell in August 1929. In the years since countless copies have been displayed by Scouting movements worldwide.

He joined the Savage Club in June 1930.

Cecil King (1881–1942) was a maritime artist whose works hang today in the National Maritime Museum in Greenwich, the Imperial War Museum in Elephant and Castle and the *Musee de Marine* in Paris, depicting many of the Royal Navy's finest vessels from the age of the Dreadnought. During the Great War, however, his service was not at sea on board one of the ironclads, but instead as a soldier on the Western Front.

King exhibited in London from 1906. Some of his drawings were accepted by the *Sphere* and the *Illustrated London News,* and he became a regular contributor to the latter. He also did a considerable amount of poster work. Besides specialising in maritime painting, he was an enthusiast for all nautical matters, and was said to have an extensive knowledge of naval lore. In 1914, drawing on his naval knowledge, he published a book entitled *A History of British Flags.*

King had been a member of the territorial forces before the war. At the turn of the century he had joined the 26th Middlesex (Cyclists) Volunteer Rifle Corps, part of the London territorials, as a second lieutenant.[52] By 1910 he had reached the rank of captain.[53]

The 25th Battalion itself – though not all of its members – served in India and the North West Frontier during the war, with a contingent also being sent to Mesopotamia. King, however, as with a few others, remained behind and was deployed to France in April 1916. The following year brought him some respite and a return to Britain, since he was nominated for membership of the Savage Club in June 1917 and elected in July.

After the war, King continued with his successful painting career and his intellectual interest in all things naval. In 1924, he designed some historical ship models to be used at an exhibition in Wembley. His painting *Dazzled Ships at Leith* depicted the distinctive 'dazzle camouflage' created during the war by another maritime artist, Norman Wilkinson, in order to confuse U-boats. Its development at the Admiralty was assisted by Brother Savage Steven Spurrier.[54]

---

52 *London Gazette,* 24 December 1901, p 9069, records him as second lieutenant in the Middlesex Cyclists.

53 *London Gazette,* 19 August 1910, p 6042.

54 Steven Spurrier (1878–1961). Born in London, he initially worked as a silversmith following his father's business but from 1900 worked as a freelance magazine illustrator. In the Second World War, he was offered a commission by the War Artists' Advisory Committee for a picture of an army discussion group, for 50 guineas. He rejoined the Savage Club in May 1943, having been a member earlier. He was made an associate member of the Royal Academy in 1945 and became a full member in 1952.

Early in the Second World War, and shortly before his death, King published two books, *His Majesty's Ships and their Forebears* (a history of the Royal Navy, published in 1940) and *Rule, Britannia* (a record of some of the early naval victories in the Second World War, with his own decorative marginal sketches, published in 1941).

The painter **Augustus John** (1878–1961) had a short but interesting time in the Great War. He was attached to the Canadian forces as a war artist and created numerous portraits of Canadian soldiers. It was intended to join them all into a giant mural for the Canadian press baron Lord Beaverbrook, but it was never completed. Since he was a war artist, John was allowed to keep his facial hair; it was said that he and George V were the only Allied officers to have beards during the conflict.

In the event, however, John only spent two months in France before being returned home in disgrace after engaging in a fight.[55] The Canadian Lord Beaverbrook managed to intervene on his behalf and save him from a court martial.

John then returned to France where he produced studies for a proposed Canadian War Memorial picture, although he only managed one substantial work, and even that was incomplete.

John was made an honorary life member of the Savage Club in 1949.

Sir Gerald Kelly (1879–1972) was one of Britain's most respected twentieth century artists. His career was well established by the time of the Great War. During the conflict he served for a time in Admiralty intelligence, in which capacity he was posted to Seville. He was a close friend of Somerset Maugham and, like Maugham, was an honorary life member of the Savage Club, in his case from 1950.[56]

The name **Heath Robinson** (1872–1944) has long been in the English vernacular as shorthand for any form of improvised, shoddy or comic-looking contraption or engineering solution, thanks to Robinson's cartoons, which became particularly well-known during the Great War.

Robinson started his artistic career illustrating books including works by Shakespeare, Hans Christian Andersen and Charles Kingsley (author of *The Water-Babies*). He also wrote and illustrated three children's books himself. In April 1911, he drew a much admired menu card for a Savage Club house dinner with Ernest Goddard in the chair,[57] though he did not join the Club until May 1924.

---

55 See his obituary in the *Times*, 6 January 1972.

56 In 1924 he painted a nude woman smoking. It was bought by Newport Town Council in 1947 but quickly withdrawn from display once the Bishop of Caerleon learned from a gallery visitor the unpalatable horror that a schoolgirl had been seen sniggering at it.

57 Norgate and Wykes, op cit, reproduced the picture in their book on the Club, noting that in

After the Great War began, he drew numerous cartoons showing improbable secret weapons supposedly possessed by the various combatants. His machines usually had some ridiculous power supply in the form of a steam boiler or candles, and a host of pulleys and levers, and were often accompanied by a stereotypical British boffin in a boiler suit.

After the war, his work found a perfect home in Norman Hunter's *Professor Branestawm* children's stories about a brilliant but comically hapless inventor.

The sculptor **Sir Charles Wheeler** (1892–1974) was unfit for active service during the Great War, but he did work on creating artificial limbs for amputee soldiers. He was made an honorary life member of the Savage Club in 1960.

The political cartoonist **George Whitelaw** (1887–1957) served in the Tank Corp during the war, working on camouflage, something discussed in more detail in the entry on the Savage artist Oliver Bernard in Chapter 7. He was for a time chairman of the Savage Club and served on the Club committee during the Second World War. As a cartoonist he was well regarded in his day, though his work has perhaps not endured as well as other Savages such as David Low. He joined the Savage Club in March 1917, while the war was still in progress.

Savage Men of Law

We already noted how remarkable the number of Savage Club lawyers existed in the early part of the twentieth century, when law was not a category of membership until after the Second World War. Their number included no fewer than three Lord Chief Justices: **Rufus Isaacs** (the Marquess of Reading), **Richard Webster** (Viscount Alverstone) and **Gordon Hewart** (Viscount Hewart), along with the Lord Chancellor **FE Smith** (Lord Birkenhead).

We encountered both Isaacs and Smith in the context of the Marconi Scandal, and Smith in his short-lived role as a wartime censor.

Neither Alverstone nor Hewart served in the Great War, and hence fall outside the scope of this book. Both appear from time to time in Savage reminiscences: Alverstone apparently had a talent for music and was known to sing the Judge's Song from Gilbert and Sullivan's *Trial by Jury* at the Club,[58] while Hewart (who was not a well-regarded Lord Chief Justice[59]) had some sympathy in the Club since he was known to have been Brother Savage Mostyn Pigott's fag at school.

One finds other random legal names in the candidate books of the time, such as Wallace Cranston Fairweather, who was the author of the slightly

---

the 'beautifully drawn and stylistically unique card' Robinson had been able 'to touch with his magic the celebration of a Brother Savage's occasion'.

58 Hambourg, *The Eighth Octave*, op cit, p 137.
59 See *Trials and Tribulations*, Ch 50.

stodgy-sounding tome *Foreign and Colonial Patent Laws* (1910), recently reprinted by Kessinger Publishing on the ground it was 'culturally important'.

Savage Men of Science

Professor **Sir Charles Lovatt Evans** FRS (1884–1968) was a member of the Savage Club from June 1928. Before the war he had been an outstanding student: among other things, he was Sharpey scholar in the Institute of Physiology, University College London, from 1911. He qualified MRCS, LRCP in 1916 and then joined the Royal Army Medical Corps (RAMC), serving in the Anti-gas Department at Millbank and later as command chemical adviser at Aldershot until demobilisation. In 1918 he was promoted to the rank of major. One of his obituaries explained:[60]

> Lovatt Evans's outstanding gifts led to his rapid advancement after the war. After a brief period as Professor of Physiology and Pharmacology at Leeds (1918-19) he worked with H.H. Dale (later Sir Henry) on the staff of the National Institute for Medical Research (1919-1922). He was Professor of Physiology at St. Bartholomew's Medical College (1922-1926) and succeeded Professor A.V. Hill as Jodrell Professor of Physiology at University College (1926-1949). He was away from University College in World War II, working at Porton on gas warfare in the Chemical Defence Establishment (1939-1944). After his retirement from the Jodrell Chair, at the age of 65, he returned to Porton, as Consultant to the Ministry of Supply, actively pursuing his researches for nearly twenty years.

Another esteemed physician was Lieutenant-Colonel **Ernest George Ffrench** (1876–1937) who served in the Royal Army Medical Corps during the Boer War and in the First World War. In the latter he was twice mentioned in despatches. After the war he worked as a Harley Street practitioner and joined the Savage Club in February 1921. He was clearly mixing with London's elite, which makes his origins all the more intriguing – it seems he was an illegitimate son, which in those days carried much unjust social stigma.

Colonel **Alfred Edward Webb-Johnson**, 1st Baron Webb-Johnson GCVO, CBE, DSO, TD, FRCS (1880–1958), was a territorial soldier and consulting surgeon in the Middlesex Hospital in London when the First World War began. He spent the conflict at a hospital at Wimereux on the French coast. He was awarded the DSO and the CBE for his distinguished work 'in connection with military operations in the field' and reached the rank of colonel, Army Medical Service. After the war, he returned to working at Middlesex Hospital. He joined the Savage Club in April 1920. A measure of the reputation he had made was

---

60 Royal College of Physicians 'Lives of the Fellows', Munk's Roll: Volume VI. Another RAMC officer was Major Robert WH Jackson, who joined the Savage Club in January 1907.

that a ward of the hospital was named after him during his lifetime. He also acted as consulting surgeon to Chesham, Southend, and Woolwich Hospitals. From 1936 to 1953 he was surgeon to Queen Mary and from 1941 to 1949 served as president of the Royal College of Surgeons. He was knighted in 1936, made a Knight Commander of the Royal Victorian Order (KCVO) in 1942 and created a Baron of Stoke-on-Trent in 1945.

Still another pioneering Savage surgeon was **John Swift Joly**, MRCS, FRCS, MB, BCh, BAO, MD, LM (1876–1944). He was believed to be a collateral descendant of Jonathan Swift, the author of *Gulliver's Travels*.

Joly was educated at Dublin High School and at Trinity College, Dublin, where he came first in his class in experimental science in 1898. His academic success continued when he was made the Stewart medical scholar in chemistry and physics, botany and zoology in 1898, and in anatomy and 'the institutes of medicine' (physiology) in 1900.

During the First World War, he was commissioned as a captain in the RAMC in July 1917. He was promoted to acting major in April 1918. He served with the Egyptian Expeditionary Force and at the 47th Stationary Hospital at Gaza in Palestine. He was also appointed operative surgeon at the Tooting Military Hospital, and later civil consulting urologist to the Royal Navy. He reached the level of senior surgeon as well as consulting urologist for the navy.[61]

For all his lifelong service to medical science, he was also clearly a man of wide interests a and sense of humour. He used to sign letters 'Yours in haste' – signifying how busy he was in life. His biography on the Royal College of Surgeons' website recorded:[62]

> Joly was a sound surgeon and an inspiring teacher, who retained through life the wide scientific outlook of his early training. He was a careful, slow operator. He had a great talent for inventing and improving instruments; his cystoscope and urethroscope were very widely used, his bladder-retractor was also well known. Quiet and reserved, but not without wit, he was a sociable member of the Savage Club and an active freemason and had served as master of the Lodge of Trinity Dublin men in London. As a young man he was a noted cross-country runner and a keen fisherman. He was an expert photographer and fond also of golf, but his favourite pastime in his last ten years was mountaineering in the Swiss Alps with his wife and their only son; he climbed the Dent Blanche, 14,300 feet, when aged 61. His collection of his own Alpine photographs was very remarkable.

61 Ibid.
62 'Joly, John Swift (1876–1943)', *Plarr's Lives of the Fellows Online*.

George Parkinson CBE, DSO, MRCS, LRCP, DPH (1880–1953), epitomised his era's values of public service as reflected by his remarkable wartime record.

Parkinson started studying medicine immediately after leaving school, but volunteered for the Imperial Yeomanry at the start of the Second Boer War, when he was just 19. He served in the 75th (Sharpshooters) Company, 18th Battalion throughout the conflict. In 1902, following the cessation of hostilities, he resumed studying medicine, and four years later he qualified as a Member of the Royal College of Surgeons (MRCS) and as a Licentiate of the Royal College of Physicians (LRCP).

When the First World War broke out, he was serving as a captain in Southern Command. He immediately joined the British Expeditionary Force and served without a break right through the entire conflict. He began as deputy assistant director of hygiene and later served as assistant director of medical services, 1st Army, receiving particular recognition for his work during the Lys Offensive of April 1918. He ended the war with the rank of lieutenant-colonel.

His awards speak for themselves: he received the DSO and was mentioned in despatches three times.[63] He was also given the French *Légion d'honneur* (Chevalier) and *Croix de Guerre*,[64] and the Portuguese Military Order of Aviz (Chevalier).[65]

Following the Armistice, he was given further recognition by the French in the form of the *Medaille de la Reconnaissance*, the official announcement appearing in the *London Gazette* of 2 March 1926.

After the war, he served as deputy assistant director of hygiene and medical officer of health in Gibraltar from 1919–23. On returning to Britain he was appointed assistant professor of hygiene at the Royal Army Medical College. He stayed in the latter capacity until being placed on the Reserve of Officers as a lieutenant-colonel in August 1928. Meanwhile, in July 1925, he joined the Savage Club.

When the Second World War began, he was recalled to the RAMC, in which he once again served with distinction, reaching the rank of brigadier.[66]

---

63 See the *London Gazette* for 1 January 1916, 29 May and 24 December 1917.

64 See the *London Gazette* for 6 November 1918.

65 See the *London Gazette* for 21 August 1919.

66 He served for a short time at Millbank before returning to the London School of Hygiene and Tropical Medicine as acting dean. In 1943, he was appointed director of the Allied military government in Sicily and Italy, and was attached to the National Headquarters of the Armistice Control Commission in Italy 1944-45. In the latter role he was given the acting rank of brigadier.

During his time with the Allied military government in Italy, he played a leading role with the American forces in controlling a typhus outbreak. In Naples, a mass delousing of the civilian populace was organised. In 1945, Parkinson was awarded the CBE and the American Typhus

He was raised to Commander in the Order of St John in 1952, a year before his death.[67]

Lieutenant-Colonel **Harold Robinson** (1889–1955) was a scientist who performed a vital role for the artillery during the Great War. Before the conflict, he studied and then taught at Manchester University, from which he graduated BSc in 1911 and MSc in 1912. During the First World War, he was commissioned into the Royal Field Artillery, and served in France from August 1915. He was promoted to captain and acted as adjutant to the 1st Field Survey Battalion.

The work of the field surveyors was of the greatest importance once the mobile phase of the war was over, since artillerymen lost much of the opportunity to observe the enemy. Field survey companies were therefore established and given the task of surveying the ground, creating maps and identifying the position of the enemy. There were four such companies formed in France in 1916 and organised as units of the Royal Engineers. Each was composed of a headquarters, topographical section, map section, observation section and sound-ranging section. Robinson worked in sound-ranging – implementing the important research by Sir William Bragg's son Lawrence. Later, the army printing sections were added so they could to organise production of the tens of thousands of maps required. Three more companies were also formed and moved to other theatres.

In May 1918, the companies in France were reorganised into field survey battalions, Robinson's company forming part of the 1st Battalion. Each battalion was made up of headquarters (including the surveying and printing sections), two artillery sections (incorporating the sound-ranging and observation sections) and a corps topographical section. One was assigned to each of the five British Armies, and for tactical purposes was placed under the Commander, Royal Artillery (CRA) in each army.[68]

Commission Medal, and in 1947 he received the Italian Red Cross *Croce al Merito*.

67 In 2007, a group of his medals were put up for auction, comprising:

> Distinguished Service Order, GVR, silver-gilt and enamels; The Order of St John of Jerusalem, Officer's (Brother's) breast badge, silvered-metal and enamel; Queen's South Africa 1899-1902, 5 clasps, Cape Colony, Rhodesia, Orange Free State, Transvaal, South Africa 1901 (15492 Tpr, 75th Coy, 18th Imp, Yeo); 1914 Star (Capt, RAMC); British War and Victory Medals, MID oak leaf (Lt-Col); 1939-45 Star; Italy Star; Defence and War Medals; Jubilee 1935; Coronation 1937; French Legion of Honour, Chevalier's breast badge, silver and enamel, gold centre; French Croix de Guerre 1914-1918; French Medaille de la Reconnaissance, silver; Portuguese Military Order of St. Avis, Chevalier's breast badge, gilt and enamel; USA, Legion of Merit, Officer's breast badge, gilt and enamel; USA, Typhus Commission Medal; Italian Red Cross, Merit Medal.

> They were quite correctly described as a 'most unusual and impressive' collection. They were sold for £2,500, https://www.dnw.co.uk/auction-archive/lot-archive/lot.php?department=Medals &lot_id=138008.

68 'The Field Survey Companies of the Royal Engineers' in *The Long, Long Trail: the History of the British Army in the Great War of 1914–1918*, http://www.longlongtrail.co.uk/army/regiments

After the war, Robinson continued with his work in physics at Manchester University, reaching the level of assistant director of the Physical Laboratory, until 1921. He then undertook a PhD in physics at Cambridge, which he was awarded in 1924.

During the Second World War, he delivered the first ever Rutherford Memorial Lecture (the lectures were converted to a medal and prize from the mid-1960s and continue as such in the present day).

Afterwards, in 1946, he was appointed vice-principal of Queen Mary College, where he stayed until retiring in 1953. From 1954 until his death the following year he served as vice-chancellor of the University of London.

AE (Albert Edward) Mortimer Woolf FRCS (1884–1957) was a surgeon who studied at Cambridge, from which he obtained the degrees BA, MD, BCh in 1911. During the First World War he was a captain in the RAMC. After the war, among other things he worked at the Queen Mary's Hospital for the East End, the London Orphan Asylum in Watford and the British Red Cross Rheumatic Clinic. He served two non-consecutive terms as president of the Hunterian Society and was widely published in medical journals. He joined the Savage Club in December 1936.

Lieutenant-Colonel **Nathan Raw** CMG, MP, FRSE (1866–1940) was a distinguished doctor in the diverse fields of tuberculosis and medical psychology. He also served for a time as a Conservative MP for Liverpool, Wavertree. During the First World War, Raw joined the Royal Army Medical Corps. He served as lieutenant-colonel and commanding officer of the last 1st Western General Hospital, Lancashire, and also as commanding officer and senior physician of the Liverpool Hospital of the BEF in France. He was appointed a Companion of the Order of St Michael and St George in the 1918 New Year Honours.

Raw had two stints as a Savage Club member, the first from February 1925 and the second beginning in October 1936.

In other scientific fields, one finds among the Savages Lieutenant-Colonel **Sir Philip Wigham Richardson** (1865–1953), who joined the Club in June 1941, towards the end of his long life. He was educated at Rugby and King's College, Cambridge, before joining his father's Tyneside shipbuilding company. By 1891 he was a director of the company, a position he retained after it merged with CS Swan and Hunter, Ltd to form Swan, Hunter and Wigham Richardson, Ltd.

Richardson was an expert shot with the rifle. As well as competing at Wimbledon and Bisley, he represented Britain in the 1908 Summer Olympics and 1912 Summer Olympics, winning a silver medal in the team military rifle event in 1908. He was thus able to bring much relevant expertise to training

-and-corps/the-corps-of-royal-engineers-in-the-first-world-war/the-field-survey-companies-of-the-royal-engineers/.

soldiers during the Great War, though he was too old for frontline infantry service. He was awarded an OBE in 1919 for his 'services towards improving the standard of musketry'.[69]

After the war he served as the MP for Chertsey from 1922 until 1931. He was knighted in 1921 and created a baronet in 1929.

Edward Neville da Costa Andrade (1887–1971) was a polymath and public intellectual. Before the war he worked with Ernest Rutherford on the wavelength of a type of gamma radiation. During the war, he served in the Royal Artillery. He joined the Savage Club in February 1919. After the war, he served in many important academic posts, though he was removed from the Royal Institution after a vote of no confidence in his proposed reforms. In later life he appeared on the BBC programme *The Brains Trust* with Brother Savage Cyril Joad.

We have already discussed Lord Moulton's invaluable work on explosives during the war. Working in the same field was **John Percy 'Jack' Blake** (1874–1950), an Olympic fencer, amateur boxer, water polo enthusiast and local politician. During the Great War, he was in charge of the priority section of the High Explosives Section of the Ministry of Munitions.[70] He represented Britain in the 1908, 1912 and 1920 Summer Olympics in fencing, and won a silver medal in the 1912 épée team event. He was a life member of the Savage Club from 1914.

The engineer **Charles Hitchins** (1872–1959) was born in Australia, but his family moved to Britain before the close of the nineteenth century. He joined the Institution of Mechanical Engineers before the First World War. During the war, he commanded the 2/5th Battalion Loyal North Lancashires from 5 July 1916 to the end of the war.[71] In his memoir *The Fateful Battle Line*, Captain Henry Ogle MC recalled:[72]

> Lieutenant-Colonel Charles Hitchins, the Commanding Officer, had a reputation as a formidable man. He was big, dark and powerful with the loud voice and confident manner of one accustomed to dominate any board meeting or assembly of men. I heard that he was managing director of a firm of agricultural implement manufacturers in Kent. With his battalion he had endured one of the heaviest attacks on

---

69 Obituary, *Grace's Guide to British Industrial History*, https://www.gracesguide.co.uk/Philip_Wigham_Richardson.

70 See his obituary in *The Times*, 21 December 1950. The minister of munitions was created in response to the Shell Crisis of 1915, and David Lloyd George was the first to hold the post. See further Ralph Adams, *Arms and the Wizard: Lloyd George and the Ministry of Munitions, 1915–1916* (Cassell, 1978).

71 See Harold Carmichael Wylly, *Loyal North Lancashire Regiment, 1914-1919* (Royal United Services Institution, 1933; Albion Press Ltd, 2016, Kindle edn). Surprisingly, Hitchins is only mentioned once in the book, in passing. He also appears twice only on the website of the regiment, once with his name incorrectly spelt 'Hitchens'. See https://www.loyalregiment.com

72 Edited by Michael Glover, Pen & Sword Books, 2014, p 157.

Passchendaele late in 1917, when I would have been with them but was laid up in hospital at Étaples. 'Charlie' was a crack shot with a service revolver and I have seen him hit three bottles, each on a fence post, in succession. He was a great dog lover and breeder of Airedales.

Hitchins won the Distinguished Service Order.[73] After the war, in February 1939, he joined the Savage Club under the category of science, proposed by H Fletcher Moulton. He died in 1959.[74]

Savage Politicians

As with the politicians considered in the main section of the book, there are representatives from several different parties, showing the broad-mindedness of the Club then as now.

The Conservative Viscount Ullswater (1855–1949) served from 1905 to 1921 as Speaker of the House of Commons under his pre-honorific name **James Lowther**. He made a notable recommendation to his profession during the Great War when, in in 1917, he advised sagely 'There are three golden rules for Parliamentary speakers: Stand up. Speak up. Shut up.' In the same year he was made an honorary member of the Savage Club.

Tom Shaw (1872–1938) was an early and influential member of the union movement in Britain. As a member of the nascent Labour Party, and a person with some sympathy to communism (though not a communist sympathiser in the term as it is ordinarily understood), he would have been atypical of most London club members of the time, again showing how the Savage was more broad-minded about its membership. He did not serve overseas during the war, but did play a part nonetheless as director of National Service for the West Midland Region. He was appointed a Commander of the Order of the British Empire in the 1919 New Year Honours. He joined the Savage Club in June 1925. The great Savage pianist Mark Hambourg recalled:[75]

Risen from mill boy to Cabinet Minister, [Shaw] was popular in the club for his rugged, rather naïve, simplicity, and had not an "H" to his name. In the card room one day he was playing bridge with Douglas Furber,

---

73 In the *Supplement to the Edinburgh Gazette* of 29 July 1918, p 2741, it is recorded 'Maj. (T./Lt.-Col.) Charles Faunce Hitchins. DSO, R W Kent R., Spec Res, attd. N. Lan R (DSO gazetted 1ˢᵗ January, 1918.)'

74 The description read: 'Colonel Charles Faunce Hitchins DSO – Knights of the Round Table silver hallmarked and enamel medal named to Colonel Charles Faunce Hitchins DSO MI Mec E 1938. Col Hitchins was also Mentioned in Despatches during WW1, he was Lt Colonel of 3ʳᵈ R. W. Kent Regt, and later 2/5ᵗʰ L.N.Lan Regt.' See https://www.the-saleroom.com/en-gb/auction-catalogues/lockdales/catalogue-id-lo10013/lot-b2fbb674-3362-4e47-a707-a3f801749225.

75 Hambourg, *The Eighth Octave*, op cit, p 137.

the successful theatrical librettist as partner, and declared, "Three 'earts." "To which do you refer, sir," called out Furber, "to music, drama, or literature?" When Shaw returned from Gibraltar where he had been to inspect fortifications [Shaw served as Minister for War in the first Labour Government], he told us proudly that he had been received by a salute of fourteen guns. "And did they all miss you," asked Furber, "you were lucky!"

AV Alexander, 1ˢᵗ Earl Alexander of Hillsborough (1885–1965) was an important figure in the early days of the co-operative movement. It is known today throughout Britain by the chain of 'Co-Op' supermarkets, though in its infancy it also had its own political party. Alexander was elected to parliament as one of its representatives in the 1920s. The Co-Op Party later merged with the Labour Party, which Alexander also joined.

During the Great War, Alexander joined the Artists Rifles. He trained in London before being commissioned into the Labour Corps in December 1917. In the event, due to health problems, he never saw active service, but remained in Britain working as a posting officer in Lancashire. In November 1918, he was promoted to captain and transferred to the General List, where he became an education officer charged with preparing wounded soldiers for civilian life. He was demobbed in late 1919.

His service in the Second World War was much more significant. He served as First Lord of the Admiralty in the coalition government under Churchill, though often found Churchill making decisions over his head, especially as Churchill himself had held the same office for a time during the First World War.

He joined the Savage Club in October 1940 – a dark time in the country's history indeed. He gave his address as 'Admiralty, SW 1.'

Sir Robert Menzies (1894–1978) was Australia's longest-serving prime minister, notable for being in office when Australia joined the Second World War. He was made an honorary Savage in 1948 and clearly enjoyed his link with the Club, as he was often to be seen wearing a Savage tie during his overseas trips.

His reputation has remained largely positive in the years since his death, but one thing that dogged him periodically during his lifetime was the fact he did not serve during the Great War, despite being of an eligible age from the beginning. He pointed out that his two brothers did serve, but they did not do so from the beginning of the war, so that did not provide an excuse for his initial decision not to enlist.

Royal Savages

Prince Arthur, Duke of Connaught was one of Queen Victoria's many grandchildren. Arthur was born in 1883. He became the first member of the royal family to attend Eton. Later he went to Sandhurst, and was commissioned as a second lieutenant in the 7th (Queen's Own) Hussars in 1901. The regiment saw action in the Second Boer War shortly afterwards.

In 1906, his family was honoured by the Savage Club with a dinner in honour of his father, HRH The Duke of Connaught. Both father and son were Club members.

When the First World War began, Prince Arthur held the rank of brevet major. He was appointed *aide-de-camp* to Sir John French and served in the same capacity for Sir Douglas Haig when Haig replaced French. The role of *aide-de-camp* meant he was not on the frontline himself, though he had administrative duties all the same.

In June 1919, he was promoted to lieutenant-colonel, but retired from active service at the end of the year. He became a colonel in the reserves in 1922. From 1920 until 1923 he served as governor-general of South Africa.

Upon the accession of George V, he and his father were the next highest-ranking male royals in Britain. He worked as an *aide-de-camp* to George V, performing a lot of royal duties when the latter was unavailable. He did not live much longer, though, dying in 1938 at the age of just 55 due to stomach cancer.

Index

A

Cases, Causes and Controversies
Fifty Tales from the Law

James Wilson

Published by Wildy, Simmonds & Hill, 2012

What do Prince Charles, Bette Davis, Sir Ian Botham, Mrs Victoria Gillick and a man whose family grave appeared in the background of a splatter horror film have in common? Each of them felt they had been wronged in some way, and each went to court to try and do something about it.

This book looks at 50 legal disputes from Victorian times to the present day, where a compelling moral or legal issue was at stake, or where the background to the case was interesting, amusing or infuriating. The disputes include civil and criminal cases. Some concerned petty insults of the most trivial importance; others raised the weightiest moral, ethical and legal questions. Some of the stories are richly ironic. Bette Davis was left penniless after losing her case in England and felt she had no option but to return to America and resume working for the studio she had unsuccessfully sued. But after doing so she became one of the richest and most acclaimed actresses in history.

Cases, Causes and Controversies will be of interest not simply to lawyers but to anyone interested in stories of great human interest and how the legal system tried to deal with them.

… a good mix of 50 tales from the courts covering murder, warfare, the press, sport and many others. The accounts of each case are interesting and include something new for everyone.
Law Society Gazette

*****

These tales are riveting
Christchurch Press

Court & Bowled
Tales of Cricket and the Law

James Wilson

Published by Wildy, Simmonds & Hill, 2012

Second edition (paperback) published by Wildy, Simmonds & Hill, 2017

'In summertime village cricket is the delight of everyone' the English judge Lord Denning famously wrote, in a case brought by someone who clearly disagreed with him. The case was but one example of how the game of cricket cannot always avoid the law. Neighbours or passers-by get hit by stray cricket balls, protesters interrupt matches, players get into fights or take drugs, and not a few involved with the game sue each other for libel.

This book looks at a number of stories where cricket or cricketers gave rise to a legal dispute. It begins with a short history of cricket as it appears in the early law reports, including the case from 1598 which contains the very first known use of the word cricket. It then turns to individual cases from Victorian times to the present day.

All of the stories demonstrate something common to both cricket matches and court cases: behind the intrigue, entertainment and amusement of both there are real people and real human stories, with all the usual human emotions and fallibility.

The book will be of interest not only to cricket fans or lawyers but anyone interested in tales of high (and low) human drama and great ethical, moral and legal dilemmas.

A surprising gem ... all in all, a thoroughly enlightening piece of work
Wisden Cricketers' Almanack 2015

*****

A thoughtful and well written book
Lord Judge, former Lord Chief Justice

*****

A must read for anyone interested in these pursuits
Robert Griffiths QC, former Chairman of the Laws Sub-committee, MCC

*****

An interesting and entertaining collection of stories and cases
Law Society Gazette

Trials and Tribulations
Uncommon Tales of the Common Law

James Wilson

Published by Wildy, Simmonds & Hill, 2015

Why are court cases such a fertile source for writers of fiction and non-fiction alike? For a start, they usually have a beginning, middle and end; and a ready cast of characters playing defined roles.

They always have an inherent crisis to be resolved. But they also contain a great deal of human interest: behind the theatrics and etiquette of the courtroom, and the often arcane language and concepts of the law, there are real people seeking answers to real-life problems.

The common law is sometimes made by faceless corporations, or rich and powerful individuals seeking to preserve their money or reputation. Just as often, however, it is made by ordinary people who are not seeking fame or wealth, but who are simply trying to right whatever they believed has been wronged.

This book is a collection of 50 stories of notable court cases spanning more than a century. Written in an accessible style with an eye to the human as much as legal interest, the book will be of interest to lawyers and non-lawyers alike.

Ethical dilemmas, nail-biting litigation, human crises - all are here. No wonder writers like the law ...

The Times, 17 December 2015

✦✦✦✦✦

... an excellent addition to the bookshelves

Phillip Taylor MBE, Amazon review

✦✦✦✦✦

A great read for any lawyer

Emeritus Professor Keith Davies, New Law Journal